Anglo-Saxon Texts

10

THE OLD ENGLISH MARTYROLOGY

Edition, Translation and Commentary

Anglo-Saxon Texts

ISSN 1463–6948

Editorial Board
MICHAEL LAPIDGE
MARY CLAYTON
LESLIE LOCKETT
RICHARD MARSDEN
ANDY ORCHARD

Anglo-Saxon Texts is a series of scholarly editions (with parallel translations) of important texts from Anglo-Saxon England, whether written in Latin or in Old English. The series aims to offer critical texts with suitable apparatus and accurate modern English translations, together with informative general introductions and full historical and literary commentaries.

Previously published volumes in the series are listed at the back of this book

Cambridge, Corpus Christi College 196, p. 24, which shows the characteristic itemised layout of almost all manuscripts of the *Old English Martyrology*. Reproduced by kind permission of the Master and Fellows of Corpus Christi College, Cambridge.

THE OLD ENGLISH MARTYROLOGY

Edition, Translation and Commentary

Edited with a translation by
CHRISTINE RAUER

D. S. BREWER

© Christine Rauer 2013

All rights reserved. Except as permitted under current legislation
no part of this work may be photocopied, stored in a retrieval system,
published, performed in public, adapted, broadcast,
transmitted, recorded or reproduced in any form or by any means,
without the prior permission of the copyright owner

First published 2013
D. S. Brewer, Cambridge
Paperback edition 2016

ISBN 978 1 84384 347 4 hardback
ISBN 978 1 84384 431 0 paperback

The publisher has no responsibility for the continued existence or accuracy
of URLs for external or third-party internet websites referred to in this book,
and does not guarantee that any content on such websites is,
or will remain, accurate or appropriate

Printed from camera-ready copy supplied by the author

This publication is printed on acid-free paper

Printed and bound by CPI Group (UK) Ltd, Croydon, CR0 4YY

Contents

Acknowledgements	ix
Abbreviations	xi
Introduction	
1 Date of Composition, Sources	1
2 Language and Origin	4
3 Historical and Literary Context	11
4 Manuscripts	18
5 Previous Editions and Editorial Policy	25
6 Note on the Translation	30
Sigla	32
Text and Translation	33
Commentary	228
Appendices	
1 Manuscript A	311
2 Manuscript E	314
3 Manuscript F	319
Glossary	321
Bibliography	362
Indices	
Persons	387
Authors and Texts	394
Place-Names and Geographical Terms	398

Acknowledgements

Whether the martyrologist compiled his encyclopaedia alone or in collaboration with others is unclear, but I could certainly not have controlled the same materials without the help of many friends and colleagues.

Advice on individual text sections was generously provided by a number of scholars with particular expertise on these topics: Mary Clayton (concerning the Marian text sections), Kees Dekker (Pentecost and The Birth of Christ), David Dumville (The Birth of Christ), Patricia Karlin-Hayter (The Forty Soldiers of Sebastea), Juliet Mullins (St Martin), Brian Ó Broin (Ascension), Patrick Sims-Williams (St Patrick), Francesca Tinti (St Cuthbert), Gordon Whatley (SS. Eugenia and Basilla), Alex Woolf (SS. Aidan, Patrick, Oswald, Columba and Fursa), and Charles Wright (The Annunciation).

Access to unpublished secondary literature was kindly granted by Sándor Chardonnens, Victoria Condie, Philip Rusche, Jacqueline Stodnick, and Alan Thacker. Other bibliographical advice I received from Rolf Bremmer, Marianne Chenard, François Dolbeau, Thomas Falmagne, John Flood, Rob Getz, Tom Hall, Peter Jackson, Michael Lapidge, and Clive Sneddon, for which I am very grateful.

I was glad to discuss some of the Old English vocabulary with two experienced lexicographers, Toni Healey of the Dictionary of Old English, University of Toronto and Inge Milfull of the Oxford English Dictionary, University of Oxford; both were patient, prompt and unfailingly informative in answering my questions.

Particular thanks are also due to two colleagues in other disciplines, who readily helped me out when I contacted them out of the blue: Andrew Cameron, School of Physics and Astronomy, University of St Andrews, who discussed with me the medieval night sky and demonstrated what *Stellarium* could do for me, and Arie Zwiep, Faculteit der Godgeleerdheid, Vrije Universiteit Amsterdam, who gave me his opinion on the Ascension section and managed to link it to several more patristic sermons.

Paul Harvey, Department of History and Religious Studies, Pennsylvania State University was kind enough to advise me on Jerome's *Vita S. Hilarionis* and *Vita S. Pauli* and the contents of his forthcoming edition of these texts. Dorothea Weber of the ÖAW Kirchenväter-Kommission provided information on Augustine's newly discovered Sermo 282. Paola Moretti, Dipartimento Scienze dell'Antichità, Università degli Studi di Milano, kindly checked manuscript readings in the *Passio S. Anastasiae* for me. I was also glad to talk to Mary Whitby, editor of Translated Texts for Historians, Liverpool University Press, who shared with me her expertise on translation policies and on a number of Eastern saints. Peter Bierbaumer, Karl-Franzens-Universität Graz, provided information on the topic of Germanic plant names. Many thanks to all of them.

I am grateful to several institutions which have supported my work on the *Old English Martyrology* over the years: the Universities of St Andrews, Oxford and Birmingham, and Corpus Christi College, Oxford. I am indebted to the British Academy for assisting me with a grant from the Neil Ker Memorial Fund, and I would also like to thank two Heads of School, Nicholas Roe and Lorna Hutson, for granting me two semesters of research leave.

Of the many librarians and technicians in Cambridge, Oxford, London, and St Andrews who helped me in various ways and often beyond the call of duty, I particularly need to acknowledge the assistance of Chris Lee, Imaging Services, British Library, for his help with ultraviolet imaging, Gill Cannell, Corpus Christi College Cambridge, for her help with the Corpus manuscripts, and the Interlibrary Loan staff at the University of St Andrews for tracing far-flung publications for this project.

I have enjoyed discussing the *Old English Martyrology* with many students in the institutions mentioned, but two research assistants must to be mentioned for more active contributions: Petra Hofmann, who assisted in the compilation of the glossary, and Jennifer Key, who contributed expert editing when it was needed most. I was also glad to have Mitchell Papish and Ruth Mullett as amanuenses.

Claire Ruben, my copy editor, and Caroline Palmer and other Boydell and Brewer staff saw the book safely through its production and saved me from many errors; I am very grateful to them, and also to the series editor Michael Lapidge: this book was much improved by his many wise suggestions. For general advice and congeniality over many years I would like to thank Andy Orchard, Gordon Whatley, Malcolm Godden, Joyce Hill, Rolf Bremmer, Don Scragg, Tom Duncan, Eric Stanley, Sharon Rowley, Fred Biggs, Kurt Bornhauser, Catherine and David Fraser, Iris Netzle, and the members of the *Fontes Anglo-Saxonici* Management Committee under whose patronage I first began my work on the *Old English Martyrology*. A debt of a special kind is owed to the late Sir Hugh Thomas Munro for compiling the greatest of all martyrologies.

My most profound thanks, of course, go to Kees, who discussed Germanic phonology, commented diplomatically on editorial decisions, and took me off to Alpine slopes and Roman ruins. It has been wonderful to have his support.

St Andrews, November 2012

Abbreviations

AASS	Acta Sanctorum, 1st edn, 68 vols., ed. Bollandists (1643–1940)
AB	*Analecta Bollandiana*
ASE	*Anglo-Saxon England*
ASPR	Anglo-Saxon Poetic Records
BCLL	*Bibliography of Celtic-Latin Literature 400–1200*, ed. M. Lapidge and R. Sharpe (Dublin, 1985)
BHL	*Bibliotheca Hagiographica Latina*, ed. Bollandists, 2 vols. (Brussels, 1899–1901) and H. Fros, *Novum Supplementum* (Brussels, 1986)
BL	London, British Library
BnF	Paris, Bibliothèque nationale de France
BRASE	Basic Readings in Anglo-Saxon England
BSS	*Bibliotheca Sanctorum*, ed. F. Caraffa, 13 vols. (Vatican, 1961–70)
CCCC	Cambridge, Corpus Christi College
CCCM	Corpus Christianorum Continuatio Mediaevalis
CCSL	Corpus Christianorum Series Latina
CSASE	Cambridge Studies in Anglo-Saxon England
CSEL	Corpus Scriptorum Ecclesiasticorum Latinorum
DMLBS	*Dictionary of Medieval Latin from British Sources*, ed. R. E. Latham *et al.* (London, 1975–)
DOE	*Dictionary of Old English: A-G on CD-ROM*, ed. A. diPaolo Healey *et al.* (Toronto, 2008)
DOEC	*Dictionary of Old English Corpus*, ed. A. diPaolo Healey *et al.* (Toronto, 2005), http://quodlib.umich.edu/o/oec
EETS	Early English Text Society
os	original series
ss	supplementary series
ePL	Patrologia Latin Database, http://pld.chadwyck.co.uk
Fabricius	J. A. Fabricius, *Codex apocryphus novi testamenti*, 2nd edn, 2 vols. (Hamburg, 1719, 1743)
Gneuss	H. Gneuss, *Handlist of Anglo-Saxon Manuscripts: A List of Manuscripts and Manuscript Fragments Written or Owned in England up to 1100*, MRTS 241 (Tempe, 2001)
HBS	Henry Bradshaw Society
Herzfeld	G. Herzfeld, ed., *An Old English Martyrology*, EETS os 116 (London, 1900)
Ker	N. R. Ker, *Catalogue of Manuscripts Containing Anglo-Saxon* (Oxford, 1957)
Kotzor	G. Kotzor, ed., *Das altenglische Martyrologium*, Abhandlungen der Bayerischen Akademie der Wissenschaften, phil.-hist. Kl. ns 88.1–2, 2 vols. (Munich, 1981)

LLASE	*Learning and Literature in Anglo-Saxon England: Studies Presented to Peter Clemoes on the Occasion of his Sixty-Fifth Birthday*, ed. M. Lapidge and H. Gneuss (Cambridge, 1985)
MÆ	*Medium Ævum*
MGH	Monumenta Germaniae Historica
AA	Auctores antiquissimi
SRLI	Scriptores rerum Langobardicarum et Italicarum
SRM	Scriptores rerum Merovingicarum
MJ	*Mittellateinisches Jahrbuch*
Mombritius	B. Mombritius, *Sanctuarium seu vitae sanctorum*, 2nd edn, 2 vols. (Paris, 1910)
MRTS	Medieval and Renaissance Texts and Studies
NM	*Neuphilologische Mitteilungen*
NQ	*Notes and Queries*
ODNB	*Oxford Dictionary of National Biography*, ed. H. C. G. Matthew and B. Harrison (Oxford, 2004), http://www.oxforddnb.com
PASE	*Prosopography of Anglo-Saxon England*, ed. J. L. Nelson, S. Keynes *et al.*, http://www.pase.ac.uk (cited by saint's name)
PL	Patrologia Latina, ed. J.-P. Migne, 221 vols. (Paris, 1844–64)
Rauer, *Fontes*	C. Rauer, 'The Sources of the *Old English Martyrology* (Cameron B.19)', 1999, *Fontes Anglo-Saxonici: World-Wide Web Register*, http://fontes.english.ox.ac.uk/
RES	*Review of English Studies*
SASLC	*Sources of Anglo-Saxon Literary Culture: A Trial Version*, ed. F. M. Biggs, T. D. Hill and P. E. Szarmach, MRTS 74 (Binghamton, 1990)
SChr	Sources chrétiennes
SH	Subsidia Hagiographica
TU	Texte und Untersuchungen zur Geschichte der altchristlichen Literatur
Whatley	Whatley, E. G., 'Acta Sanctorum', *Sources of Anglo-Saxon Literary Culture: Volume One*, ed. F. M. Biggs *et al.* (Kalamazoo, 2001), pp. 22–548

References to the *Old English Martyrology* are in bold print and indicate section numbers (eg. **45**).

Introduction

The *Old English Martyrology* is one of the longest and most important prose texts written in Anglo-Saxon England; it also represents one of the most impressive examples of encyclopaedic writing from the European Middle Ages. Probably intended as a reference work, it experienced more than 200 years of transmission and usage. Its principal aim must have been to educate Anglo-Saxon readers in their cults of native and foreign saints, but it also presents detailed information on time measurement, the seasons of the year, biblical events, and cosmology. Its range is impressive even by modern standards: the text makes reference to roughly 450 historical and legendary characters, covering more than 6000 years of political, ecclesiastical and saintly history, as the events described range from the creation of the world in the year 5199 before Christ to contemporary cosmological phenomena still observed by the author himself. Geographically, the text covers the British Isles to western, central, and southern Europe, the Middle East, Northern Africa, and India. The complete set of data contained in this encyclopaedia is collected in no other surviving literature from the early Middle Ages, although constituent parts of this information can be found in some 250 earlier texts, many of which may directly have influenced the composition of the *Old English Martyrology*. It is hard to imagine today what difficulties its author or authors must have overcome in the compilation of this knowledge, and even now, in an age where information travels fast and electronically, one is struck by the range and comprehensive nature of this hagiographical database.

1 Date of Composition, Sources

Attempts to identify the likely date of composition (together with the location of composition and the author's ethnicity) have often concentrated on the respective inclusion or exclusion of certain saints or feasts in the *Old English Martyrology*.[1] The recognition that the text seems to attempt an inclusive and comprehensive approach in the selection of its saints has, however, made it harder to base such arguments on the inclusion of given saints; arguments *e silentio*, based on the omission of certain saints, are on the other hand made difficult by the fact that even hagiographical texts which can be securely dated often present unexpected omissions that run counter to their known date of composition.[2]

Less controversial dating criteria can be gained from the earliest manuscripts of the text. Two early manuscript fragments of the *Old English Martyrology*, London, BL Add. 23211 (s. ix ex.) and London, BL Add. 40165 A2. (s. ix / x), provide an

---

[1] The inclusion of All Saints has often been noted, as well as the omission of several West Saxon saints such as Birinus, Aldhelm and Boniface; see Kotzor, I, 19–20, 22–3, 27–8, 446–8, and 450–54. For a more comprehensive list of secondary literature relating to a possible date of composition, see Rauer, 'An Annotated Bibliography', s. vv. 'Date, Historical Background' and 'Manuscripts'.

[2] Rauer, 'The Sources of the *Old English Martyrology*', pp. 93–4. For saints unexpectedly omitted by Ælfric, see Lapidge, 'Ælfric's Sanctorale', pp. 119–22; for Aldhelm's omissions in his *De uirginitate*, see Lapidge and Herren, trans., *Aldhelm: The Prose Works*, pp. 57–8.

upper limit for its composition, demonstrating that the text was already in circulation by *c.* 900.[3] These two earliest copies, moreover, belong to quite distinct branches of manuscript transmission, and it is therefore possible to say that the text had already experienced an eventful transmission history, and perhaps even a systematic stylistic revision, by the time the two earliest witnesses were copied out. These early manuscripts already present the characteristic structure and wording which the text displays in its later and fuller copies, and there is no reason to doubt that the *Old English Martyrology* existed in what we now know as its full length and detail at the end of the ninth century.

An early limit for a date of composition is sometimes suggested by a number of relatively late historical events mentioned in a text, and the dates of composition of those primary sources on which an author drew to describe these events. But this method brings its own problems. The deaths of a number of saints mentioned in the text are thought to have occurred in the late seventh or early eighth century: John of Beverley (721), Bertinus (698), Audomarus (*c.* 690), Winnocus (*c.* 717). For his entries on the last three saints, the martyrologist is thought to have relied, directly or indirectly, on the *Vita S. Bertini* (*BHL* 763), the *Vita S. Audomari* (*BHL* 763), and the *Vita S. Winnoci* (*BHL* 8952), as Günter Kotzor demonstrated.[4] These three texts, which were often, but not always, transmitted together, form a composite tripartite *vita*, thought to have been composed by a single author *c.* 800. This date of composition has not been reliably established, but would at least for the moment seem to point to the late eighth or even early ninth century as the point when an English author could plausibly have accessed this material at the earliest. Two other texts probably used by the martyrologist, the second *Passio S. Afrae* (*BHL* 108–9), composed *c.* 770, and the sermon on the feast of All Saints known as 'Legimus in ecclesiasticis historiis', which has in recent years more reliably been assigned to Helisachar of Trier (d. 833x840), would also seem to point to the late eighth or early ninth century as the time when information used by the martyrologist in the composition of his text would first have been available.[5] Extensive and detailed usage of another relatively late text, the *Vita S. Mariae Magdalenae* (*BHL* 5453), which has been thought to date from the ninth century, would again support a ninth-century date of composition, and the same could be said for the inclusion of a feast for St Michael on 8 May (which is thought to be a later addition to other, earlier, feasts for that saint).[6]

In his numerous publications on the *Old English Martyrology*, James Cross identified large numbers of Latin hagiographical texts as sources, and was in many cases even able to single out specific text variants as particularly close to the wording in the *Old English Martyrology*. In doing so, he noticed that many of the earliest

---

[3] See Kotzor, I, 52–4, 115–116, and 449–50 and pp. 18–25 below for further discussion of all manuscripts.
[4] See Rauer, 'Female Hagiography'; and Kotzor, I, 452–3 and II, 347–8, 350, and 367–8 for surveys of dating criteria.
[5] Rauer, 'Female Hagiography'.
[6] For Mary Magdalen, see Rauer, 'Female Hagiography'; for feasts of St Michael, see the summary in Whatley, s. v. 'Michael archangelus' and the literature cited there.

manuscripts of a relevant text variant dated from the late eighth or early ninth centuries. This reinforced Cross's belief that the source material necessary for the compilation of the *Old English Martyrology* would have been complete at some point during the first half of the ninth century, and that a composition in the first half of the ninth century could therefore be just as, or even more, plausible than one assigned to the late eighth century or the second, more 'Alfredian', half of the ninth century.[7] It is important to remember that periods of poor book survival in earlier centuries could at least have been partially responsible for the fact that so much of the Latin hagiography identified as closest in wording to the *Old English Martyrology* seems to date from the late eighth or earlier ninth century and that no earlier or later manuscripts seem to offer parallels of significant interest. Nevertheless, the cumulative evidence of relatively late source texts, feasts which are relatively late innovations, and text variants which often only appear at a relatively late point make a composition of the *Old English Martyrology* in the late eighth century or ninth century most likely. The earlier arguments presented by Cross and Kotzor have in that sense largely been confirmed by further source studies during recent decades. A relevant caveat, however, arises from the fact that it is in many cases difficult to date anonymous saints' lives; moreover, many of the Latin texts in question have not even been edited reliably. These problems show that the last word may not have been spoken regarding the text's date of composition. At the current stage of research, it would therefore be cautious to suggest that the *Old English Martyrology* was probably composed sometime between *c.* 800 and *c.* 900.

The process of composition has likewise been a topic of discussion. One of the most interesting features of the *Old English Martyrology* is its combination of a calendrical arrangement of feastdays and saints' names with substantial narrative material, including vast numbers of abbreviated miracle stories and frequent instances of direct speech.[8] The register of feastdays and saints' names ultimately derives from one or more liturgical sources (martyrologies, calendars, sacramentaries).[9] The narrative component can be shown to have been summarised from between 200 and 300 Latin source texts (especially anonymous *passiones* of Continental origin), most of which were identified by James Cross.[10] Michael Lapidge has argued that this summarised narrative material and the calendrical grid of feastdays and saints' names reached the martyrologist already combined in a hypothetical lost Latin text

---

[7] See, for example, Cross, 'Mary Magdalen', p. 20; Cross, 'The Apostles', pp. 42–3; Cross, 'Popes of Rome', p. 204; Cross and Tuplin, 'An Unrecorded Variant', p. 168; Cross, '*Passio Symphoriani*', pp. 269 and 275; Cross, 'Cosmas and Damian', p. 18; Cross, 'Pelagia in Mediaeval England', p. 282; and Cross, 'The Use of a *Passio S. Sebastiani*', pp. 39–40.

[8] See Rauer, 'Usage of the *Old English Martyrology*', p. 133 and the literature cited there for similar Continental examples of the *légendier-martyrologe*.

[9] See Rauer, 'The Sources of the *Old English Martyrology*', p. 90 and the literature cited there.

[10] The precise number depends on definitions of what should be classified as a separate text (as opposed to a text variant) and on whether possible, probable and antecedent sources should all be regarded as sources. See the Commentary section below for the most comprehensive list of source texts to date; earlier surveys can be found in Rauer, *Fontes*; Rauer, 'The Sources of the *Old English Martyrology*', pp. 103–9; and Lapidge, *The Anglo-Saxon Library*, pp. 233–7. Secondary reading on the topic is collected in Rauer, 'An Annotated Bibliography', s. v. 'Sources, Composition'.

composed in eighth-century Northumbria, which the ninth-century martyrologist then translated into Old English, as a *Vorlage* for his own vernacular text.[11] Lapidge further explored the composition of that lost Latin text, and identified a number of texts on which this hypothetical source in its turn would have been based; these include the martyrologies of Pseudo-Jerome and Bede, from which the feastdays and saints' names in the *Old English Martyrology* would thus ultimately have been derived.[12] The lost text would also have contained abbreviated narrative material from *passiones* available in early Northumbria. As a scenario of composition for this lost Latin source text, Lapidge suggested that it was composed by Acca of Hexham, sometime between 731 and 740, since Acca is known to have had access to large numbers of *passiones*.[13] Lapidge also made a case for other material, such as excerpts from Bede, *Historia ecclesiastica* and *De temporum ratione*, Adomnán, *De locis sanctis*, and excerpts from a sacramentary to have been integrated in the hypothetical Latin text, material which in that case would not have been used directly by the martyrologist, but indirectly, embedded in the lost text in an abbreviated format.[14] Given this hypothetical component in the composition of the *Old English Martyrology*, it is important to bear in mind that the sources identified for the Old English text (which are listed and discussed in the Commentary below) could have been used directly or indirectly by the martyrologist. An unknown proportion of the source texts identified so far should in that case technically be regarded as so-called antecedent sources, rather than as texts which were directly known to the martyrologist.

2 Language and Origin

Various aspects of the martyrologist's language have already been examined systematically. Given the constraints of this editorial introduction, the aim here is to give an outline of the linguistic research undertaken to date and to indicate where further work is required. The principal focus of linguistic study so far has been phonological, lexicological, and morphological, and has resulted in a longstanding debate regarding the dialectal origin of the text. It was Eduard Sievers (1884) who first suggested an Anglian original for the *Old English Martyrology*; other linguistic observations were made by Georg Herzfeld (for his edition of the text, 1900), by commentators responding to Herzfeld's edition, and by Franz Stossberg (in a short monograph, 1905).[15] The first systematic and reliable linguistic study, however, was undertaken by Kotzor, who examined both the earlier and later manuscripts of the

---

[11] Lapidge, 'Acca of Hexham'; for the term *Vorlage* ('model', 'source') used by Lapidge, see the editorial introduction of Kotzor, I, 21n, 35, 39n, 250–1, and 448. See also Gretsch, 'Æthelthryth of Ely', pp. 166–8 for more information on this text.
[12] Lapidge, 'Acca of Hexham', pp. 44 and 57–8.
[13] Lapidge, 'Acca of Hexham', pp. 66–9.
[14] Lapidge, pers. comm.
[15] Sievers, 'Miscellen zur angelsächsischen Grammatik', p. 299; Stossberg, 'Die Sprache des altenglischen Martyrologiums'; Herzfeld, pp. xi–xxxii. For a survey of early linguistic research on the *Old English Martyrology*, see Kotzor, I, 15–25; further secondary literature on the martyrologist's language can be located with the help of Rauer, 'An Annotated Bibliography', s. vv. 'Language, Style' and 'Reviews'.

text for their phonology, morphology, syntactical features and dialect vocabulary, and distinguished diverging practices between their scribes. Kotzor applied the dialectological work of Franz Wenisch and Hans Schabram to the vocabulary of the *Old English Martyrology*, and was able to paint a more nuanced picture of the Anglian lexis of the text, by distinguishing between lexical items originally Anglian which later acquired a more supraregional character, and items which more consistently seem to indicate Anglian dialect even throughout the later stages of the Anglo-Saxon period.[16] Syntactical features examined by Kotzor include the usage of *mid*, in the *Old English Martyrology* used variously with dat. or acc., with the latter as an indicator of possible Anglian origin. Among the morphological features considered to be indicative in terms of dialect are the formation of abstract nouns (variously from participles or verb stems, the latter being associated with Anglian usage) and the suffix formation of abstract nouns (varying between *-nes* or *-nis*, with the latter as a possible Anglian feature). Syncope in inflectional morphology was also examined by Kotzor, as unsyncopated forms have been regarded as characteristically Anglian, and another feature investigated by Kotzor was allomorphic variation in the conjugation of *seon*. His phonological analysis included an examination of ă / ŏ before nasals (with ŏ as the predominant feature in Anglian texts) and retraction of ǣ to ă before l + consonant, instead of breaking to ĕa (with the retracted form characteristic of Anglian).[17] Of particular importance in Kotzor's study is also the linguistic analysis of the earliest two manuscripts, A and E, which he examined for West Saxon features, such as the retention of Germanic ǣ in West Saxon (as opposed to ē in Anglian and Kentish), palatal diphthongisation, and the absence of Anglian smoothing. Kotzor also re-examined instances of possible Kentish features cautiously posited earlier by Celia Sisam.[18]

Taken collectively, Kotzor's results indicate that the original text of the *Old English Martyrology* is likely to have been predominantly Anglian, although a West Saxon component even in the language of the original cannot be ruled out, as even the earliest surviving manuscripts, A and E, already present a mixture of Anglian and West Saxon features. The picture differs slightly for the later manuscript B (s. x / xi) which shows even more West Saxon features; the language of C (s. xi²) appears to be the most West Saxonised of all the copies. In sum, the Anglian component seems to have decreased and the West Saxon component seems to have increased during the transmission of the text. Some of this West Saxonisation seems to have gone hand in hand with a radical stylistic revision.[19]

Several caveats need to be added. The Anglian group of dialects has traditionally been subdivided into Mercian and Northumbrian. Specifically Northumbrian dialectal features seem to be absent from the *Old English Martyrology*;

---

[16] Wenisch, *Spezifisch anglisches Wortgut*; Schabram, *Superbia*. Vocabulary thought to have been Anglian either at the stage of composition or later during transmission is listed in Kotzor, I, 329–67, and Rauer, 'An Annnotated Bibliography', s. v. 'Glossary'.
[17] Kotzor, I, 367–96.
[18] Kotzor, I, 396–400 and 403; Sisam, 'An Early Fragment', p. 215; for dialectal features of individual manuscripts, see also pp. 18–25 below.
[19] See pp. 7, 9–10, 20 and 24–5 below.

the Anglian features in the text are not necessarily distinctively Mercian; and the manuscript transmission of the text known to modern scholarship is entirely restricted to the south of England. Celia Sisam first pointed out that the north is referred to in the text as a distant and unfamiliar place.[20] Taken together, these factors make it unlikely that there is a Northumbrian component in the composition of the *Old English Martyrology*, although it cannot be ruled out entirely.

Moreover, it is clear that the dialectal character of a word or other linguistic feature can change through time, in the sense that a word originally belonging to one dialect can over time become supradialectal, and vice versa. Modern scholarship is trying to establish the dialectal characteristics of a ninth-century text from ninth-, tenth-, and eleventh-century manuscripts, and it is clear that this is difficult.[21] From an editorial point of view, it is in any case important not to remove features silently from the text which could testify to the presumed early mixture of Anglian, West Saxon and possibly also Kentish features.[22]

Moreover, in view of Kotzor's extremely cautious assessment of the phonology and dialect vocabulary of both the presumed author of the *Old English Martyrology* and the scribes of the surviving manuscripts, it is important to remember that it is hard to draw conclusions from the text's dialect features as to its place of composition.[23] The intertwined politics of ninth-century Mercia and Wessex, together with the Mercian political influence in Kent, can easily explain why a ninth-century southern English text should present no clear-cut dialectal picture, and could have been formed by varying influence from its author, his patron, and the text's place of composition.[24] In sum, it can cautiously be said that the *Old English Martyrology* presents all the phonological features which one could expect from a text suspected to have been composed in a ninth-century environment where persons of Mercian and West Saxon and possibly Kentish linguistic origin mingled. Possible reasons which could account for dialectally ambiguous language include composition by an author whose biography took him through a variety of dialect areas, or an author originating from a dialectal border area, or even an author who wrote in a supradialectal medium mixing Mercian and West Saxon features, as has been suggested for the Junius Psalter gloss by Mechthild Gretsch.[25] The difficulty of establishing clear boundaries between ninth-century dialects, particularly in the south and south-east of England,

---

[20]For the southern transmission of the text, see Rauer, 'Usage of the *Old English Martyrology*', pp. 144–6; for the absence of specifically Northumbrian forms, see Kotzor, I, 400n and 445n. For textual references to the north, see, for example, **37** and **196**; Sisam, 'An Early Fragment', p. 214; and Kotzor, I, 28 and 447.

[21]For a survey of relevant research, see Kastovsky, 'Semantics and Vocabulary', pp. 338–51 and Toon, 'Old English Dialects'.

[22]For two examples, see Commentary on **41** and **226**.

[23]Kotzor, I, 445–6.

[24]For the resulting dialectal and cultural output, see esp. Gretsch, 'The Junius Psalter Gloss'; Wilson, 'The Provenance of the Vespasian Psalter Gloss'; and Brown, 'Mercian Manuscripts'; for further political background, see Keynes, 'King Alfred and the Mercians'; Gretsch, *The Intellectual Foundations*, pp. 317–25; Keynes, 'The Control of Kent'; and Keynes, 'Between Bede and the Chronicle'.

[25]Gretsch, 'The Junius Psalter Gloss', pp. 99–106 and 120–1.

and the possibility of supradialectal language, currently stand in the way of identifying the martyrologist's geographical and dialectal home.[26]

The translations of Gregory's *Dialogi* and Bede's *Historia ecclesiastica* seem to be those which are most closely related to the *Old English Martyrology* in dialectal terms; from a thematic point of view, the hagiographical interest of the *Dialogi* and the focus on British historiography in Bede's work are also shared by the *Old English Martyrology*.[27] The style of Wærferth, to whom the translation of Gregory's *Dialogi* has been ascribed, resembles that of the martyrologist to some extent: 'It is in many respects a very literal rendering, following the order of the Latin as closely as he can and imitating its structures as much as possible. Nothing of substance is added and very little removed.'[28] Wærferth's predilection for word pairs is to some degree echoed in the *Old English Martyrology*.[29] Like the *Old English Martyrology*, the Old English translation of Gregory's *Dialogi* experienced extensive stylistic and lexical revision during its later transmission, and the same characteristics apply to the Old English translation of Bede's *Historia ecclesiastica*:[30] its original is believed to have been written in an Anglian dialect, displays a preference for doublets and rare vocabulary (often formed from Latin models), and experienced a later revision with changes in lexis and syntax, and overall a greater move towards West Saxon. Given these shared characteristics between the three texts, systematic lexical and stylistic comparison of the *Old English Martyrology* and the Old English translations of the *Dialogi* and *Historia ecclesiastica* would make sense, and more research in this area still needs to be undertaken.[31]

One of the most interesting linguistic aspects of the *Old English Martyrology* is its vocabulary, particularly its more unusual components, which are now easier to survey with the help of electronic tools. The searchable electronic corpus of Old English (*DOEC*) and the progressing *Dictionary of Old English* project (*DOE*) in particular have helped in the identification of a relatively large proportion of rare vocabulary and hapax legomena in the *Old English Martyrology*, which is signalled as such in the glossary below. Although a systematic study of this rare vocabulary has not yet been undertaken, there are indications that at least some of the more unusual words or semantic preferences in the language of the martyrologist could have been influenced by related Latin vocabulary, or Latin vocabulary which he regards as

---

[26] For general background, see Hogg, 'On the Impossibility of Old English Dialectology'; Lowe, 'On the Plausibility of Old English Dialectology'; Anderson, 'The Great Kentish Collapse'; for Kentish in particular, see now Kalbhen, ed., *Kentische Glossen*, pp. 241–258.

[27] See the early remarks by Jordan, *Eigentümlichkeiten*, pp. 5–7.

[28] See Godden, 'Wærferth and King Alfred', esp. pp. 36 and 47. See also Rauer, 'Errors and Textual Problems', for further stylistic similarities.

[29] See Kotzor, I, 421–5.

[30] Godden, 'Wærferth and King Alfred', esp. 42–4; Hofstetter, *Winchester und der spätaltenglische Sprachgebrauch*, pp. 146–9; Waite, 'The Vocabulary'; Waite, *Old English Prose*, pp. 46–8; and Rowley, *The Old English Version*, pp. 41–6.

[31] For some overlap of the rare vocabulary found in the *Old English Martyrology* with that of the Old English translations of the *Dialogi* and *Historia ecclesiastica*, see Rauer, 'An Annotated Bibliography', s. v. 'Glossary'.

related.[32] One important question which will need to be addressed is whether his predilection for unusual Latinate vocabulary should be seen as an idiosyncratic trait, or whether it could be aligned with similar phenomena found in authors involved in gloss production. Lucia Kornexl has drawn attention to a number of Old English lexical coinages specific to the genre of glosses, namely coinages which seem to imitate Latin vocabulary, and the question arises whether the martyrologist's lexical predilections (together with his generally very literal translation methods and a conspicuous element of Latin vocabulary inserted into his Old English text) could be ascribed to a biographical background in the production or usage of glosses.[33] As part of his examination of Latin vocabulary inserted into the *Old English Martyrology*, Kotzor identified a number of lexical items with connections to the Second Corpus Glossary (CCCC 144, a Mercian production of the first half of the ninth century), but rightly cautioned against the positing of a direct link between the *Old English Martyrology* and the glossary.[34] With the help of electronic tools, it is now also possible to trace further rare vocabulary in the text which also appears in glosses or glossaries, but the significance of this lexical overlap still needs to be assessed.[35]

One characteristic syntactic feature found in the surviving manuscripts of the *Old English Martyrology*, which can be presumed to have been present in the original, is a conspicuous number of anacoluthic constructions, often employing recapitulatory pronouns:[36]

Se Uictor, **he** wæs Maura cynnes, **83**	That Victor — **he** was a Moor
Þa se man ðe þæt sceolde behealdan þæt hi man beheafdade, wepende ond swergende, **he** sæde þæt he gesawe heora sawla gongan ut of þæm lichoman fægre gefretwade, **64**	When the man who was supposed to watch that they got beheaded, weeping and swearing an oath — **he** said that he saw their souls leave the body beautifully adorned
Ðone Dioclitianus se casere, he wæs hæþen, **he** het hine mid strælum ofscotian, **27**	Him [ie. Sebastian] the emperor Diocletian — **he** was pagan, he ordered him to be shot dead with arrows

---

[32]Rauer, 'Errors and Textual Problems'; for two case studies, see Rauer, 'Pelagia's Cloak' and Rauer, 'Old English *blanca*'.
[33]See Kornexl, 'Sprache der Glossen', 'Unnatural Words', and 'The *Regularis Concordia*'. Gneuss describes some of the rare coinages in psalter glosses as vocabulary which 'never really lived' and 'at most migrates from one manuscript to another', and which is 'forgotten again as soon as it is coined', *Lehnbildungen und Lehnbedeutungen*, p. 156 (my translations).
[34]Kotzor, I, 250n, further discussed by Rusche, 'The *Old English Martyrology* and the Canterbury Aldhelm Scholia'.
[35]Rare vocabulary which is found in both the *Old English Martyrology* and Anglo-Saxon glosses is signalled as such in Rauer, 'The *Old English Martyrology* and Anglo-Saxon Glosses'.
[36]Herzfeld, p. xxxii, 'wherever he tries to build up a longer sentence, he fails signally'.

Þes Iacobus ærest monna Hispanius, ða elreordegan þeode ða syndon on middangeardes westdæle neah þære sunnan setlgonge, **he hi** gelærde to Cristes geleafan, **135**	This James was the first man [to introduce] Spain, the barbarian nations who live in the west of the world near where the sun sets — **he** introduced **them** to the Christian faith.
ðone Datianus se casere seofan gear mid unasegendlicu*m* witum **hine** þreade þæt he Criste wiðsoce, **67**	him [ie. George] the emperor Datianus forced **him** for seven years with unspeakable tortures to renounce Christ
On ðone ðreo ond twentegðan dæg ðæs monðes, **ðæt** bið se sexta worolde dæg, **53**	On the twenty-third day of the month — **that** is the sixth day of the world.

It is difficult to say whether constructions of this type would ever have been regarded as a satisfactory form of Old English prose, but it is in any case interesting to see that many examples of this feature are subsequently smoothed out in the revision of the *Old English Martyrology* which survives in the manuscripts CE.

Also conspicuous is the author's preference for paratactic syntax as a default, which, as Kotzor has pointed out, can partially be attributed to the sequential listing of facts inherent in the martyrological genre.[37] It is true that not all of the syntax is of this paratactic type, and that the more hypotactic passages tend to summarise Latin sources of a syntactially and narratologically more ambitious type. Nevertheless, there are some quite extreme cases of paratactic sequence:

> Ða geseah he sume Godes cyrican. Þa forlet he þa sceap ond arn to þære Godes ciricean. Þa geherde he þær rædan Godes bec. Þa fregn he ænne ealdne mon hwæt þæt wære. Þa cwæþ se ealda mann: 'Hit is monna sawla gestreon, ond þa þeawas ðe mon sceal on mynstre healdan.' Ða eode <he> sona of þære cirican to sumes haliges abbodes mynstre, **136**

> Then he saw a church of God. Then he abandoned the sheep and ran to that church of God. Then he heard God's books read there. Then he asked an old man what that was. Then the old man said: 'It is the treasure of human souls and the customs which are to be upheld in a monastery.' Then he soon went from the church to the monastery of a holy abbot.

Another syntactical feature which seems unusual is the martyrologist's positioning of pronouns. It is again noteworthy that the revised version of the *Old English Martyrology* seems to have edited out some of the more extreme examples:

---

[37]Kotzor, I, 20 and 407; Herzfeld, p. xxxii; see also pp. 30–1 below for modern reactions to the martyrologist's style.

B	ac is wen þæt englas **mid him hit** læddan to Godes neorxnawonge, **122**
C	ac is wen þæt englas **hyt myd heom** læddon to Godes neorxnawange
	but the angels probably took **it with them** to God's paradise

B	(he) het mid monige wite **hi þreagan** from Cristes geleafan, **122**
C	he het **hyg** myd manegum wytum **þreatian** fram Cristes geleafan
	(he) ordered **her** with many tortures **to be forced away** from Christ's faith

B	he het **lædan hi** feor on ðone wudu, **98**
C	he het **hig** feor on þone wudu **lædan**
	he commanded **them to be led** far into the wood

Anacoluthon and recapitulatory constructions are already apparent in the oldest surviving manuscripts A and E, and seem to go back to the earliest version of the text.[38] It is hard to believe that these features could have been considered particularly elegant by the author or his contemporary peers; as the revision of the text shows, his early readers felt the need to improve his language not just in dialectal and lexical terms, but also in terms of syntax. To some extent it would even be fair to say that the text's first editor was the author of the revised CE tradition. The question remains, however, what could have led to language with these syntactical idiosyncrasies being composed and even transmitted, and a number of possible answers suggest themselves: (1) these features could be the result of incomplete authorial editing, that is, circulation of the text before its composition was considered complete by its author; (2) serious difficulties during the translation, encountered by an author who was struggling to summarise long hagiographical texts and translated phrase by phrase, arranging the resulting gobbets in the order in which he translated them; (3) an author not entirely proficient in the target language, such as a non-native speaker of Old English; (4) an author accustomed to working in a medium where idiomatic translation is not necessarily considered to be desirable, in the same way as Anglo-Saxon glossators are known to have tolerated a considerable Latinate element in their choice of Old English vocabulary and syntax.[39] The last two possibilities would also account for some of the exotic lexis found in the *Old English Martyrology* and would

---

[38] For features of this type in A and E, see, for example, **67** (A), **76** (E) and **83** (E).
[39] In interlinear vernacular glossing of Latin texts, for example, anglicised word order tends to be the exception, not the norm; see Crowley, 'Anglicized Word Order'.

probably repay further investigation but, at the present state of research, all possible scenarios still need to be considered.[40]

The text of the *Old English Martyrology*, as it is found in the seven surviving manuscripts, is in many places defective.[41] This is hardly surprising, given a period of 150–250 years of transmission, but another contributing factor should be seen in the unusual vocabulary used by the martyrologist, which can be shown to have caused problems of comprehension already for Anglo-Saxon readers. The editorial principle of *lectio difficilior potior* usually only makes sense if an original text was linguistically particularly difficult to start with, as is the case, for instance, with poetic texts (often characterised by unusual syntax and specialised lexis), or texts with very complex prose syntax. It is therefore interesting to see that the *Old English Martyrology*, for all its pedestrian prose syntax and relatively concrete narrative content, seems to have been a surprisingly difficult text for Anglo-Saxon scribes and readers, and that mainly because of its lexis.[42]

3 Historical and Literary Context

The availability of possible source texts and libraries (as discussed above) is an important criterion in identifying historical contexts which could have produced the *Old English Martyrology*, but other factors also need to be considered.

That some ninth-century Old English prose texts are the product of a concerted translation project directed by King Alfred is suggested by several early medieval authors, including Asser, Ælfric and William of Malmesbury.[43] Although the *Old English Martyrology* is not among the texts explicitly linked by early medieval sources to Alfred's circle, it has often been compared and associated with the ninth-century translations ascribed to Alfred's circle.[44] What could be seen to support a link to an Alfredian milieu, as conventionally understood, is the educational aim of the *Old English Martyrology*, with its wide and seemingly comprehensive hagiographical, geographical and literary range, and its flavour of a systematically compiled encyclopaedia.[45] The conservative and in some ways even antiquarian interests apparent in its selection of materials would also seem to match the backward-looking materials of the texts associated with Alfred's educational programme.[46] Given its mixture of West Saxon and Anglian language features, with a possible Kentish component, it would not seem far-fetched to link the text with an intellectual circle which had Canterbury, Winchester and Worcester as its most

---

[40]Herzfeld, p. xxxii, suggests that the martyrologist's syntactical problems should be seen as an indication of a pre-Alfredian composition, but this seems unconvincing.
[41]See Rauer, 'Errors and Textual Problems', for a survey.
[42]Idiosyncratic lexis, textual error and the resulting editorial problems will be discussed in Rauer, 'Errors and Textual Problems'.
[43]Keynes and Lapidge, trans., *Alfred the Great*, pp. 26–35 and 45.
[44]Rauer, 'The Sources of the *Old English Martyrology*', esp. pp. 98–102; Kotzor, I, 449–55; Bately, 'Old English Prose'; Bately, 'Did King Alfred'; and Pratt, 'Problems of Authorship'; for further reading, see Rauer, 'An Annotated Bibliography', s. v. 'Studies: Date, Historical Background'.
[45]For explicit source references in the text, see Kotzor, I, 252–66; for Latin factoids, see Kotzor, I, 245–8.
[46]Rauer, 'Female Hagiography'.

important centres; that the text is based on Continental, English and Irish sources would, on a very basic level, also match the circle of Mercian, Frankish, Saxon, and Irish collaborators at Alfred's court. Some copies of the *Old English Martyrology* were transmitted side by side with other ninth-century materials.[47] Internal evidence, such as dialectal and lexical similarities, suggests that some ninth-century texts are more closely related than others, and modern commentators have tended to accept the idea of an Alfredian cluster of texts which share the same intellectual origin. As indicated above, further comparative studies, particularly of the language and transmission of the *Old English Martyrology*, the Old English Bede and the Old English translation of Gregory's *Dialogi* ascribed to Wærferth, could be useful for our notion of this cluster of texts.

But Wærferth is not the only ninth-century scholar whose profile is of relevance for the study of the *Old English Martyrology*. Several other persons traditionally associated with King Alfred's circles present either ethnic, linguistic, literary, or biographical characteristics which one could expect to find in the martyrologist. Thus, Plegmund and the priests Wærwulf and Æthelstan were all of Mercian origin; Asser, Grimbald, and John the Old Saxon are all thought to have had scholarly reputations at the time of their selection and could have been able to provide access to foreign textual materials.[48] There are many reasons, therefore, for furthering comparisons between the *Old English Martyrology* and other ninth-century prose texts.

That the *Old English Martyrology* was probably composed sometime between *c.* 800 and *c.* 900 equally allows for an alignment with possible literary contexts earlier in that century. Little is known, for example, about the literary interests or talents of Wærferth, Plegmund, Wærwulf, and Æthelstan *before* they entered Alfredian circles, and about the qualities which highlighted them as candidates for a scholarly advisory board, if such a thing really existed. The question arises whether they would have been acquainted with the Mercian prose traditions of the earlier ninth century, such as those surviving in the Vespasian Psalter glosses, the glosses to Bede's *Historia ecclesiastica*, the Life of Chad, and the Corpus Glossary.[49] The Life of Chad and the glosses to Bede's *Historia ecclesiastica* have obvious thematic parallels with the *Old English Martyrology*, and affinities between the martyrologist's working methods and those at work in glosses and glossaries are still emerging. That

---

[47]Rauer, 'Usage of the *Old English Martyrology*', pp. 141–2.

[48]Asser, *Life of King Alfred*, 77–9; Keynes and Lapidge, trans., *Alfred the Great*, pp. 26–8; Bately, 'Grimbald of St. Bertin's'; *ODNB*, s. vv. 'John the Old Saxon', 'Asser', and 'Grimbald'; and PASE, s. vv. 'Æthelstan', and 'Wærwulf'. For Grimbald, see also Gretsch, 'The Junius Psalter Gloss', pp. 113–19.

[49]Psalter glossing may even have been a school activity; see Gretsch, 'The Junius Psalter Gloss', pp. 87–8; for general background on Mercian psalter glossing, see Sisam, 'Canterbury, Lichfield'; Wilson, 'The Provenance of the Vespasian Psalter Gloss'; and Kuhn, 'The Dialect of the Corpus *Glossary*' for Mercian contributions to the compilation of glossaries. Details of texts regarded as of Anglian or Mercian authorship can be found in Wenisch, *Spezifisch anglisches Wortgut*, pp. 19–82. The hypothesis of an extensive Mercian Schriftsprache dominant throughout ninth-century England, first posited by Vleeskruyer, ed., *The Life of St. Chad*, is now treated with more caution; see Kotzor, I, 30–3 and Rowley, *The Old English Version*, pp. 41–6.

the *Old English Martyrology* is regarded as a Mercian text is based on its dialectal features, but it is interesting that the text also fits very plausibly into the history of Mercian literary production for other reasons. The Canterbury connection of some of the more prominent Mercian productions, such as the Vespasian Psalter glosses and the Corpus Glossary, and Plegmund's later career as archbishop of Canterbury, serve as an important reminder that Mercian literature need not have been produced in the Mercian heartland.[50] If Canterbury had a history of using and producing glosses and glossaries, it is also one of the few places where early legendaries, and rare and obsolete information on the Italian sanctorale, are known to have been available in Anglo-Saxon England.[51] In that sense, Canterbury ticks many boxes in the search for a possible centre which could have produced the *Old English Martyrology*. But an important caveat would be that our knowledge of ninth-century literary Canterbury is better informed than that of other centres. In literary history, the most easily understandable scenario does not always apply.

Nor is it clear that an Alfredian project ever existed in the form in which modern literary historians have hypothesised. How much literal weight should be given to the remarks made by medieval commentators like Asser, Ælfric, and Alfred himself remains a matter of dispute, and it would be difficult to say decisively which ninth-century prose texts could be seen as Alfredian productions, and what the king's personal input would have been for each translation.[52] Malcolm Godden has recently painted an alternative scenario of an early prose production more dissociated from a central figure: 'a variety of prose works, written by various people at different times over the ninth and early tenth centuries and in different contexts, people whom we cannot currently identify, and perhaps never will'.[53]

In that respect, figures like Wærferth, Plegmund, Wærwulf, Æthelstan, and to a lesser extent Grimbald and Asser, who seem to represent good candidates for an identification with the martyrologist, may just conform to a modern predilection for linking the composition of a text to known historical figures or events. There is no reason for ruling out the idea that the martyrologist could have been 'a less well-known figure whom we cannot currently identify, and perhaps never will'.

There are several other, less obvious, scenarios which present themselves as possible historical and intellectual backgrounds which could have produced the *Old English Martyrology*. Early canonical communities, for example. Manuscripts C and D of the *Old English Martyrology* can be linked in the eleventh century with Leofric, bishop of Exeter, and thus to a canonical environment with an interest in translation, lay preaching, and the recovery of traditional materials. CCCC 196, manuscript C of the *Old English Martyrology*, is thought to have been produced as a companion

---

[50]The connection between the *Old English Martyrology* and Canterbury glosses was explored in an unpublished paper by Rusche, 'The *Old English Martyrology* and the Canterbury Aldhelm Scholia'.
[51]Hohler, 'Theodore and the Liturgy', pp. 227–8; for legendaries in Canterbury, see Brown, 'Paris, Bibliothèque Nationale, lat. 10861'.
[52]See Godden, 'Did King Alfred Write Anything?'.
[53]Godden, 'The Alfredian Project and its Aftermath', esp. pp. 119–22; and Godden and Irvine, ed., *The Old English Boethius*, I, 145–6.

volume to CCCC 191 and CCCC 201, pp. 179–272, all from Exeter.[54] CCCC 191 contains a bilingual copy of the Rule of Chrodegang; CCCC 201 the bilingual version of the *Theodulfi Capitula*, an instructional work for parish priests compiled *c.* 800 by Theodulf, bishop of Orléans. Erika Corradini has pointed out that the constellation of texts contained in CCCC 196, 191 and 201 has parallels in similar books produced on the Continent. One of them, Bern, Burgerbibliothek 289, produced in Metz in the early ninth century, similarly juxtaposes a martyrology, a Rule of Chrodegang and the *Theodulfi Capitula*.[55] There is a possibility that the original Rule of Chrodegang, composed in Metz *c.* 755, had reached the community of Christ Church Canterbury under Wulfred (*d.* 832) by the early ninth century.[56] If he used Chrodegang's Rule for the reform of his community, one wonders whether, like his Continental models, he would have regarded a martyrological handbook (in the vernacular or Latin) as an essential tool for the education of his community, particularly one that would present more information than was contained in conventional martyrologies, and one that was backward-looking and easily accessible.

It needs to be stressed that there is no firm evidence which would link the composition of the *Old English Martyrology* to such a background. But it is important to show that a scenario involving a later ninth-century composition is not the only possibility; an earlier ninth-century composition, for example by one of Alfred's Mercian associates before his appointment to Alfred's circles, or an even earlier composition, for example at Wulfred's behest, are also possibilities. Further scenarios could still present themselves. For example, the *Old English Martyrology* presents a very distinctive Irish element in its source profile and thematic interests, and it may still be possible to link this element to other, known, areas of Irish activity in Anglo-Saxon England, particularly in the areas of homiletic writing or the use of biblical commentaries. As another scenario, the question regarding the potential authorship of Cynewulf needs to be addressed. This author is known to have had hagiographical interests, is associated with an Anglian linguistic background, and has been assigned to the ninth century by most commentators.[57] Or, to consider another possibility, it may be the case that the composition of the *Old English Martyrology* is linked to the tradition of the so-called Cotton-Corpus Legendary: this eleventh-century legendary is thought to be descended from a much earlier northern French import, believed to have entered England sometime between the later ninth and the

---

[54]The literature on these volumes and their connection is summarised in Rauer, 'Usage of the *Old English Martyrology*', pp. 129–30.

[55]Corradini, 'Leofric of Exeter', pp. 216–17; Hagen, *Catalogus codicum*, no. 289; Gretsch, 'Æthelthryth of Ely', p. 162; Bertram, ed., *The Chrodegang Rules*, p. 24. It is hard to determine the date at which the *Theodulfi Capitula* entered Anglo-Saxon England; see Sauer, ed., *Theodulfi Capitula* in England, pp. 71–5, and p. 21 for Burgerbibliothek 289.

[56]Langefeld, '*Regula canonicorum* or *Regula monasterialis uitae*?', and Langefeld, ed., *The Old English Version of the Enlarged Rule of Chrodegang*, pp. 15–20; Foot, *Monastic Life*, pp. 58–69; Corradini, 'Leofric of Exeter', pp. 214–23; *ODNB*, s. v. 'Wulfred'; and Brooks, *The Early History of the Church of Canterbury*, pp. 155–71.

[57]Cross, 'Cynewulf's Traditions about the Apostles'; McCulloh, 'Did Cynewulf Use a Martyrology'; Fulk, 'Cynewulf: Canon, Dialect, and Date'.

later tenth centuries.[58] If the precursor of the Cotton-Corpus Legendary and its importation to England could indeed be traced to the ninth rather than the tenth century, a link with a late ninth-century composition of the *Old English Martyrology* (the author of which could conceivably have used that legendary, or one that was related, as a source) would become more interesting.

More general characteristics regarding the authorship of the *Old English Martyrology* remain open. Although male authorship is more likely in view of general Anglo-Saxon patterns of literary production, the text could theoretically have been written by a female author; it could theoretically have been composed by more than one person. The text sections follow a more or less rigid pattern which could easily have been communicated to an author's research assistants or a production committee.[59] The text contains no internal cross-references or other identifying links where one would perhaps expect them. Whatley points out, for example, that Vitalis (**72**), who is given a text section of his own, also appears in the section dedicated to Ursicinus (**236**), anonymously as 'a Christian man'; the two sections are based on the same source, the *Passio S. Geruasii* (*BHL* 3514).[60] Similarly, Valerianus, husband of Caecilia, remains anonymous in his wife's text section (**227**), although he is named in his own (**64**); both sections are based on the *Passio S. Caeciliae* (*BHL* 1495). It could therefore be said that the text sections remain relatively independent of each other. Whether that should be interpreted as a sign of multiple authorship, or a sign of one author's determination to focus on one section at a time, remains open.

Certain phrases occur throughout the text; Alexandria, for example, is called 'the great city of Alexandria' in three of the four sections which refer to it; Carthage is called 'the great city of Carthage' in two out of three sections; but similar phrasing occurs in other texts, and could have been used by more than one author. Other consistent or inconsistent phraseology could be listed here, but the fact remains that inconsistent usage can also arise from a single author's work, and consistent phraseological features could also represent the shared language of more than one author, or the language of an Anglo-Saxon editor standardising the work of several assistants. A connected question, namely whether the *Old English Martyrology* could have been accumulated over a long period of time, by more than one author, is similarly difficult to answer.

Several text sections stand out as particularly short and unhelpful. There is a suggestion that these sections are unfinished, and it may be that the martyrologist set out in his task hoping to find detailed narrative information regarding all of his saints, but was in some cases disappointed in his search for relevant literature. It is mainly these shorter sections which lead to the current assumption that the composition of the *Old English Martyrology* began with a list of saints' names and feasts (such as

---

[58] Jackson and Lapidge, 'The Contents of the Cotton-Corpus Legendary', p. 134; see also Kotzor, I, 277–8, who points to the fact that the Cotton-Corpus Legendary also preserves the lives of Bertinus, Audomarus and Winnocus, and the 'Legimus' sermon, which are likely to have been among the martyrologist's sources. See also above n. 48 for Grimbald's origin.

[59] For a survey of the formulae used, see Kotzor, I, 409–21.

[60] Whatley, s. vv. 'Gervasius et Protasius'.

could be found in one or more martyrologies or calendars) which were then fleshed out with narrative material derived from other sources.

Some features seem to indicate that the sections were not composed in a linear way, that is, not in the order in which they are preserved in the text. In a small number of cases, the martyrologist seems to be influenced by information which he probably encountered in his work on later text sections. For example, two separate personages called Datianus are referred in the text, one as the persecutor of Vincent and Eulalia (**31, 234**), the other as the persecutor of George and Alexandria (**67, 71**). In his entry for Vincent, the martyrologist refers to the persecutor as 'emperor Datianus', 'Datianus se casere'. But only in the Latin hagiography of George and Alexandria is the man of that name referred to as an emperor.[61] If the martyrologist had got that idea from the Latin texts used for his entries on George and Alexandria, the suggestion would be that, in composing a text section which occurs earlier in the text, he was using material which he needed for a text section placed further towards the end of the text. Given the scale of the text in question, it would not seem surprising if the martyrologist fleshed out his text sections in the order in which he accessed their sources, rather than in the order in which the sections occur in the text, which would instead have required him to keep going back to the same source texts. This also means that the martyrologist would not necessarily have needed repeated access to his source texts, but could conceivably and without major problems have collected materials in more than one literary centre.

The *Old English Martyrology* has been aligned with other examples of the martyrological genre, and it is true that it shares many characteristics with Latin martyrologies: the skeletal structure of each section, which tends to provide information about the name of the saint and associated figures, his or her geographical origin, place and nature of the martyrdom, and details of any place of burial.[62] The arrangement of the entries by feastday, and the fact that not all days are allocated a text section whilst other have several, are also common characteristics of martyrological texts. But the *Old English Martyrology* goes beyond what is normally contained in a martyrology: many entries are concerned with time measurement and cosmology, interests which are frequently found in calendars.[63] Like the *Old English Martyrology*, the calendar in Oxford, Bodleian Library, Digby 63, for example, presents parallels for the birth of Adam, astronomical and cosmological events, feasts of the Easter cycle, the beginning of summer and winter, and the length of day and night in a given month (e.g. 'nox horas .xiiii. dies x', end of February), in sum, a mix of information also reminiscent of early modern almanacs.[64]

The narrative detail of the *Old English Martyrology*, with its frequent direct speeches (as one can find in saints' lives), and its habit of interpolating explanations

---

[61] From a historical point of view, neither Datianus was in fact an emperor; see de Gaiffier, '*Sub Daciano praeside*' and Kotzor, I, 287 and 302.
[62] Kotzor, I, 290–311 and 'The Latin Tradition of Martyrologies'; McCulloh, 'Historical Martyrologies'.
[63] Rauer, 'Usage of the *Old English Martyrology*', pp 132–3. For further secondary reading, see also Rauer, 'An Annotated Bibliography', s. v. 'Studies: Hagiography, Liturgy, Function'.
[64] For further discussion, see Rauer, 'Usage', pp. 132–3; on almanacs, see Chapman, 'Reforming Time'.

of difficult vocabulary in a second language, are also not often encountered in martyrologies; as a consequence, the communal or ceremonial reading which other martyrologies experienced seems less likely in the case of the *Old English Martyrology*.[65] It seems doubtful that the sanctorale of the *Old English Martyrology* reflects the liturgical practice of any single Anglo-Saxon religious house. Whatever the martyrologist's aim was, there can be no doubt that he must have used one or more Latin martyrologies as a model and starting point, but went well beyond a martyrological scope in the composition of his text.

If the *Old English Martyrology* presents features from more than one genre, such as martyrology, calendar, saints' life, and glossary, its usage may have been similarly versatile, both at the point of composition and during its long transmission. Herzfeld suggested that the text was intended as a collection of materials for preachers, and although there are signs that the text was used by homilists, it would be difficult to show that it had been intended and composed specifically for such a readership.[66] Similarly, the modest evidence that there is for the usage of the *Old English Martyrology* seems to suggest that the text was used by relatively competent Latinists, but this again need not mean that it was intended or composed for such a group.[67] Ado thought of his own ninth-century martyrology as a one-volume devotional reader intended for clerics who could not manage to read more extensively, and in that sense the collection of materials in the *Old English Martyrology* compares very well with its compact format.[68]

The inclusive approach to the selection of saints, which has already been mentioned, makes it hard to identify geographical points of gravity. Similarly problematic for enquiries into the text's historical origin is the fact that its thematic focus would seem to fit into a vast multitude of possible backgrounds. The most common nouns used in the text relate to the saints themselves, their persecutors, feastdays and martyrdoms, as could be predicted for a text with a martyrological focus. But particularly common are also references to the Holy Spirit ('gast', *c.* 60 occurrences), heaven ('heofon', *c.* 50 occurrences), pagans ('hæþen', *c.* 50 occurrences), miracles ('wundor', *c.* 50 occurrences), night ('niht', *c.* 50 references), belief ('geleafan', *c.* 50 occurrences), prayer ('gebed', *c.* 40 occurrences) and angels ('engel', *c.* 40 occurrences); Kotzor also pointed to the frequent miraculous appearance of voices from heaven, angels leading souls to the next world, doves, pleasant smells and heavenly lights.[69] It is interesting that even in very short text sections, which give very little information on a saint, the martyrologist frequently reassures the reader of the saints' general association with miracles, either during their lifetime, or posthumously at their place of burial: **7, 36, 72, 81, 98, 129, 141,**

---

[65] But see Dolbeau, 'Notes sur l'organisation' for other hybrid texts and books combining features of the martyrology, the saint's life, and the calendar. For speech patterns in the text, see Rauer, 'Direct Speech, Intercession, and Prayer'.
[66] Herzfeld, p. xi; and Rauer, 'Usage of the *Old English Martyrology*'.
[67] Rauer, 'Usage of the *Old English Martyrology*', pp. 135–7.
[68] de Gaiffier, 'De l'usage', pp. 57–8.
[69] See Kotzor, I, 408–9. I am currently preparing a comprehensive motif index for the *Old English Martyrology*.

171, **201**. Also conspicuous are a number of long appeals, in the form of prayers, given by George (**67**), Christopher (**73**), Marina (**122**), and Cyricus and Iulitta (**127**).[70] Shortly before their martyrdom, these saints request reassurance from God that future believers appealing to them (in case of need, danger or distress) will be rewarded. These prayers may have been expanded from their source, and seem to have been particularly important to the author as examples of potential interaction between worshippers and saints, notwithstanding the somewhat suspect character of these prayers in theological terms. In sum, all of these characteristics tell us something about the author's interest in numinous revelations, or the 'spectacularly miraculous', as David Rollason put it. But such an interest in the miraculous can be suspected to have been at work in many religious houses in Anglo-Saxon England, where audiences and readers had to be enthused for their interaction with the saintly world.[71]

4 Manuscripts

Six medieval manuscripts (ABCDEF) and one early modern witness (C*), survive of the *Old English Martyrology*.[72] All manuscripts are fragments; A, B, C, and E seem to have been accidentally fragmented in the course of transmission, whereas the text appears to have been left incomplete intentionally in D and F. The fact that all but two text copies are acephalous has made it difficult to determine the intended beginning of the text, which may be 25 December (based on internal evidence and as presented in D), or 1 January, for which there are also internal indications; it may also be the case that the text was formulated to allow either of these two dates to function as the opening of the text.[73] All manuscripts except for C* and F present the same characteristic layout of the text, which allocates a new line and large initial for the opening of most text sections.[74]

Put together, the manuscripts present contents for almost the entire course of the year, except for apparently lost parts from 25 January to ?27 February and perhaps also late December. It is hard to speculate what could have been contained in any lost sections, but arguments have been put forward for a number of saints with feastdays in the relevant months: Agatha, Brigida, Candida, Dorothy, Juliana, Scholastica, Victoria, Crispinus, Eutychianus, Fructuosus, Polycarp, Polychronius, Valentinus

---

[70] For further discussion of these passages, see Rauer, 'Direct Speech, Intercession, and Prayer'. On the general overlap between the genres of prayers and charms or magic, see the interesting studies by Fisher, 'Genre, Prayers and the Anglo-Saxon Charms' and 'Writing Charms', esp. pp. 7–37.
[71] Rollason, Review of Kotzor, p. 224.
[72] Rauer, 'An Annotated Bibliography', s. v. 'Manuscripts'; for the conspectus of manuscript contents, see the same website, s. v. 'An Index of Reference Nos., Saints, Feasts and Manuscript Contents'. For the sake of convenience, this edition uses the sigla which have been used since the first critical edition, see Herzfeld, pp. xi–xviii.
[73] 'On þone forman dæig on geare', **1** (25 December); 'Þæt bið se æresta geares monað mid Romwarum ond mid us', **8a** (1 January); Rauer, 'Usage of the *Old English Martyrology*', pp. 143–4; and Tupper, 'Anglo-Saxon Dæg-Mæl', pp. 208–12.
[74] See the facsimile pages of individual manuscripts cited below; F has a thematic arrangment and C* is an early modern transcript.

Interamnensis, Valentinus Presbiter, Vedastus, and the Purification of Mary.[75] These saints (and possibly others with feastdays in the relevant portions of the liturgical year) may have been included in the original *Old English Martyrology*.

Since detailed descriptions already exist for all manuscripts, only brief introductions are given below, together with updated bibliographical references.

A: London, BL Add. 23211 (c. 871x899), fol. 2; Ker no. 127; Gneuss no. 282
A is a damaged fragment which contains only a short sequence of text from the *Old English Martyrology*: 14, 18, 21 and 23 April.[76] The importance of this witness lies in the fact that it represents one of the two earliest manuscripts of the *Old English Martyrology*, and seems to have been copied not long after the presumptive composition of the text in the ninth century. In this fragment, the text is transmitted alongside computistical verse and genealogies of West Saxon and East Saxon kings; the copying of this manuscript has conventionally been dated to 871 x 899.[77] David Dumville has urged caution, however, emphasising that the dating is based on the 'not wholly conclusive evidence of its text of the West Saxon Genealogical Regnal List to the reign of Alfred of Wessex (it could in principle be later than his time)'.[78]

The few fragmented entries of the *Old English Martyrology* contained in this manuscript are in any case not thought to be directly copied from the original o, or the archetype z.[79] Comparison of its content and phrasing with those found in the later manuscripts shows an overwhelming agreement with the later tradition. The language of the fragment (copied by a single scribe) can be regarded as largely Anglian, but Kotzor importantly points to an admixture of West Saxon features, possibly also a small number of Kentish characteristics.[80] A mixture of Anglian and West Saxon features with possible traces of Kentish features has also been postulated for the presumptive original Old English text, and the assumption is that manuscript *A* represents a relatively accurate line of transmission. Because its early phonology and orthography differ so much from those of the later and more complete manuscripts, most editors have chosen to edit the entire fragment separately, a tradition which is followed here (see Appendix 1 below). The fragment was used, in post-medieval times, as a paste-down in an octavo volume, and suffered truncation on three sides. The written space is damaged particularly on one side.[81]

---

[75]See Rauer, 'Female Hagiography'; Lapidge, 'Acca of Hexham', p. 39n; Rauer, 'The Sources of the *Old English Martyrology*', p. 94; and Whatley (under the names of the saints mentioned).

[76]For the most detailed assessment of this fragment of the *Old English Martyrology*, see Kotzor, I, 43–55; for more recent secondary literature and a complete bibliography, see Rauer, 'An Annotated Bibliography', s. v. 'Manuscripts'.

[77]For a summary of dating criteria, see Kotzor, I, 52–54. More recent discussions include Dumville, 'The West Saxon Genealogical Regnal List', pp. 2–3 and Dumville, 'English Script in the Second Half of the Ninth Century'.

[78]Dumville, 'English Script in the Second Half of the Ninth Century', p. 310.

[79]Kotzor, I, 143 and 444; see also the *stemma codicum* below, p. 24.

[80]Kotzor, I, 323–4, 396–405 and 445–6, and Sisam, 'An Early Fragment', pp. 216–17.

[81]A microfiche facsimile of this manuscript can now be found in Doane, *Saints' Lives, Martyrologies*; for facsimile pages see Kotzor, I, 46, and Dumville, 'The West Saxon Genealogical Regnal List', p. 3 (genealogy only). Codicological and palaeographical descriptions can be found in Kotzor, I, 45–52,

INTRODUCTION

B: London, BL Cotton Julius A. x (s. x/xi), fols 44–175; Ker no. 161; Gneuss no. 338
B represents the most extensive of the surviving manuscripts of the *Old English Martyrology*, containing 229 text sections (31 December to 25 January, ?27 February to 13 March, 18 March to 24 June, 2 July to 11 November; the textual gaps are due to missing leaves).[82] B presents a text which is thought to be closer to the original than the revised version transmitted in C and E. For this reason, B has formed the *Leithandschrift* for the editions by Herzfeld and Kotzor, and is also used as such here. It should be remembered, however, that B too has its textual problems, some of which can be solved with recourse to the CE branch of transmission. The other contents of this manuscript were added in early modern times, and provide no information on the codicological context for this copy of the *Old English Martyrology*, but internal evidence points to Glastonbury as a possible provenance or origin for B.[83] Kotzor was able to distinguish four different pre-Conquest hands responsible for the copying of the original text (Ba, Bb, Bc, Bd), and two further pre-Conquest hands inserting corrections (Be, Bf); dialectal differences between the scribes were also traced by Kotzor.[84] The manuscript contains numerous marginalia from medieval and early modern times which provide clues concerning the post-Conquest reception of the *Old English Martyrology*.[85]

C: CCCC 196 (s. xi², Exeter), pp. 1–110; Ker no. 47; Gneuss no. 62
C contains 207 sections of the *Old English Martyrology* (19 March to 21 December), and, like B, represents one of the more complete witnesses; the text was probably copied by a single scribe.[86] C is thought to belong to a branch of transmission which presents an early revision of the text, and details of this stylistic, lexical and dialectal revision can be identified through comparison of AB and CE. Although most variants in C seem to be due to this revision, it must not be forgotten that C also preserves a number of readings which appear to be original and which can be used to highlight textual problems in B. The codex, which has been associated with Bishop Leofric, also contains the *Vindicta Saluatoris* (pp. 111–22) and was probably produced as a companion volume to CCCC 191 (containing the Bilingual Rule of Chrodegang) and CCCC 201, pp. 179–272 (containing the *Capitula Theodulfi*, and a fragment of Usuard, *Martyrologium*). Most of the recent literature on this manuscript has

---

Doane, *Saints' Lives, Martyrologies*, pp. 1–4, and Ker, p. 160.
[82]For a systematic description of this manuscript, see Kotzor I, 56–74, and Doane, *Saints' Lives, Martyrologies*, pp. 37–50. Rauer, 'An Annotated Bibliography', s. v. 'Manuscripts' lists related secondary literature. For a facsimile page, see Kotzor, I, 60–3; and Roberts, *Guide to Scripts*, p. 72; the entire text can now be found on microfiche facsimile in Doane, *Saints' Lives, Martyrologies*.
[83]Rauer, 'Usage of the *Old English Martyrology*', pp. 130–1.
[84]Kotzor, I, 58–71, and 404. Rob Getz points out (pers. comm.) that scribe *Ba* distinguishes himself with a number of phonological features which could be interpreted as south-eastern, including æ before nasal, see Campbell, *Old English Grammar*, §193d. Unfortunately, no connection can at this stage be made between *Ba*'s phonology and the origin of *B* or the *Old English Martyrology*.
[85]Kotzor, I, 56–7; Rauer, 'Usage of the *Old English Martyrology*', pp. 137–8; Ker, p. 206.
[86]See Kotzor, I, 75–88 for a very detailed palaeographical analysis of this manuscript; cp. also Treharne's description for the project *The Production and Use of English Manuscripts 1060–1220*; Rauer, 'An Annotated Bibliography', s. v. 'Manuscripts' lists related secondary literature.

concentrated on the relationship between these manuscripts and possible lay or parish usage. An online digital version of this witness has recently been made accessible to researchers.[87]

C*: *London, BL Cotton Vitellius D. vii. (s. xvi), fols 131r–132r*
C* is an early modern transcript made by John Joscelyn (1529–1603) of parts of manuscript C.[88] The transcript is contained in Joscelyn's notebook of transcriptions known as the *Collectanea Joscellini* and consists of 24 text sections which are transcribed wholly or partially: The End of March, The Beginning of April, The Beginning of May, The Beginning of Summer, The End of May, The Beginning of June, Summer Solstice, The End of June, The Beginning of July, The End of July, The Beginning of August, The End of August, The Beginning of September, The End of September, The Beginning of October, The End of October, The Beginning of November, The Beginning of Winter, The End of November, The Beginning of December, and 17 March.[89] The last entry, that for St Patrick, is transcribed twice and is of particular importance, as this text section survives in no other witness. Joscelyn is thought to have copied this entry from an already loose leaf in C which was subsequently lost.[90] It was Kotzor who first recognised the connection between Joscelyn's transcript and C.

D: CCCC 41 (s. xi^1 – xi med., prob. S England, prov. Exeter by s. $xi^{3/4}$), pp. 122–32; Ker no. 32; Gneuss no. 39
Manuscript D contains only a brief sequence of text sections (25 to 31 December) and is perhaps the most idiosyncratic of the six witnesses. The text of the *Old English Martyrology* is copied (together with other texts) probably by single scribe into the margins of an Old English Translation of Bede's *Historia ecclesiastica*.[91] Previous commentators have perhaps not sufficiently emphasised how careless the copying appears to be: although all manuscripts present their own textual problems, D presents the greatest density of errors, which range from missing initials and chaotic corrections to textual lacunae, defective concordance, missing endings, nonce words, calendarial confusion and names which are garbled to the point of causing

---

[87] *Parker Library on the Web*, http://parkerweb.stanford.edu; a printed facsimile page can also be found in Kotzor, I, 78.
[88] *ODNB*, s. v. 'Joscelin, John'; secondary literature relating to this manuscript is listed in Rauer, 'An Annotated Bibliography', s. v. 'Manuscripts'. See also Kotzor, I, 75, 87–8; Kotzor, 'St. Patrick in the Old English "Martyrology"; and Page, 'The Lost Leaf of MS. C.C.C.C. 196' regarding its relationship with C.
[89] See Sanders Gale, 'John Joscelyn's Notebook', pp. 216–18; and Rauer, 'Usage of the *Old English Martyrology*', pp. 139–40.
[90] Sisam, Review of Kotzor, p. 68, speculates that the leaf may have been loosened by 'constant thumbing in Glastonbury'.
[91] Kotzor, I, 89–108, presents a detailed description of the *Old English Martyrology* sections in this manuscript; see also Jolly, 'On the Margins of Orthodoxy' for a recent survey of the codicological and literary context. Rauer, 'An Annotated Bibliography', s. v. 'Manuscripts' lists related secondary literature. For the unusual layout and digital images, see now the *Parker Library on the Web*, http://parkerweb.stanford.edu; a facsimile page can also be found in Kotzor, I, 95.

misunderstandings.[92] Despite its poor standards of copying, D is an important witness, as it alone preserves the text sections for the Christmas Octave. The relationship between D and other witnesses remains unclear, as there is no overlapping content between D and other witnesses; D is for this reason usually excluded from the *stemma*. Recent research on this witness has focused on the thematic or generic connections between the marginalia, several of which may point to an Irish component in their composition or transmission.[93] The codex is one of the books given to Exeter by Bishop Leofric.

E: London, BL Add. 40165 A.2, fols. 6–7; Ker no. 132; Gneuss no. 298
E represents a badly damaged, short fragment of the *Old English Martyrology*;[94] part of its text was lost when the top part of the written space was cut down to a smaller size. The manuscript was in medieval times also used as a paste-down, and much of the written space was damaged and made partly illegible when glue or a similar substance was applied.[95] The fragment contains only eleven entries of the *Old English Martyrology*, copied by a single original scribe (Ea), with corrections in what seems to be a second hand (Eb); the text sections are those for 2 and 3 May, Rogation Days, and 5, 6, 7, 8, 9 and 10 May. It was Celia Sisam who discovered the manuscript and first noted that, notwithstanding its minimal length, the text preserved in E is important in establishing several original readings, mainly by supporting readings in C against B.[96] The survival of E is also important on account of its late ninth- or early tenth-century date of production, which, together with A, confirms a ninth-century composition of the *Old English Martyrology*.[97] The linguistic characteristics of the text fragment preserved in *E* can be regarded as largely Anglian, although West Saxon and possibly Kentish features are also attested.[98] Because the language of the fragment differs substantially in its phonology and orthography from the later and more substantial manuscripts which preserve the bulk of the *Old English Martyrology*, E has several times been edited separately, which is also the case here (see Appendix 2 below).

F: London, BL Harley 3271 (s. xi¹), fol 92v; Ker no. 239; Gneuss no. 435
The text of the *Old English Martyrology* contained in F consists of parts of two short entries only, 9 May (The Beginning of Summer) and 7 November (The Beginning of

---

[92]See Commentary below, sections 1–7.
[93]See particularly Olsen, 'Thematic Affinities'; and Jolly, 'On the Margins of Orthodoxy'; for a recent study of the use of this manuscript, see Rowley, *The Old English Version*, pp. 164–73.
[94]For the fullest description, see Kotzor, I, 109–17, Sisam, 'An Early Fragment', and Doane, *Saints' Lives, Martyrologies*, pp. 5–13. A facsimile page can be found in Kotzor, I, 111, and the entire manuscript is now available in manuscript microfiche in Doane, *Saints' Lives, Martyrologies*. Secondary reading is listed in Rauer, 'An Annotated Bibliography', s. v. 'Manuscripts'.
[95]Ker, pp. 163–4.
[96]See the Commentary section, and the *stemma codicum* on p. 24; Sisam, 'An Early Fragment', and Kotzor, I, 26–30, for an assessment of Sisam's work.
[97]Kotzor, I, 115–16.
[98]Kotzor, I, 323–4, 396–405; Sisam, 'An Early Fragment', 214–17.

Winter), copied by a single hand.[99] Both of these text sections survive in several other manuscripts, and F is therefore of modest value for the reconstruction of the text. The manuscript is, however, an important indicator for the usage and codicological context in which the *Old English Martyrology* was transmitted.[100] It is interesting to see that this manuscript juxtaposes two text sections which are situated far apart in the *Old English Martyrology*, and it is clear that their position within Harley 3271 is linked to their thematic content, since in that manuscript they are preceded and followed by other items which also concern themselves with chronology and the sequence of months and seasons.[101] In the *Old English Martyrology*, the two entries are preceded by an introductory formula which links the information given to a day of the month ('On the ninth day of the month is the beginning of summer'; 'On the seventh day of the month is the beginning of winter'); this formula is not attached to the entries in Harley 3271, as the surrounding texts have no calendarial arrangement. A Winchester origin has been suggested for this manuscript, whose relationship with other manuscripts remains unclear; F is therefore excluded from the *stemma* here.

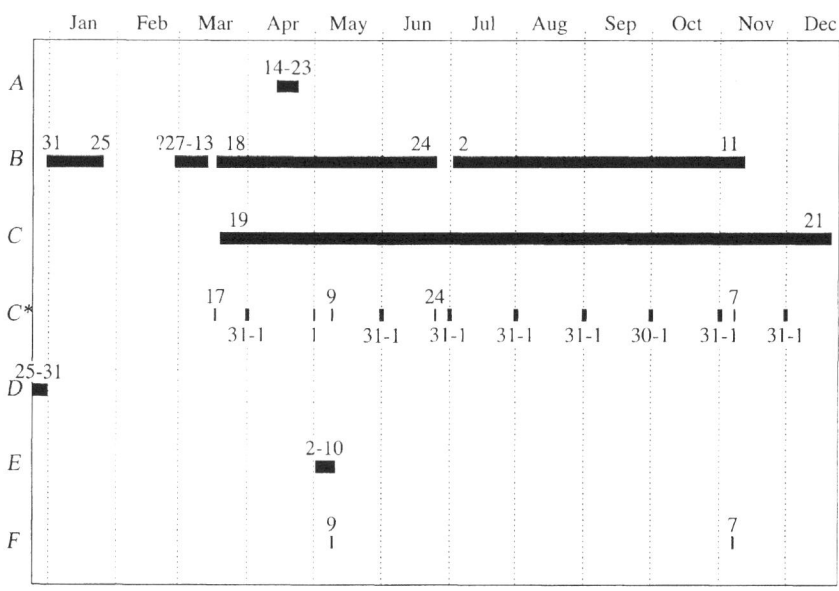

---

[99] Previously edited in Henel, 'Altenglischer Mönchsaberglaube'. Since this edition is now relatively inaccessible, the text of F is presented separately in Appendix 3 below. The manuscript was known to Kotzor, without being classified by him as a separate witness, see Kotzor, I, 3n. The *DOE* refers to F under the name 'Mart 6 (Henel)'; it is listed as B.19.6 in Frank and Cameron, *A Plan for the Dictionary of Old English*.

[100] See Rauer, 'An Annotated Bibliography', s. v. 'Manuscripts'.

[101] A detailed list of its contents can be found in Chardonnens, 'London, British Library, Harley 3271', pp. 28–34.

INTRODUCTION

As the diagram of manuscript contents demonstrates, B and C represent the two most important witnesses in terms of textual extent.[102] Following her discovery of E, Sisam corrected Herzfeld's *stemma codicum* to the one on which this edition is based.[103] The current hypothesis is that there are two main branches of transmission (AB and CE), both derived from lost hyparchetypes (x and y) sharing a lost common ancestor z, which is not thought to have been the original (o). The hypothesis which was first put forward by Sisam is based on shared readings and errors, and was corroborated in Kotzor's detailed comparison of variants.[104]

It is important to stress that the relationships between the witnesses need not be direct; further copies could have functioned as intermediaries. An eleventh-century booklist contained in CCCC 367 refers to a text of the *Old English Martyrology* apparently kept at Worcester, which could represent a copy unknown to modern scholarship.[105]

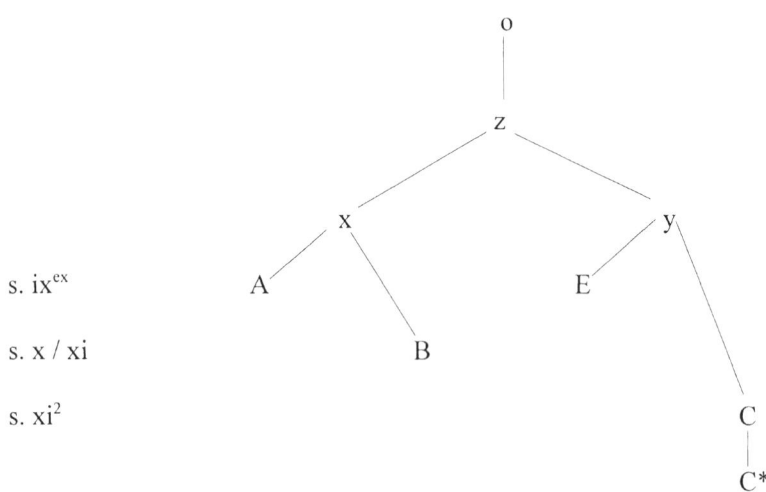

One of the most interesting features of the *Old English Martyrology* and its transmission is the notion that it underwent an early and major revision (resulting in the branch represented by CE), which seems to have gone far beyond the normal degree of reinterpretation inherent in the manual copying of medieval texts. The text presented in CE is frequently clearer in style, often edits out difficult lexis and clumsy syntax, and has a greater West Saxon dialectal component in its language than the tradition preserved in AB.[106] Several revised features are shared by both C and E; the revision is therefore thought to have occurred before the production of E (and thus

---

[102]The diagram is adapted from Kotzor, I, 167.
[103]Sisam, 'An Early Fragment'; see also Kotzor, I, 26–30 for an assessment of Sisam's work.
[104]Kotzor, I, 118–44.
[105]Lapidge, 'Surviving Booklists from Anglo-Saxon England', pp. 62–4; and Wilson, *The Lost Literature of Medieval England*, pp. 81–2.
[106]Kotzor, I, 133–65. To what extent this stylistic and dialectal revision resembles later revisions of other ninth-century Old English prose texts, such as the Old English translations of Bede's *Historia ecclesiastica* and Gregory's *Dialogi*, has not yet been explored.

at an early stage), but the process of West Saxonisation seems to have progressed further in C. As a consequence of this revision, the CE tradition is less prone to misunderstandings by the reader, but also represents a text further removed from the presumed original and the Latin source material.[107] It is hard to speculate on the possible historical context for such a revision. Given how early this redaction was apparently undertaken, it is worth considering whether the author himself, or persons in the author's circle, were responsible for producing a revised version, perhaps as a planned part of the translation project, which could have consisted of a first stage of translation from Latin, where accuracy was an important criterion, followed by a second stage of editing and smoothing over of the text in the new target language. Such a scenario, which places the two versions close together, however, has to deal with the fact that the revision in several places appears to have problems understanding the original text, and presents reinterpretations of the text which are in themselves elegant, but have only little to do with the older Old English version or the Latin sources. In other words, the communication between the original author and the reviser seems to have been problematic at least in some ways, and for this reason it is perhaps unlikely that the author himself or a person in his closer literary or linguistic environment is responsible for the revision. It is important to bear in mind that the revision could have been triggered either by dissatisfaction with the sometimes very difficult lexis, syntax and style of the first version, or by the needs of a new audience, or indeed by both factors. A redaction of an Anglo-Saxon text need not be linked to a historical movement known to modern scholarship, and could have been motivated by nothing more than the initiative of a single reader.

This raises the interesting question of which version should be regarded as the real *Old English Martyrology*. It is clear that a text based on B as a *Leithandschrift*, like the one presented here and in previous editions, is closer to the Latin sources, and therefore to the intentions of the author of o.[108] If the revised version really does originate from an environment which was no longer in touch with the author of the original, the revised version has to be regarded as derivative. Given that the two versions are the same for long stretches of text, a separate edition of the CE tradition is probably not justified, although its deviations from the AB tradition certainly present interesting areas for further study.

5 Previous Editions and Editorial Policy

Modern interest in the text of the *Old English Martyrology* started early, often concentrating on the non-hagiographical text sections (especially those related to Anglo-Saxon time measurement and medieval English historiography). Thus, early partial transcripts were made by John Joscelyn (1529–1603, from C) and Francis Junius (1591–1677, from B and C).[109] A complete text of the *Old English Martyrology* was assembled for the first time in 1869 by Thomas Oswald Cockayne

---

[107]For examples, see Rauer, 'Errors and Textual Problems'.
[108]Kotzor, I, 144–65.
[109]Kotzor, I, 9–12; for more recent literature on Joscelyn, see above nn. 88–9; for a contextualisation of Junius' transcriptions, which were intended to aid Old English lexicography, see Dekker, 'That Most Elaborate One'.

(1809–1873), although this publication too resembles a transcript more than a critical edition.[110] Cockayne's text did not draw on the manuscripts E and F, and presented no systematic collation of the manuscripts that were known to Cockayne. A particular focus of his publication was source study, which, despite Cockayne's overestimation of Eastern influences, led to many correct source identifications still regarded as valid today. Cockayne recognised the ninth-century date of the text and posited a link to Alfredian circles, referring to the *Old English Martyrology* as 'King Ælfred's Book of Martyrs'.[111] Cockayne's edition leaves a very eccentric impression today, but its influence should not be underestimated; it was Cockayne's text which was used by Eduard Sievers for his phonological and morphological work, by Thomas Northcote Toller for his *Dictionary of Anglo-Saxon* (1882–98, based on the work of Joseph Bosworth), and by John Clark Hall for his *Concise Anglo-Saxon Dictionary* (1894).[112] The *Supplement* to Bosworth and Toller's Dictionary (1908–21) was already based on a new edition of the *Old English Martyrology* which could be said to be the first critical edition, namely that undertaken by Georg Herzfeld for the Early English Text Society (1900), although that editor too remained unaware of E and F.[113] Herzfeld's edition was seen in the years following its publication as something of a curate's egg, but it would be fair to say that it did not deserve the critical reaction it received and still represents a considerable achievement, given the research tools available to scholars working at the time.[114] Without the help of the *Bibliotheca Hagiographia Latina* (published 1899–1901), Herzfeld nevertheless identified an impressive number of Latin texts which seemed to resemble sections of the *Old English Martyrology* in content and wording.[115] Although his linguistic and editorial approach was in many ways unsystematic, Herzfeld also delivered a good number of informed textual conjectures, not all of which have so far received the necessary attention. Herzfeld correctly identified many corrupt passages in the text, and attempted relatively useful emendations. He also speculated about the possible use of the text by homilists, an idea which has more recently received support from emerging links with homiletic texts, traced with the help of the *Fontes Anglo-Saxonici* project.

The edition published by Günter Kotzor as an Abhandlung of the Bayerische Akademie der Wissenschaften (1981) was based on his doctoral dissertation and can certainly be regarded as exemplary for the time at which it was published, both in its careful detail and the wide range of textual aspects it covers. Particularly systematic

---

[110]Cockayne, ed., *The Shrine: A Collection of Occasional Papers on Dry Subjects*, with editions of A, B, C (pp. 46–156) and D (pp. 29–33). A fascinating biographical account of Cockayne can be found in Van Arsdall, *Medieval Herbal Remedies*, pp. 1–34. For a list of incomplete editions, see Rauer, 'An Annotated Bibliography', s. v. 'Editions and Translations'.

[111]Kotzor, I, 12–14.

[112]Sievers, *Angelsächsische Grammatik*, p. 270, and see above, n. 15 for 'Miscellen zur angelsächsischen Grammatik', p. 299; Bosworth and Toller, *An Anglo-Saxon Dictionary*, p. xi; and Hall, *A Concise Anglo-Saxon Dictionary*, p. xi.

[113]Toller, *An Anglo-Saxon Dictionary Supplement*, p. iii; Herzfeld, ed., *An Old English Martyrology*.

[114]For reviews of Herzfeld's edition, see Rauer, 'An Annotated Bibliography', s. v. 'Reviews'. See Kotzor, I, 5–6 and 16–23, for a detailed summary and critique of Herzfeld's work.

[115]Herzfeld, pp. xxxvi–xlii, presents a list of sources which is now largely superseded, but represented a great step forward in the study of the *Old English Martyrology*.

and to this day not superseded are Kotzor's palaeographical and codicological examinations of the manuscripts and scribal hands, and his work on the language of the text, which included systematic studies on dialectal features, vocabulary, and phonology.[116] Kotzor also identified a good number of further sources and produced the first stylistic studies of the text. It is unfortunate that Kotzor's editorial work and Cross's source work coincided, so that in the reconstruction of his text Kotzor was not able to draw on the full range of Latin sources which were then being identified by Cross, who in turn was unable to use Kotzor's accurate text.

The need for a new edition of the *Old English Martyrology* at this stage arises from the substantial amount of research which has been undertaken since the publication of Kotzor's edition. Cross's work on the Latin sources of the text has furthered modern knowledge of the text considerably. Consulting vast numbers of unprinted versions of Latin saints' lives, Cross was able to identify not only related source texts, but particular versions of such texts, which testifies to the unusually close translation technique of the martyrologist.[117]

Since the completion of Kotzor's editorial work, many important new research tools have become available, several of them electronic. The availability of a searchable *Dictionary of Old English Corpus* has greatly facilitated lexical, morphological and syntactical comparison.[118] The ongoing *Dictionary of Old English* project is able to provide authoritative interpretation and contextualisation of at least part of the text's vocabulary. The searchable corpus of Latin material accessible through the electronic *Acta Sanctorum* and *Patrologia Latina* databases have similarly contributed to a refining of previously known Latin sources.[119] The many new editions and related publications which have emerged in the field of Anglo-Saxon saints' lives since the early 1980s can now be controlled with the help of the compendious 'Acta Sanctorum' by Gordon Whatley, the product of another collaborative research probject, *Sources of Anglo-Saxon Literary Culture*.[120] Other more recent developments in hagiographical research include new editions of Anglo-Saxon litanies and calendars, both published by the Henry Bradshaw Society, and a supplement volume to the *Bibliotheca Hagiographia Latina*.[121] The electronic database produced by the project *Fontes Anglo-Saxonici* has for the first time collected all source references to the *Old English Martyrology* in one place, facilitating access and enabling fresh searches and comparisons.[122] Publications on the text have tended in recent decades to focus on individual sections of text rather than the *Old English Martyrology* as a whole, and a comprehensive new bibliography

---

[116] Kotzor, I, 43–117.
[117] See esp. Cross, 'On the Library' and 'The Latinity' and his publications cited in the Bibliography below. For a recent study of the martyrologist's translation skills, see Rauer, 'Errors and Textual Problems'.
[118] diPaolo Healey, ed., *Dictionary of Old English Corpus*.
[119] *Acta Sanctorum* at http://acta.chadwyck.co.uk and *Patrologia Latina* at http://pld.chadwyck.co.uk
[120] Whatley, 'Acta Sanctorum'.
[121] Lapidge, ed., *Anglo-Saxon Litanies of the Saints*; Rushforth, ed., *Saints in English Kalendars before A.D. 1100*.
[122] Rauer, *Fontes*; for further information on the project, see *Fontes Anglo-Saxonici: World-Wide Web Register*, http://fontes.english.ox.ac.uk/.

in electronic format now makes it possible to remain up to date on research relating to the *Old English Martyrology*.[123]

The aim of this new edition is make use of these recent resources in the reconstruction of the text, with particular focus on the many Latin texts which have been linked to the *Old English Martyrology*. The text that follows is based on a re-examination of the text, combined with a fresh comparison with some 200 Latin texts which have been identified as containing the closest verbal correspondences with the Old English wording.[124] The intention is to present the results in a single volume, together with a new translation, updated textual and explanatory notes, appendices containing separate editions of the shorter manuscripts, a glossary, and indices for persons, texts and geographical terms.

The editorial policies which govern this edition can be outlined as follows. I have used all seven manuscripts ABCC*DEF to reconstruct the main text; separate editions of manuscripts A, E and F are presented in appendices, in the case of A and E on account of their ninth-century phonology which would render systematic reporting difficult in the apparatus of the main text, and in the case of F because this witness is not easily accessible in previous editions. For the reconstruction of the main text, B is used as the *Leithandschrift*; all variant readings contained in C are reported in the apparatus. Variants in A, E, and F are reported only in cases of textual uncertainty; interested readers can consult the relevant appendices for the complete text of these manuscripts. The diagram above shows which text sections are preserved in each manuscript.[125] Changes of manuscripts are indicated both in the page headers of the main text below, and in more detail also in the apparatus.

I have presented the apparatus criticus without subdivision into sections for textual notes, lexical variants and other variants. Although a subdivided system does have its merits (particularly with regard to lexicography and the ongoing production of a *Dictionary of Old English*), and certainly presents a maximum of information in relatively clear terms, it also creates problems of classification which may not always be appreciated by the reader; it also presents no advantage for the reconstruction of the edited text. Other editors working in Anglo-Saxon studies have more recently highlighted the difficulties inherent in following such a system, and the priority here is to be economical in presenting information in a more compact type of apparatus.[126] The apparatus is thus intended to indicate textual content of the various manuscripts, to record palaeographical and codicological features where they impinge on the reconstruction of the text, and to signal points where the text deviates from that of previous editors.

The editorial principle here involves negative reporting in the apparatus, which is unproblematic in the case of a text that is preserved in a maximum of four

---

[123]Rauer, 'An Annotated Bibliography'.

[124]See Rauer, 'Errors and Textual Problems' and Torkar, 'Die Ohnmacht der Textkritik' for the importance of source study in textual criticism.

[125]A list of text sections and the manuscripts in which they are preserved can also be found in Rauer, 'An Annotated Bibliography', s. v. 'An Index of Reference Nos., Saints, Feasts and Manuscript Contents'.

[126]See Gneuss, 'Guide to the Editing and Preparation of Texts', pp. 8–9, and Kotzor, I, 458–61.

manuscripts for any given passage. As indicated above, the reporting of all variants is important particularly for our knowledge of the CE tradition, since the revised version of the text could be seen as a text in its own right.[127] Positive reporting is here used only selectively in cases of textual controversy (e.g. to signal supporting readings of previous editors or the reading of a third manuscript in case of crucial differences between B and C). Variant readings (including orthographical ones) are given in the apparatus criticus, except for variant spellings of i / y, þ / ð, and *and / ond* (where these are spelled out as words). Although such information would prove useful in research on late Anglo-Saxon spelling, it is perhaps less important to present an apparatus which accounts for all spelling variations, given the improving electronic access to manuscripts.[128] Readings which deviate from Kotzor's edited text of the *Old English Martyrology* are consistently flagged up in the apparatus criticus (Ko); deviating content in Herzfeld's text is signalled only in cases where it sheds further light on a particular reading (Herz). Minor deviations from Kotzor's or Herzfeld's punctuation are not reported. Where I disagree with Kotzor's readings of variants in C which do not affect the reconstruction of the main text, I do not signal such disagreement (e.g. **65** 'lymu' C, where Ko reports the reading in C as 'limu'). I have not used the apparatus criticus to indicate the line layout found in the manuscripts.

Like previous editors, I have used B as a *Leithandschrift* for those parts of the text which are transmitted in more than one manuscript; textual deviations from B in the form of conjectures appear in angular brackets < >; material removed from the text is signalled only in the apparatus. Emendations are made wherever it is clear that a textual problem exists and where an alternative presents itself, either in the form of a variant from another manuscript, or a conjecture based on source material, or a liguistic precedent. If no direct emendation can be made, the textual problem and potential solutions are outlined in the Commentary. Lost or illegible passages are indicated by three dots enclosed in parentheses (...); I have not attempted to calculate the number of missing letters in erasures. I have on the whole followed the useful section numbering introduced by Kotzor and have made only minor changes to previous headings of individual text sections.[129]

Spelling variations in the Old English text have not been standardised; personal names and place-names have, however, been levelled in the modern English translation and the Indices. I have introduced modern capitalisation and paragraphing which do not reflect those found in the manuscripts. Abbreviations are expanded silently; the tironian note used for the abbreviation of *and* is also silently expanded, namely to either *ond* (in text from manuscripts ABE), or *and* (for manuscripts

---

[127]There is a considerable amount of secondary literature discussing the theory of editing Anglo-Saxon texts; the implications arising from editions of the *Old English Martyrology* for modern textual criticism will be discussed in Rauer, 'Difficult Readings'.

[128]For some statistical data regarding i / y variants in manuscripts of the *Old English Martyrology*, see Kotzor, I, 435–8.

[129]List of numbers and titles can be found in Rauer, 'An Annotated Bibliography', s. v. 'An Index of Reference Nos., Saints, Feasts and Manuscript Contents'.

CC*DF).[130] In line with the conventions of the series, roman numerals are spelt out in words. Suprascript, subscript and intralinear insertions in the manuscripts (whether made by the original scribe or a later hand) are signalled in the apparatus, but not in the text. Erasures in the manuscripts are signalled only in case of uncertain or disputed readings. I have not generally indicated unusual letter forms in the apparatus criticus; instances of *e caudata* are reproduced as 'æ' in Old English words and 'ae' in Latin ones. Page or folio breaks are not marked in the text.[131] Accents are generally not reproduced here, and are signalled in the Commentary only in exceptional cases, when they are perceived to help establish a particular reading.[132]

6 Note on the Translation

The last complete translation of the *Old English Martyrology* was published more than a century ago, and I hope to stimulate new interest in the text by presenting it with a modern translation on the facing page.[133] Three of the stylistic features discussed above require further commment here on account of the difficulties that they pose for a modern translator: extreme parataxis, anacoluthon, and what could be seen as ungrammatical syntax.

In modern styles of writing, parataxis is often associated with clear but simple thinking, and tends to be accompanied by more complex hypotactic structures intended to show up the complexity of a particular point. The martyrologist, by contrast, comes across as almost indifferent towards the simplistic impression which his style could leave, and more concerned with narrating sequential events in the correct order, as if intentionally avoiding any kind of further reasoning, justification, subordinated syntax or stylistic variation. In my translation, I have largely tried to echo such a style, even though the resulting text could be seen to violate modern stylistic taste. In his translation of the *Old English Martyrology*, Herzfeld opted for a more varied translation policy, and recent translators of other Old English texts have similarly recommended the insertion of subordination, syndetic devices, and a somewhat softer punctuation.[134] But such a departure from the Old English style would here substantially change the character of what is an encyclopaedic work of reference, whose prose style was probably never intended to be particularly elegant or varied. Nevertheless, the martyrologist's general linguistic competence is not in doubt, and it is important to note that his prose style should not be seen as a sign of intellectual inferiority, but more as a consequence of his faithfulness to the information given in his sources, which he is trying to convey in its barest form.

---

[130]See also Kotzor, I, 456.
[131]For contents of individual folios and manuscript pages, see Rauer, 'An Annotated Bibliography', s. v. 'Manuscripts'.
[132]Readers interested in accent usage are referred to Kotzor's edition, where accents in B are signalled in the main text, and where a convenient list of accents in C can be found; see Kotzor, II, 269–70.
[133]Herzfeld, pp. 3–223; for further partial translations, see Rauer, 'An Annotated Bibliography', s. v. 'Editions and Translations'.
[134]Mitchell and Robinson, *A Guide to Old English*, §182; and Mitchell, *Old English Syntax*, §1685. Compare **136** in the translation of Herzfeld, p. 129, 'When he saw a certain church of God, he left the sheep and hastened to the church of God. When he heard the gospel being read there, he asked an old man what it was. The old man said (...). Then at once he went away (...).'

Another stylistic idiosyncrasy is the author's predilection for anacoluthic syntax, especially recapitulatory pronouns. Again the problem for a translator lies in the fact that modern readers tend to associate this feature with poor reasoning (often at oral level) and incomplete editing. 'In their attempts to explain complicated ideas, Anglo-Saxon writers often had recourse to a device similar to that used by some modern politician who has the desire but not the ability to be an orator, ie. the device of pausing in mid-sentence and starting afresh with a pronoun or some group of words which sums up what has gone before'.[135] Herzfeld tended to avoid these changes of construction in his translation, whereas I have tried to retain them where that is possible without causing misunderstandings.[136] I have tried in such cases to use the long dash to mark such changes of construction, —.

There is only a fine line between anacoluthic syntax and ungrammatical syntax: the distinction lies in the notion that ungrammatical syntax is unlikely to be authorial and is more likely to be the result of a textual defect, caused, for instance, by careless transmission. Since it would be wrong to reproduce faulty syntax of this type in a modern translation, I have in such cases used square brackets [ ] to signal a conjectural translation based on uncertain or ambiguous text.

---

[135] Mitchell and Robinson, *A Guide to Old English*, §148; Mitchell, *Old English Syntax*, §§3878–3886.
[136] See Herzfeld's translation, p. 56, ll. 17–19 and p. 76, ll. 18–21, for example.

Sigla

Manuscripts

A	London, British Library, Add. 23211, fol. 2
B	London, British Library, Cotton Julius A. x, fols. 44–175
C	Cambridge, Corpus Christi College 196, pp. 1–110
C*	London, British Library, Cotton Vitellius D. vii, fols. 131r–132r
D	Cambridge, Corpus Christi College 41, pp. 122–32
E	London, British Library, Add. 40165 A.2, fols. 6–7
F	London, British Library, Harley 3271, fol. 92v

Scribes, Insertions and Corrections

For details of the text sections copied by each individual scribe, see the references below.

Aa	Original scribe, Manuscript A, see Kotzor, I, 47–54
Ba	Original scribe, Manuscript B, see Kotzor, I, 58 and 404
Bb	Original scribe, Manuscript B, see Kotzor, I, 58 and 404
Bc	Original scribe, Manuscript B, see Kotzor, I, 58 and 404
Bd	Original scribe, Manuscript B, see Kotzor, I, 58 and 404
?Be	Later corrector, date uncertain, see Kotzor, I, 58–9
?Bf	Later corrector, s. xii, see Kotzor, I, 58–9
Ca	Original scribe, Manuscript C, see Kotzor, I, 76–82
Da	Original scribe, Manuscript D, see Kotzor, I, 94–101
Ea	Original scribe, Manuscript E, see Kotzor, I, 110–15
Eb	Later corrector, date uncertain, see Kotzor, I, 110
Fa	Original scribe, Manuscript F, see Ker, pp. 311–12

Previous Editions

Co	T. O. Cockayne, *The Shrine: A Collection of Occasional Papers on Dry Subjects* (London, 1869), pp. 29–156
Herz	G. Herzfeld, ed., *An Old English Martyrology*, EETS os 116 (London, 1900), pp. 1–223
Ko	G. Kotzor, ed., *Das altenglische Martyrologium*, Abhandlungen der Bayerischen Akademie der Wissenschaften, phil.-hist. Kl. ns 88.1–2, 2 vols. (Munich, 1981), II, 1–266
Si	C. Sisam, 'An Early Fragment of the *Old English Martyrology*', *Review of English Studies* 4 (1953), 209–20, at 217–20

Text and Translation

25 December: The Birth of Christ

1. On[a] þone forman dæig on geare, þæt is on þone ærestan geoheldæig, eall Cristen folc worþiað Cristes acennednesse. Sancta Maria hine acende on þære nihte on anum holum stanscræfe beforan Beth<l>em[b 1] ðære ceastre; and sona ða he acenned wæs, heofanlic leoht scean ofer eall þæt land; and Godes engel ætiwde sc<e>aphirdon[c] on anre mile [d]be eastan[d] þære cestre and him sæde þæt eallra folca Hælend wære acenned; and ða hirdas gehirdon micelne engla sang on eorðan. [e]Þa wæs[e] agangen fram middangeardes fruman fif þusend geara and ane geare læs þonne twa hund, ða Crist was acenned. On þam geare þa he wæs acenned, þa æteowdon swilc tacn mannum swilce ær næron, ne næfre siðan[2]. <Ð>y[f] geare men gesawon þreo[g] sunnan and oþre siðe þrie[h] monan, and Romanan[i] gesawon firen cleowen feallan of heofnum, and oþre siþe gilden cleowen. And þi geare man geseah hwætes <ear><j> weaxan on treowum; and on sumere mæigðe þonne hi hira hlaf bræcon æt mete, þonne fleow þæt blod of þam hlafe, swa of mannes lichaman deð þonne he gewundod bið. And þi geare man geseah meoloc rinan of heofnum, and lamb spæcan on mennisc gecinde mid Egiptum. And oxa spæc on Rome to þam ergendum, and he cwæð: 'Tohwon sticast þu me? God hwæte geweaxeð togeare, ac ne bist ðu þonne, ne his ne abitest.' Eall þis tacnode þæt seo clæne fæmne cende sunu swa[3] hire næfre wer ne gehran, ac se ðe hæfde fæder on heofnum butan meder, and hæfde þa modur on eorðan butan fæder.[4] Þæt bæð þæt Sancta Maria þæt cild on baþode, þurh ðæt manige untrume men þæron wurdon gehælede.

1. [a] D starts here; [b] Bethem D, Beth<leh>em Ko, beth<l>em Co; [c] sceeaphirdon D, Ko; [d-d] beeastan Ko; [e-e] suprascript Da; [f] planned initial missing, y D, Ðy Ko; [g] .iii. D; [h] .iii. D; [i] a subscript below the second n Da; [j] eare D, Ko.

25 December: Anastasia

2. On þone ilcan dæig Cristes acennednesse Godes circean arworðiað Sancta Anastasiam gebird <þæs>[a] halegan gesiðwifes; seo wæs swiðe æþele for worulde and micele betere for Gode. Diocletianus se hæþena casere hi sealde his gereua<n>[b 5] þæt hi sceolde mid witum bregean þæt heo Criste wiðsoce and hæþengild gulde. Þa het se gerefa[c] hi belucan in carcerne sixtig daga and nihta, and hire man ne sealde ne hlaf ne wæter, ne nanne eorðlicne mete. Hire com ælce niht sumes haliges wifes gast to, seo wæs haten Sancta Theodote, and broht<e>[d] hire heofonlicu gereordu, and sæde hire be þære heofonlican fægernesse, and wunode mid hire oð hanasang, and eft ferde to heofnum. Ða æfter syxtigum[e] dagum, þa heo [f]ut eode[f] of þam <carcerne>[g], þa wæs hire ansin swa reod[6] and swa fæiger[h] [i]s<wa> winsummestan[i] fæmnan þonne heo fægerost bið. Þurh wuldorlicne martyrdom heo forlet þis andwearde lif, and hire lichama resteð nu on Romebirig.

2. [a] þære D, Ko, þæs Herz; [b] gereuas D, Ko, gerefan Herz; [c] re suprascript Da; [d] broht D, Ko, brohte Herz; [e] tigum suprascript Da; [f-f] uteode Ko; [g] carcercerne D; [h] i suprascript Da; [i-i] swinsummestan D.

25 December: The Birth of Christ

1. On the first day of the year, that is on the first day of Christmas, all Christians celebrate Christ's birth. St Mary gave birth to him during that night in a rocky cave outside the town of Bethlehem; and as soon as he was born, a heavenly light shone over the entire land; and God's angel appeared to shepherds one mile to the east of the town and told them that the Saviour of all men was born; and the shepherds heard much angelic song on earth. 5199 years had passed since the beginning of the world, when Christ was born. In the year in which he was born, such portents appeared to men as there had never been before, nor since. In that year men saw three suns, and on another occasion three moons; and the Romans saw a fiery ball fall from the sky, and another time a golden ball. And in that year people saw ears of wheat growing on trees; and when in one country bread was broken at mealtime, blood flowed from the loaf, as from a human body when it is injured. And in that year people saw milk flowing from the sky, and a lamb speaking like a human being among the Egyptians. And an ox spoke to the ploughman in Rome, and said: 'Why do you poke me? Good wheat will grow in this year, yet you will not live to eat it.' All this signified that the pure virgin had given birth to a son in such a way that no man ever touched her, except he who had a father in heaven without a mother and had a mother on earth without a father. In the water in which St Mary bathed her child many sick people were healed.

25 December: Anastasia

2. On the same day as The Birth of Christ, God's churches celebrate the birth of the holy lady St Anastasia, who was very noble in the world, and even more so before God. The pagan emperor Diocletian handed her over to his reeve, so that under torture he might terrorise her into renouncing Christ and worshipping pagan gods. Then the reeve commanded her to be locked up in prison for sixty days and nights, and she was given neither bread nor water, in fact no earthly food at all. Every night the spirit of a holy woman, who was called St Theodota, visited her, and brought her a heavenly meal, and talked to her about heavenly beauty, and stayed with her until cock-crow, and then went back to heaven. Then after sixty days, when she left prison, her face was as red and as beautiful as that of the prettiest virgin at her most beautiful. She left the present life through a glorious martyrdom, and her body now rests in the city of Rome.

25 December: Eugenia

3. <O>n[a] ðone forman dæig bið Sancta Eu<g>e<n>ian[b 7] tid þære æþelan fæmnan; seo wæs on Commodes dagon þæs caseres, and heo lufode Crist ær heo gefullod wære. Heo was swiðe mæres weres dohtur, se wæs haten Philippus. He wæs þære mæran burge gereua þe hatte Alexsandria, and ealle Egipta þeode him hirdon. Þa þæt mæden wæs fiftene[c] gear, þa wolde se fæder hi sellan sumum æþelon men to bryde. Þa on niht bescear heo hire feax swa weras and onfeng weres gegyrlan and gewat of hire fæder rice mid twam cnihton. Þa eode heo on wera minster[d], þer nan wifman ær ne com, and heo onfeng fulwihte and Gode þenode and þeowode, and mid þam wu<n>ode[e] þæt nan man ne mihte onfindan þæt heo wæs fæmne. And binnan þreo[f] gearum heo wearð þæs minstres abbud, and heo was swa mihtegu wið God þæt heo sealde [g]blindum mannum[g] gesihðe and deofulseoce gehælde.[8] And þa æfter manegum gearum heo wæs fram hire fæder ongitenu and broþrum, and siððan heo wunode mid fæmnum on hira hiwe. And æfter hire fæder <deaðe>[9] heo gewat mid hire meder to Rome and þær geþrowode mar<tir>dom[h] for Criste. Þær Necittius, Romeburge[i] gereua, hi nidde þæt heo Criste wiðsoce and deofulgild gelifde. Þa heo þæt nolde, þa het he bindan hire stan to[j] þam swuran,[10] and worpan on Tifre flod. Þa tobærs<t>[k 11] se stan, and heo [l]fleat ofer[l] þæt wæter to lande. And þa het hi eft sendan on birnendne ofon, and se acolode sona. Þa het hie[12] don on carcern, and heo wæs þær tyn[m] niht and dagas butan mete. Þa æteowde hire[n] Drihten silfa on þa ilcan niht æt his acennisse and cwæð to hire: 'Ic þe nime, Eugenie, and ic eom se þe þu lufodest. Þi illcan dæge ic to heofnum astah þe þe ic to eorþan com.'[13] And þi illcan dæig heo onsende hire gast to Gode, and hire lichama resteð wið Romebirig on þam wege þe ma<n>[o 14] nemneð Latina.

3. [a] planned initial missing, n D; [b] eufemian D; [c] xv D; [d] r suprascript Da; [e] wuwode D; [f] iii D; [g-g] blindu D followed by suprascript abbreviation mark and suprascript m again with abbreviation mark, blindum men Ko; [h] mardom D; [i] ge suprascript Da; [j] t suprascript Da; [k] tobærs D, Ko, tobærst Herz; [l-l] fleat aweg ofer D with aweg expunged by same hand, fleat <aweg> ofer Ko, fleat ofer Herz; [m] x D; [n] hire suprascript Da; [o] ma D.

25 December: Eugenia

3. On the first day is the feast of the noble virgin St Eugenia, who lived at the time of emperor Commodus, and she loved Christ even before she was baptised. She was the daughter of a distinguished man called Philippus. He was the reeve of the famous city of Alexandria, and the entire Egyptian nation obeyed him. When the girl was fifteen years old, her father wanted to give her to a nobleman as a bride. During that night she cut off her hair, as men do, and put on men's clothes and left her father's domain with two servants. She then joined a male monastery which no woman had ever entered, and she received baptism and served and ministered to God, and lived with them in such a way that nobody was able to notice that she was a woman. And within three years she became the monastery's abbot, and she was so powerful before God that she gave sight to blind men and healed those possessed by the devil. And then after many years she was recognised by her father and brothers, and after that she lived among women, looking like them. And after her father['s death], she went to Rome with her mother, and suffered martyrdom for Christ there. There Necitius, the reeve of the city of Rome, forced her to abandon Christ and believe in devil worship. When she resisted, he had a stone tied to her neck and had her thrown into the River Tiber. Then the stone broke apart, and she drifted through the water to the bank. And then [he] had her put into a burning oven, but that promptly cooled down. Then [he] had her put into prison, and she was there for ten nights and days without food. Then the Lord himself appeared to her during the night of his birth and said to her: 'I am taking you away, Eugenia, and I am the one whom you have loved. [I will receive you in heaven on the same day as I came to earth.'] And on the same day she gave up the ghost to God, and her body rests near the city of Rome by the road which is called [the Via] Latina.

26 December: Stephen

4. <O>n[a] þone æfteran dæig Godes circean arworðiað Sanctus Stefanus gemind þæs ærestan diacones and[b] þæs ærestan martires æfter Cristes þrowunge. Þone halgan Stefanus Cristes þegnas gehalgodon to diacone, ac Iudeas hine eft mid stanum ofwurpon, forþan þe he mid micelre baldnisse ciðde þæt se Hælend wære soð Godes sunu, se ðe hi on rode onhengon. And þa hi Stefanus to þære stæninge læddon, þa mihte he locian on heofnas, and he geseah þone Hælend silfne standan on his godþrimme, and he hit þam Iudeum sæde. And hi him micle þe reðran on[c] wæron, and þe raþor hine oftorfod hæfdon. Þa leton hi his lichaman licgan butan Hierusalem þære ceastre and woldon þæt hine fuglas tobæron; þa bebirigde hine sum geleafful man, se was haten Gamaliel. And þa æfter manegum gearum was se lichama geciðed þurh heofonlicu tacn, and þær wæs swete stenc, and menig untrume man þær his hælo onfeng þa hine man of eorþan up dide, and miclon lofsange læddon to Hierusalem.[15] Þæt wæs Sanctus Stef<h>anus[d] wundra sum þæt an plegende cild arn under wænes hweowol and wearð sona dead. Þa nam þæs cild<es>[e][16] modor þone deadan lichaman and wearp[f] on Sanctus Stefhanus circean, þær his reliquia sum dæl inne wæs. Þa heo eft com, þa mitte heo hire cild lifiende and gesund.

4. [a] planned initial missing, n D; [b] and þæs ærestan diacones and D; [c] suprascript Da; [d] Stefnanus D; [e] cild D, Ko, cildes Herz; [f] r over erased p D.

27 December: John the Evangelist

5. <O>n[a] þone þriddan[b] dæig bið Sancte Iohannes tid þæs godspellres[c]; se wæs Criste leof ofer ealle oþre men þe he on middangearde gemette. And he wæs him swa leof þæt he æt gereordum hlenode on þæs Hælendes bearme and ofer his breost. And he aweahte men of deaþe; and he gesen<ode>[d] twa[e] birþena gyrda, and hie wurdon sona to þam golde þe man hateð abritsum, þæt is [f]smæte gold[f]. And twegen[g] beorgas litelra stana he gesenod<e>[h] to æþelum gymmum. And rice hæþene men hine <niddon>[i][17] þæt he dranc ator; on þam was ælces cynnes wirm, oððe ban oððe blod, and ne ablacode he. And his birgen is mid Grecum on Effessio þære ceastre; æt þære byrgenne[j] bið [k]well micel[k] wundor gesewen and gehired: Hwilon heo eðað swa lifiende man slape; hwilon þonne man þa byrgine sceawað, þonne ne bið þær nan lichoma gesewen, ac bið micel swetnisse stenc. Forþam nat nænig man hwæþer se Iohannes si þe cwicu þe dead.

5. [a] n D; [b] iii D; [c] r suprascript Da; [d] geisenonde D; [e] ii D; [f-f] smætegold Ko; [g] ii D; [h] gesenodo D, with first o suprascript Da; [i] snidon D, atypical use of round s; [j] byrgenne D with en expunged and suprascript i Da, byrgine Ko; [k-k] wellmicel Ko.

26 December: Stephen

4. On the second day God's churches celebrate the memory of St Stephen, the first deacon and first martyr after Christ's passion. Christ's followers ordained St Stephen a deacon, but the Jews then stoned him to death, because he announced with great courage that the Saviour whom they had hanged on the cross was the son of God. And when they led Stephen to his stoning, he could see into heaven, and he saw the Saviour himself stand amid all his divine glory, and said so to the Jews. And they were even more cruel to him therefore, and had him stoned even sooner. Then they left his body lying just outside the city of Jerusalem, for the birds to take it away; then a believing man called Gamaliel buried him. Many years later the body was revealed through a sign from heaven; there was a sweet smell, and many a sick man regained health in that place when he was exhumed and brought to Jerusalem with great festivity. It was one of St Stephen's miracles that a child playing outside ran under the wheel of a wagon and was killed outright. Then the child's mother took the dead body and wept over it in St Stephen's church, which contained some of his relics. When she came out again, she found her child alive and well.

27 December: John the Evangelist

5. On the third day is the feast of St John the Evangelist; he was dearer to Christ than all the other men he knew on earth. And he was so dear to him that during the meal he leaned on the Saviour's bosom and across his chest. And he resuscitated men from death; and he made the sign of the cross over two bundles of sticks, and they immediately turned into the type of gold which is called *obryzum*, that is refined gold. And two piles of pebbles he turned into precious stones by making the sign of the cross. And powerful heathens [forced] him to drink poison containing the blood or bones of all manner of vermin, and he did not even turn pale. And his burial place is among the Greeks in the city of Ephesus; at the tomb a quite extraordinary miracle can be seen and heard: sometimes it breathes as if a living man is asleep; sometimes when one looks at the tomb, no body is to be seen there, only a very sweet smell. Therefore nobody knows whether John is alive or dead.

28 December: The Holy Innocents

6. On þone feorþan dæig <b>ið[a] þara haligra cilda tid þe Herodes acwealde for Criste on Bethlem[b][18] þære ceastre, ealle þa cnihtcild þe wæron twam gearum geborene oððe anre nihte eald cild, forþan þe he wolde Crist acwellan on þæra cilda gemange. Herodes[c] het tion ða cild of hira modor breostum and bosmum; and þonne man þa cild cwalde, þonne spiwon hi þa meoloc[d] ær þæt blod. Þa wæron þa cild mid hira blode gefullode, and þa modor mid þam tearum gefullode for þam sare þe æt þam cildon gesawon. Þæra cild<a>[e] wæs tu hund[f] and feowertig[g] and feower[h] mille.[19] And Erodes forwearð æfter þæra cilda cweallme, and he ofstang hine silfne mid his agenre handa.

6. [a] þið D; [b] l corrected from e Da, Bethlehem Ko; [c] subscript Da; [d] second o suprascript Da; [e] cildea D, Ko, cilda Herz; [f] cc D; [g] xl D; [h] iiii D.

31 December: Pope Silvester I

7. On þone seofoþan[a] [b]dæg[20] bið[b] Sancte Siluestres tid þæs halgan papan, þæs lichoma resteð on Romebirig; se dide fela wundra ær he papa wære. Tarquinius hatte Romeburge gereua; he þreatode hine to hæþenscipe. Þa nolde he þæt. Þa het hine man gebindan and lædan to carcerne. Þa cwæt Sanctus Silluester to him: 'Disega, on þisse nihte þe bið þæt feorh afirred.' And þæt gelamp[c].

7. [a] vii D; [b-b] dæg þæs monþes bið D, Ko, with þæs monþes underlined by unknown hand; [c] D breaks off after gelamp.

31 December: Columba

8. (...) Þa[a] he ða ineode on þæt carcern ond hire [b]to genealæhte[b], þa com ðider in ursa þæt deor, þæt is on ure geðeode byren, ond awearp hine to eorðan, ond locade to þære Godes fæmnan hwæþer heo sceolde hine cucene þe deadne.[21] Ond þa bebead seo Godes fæmne þære byrene þæt heo læge on þæs carcernes duru. Ond heo ongan læran þone leasere þæt he gelyfde on Crist, ond he þæt geþafade. Ond seo byren hine let gangan of þæm carcerne. Ond he þa sona clypode þurh ealle þa ceastre ond cwæþ: 'Se an God is soð God, þone Columbe seo fæmne begangeð, ond nis ænig oþer butan þam.'

8. [a] B starts here; this entry is acephalous; [b-b] togenealæhte Ko.

28 December: The Holy Innocents

6. On the fourth day is the feast of the holy children whom Herod killed in place of Christ in the city of Bethlehem, all male babies between two years and one night old, because he wanted to kill Christ among that group of children. Herod had the children torn away from their mothers' breasts and bosoms; and when the children were killed, they spewed milk before they spewed blood. The children were thus baptised with their blood, and the mothers were baptised with tears for the suffering which they saw in their children. There were 244,000 children. And Herod died after the massacre of the children, and he stabbed himself to death with his own hands.

31 December: Pope Silvester I

7. On the seventh day is the feast of the holy pope St Silvester, whose body lies in the city of Rome. He worked many miracles before he became pope. The reeve of the city of Rome was called Tarquinius. He forced him into the pagan religion, but he refused. Then they had him tied up and led to prison. Then Silvester said to him: 'You fool, your life will be taken away this very night.' And that is what happened.

31 December: Columba

8. (...) When he entered the prison cell and approached her, an animal called *ursa*, in our language 'female bear', came in, and threw him to the ground, and looked at God's virgin [as if asking] whether she wanted him alive or dead. And God's virgin then commanded the bear to lie beside the cell door. And she began to teach that thug to believe in Christ, and he agreed to that. And the bear allowed him to walk out of the cell. And he soon called throughout the entire city: 'The one God is the true God, whom the virgin Columba worships, and there is no other beside Him.'

The Beginning of January

8a. On ðone eahteþan geohheldæg bið þæs monðes fruma þe mon nemneð Ianuarius, þæt is on ure geðeode se Æftera Geola. Þæt bið se æresta geares monað mid Romwarum ond mid us. On ðæm monðe bið an ond þritig daga.

1 January: Octave of Christ and Mary (The Circumcision of Christ)

9. On þone ærestan dæg þæs monðes bið Cristes eahteða dæg ond Sancta Marian. On ðæm dæge Crist onfeng ða ealdan ymbsnidenysse ond ða ealdan clæsnunge Iudea folces. Þæt þonne wæs þæt hie æghwelcum cnihtcilde ymbsnidon þæt werlice lim on ðæm eahteþan dæge æfter his acennysse, ond seo clæsnung him wæs swa halig swa us is fullwiht. Ond Crist forðon þa clæsnunge onfeng þæt he us mid þy getacnode þæt we sceolan aceorfan fram usse heortan unclæne geðohtas, ond from lichoman unalefde dæde, gif we willað habban lif mid Gode. Ond on þone eahteþan dæg menn sceopan Criste naman æfter ealdre wisan. Se nama wæs on Iudisc Ihesus, ond on Grecisc Soter, ond on Læden Saluator, ond on ure geðeode Hælend.[22] Þone naman hæfde se engel Sancta Marian gesæd, ær ðon þe heo geeacnad wære.

3 January: Pope Anteros

10. On ðone þriddan dæg ðæs monðes bið þæs halgan papan tid þe is nemned Sancte Antheri. He wæs Grecisces cynnes mon, ond he sæt on Sancte Petres setle on Rome þreottyne gear on Maximianus dagum þæs caseres. Ond he geþrowade martyrdom for Criste, ond his lichoma is bebyrged on ðæm mynstre ðe we nemnað Calistes mynster.[23]

5 January: Emiliana

11. On ðone fiftan dæg þæs monðes bið Sancte Emelianan tid ðære fæmnan, þæt wæs Sancte Gregorius faðe, ðæs þe us fulwiht onsænde. Hire ætywde on nihtlicre gesyhðe hire swyster gast ond cwæþ to hire: 'Butan þe ic dede þone halgan dæg æt Drihtnes acennisse, ac ic do mid þe ðone halgan dæg æt Drihtnes ætywnesse, þæt is se Drihtnes halga twelfta dæg, Drihtnes fullwihtes dæg.'

The Beginning of January

8a. On the eighth day of Christmas is the beginning of the month which is called *Januarius*, which in our language is 'Æftera Geola' [The Latter Month of Yule]. It is the first month of the year for the Romans and for us. This month has thirty-one days.

1 January: Octave of Christ and Mary (The Circumcision of Christ)

9. On the first day of the month is the octave of Christ and St Mary. On that day Christ received the traditional circumcision and the traditional purification of the Jewish people. It was then that they used to circumcise the male member of every male child on the eighth day after his birth, and that purification was as holy to them as baptism is to us. And Christ therefore received the purification in order to show us through it that we should cut out unchaste thoughts from our heart, and illegitimate actions from our body, if we want to have a life with God. And on the eighth day men gave Christ his name according to the old custom. His name in Hebrew was Jesus, in Greek *Soter*, and in Latin *Saluator*, and in our language 'Healing One' [Saviour]. That name had been passed on to St Mary by the angel, before she conceived.

3 January: Pope Anteros

10. On the third day of the month is the feast of the holy pope who is called St Anteros. He was a man of Greek origin, and he sat on the throne of St Peter in Rome for thirteen years in the days of emperor Maximian. And he suffered martyrdom for Christ, and his body is buried in the church which we call the church of Callistus.

5 January: Emiliana

11. On the fifth day of the month is the feast of the virgin St Emiliana. That was the paternal aunt of St Gregory, who sent us baptism. In a vision at night her sister appeared to her and said to her: 'I celebrated the feast at the Lord's birth without you, but I will celebrate with you the feast at the Lord's showing [Epiphany], that is the Lord's holy twelfth day, the day of the Lord's baptism.'

6 January: Epiphany, The Baptism of Christ etc.

12. On ðone sextan dæg þæs monðes bið se micla ond se mæra dæg þone Grecas nemnað Epiphania; ond Romware hine nemnað Aparitia Domini, þæt is on ure geþeode Drihtnes ætywnesse dæg. On ðam dæge he gecyþde mid þæm mæstum wundrum feowerum þæt he wæs soð God. Þæt æreste wundor wæs þæt þreo tungolcræftegan coman fram eastdæles mægðum to Criste þa þa he wæs cild, ond him mon brohte gold to gefe; on ðæm wæs getacnod þæt he wæs soð cyning. Oðer him brohte recels; on ðæm wæs getacnod þæt he wæs soð God. Se þridda him brohte myrran þa wyrt;[24] on þon wæs getacnod þæt he wæs deadlic mon, ond þæt he þurh his anes deað ealle geleaffulle men gefreode fram ecum deaðe. Ond on ðone ylcan dæg Crist onfeng fulwihte on Iordane fram Iohanne þæm fulwere. Ond he wæs þa on ðritiges geara ylde se Hælend, þa he þæm fulwihte onfeng. Ond on þone dæg æt sumum brydþingum Crist gecerde sex fatu full wætres to ðæm betestan wine; on æghwelc þara fata mihte twegen mittan oþþe ðreo.[25] Ond on ðone ylcan dæg Crist gereorde fif ðusenda wera of fif hlafum ond of twam fixum, eac wifum ond cildum þara wæs ungerim, ond þara hlafgebroca wæs to lafe twelf binna fulle.

6 January: Julian and Basilissa

13. On ðone ylcan dæg bið þæs æþelan weres þrowung se is nemned Sanctus Iulianus, ðæs[a] lichoma resteð in Antiochia þære ceastre; se sona on his cnihthade ðeowade Gode on clænnesse. Ond his yldran hine þa genyddon on his geogoðe, þæt he onfeng æþele bryd, seo wæs on naman Basilissa. Ond ða þære forman brydniht, þa hi twa wæron on ðæm brydbure, þa com þær ærest wundorlic stenc, ond æfter ðæm stence heofonlic leoht, ond æfter þæm leohte Crist self þær ætewde mid engla werede. Ond ða for þære gesihðe fægernesse ðe hi gesawon, ond ðæm wordum ðe hi gehyrdon, hi wunedan a clæne, he mid werum ond heo mid fæmnum. Þes Iulianus awehte hæþenne man of deaðe, ond se wæs siððan gefullad. Se man sæde fram helle siðfæte swylc sarspell swylce næfre ær on men ne becom, ne naht oft siððan.

13. [a] þæs Ko.

6 January: Pope Telesphorus

14. On ðone ilcan dæg bið þæs papan tid þe is nemned Ðelesfor; se wæs Grecisces cynnes. He sæt on ðæm papsetle ændlefen gear ond þry monað on þara casere[a] [26] dagum Antonius ond Marcus.[27] Ond ðes papa wæs eft Cristes martyr, ond his lichoma resteð neah Sancte Petres lichoman. Þes papa gesette ærest manna þæt man fæste on Rome syfon wucan ær eastran. Ond he gesette ærest þæt man sang Gloria in excelsis Deo þone lofsang foran to mæssan.

14. [a] casere B, Ko, casera Herz.

6 January: Epiphany, The Baptism of Christ etc.

12. On the sixth day of the month is the important and celebrated day which the Greeks call *epiphania*; and the Romans call it *apparitio Domini*, which in our language is 'the day of the Lord's appearance'. On that day he showed with the four greatest miracles that he was the true God. The first miracle was that three astronomers came from Eastern countries to Christ when he was a baby, and gold was brought to him as a gift; that signified that he was the true king. The second one brought him incense; that signified that he was the true God. The third brought him myrrh, the plant; that signified that he was a mortal human being, and that he through the death of him alone liberated all believers from eternal death. And on the same day Christ received baptism in the [River] Jordan from John the Baptist. And he was then thirty years old, our Saviour, when he was baptised. And on that day at a wedding Christ turned six pots full of water into the best wine; each of the pots would have held about two or three *mittan*. And on the same day Christ fed five thousand men with five loaves and two fish, on top of that women and children of whom there was an incalculable number, and the leftovers from the bread filled twelve baskets.

6 January: Julian and Basilissa

13. On the same day is the passion of the nobleman who is called St Julian, whose body rests in the city of Antioch. Even as a young boy he served God in chastity. And his parents then forced him in his youth to marry a noblewoman, who was called Basilissa. And in the wedding night, when the two were in the bedroom, there first appeared a wonderful smell, and after the smell a heavenly light, and after the light Christ himself appeared there with a host of angels. And on account of the beauty of the vision which they saw, and the words which they heard, they later always lived chaste lives, he amongst men and she amongst women. This Julian revived a pagan man from death, and he was then baptised. That man told such a horror story from his journey to hell as had never reached people before, and has not often since then.

6 January: Pope Telesphorus

14. On the same day is the feast of the pope called Telesphorus, who was Greek. He was on the papal throne for eleven years and three months in the days of emperors Antoninus and Mark. And this pope later became a martyr of Christ, and his body rests near that of St Peter. It was this pope who first amongst men established that people should fast in Rome the seven weeks before Easter. And it was he who first established that people should sing *Gloria in excelsis Deo*, the hymn of praise, during mass.

9 January: Pega

15. On ðone nygeðan dæg ðæs monðes bið Sancte Pegean geleornes ðære halgan fæmnan; heo wæs Sancte Gutlaces[28] swyster þæs ancran. Ond æfter his geleornisse heo dyde blindum men þæt sealt on eage þæt he ær gehalgode, ond he mihte sona geseon.

16. [a-a] oþþæt Ko; [b-b] ætnehstan Ko.

10 January: Paul the Hermit

16. On ðone teoþan dæg þæs monðes bið Sancte Paules tid; se wæs sextyne geara þa he ærest on þæt westen gewat, ond he wunade þær [a]oþ þæt[a] he hæfde ðreo ond hundændleftig wintra. Þær he næfre naht oþres ne geseah ne ne gehyrde butan leona grymetunge ond wulfa gerar,[29] ond æt þæs westenes æppla[30] ond ðæt wæter dranc of his holre hand.[31] Ond ða [b]æt nehstan[b] fedde hine an hræfn sextig geara, se him brohte æghwelce dæge healfne hlaf. Ond ða hwæne ær his ende com him to Sanctus Antonius se ancra, ond ða sona brohte him se hræfn gehalne hlaf. Se Antonius geseah ðæs Paules saule swa hwite swa snauw stigan to heofonum betweoh engla þreatas, ond haligra manna þreatas. Ond twegen leon adulfan his byrgenne on ðæs westenes sande; þær resteð Paules lichoma mid yfelice duste bewrigen, ac on domesdæge he ariseð on wuldor.

12 January: Benedict Biscop

17. On <ðone>[a] twelftan dæg þæs monðes bið Sancte Benedictes tid þæs halgan abbodes; se wæs angelcynnes man. He wæs swiðe æþele for worolde ond micle æþelra for Gode. Ond ða he wæs on fif ond twentigum geara, þa ferde he to Rome, ond ðær ond on oðrum manegum æþelum mynstrum he leornade gastlice ðeodscipas. Ond he onfeng preosthades scare on ðæs ealandes mynster[32] ðe is nemned Lerinensi, ond he hwerfde eft to eþle. Ond he getimbrade on Brytene æþele mynster on ðære stowe þe is cweden æt Wiremuðan, ond ðæt gehalgode Gode ond Sancte Petre, ond ða ciricean æþellice gefretwade ge mid godcunde wisdome ge mid woroldlicum frætwum ofersæwiscum. Ond ða ðæs æfter sextene gearum, þa forlet he þone læmnan ofn ðæs mænniscan lichoman, ond se gast fleah freo[33] to ðam upplican[b] wuldre.

17. [a] om. B, Ko, þone Herz; [b] upplican upplican B.

13 January: Hilary of Poitiers

18. On ðone ðreotte<oþ>an[a] [34] dæg þæs monðes bið ðæs halgan biscopes gemynd Sancte Hilaries; he wæs on ðære ceastre Pictauie. Se wæs Sancte Martines lareow, ond he awehte deadne man of deaðe.

18. [a] ðreottegan B.

9 January: Pega

15. On the ninth day of the month is the death of the holy virgin St Pega. She was the sister of the hermit St Guthlac. And after his death she put the salt which he had blessed earlier in the eyes of a blind man, and he could see straightaway.

10 January: Paul the Hermit

16. On the tenth day of the month is the feast of St Paul; he was sixteen years old when he first went into the desert, and he stayed there until he was 113 years old. There he never saw anything or heard anything apart from the roaring of the lions and the howling of the wolves, and he ate the fruit of the desert and drank water from his hollow hand. And eventually a raven fed him for sixty years; he brought him half a loaf of bread every day. And when a short while before his end St Antony the hermit came to him, the raven promptly brought him an entire loaf. Antony saw Paul's soul, as white as snow, ascend to heaven among hosts of angels, and hosts of saints. And two lions dug his grave in the desert sand; there Paul's body rests covered with vile dust, but on Doomsday he will arise in glory.

12 January: Benedict Biscop

17. On the twelfth day of the month is the feast of the holy abbot St Benedict, who was English. He was very noble before the world and still nobler before God. And when he was twenty-five years old, he travelled to Rome, and there and in many other distinguished monasteries he underwent religious instruction. And he received the tonsure of priesthood in the island monastery of Lerina [i.e. Lérins], and afterwards he travelled back home. And in Britain he built a glorious monastery in the place which is called Wearmouth, and dedicated it to God and St Peter, and he splendidly adorned the church both with spiritual wisdom and with worldly ornaments from abroad. And then later, after sixteen years, he left behind the clay furnace of the human body, and his soul flew to the heavenly glory, liberated.

13 January: Hilary of Poitiers

18. On the thirteenth day of the month is the commemoration of the holy bishop St Hilary; he lived in the city of Pictauia [i.e. Poitiers]. He was the teacher of St Martin, and he revived a man from death.

14 January: Felix

19. On ðone feowerteogðan dæg þæs monðes bið Sancte Felices [a]tid mæssepreostes[a][35] on Rome, on ðære stowe þe Pincis is nemned; þone rice men hæþne ðreadon þæt he Criste wiðsoce ond hæþengeldum gelyfde. Þa he þæt nolde, he wæs [b]nacod ond[b] [36] on carcern onsænded, ond þær wæs understregd mid sæscellum ond mid scearpum stanum. Ond þa Godes engel on ðære ilcan niht tobræc ðæs carcernes duru ond hine þonan alædde.

19. [a–a] tid þæs mæssepreostes Herz; [b–b] nacod He.

16 January: Pope Marcellus

20. On ðone sexteoðan dæg ðæs monðes þonne bið Sancte Marcelles tid þæs papan. Ðone papan Maxentius, Romeburge ealdormon, nedde þæt he his fullwihte wiðsoce ond deofolgeldum gelyfde. Da he þæt ne geðafode, þa het he on ðæs papan ciericean gestællan his blancan[37] ond monig oðer neat, ond he genydde þone papan þæt he þæm þenade, ond on ðæm ðeowdome he geendade his lif. Ond his lichoma resteð arwyrðlice on ðæm mynstre[38] Priscille on ðæm wege Salariae.

16 January: Fursa

21. On ðone ilcan dæg bið þæs mæssepreostes geleornis, se wæs nemned Sancte Furseus; se wæs acenned in Hibernia mægðe, þæt is on Scotta lande. Þæs gast wæs neahterne of lichoman alæded, ond he geseah ma ondry<sn>lices[a] [39] ond eac wuldorlices þonne he mihte monnum asecgan. Ond seo gesihð him wæs on swa micelre gemynde þæt he on ðæm miclan wintres cele, þonne he ymb þæt þohte oþþe spræc, ðonne aswætte he eall. Ond eft on ðære miclan sumeres hæte, ðonne he his siðfæt gemunde, þonne ablacode he eall ond abifode. Ond ða ða Godes englas eft his gast brohtan to þæm lichoman, þa locade he on his agenne lichoman swa swa on uncuðne hræw, ond he nolde næfre eft on ðone lichoman gif he nyde ne sceolde. Þes Fursing[40] gewat eft of Scottum on Brytone, ond on Eastengla mægðe he getimbrede fæger mynster þæt is geceged Cnofesburh[41]; ðæt he dyde on Sigeberhtes dagum þæs cyninges. Ond þanon he gewat ofer sæ in Gallia mægðe to Clodfeo[42], Fra<n>cna[b] cyninge, ond ðær his dagas geendade. Ond his lichoma resteð on ðæm tune Ferano[43], ond his geearnunga þær wæron oft beorhte gecyþed.

21. [a] ondryrrlices B, Ko, ondrysnlices Herz, Cross, 'The Influence of Irish Texts and Traditions'; [b] Fracna B, Ko, Francna Herz, Cross, 'The Influence of Irish Texts and Traditions'.

14 January: Felix

19. On the fourteenth day of the month is the feast of the priest St Felix, in Rome in the place which is called Pincian [Hill]; powerful pagans forced him to renounce Christ and to adopt the pagan religion. When he refused he was sent to prison naked, on a floor of sea-shells and sharp stones. And then God's angel broke the prison door open that night and led him away.

16 January: Pope Marcellus

20. On the sixteenth day of the month then is the feast of Pope St Marcellus. Maxentius, the governor of the city of Rome, forced the pope to renounce his baptism and adopt devil worship. When he refused, he commanded his steeds [or 'steed'] and many other animals to be stabled in the pope's church, and he forced the pope to look after them, and in that service he ended his life. And his body rests with dignity in the church of Priscilla on the Via Salaria.

16 January: Fursa

21. On the same day is the death of the priest who was called St Fursa; he was born in the country of Ireland, that is in the land of the Gaels. His soul was led from his body for one night, and he saw more horror and marvels than he was able to relate to men. And the vision was so vivid in his mind that even in the great cold of winter he really began to sweat when he thought and talked about it. And then in the great heat of summer, when he recalled his journey, he turned really pale and trembled. And when God's angels then brought his soul to his body, it looked down on his own body as if on an unknown corpse, and it would never have entered his own body again except that it willy-nilly had to. This Fursing later came from the Gaels to Britain, and among the East Angles he built a magnificent monastery which is called Cnobheresburh; he did that in the days of King Sigeberht. And from there he travelled overseas to Clovis, king of the Franks, in Gaul, and ended his days there. And his body rests in the town of Peronna [i.e. Péronne], and his merits were often gloriously revealed there.

17 January: Antony the Hermit

22. On ðone seofenteoþan dæg þæs monðes bið seo geleornes þæs halgan munuces Sancte Antonies; se gewat on westen ða he wæs on twentigum geara, ond on ðæm he wunade ᵃoþ þætᵃ he wæs on fif ond hundteontigum geara. Ond on fruman he þær wunade twentig geara, swa⁴⁴ he nænigne oþerne mon ne geseah. Ðær he fæste hwilum twegen dagas, hwilum þry tosomne; ond ðonne he mete þigde, ðonne wæs þæt hlaf ond sealt ond lytel wætres drync. Ond hine þær deofla⁴⁵ costodon mid ofermæte unclæne luste, efne swa þæt hi eodon on niht to him on geglengedra wifa hiwe. Ðær he geseah eac þone fulan gast þe men lærð unalyfede lustas. Þæt wæs sweart cniht ond lytel ond egeslic, ond he him sæde sylf þæt his nama wære spiritus fornicationis, þæt is dernes geligeres gast. Hwilum ða deofol hine swungan þæt he ne mihte hine astyrigean ne noht cwedan. Hwilum hi hine bylgedon on swa fearras, ond ðuton eallswa wulfas. Hwilum hi him bæron to gold ond seolfer, ond him ætywdon in arwyrðestan hiwe, ond hi him bæran mettas to ond hine bædon þæt he þa þigde. Þonne sænade he hine, þonne glad þæt deofol⁴⁶ ut mid his leasunge, swa swa smyc æt his eagdura. Antonius wunade on ðæm ytemestan ænde eorðan ymbhwyrftes on Egypta westenne, ond he wæs hwæþre mære geond ealne middangeard. Ond þa he his dagas geendade, þa ongeatan þæt his þegnas twegen þæt hine openlice englas læddon to heofenum; ond his lichoma resteð on ðære miclan ceastre Alexandria.

22. ᵃ⁻ᵃ oþþæt Ko.

17 January: Speusippus, Eleusippus and Meleusippus

23. On ðone ilcan dæg bið þreora cnihta tid þa wæron getwinnas, ond hi wæron nemde Sanctus Speosippus ond Sanctus Elasippus ond Sanctus Melasippus. Þa hæfdon Cristene modar ond hæþenne fæder, ond þurh heora yldran modor lare hi gelyfdon Gode. Ond hwæþre næron hi na gefulwade, forðon hæðne caseras hæfdon ofslegen ealle biscopas ond mæssepreostas. Þas cnihtas þry fram þrym deman wæron nedde, þæt hi Godes geleafan wiðsocan. Þa hi þæt ne geþafedon, þa heton þa deman micel fyr onbærnan, ond ða cnihtas ahon on an treow ond byran⁴⁷ to þæm fyre. Ða cwædon hi to heora yldran medder: 'Beo þu nu ure gemyndig on þinum gebedum. Ond þonne þu hlaf brece ond metes onfo, þonne sæna þu þa cruman for us ðe of þinum beode feallen, þæt we moton bergan of þæs heofonlican cyninges gereordum, þeah ðe we næron mid fulwihte her on eorðan onðwægen.' Da cwæð seo yldre modar: 'Cnihtas, beoð orsorge. Eower blod eow fulwað, ond eower martyrdom eow gelædeþ to Cristes gereordum.' Þa wæron þa cnihtas on ðæt fer onsænded. Da ne onhran þæt fyr him no, ac hi onsændon heora gast to Gode swa swa þreo lamb. Ond seo cierece, on ðære þe heora lichoma resteð, is neah ᵃLingona byrigᵃ; þa man nemneð æt Sanctos Geminos,⁴⁸ æt þæm halgum getwinnum.

23. ᵃ⁻ᵃ Lingonabyrig Ko.

17 January: Antony the Hermit

22. On the seventeenth day of the month is the death of the holy monk St Antony; he went into the desert when he was twenty years old, and he lived there until he was 105 years old. And initially he lived there for twenty years without seeing anybody else. There he sometimes fasted for two days in a row, sometimes three; and when he did take food it was bread and salt and just a little water. And devils tempted him there endlessly with dirty lecherousness, even to the point where they visited him at night in the appearance of dressed-up women. There he also saw the foul spirit which incites men to illicit lust. That was a black boy, small and horrible, and he himself told him that his name was *spiritus fornicationis*, which means 'spirit of illicit sex'. Sometimes the devils beat him so that he was unable to move or talk. Sometimes they bellowed at him like bulls and howled like wolves. Sometimes they brought him gold and silver, and showed themselves to him in the most respectable appearance, and they brought him food and asked him to eat. Then he made the sign of the cross over himself, and the devil with his artifice slipped outside, like smoke through his window. Antony lived at the outmost end of the earth within the Egyptian desert, but he was nevertheless famous throughout the whole world. And when he ended his life, two of his men saw angels evidently leading him to heaven; and his body rests in the great city of Alexandria.

17 January: Speusippus, Eleusippus and Meleusippus

23. On the same day is the feast of three boys who were triplets, and they were called St Speusippus, St Eleusippus and St Meleusippus. They had a Christian mother and a pagan father, and through their grandmother's teaching they believed in God. But they were not at all baptised, because the pagan emperors had killed all bishops and priests. These boys were by three judges forced to renounce God's religion. When they refused, the judges had a great fire lit, and had the boys hanged on a gallows and brought to the fire. Then they said to their grandmother: 'Remember us now in your prayers. And when you break bread and eat, bless the crumbs for us which fall from your table, so that we may taste the heavenly king's food, even though we were not cleansed with baptism here on earth.' Then the grandmother said: 'Boys, you can be certain of that. Your blood will baptise you, and your martyrdom will lead you to Christ's communal meal.' Then the boys were consigned to the flames. The fire did not then touch them at all, but they gave up the ghost to God like three lambs. And the church, in which their bodies rest, is near the town of Lingones [Langres]; it is called St Gemini, 'the Holy Twins'.

18 January: Prisca

24. On ðone eahtateoþan dæg <þæs monðes> bið ðære halgan fæmnan Sancte Prisce <geleornes>;[49] ðære lichoma resteþ on Rome, ond hire gemynd sceal beon mærsod on eallum cierecum.

18 January: The Consecration of St Peter's Church

25. On<d>[a] ðy ilcan dæge[50] Sancte Peter gehalgode ærest cierecean on Rome.

25. [a] On B, Ko, Herz.

19 January: Ananias, Petrus etc.

26. On ðone nigonteoþan dæg þæs monðes þonne bið þæs mæssepreostes gemynd Sancte Annani, in Biððinie ðære mægðe,[51] on Dioclitianus dagum þæs hæþenan caseres. He wæs on carcern sænded twelf dagas butan mete, ond þa æfter twelf dagum com se carcernweard; se wæs nemned Petrus. Þa geseah he sittan ðone halgan gast on culfran hiwe on ðæs carcernes eagdura, ond spræc<an>[a 52] to Annani þæm Godes men, ond eft fleogan to heofonum. Þa gelefde se carcernweard Gode. Þa het sum hæþen gerefa hi begen belucan on fyrenum bæþe, ond ymb þreo niht hi eodon gesunde of ðæm. Ða gesegon þæt seofon cæmpan; þa gelyfdon þa for ðæm wundre. Þa het se gerefa heora ælcum gebindan leades bloman on heora swyran ond sændon[53] on widsæwes grund. Þa toburstan þa bendas ond afeoll ðæt lead of him, ond hi onsendon heora gastas to Gode, ond þa lichoman coman to þam waroðe. Ðær Cristene men hi bebyrgdon mid micelre are; ond þær wæron siððan on ðære stowe monegu wundor. Ond se gerefa þe hi cwellan het, se wæs sona mid swa miclum sare gewitnad þæt he nolde læng libban, ac he het his agene men hine sændan on ðone sæ; ond þa sædeor hine sona forswulgon þæt his ne com þy furðor an ban to eorðan.

26. [a] spræc B, Ko.

20 January: Sebastian

27. On ðone twentigþan dæg ðæs monðes bið Sancte Sebastianes tid þæs æþelan martyres. Ðone Dioclitianus se casere, he wæs hæþen, he het hine mid strælum ofscotian,[54] þæt he wæs ðara swa full swa igl þæt deor bið byrsta. Ond mid ðy he hine ne mihte swa acwellan,[55] ða het he hine mid stengum ðyrcsan, [a]oþ þæt[a] he his gast onsende. Ond his lichoma wæs gebyrged æt Rome on ðære stowe Catacumbe.

27. [a-a] oþþæt Ko.

18 January: Prisca

24. On the eighteenth day [of the month] is [the feast] of the holy virgin St Prisca; her body rests in Rome, and her commemoration shall be celebrated in all churches.

18 January: The Consecration of St Peter's Church

25. And on the same day St Peter first consecrated a church in Rome.

19 January: Ananias, Petrus etc.

26. On the nineteenth day of the month is the commemoration of the priest St Ananias, [who was martyred] in the country of Bithynia, in the days of the pagan emperor Diocletian. He was sent to prison for twelve days, without food, and then after twelve days the prison-guard came, who was called Petrus. He then saw the Holy Spirit in the shape of a dove sitting in the window of the prison, and speak to Ananias the man of God, and afterwards fly into the sky. Then the prison-guard believed in God. Then a pagan reeve commanded that both be locked into a fiery bath, and after three nights they left it unharmed. Then seven soldiers witnessed this and then they became believers because of that miracle. Then the reeve commanded that each of them should have a leaden weight attached to his neck and be sent to the bottom of the open sea. Then the bonds burst, and the lead fell from them, and they gave up the ghost to God, and the bodies were washed up on the shore. Christians buried them there with great reverence, and since then many miracles have occurred in that place. And the reeve who had sentenced them to death was shortly thereafter racked with such great pain that he no longer wanted to stay alive, and he commanded his own men to throw him into the sea, and the wild beasts in the sea swiftly devoured him so that not a single bone of his body reached dry land.

20 January: Sebastian

27. On the twentieth day of the month is the feast of St Sebastian, the noble martyr. The emperor Diocletian – he was pagan; he commanded that he be shot to death with arrows, so that he was as fully covered with them as that animal called 'hedgehog' is with its bristles. And when he could not kill him in this way, he then had him battered with poles until he gave up the ghost. And his body was buried in Rome in the place called 'Catacombs'.

20 January: Pope Fabian

28. On ðone ilcan dæg bið Sancte Fabianes tid þæs halgan papan; þæm wæs þurh haligne gast getacnod þæt he onfenge Romeburge biscopdome: Culfre com fleogan of heofonum ond gesæt ofer his heafde. Ond he hæfde ðære burge biscopdom þreottyne gear ond ændlefen monað ond twelf dagas. Ond he geðrowade eft on Decies dagum þæs caseres martyrdom for Criste, ond his lichoma resteð in Calistes mynster[56] æt Rome.

20 January: Marius, Martha, Audifax and Abacuc

29. On ðone ilcan dæg bið þara haligra gesinhina tid þa coman of Perscwara mægðe to Rome ond ðær geþrowadan æþelne martyrdom for Criste, ond heora suna twegen mid him. Þæs weres nama wæs Marius, ond þæs wifes nama wæs Marða, ond ðara suna naman wæron Audifax ond Abbacuc.

21 January: Agnes

30. On ðone an ond twentigðan dæg bið Sancta Agnan þrowung ðære halgan fæmnan, seo geþrowade martyrdom for Criste þa heo wæs þreottene geara. Þa fæmnan Simfronius, Romeburge gerefa, ongan þreatian his suna to wife. Þa heo þæt nolde, þa het he hi nacode lædan to sumum scandhuse. Þær hire brohte Godes engel swylcne gerelan swylcne næfre nænig fulwa, þæt is nænig webwyrhta, þæt mihte don on eorðan. Ðæs burhgerefan sunu wolde ræsan on hi on ðæm scandhuse ond hi bysmrian, ac fram deoflum forbroden he <aswalt>[a][57]. Þa cwædon Romware þæt heo wære dryegge ond scinlæce, ond hire man bestang sweord on ða hracan, ond ðus heo onsende hire gast to Gode. Ond hire lichoma resteð neah Romebyrig, on ðæm wege þe hi nemnað Numentana. Ond naht lange æfter hire þrowunge, heo ætywde hire yldrum on middeniht þær hi wacedon æt hire byrgenne, ond heo cwæþ to him: 'Ne wepað git me na swa ic dead sy, ac beoð me efenbliðe, forðon þe ic eom to Criste on heofonum geþeoded ðone ic ær on eorðan lufade.'

30. [a] aslat B, Ko, Herz.

20 January: Pope Fabian

28. On the same day is the feast of the holy pope St Fabian; it had been signified to him by the Holy Spirit that he would receive the episcopate of the city of Rome: a dove came flying from the sky and settled on his head. And he held the city's episcopate for thirteen years, eleven months and twelve days. And he later suffered martyrdom for Christ in the days of emperor Decius, and his body rests in the church of Callistus in Rome.

20 January: Marius, Martha, Audifax and Abacuc

29. On the same day is the feast of the holy couple who came from Persia to Rome and suffered a magnificent martyrdom for Christ there, and their two sons with them. The man's name was Marius, and the wife's name was Martha, and their sons' names were Audifax and Abacuc.

21 January: Agnes

30. On the twenty-first day is the passion of the holy virgin St Agnes, who suffered martyrdom for Christ when she was thirteen years old. Symphronius, the reeve of the city of Rome, tried to force that virgin upon his son, as a wife. When she refused, he had her led to a brothel, naked. There one of God's angels brought her a garment such as no fuller, that is no cloth-worker, could ever have produced on earth. The reeve's son tried to assault her in the brothel and rape her, but, dragged about by devils, he [?died]. Then the Romans said that she was a witch and a sorceress, and they thrust a sword down her throat, and she thus gave up the ghost to God. And her body rests near the city of Rome, on the road which they call [the Via] Nomentana. And not long after her martyrdom, she appeared to her parents in the middle of the night when they were keeping watch at her grave, and she said to them: 'Please do not weep for me as if I was dead; but be happy together with me, because I am united with Christ in heaven, whom I loved earlier on earth.'

22 January: Vincent

31. On ðone twa ond twentigðan dæg þæs monðes bið Sancte Uincentes ðrowung þæs diacones, se þrowade in Hispania ðære mægðe on ðære ceastre Falentia. Þær Datianus se casere[58] nydde Ualerium þone biscop ond ðone ylcan diacon Uincentium to hæþenscipe. Þa swygode se biscop. Ða cwæþ se diacon to þam biscope: 'Clypa ongen þissum deofles hunde þe þe on beorceð[a].' Þa het se casere forlætan ðone biscop, ond ðone diacon miclum witum underþeodan, ac ne mihte he mid nænge þara hine acwellan, ne hine genydan þæt he Criste wiðsoce. Ac he mid micelre blisse ðone sigefæstan gast to Gode onsænde. Ond se casere þa bebead þæt hine man forlete unbyrgedne, þæt hine fuglas ond wilde deor forswulgon. Ða com þærto blæc fugel, hæfde micele feðra, ond swift, se adraf ealle þa oþre fuglas[59] ond þa wildan deor fram þæm lichoman. Ða het se casere hine wurpan on widsæ. Ða ferede hine Godes hand þider þær hine Cristne men siððan a wulderlice aredon.

31. [a] onbeorceð Ko.

22 January: Anastasius

32. On ðone ilcan dæg bið þæs halgan weres ðrowung Sancti Anastas<i>[a][60], se wæs ærest dry in Persida mægðe, ond ða æfter þon gelyfde Criste. Ond Cossra, Persida cining, hine het ahon be oþerre hand ond hine nydde þæt he wiðsoce Godes geleafan. Þa he þæt ne geðafade, þa het se cining hine beheafdian. Þa Heraclius se casere genam his lichoman mid herge in Persida mægðe ond lædde to Rome; ond he resteð þær on Sancte Paules mynstre, æt þæm wætrum þe hi nemnað Aquas Saluias. Ond þær mon byrð his heafod on ðas dagas Cristenum mannum to reliquium[b].

32. [a] one or more letters partially erased, remainder used to serve as i B; [b] second i suprascript Ba.

23 January: Emerentiana

33. On ðone ðreo ond twentigðan dæg bið þære halgan fæmnan tid Sancte Emerentiane, seo wæs afeded mid Sancte Agnan þære halgan fæmnan. Ond swiðe anrædlice heo ætwat ðæm hæþnum on Rome heora dysignesse. Ond heo wæs stæned fram him [a]oþ þæt[a] heo hire gast onsænde. Ond þa sona com þunerrad ond legetsleht ond ofsloh ðone mæstan dæl þæs hæþnan folces þe hi stænde. Ond hire lichoma resteþ on ðære ylcan ciricean on Rome þær Sancte Agnan lichoma resteð.

33. [a-a] oþþæt Ko.

22 January: Vincent

31. On the twenty-second day of the month is the passion of the deacon St Vincent, who suffered in the country of Spain in the city of Valencia. There emperor Datianus forced Bishop Valerius and also that deacon Vincent to worship pagan gods. Then the bishop remained silent. Then the deacon said to the bishop: 'Call out against this devil's dog which barks at you.' Then the emperor commanded the bishop to be left alone and the deacon to be subjected to terrible torments, but he could not kill him with any of them, nor force him to renounce Christ. But with great joy he gave up his victorious spirit to God. And the emperor then decreed that one should leave him unburied, so that the birds and wild animals would devour him. Then there arrived a black bird, which had enormous wings, and being swift, it drove away all the other birds and the wild animals from the body. Then the emperor had him thrown into the open sea. Then God's hand transported him to a place where Christians have since always honoured him gloriously.

22 January: Anastasius

32. On the same day is the passion of St Anastasius, who was originally a sorcerer in the country of Persia, and then later came to believe in Christ. And Chosroes, the king of Persia, had him suspended by one hand and forced him to renounce his faith in God. When he refused, the king then had him beheaded. The emperor Heraclius seized his body with an army in the country of Persia and brought it to Rome; and it rests there in St Paul's minster, at the waters which they call Aquae Saluiae. And these days they carry his head about as a relic for Christians.

23 January: Emerentiana

33. On the twenty-third day is the feast of the holy virgin St Emerentiana, who was brought up together with the holy virgin St Agnes. And she very resolutely criticised the pagans in Rome for their error. And she was stoned by them until she gave up the ghost. And suddenly there was thunder and lightning which killed most of the pagans who had stoned her. And her body rests in the same church in Rome where St Agnes's body rests.

24 January: Babylas etc.

34. On ðone feower ond twentigðan dæg þæs monðes bið Sancte Babylles tid þæs halgan biscopes in Antiochia þære ceastre. Se biscop mid Cristene folce forstod cirican [a]duru <Numeriane>[a][61] ðæm hæþnan kasere. He cwæþ to him: 'Ne gang þu na on Godes hus; ðu hafast besmitene handa, ond þu eart deofles wulf.' Ond þa het se kasere hine beheafdian, ond his cnihtas þry mid hine. Þara wæs an twelf geara, oþer nigan geara, ond se þridda seofan geara. Ond ðara cnihta naman wæron Urbanus, Prilidanus, Epolanus. Ðis wæs swiðe clæne biscop, ond his clænnes swiðe mære wæs.

34. [a-a] duru a Numer<i> B, letters erased after a B, letters partially erased after Numer-, remainder left to serve as i B.

25 January: The Conversion of St Paul

35. On ðone fif ond twentigðan dæg þæs monðes bið Sancte Paules gehwerfnes[a] to Criste. Se wæs ær nemned Sauwlus, ond he wæs Cristenra manna ehtere ær ond cwellere. Ond ða færinga on midne dæg com leoht ofer hine of heofonum, ond stefn clypade, þus cweðende: 'Sawlus, Saulus, hwæt ehtes<t>[b] ðu me? Ic eom Ihesus' (ðæt is Hælend),[62] 'þone þu ehtest.' Ond þa æfter ðissum he onfeng fullwihte, ond his nama wæs Paulus geciged, ond he wæs ealra Cristenra ðeoda lareow. Forðon he is nemned ofer ealle oðre se æþela ðeoda lareow[c].

35. [a] r suprascript Ba; [b] ehtes B, Ko; [c] B breaks off after this word, gap is due to loss of leaves.

< . . . . . >

February: The Discovery of the Head of St John the Baptist

36. ...Sanctus[a] Iohannes[63] hine þæm men on niht, ond hine het gewitan mid þy heafde on Fenice þære mægðe, on ða burh Emisena. Swa þæt Iohannes heafod ferde: Hwilum hit hæfdon geleaffulle men, hwilum swiðe ungeleaffulle, ond æghwær hit scan mid godcundum wundrum.

36. [a] B resumes here.

The End of February

36a. Ðonne se Solmonað bið geendod, þonne bið seo niht feowertyne tida lang, ond se dæg tyn tida.

The Beginning of March

36b. On ðæm þriddan monðe on geare bið an ond þrittig daga. Ond se monð is nemned on Læden Martius, ond on ure geþeode Hredmonað.

24 January: Babylas etc.

34. On the twenty-fourth day of the month is the feast of the holy bishop St Babylas in the city of Antioch. Together with other Christians the bishop blocked the doorway of the church against the pagan emperor [Numerian]. He said to him: 'You cannot enter God's house; you have polluted hands, and you are the devil's wolf.' And then the emperor had him beheaded, and his three boys with him. One of them was twelve years old, the second nine years and the third seven years. And the boys' names were Urbanus, Prilidianus and Epolanus. This was a very chaste bishop, and his chastity was quite famous.

25 January: The Conversion of St Paul

35. On the twenty-fifth day of the month is St Paul's conversion to Christ. He first used to be called Saulus, and originally he was a persecutor and murderer of Christians. And then suddenly in the middle of the day a light came over him from the sky, and a voice called, saying: 'Saulus, Saulus, why do you persecute me? I am Jesus' (that means 'the Saviour'), 'whom you persecute.' And after this he received baptism, and he was called Paulus, and he was the teacher of all Christian nations. For that reason he is called above all others 'the noble teacher of nations'.

< . . . . . >

February: The Discovery of the Head of St John the Baptist

36. ... St John to that man at night and told him to travel together with the head to the country of Phoenicia, to the city of Emesa. That head of John's travelled like this: sometimes believers had it, sometimes hardened non-believers, and everywhere it shone with divine miracles.

The End of February

36a. When the 'Solmonað' is over, the night is fourteen hours long, and the day ten hours.

The Beginning of March

36b. In the third month of the year there are thirty-one days. And in Latin the month is called *Martius*, and in our language 'Hredmonað'.

2 March: Chad

37. On þone æfteran dæg þæs monðes bið þæs biscopes geleornes Sancte Ceaddan. Ond þæs wundor ond lif Beda se leornere wrat on Angelcynnes bocum. Ðone Ceaddan ðyder[64] se ercebiscop nam be norðan gemære, on ðæm mynstre Læstenga yge, ond hine asænde Myrceon to biscope ond Middelenglum ond Lindesfarum. Ond openlice Godes englas læddon hine mid wynsume sange to heofonum; ond þæt gehyrde his Godes þeow sum[65] þæs nama wæs Owine. Ond Sancte Ecgberht se ancra sægde Higebalde þæm abbode, þæt Ceaddes sauwl ðæs biscopes come of heofonum mid engla weorode, ond fette his broþor sawle to heofonum. Þæs biscopes lichoma resteþ æt Licettfelda on ðæm mynstre.

4 March: Adrian and Natalia

38. On ðone feorðan dæg þæs monðes bið Sancte Adrianes ðrowung þæs æþelan weres; se wæs ðæs caseres ðegnscipes ealdorman, ðe Maximianus wæs nemned. Ða geseah he hu anræde þa Cristenan men wæron, þa gelyfde he Criste ond þrowade micelne martyrdom for Criste. Adrianus wæs geong ond ænlic on eahta ond twentigum geara, ond he hæfde æþele bryd seo wæs on naman Nataleae, ond syxtyne monað hi wæron somod. Seo hine lærde þæt he næfre Godes geleafan forlete, ond þæt nænig woruldfægernes æfre his geðoht oncerde. Ond æfter þan ðe he hæfde martyrdom geðrowad for Gode, ða genam heo Sancte Adrianes hand seo him wæs ªof acorfenª, ond heo begeat þa mid deorwyrðum wyrtum ond bewand on godwebbe[66] ond asette æt hire heafdum on hire ræste ond hire hæfde þa to hihte. Þa ongan oðer rice man hæþen hi laðian to his gesynscipe. Þa weop heo ond cwæð: 'Drihten God, gefultuma me, þinre þeowenne, þæt ic næfre gewemme Adrianes brydræste ðines martyres.' Ond ða genam heo þa hand ane ond astag on scip ond lað of Nicomedia ceastre in Bisantiam ðone tun ofer ðone sæ, þyder Cristne men hæfdon gelæded Adrianus lichoman. Ða on middeniht, ða oncierde þæt scip on wonne siðfæt þurh deofles beswicennesse. Ða ætywde þær sona Adrianus, sittende on medmiclum scipe, ond clypade on þæt scip þe þæt wif on wæs mid þære hand ond cwæð: 'Ferað nu swa swa eowre seglas sendon geseted; se wind eow lædeþ.' Þa aras Natalia ond geseah þæt Sanctus Adrianus him lað beforan. Heo þa gefeonde cwæþ: 'Ecce dominus meus. Hona la min hlaford.' Ond þa sona ne mihte heo hine geseon. Heo þa lað on ðone tun þær se lichoma wæs ond asette þa hand to þæm lichoman ond hire þær gebæd ond þa hwon onslep, forðon þe heo wæs on þære sæ swiðe geswenced. Ða ætywde Sanctus Adrianus hire on ðæm slæpe ond cwæð hire to: 'Wel þu come.[67] Ac cum to us on ece reste.' Ond ða sona onsende heo hire gast to Gode.

38. ª⁻ª ofacorfen Ko.

2 March: Chad

37. On the second day of the month is the death of the bishop St Chad. And Bede the scholar wrote about his miracles and life in the books about the English. The archbishop took Chad in the north, in the monastery of Lastingham, to that place, and sent him to the Mercians as their bishop, and to the Middle Angles and the people of Lindsey. And God's angels openly led him under jubilant song to heaven, and one of his servants of God, whose name was Owine, heard that. And the hermit St Ecgberht told Abbot Higebald that Bishop Cedd's soul had come from heaven with a host of angels, and had fetched his brother's soul to heaven. The bishop's body rests in the monastery of Lichfield.

4 March: Adrian and Natalia

38. On the fourth day of the month is the passion of the famous man St Adrian; he was head of the guard of the emperor called Maximian. When he saw how resolute the Christians were, he believed in Christ and suffered a renowned martyrdom for Christ. Adrian was young and handsome at twenty-eight years of age, and he had a noble spouse who was called Natalia, and they were together for sixteen months. She taught him never to abandon his belief in God, and never to allow any worldly beauty to change his way of thinking. And after he had suffered martyrdom for God, she then took St Adrian's hand which had been cut off, and she covered it with precious herbs and wrapped it in expensive fabric and put it on her bed next to her head and kept it to console herself. Then another powerful pagan man proposed to marry her. Then she cried and said: 'Lord God, help me, your servant, that I should never defile the marriage bed of your martyr Adrian.' And she then took that one hand and boarded a ship and sailed from the city of Nicomedia to the town of Byzantium across the sea, where Christians had taken the body of Adrian. Then in the middle of the night, the ship then veered off course through the devil's deception. Then suddenly Adrian appeared there, sitting in a small boat, and called towards the ship on which his wife was with his hand and said: 'Sail now just as your sails are set; the wind will lead you.' Then Natalia stood up and saw that St Adrian was sailing ahead of them. Then she was glad and said: '*Ecce dominus meus*. Look, there is my lord.' And shortly afterwards she could no longer see him. She then sailed into the town where his body was and put the hand to the body and prayed there and then fell asleep for a while, because she had become very tired at sea. Then St Adrian appeared to her in her sleep and said to her: 'Welcome. Now come to us in eternal rest.' And shortly afterwards she sent the ghost to God.

7 March: Perpetua and Felicity

39. On ðone seofoðan dæg þæs monðes bið þara haligra wifa gemynd Sancta Perpetuan ond Sancta Felicitatis, ðara lichoma resteþ[68] on Cartagine þære miclan ceastre on Affrica mægðe. Þære Perpetuan mætte þa[a] heo wæs on mædenhade þæt heo wære on wæres hiwe, ond ðæt heo hæfde sweord on handa, ond ðæt heo stranglice fuhte mid þy. Þæt wæs eall eft on hire martyrdome gefylled, ða heo mid werlice geðohte deofol oferswiðde ond þa hæþnan ehteras. Ðonne wæs seo Felicitatis cristenwif[b][69], ond heo wæs mid bearne ða heo wæs for Criste on carcern onsænded. Þa woldan þa ehteras hi forþon forlætan. Da weop heo ond bæd God þæt he hire ðæt bearn [c]fram adyde[c], ond þa acende heo hit on ðære ylcan niht, on ðone seofoðan monað þæs beorðres. Ond heo geþrowade martyrdom for Criste.

39. [a] a subscript Ba; [b] Cristen wif Ko; [c-c] framadyde Ko.

7 March: Eastorwine

40. On ðone ilcan dæg bið þæs halgan abbodes geleornes se wæs nemned Eastorwine, se wæs her on Brytene on Sancte Petres mynstre æt Wiremuðan. Þæt wæs swiðe æþele wer for worolde, ond for Gode micle æþelra. He wæs Ecgferðes þegn ðæs cyninges, ac he forlet þa wæpna ond ða woruldlican wisan ond eode on þæt mynster ond wæs þær mæssepreost ond abbod. Ond hweþre he wæs for Gode swa eaðmod þæt he sulh heold, ond on iren sloh, ond corn ðærsc ond þæt windwode, ond ewa mealc, ond ða cealfas to cuum lædde, ond hlafas brædde, ond leac sette. Ond þa he wæs on feower ond twentigum geara,[70] æfter twelf gearum ðæs þe he wæs on ðæm mynstre, ða forlet he þa eorðlican lima ond gesohte þa heofonlico rico. Ond þy dæge þe he his gast on niht onsænde, he sæt ute on sunnan ond eallum ðæm wependum broðrum ond gnorniendum he sealde sibbe coss.

9 March: Forty Soldiers of Sebastea

41. On ðone nygeðan dæg ðæs monðes bið feowertiges cæmpena ðrowung on Sebastia ðære ceastre on Licinis tidum ðæs cyninges; þæt wæron strange weras ond sigefæste on woroldgefeohtum ond hwæþre arwyrðlice Gode herdon. Ða ongan þære burge gerefa, se wæs on naman Agriculaus, ond ðara cæmpena ealdorman, se wæs on naman Lyssiarchus[71], hi neddon[72] þæt hi Criste wiðsocan. Þa hi þæt ne geðafedan, þa hetan hi on æfenne on swiðe cealdum winde weorpan hi on deopne mere. On ðæm mere wæs micel is ond yfel, ond þær wæs hat bæþ bi þæm mere, þæt gif heora hwilc on his geleafan getweode, þæt he gebuge to þæm. Þa on forewearde niht snað þæt is ðara haligra lichoman; þa getweode heora an on his mode ond arn to þæm hatan baðe ond wæs sona dead ond him þa lima ealle tofeollan. Ða on niht com leoht of heofonum, swa hat swa sunne bið on sumera, ond þæt is gemelte ond þæt wæter

7 March: Perpetua and Felicity

39. On the seventh day of the month is the feast of the holy women St Perpetua and St Felicity, whose bodies rest in the great city of Carthage in the province of Africa. When she was a girl, Perpetua dreamed that she looked like a man, and that she carried a sword in her hands, and that she fought fiercely with it. That was all later fulfilled at her martyrdom, when she overpowered the devil and the pagan persecutors with masculine determination. Then there was the Christian woman Felicity, and she was pregnant when she was sent to prison for Christ. Then the persecutors wanted to let her go because of that. Then she wept and asked God that he would remove the baby, and then she gave birth to it in the same night, in the seventh month of pregnancy. And she suffered martyrdom for Christ.

7 March: Eastorwine

40. On the same day is the death of the holy abbot who was called Eastorwine, who lived here in Britain in St Peter's monastery at Wearmouth. He was a very noble man before the world, and even nobler before God. He was a thegn of King Ecgfrith, but he gave up his weapons and his secular life and joined the monastery and was a priest there and an abbot. But before God he was so humble that he held the plough, and forged iron, and threshed the corn and winnowed it, and milked the ewes, and brought the calves to the cows, and baked loaves of bread, and grew vegetables. And when he was twenty-four years old, after he had been in the monastery for twelve years, he left his earthly body behind and sought the heavenly kingdom. And on the day before he gave up the ghost at night, he sat outside in the sunshine and gave all the weeping and grieving brothers the kiss of peace.

9 March: Forty Soldiers of Sebastea

41. On the ninth day of the month is the passion of forty soldiers in the city of Sebastea in the days of King Licinius; they were strong men and victorious in worldly battles and nevertheless worshipped God reverently. Then the town reeve, who was called Agricolaus, and the soldiers' officer, whose name was Lysias, began to force them to renounce Christ. When they refused, they commanded that they be thrown into a deep lake, in the evening, in a very cold wind. In the lake there was a lot of nasty ice, and there was a hot tub by the lake, so that, if any of them were to have doubts about his faith, he could cross over to it. Then in the early hours of the night the ice was lacerating the bodies of the saints; then one of them changed his mind and ran to the hot tub and died straightaway and all his limbs came off. Then at night a light came from heaven, as hot as the sun is in the summer, and the ice melted and

wearð wearm, ond þara wearda sum geseah ðæt of heofonum com an læs feowertig wuldorbeaga[73] ofer þa cæmpan. Þa ongeat he þæt se wæs Gode wiðcoren, se þe on ðæt bæþ eode. Þa gecerde se weard to Criste, ond awearp his hrægl him of, ond hleop on ðone mere, ond stod on ðara midle, ond mid him þurh martyrdom his gast to Gode onsænde.

12 March: Pope Gregory the Great

42. On ðone twelftan dæg ðæs monðes bið Sancte Gregori<u>s[a] [74] geleornes ures fæder, se us fullwiht onsænde on ðas Brytene. He is ure altor ond we syndan his alumni: Ðæt is ðæt he is ure festerfæder on Criste, ond we syndon his festerbearn on fullwihte. Gregorius geþingade mid his tearum ond mid his gebedan Traianus sauwle ðæs hæþnan caseres, þæt hine God of helle gefreode ond on reste gelædde. Ond Gregorius cnihta sum geseah hwite culfran of heofonum[75] ond sittan on Gregorius heafde, ond him eþode on ðone muð þone godcundan wisdom þe he on bocum wrat.

42. [a] Gregories B with v suprascript above second e Ba, Gregori<u>s Ko.

13 March: Macedonius, Patricia and Modesta

43. On ðone þreotegðan dæg ðæs monðes bið þæs mæssepreostes tid Sancte Macedones, ond his wifes, seo wæs nemned Patricie, ond his dohtar, ðære nama wæs Modestae[a].

43. [a] B breaks off after this word, gap is due to loss of leaves.

< . . . . . >

17 March: Patrick

44. On ðone[a] seofonteoðan dæg ðæs [b]monðes byð[b] Sancte Patrices tyd ðæs halgan bisceopes, se gelærde ða mægðe to geleafan Hiebernia, þæt is Scotta mægðe. His fæder nama wæs Calpurne, and his modor nama wæs Contablata[76]. And he sylf wæs on hundteontigum geara and on an and ðrytegum ða he his gast ageaf. And ær ðam ðe he come on Scotta mægðe, ða cyld clypedon and cwædon: 'Cum, Sancte Patrice, and gehæle us ec.'

44. [a] ðon C* fol. 132a, ðone C* fol. 131b; [b-b] monðes Martii bið C* fol. 132a, monðes byð C* fol. 131b.

18 March: The First Day of Creation

45. ...ond[a] tosced on twa dæg ond niht.

45. [a] B resumes here.

the water warmed up, and one of the guards saw that from heaven there came thirty-nine crowns of glory over the soldiers. Then he realised that he who had gone into the bath had been rejected by God. Then the guard converted to Christ, and threw his clothes off, and leapt into the lake and stood in their midst, and gave up the ghost to God in martyrdom with them.

12 March: Pope Gregory the Great

42. On the twelfth day of the month is the death of our father St Gregory, who sent us baptism here to Britain. He is our *altor* and we are his *alumni*: that means that he is our fosterfather in Christ, and we are his fosterchildren in baptism. Gregory interceded with his tears and with his prayers for the soul of the pagan emperor Trajan, so that God might release him from hell and take him to rest. And one of Gregory's boys saw a white dove [come down] from heaven and sit on Gregory's head, and it breathed into his mouth religious wisdom which he recorded in books.

13 March: Macedonius, Patricia and Modesta

43. On the thirteenth day of the month is the feast of the priest St Macedonius and that of his wife who was called Patricia, and that of his daughter whose name was Modesta.

< . . . . . >

17 March: Patrick

44. On the seventeenth day of the month is the feast of the holy bishop St Patrick, who instructed the country of Hibernia in the Christian faith, that is the country of the Gaels. His father's name was Calpurnius, and his mother's name was Contablata. And he himself was 131 years old when he gave up the ghost. And before he came to the country of the Gaels, the children had called and said: 'Come, St Patrick, and heal us too'.

18 March: The First Day of Creation

45. ... and separated day and night.

19 March: The Second Day of Creation

46. On ðone nygonteogðan dæg <þæs>[a][77] monðes bið se æftera worolde dæg. On ðæm dæge God gescop ðone rodor betweoh heofone ond eorðan, ond betweoh ðæm twam sæum, ðæm uplican ond þæm niðerlican. Se uplica sæ[b] is to [c]þæm geseted[c] þæt he celeð ðære[d] tungla hæto, ðy læs heo[e] to swiðe bærne[f] þas nyþerlican gesceafte. [g]Ond se rodor ymbfehð utan eall ðas niðerlican gescæfte[g], sæ ond eorðan, swa seo scell[h] ymbfehð[i] þæt æg, swa leorneras secgað.

46. [a] om. B, Ko, <þæs> Herz; [b] se C, C starts here; [c-c] þam geset C; [d] þæra C; [e] hig C; [f] bærnon C; [g-g] om. C; [h] scyll C; [i] utan ymbfehð C.

19 March: Gregory Nazianzen

47. On ðone ilcan dæg bið Sancte Gregories tid þæs clænan[a] biscopes[b], se wæs on ðære ceastre Nazasene[c]. [d]Ðæm biscope[d] æteawdon[e] on his geogoðe ðurh nihtlice gesihð<e>[f78] [g]fægre fæmnan[g][79] ond cwædon[h] to him: 'Wit sendon[i] ðine sweostra[j], ond Crist unc sende to þe. Ond wit sceolon a [k]beon mid þe[k] þenden[l][80] ðu leofast. Ond uncer oðer hatte Sapientiae[m], oðer Castitas', þæt is ðonne 'Godcund Snyttro[n]' ond 'Clænnes[o]'.

47. [a] halgan C; [b] bisceopes C; [c] nazarene C; [d-d] þam bisceope C; [e] ætywde C; [f] gesihð B, Ko, gesyhðe C; [g-g] twa fægre fæmnan C; [h] þa cwædon C; [i] syndon C; [j] swustor C; [k-k] myd þe beon C; [l] þa hwile C; [m] sapientia C; [n] snytro C; [o] clænnys C.

20 March: The Third Day of Creation

48. On ðone twentegðan[a] dæg þæs monðes bið se þridda worolde[b] dæg. On ðæm[c] dæge God tosced[d] on twa eorðan ond sæ. Ond ðone sæ he gesette toþon þæt se[e] sceolde fixas[f] fedan, ond of þæm[g] [h]sceoldan regnas[h] ofer eorðan cuman, forðon[i] ðære lyfte gecynd is þæt heo tehð[j] to þa renas of ðæm[k] sealtan sæ, ond þurh hire mægen heo fersc<e>[l81] sendeþ to eorðan. Ond on ælcum anum geare weaxeð[m] þæt [n]flod ðæs sæs[n] feower ond twentigum siða, ond swa oft wanað[o]. Fylleþflod[p] bið [q]<nemned on>[q] Læden[r] malina, ond se [s]nepflod ledo[s].

48. [a] twentigoðan C; [b] worulde C; [c] þam C; [d] gescyrede C; [e] he C; [f] fiscas C; [g] þam C; [h-h] sceoldon renas C; [i] forþam C; [j] tyhð hyre C; [k] þam C; [l] fersc B, Ko, hig fersce C, Herzfeld, p. 227; [m] geweaxeð C; [n-n] sæflod C; [o] gewanað C; [p] se fylled C; [q-q] nemned on C, Herz, nemned ond on B, Ko; [r] leden C; [s-s] epflod leda C.

19 March: The Second Day of Creation

46. On the nineteenth day of the month is the second day of the world. On that day God created the sky between heaven and earth, and between the two oceans, the upper and the lower one. The upper ocean is positioned in such a way that it cools down the heat of the stars, so that it does not scorch the creatures down below too much. And the sky surrounds all the creatures down below on the outside, sea and earth, like a shell surrounds an egg on the outside, as scholars say.

19 March: Gregory Nazianzen

47. On the same day is the feast of the chaste bishop St Gregory, who lived in the city of Nazianzus. In his youth beautiful women appeared to the bishop in a dream at night, and spoke to him: 'We are your sisters, and Christ sent us to you. And we shall always be with you for as long as you live. And one of us is called Sapientia and the other Castitas', which thus translates as 'Religious Wisdom' and 'Chastity'.

20 March: The Third Day of Creation

48. On the twentieth day of the month is the third day of the world. On that day God separated earth and sea. And he made the sea so that it should feed the fish, and from it rains should come over the earth, because it is the nature of the air that it draws up the rains from the salty sea, and through its force sends fresh ones to the earth. And in any one year the force of the tide peaks twenty-four times and then decreases as often. Spring tide is called *malina* in Latin, and neap tide *ledo*.

20 March: Cuthbert

49. On ðone ilcan dæg bið Sancte Cuthberhtes[a] geleornes[b] ðæs halgan biscopes[c], se wæs on þysse Brytene on þære mægðe þe is nemned Transhumbrentium, ðæt is Norðanhymbra[d] ðeod. Ðone[e] wer oft englas sohtan, ond him tobrohtan heofonlico gereordo. Ond he hæfde þa [f]miht þæt he[f] mihte geseon manna sawle[g], [h]þa clænan[h] ond[i] ða oþre, þonne heo[j] [82] of [k]þæm lichoman[k] leordon[l]; ond ealle untrumnesse[m] he mihte hælan[n] mid his gebedum. Þæt wæs his wundra sum þæt he wæs æt gereordum on sumre[o] æþelre abbadissan[p] mynster[q] [83]. Ða he aras on dæge[r] of undernræste[s], ða sæde he þæt hine ðyrste ond het him beran wæter to, þæt he mihte onbergean[t]. Ða bletsode he þæt wæter ond his onbergde[u] ond sealde his mæssepreoste, ond he[v] hit sealde [w]heora þene[w]; heora[x] þen[y] wæs ðæs ilcan mynstres mæssepreost. Ða ondranc se þæs wætres[z] [a]ond sealde[a] hit þæm[b] breðer ðe [c]him ætstod[c], [d]ðæs mynstres profoste[d] [84]. Ond se ondranc eac þæs wætres[e], ond hi[f] gefeldan[g] begen þæt þæt[h] wæs ðæt betste win. Ond þa hi[i] þa tid hæfdon ymb[j] þæt to sprecanne[k], þa [l]ondette heora[l] ægðer oþrum þæt hi[m] næfre ær selre wiin[n] ne druncon.

49. [a] cuðberhtes C; [b] gewytennys C; [c] bisceopes C; [d] norðhymbra C; [e] and ðone C; [f-f] om. C; [g] sawla C; [h-h] ge þa clænan C; [i] ge C; [j] hig C; [k-k] þam lichaman C; [l] gewiton C; [m] untrumnyssa C; [n] gehælan C; [o] sumere C; [p] abbudessan C; [q] mynstre C; [r] dæg C; [s] undernreste C; [t] onbyrgean C; [u] onbyrgde C; [v] se C; [w-w] hyra þegne C; [x] and se hyra C; [y] þegen C; [z] wæteres C; [a-a] þa sealde se C; [b] þam C; [c-c] ðær æt hym stod C; [d-d] þæt wæs þæs mynstres prauast C; [e] wæteres C; [f] hig C; [g] gefeldon C; [h] hyt C; [i] hig C; [j] ymbe C; [k] sprecanne C; [l-l] andette hyra C; [m] hig C; [n] win C, Herz.

21 March: The Fourth Day of Creation

50. On ðone an ond twentegðan[a] dæg[b] [85] bið se feorða worolde[c] dæg. On ðæm[d] dæge God gesette on heofones rodor sunnan ond monan. Þa[e] wæs seo sunne seofon siðum beorhtre ðonne heo nu is, ond se mona hæfde ða ða beorhtnesse[f] þe seo sunne nu hafað[g]. Ac þa Adam ond Eua on [h]neorxnawonge gesyngodan[h], ða wæs þæm[i] tunglum [j]gewonad heora beorhtnes[j], ond hi[k] næfdon na siððan butan[l] þone seofoðan[m] [86] dæl heora[n] leohtes. Ac on domesdæge, þonne ure Drihten edniwað ealle gesceafte[o], ond eall mænnisc[p] cynn eft ariseð, ond hi[q] næfre ma ne gesyngiað[r], þonne scineð seo sunne seofon siðum[s] beorhtre[t][87] ðonne heo nu do, ond heo næfre on setl gangeþ[u]. Ond se mona scineð [v]swa swa nu seo sunne[v] deþ, ond he [w]næfre ma[w] wonað[x] ne ne weaxeð, [y]<ac he standeð a>[y] on his endebyrdnesse[z], þenden[a] þa tunglu her lyhtaþ on ðysse deadlican worolde[b]. Symble[c] ðonne se mona gangeþ æfter ðære sunnan, ðonne weaxeð his leoht; [d]<þonne he byð beforan hyre, þonne wanað hys leoht>[d] [88]. Ond swa he bið þære sunnan near, swa bið his leoht læsse; ond swa he bið hire fyrr, swa[89] bið his leoht mare; ond hwæðre he bið symble[e] þurh þa sunnan onlyhted.

50. [a] twentigoðan C; [b] dæg þæs monðes C, Herz; [c] worulde C; [d] þam C; [e] and þa C; [f] byrhtnysse C; [g] hæfð C; [h-h] neorxnawonge gesingodon C; [i] þam C; [j-j] heora beorhtnys gewanod C; [k] hig C; [l] buton C; [m] þryddan C; [n] hyra C; [o] gesceafta C; [p] mennisc C; [q] hig C; [r] singiað and C; [s] syðon C; [t] beorhtre Ko, beorhtor C, Herz; [u] ne gangeð C; [v-v] swa seo sunne nu C; [w-w] na ne C; [x] wanað C; [y-y] C, Herz, om. B, Ko; [z] endebyrdnysse C; [a] Herz, ac þenden B, Ko, æfre þa hwile C; [b] worulde C; [c] symle C; [d-d] þonne...leoht C, Ko, om. B; [e] symle C.

68

20 March: Cuthbert

49. On the same day is the death of the holy bishop St Cuthbert, who lived here in Britain in the province which is called Transhumbrentium ['land of those beyond the Humber'], that is Northumbria. Angels frequently visited that man and brought him heavenly food. And he had the capacity of seeing the souls of men, the chaste ones and the others too, when they left the body; and he could heal any illness with his prayers. One of his miracles was that he was receiving hospitality in the monastery of a noble abbess. When he got up from his lunchtime nap, he mentioned that he was thirsty and asked to be given water, for a drink. Then he blessed the water, and drank from it, and gave it to his priest, and he gave it to the man who was looking after them; that man was the monastery's priest. He then drank from the water and gave it to the brother who stood next to him, the monastery's provost. And he too drank from the water, and they both realised that it was the best wine. And when they had the opportunity to discuss this, they both then admitted to each other that they had never before had better wine.

21 March: The Fourth Day of Creation

50. On the twenty-first day is the fourth day of the world. On that day God positioned the sun and the moon in the heavenly sky. The sun then was seven times brighter than it is now, and the moon had the brightness that the sun has now. And when Adam and Eve sinned in Paradise, the brightness of the heavenly bodies was then dimmed, and since then they have only had one seventh of their former brightness. And on Doomsday, when our Lord will renew all of creation, and all humankind will be resurrected and they will sin no more, the sun will then shine seven times brighter than it does now, and it will never set. And the moon will shine like the sun does now, and it will never after that wax and wane, but it will always remain in its place, for as long as the heavenly bodies shine here in this mortal world. Always when the moon follows the sun, then its light grows; when it is ahead of it, then its light decreases. And by as much it is nearer the sun, by that much is its light less; and by as much as it is far away from it, by that much is its light more intense. And it is, however, illuminated always by the sun.

21 March: Benedict of Nursia

51. On ðone ilcan dæg bið Sancte ᵃBenedictes geleornesᵃ ðæs halgan abbodesᵇ; se wæs acenned on Nursiaᶜ ðære mægðe,⁹⁰ ond sona on his cnihthade he wilnadeᵈ þæt he Gode anum licadeᵉ. Ond on sumum þaraᶠ mynstra þe he ofergeseted wæs, þa broðorᵍ him woldon syllanʰ attor drincan, ⁱ⁻ⁱforðon þeⁱ hiʲ ne mostanᵏ for him nahtˡ unalyfedlices begangan. Ðaᵐ he þa senadeⁿ þæt fæt þe þæt attor on wæs, ða tobærst hit, swæᵒ þær mon stan ᵖon wurpeᵖ. Ond heᑫ mid bliðe mode fo<r>letʳ ðaraˢ broðra onwaldᵗ ond eft toᵘ his oðrum mynstre ferdeᵛ. Wæs his Godes þeowʷ sum⁹¹ se ˣæt nænigre gebedtide woldeˣ on ðære ciricanʸ wunianᶻ, ðæt he mid þæmᵃ oþrumᵇ his gebed gefylde. Ða geseah se abbodᶜ ðæt sum lytel ᵈcniht sweartᵈ teah þone broðor be his hrægle ᵉof þære cirican utᵉ. Se abbodᶠ þa sume dæge ᵍut gangendeᵍ sloh ðone broðor mid gyrde, ond ʰþa wæs se feond mid þy geflymedʰ, <s>waⁱ he hine sloh; ond se broðor siþþan a wunode æt his gebede. ʲDy dægeʲ ðe se abbodᵏ geleordeˡ, his broðra twegen geseagonᵐ ænne weg fram his mynstre rihte east on ðone heofon; seⁿ wæs bebræded mid hwitum ryftumᵒ ⁹², ond þær wæs ᵖon unrimᵖ scinendra leohtfata, ond þær stod an beorht wer ond cwæþ to him: 'Þis is se weg ᑫmid þy þeᑫ Drihtnes⁹³ se leofa Benedictus astagʳ on heofon.'

51. ᵃ⁻ᵃ Benedictus gewytennys C; ᵇ abbudes C; ᶜ nursio C; ᵈ gewylnode C; ᵉ lycode C; ᶠ þæra C; ᵍ broþru C; ʰ syllan C; ⁱ⁻ⁱ for þam ðe C; ʲ hig C; ᵏ moston C; ˡ nan þing C; ᵐ om. C; ⁿ gesenode C; ᵒ swa C; ᵖ⁻ᵖ onwurpe Ko, Herz; ᑫ he þa C; ʳ folet B, forlet C; ˢ þær C; ᵗ anweald C; ᵘ on C; ᵛ om. C; ʷ þeowa C; ˣ⁻ˣ nolde æt nanre gebedtyde C; ʸ cyrcan C; ᶻ gewunian C; ᵃ þam C; ᵇ oðrum broðrum C; ᶜ abbud C; ᵈ⁻ᵈ sweart cnyht C; ᵉ⁻ᵉ ut of þære cyrican C; ᶠ abbud C; ᵍ⁻ᵍ utgangende Ko; ʰ⁻ʰ se feond wæs þa myd þam aflymed C; ⁱ <s>wa Ko, þa Herz, erasure preceding wa B, swa C; ʲ⁻ʲ oð þæne dæg C; ᵏ abbud C; ˡ gewat C; ᵐ gesawon C; ⁿ and se C; ᵒ reafe C; ᵖ⁻ᵖ ungerym C; ᑫ⁻ᑫ myd þig C; ʳ astah C.

22 March: The Fifth Day of Creation

52. On ðone twa ond twentegðanᵃ dæg ðæs monðes bið se fifta ᵇdæg woroldeᵇ ⁹⁴. On ðæmᶜ dæge God gescopᵈ of wætere eall fleotendra fixaᵉ cyn ond fleogendra fuglaᶠ. Woroldsnottreᵍ men secgað þæt þa ficsasʰ syn on sæ hundteontiges cynna ond ðreo ond fiftiges, ond nis ænig mannaⁱ þæt he wite hwæt þaraʲ ᵏfugla cynnaᵏ syˡ ofer eorðan. Ond hwæðre æghwelcᵐ fugalⁿ wunað ᵒðæt ðætᵒ he of gesceapen wæs: Ða swimmaþ nu ᵖ<a on> sealtumᵖ yþum⁹⁵ ða þe of ðæmᑫ gesceapenʳ wæron, ond ða wuniað on merum ond on flodum þa þe of ðæmˢ ferscum wætreᵗ gescæpeneᵘ wæron, ond þa sittaþ on feldumᵛ ond ne magon swimman ða þe of þæs græses deawe geworhtʷ ⁹⁶ wæron, ond þa wuniað on wudum ða þe of þaraˣ treowa dropum gehiwode wæron, ond þa wuniað on fænneʸ þa þe gewurdon of þæs fænnesᶻ wætan.

52. ᵃ twentigoðan C; ᵇ⁻ᵇ worulde dæg C; ᶜ þam C; ᵈ gesceop C; ᵉ fisca C; ᶠ fugla cyn and C; ᵍ woruldsnotere C; ʰ fiscas C; ⁱ man C; ʲ þæra C; ᵏ⁻ᵏ fugelcynna C; ˡ sig C; ᵐ æghwylc C; ⁿ fugel C; ᵒ⁻ᵒ on þam ðe C; ᵖ⁻ᵖ sealtum B, Ko, a on sealtum C, Herz; ᑫ þam C; ʳ gesceapene C; ˢ om. C; ᵗ wæterum C; ᵘ gesceapene C; ᵛ felda C; ʷ geworhte C; ˣ þæra C; ʸ fenne C; ᶻ fennes C.

21 March: Benedict of Nursia

51. On the same day is the death of the holy abbot St Benedict; he was born in the region of Nursia, and even as a child he yearned that he might please only God. And in one of the monasteries over which he presided, the brothers tried to give him poison to drink, because with him they were not allowed to do anything illicit. When he then blessed the vessel which contained the poison, it then broke to pieces, as if one had thrown a stone against it. And he happily left the brothers to their own devices and went back to his other monastery. There was one of his servants of God who never wanted to stay in church at prayer-time, to perform his prayer with the other brothers. Then the abbot saw that a little black boy pulled the brother by his clothes out of the church. One day, on his way out, the abbot beat the brother with a stick, and as he hit him, the demon was driven out by that, and the brother always stayed for prayer from then on. On the day when the abbot died, two of his brothers saw a path from his monastery due east to heaven; it was covered with white vestments, and there were innumerable shining lights, and there stood a radiant man and said to him: 'This is the way by which the beloved of the Lord, Benedict, ascended to heaven.'

22 March: The Fifth Day of Creation

52. On the twenty-second day of the month is the fifth day of the world. On that day God created from water all species of swimming fish and flying birds. Men who know about the world say that there are 153 different types of fish in the sea, and there is nobody who would know how many types of bird there are on earth. But every bird lives in the place from which it was created: those which were created from the salty waves now always float on them, and those which were created from fresh water live on lakes and streams, and those which were created from the dew of the grass sit in the fields and cannot swim, and those which were shaped from the drops from the trees live in the woods, and those which were made from the moisture of the fen now live in the fen.

23 March: The Sixth Day of Creation, Adam and Eve

53. On ðone ðreo ond twentegðan[a] dæg ðæs monðes, ðæt[b] bið se [c]sexta worolde[c] dæg. On ðæm[d] wæs Adam gescæpen[e] se æresta man, ond Eua his [f]wif wæs gescæpen[f] of his ribbe. Hi[g] wæron swa gescæpene[h] ðæt hi[i] ne mihte fyr bærnan, ne wæter dræncean[j], ne wildeor[k] slitan, ne þorn stician[l]. Ne hi[m] ne mihtan[n] næfre forealdian, ne deade[o] beon, gif hi[p] Godes [q]bebod geheoldan[q]. Ac þa hi þæt [r]ne geheoldan[r], ða underðeoddon hi[s] selfe[t] ond eall ðæt[u] mænnisce[v] cynn to sare ond eldo[w] ond to deaðe. Adam lifde her on wræcsiðe nigan[x] hund geara [y]ond ðritig geara[y], ond his ban syndon bebyrged[z] [a]noht feorr[a] [b]be eastan[b] ðære byrig ðe is nemned Cebron[c], ond him is ðæt heafod suð gewend[d] ond þa fet norð,[97] ond seo byrgen is bewrigen mid dimmum stanum ond yfellicum.

53. [a] twentigoðan C; [b] om. C; [c-c] syxta worulde C; [d] þam dæge C; [e] gesceapen C; [f-f] wif seo wæs gesceapen C; [g] hig C; [h] gesceapene C; [i] hig C; [j] drencan C; [k] wylddeor C; [l] stingan C; [m] hig C; [n] myhton C; [o] dede C; [p] hig C; [q-q] bebodu geheoldan B, Ko, bebod geheoldon C; [r-r] ne geheoldon C; [s] hig hig C; [t] sylfe C; [u] þys C; [v] mennisce C; [w] to yldo C; [x] nygon C; [y-y] om. C; [z] gebyrged C; [a-a] naht feor C; [b-b] beeastan Ko; [c] om. C; [d] gewended C.

23 March: Theodoret

54. On ðone ylcan dæg bið þæs halgan mæssepreostes ðrowung se wæs nemned Þeodorotos[a]. Se þrowade[b] monigfealdne[c] martyrdom for Criste on Antiochia þære ceastre on Iulianus dagum þæs hæþnan[d] caseres, ond[e] [f]æt nyhstan[f] he wæs beheafdod. Ond ða þære ylcan niht ða <swealt>[g] se dema þe hine cwellan het mid unasecgendlicum sarum, efne swa[98] þæt he spaw his innoð ut[h] þurh his muð.

54. [a] theodoratus C; [b] þrowode C; [c] manigne C; [d] om. C; [e] and þa C; [f-f] ætnyhstan Ko, æt niehstan C; [g] om. B, swealt C, Herz, Ko; [h] om. C.

24 March: The Seventh Day of Creation

55. On ðone feower ond twentegðan[a] dæg þæs monðes, ðæt[b] bið se seofoða worolde[c] dæg. On ðæm[d] dæge God gereste fram[e] his weorce ond þone gehalgode.

55. [a] twentigoðan C; [b] om. C; [c] worulde C; [d] þam C; [e] from C.

25 March: Annunciation Day, The Crucifixion

56, 56a. On ðone fif ond twentegðan[a] dæg þæs monðes com Gabrihel[b] ærest to Sancta Marian mid Godes ærende, ond on ðone <dæg>[c] Sancta Maria wæs eacen geworden on Nazareth[d] ðære ceastre þurh þæs engles word ond þurh hire earena gehyrnesse[e], swa þas treowa ðonne hi[f] blostmiað þurh þæs windes blæd. On ðære ylcan

56, 56a. [a] twentigoðan C; [b] gabriel se engel C; [c] om. B, dæi suprascript Be, dæg C; [d] nazarenet C; [e] gehyrnysse C; [f] hig C;

23 March: The Sixth Day of Creation, Adam and Eve

53. On the twenty-third day of the month – that is the sixth day of the world. On that day Adam was created as the first man, and Eve his wife was created from his rib. They were made in such a way that fire could not burn them, nor water drown them, nor any wild animal tear them to pieces, nor any thorn pierce them. Nor could they ever grow old, or die, if they were to obey God's commandment. But when they did not obey it, they then subjected themselves and all of humankind to pain and old age and to death. Adam lived here in exile for nine hundred and thirty years, and his bones are buried not far east of the city called Hebron, and his head is pointing south and his feet north, and the grave is covered with horrible dark stones.

23 March: Theodoret

54. On the same day is the passion of the holy priest called Theodoretus. He suffered various types of martyrdom for Christ in the city of Antioch in the days of the pagan emperor Julian, and eventually he was beheaded. And then in the same night the judge who had commanded him to be killed died amid unspeakable pains, which reached the point where he spewed his entrails out through his mouth.

24 March: The Seventh Day of Creation

55. On the twenty-fourth day of the month, that is the seventh day of the world. On that day God rested from his work and sanctified it.

25 March: Annunciation Day, The Crucifixion

56, 56a. On the twenty-fifth day of the month Gabriel first came to St Mary with God's message, and on that day St Mary became pregnant in the city of Nazareth through the angel's word and through the hearing of her ears, like these trees when they blossom through the blowing of the wind. In the same place where her house

stowe þær hire hus ða wæs, þa[g] se engel hi[h] ane gemette, Cristne[i] men timbredon micle[j] cirican[k]. Ond ða æfter twa ond ðritegum[l] geara ond æfter ðrym monðum wæs Crist ahangen on rode on ðone ylcan dæg. Ond sona swa he on ðære rode[m] wæs, ða gescæfta[n] tacnedon þæt he wæs soð God. Seo sunne asweartade[o], ond se dæg wæs on þeostre[p] niht gecierred[q] fram midne[r] dæg oð non. Þa he æt þæm[s] none his gast onsænde[t], þa byfode[u] seo eorðe, ond stanas burstan[v], ond stanweallas tofeollan[w], ond deadra manna byrgenna[x] wurdon opene, ond monige [y]menn gesegon[y] þæt þa deadan arison of [z]þæm byrgennum[z] ond eodon geond[a] ða halgan burh on Hierusalem, [b]oþ þæt[b] Crist eft aras. Þa gewiton hi[c] mid hine[d] ge mid lichoman[e] ge mid sawle on ece wuldor, þæt we [f]þy untweogendran[f] be us gelyfden[g] ðæt we be þæm[h] leorniað. Seo Cristes rod, on þa[i] he wæs ahongen[j], is on ðære byrig Constantinapole[k] on cirican[l], ond[m] on treowenre ceste[n] belocen. Ond ðonne seo cest[o] bið onlocen[p], þonne cymð ðær [q]upp wunderlic[q] stenc [r]ond swa[r] wynsum, [s]swa þærs[s] syn ealle[t] blostman gesamnod[u]. Ond of þæm[v] ostum[99] ðæs treowes floweð[w] ut swetes stences wæte[x 100], se<o>[y] hafað eles onlicnesse[z]. Gif[a] mon [b]ðæs wætan ænne lytelne dropan seleð untrumum mæn[b], him bið sona sel.

[g] om. C; [h] hig C; [i] cristene C; [j] om. C; [k] cyrcan C; [l] þryttigum C; [m] om. C; [n] gescæfte B, with e expunged, and a suprascript Ba, gescæafta C; [o] aþystrode and asweortode C; [p] þystre C; [q] gecyrred C; [r] myddum C; [s] þam C; [t] onsende C; [u] abyfode C; [v] burston C; [w] tofeollon C; [x] byrgena C; [y-y] men gesawon C; [z-z] þam byrgenum C; [a] eond C; [b-b] oþþæt Ko; [c] hig C; [d] hym C; [e] lichaman C; [f-f] untweogende C; [g] n suprascript above second e Ba, gelyfdon C; [h] þam C; [i] re suprascript Be, þære C; [j] ahangen C; [k] constantinum polim C; [l] cyrcan C; [m] om. C; [n] cyste C; [o] cyste C; [p] unlocen C; [q-q] up wundorlic C; [r-r] and se byð swa C; [s-s] swylce þær C; [t] om. C; [u] ingesamnode C; [v] þam C; [w] flowað C; [x] originally wæte B with e expunged and suprascript a Ba, wæt`a´ Ko; [y] o erased after se B, and seo C, se Ko; [z] anlycnysse C; [a] and gif C; [b-b] sylð untrumum menn of þam wætan anne lytelne dropan C.

26 March: Christ's Descent into Hell

57. On ðone syx ond twentegðan[a] dæg ðæs monðes, on þone dæg Crist [b]reste dead on byrgenne[b] for us, ond his [c]sawl somod ond his godcundnes somod hergode[c] geond[d] hellegrund ond sloh þara[e] feonda weorod[f] mid his godcunde[g] sweorde ond draf on hellegrund ond hi[h] þær geband.[101] Þær hine ongeatan[i] weras ond wif ealle þa þe hine[j] æfre ær gelyfdon, ond hi[k] of þæm[l] witum [m]forð ræsdon[m] ond wepende him to fotum luton ond þis[n 102] cwædon: 'Help ure la, Hælend, nu þu hider come, ðeah ðe hit late wære. A[o] we gehyhton[p] to þinum cyme[q], ac adwæsc nu ðas gebeot[r] ond ðas wopas tobrec ond gecyþ þinne þrymm[s] on helle swa þu dydest[t] on eorðan, þær þu alysdest cuce[u] men mid þinre rode; [v]genere nu[v 103] us deadan[w] mid þine[x] deaðe.' Ðær[y] hine eac ongeaton Adam ond Eua, þær [z]hi asmorede[z] wæron mid deopum ðeostrum[a]. Ða ða hi[b]

57. [a] twentigoðan C; [b-b] dead C; [c-c] sawl somod and hys godcundnys samod hergode C, ond inserted before hergode Bf, Herz; [d] eond C; [e] þæra C; [f] werod C; [g] godcundan C; [h] hig C; [i] ongeaton C; [j] on hyne C; [k] hig C; [l] þam C; [m-m] forðræsdon Ko; [n] þus C; [o] æfre C; [p] gehyhtað C; [q] tocyme C; [r] beot C; [s] þrym C; [t] nu dydest C; [u] cwyce C; [v-v] genera C; [w] eac C; [x] þynum C; [y] and þær C; [z-z] hig asmorode C; [a] þrystrum C; [b] hig C;

then was, when the angel met her alone, Christians built a mighty church. And then after thirty-two years and three months Christ was crucified on the cross on the same day. And as soon as he was on the cross, the creation demonstrated that he was the true God. The sun grew black, and day was turned into dark night from midday to the ninth hour. When he gave up the ghost at the ninth hour, the earth then trembled, and stones broke apart, and stone walls collapsed, and the tombs of the dead opened up, and many people saw that the dead arose from their graves and walked around the holy city in Jerusalem, until Christ was resurrected. Then they went with him both in body and in spirit into everlasting glory, so that the more unwavering we would believe for ourselves, that we would learn from it. Christ's cross, on which he was hanged, is in the city of Constantinople in a church, and shut away in a wooden box. And when the box is opened, a wonderful smell comes out, so pleasant as if there were all blossoms gathered together. And from the knots of the tree trickles a sweet-smelling liquid, which is similar to oil. When you give one small drop of the liquid to a sick man, he recovers immediately.

26 March: Christ's Descent into Hell

57. On the twenty-sixth day of the month, on that day Christ was resting dead in his tomb for us, and together with his soul and together with his divinity harrowed the entire depth of hell, and killed a host of devils there with his divine sword and drove them into lowest hell and bound them up there. All men and women who had ever believed in him before saw him there, and they rushed forth from the torments and threw themselves at his feet, weeping, and said this: 'O help us, Saviour, now that you have come here, even though it may be late. We had always hoped for your coming, but put an end to these afflictions now and stop the wailing and make known your power in hell as you did on earth, where you redeemed living men with your cross: save us, the dead, now with your death.' Adam and Eve also saw him there, where they were stuck in deep darkness. When they then saw his bright light after that

gesawon his þæt beorhte leoht æfter þære langan worolde^c, þær Eua hine halsode for Sancta Marian mægsibbe ðæt he hire miltsade^d. Heo cwæþ to him: 'Gemyne, min Drihten, þæt seo wæs ^eban of minum banum, ond flæsc of minum flæsce^e.[104] Help^f min forþon^g.' Ða Crist hi^h butu ðonanⁱ alysde ond unrim^j bliðes folces him beforan onsende, ða he wolde gesigefæsted^k [105] eft siðian to ^lþæm lichoman^l.

^c worulde C; ^d myltsode C; ^{e-e} flæsc of mynum flæsce and ban of mynum banum C; ^f gehelp C; ^g forþam C; ^h hig C; ⁱ þanon C; ^j eac unrym C; ^k gesigefæst C; ^{l-l} þam lychaman C.

27 March: The Resurrection

58. On ðone ^aseofon ond twentegðan^a dæg þæs monðes bið se dæg on þone ure^b Drihten of deaðe aras, ond æfter^c his æriste hine tyn siðum monnum^d ætywde, swa hit on his godspelle awriten is, ond mid his þegnum æt^e gebrædne fisc ond huniges beobread, ond him ætywde^f ^gða wunda on his handum ond on his fotum ond^g þa gewundedan^h sidan, þæt ⁱhi þyⁱ soðlicor ongeaton þæt hit wæs soðlice his agen lichoma^j ðæt þær of deaðe aras. Seo byrgen is on Hierusalem þe he of aras; ðæt is sinowalt^k hus acorfen of anum stane. On ðæm^l magon nigon men standende him gebiddan. Ond hit is swa heah þæt hit bið mannes^m [106] oðres healfes fotes gemet bufan ðæmⁿ heafde. Ond se ingang is eastan in, ond on ða swiðran healfe ^oþæm ingange, þæt is on ða norðhealfe^o, is stænen bedd^p, seofon fota lang, þrym^q mundum hierr<e>^r [107] þonne þæs huses flor. On ðæm^s bedde reste Drihtnes lichoma^t on scetan^u bewunden, ða he wæs dead for us.

58. ^{a-a} seofen and twentigoðan C; ^b dæg C; ^c þa æfter C; ^d mannum C; ^e he æt C; ^f ywde C; ^{g-g} om. C; ^h gewundodan C; ⁱ⁻ⁱ hig þe C; ^j lychama C; ^k synewealt C; ^l þam C; ^m medemum men C; ⁿ þam C; ^{o-o} om. C; ^p bed C; ^q and þrym C; ^r hierra B, Ko, hierre C, Herz; ^s þam C; ^t lichama C; ^u scytan C.

The End of March

58a. Ðonne se Hreðmonað bið agan, þonne bið seo niht twelf tida lang, ond se dæg þæt^a ilce.

58a. ^a byð þæt C.

The Beginning of April

58b. On ðæm^a feorðan monðe^b on geare bið þritig^c daga. Þone monað^d man nemneð on Læden^e Aprelis, ond on ure geþeode Eastermonaþ.

58b. ^a þone C; ^b monað C; ^c .xxx. C; ^d om. C; ^e leden C.

long period, Eve begged him there for the sake of her kinship with St Mary to have mercy on her. She said to him: 'Remember, my Lord, that she was bone of my bones and flesh of my flesh. Help me therefore.' Then Christ released them both from there and also sent a countless number of joyful people before them, when, crowned with victory, he set out to return to his body.

27 March: The Resurrection

58. On the twenty-seventh day of the month is the day on which our Lord rose from death, and after his resurrection showed himself ten times to men, as it is written in his gospel, and with his disciples ate grilled fish and honeycomb, and showed them the wounds on his hands and on his feet and the pierced side, so that they might more genuinely understand that it was truly his own body that had arisen from death there. The tomb from which he arose is in Jerusalem; that is a round building carved out of one stone. Inside that, nine men standing up can pray to him. And it is so high that there is one and a half foot of space above one's head. And the entrance is from the east, and to the right of the entrance, that is on the north side, is a bed made of stone, seven feet long, three hands higher than the floor of the building. On that bed the Lord's body rested wrapped in a sheet, when he had died for us.

The End of March

58a. When the 'Hreðmonað' has passed, the night is twelve hours long, and the day also.

The Beginning of April

58b. The fourth month of the year has thirty days. That month is called *Aprilis* in Latin and 'Eastermonaþ' ['Easter month'] in our language.

3 April: Agape, Chionia and Irene

59. On ðone þriddan dæg þæs monðes bið þara[a] haligra fæmnena gemynd[b] ond ðara[c] eadigra gesweostra[d] Sancta[e] Agape ond Sancte Choniae[f] ond Sancte Hirena. Þis syndon[g] swiðe mære[h] fæmnan on De Uirginitate, ðæt is on fæmnena bocum. Ðas fæmnan [i]on Dioclitianus dagum ðæs caseres ðrowedon mærne martyrdom for Criste[i]. Se casere [j]hi sealde[j] his gerefan, þæs nama wæs Dulcitius, þæt [k]se hi genedde[k] þæt hi[l] Criste wiðsocan[m]. Ða sona swa he þa fæmnan geseah, ða wæs he[n] onstered[o] mid scondlice[p] luste. Ond he eode on nihtlice tid on þæt hus ðær[q] þa fæmnan [r]to Criste hi[r] gebædon, ond he þohte þæt he hi[s] gebismrode. Ðær[t] wæron inne geseted hweras ond pannan, ond he þa þurh Godes miht wæs oncierred[u] fram þæm[v] fæmnum ond clypte[w] ða hweras ond cyste[x] ða pannan, ðæt he wæs eall sweart [y]ond behrumig[y] [108]. Ond þa he [z]ut eode[z], þa flogon[a] hine his agene mæn[b], ond wendon þæt hit wære larbo, þæt is egesgrima. Þyssa fæmnena twa [c]Sisinnius se gesið het[c] sendan on fyr, [d]Agapan ond Chonie[d]. Ond þa þæt fyr wæs gemelted[e], þa wæron ða fæmnan [f]to Criste geleored[f], ond ða lichoman[g] wæron swa gesunde, þæt him næs forbærned ne feax ne hregl[h].

59. [a] þæra C; [b] om. C; [c] þæra C; [d] geswustra C; [e] sancte C; [f] chionie C; [g] synd C; [h] mære mære C; [i-i] geþrowedon mærne martyrdom for cryste on dioclitianes dagum þæs caseres C; [j-j] hig gesealde C; [k-k] se hig sceolde genyddan C; [l] hig Criste C; [m] wiðsocon C; [n] om. C; [o] onstyrod C; [p] sceandlice C; [q] þar C; [r-r] hig to criste C; [s] hig C; [t] þar C; [u] oncyrred C; [v] þam C; [w] he clypte C; [x] he cyste C; [y-y] om. C; [z-z] uteode Ko; [a] flugon C; [b] geferan C; [c-c] het sisninius se syð C; [d-d] þæt wæs agapan and chionian C; [e] gemylted C; [f-f] gewiten to cryste C; [g] lichaman C; [h] hrægel C.

5 April: Ambrose of Milan

60. On ðone fiftan dæg ðæs monðes bið þæs halgan biscopes[a] geleornes[b] Sancte Ambrosies[c]. He[d] wæs ðære burge biscop[e] Mediolana[f], ond[g] þær resteð his lichoma[h]. Þyses biscopes[i] ende gelamp on ðone sæternesdæg ær eastran[j], ond hwene [k]ær ðon ðe[k] he his gast ageafe[l], he sæde þæt he gesawe Crist selfne[m], ond þæt he him hloge to. Ðes biscop[n] is swiðe mihtig on frecnum wisum gescyldnesse[o] to biddanne. Þæt wæs gecyþed sumum heretogan, se ferde fram[p] Rome to gefeohte wið strangre þeode. Ða[q] gecyrde[r] he to þæs[s] biscopes[t] lice ond him þær gebæd. Þa[u] þære ylcan niht æteawde[v] he him on swefne, stondende[w] on lytlum[x] hylle on sumum felda, ond he sloh ðriwa mid his cricce on ða eorðan ond cwæþ: 'Hic, hic, hic. Her, her, her.' Ða se heretoga com ongean ðæm[y] reþan herge[z], þa gemitte[a] he þær swelcne[b] feld ond on [c]ðæm swylcne hyll, swa[c] [109] him ær on swefne ætywed wæs. Ond he gestod on ðæm[d] hylle ond hæfde his sweord on handa, ond [e]sona he wæs, se reða here[e],[110] on fleam gecierred[f].

60. [a] biscopes C; [b] gewitennes C; [c] ambrosi C; [d] and he C; [e] bisceop C; [f] þe mediolana hatte C; [g] om. C; [h] lychama C; [i] bisceopes C; [j] eastron C; [k-k] ær þam ðe C; [l] ageaf and onsende C; [m] sylfne C; [n] bisceop C; [o] gescyldnysse C; [p] from C; [q] and þa C; [r] gecyrde B, with y expunged and e suprascript Ba, gecyrde C, gec`e´rde Ko; [s] þyses C; [t] bisceopes C; [u] and þa C; [v] þa ætywde C; [w] standende C; [x] lytelre C; [y] þam C; [z] here C; [a] gemette C; [b] swylcne C; [c-c] þam felda swylce hylle swylce C; [d] þære C; [e-e] þa sona wæs se reða here C; [f] gehwyrfed C.[u]

3 April: Agape, Chionia and Irene

59. On the third day of the month is the commemoration of the holy virgins and blessed sisters St Agape, St Chionia and St Irene. These are very famous virgins in the *De uirginitate*, that is in the Books of Virgins. These virgins suffered a famous martyrdom for Christ in the days of emperor Diocletian. The emperor handed them over to his reeve, whose name was Dulcitius, so that he might force them to renounce Christ. As soon as he saw the virgins, he was seized by sexual lust. And at nighttime he went to the house where the virgins were praying to Christ and wanted to dishonour them. Inside there were pots and pans stored, and through the power of God he was diverted from the virgins and hugged the pots and kissed the pans, so that he was all black and sooty. And when he came outside, his own men ran away from him, thinking that it might be a *larua*, that is a horror creature. Sisinnius the reeve had two of these virgins, Agape and Chionia, sent into the fire. And when the fire had died down, the virgins had departed to Christ, and the bodies were so intact, that neither their hair nor clothes had been burned at all.

5 April: Ambrose of Milan

60. On the fifth day of the month is the death of the holy bishop St Ambrose. He was the bishop of the city of Mediolana [i.e. Milan], and his body rests there. The death of this bishop occurred on the Saturday before Easter, and just before he gave up the ghost, he said that he could see Christ himself, and that he was smiling at him. This bishop is very powerful when prayed to for protection in dangerous situations. That was revealed to a general, who was advancing to battle from Rome, against a more powerful nation. Then he turned to the bishop's body and prayed there. Then in the same night he appeared to him in a dream, standing on a small hill in a field, and he struck the ground three times with his crosier and said: '*Hic, hic, hic*. Here, here, here.' When the general went to meet the formidable army, he found such a field there and in it such a hill, as had appeared to him in the dream. And he stood on the hill, sword in hand, and soon it (that is the terrible army) had been turned to flight.

5 April: Irene

61. On ðone ylcan dæg bið Sancta[a] Hirenan tid ðære halgan fæmnan. [b]Ða fæmnan[b] Sisinnius se gesið sealde[c] his cæmpum[d] to bismrienne. Ða [c]hi þa hi[e] læddon to þære scondlican[f] stowe, ða ætywdon þær twegen Godes englas[111] on cæmpena[g] hiwe ond genamon ða fæmnan ond [h]hi gelæddan[h] on swa heanne[i] munt, þær hire ne mihte [j]nænig mon[j] [k]to genealæcean[k],[112] ond heo þær hire gast onsænde[l].[113] Ond hire lichoma[m] rested on Ðæssalonica[n] ðære ceastre, ðær hire sweostra[o] lichoman[p] syndon, Agapan ond Chonian[q].

61. [a] sancte C; [b–b] om. C; [c] hig sealde C; [d] cempum C; [e–e] hig hig C; [f] sceandlican C; [g] cempena C; [h–h] gelæddon hig C; [i] heahne C; [j–j] nan man C; [k–k] togenealæcean Ko, to genealæcan C; [l] onsende C; [m] lychama C; [n] tessalonica C; [o] swustra C; [p] lychaman C; [q] chionian C.

9 April: Seven Women at Sirmium

62. On ðone nigeðan[a] dæg ðæs monðes bið seofon fæmnena tid, þa þrowedon[b] martyrdom for Criste on Syria mægðe.[114] [c]Þara naman syndon[c] Saturnina, Hilarina, Dominando, Rogantina, Serotina[d], Donata, Paulina.

62. [a] nygoðan C; [b] geþrowedon C; [c–c] and þæra nama wæron C; [d] sorotina C.

11 April: Guthlac

63. On ðone ændleftan[a] dæg þæs monðes bið Sancte Guthlaces[b] geleornes[c] ðæs anceran[d] on Brytone[e], þæs lichoma[f] rested on þære stowe [g]ðe is cweden[g] Cruwland. His nama is[h] on [i]Læden belli munus[i],[115] ond his halignes[j] wæs sona getacnad[k] æt his acennisse[l] mid heofonlicum[m] tacnum. Men gesegon[n] cuman fægre[o] hand of heofonum[p] ond gesegnian[q] þæs huses duru[r] ðe he wæs on acenned, ond eft to heofonum[s] gewat. Ond ymb[t] an gear ðæs þe he on [u]ancorsetle wunade[u], he geearnade[v] ðæt him spræc an Godes engel to æghwelce[w] æfenne ond eft on ærnemergen[x], ond him sæde [y]heofonlico geryno[y].

63. [a] endlyftan C; [b] guðlaces C; [c] gewytennys C; [d] ancran C; [e] brytene C; [f] lychama C; [g–g] om. C; [h] wæs C; [i–i] leden belli minus C; [j] halignys C; [k] getacnod C; [l] acennednysse C; [m] heofonlicum C; [n] gesawon C; [o] fægere C; [p] heofenum C; [q] gesenian C; [r] dura C; [s] heofenum C; [t] þa ymbe C; [u–u] ancersetle wunode C; [v] geearnode C; [w] æghwylce C; [x] mergen C; [y–y] heofenlicu gerynu C.

14 April: Valerianus, Tiburtius and Maximus

64. On ðone feowerteoðan[a] dæg þæs monðes bið þara[b] haligra gebroðra[c] tid Sancte Ualerianes[d] ond Sancte Tiburties[e]; ða Allmachius[f][116], Romeburge gerefa, nedde[g] mid witum ðæt hi[h] Criste wiðsocan[i]. Ða hi[j] þæt ne geþafodan[k], þa het he hi[l] beheafdian.

64. [a] feorteoðan C; [b] þæra C; [c] broðra C; [d] Ualeriane C; [e] tiburtii C; [f] almatheus C; [g] nydde C; [h] hig C; [i] wyðsocon C; [j] hig C; [k] geþafedon C; [l] hig C;

5 April: Irene

61. On the same day is the feast of the holy virgin St Irene. Sisinnius the reeve handed that virgin over to his soldiers to have her put to shame. When they then led her away to the place of her humiliation, two of God's angels appeared there in the shape of soldiers, and took the virgin and led her up such a high mountain that nobody could get near her, and she gave up the ghost there. And her body rests in the city of Thessalonica, where the bodies of her sisters Agape and Chionia are.

9 April: Seven Women at Sirmium

62. On the ninth day of the month is the feast of seven women who suffered martyrdom for Christ in the province of Syria. Their names are Saturnina, Hilarina, Dominanda, Rogatina, Serotina, Donata, Paulina.

11 April: Guthlac

63. On the eleventh day of the month is the death of the hermit St Guthlac in Britain, whose body rests in the place called Crowland. His name means *belli munus* in Latin, and his sanctity was revealed early on, at his birth, through heavenly signs. Men saw a beautiful hand come down from heaven and bless the door of the house in which he was born, and then disappeared back to heaven. And after he had lived in his hermitage for one year, he merited that an angel of God spoke to him every evening and also early in the morning, and told him heavenly mysteries.

14 April: Valerianus, Tiburtius and Maximus

64. On the fourteenth day of the month is the feast of the holy brothers St Valerianus and St Tiburtius; Almachius, the reeve of the city of Rome, forced them under tortures to renounce Christ. When they refused, he commanded them to be beheaded.

Þa se man ðe þæt sceolde behealdan þæt ᵐhi man beheafdadeᵐ, wepende ond swergende he sæde þæt he gesawe heoraⁿ sawla gongan° ut of ᵖþæm lichomanᵖ fægre gefretwadeᑫ,¹¹⁷ ond þæt he gesawe Godes englas swa scinende swa sunne, ond þa hiʳ bæron to heofonumˢ midᵗ ᵘheora feþeraᵘ flihte. Ond se man þa gelyfde Godᵛ, ond he wæs ofswungen on deað for Criste, ond his nama wæs Maximus.

ᵐ⁻ᵐ hig mon beheafdode C; ⁿ hyra C; ° gangan C; ᵖ⁻ᵖ þam lichaman C; ᑫ gefrætwode C; ʳ hig C; ˢ heofenum C; ᵗ A starts here; ᵘ⁻ᵘ hyra fyðra C; ᵛ on god C.

18 April: Eleutherius, Antia

65. On ðone eahtateogðanᵃ dæg ðæs monðes ᵇbið þæsᵇ halganᶜ biscopesᵈ tid Sancte Eleutheriᵉ ond his modorᶠ, ðære nama wæs ᵍSancta Anthiaeᵍ. Heʰ wæs þære burge biscopⁱ ðe is nemned Mechaniaʲ¹¹⁸, ᵏin Apulia þære mægðeᵏ, ac he geðrowadeˡ eft on Rome martyrdom for Criste. Adrianus se casere hine ðreatadeᵐ þæt he Criste wiðsoce. Ða he þæt ne wolde, þa het se casere gesponnanⁿ feower wilde hors to scride° ond hine gebundenne on þæt scridᵖ asettan, þæt þa wildan hors sceoldanᑫ yrnan on hearde wegas on westene ond him þa limaʳ eall tobrecan. Þa com Godes engel of heofonumˢ ond gestilde ðæmᵗ horsum, ond hi gelæddon þæt scrid on hea dune, þær him comanᵘ to monigraᵛ cynna wilddeor ond wunedon mid hineʷ. Ond þonne he ˣhof his handa uppˣ to heofonumʸ, ðonne hofanᶻ ða deor heoraᵃ fet uppᵇ ¹¹⁹ ond heredon God mid hineᶜ. Þa het se casere ᵈhis huntanᵈ ¹²⁰ hine ðær gefecceanᵉ ond hine midᶠ sweorde ofslean. Ða com stefnᵍ of heofonumʰ ond cwæð: 'Cum, min þeow Eleuðeriusⁱ, mine englas ðe lædaðʲ on ða heofonlicanᵏ Hierusalem.' Þa feollˡ his modorᵐ ⁿufan onⁿ his lichoman° ond cwæþ: 'Min sunu, gemyneᵖ þu me on þære eceanᑫ reste.' Ond se casere hiʳ het gemartyrian, ond God wuldriendeˢ heo ageaf hire gast.

65. ᵃ eahtateoðan C; ᵇ⁻ᵇ byð þæs byð þæs C; ᶜ om. C; ᵈ bisceopes C; ᵉ eleutherii C; ᶠ moder C; ᵍ⁻ᵍ anthie C; ʰ and he C; ⁱ bysceop C; ʲ mecherie C; ᵏ⁻ᵏ and on þære mægðe þe ys nemned apolina C; ˡ geþrowode C; ᵐ þreatode C; ⁿ gespannan C; ° scriðe C; ᵖ scryð C; ᑫ sceoldon C; ʳ lymu C; ˢ heofenum C; ᵗ þam C; ᵘ comon C; ᵛ manigra C; ʷ hym C; ˣ⁻ˣ hys handa hof up C; ʸ heofenum C; ᶻ hofon C; ᵃ hyra C; ᵇ up C; ᶜ hym and C; ᵈ⁻ᵈ om. C; ᵉ gefeccan C; ᶠ om. C; ᵍ stefen C; ʰ heofenum C; ⁱ eleutherius C; ʲ gelædað C; ᵏ heofenlican C; ˡ feol C; ᵐ moder C; ⁿ⁻ⁿ onufan C; ° lychaman C; ᵖ gemun C; ᑫ ecan C; ʳ hig C; ˢ wuldrigende C.

21 April: Æthelwald

66. On ðone an ond twentegðanᵃ dæg ðæs monðes bið þæs halgan anceranᵇ geleornesᶜ Sancte Æþelwaldes, se gesetᵈ ancersetl on Fearne ᵉðæm ealondeᵉ ærest æfter Cuthbrihteᶠ ᵍðæm halgan biscopeᵍ. Ond ʰæfter þon þeʰ he twelf gear ðær wunode, þa eode he on ðone gefean ðære ⁱecean eadignesseⁱ.¹²¹ Ðæs Aþeuualdesʲ wunder wæs þæt

66. ᵃ twentigoðan C; ᵇ ancran C; ᶜ gewytennys C; ᵈ gesæt C; ᵉ⁻ᵉ þam ealande C; ᶠ sancte cuðberhte C; ᵍ⁻ᵍ þam bisceope C; ʰ⁻ʰ æfter þam þe C; ⁱ⁻ⁱ ecan eadignysse C; ʲ æðelwaldes C;

Then the man who was supposed to see that they got beheaded, weeping and swearing an oath – he said that he saw their souls leave the body beautifully adorned, and that he saw God's angels as radiant as the sun, and carried them to heaven with the flying of their wings. And the man then believed in God, and he was beaten to death for Christ, and his name was Maximus.

18 April: Eleutherius, Antia

65. On the eighteenth day of the month is the feast of the holy bishop St Eleutherius, and that of his mother, whose name was St Antia. He was bishop in the city called [Aecae], in the province of Apulia, but he later suffered martyrdom for Christ in Rome. Emperor Hadrian forced him to renounce Christ. When he refused, the emperor had four wild horses harnessed to a chariot and had him put on the chariot, tied up, so that the wild horses would run on rough tracks in the desert and smash his limbs to pieces. Then God's angel came from heaven and calmed down the horses, and they took the chariot up a high hill, where many wild animals joined him and lived with him. And when he raised his hands up to heaven, the animals raised their paws up and worshipped God with him. Then the emperor commanded his hunters to fetch him from there and to kill him with the sword. Then a voice came from heaven and said: 'Come, my servant Eleutherius, my angels will lead you into the heavenly Jerusalem.' Then his mother fell on his body and said: 'My son, remember me in eternal rest.' And the emperor had her martyred, and, praising God, she gave up the ghost.

21 April: Æthelwald

66. On the twenty-first day of the month is the death of the holy hermit St Æthelwald, who was the first to set up his hermitage on Farne Island after the holy bishop Cuthbert. And after he had lived there for twelve years, he then entered the joy of eternal bliss. Æthelwald's miracle was that he was talking to one of his pupils and

he spræc to ᵏhis leornera sumumᵏ ond þa færinga oðswigdeˡ he, swaᵐ he hwæshwugunⁿ hercnadeᵒ. Ða fregnᵖ se his þegn hine, forhwonᑫ he swa dyde. Ða cwæþ he: 'Hu mihte ic buʳ somodˢ ge on heofonᵗ geheranᵘ ge her sprecan?'

ᵏ⁻ᵏ sumum hys leornera C; ˡ ætswigde C; ᵐ swylce C; ⁿ hwæs C; ᵒ hlyste and C; ᵖ frægn C; ᑫ forhwan C; ʳ butu C; ˢ samod C; ᵗ heofenum C; ᵘ gehyran C.

23 April: George

67. On ðone ðreo ond twentegðanᵃ dæg þæs monðes bið Sancte Georgiusᵇ tid ðæs æþelan weresᶜ; ðone¹²² Datianus¹²³ se casere seofanᵈ gear mid unasegendlicum witum hine þreadeᵉ þæt he Criste wiðsoce, ond he <næfre>ᶠ¹²⁴ hine oferswiðan mihteᵍ; ond ða æfterʰ seofon gearum het he hine beheafdian. Ða he þa wæs lædedⁱ to þære beheafdungaʲ, þa com fyr of heofonumᵏ ond forbærnde ðone hæðanˡ casere ond ealle þa þe mid hineᵐ ær tintergedonⁿ þone halgan wer. Ond ᵒhe, Sanctusᵒ Georgiusᵖ, him to Drihtne gebæd ond ðus cwæð: 'Hælendeᑫ Crist, onfoh minum gaste. Ond ic þe bidde þæt swa hwilc man ðeʳ min gemynd on eorðan do, þonne afyrr þuˢ fram þæs mannes husumᵗ ælce untrumnesseᵘ; ne him feond sceþþeᵛ, ne hungor, ne mancwyldʷ. Ond gif monˣ minne namanʸ nemneð on ænigre frecennesseᶻ, oððe on sæ oþþe on siðfæteᵃ, þonne gefylgeᵇ se þinreᶜ mildheortnesseᵈ.'¹²⁵ Ða com stefnᵉ of heofonumᶠ ond cwæð ᵍto himᵍ: 'Cum, þu gebletsoda. ʰSwa hwelcʰ¹²⁶ swa on ænigre frecennesseⁱ minne naman þurh þe gecegðʲ, ic hine gehereᵏ.' Ond siððan þissesˡ halgan weres mihta wæron oft micleᵐ gecyþed; ⁿþæt mægⁿ ongetanᵒ se þe rædeþ Sancte Arculfes boc, þæt se man wæs stranglice gewitnadᵖ ᑫ⁻ᑫse geunaradeᑫ ¹²⁷ Sancte Georgiesʳ anlicnesseˢ, ond se wæs wið his feondum gescildedᵗ ᵘ⁻ᵘbetweoh micle frecennisseᵘ se þe ʷhi to geþingungᵛ¹²⁸ sohteʷ.

67. ᵃ twentigoðan C; ᵇ georius C; ᶜ martyres C; ᵈ seofen C; ᵉ þreatode C; ᶠ næfre A, C, Herz, no hwæþre B, nohwæþre Ko; ᵍ ne mihte C; ʰ æfter þam C; ⁱ gelæd C; ʲ beheafdunge C; ᵏ heofenum C; ˡ hæðenan C; ᵐ hym C; ⁿ tyntregodon C; ᵒ⁻ᵒ sancte C; ᵖ georius C; ᑫ hælend C; ʳ swa C; ˢ om. C; ᵗ huse C; ᵘ untrumnysse C; ᵛ ne sceððe C; ʷ mancwealm C; ˣ man C; ʸ nama C; ᶻ frecednysse C; ᵃ oðrum siðfæte C; ᵇ fylge C; ᶜ A breaks off after þinre; ᵈ myldheortnysse C; ᵉ stefen C; ᶠ heofenum C; ᵍ⁻ᵍ om. C; ʰ⁻ʰ and swa hwylc man C, swa hwelc mon Herz; ⁱ stowe and frecednysse C; ʲ cygð C; ᵏ gehyre C; ˡ þyses C; ᵐ mycele C; ⁿ⁻ⁿ þa mæg C; ᵒ ongytan C; ᵖ gewytnod C; ᑫ⁻ᑫ se ðe geunarode C, se þe geunarade Herz; ʳ georius C; ˢ anlycnysse C; ᵗ gescyld C; ᵘ⁻ᵘ betweox mycelre frecednysse C; ᵛ geþingum Ko; ʷ⁻ʷ hym þa anlycnysse to þyngunge gesohte C.

24 April: Wilfrid

68. On ðone feower ond twentegðanᵃ dæg þæs monðes bið Sancte Willferðesᵇ geleornesᶜ ðæs halgan biscopesᵈ, ðæs halignesᵉ wæs sona æt his acennisseᶠ gecyþed. Þæt hus þæt he wæs on acenned, þæt wæs byrnende gesæwenᵍ ʰeallum þæm neahmonnumʰ, ond se legⁱ sloh to heofonumʲ. Ond hiᵏ þær ˡto urnonˡ ond woldon mid wætreᵐ dwæscan ðone bryne æfter monnaⁿ þeaweᵒ. Ond þa hiᵖ ᑫþær to comonᑫ, ða ne

68. ᵃ twentigoðan C; ᵇ wylferðes C; ᶜ gewytennys C; ᵈ bysceopes C; ᵉ halignys C; ᶠ acennednysse C; ᵍ gesewen C; ʰ⁻ʰ þam mannum þe ðær neah wæron C; ⁱ lig C; ʲ heofenum C; ᵏ hig C; ˡ⁻ˡ tournon Ko; ᵐ wætere C; ⁿ manna C; ᵒ þeawum C; ᵖ hig C; ᑫ⁻ᑫ to urnon C, þær tocomon Ko;

then suddenly went quiet, as if he was listening to something. Then that man of his asked him, why he was behaving like that. Then he said: 'How could I both at once listen into heaven and speak here?'

23 April: George

67. On the twenty-third day of the month is the feast of the noble man St George; emperor Datianus forced him for seven years with unspeakable tortures to renounce Christ, but he could never overpower him; and then after seven years he ordered him to be beheaded. When he was being led to the execution, fire came from heaven and burnt the pagan emperor to death, and all those who had earlier tortured the holy man with him. And he, St George, prayed to the Lord and spoke thus: 'Saviour Christ, receive my spirit. And I ask you that whichever man may celebrate my memory on earth, remove then from this man's dwellings every illness; let no enemy harm him, nor hunger, nor pestilence. And if anyone mentions my name in any danger, either at sea or on a journey, may he obtain your mercy.' Then a voice came from heaven and said to him: 'Come, you blessed one. Whoever calls upon my name through you in any danger, I will hear him.' And afterwards the powers of this holy man were often made widely known; anyone who reads St Arculf's book will realise that, [namely] that the man who dishonoured George's image was severely punished, and he who sought it for intercession was protected from his enemies in great danger.

24 April: Wilfrid

68. On the twenty-fourth day of the month is the death of the holy bishop St Wilfrid, whose holiness was made known even at his birth. The house in which he was born was seen burning by all the neighbours, and the flames rose up to the sky. And they came running there and tried to extinguish the fire with water, as people do. And

gemitton hi^r ^(s)þær nænigne^s bryne. ^tOnd þissum biscope onsundrum ætywde Sanctus Michahel ond him^t sæde hu andfænge^u his dæda^v wæron, ond hu lange his lif sceolde beon. Ond þa^w he his gast ageaf^x, ða com sweg suðaneastan of ðære lyfte ^yswa swa^y micelra fugla^z sweg, ond gesetton on þæt hus ðær he inne wæs. Þæt wæs ðara^a engla flyht þe hine to heofonum^b læddon.

^r hig C; ^(s–s) nænne C; ^(t–t) ac sancte michael ætywde þysum bysceope and hym onsundrum C; ^u andfenge C; ^v dæda gode C; ^w þan C; ^x onsende and ageaf C; ^(y–y) swylce C; ^z fugola C; ^a þæra C; ^b heofenum C.

25 April: Rogation Day

69. On ðone fif ond twentegðan^a dæg ðæs monðes bið seo tid on Rome ond on eallum Godes ciricum^b seo is nemned Laetania^c Maiora, þæt is þonne micelra bena dæg. On ðæm^d dæge eall Godes folc mid eaðmodlice^e relicgonge sceal God biddan þæt he ^fhim forgefe^f ðone gear siblice tid ond ^gsmyltelico gewidra^g ond genihtsume wæstmas ond ^hheora lichoman^h trymnysse. Ðone dæg Grecas nemnað zymologesin^i, þæt is þonne hreowsunge dæg ond dædbote.

69. ^a twentigoðan C; ^b circum C; ^c letania C; ^d þam C; ^e eaðmodum C; ^(f–f) heom forgife C; ^(g–g) smyltelice gewydru C; ^(h–h) hyra lychaman C; ^i decimologesin C.

25 April: Mark

70. On ðone ilcan dæg bið Sancte Marcus ðrowung þæs godspelleres. He wæs Sancte Petres godsunu on fulwihte, ond he leornode æt him. Ond þæt Sanctus Petrus ^aon dæge folce be Criste sæde^a, þonne wrat ^bSanctus Marcus þæt^b on niht. Ond he ^cþæt hæl^c ærest Sancte Petre, forðon his godspell^d is ^eswa cweden^e furtum laudabile, ^fhergendlico stalo^f. He wæs ærest Cristenra biscopa^g on Alexandreae^h ðære miclan^i ceastre; ond he gecerde^j ærest to Godes geleafan Egypta mægþe, ond Libia mægðe, ond Armarice, ond Pentapalim^k. On þissum^l mægðum^m wæron ær swa unclæne men þæt hi^n guldon deofolgildum ge^o astorfen æton. Ðes Sanctus Marcus hælde untrume men ond hreofe, ond deade^p men of deaðe awehte. Ac þa æfestgodon^q þæt sume godwrece^r men^s eodon þa ^ton ciricean^t ^uon þy^u ærestan easterdæge þær he mæssan sang, ond brudon^v rap ^won his^w sweoran ond hine^x drogon^y ut æfter^129 þæm^z stanum ^aon ðære eorðan^a, swa þæt his flæsc cleofode on þære eorðan, ond ða stanas wæron gebaswad^b mid his blode. Ond þa on æfen^c dydon hi^d hine on carcern; þær him on niht ætywde^e Godes engel ond him sæde þæt he sceolde þæs on ^fmergen leoran^f on ða ecean^g reste. Ond þa ^hæt nehstan^h Crist seolfa^i him ætywde ond him ^jcwæd to^j: 'Sibb^k sy^l þe, ure godspellere^m Marcus.' Ða on ^n mergen drogan^n þa hæþnan^o hine mid þy^p

70. ^(a–a) sæde on dæg þam folce be cryste C; ^(b–b) þæt sanctus marcus C; ^(c–c) hæl þæt C; ^d godspel C; ^(e–e) gecweden C; ^(f–f) þæt ys hergendlicu stalu and C; ^g bysceop C; ^h alexandria C; ^i cynelican C; ^j gecyrde C.^k pentapolim C; ^l þysum C; ^m om. C; ^n hig C; ^o and C; ^p unlyfigende C; ^q æfstegodon C; ^r godwræce C; ^s weras C; ^(t–t) in þa cyrcan C; ^(u–u) þig C; ^v hig þa brudon C; ^(w–w) hym on C; ^x hyne þa C; ^y drogon C; ^z þam C; ^(a–a) om. C; ^b gebaswode C; ^c æfenne þa C; ^d hig C; ^e ætyowde C; ^(f–f) morgenne gewitan C; ^g ecan C; ^(h–h) ætnehstan Ko, æt nyhstan C; ^i sylfa C; ^(j–j) to cwæð C; ^k syb C; ^l om. C; ^m godspelre C; ^(n–n) morgen drogon C; ^o hæðenan C; ^p þig C;

when they got there, they found no fire there. And St Michael appeared more than once to this bishop and told him how fitting his deeds were, and how long his life would be. And when he gave up the ghost, a noise came from the southeast in the air, like the noise of large birds, and they settled on the house in which he was. That was a host of flying angels who took him to heaven.

25 April: Rogation Day

69. On the twenty-fifth day of the month is the feast in Rome and in all of God's churches which is called *Litania Maior*, which is the day of the Greater Litany. On that day all people of God shall beseech God with humble processions that he may grant them during that year a peaceful period and mild weather and plentiful crops and physical health. The Greeks call this day [*Exomologesis*], which is the day of repentance and penance.

25 April: Mark

70. On the same day is the passion of St Mark the Evangelist. He was St Peter's godson in baptism, and he learned from him. And what St Peter said to people about Christ during the day, that St Mark then wrote down at night. And he first concealed that from St Peter, wherefore his gospel is thus called *furtum laudabile*, praiseworthy theft. He was the first Christian bishop in the great city of Alexandria; and he first converted to God's faith the province of Egypt and the province of Libya, and Marmarica, and Pentapolis. In these countries there used to be people so unclean that they worshipped devils and ate carrion. This St Mark healed sick people and lepers, and resuscitated dead people from death. But then some impious men became envious of that [and] went to a church on the first day of Easter when he was celebrating mass, and tied a rope around his neck and dragged him out across the stones on the ground, in such a way that his flesh stuck to the ground and the stones were stained crimson with his blood. And then in the evening they put him into prison; there God's angel appeared to him at night and said to him that the next morning he would depart to eternal rest. And finally Christ himself appeared to him and said to him: 'Peace be with you, our Evangelist Mark.' Then in the morning the

rape, ⁹⁻⁹oð ðæt⁹ he his gast onsende ʳto Godeʳ. Ðaˢ woldon hiᵗ his lichoman forbærnan. Ða comᵘ þunor ond regnᵛ ofslogonʷ monige þaraˣ hæþenra, ond þa oþre flugon onweg. Ond æfesteʸ weras bebyrgdon his lichomanᶻ on micelre ond mærreᵃ cierecean ᵇ seo is on Alexandria ceastreᶜ.

⁹⁻⁹ oððæt Ko; ʳ⁻ʳ om. C; ˢ and þa C; ᵗ hig C; ᵘ com þær C; ᵛ ren C; ʷ and ofsloh C; ˣ þæra C; ʸ æfæste C; ᶻ lychaman C; ᵃ on mærre C; ᵇ cyrcan C; ᶜ þære ceastre C.

27 April: Alexandria

71. On ðone seofon ond twentegðanᵃ dæg þæs monðes bið þære halgan cwene tid Sancta Alexandreaᵇ; seo wæs Datianus cwen ðæs hæðnanᶜ caseres,¹³⁰ se wæs ealra eorðcyninga ealdorman. Ac heo gelyfde Godeᵈ þurh Sancte Georgiusᵉ lare ðæs martyres. Ða se casere ðæt ongeatᶠ þæt heo Cristeᵍ gelyfde, ʰ⁻ʰþa cwæð heʰ: 'Wa me, Alexandreaeⁱ; þu eart beswicen mid Georgiusʲ scinlacum. ᵏ⁻ᵏForhwon toweorpestᵏ þu min rice. Oþþe tohwonˡ forlætestᵐ þu me?' Þa he þa ne mihte hiⁿ mid his wordum oncerranᵒ, þa het he hiᵖ ahon be hire loccum ond ⁹⁻⁹hi þreagean⁹ mid missenlicum witum. Ða he þa ʳne mihte mid þæm hiʳ oferswiðan, þa het he ˢhi lædanˢ to beheafdianneᵗ. Ða bedᵘ heo þa cwelleras ðæt hiᵛ ʷ⁻ʷhire geanbidedan medmicleʷ hwile. Þa eode heo on hire palatium, þæt is on hire healle, ond anhofˣ hire eagan uppʸ to heofonumᶻ ond cwæð: 'Geseoh, Drihtenᵃ, þæt ic forlæte nu mine healle opene mid eallum minum goldhordum for þinum ᵇ⁻ᵇðæm halgumᵇ naman. Ac ðu, min Hælend, ontyn me nu ᶜ⁻ᶜþin neorxnawongᶜ¹³¹.' Ond ða gefylde heo hire martyrdom mid Cristes geleafan.

71. ᵃ twentigoðan C; ᵇ alexandria C; ᶜ hæðenan C; ᵈ on god C; ᵉ georius C; ᶠ onget C; ᵍ on cryst C; ʰ⁻ʰ om. C; ⁱ alexandria þæt C; ʲ georius C; ᵏ⁻ᵏ forhwan towyrpst C; ˡ forhwon C; ᵐ forlætst C; ⁿ hyg C; ᵒ oncyrran C; ᵖ hig C; ⁹⁻⁹ þreatian hig C; ʳ⁻ʳ myd þam hig ne myhte C; ˢ⁻ˢ lædan hig C; ᵗ beheafdunnge C; ᵘ bæd C; ᵛ hig C; ʷ⁻ʷ ðoledon ane medemlice C; ˣ onhof C; ʸ up C; ᶻ heofenum C; ᵃ dryhten myn C; ᵇ⁻ᵇ halgan C; ᶜ⁻ᶜ þynne neorxnawang C, þinne neorxnawong Herz.

28 April: Vitalis

72. On ðone ᵃeahta ond twentegðanᵃ dæg ðæs monðes bið Sancte Uitales tid þæs martyres, se resteþ ᵇ⁻ᵇon Uicolongeᵇ, ᶜ⁻ᶜþæt isᶜ on ðæmᵈ langan tune. Se wæs ærest caseres cæmpaᵉ under Paulino ðæmᶠ deman ᵍ⁻ᵍon Rauennaᵍ ðære ceastre, ac he þa gelyfde on Crist ond oðre men lærde to Cristes geleafan. Þa yrsode se dema forþon ond hine þa nydde to ʰ⁻ʰdeofolgylde¹³² begongeʰ. Þa he þæt ne geþafode, þa het se dema adelfan deopne seað ond hine cwicne on ðone ansændanⁱ ond hineʲ fyllan ᵏ⁻ᵏufon midᵏ eorðan ond ˡ⁻ˡmid stanumˡ, ᵐ⁻ᵐoþ þætᵐ he his gast onsændeⁿ. On ðære stowe wæron oft siððanᵒ ᵖ⁻ᵖheofonlico wundroᵖ.

72. ᵃ⁻ᵃ ehta and twentigoðan C; ᵇ⁻ᵇ in uicolongo C; ᶜ⁻ᶜ om. C; ᵈ þam C; ᵉ cempa C; ᶠ þam C; ᵍ⁻ᵍ in Rauenna C; ʰ⁻ʰ deofolgylda bigange C; ⁱ weorpan C; ʲ hym C; ᵏ⁻ᵏ onufan þa C; ˡ⁻ˡ stanas C; ᵐ⁻ᵐ oþþæt Ko; ⁿ to gode onsende C; ᵒ om. C; ᵖ⁻ᵖ heofenlicu wundru C.

pagans dragged him with the rope, until he gave up the ghost to God. Then they wanted to incinerate his body. Then came thunder and rain [and] killed many of the pagans, and the others ran away. And devout men buried his body in a great and wonderful church which is in the city of Alexandria.

27 April: Alexandria

71. On the twenty-seventh day of the month is the feast of the holy queen St Alexandria; she was the queen of the pagan emperor Datianus, who was the head of all earthly kings. But she believed in God through the teaching of the martyr St George. When the emperor realised that, that she believed in God, he said: 'Woe is me, Alexandria; you are bewitched by the tricks of George. Why are you destroying my authority. Or why are you leaving me?' When he could not change her mind with his words, he had her suspended by her hair and punished with various tortures. When he could not overcome her with those, he had her led away to be beheaded. Then she asked the executioners that they should give her a little more time. Then she went to her *palatium*, that is to her hall, and lifted up her eyes to heaven and said: 'See, Lord, that I now leave my hall open with all my treasures for your holy name. But you, my Saviour, open now your paradise to me.' And then she fulfilled her martyrdom with faith in Christ.

28 April: Vitalis

72. On the twenty-eighth day of the month is the feast of the martyr St Vitalis, who rests in the Vicus Longus, that is the long town. He was initially one of the emperor's soldiers under judge Paulinus in the city of Ravenna, but he then believed in Christ and converted others to Christ's religion. Then the judge got angry therefore, and forced him to practise devil-worship. When he refused, the judge had a deep pit dug out and him thrown down there alive and had it filled to the top with earth and stones, until he gave up the ghost. In that place heavenly miracles happened often afterwards.

28 April: Christopher

73. On ðone ylcan dæg bið Sancte Cristofores ðrowung[a] þæs miclan martyres; se com on Decies dagum þæs caseres on[b] ða ceastre þe [c]Samo is nemned[c], of þære þeode þær men habbað hunda heafod, ond of þære eorðan on ðære æton[d] men [e]hi selfe[e]. He[f] hæfde hundes heafod, ond his loccas wæron [g]ofer gemet[g] side, ond his eagan scinon swa leohte swa morgensteorra[h], ond his teþ wæron swa scearpe swa eofores tuxas. He[i] wæs [j]Gode geleaffull[j] on his heortan, ac he ne mihte[k] sprecan [l]swa mon[l]. Ða bæd he God ðæt he him sealde monnes[m] gesprec[n]. Ða[o] stod [p]him æt[p] sum wer on hwitum gegirelan[q] ond eðode him on ðone muð; ða mihte he siððan sprecan [r]swa mon[r]. Ða sænde[s] se casere twa hund cæmpena[t] [u]þæt þa hine gelæddan[u] to him, gif he þonne nolde to[v] him cuman, þæt hi[w] hine ofslogon ond him brohtan[x] þæt heafod to, þæt he [y]gesege hulic[y] þæt wære. Ða ða cempan him [z]to coman[z], ða ne [a]dorstan hi[a] no[b] him genealæcean[c], ond þa hwæþre[d] ferde he mid him. Þa he [e]þa com[e] to þæm[f] casere ond he geseah his onsyne[g], þa wundrade[h] he swa[i] ðæt he feoll[j] of his ðrymsetle. Ða bead se casere him gold ond seolfor ðæt [k]<he> hine[k] oncerde[l] fram Cristes geleafan. Þa he þæt ne geþafade[m], þa het he hine tintergian[n] mid missenlicum[o] witum. Ða[133] he [p]þa ne mihte mid þæm hine[p] oferswiðan, ða bebead he þæt hine man[q] lædde to beheafdunga[r]. Ða gebæd Cristoforus him[s] to Drihtne ond bæd God ðæt [t]æghwelc ðara[t] manna þe his reliquia aht[u] hæfde, þæt he næfre hi[v] fordemde on heora synnum, ne þæt[w] Godes yrre ofer hi[x] come, ne him wære[y] [z]hwæ<te>s gneað<n>es[z][134] ne [a]oþerra worldwisena[a].[135] Þa com stefn of heofonum[b] ond seo[c] cwæd: 'Swa hit bið, [d]swa swa[d] þu bidest[e]. Ond ic þe soðlice secge: Gif hwilc man[f] on micelre neadþearfnesse[g] bið þin gemyndig, ond he geceð[h] him to geþingung[i][136] ðinne ðone medoman naman, ic þonne gefremme þæs mannes nedðearfnesse[j].' Ða geendode Cristoforus his martyrdom. Ða gebohte an biscop[k] his lichoman[l] mid feo, se wæs on naman Petrus, ond hine gelædde on his ceastre ond hine gesette æt sumum mere, of þæm[m] fleow ær flod ond gehwerfde[n] ða ceastre[o], ond siððan wæs seo ceaster wið þæm[p] flode gehealden on[q] Godes wuldor.

73. [a] tyd and ðrowung C; [b] in C; [c-c] ys gehaten samo C; [d] hig æton C; [e-e] hig sylfe C; [f] and he C; [g-g] ofergemet Ko; [h] morgesteorra C; [i] and he C; [j-j] swa þeah on god gelyfed C; [k] myhte na C; [l-l] swa swa men doð C; [m] mannes C; [n] spræce C; [o] þa C; [p-p] æt hym C; [q] gegyrlan C; [r-r] on mennisc C; [s] sende C; [t] cempena C; [u-u] and het hyne lædan C; [v] myd C; [w] hig C; [x] brohton C; [y-y] sawe hwylc C; [z-z] tocoman Ko, to comon C; [a-a] dorston hig C; [b] om. C; [c] to genealæcan C; [d] om. C; [e-e] com C; [f] þam C; [g] ansyne C; [h] wundrode C; [i] ðæs swa swyðe C; [j] afeoll C; [k-k] he hyne C, scratched he in the margin left of hine B; [l] gecyrde C; [m] geþofode C; [n] tyntegrian C; [o] myssenlicum and unasecgendlicum C; [p-p] myd þam hyne ne myhte C; [q] mon C; [r] beheafdunge C; [s] hyne C; [t-t] æghwilc þæra C; [u] awyht C; [v] hig ne C; [w] þæt næfre C; [x] hig ne C; [y] nære C; [z-z] hwæs gneaðes B, Ko, hwætes gneðnys C, hwætes gneaðnes Herz; [a-a] oðra woruldwelena C; [b] heofenum C; [c] om. C; [d-d] swa C; [e] byddest C; [f] mon C; [g] nedþearfnysse C; [h] cygð C; [i] geþingum Ko; [j] nydþearfnysse C; [k] bysceop C; [l] lychaman C; [m] þam C; [n] gehwyrfde C; [o] ceaster C; [p] þam C; [q] in C.

The End of April

73a. [a]Þonne se monað bið geendad ðe we nemnað Eastermonað, þonne bið seo niht tyn tida lang, ond se dæg feowertyne[b] tida[a].

73a. [a-a] om. C; [b] .xiiii. B.

28 April: Christopher

73. On the same day is the passion of the great martyr St Christopher; he came in the days of the emperor Decius into the city which is called Samos, from the country where men have dogs' heads, and from the region where people eat each other. He had the head of a dog, and his hair was long beyond measure, and his eyes shone as brightly as the morning star, and his teeth were as sharp as the tusks of a wild boar. He was faithful to God in his heart, but he could not speak like a man. Then he asked God that he might give him human language. Then a man dressed in white appeared beside him and breathed into his mouth; then afterwards he could speak like a man. Then the emperor sent two hundred soldiers that they might lead him to him, if he did not want to come to him that they were to kill him and bring his head to him, that he might see what it might be like. When the soldiers came to him, they dared not at all approach him, and he still came with them. When he came to the emperor and he saw his appearance, he was so amazed that he fell off his throne. Then the emperor offered him gold and silver that he might convert him from his belief in Christ. When he refused, he had him punished with many tortures. When he could not overcome him with those, he commanded him to be led to his beheading. Then Christopher prayed to the Lord and asked God that any man who had any of his relics – that he would never condemn them for their sins, nor that God's anger would come over them, nor that there would be any [shortness of wheat] or any other worldly things. Then a voice came from heaven and it spoke: 'It shall be as you request. And I tell you truly: if any man in great distress remembers you, and he invokes your worthy name for intercession, I will fulfil that man's need.' Then Christopher completed his martyrdom. Then one bishop bought his body with money, he was called Petrus, and took it to his city and placed it by a lake, from which a flood had recently poured forth and had damaged the city, and since then the city was safe against the flood in God's glory.

The End of April

73a. When the month has passed which we call 'Eastermonaþ' ['Easter month'], the night is ten hours long, and the day fourteen hours.

The Beginning of May

73b. Þonne[a] on þone [b]fiftan monað[b] on geare bið an ond þritig[c] daga. Se monað is nemned on Læden[d] Maias[e], ond on ure geðeode Ðrymylce, forðon[f] swylc genihtsumnes[g] wæs geo[h] on Brytone[i] ond eac on Germania lande, of [j]ðæm Ongla[j] ðeod com on ðas Breotone[k], þæt hi[l] on þæm[m] monðe þriwa on dæge[n] mylcedon[o] heora neat.

73b. [a] om. C; [b-b] fiftan monðe C; [c] þryttig C; [d] leden C; [e] maius C; [f] forþam C; [g] genyhtsumnys C; [h] om. C; [i] brytene C; [j-j] þam engla C; [k] brytene C; [l] hig C; [m] þam C; [n] dæg hig C; [o] meolcodon C.

1 May: Philip

74. On ðone ærestan dæg þæs monðes bið Sancte [a]Philippes tid[a] þæs apostoles ond ðæs Godes ærendwrecan[b]. His nama is gereht on Læden[c] *os lampadis*, þæt is on ure geþeode leohtfætes[d] muþ; he getacnað ða gastlican lareowas Godes cyrecena[e]. Ure Hælend geceas ðysne Philippum him[f] to þegne on Galilea mægðe fram Bethsaida[g] ðære ceastre; Bethsaida[h] is gereht *domus uenatorum*, ðæt [i]þonne is[i] huntena hus. Ðes Philippus æfter þæs Hælendes[j] uppastignesse[k] he bodade[l] Cristes[m] godspell[n] on Sciðia[o] mægðe; ðær he awehte[p] ðry men of deaðe. Ond[q] his lichoma[r] resteð nu[s] on Hierapole[t] þære ceastre on Frygia mægðe, ond his dohtra[u] twa, þa halegestan[v] fæmnan, syndon ðær bebyrgde[w] on twa healfe[x] his.

74. [a-a] philippus C; [b] ærendracan C; [c] leden C; [d] leohtfates C; [e] cyrcena C; [f] om. C; [g] bedzaida C; [h] bedzaida C; [i-i] ys þonne C; [j] h suprascript Ba; [k] upastigenysse C; [l] bodude C; [m] om. C; [n] godspel C; [o] sumre C; [p] awrehte C; [q] om. C; [r] lychama C; [s] om. C; [t] hieropolim C; [u] dohtor C; [v] halgestan C; [w] bebyrgede C; [x] healfa C.

2 May: Athanasius

75. On[a] ðone æfteran dæg þæs monðes bið þæs halgan biscopes[b] gemynd Sancte Athanasi; he wæs biscop[c] on ðære miclan ceastre Alexandriae[d]. His halignes[e] wæs sona[f] foretacnod on his cnihthade. Ðære burge biscop[g] [h]ær him[h] wæs nemned Alexander[i]; se sæt sume symbeldæge on ðære cierecan[j], ond þa geseah he þurh þa eagduru[k] plegan micel cnihta weorod[l] be sæs waroðe; þara[m] wæs an Athanasius[n]. Ða ongan he fullwian[o] ða oðre cnihtas on ðæs sæs yðum, ond hip[p] eodon him under hand, swa he biscop[q] wære. Ond þa sona het se biscop[r] ðone cniht [s]him to gelædan[s], ond hine lærde gastlicne wisdom. Ond he wæs eall mid Godes snyttro[t] gefylled.

75. [a] E starts here; [b] bisceopes C; [c] bisceop C; [d] alexandria C; [e] halignis C; [f] om. C; [g] bysceop C; [h-h] om. C; [i] alexandre C; [j] circan C; [k] ehþyrl C; [l] werod C; [m] þæra C; [n] aðanasius C; [o] fullian C; [p] hig C; [q] bisceop C; [r] bisceop C; [s-s] him togelædan Ko, to hym gelædan C; [t] snytro C.

The Beginning of May

73b. Then in the fifth month of the year there are thirty-one days. The month is called *Maius* in Latin, and in our language 'Þrimilce' ['Three Milkings'], because there used to be such abundance in Britain and also in Germany, from where the Angles came to this Britain, that in that month they milked their cattle three times a day.

1 May: Philip

74. On the first day of the month is the feast of St Philip the apostle and God's emissary. His name translates into Latin as *os lampadis*, that is in our language 'the mouth of a lamp'; he represents the spiritual teachers of God's churches. Our Saviour chose this Philip as his disciple in the province of Galilee from the city of Bethsaida; Bethsaida translates as *domus uenatorum*, and that is 'the house of the hunters'. This Philip, after the Saviour's ascension, he preached Christ's gospel in the country of Scythia; there he revived three men from death. And his body now rests in the city of Hierapolis in the country of Phrygia, and his two daughters, the holiest of virgins, are buried there on either side of him.

2 May: Athanasius

75. On the second day of the month is the commemoration of the holy bishop St Athanasius; he was a bishop in the great city of Alexandria. His holiness was prefigured even in his childhood. The bishop before him in that city was called Alexander; one holiday, he sat in the church, and then he saw through the window a large group of children playing by the seashore; one of them was Athanasius. Then he began to baptise the other boys in the waves of the sea, and they submitted themselves to him, as if he was a bishop. And the bishop quickly had the boy brought to him, and taught him spiritual knowledge. And he was completely filled with God's wisdom.

3 May: Pope Alexander I, Eventius and Theodolus

76. On ðone ðriddan dæg þæs monðes bið Sancte Alexandres þrowung ðæs geongan papan on Rome ond twegra mæssepreosta mid hine[a], ða wæron nemde[b] Sanctus Euensius[c] ond Sanctus Theodolas[d]. Þa Aurelianus se gesið, se þær cwealde Cristne[e] men, [f]he ongan hi nedan[f] þæt [g]hi Criste wiðsocan[g]. Da hi[h] þæt ne geðafodon[i], þa het he sendan hi[j] ealle ðry on [k]byrnendene ofn[k]; ða nolde hi[l] þæt fyr bærnan[m]. Þa het he þa mæssepreostas beheafdian, ond ðone[n] papan ofstician. Ða sona com stefn of heofonum[o] ond seo[p] cwæþ: 'Aurelianus, ðysum monnum[q] þe þu her bismrodest, him is Godes neorxnawong[r] ontyned, ond þe syn[s] helletintergu[t] ontyned.' Ða swealt[u] he sona [v]þære ilcan niht[v] mid egeslice[w] deaðe. Ond his wif, seo wæs on naman Seueriane, heo bebyrgde[x] ðæs papan lichoman[y] ond þara[z] mæssepreosta arweorðlice on þære seofoðan mile fram Romebyrg[a] on ðæm[b] wege Numentana[c]. Ðes Sanctus Alexander wæs se fifta papa æfter Sancte Petre.

76. [a] m suprascript Be, hym C; [b] nemnede C; [c] Euentius C; [d] theodolus C; [e] crystene C; [f-f] þa ongan he hig nydan C; [g-g] hig criste wiðsocon C; [h] hig C; [i] geðafedon C; [j] hig C; [k-k] byrnendne ofen C; [l] hig C; [m] bærnan na and C; [n] þæne C; [o] heofonum C; [p] om. C; [q] mannum C; [r] neorxnawang C; [s] syndon C; [t] helletyntrega C; [u] sweolt C; [v-v] on þære ylcan nyhte C; [w] egeslicum C; [x] bebyrgede C; [y] lychaman C; [z] þæra C; [a] romebyrig C; [b] þam C; [c] þe hatte nu(....)ia C.

3 May: The Discovery of the Holy Cross

77. On ðone ilcan dæg bið seo tid þæt[a] Cristes rod wæs gemeted ærest, swa us þa halgan gewritu secgað, on ðone dæg þe we nemnað Quinta Nonas Maius. Ðær com upp[b] of ðære eorðan wynsumes stences rec; [c]ðær seo rod wæs gemeted[c].[137] Ond ðy ilcan dæge þe seo rod wæs gemeted,[138] þæt treow wæs geseted[d] ofer deades mannes lichoman[e] [139], ond se sona aras. [f]Ond þurh[f] ðæt wundor wæs gecyþed [g]þæt þæt[g] wæs [h]soðlice Cristes rod[h].

77. [a] þe C; [b] up C; [c-c] om. C; [d] aseted C; [e] byrgenne and hys lychoman C; [f-f] om. C; [g-g] þæt C; [h-h] crystes rod soðlice C.

Rogation Days

78. Ymb þas dagas utan, hwilum ær, hwilum æfter, beoð þa þry dagas on ðæm[a] Godes ciric<an>[b] [140] ond Cristes folc mærsiað Laetanias[c], [d]þæt is þonne bene ond relicgongas[d][e] foran to Cristes uppastignesse[f]. On ðæm[g] ðrym dagum sceolon cuman to Godes cirican[h] ge weras ge wif, ge ealde men ge geonge, ge þeowas ge ðeowenne[i], to ðingianne to Gode, forðon ðe Cristes blod wæs gelice agoten for eallum monnum[j]. On ðæm[k] þrym dagum Cristne[l] men sceolon alætan heora[m] ða woroldlican[n] weorc on ða þriddan tid dæges, ðæt is on undern, ond [o]forð gongen[o] mid þara[p] haligra reliquium oð ða nigeðan[q] tid, þæt is þonne non. Ða dagas syndon rihtlice to fæstenne[r], ond

78. [a] þam C; [b] ciricum B, cyrcan C, ciercean E; [c] letanias C; [d-d] om. C; [e] quia suprascript Be; [f] upastigenysse C; [g] þam C; [h] cyrcean C; [i] þeowena C; [j] mannum C; [k] þam C; [l] crystene C; [m] hyra C; [n] woruldlican C; [o-o] forðgongen Ko, forð gangan C, forð gonge E; [p] þæra C; [q] nygoðan C; [r] gefæstanne C.

3 May: Pope Alexander I, Eventius and Theodolus

76. On the third day of the month is the passion of the young pope St Alexander in Rome and also of two priests, who were called St Eventius and St Theodolus. Then Aurelianus the reeve, who was killing Christians there – he began to force them to renounce Christ. When they refused, he had all three of them thrown into a burning oven; then the fire would not burn them. Then he had the priests beheaded, and the pope stabbed to death. Then suddenly a voice came from heaven and said: 'Aurelianus, God's paradise is opened for these men – for the ones you put to shame here, and for you the torments of hell are opened.' Then straightaway the same night he died a terrible death. And his wife, whose name was Severiana, she buried the bodies of the pope and the priests in a dignified manner seven miles from the city of Rome on the Via Nomentana. This St Alexander was the fifth pope after St Peter.

3 May: The Discovery of the Holy Cross

77. On the same day is the feast on which Christ's cross was first found, as the holy writings tell us, on the day which we call the fifth Nones of May. The scent of a wonderful smell came out of the ground there; there the cross was found. And on the same day as the cross was found, the tree was placed over the body of a dead man and he immediately arose. And through that miracle it was revealed that that was truly Christ's cross.

Rogation Days

78. Round about these days, sometimes earlier, sometimes later, are the three days on which God's churches and the people of Christ celebrate *Litaniae*, and that is the prayers and relic processions before Christ's Ascension. On those three days both men and women shall come to God's church, both old people and the young ones, both male and female servants, to ask favour with God, because Christ's blood was equally shed for all men. On those three days Christians shall leave behind their worldly occupation at the third hour of the day, that is at 'undern', and process with the relics of the saints until the ninth hour, and that is 'non'. Those days are rightly

þara[s] metta to brucenne ðe menn[t] brucað on ðæt feowertiges nihta fæsten[u] ær eastran[v]. Ne[w] bið alefed[x] on ðyssum[y] dagum ðæt mon[z] blod læte oððe <cl>æsnungdrenceas[a] [141] drince oððe aht feorr[b] gewite for woroldlicre[c] bysgunge[d] fram ðære stowe ðe he sceal Gode ætþeowian. Ðas ðry dagas syndon mannes sawle læcedom ond gastlic wyrtdrenc; forðon [c]hi sendon[e] to healdanne[f] mid heortan onbryrdnesse[g], þæt is mid wependum gebedum ond mid rumedlicum[h] ælmessum ond fulre blisse ealra mænniscra[i] feonda, [j]forþon ðe[j] God us forgyfeð[k] his erre[l], gif we ure [m]monnum forgeofað[m].

[s] þæra C; [t] men C; [u] fæstene C; [v] eastron C; [w] and ne C; [x] alyfed C; [y] þysum C; [z] mon hym C; [a] a æsnungdreceas B, clænsung in the margin Be, clæsnungdrencas C, E, a <cl>æsnungdrenceas Ko; [b] feor C; [c] woruldlicre C; [d] abysgunge C; [e–e] hig syndon C; [f] healdenne C; [g] onbryrdnysse C; [h] rummodlicum C; [i] menniscra C; [j–j] for C; [k] forgyfð C; [l] yrre C; [m–m] mannum forgyfað C.

5 May: The Ascension of Christ

79. On ðone fiftan dæg þæs monðes bið se dæg þe ure Dryhten to[a] heofonum astag[b]. Ðy[c] dæge hine [d]gesegon nyhst[d] his þegnas on Oliuetes done[e]; ðær he [f]bletsade hi[f] ond ða gewat mid þy lichoman[g] on heofonum[h]. Ðy[i] dæge eode seo eorðe on heofon, ðæt is se mon[j] ofer engla ðrym. Ond on Oliuetes dune syndon nu gyt ða swæþe[k] Drihtnes fotlasta. Ymb[l] þa Drihtnes fotlastas timbredon Cristne[m] men [n]seonewealte cirican wunderlice[n]. Ne[o] mihte seo his swaðu næfre mid nænigre oðre wisan beon þæm[p] oðrum florum geonlicod[q] ond gelice gehiwad[r]. Gif þær mon hwæt mænnisces[s] [t]on asette[t], ðonne [u]<nolde seo eorðe him onfon>[u] [142]; ðeah hit wære marmarstanas[v], ða [w]wæron aswengde[w] on ðara[x] onsyn[y] þe[z] [143] þær [a]on sæton[a] [144]. Ðæt dust ðæt God[b] ðær [c]on træd[c], ond þa his swaða[d] ðe þær [e]on þricced[e] sendon[f], [g]ða syndon[g] monnum[h] to ecre[i] lare. Ond dæghwamlice geleaffulle men[j] nimað ðæt sand, ond þær hwæðre ne bið nænig wonung[k] on þæm[l] sande ðære[m] [145] Drihtne<s>[n] [146] fotswaða[o]. Sanctus[p] Arculfus sæde þæt þær ne mihte nænig hrof [q]on beon[q] on ðære cirican[r] on ðære stowe ðe ure Drihten on stod þa he to [s]heofonum astag[s], ac þæt se weg ðær wære a to heofonum[t] open þara[u] monna[v] eagum þe him þær gebædan[w] on ðære ylcan stowe. Ond he sæde þæt þa Drihtnes fotlastas wæron beworht[x] mid [y]ærne hweole[y], ond þæs heanes[z] wære oð [a]monnes swyran[a], ond þæt þær wære ðyrel[b] [c]onmiddum[c] [d]þæm hweole[d], ðurh þæt [e]mihton men[e] ufan beorhtlice sceawian Drihtnes fota swaðe, ond

79. [a] on to C; [b] astah C; [c] þig C; [d–d] gesawon nehst C; [e] dune C; [f–f] bletsode hig C; [g] lychaman C; [h] heofon C; [i] þig C; [j] man C; [k] swaðu C; [l] ymbe C; [m] crystene C; [n–n] synewealte cyrcean wundorlice C; [o] and ne C; [p] þam C; [q] geanlycod C; [r] gehywod C; [s] mennisces C; [t–t] onasette Ko; [u–u] He, seo eorðe him onufan scealde B, Ko, nolde seo eorðe hym onfon C, nolde sio eorðe him onfon E; [v] marmanstanas C; [w–w] swengdon C; [x] originally ðære B and then corrected to ðara Ba, þæra C; [y] ansyne C; [z] þe hig C, þe ða E; [a–a] onsæton Ko, on asetton C; [b] he C; [c–c] ontræd Ko; [d] swaðe C; [e–e] onþricced Ko, on aðricced C; [f] syndon C; [g–g] beoð C; [h] mannum C; [i] om. C; [j] menn þær C; [k] wanung C; [l] þam C; [m] þara C; [n] drihtne B, Drihtne<s> Ko, Herz, dryhtnes C; [o] fota swaðe C; [p] sancte C; [q–q] beon C; [r] cyrcan C; [s–s] heofenum astah C; [t] heofenum C; [u] þæra C; [v] manna C; [w] gebædon C; [x] beworhte C; [y–y] ærene hweowle C; [z] heahnes C; [a–a] mannes sweoran C; [b] þyrl C; [c–c] onmyddan C; [d–d] þam hweowle C; [e–e] men men myhton C;

there for fasting and for the use of those foods which are used during the fast of forty days before Easter. During these days it is not permitted that blood be let or purgative drinks be drunk, or that one should travel at all far for worldly affairs from the place where one is supposed to serve God. These three days are the medicine of man's soul and a spiritual potion; they are therefore to be kept with compunction of the heart, that is, with weeping prayers and with generous alms and the complete benevolence of all human enemies, because God will spare us his anger, if we forgive our people.

5 May: The Ascension of Christ

79. On the fifth day of the month is the day on which our Lord ascended to heaven. On that day his disciples last saw him on the Mount of Olives; there he blessed them and then he went to heaven together with his body. On that day the earth migrated to heaven, that is the man over the host of angels. And even now there are the tracks of the Lord's footprints on the Mount of Olives. Around the Lord's footprints Christians built a beautiful round church. In no way could his trace ever be levelled to the rest of the ground, nor made alike in profile. If something is put on it by people, the ground would not tolerate it; even if it might be marble rocks, they would come flying back into the face of the people who had put [them] there. The dust on which God walked there, and his tracks which are imprinted in it, are there as an eternal reminder to people. And believers daily take away the sand, and still there is no reduction in the sand of the Lord's tracks. St Arculf said that there could not be any roof on the church in the place where our Lord stood when he ascended to heaven, but that the way to heaven there was always open for the eyes of the people who were praying there in the same place. And he said that the Lord's footprints were covered by a round barrier made of brass, and its height was up to men's necks, and that there was a hole in the middle of the barrier, through which people could clearly see the Lord's

þæt hi[f] mihton mid heora[g] handum ræcean[h] ond niman þæs halgan[i] dustes dæl. Ond Sanctus[j] Arculfus sæde þæt þær hangade[k] u<n>mæte[l] leohtfæt, ond ð<æt>[m] wære byrnende[o] dæges ond nihtes ofer þara[p] Drihtnes fota swaða[q] [147]. Ond he sæde þæt æghwelce[r] geare ðy[s] dæge æt Cristes uppastignesse[t] on midses dæges tide[u], æfter þon þe mæssesangas wæron geendode on þære ylcan cirican[v], þæt þær [w]to come[w] þæs strongestan[x] windes yste[y], ond þæt se swa stronglice[z] hrure[a] on þa circan[b], þæt þær ne mihte nænig mon[c] [d]ænge gemete[d] on ðære circean oððe on [e]hire neahstowe[e] gestandan oþþe gesittan, ac þæt ealle þa men, ðe þær þonne wæron, lagon aþænede[f] on þære eorðan mid [g]ofdune healdum[g] ondwleotan[h], [i]oþ þæt[i] seo ondry<sn>lice[j] [148] yst forðgeleoreð[k]. Se ondrysnlica wind þæt deð þæt se dæl ðære ciricean[l] ne mæg habban ðone hrof ðær þæs Hælendes [m]fotlastas syndon under[m]. Sanctus[n] Arculfus sæde þæt he self[o] ðær wære ondweard æt þære ylcan cyricean[p] ðy dæge æt Cristes uppastignesse[q], ða se stranga ond se forhtlica wind þær[r] onræsde.

[f] hyg C; [g] hyra C; [h] ræcan C; [i] om. C; [j] sancte C; [k] hangode C; [l] uþmæte B, Ko, unmæte C, Herz; [m] Ko, ð B; [o] a byrnende C; [p] þæra C; [q] swaðe C; [r] æghylce C; [s] þig C; [t] upastigenysse C; [u] tyd C; [v] cyrcean C; [w-w] tocome Ko; [x] strangestan C; [y] blæd C; [z] stranglice C; [a] gehrure C; [b] cyrcean C; [c] man C; [d-d] nænige mete C; [e-e] þære neaweste myhte C; [f] aðenede C; [g-g] ofdunehealdum Ko, ofdun ahyldum C; [h] andwlytan C; [i-i] oþþæt Ko; [j] ondrynslice B, Ko, ondryslice C; [k] forðgewyteð C; [l] cyrcean C; [m-m] fotlas under syndon C; [n] sancte C; [o] sylf C; [p] cyrcean C; [q] upastygenysse C; [r] om. C.

6 May: Eadberht

80. On ðone sextan[a] dæg þæs monðes bið Sancte Eadberhtes[b] geleornes[c] ðæs arwyrðan[d] fæder, se wæs biscop[e] on Brytone[f] æfter Sancte Cuthberhte[g] on ðæm[h] halgan mynstre ðe is nemned Lindesfarna[i] yg[j]. [k]Þæm Eadberhte[k] wæs gewunelic þæt he symble[l] feowertig daga ær eastran[m] ond[n] feowertig daga ær Cristes acennisse[o], þæt is ær [p]geolum, þæt[p] he wunode on dygolre[q] stowe on his gebedum ond on gastlicum weorcum, ond seo stow wæs ymburnen[r] mid [s]sæs streamum[s]. Þa on ð<æt>[t] lencenfæsten [u]on ðæm[u] ðæs mynstres broðra[v] dydon Sancte Cuthberhtes[w] liic[x] of eorðan[y], ond hi[z] þæt gemetton swa gesund swa[a] he þa gyt lifde[b], æfter ændlefan[c] gearum ðæs þe [d]<he> wæs[d] bebyrged. Ða bæron hi[e] þæs lichrægles dæl to [f]Eadberhte þæm biscope[f], ond he þæt cyste mid clænre[g] [149] lufan, [h]ond weop[h], þæt he mihte uneaðe ænig word [i]gecweþan, ond[i] cwæþ: 'Hwilc man mæg areccean[j] Drihtnes gefe[k]? He þæt seleð[l] ðæm[m] þe hine lufiað[n], þæt þa sawla lifgað[o] a[p] on ðære heofonlican heannesse[q], ond he healdeþ ða deadan lichoman[r] ungemolsnode under eorðan, [s]oþ þæt[s] hi[t] eft cuce[u] arisað, þonne þes middangeard byfað ond engla byman ufan singað.' He[v] cwæð: 'Ic wat cuðlice þæt seo stow ne bið [w]noht longe æmettugu[w] [x]on ðære[x] Sancte Cuthberhtes[y] lichoma[z] resteþ, ond þæt bið swiðe eadig [a]mon þæm[a] þe Drihten

80. [a] syxtan C; [b] eadbyrhtes C; [c] gewytennys C; [d] arweorðan C; [e] biscop C; [f] brytene C; [g] cuðberhte C; [h] þam C; [i] lindesferena C; [j] ea C; [k-k] þam eadbyrhte C; [l] fæste symle C; [m] eastron C; [n] and eac C; [o] acennednysse C; [p-p] gyhhelum C; [q] dygelre C; [r] utan ymburnen C; [s-s] sæstreamum C; [t] Ko, ð B; [u-u] þa C; [v] broðras C; [w] cuðberhtus C; [x] lic C; [y] e suprascript Ba; [z] hig C; [a] swylce C; [b] lyfode and þæt wæs C; [c] endlyfen C; [d-d] wæs B, Ko, he wæs C, E, Herz; [e] hig C; [f-f] eadbyrhte þam bisceope C; [g] mycelre C, E; [h-h] and he weop C; [i-i] cweðan and he C; [j] areccan C; [k] gife C; [l] syleð C; [m] þam C; [n] lufað C; [o] lyfiað C; [p] a in ecnysse and C; [q] heahnysse C; [r] lychaman C; [s-s] oþþæt Ko; [t] hig C; [u] cwyce C; [v] and he C; [w-w] naht lange æmtig C; [x-x] þe C; [y] cuðberhtes C; [z] lychama on C; [a-a] man þam C;

footprints from above, and that they could reach down with their hands and take some of the holy sand away. And St Arculf said that there was an enormous lamp hanging there, and that was burning day and night over the Lord's footprints. And he said that each year on the day of Christ's Ascension at midday, after mass had been sung in the same church, that the strongest of winds would start to blow there, and that it would hit the church so hard, that nobody in the church or in its vicinity might be able to stand or sit there for any length of time, but that all people, who were there then, would be lying flat on the ground, face down, until the terrible blast goes away. The terrible wind is responsible for the fact that that part of the church, under which the Saviour's footprints are, has no roof. St Arculf said that he himself was present there at the same church on the day of Christ's ascension, when the strong and terrible wind was raging there.

6 May: Eadberht

80. On the sixth day of the month is the death of the venerable father St Eadberht, who was a bishop in Britain after St Cuthbert in the holy monastery which is called Lindisfarne. Always forty days before Easter and forty days before Christ's birth, that is before Christmas, Eadberht used to stay in a secret place in prayer and spiritual life, and the place was surrounded by sea currents. Then one Lent, the monastery's brothers exhumed St Cuthbert's body, and they found it as healthy as if he was still alive, eleven years after he had been buried. Then they took some of the funeral garment to Bishop Eadberht, and he kissed it with chaste affection, and wept that he could hardly say a word, and said: 'Which man can recount the Lord's gifts? He grants that to them who love him, that the souls live eternally in heaven on high, and he preserves the dead bodies undecayed under the earth, until they are resurrected alive, when this earth will tremble and the angels' trumpets will sound from above.' He said: 'I certainly know that the place in which St Cuthbert's body rests will not be empty for long, and that will be a very blessed man to whom the Lord grants rest

forgyfeð[b] [c]þæt on ðære stowe resteþ[c] [150].' Ða [d]noht longe[d] æfter þissum[e], ða[f] geuntrumade[g] Godes[h] se leofa Eadberht[i] bisceop, ond þæs[j] æfter seofon[k] ond feowertig[l] daga he onsende his gast[m], ond his lichoma[n] wæs geseted on þa ylcan stowe ðær Sancte [o]Cuthberhtes lichoma[o] ær reste[p].

[b] forgyfð C; [c-c] on þære stowe reste and C, on ðære stowe ræste E; [d-d] naht C; [e] þysum C; [f] om. C; [g] geuntrumode C; [h] gode C; [i] eadbyrht C; [j] þæs ða C; [k] seofan C; [l] feowertygum C; [m] gast to gode C; [n] lychama C; [o-o] cuðberhtes lychama C; [p] on reste C.

7 May: John of Beverley

81. On ðone seofoðan dæg þæs monðes bið Sancte Iohannes geleornes[a] [151], se wæs biscop[b] on Brytone[c] on Norðanhymbra[d] ðeode. Se gedyde dumbum men spræce, ond his wundor syndon[e] awritene on Istoria[f] Anglorum [g]ðæm bocum[g]. Ond his lichoma[h] ðær resteð on ðære stowe ðe [i]mon nemneð Derewudu[i].

81. [a] gewytennys C; [b] byscep C; [c] brytene C; [d] norðhymra C; [e] synd C; [f] hystoria C; [g-g] on ðære bec C; [h] lychama C; [i-i] ys nemned derawudu C.

8 May: The Discovery of St Michael's Church

82. On ðone eahteþan[a] dæg þæs monðes bið þæt[b] [c]Sancte Michaheles cirice[c] ærest funden wæs on ðæm[d] munte Gargano[e], þær se mon[f] wæs ofscoten mid his agenre stræle, mid þy[g] þe he wolde ðone fearr[h] sceotan[i], se stod on þæs scræfes dura.

82. [a] ehtoðan C; [b] se dæg þe C; [c-c] michaeles cyrce C; [d] þam C; [e] gargana C; [f] man C; [g] þig C; [h] fear C; [i] om. C.

8 May: Victor Maurus

83. On ðone ylcan dæg bið Sancte Uictores ðrowung ðæs martyres, ðæs lichoma[a] resteð on Mediolane[b] ðære ceastre. Se Uictor he wæs Maura cynnes, ond he wæs Maximianus[c] cæmpa[d] ðæs hæðnan[e] caseres, ac he wæs Cristen[f]. Þa lærde se casere hine þæt he forlete Cristes geleafan. Ða he þæt ne geþafade[g], ða þreade [h]hine man[h] mid witum. He het hine begeotan mid weallende leade, ac him þæt no[i] ne derede ðon[j] ma ðe ceald wæter. Þa het he his leaseres[k] hine lædan to þæm[l] wuda, se is [m]gecegd Dulnus[m], ond hine þær beheafdian. Ða cwæþ he to þæm[n] þe hine læddon: 'Secgað ge Maximiane þæm[o] casere þæt he bið togeare dead, ond him beoð þa scancan[p] forbrocen[q] [r]ær þon[r] he sy[s] bebyrged[t].' Þa bebead se casere þæt [u]nænig mon þone lichoman[u] bebyrgde[v] siððan he wæs[w] beheafdod, ac[x] þæt hine scolden[y] [z]forswelgan wilde deor ond wyrmas[z]. Ða [a]coman þyder tu wilddeor[a] ond heoldan[b] ðone lichoman[c],

83. [a] lychama C; [b] mediolana C; [c] maximianes C; [d] cempa C; [e] hæðenan C; [f] crystes þegn C; [g] geþafode C; [h-h] he hyne C; [i] naht C; [j] þe C; [k] leogeras C, with cweleras suprascript; [l] þam C; [m-m] gecyged dulmis C; [n] þam C; [o] þam C; [p] sceancan C; [q] forbrocene C; [r-r] ær þon ðe C; [s] syg C; [t] byrged and C; [u-u] nan man hys lychaman C; [v] ne bebyrigde ac C; [w] wære C; [x] om. C; [y] sceoldon C; [z-z] wyldeor and wyrmas forswelgan C; [a-a] comon twa wylde deor C; [b] heoldon C; [c] lychaman C;

100

in that place.' Then not long afterwards, God's dear Bishop Eadberht was taken ill, and after forty-seven days he gave up the ghost, and his body was buried in the same place where St Cuthbert's body rested before.

7 May: John of Beverley

81. On the seventh day of the month is the death of St John, who was a bishop in Britain, among the Northumbrians. He gave speech to a dumb man, and his miracles are written down in the books called *Historia anglorum*. And his body rests there in the place which is called Derewudu [i.e. ?Beverley].

8 May: The Discovery of St Michael's Church

82. On the eighth day of the month is when St Michael's church was first found on Mount Gargano, where that man was shot with his own arrow, when he tried to shoot the bull, which was standing at the entrance of the cave.

8 May: Victor Maurus

83. On the same day is the passion of the martyr St Victor, whose body rests in the city of Mediolana [i.e. Milan]. That Victor – he was a Moor, and he was a soldier of the pagan emperor Maximian, but he was a Christian. Then the emperor lectured him to renounce Christ's faith. When he refused, he was forced with tortures. He commanded boiling lead to be poured over him, but it did not harm him any more than cold water. Then he commanded his guards to lead him to the wood which is called Ad Ulmos and to behead him there. Then he said to those who were escorting him: 'Tell emperor Maximian that he will be dead within a year, and that his legs will be crushed before he will be buried.' Then the emperor commanded that nobody should bury the body after he was beheaded, but that wild animals and worms should devour it. Then two wild animals came to that place and guarded the body, one at its

oþer æt þæm[d] heafdum[152], oþer æt þæm[e] fotum, [f]oþ þæt[f] þær [g]com to[g] Sanctus Maternus se biscop[h] ond hine[i] arweorðlice bebyrgde.

[d] þam C; [e] þam C; [f-f] oþþæt Ko; [g-g] to com C; [h] bysceop C; [i] hyne þa C.

9 May: The Beginning of Summer

83a. On ðone nygeþan[a] dæg ðæs monðes bið sumeres[b] fruma. Se sumor[c] hafað hundnygontig[d] daga; þonne[e] gangað þa seofon[f] steorran on uhtan upp[g], ond on æfen[h][153] on setl[i].

83a. [a] nygoðan C; [b] sumores C; [c] F starts here; [d] hundnigantig F; [e] and þonne C; [f] seofan F; [g] up C; [h] undern C; [i] F breaks off after setl.

10 May: Gordianus

84. On ðone teogþan[a] dæg ðæs monðes bið þæs martyres tid Sancte[b] Gordianes[c], þæs lichoma[d] resteð æt Rome, ond his gemynd sceal beon mærsad[e] mid mæssesongum[f] on eallum ciricum[g].

84. [a] teoðan C; [b] Sancti C; [c] Gordiani C; E breaks off after Gordianes; [d] lychama C; [e] mærsod C; [f] mæssesangum C; [g] cyrcum C.

10 May: Calepodius

85. On ðone ylcan dæg bið þæs ealdan[a] mæssepreostes þrowung Sancti[b] Calepodi.

85. [a] om. C; [b] sancte C.

12 May: Pancras

86. On ðone twelftan dæg þæs monðes bið Sancte Pancrates ðrowung þæs æþelan cnihtes, se wæs [a]fiftene geara[a] ða he for Cristes geleafan deað geðrowade[b]. He wæs acenned on Frigia[154] ceastre of æþelum cynne; his fæder nama wæs Cledones ond his modor[c] noma[d] wæs Cyriade, ac he wæs gefullwad[e] æt Rome fram Sancte Cornelie ðæm[f] papan. Ða[g] ongan Dioclitsianus[h], se hæþna[i] casere, hine læran, þæt he Criste wiðsoce, ond cwæð, þæt he hine ðonne wolde swa welinge gedon, swa he his sunu wære. Þa he þæt ne geþafade[j], ða het he hine beheafdian on ðæm[k] wege ðe æt Rome is nemned Aurelia. Ðær is his lichoma[l] bebyrged, ond his cirice[m] getimbred oð þysne ondweardan[n] dæg.

86. [a-a] .xv. geare C; [b] geþrowode C; [c] moder C; [d] nama C; [e] gefullod C; [f] þam C; [g] and þa C; [h] dioclitianus C; [i] hæþena C; [j] geþafode C; [k] þam C; [l] lychama C; [m] cyrce C; [n] andweardan C.

head and one at its feet, until Bishop St Maternus arrived there and buried it honourably.

9 May: The Beginning of Summer

83a. On the ninth day of the month is the beginning of summer. Summer is ninety days long; at that time the Seven Stars [i.e. Pleiades] rise at dawn and set in the evening.

10 May: Gordianus

84. On the tenth day of the month is the feast of the martyr St Gordianus, whose body rests in Rome, and his commemoration is to be celebrated with masses in all churches.

10 May: Calepodius

85. On the same day is the passion of the old priest St Calepodius.

12 May: Pancras

86. On the twelfth day of the month is the passion of the noble boy St Pancras, who was fifteen years old when he suffered death for his Christian faith. He was born into a noble family in the city of Phrygia; his father's name was Cleonius and his mother's name was Cyriada, but he was baptised in Rome by Pope St Cornelius. Then the pagan emperor Diocletian began to put pressure on him to renounce Christ, and said that he would then make him as wealthy, as if he was his son. When he refused, he commanded him to be beheaded on the road which in Rome is called [the Via] Aurelia. There, his body is buried, and his church stands until the present day.

14 May: Victor and Corona

87. On ðone feowerteogðan[a] dæg þæs monðes bið[b] þara[c] haligra martyra ðrowung [d]Sancte Uictores[d] ond [e]Sancte Coronan[e]. Se Uictor[f] wæs from[g] Cilicia ðære mægðe, ond he wæs Antoninus[h] [155] cæmpa[i] þæs caseres, ac he gelyfde on Crist. Ða[j] Sabastianus[k], se [l]hæðna Ægypta[l] gesið, ongon[m] hine nedan[n] to deofolgelde[o]. Þa he þæt ne geðafede[p], þa het he sumne scinlæcan him sellan[q] etan þæt flæsc ðæt wæs geættred mid þy werrestan[r] attre, ond him þæt ne sceðede[s]. Ða het he [t]hine eft[t] cwicne beflean. Ða wæs oðres cempan wif, [u]seo wæs on naman[u] Corona, seo wæs geong [v]ond wæs[v] an gear gebrydod[w] ond feower monað. Seo cwæð to him: 'Eadig eart þu, Uictor[x], ond ðin[y] þa halgan weorc sendon[z] eadige. Ic geseo twegen beagas cuman of heofonum[a], se mara is þin ond se læssa is min.' Ond ða for þære gesyhþe[b] gelyfde þæt wif on Crist. Ond þa het se gesið [c]hi buta[c] gemartyrian[d].

87. [a] feowerteoðand C; [b] om. C; [c] þæra C; [d-d] sancti uictories C; [e-e] sancti corona C; [f] uictorius C; [g] fram C; [h] Antoninus B, Herz, Antonius C, Ko; [i] cempa C; [j] and þa C; [k] sebastianus C; [l-l] hæðena egypta C; [m] ongan C; [n] nydan C; [o] deofolgylde C; [p] geþafode C; [q] syllan C; [r] wyrstan C; [s] derede and C; [t-t] eft hyne C; [u-u] þære nama wæs C; [v-v] and heo wæs C; [w] bryd C; [x] uictorius C; [y] þyne C; [z] syndon C; [a] heofonum C; [b] h suprascript Ba; [c-c] hyg butu C; [d] martyrian C.

15 May: Pentecost

88. On ðone fifteogðan[a] dæg þæs monðes bið se micla dæg [b]ðe is nemned[b] Pentecosten. Se dæg wæs mære on ðære ealdan æ ær Cristes cyme, [c]forþon ðe[c] [156] God spræc to Moyse of[d] [e]heofonum, geherendum[e] eallum Israhela folce. Ond ðy dæge God sealde his æ ond his bebodu ðæm[f] ylcan folce on twam stænenum bredum awritene, [g]on Sinai ðære dune[g]. Ond eft æfter Cristes uppastignesse[h] to heofonum[i], ðy[j] ilcan dæge he onsænde[k] his þegnum[l] ðone halgan gast, ond ealra þara[m] monna[n] wæs on anum huse [o]hundteontig ond twentig[o]. Þa færinga wæs geworden sweg[p] of heofonum[q] [r]swa swa stranges[r] windes sweg, ond se sweg gefylde ðæt hus ðær hi[s] sæton ond ofer heora[t] ælcne onsundran[u] sæt swa swa fyr. Ond hi[v] mihton sona[w] sprecan on [x]æghwelc þara[x] geðeoda[y] þe under heofonum[z] is, ond þa[a] Hælend<e>s[b] [157] þegnas mihtan[c] siþþan don [d]heofonlico wundor[d] ðurh þone gast[e]. Ðæm[f] gaste æghwelc[g] gefullwad[h] man nu[i] onfehð þurh biscopa[j] handa onsetenesse, ond se gast wunað mid [k]æghwelcne þara[k] þe god deþ. Ond he gefyhð[l] on ðæs clænan mannes heortan swa swa culfre ðonne heo [m]baðað him[m] on smyltum[n] wætre[o] on [p]hluttere wællan[p].

88. [a] fyfteoðan C; [b-b] om. C; [c-c] forþon on þone dæg C; [d] on C; [e-e] heofenum gehyrendum C; [f] þam C; [g-g] in monte synai C; [h] upastygenysse C; [i] heofenum C; [j] on þam C; [k] onsende C; [l] þegenum C; [m] om. C; [n] manna C; [o-o] .xx. and hundteontig C; [p] om. C; [q] heofenum C; [r-r] swylce strang C; [s] hig ynne C; [t] hyra C; [u] onsundrum C; [v] hig C; [w] þa sona C; [x-x] æghwylc þæra C; [y] þeoda C; [z] heofenum C; [a] þæs C; [b] hælendas B, hælendes C; [c] myhton C; [d-d] heofonlicu wundru C; [e] halgan gast C; [f] þam C; [g] æghwylc C; [h] gefullod C; [i] ufan C; [j] bysceopa C; [k-k] æghwylc þæra manna C; [l] gefehð C; [m-m] hig baðað C; [n] clænum and on smyltum C; [o] wætere C; [p-p] hluttorum wylle C.

14 May: Victor and Corona

87. On the fourteenth day of the month is the passion of the holy martyrs St Victor and St Corona. That Victor was from the country of Cilicia, and he was a soldier of the emperor Antoninus, but he believed in Christ. Then Sebastianus, the pagan reeve of the Egyptians, tried to force him into devil-worship. When he refused, he then commanded a sorcerer to give him meat to eat, which was spiked with the strongest poison, and it did not harm him. He then commanded that he be flayed alive. There was the wife of another soldier, who was called Corona, who was young and had been married for one year and four months. She said to him: 'You are blessed, Victor, and your holy deeds are blessed. I can see two crowns coming from heaven; the larger one is yours and the smaller one is mine.' And because of that vision that woman believed in Christ. And then the reeve commanded them both to be beheaded.

15 May: Pentecost

88. On the fifteenth day of the month is the great day which is called Pentecost. That day was a great occasion according to the old law [or 'Old Testament'] before the advent of Christ, because God spoke to Moses from heaven, while all the people of the Israelites were listening. And on that day God handed over his law and his Commandments written on two stone tablets to the same people, on Mount Sinai. And then after Christ's ascension to heaven, he sent his disciples the Holy Spirit on the same day, and there were as many as 120 men in one house. Then suddenly there came a noise from heaven like the noise of a strong wind, and the noise filled the house in which they sat and above each single one of them there rested something like fire. And they could suddenly speak in any language which exists under the heavens, and the Saviour's disciples could afterwards work heavenly miracles by force of the Spirit. Every baptised person now receives the Spirit through the laying on of the bishop's hands, and the Spirit stays with all those who do good. And it rejoices in the heart of the pure man like the dove does when it bathes in calm water in a clear pool.

18 May: Pope John I

89. On ðone eahtateogðan[a] dæg þæs monðes bið Sancte Iohannes tid ðæs papan ond ðæs martyres, se gedyde ðurh Godes miht blindum men gesihðe. Ðone Iohannem ofsloh[b] for æfestum[c] [d]Þeodoric<us>, Gotona[d] cyning[158], on[e] Rauenna ðære ceastre. Ond sum westensettla[f] on ðæm[g] ealande, ðe [h]Liparus is nemned[h], sæde scipliðendum monnum[i] þæt he gesege[j] Iohannes sawle ðæs papan lædon[k][159] þone cyning, þe hine ofslog[l], gebundenne on [m]ece wite[m]. He cwæþ, se Godes þeow, to þæm[n] scipliðendum: 'Gerstandæge[o] on ða nygeðan[p] tid dæges, þæt is on ðone non, Ðeodoricus[q] wæs gelæded, [r]ond ungyred[r][160] ond unscod[s], [t]ond gebunden[t] be þæm[u] handum, betweoh Iohanne þæm[v] papan ond Simachum[w] [x]ðone ealdormon[x]. Ond he wæs fram him[y] aworpen on byrnende seað on ðysum neahealande, [z]þæt is[z] nemned Ulcani[a].' Ða [b]scipliðende þæt[b] geherende[c] [d]behydelice hi mearcedon[d] ðone dæg ond cerdon[e] eft to Ete<l>wara[f] mægðe, þær hi[g] ðone cyning ær lifiende[h] wiston[i]. Ond [j]hi þa[j] hine [k]gemetton deadne[k] þy ilcan dæge, ðe his wite þæm[l] Godes þegne[m] ætewed[n] wæs. Þæt wæs swiðe riht, þæt he fram [o]þæm mannum twæm[o] wære sended on ðæt ece fyr, þa[p] he ær[q] unrihtlice ofsloh on ðyssum[r] life. Þæt wæs Ðeodoricus se cyning, ðone we nemnað Ðeodric.

89. [a] ehtateoðan C; [b] om. C; [c] æfestum C; [d-d] Þeodoricost gotona B, Þeodoric Ostgotona Ko, theodricus se wæs gotena C; [e] in C; [f] westensetla C; [g] þam C; [h-h] ys nemned lipanus he C; [i] mannum C; [j] gesawe C; [k] lædan C, Herz; [l] ofsloh C; [m-m] ecum wytum C; [n] þam C; [o] gyrsandæg C; [p] nygoðan C; [q] þeodricus C; [r-r] ungyrd C, Herz; [s] unsceod C; [t-t] and eac gebunden C; [u] þam C; [v] þam C; [w] finianum C; [x-x] þam ealdormen C; [y] heom C; [z-z] and þæt ys C; [a] ulcania and C; [b-b] scyplyðende þa þæt C; [c] gehyrende C; [d-d] hig ymbhydelyce amearcodon C; [e] hym þa cyrdon C; [f] etenwara B, etelwara C; [g] hig C; [h] lyfigende C; [i] forleton C; [j-j] hig þa eft C; [k-k] þær deadne gemetton C; [l] þam C; [m] þeowe C; [n] ætywed C; [o-o] þam twam mannum C; [p] þa ðe C; [q] her C; [r] þysum C.

20 May: Basilla

90. On ðone twentegðan[a] dæg ðæs monðes bið Sancta[b] Basillan tid ðære cynelican fæmnan, seo wæs on Rome, ond heo onfeng Godes geleafan ðurh Sancte Eugenian lare ðære halgan fæmnan. Ac heo wæs ær beweddad[c] sumum æþelum hæþnan[d] were, se wæs on [e]noman Pompeius[e]. Da he þa[f] gehyrde þæt heo wæs Cristenu[g], ða ferde he to hire huse ond forbead ðæm[h] duruweardum[i] þæt heo[j] hine hire gesægde[k].[161] Þa onbead Basilla him ond cwæþ: 'Ongytt[l] þu þis, þæt [m]ic næbbe[m] nænigne intingan þe to geseonne ne þe to gegretanne[n].' He þa wæs swiðe gedrefed, ond ferde to ðæm[o] casere Galliena, ond hine aðenede beforan ðæm[p], ond cwæð: '[q]Fultumað eowrum Romwarum[q]. Mid [r]hwelcum monnum[r] magon ge [s]onheldon[162] eowerra[s] feonda swyrban[t], gif we usse[u] bryde anforlætað[v]?' Þa gedemde se casere, þæt Basilla onfenge þone brydguman oþþe mid[w] sweorde forwurde. Da heo þa[x] wæs neded[y] to him, ða cwæð heo: 'Ic hæbbe brydguman, þæt is Crist, cininga cyning.' Ða wæs heo sona ofslegen[z] mid sweorde for Criste.

90. [a] twentygoðan C; [b] sancte C; [c] beweddod C; [d] hæðenum C; [e-e] naman pompeiius C; [f] om. C; [g] crysten C; [h] þam C; [i] dureweardum C; [j] hig C; [k] gesædon C; [l] ongitst C; [m-m] ys næbbe ic; [n] gretanne C; [o] þam C; [p] hym C; [q-q] fulltemiað eowre romwara C; [r-r] hwylcum mannum C; [s-s] onhyldan eowra C; [t] sweorban C; [u] ure C; [v] forlætað C; [w] heo myd C; [x] om. C; [y] genydd C; [z] ofslagen C.

18 May: Pope John I

89. On the eighteenth day of the month is the feast of the pope and the martyr St John, who gave sight to a blind man through God's power. Theoderic, the king of the Ostrogoths, killed John out of hatred in the city of Ravenna. And a desert hermit on the island, which is called Lipara, told sailors that he could see the soul of Pope John leading the king, who had killed him, tied up in eternal torment. He, that servant of God, said to the sailors: 'Yesterday at the ninth hour of the day, that is at 'non', Theoderic was led, with neither his armour nor his shoes on, and with his hands tied, between Pope John and the governor Symmachus. And they threw him into a burning pit on this neighbouring island, which is called Vulcania.' The sailors, when they heard that, they carefully noted the day and then returned to the country of the Italians, where they had previously known the king to be alive. And then they found out that he had died on the same day, on which his torment had been revealed to the servant of God. That was quite right, that he had been sent into the eternal fire by those two men, whom he had unjustly killed earlier in this life. That was King Theoderic, whom we call 'Ðeodric'.

20 May: Basilla

90. On the twentieth day of the month is the feast of the royal virgin St Basilla, who was in Rome, and she received God's faith through the teaching of the holy virgin St Eugenia. But she had earlier been bethrothed to a pagan nobleman, whose name was Pompeius. When he then heard that she was a Christian, he went to her house and [told the doorkeepers that they should announce him to her]. Then Basilla sent him a message, saying: 'Understand this, that I am not interested in seeing you, nor in speaking to you.' He was then very upset, and went to the emperor Gallienus, and flung himself to the ground before him, and said: 'Help your Roman citizens. With which men can you bow down the necks of your enemies, if we give up on our brides?' Then the emperor decreed that Basilla should accept the bridegroom or else die by the sword. When she was then forced to go to him, she said: 'I have a bridegroom, that is Christ, the king of kings.' Then she was promptly killed with the sword, for Christ.

25 May: Pope Urban I

91. On ðone fif ond twentegðan[a] dæg ðæs monðes bið Sancte Urbanes gemynd ðæs papan, se wæs feower gear [b]on Rome papa[b] ond þreo[c] monað ond fif ond twentig daga. Ond monigne æþelne mon[d] he gecierde[e] to Cristes geleafan, ond he is bebyrged on ðæm[f] mynstre[163] ðe hatte Praetectati[g], ond[h] on ðæm[i] wege þe Appiae[j] is nemned.

91. [a] twentigoðan C; [b-b] papa on rome C; [c] þry C; [d] man C; [e] gecyrde C; [f] þam C; [g] pretectati C; [h] om. C; [i] þam C; [j] appia C.

26 May: Augustine of Canterbury

92. On ðone [a]sex ond twentegðan[a] dæg ðæs monðes bið Sancte Augustines[b] gemynd ðæs biscopes[c], se [d]ærest fullwiht brohte[d] on ðas Breotone[e] on Angla[f] þeode; ond his biscopsetl[g] wæs on [h]Dorobernensis ðære ceastre[h], þæt wæs on Cantwarabyrg[i]. Ond his wundor wæs þæt he sealde blindum menn[j] gesihðe. Ond his siðfatas ealle to Breotone[k] ond his [l]gastlice lare[l] syndon awritene on [m]Ongelcynnes steore[m], þæt is [n]on Historia Anglorum[n].

92. [a-a] syx and twentigoðan C; [b] agustinus C; [c] bysceopes C; [d-d] brohte ærest C; [e] Brytene C; [f] engla C; [g] bysceopsetl C; [h-h] þære ceastre dorobernis C; [i] cantwarebyrig C; [j] om. C; [k] brytone C; [l-l] gastlican lara C; [m-m] angelcynnes stere C; [n-n] istoria anglorum on þam bocum C.

29 May: Sisinnius, Martyrius and Alexander

93. On ðone [a]nygan ond twentegðan[a] dæg ðæs monðes bið [b]þara halegra[b] martyra tid Sancti Sisinni [c]ond Sancti Martyri[c] ond Sancti Alexandri, ða þrowedan[d] wuldorfæstne[e] martyrdom for Criste.

93. [a-a] nygon and twentigoðan C; [b-b] þæra haligra C; [c-c] om C; [d] þrowedon C; [e] wundorlicne C.

31 May: Petronilla

94. On ðone an ond þritegðan[a] dæg þæs monðes bið Sancta[b] Petranellan[c] tid ðære fæmnan. Heo wæs Sancte Petres dohtor, ðara[d] apostola aldres[e], ond heo wæs swiðe wlitegu[f] fæmne on Rome. Ða ongann[g] þære burge gerefa hire biddan to wife, se wæs on noman[h] Flaccus; þa onbead heo him, þæt he þæs æfter seofan[i] dagum hire[j] to onsænde[k] all[l][164] ða gesiðwif ond ða æþelan fæmnan, þe[m] þær wæron, þæt heo mid þæm[n] mihte feran to þæm[o] brydþingum. Þa stod heo ealle þa seofon dagas on gebedum ond [p]God bæd[p], þæt heo on mægðhade hire lif geendade[q]. Ða on þæm[r] seofoðan dæge com hire to Nicomedes[s] se mæssepreost ond hire sealde[t] husl, ond heo sona[u] onsende hire gast to Gode. Ond eall[v][165] þa gesiðwif ond ða fæmnan, ðe [w]þær to[w] coman[x], dedan[y] hire licþenunge ond læddon hi[z] to byrgenne.

94. [a] þryttygoðan C; [b] sancte C; [c] petronellan C; [d] þæra C; [e] ealdores C; [f] wlitig C; [g] ongan C; [h] naman C; [i] seofon C; [j] hyg C; [k] onsende C; [l] ealle C; [m] þa ðe C; [n] þam C; [o] ðam C; [p-p] bæd god C; [q] geendode C; [r] þam C; [s] nicodemus C; [t] gesealde C; [u] þa sona C; [v] ealle C; [w-w] þærto Ko; [x] comon C; [y] dydon C; [z] hig C.

25 May: Pope Urban I

91. On the twenty-fifth day of the month is the commemoration of Pope St Urban, who was pope in Rome for four years, three months and twenty-five days. And he converted many a noble person to Christianity, and he is buried in the church which is called [that of] Praetextatus, and on the road which is called the Via Appia.

26 May: Augustine of Canterbury

92. On the twenty-sixth of the month is the commemoration of Bishop St Augustine, who first introduced baptism here to this Britain, to the English; and his episcopal seat was in the city of Dorobernia, that is in Canterbury. And his miracle was that he gave sight to a blind man. And all his journeys to Britain and his religious teaching are described in the history of the English, that is in the *Historia anglorum*.

29 May: Sisinnius, Martyrius and Alexander

93. On the twenty-ninth day of the month is the feast of the holy martyrs St Sisinnius, St Martyrius and St Alexander, who suffered glorious martyrdom for Christ.

31 May: Petronilla

94. On the thirty-first day of the month is the feast of the virgin St Petronilla. She was the daughter of St Peter, the first of the apostles, and she was a very beautiful virgin in Rome. Then the reeve of the city, who was called Flaccus, asked for her hand to marry her; then she asked him, that after seven days he should send her all the noblewomen and the noble virgins who were there, so that she might go to her wedding ceremony with them. Then she spent all of seven days standing in prayers, asking God, that she might end her life in virginity. Then on the seventh day the priest Nicomedes came to her and gave her the Eucharist, and she gave up the ghost to God soon thereafter. And all the noblewomen and the virgins, who had arrived there, organised her funeral and led her to her grave.

The End of May

94a. Þonne[a] [b]þrymelces monað[b] bið geendod, ðonne bið seo niht eahta[c] tida lang, ond se dæg sextene[d] tida.

94a. [a] And þonne C; [b-b] þrymylces monoð C; [c] ehta C; [d] syxtene C.

The Beginning of June

94b. On ðæm[a] syxtan monðe on geare bið þritig[b] daga. Se monað[c] is nemned on Læden[d] Iunius, ond on ure geþeode se Ærra Liða, forðon[e] seo lyft [f]bið þonne smylte ond ða windas[f]. Ond monnum[g] bið ðonne gewunelic, ðæt hi[h] [i]liðað[166] ðonne[i] on sæs bryme.

94b. [a] þam C; [b] þryttig C; [c] monoð C; [d] leden C; [e] forþon he ys nemned liða forþon þe C; [f-f] and þa wyndas beoð þonne smylte C; [g] mannum C; [h] hig C; [i-i] liðað C.

1 June: Priscus and Nicomedes

95, 96. On ðone ærestan dæg þæs monðes belimpað twegen mæssesongas[a]. Se ærra bið on [b]ðæm ealdan sacramentorium[b][167], þæt [c]is on ðæm[c] ealdan mæssebocum, on Sancte Prisces gemynd ðæs martyres; oþer bið on [d]ðæm niwran[d][168] bocum, on [e]Sancte Nicomedes[e] gemynd ðæs martyres.

95, 96. [a] mæssesangas C; [b-b] þam ealdan sacramentorum C; [c-c] ys on þam C; [d-d] þam nywan C; [e-e] sancti nicomenius C.

2 June: Erasmus

97. On ðone æfteran dæg þæs monðes bið Sancte Herasmis[a] tid, se wæs biscop[b] on Antiochia ceastre. He wæs fæger on ansyne ond <engellic>[c][169], ond his eagan wæron swelce[d] [e]sunnan leoma[e][170]. Ða on ða tid bebead Dioclitianus se casere, ðæt Cristne[f] men [g]guldan deofolgeldum[g]. Ða gewat se biscop[h] on westen ond þær eardade[i] seofon gear, ond him þær bær hræfn[j] mete to, ond misenlico[k] wilddeor[l] [m]him comon[m] to ond hine weorðedon[n]. Ða com him Godes engel to ond hine alædde ðanon on[o] Italia mægðe, þæt is on Etelwara londe[p], in Ludican[q][171] ðære ceastre. Ðær he awehte deadne mon[r] of deaðe, ond þurh þæt wundor eall ðæt folc onfeng fullwihte[s]. Ða het Maximianus se casere hine lædan to his deofolgelde[t], þæt he þæm[u] gulde. Þa stod þær [v]gyldenu onlicnes[v], twelf elna heah[w], ond of þære com gan micel draca ond abat ðone þriddan dæl ðæs hæðnan[172] folces beforan [x]ðæm biscope[x]. Þa het se casere hine don on carcern; þa [y]æt midre niht[y] ætywde hine Michahel[z] se heahengel ond hine ut

97. [a] Herasmus C; [b] bysceop C; [c] ænlic B, Ko, Herz, engellic C; [d] swylce C; [e-e] sunnan leoman C, sunnanleoma Ko, sunnan leoma Herz; [f] cristene C; [g-g] guldon deofolgyldum C; [h] bysceop C; [i] eardode C; [j] hrefen C; [k] myssenlico C; [l] wylde deor C; [m-m] hym þær comon C; [n] weorðodon C; [o] in C; [p] mægðe and on þam lande C; [q] lucridam C; [r] man C; [s] fulwyhte C; [t] deofolgylde C; [u] þam C; [v-v] gylden anlycnys C; [w] heh C; [x-x] þam bysceope C; [y-y] on myddenyht C; [z] sanctus mychael C;

The End of May

94a. When the month of 'Þrimilce' ['Three Milkings'] comes to an end, the night is eight hours long, and the day sixteen hours.

The Beginning of June

94b. There are thirty days in the sixth month of the year. This month is called *Junius* in Latin, and Ærra Liða ['Earlier Mild (Month)'] in our language, because the air is tranquil then, and the winds too. And it is then that people normally travel across the water of the sea.

1 June: Priscus and Nicomedes

95, 96. On the first day of the month there should be two masses. The first is in the old sacramentaries, that is the old massbooks, for the commemoration of the martyr St Priscus; the second is in the more recent books, for the commemoration of the martyr St Nicomedes.

2 June: Erasmus

97. On the second day of the month is the feast of St Erasmus, who was a bishop in the city of Antioch. He was good-looking in appearance and angelic, and his eyes were like rays of sunshine. Then at that time the emperor Diocletian commanded that Christians should worship devils. Then the bishop went into the wilderness and lived there for seven years, and a raven brought him food there, and various wild animals came to him and adored him. Then an angel of God came to him and led him away from there to the country of Italy, which is the country of the Italians, in the city of [?Ludica]. There he awakened a dead man from death, and because of that miracle all of that population received baptism. Then the emperor Maximian commanded that he should be led to his devil image, so that he would worship it. Then there stood a golden idol, twelve cubits high, and from that a great dragon emerged and savaged a third of the pagan population in front of the bishop. Then the emperor commanded that he be put into prison; then in the middle of the night Michael the archangel

alædde of þære ceastre. Ond þa gemette he scip, ond he astag[a] on [b]þæt scip[b] ond mid ðy oferlað[c] ða mægðe, ðæt[d] he com on oþre mægðe to þære ceastre ðe Formeae[e] is nemned. Ðær he gereste seofon dagas, ond þær com stefn of heofonum[f] ond hine cede[g] to þære ecan reste. Þa bæd he God, þæt [h]æghwelc mon[h] þe him gebæde on þære stowe, ðær his eardung wæs, þæt he þæs hæfde mede [i]wið God[i], [j]ond þæt[j] his gast [k]æghwelce sæternesdæg ond sunnan<dæg>[l] moste beon[k] on þære ilcan stowe. Þa cwæþ seo stefn eft of heofonum[m]: 'Eall hit bið swa þu bidest[n].' Ond þa onsende he his ðone sigefæstan gast to Gode.

[a] astah C; [b-b] þæt C; [c] oferfor C; [d] ða C; [e] formea C; [f] heofenum C; [g] cigde C; [h-h] æghwylc man C; [i-i] myd gode C; [j-j] and C; [k-k] moste beon æghwylce sæternesdæg and sunnandæg C; [l] sunnan B, sunnandæg C Herz, sunnan<dæg> Ko; [m] heofenum C; [n] byddest C.

2 June: Marcellinus and Peter

98. On ðone ilcan dæg bið þara[a] eadigra weora[b] tid Sancte Marcellines[c] þæs mæssepreostes ond Sancte Petres ðæs cristneres[d 173]; ða dydon [e]manego wundor[e] on Rome ond ðrowedon monigfealdne[f] martyrdom under þæm[g] deman ðe [h]Serenus wæs nemned[h]. [i]Æt nehstan[i] he het [j]lædan hi feor on ðone wudu[j] se wæs genemned[k] Silua Nigra, se swearta wudu, ond he is nu[l] nemned for þyssa haligra are Silua Candida, se hwita wudu. [m]He bead[m] þæt [n]hi mon[n] þær beheafdade[o], ond [p]hi þa hi[p] gecyston, ond [q]þa wæron hi[q] beheafdade[r]. Ond þa sægde[s] se mon[t] eallum folce, se þe [u]hi beheafdade[u], þæt he [v]gesege heora[v] sawle, ða hi[w] [x]ut eodon[x] of [y]þæm lichoman, swelce[y] heo[z 174] wæren[a] mid gimmum gefretwade[b] ond mid [c]golde, beorhtum hreglum[c] gegerede[d], [175] ond englas mid heora [e]hondum heo[e] gefeonde[f] bæren[g] to heofonum[h]. Þæs monnes[i] nama wæs, se þe [j]hi beheafdade[j], Dorotheos[k], ond he þæs dyde hreowsunga ond onfeng fullwihte[l] ond wæs to Gode gecierred[m].

98. [a] þæra C; [b] wera C; [c] marcelline C; [d] crystenan weres C; [e-e] manege wundru C; [f] mænifealdne C; [g] þam C; [h-h] wæs nemned serenus and þa C; [i-i] æt nystan C, Ætnehstan Ko; [j-j] hig feor on þone wudu lædan C; [k] nemned C; [l] om. C; [m-m] and he bebead C; [n-n] hig man C; [o] beheafdode C; [p-p] hig þa hig C; [q-q] wæron þa C; [r] beheafdode C; [s] sæde C; [t] man C; [u-u] hig beheafdode C; [v-v] gesawe hyra C; [w] hig C; [x-x] uteodon Ko; [y-y] þam lychaman swylce C; [z] heo B, Herz, hig C, Ko; [a] wære B with n suprascript Ba, wæron C; [b] gefrætwode C; [c-c] beorhtum golde C, goldebeorhtum hreglum Ko; [d] gegyrede C; [e-e] handum hig C; [f] fægnigende C; [g] bæron C; [h] heofenum C; [i] mannes C; [j-j] hig beheafdode C; [k] dorotheus C; [l] fulwyhte C; [m] gecyrred C.

2 June: Artemius, Candida and Virgo

99. On ðone ylcan dæg ðrowade[a] martyrdom for Criste Sanctus Arthemius[b], se wæs ær carcernweard, ac [c]he gelyfde hwæþre to Gode[c] for þæm[d] wundrum ðe he geseah æt þyssum[e] halgum weorum[f] Marcellini ond Petre. Ond his wif gelefde[g] mid hine[h], þære [i]naman wes[i] Candida, ond [j]heora dohter[j], [k]þare noma[k] wæs Uirgo. Ða het se

99. Water damage to B on 105v, with some letters apparently refreshed, resulting in a number of unusual spellings and forms; [a] þrowude C; [b] arthemus C; [c-c] hwæðere he gelyfde on god C; [d] þam C; [e] þysum C; [f] werum C; [g] gelyfde C; [h] hym C; [i-i] nama wæs C; [j-j] hyra dohtor C; [k-k] þære nama C;

appeared to him and led him out of the city. And he found a ship, and he boarded the ship and with that crossed the country, so that he came to another country to the city which is called Formiae. There he rested for seven days, and there came a voice from heaven and summoned him to eternal rest. Then he asked God, that everybody who would pray in the place where his dwelling had been, that he should be rewarded for this by God, and that his spirit would be allowed to be in the same place every Saturday and Sunday. Then the voice from heaven answered: 'It will all be as you ask.' And then he gave up the victorious ghost to God.

2 June: Marcellinus and Peter

98. On the same day is the feast of the blessed men St Marcellinus, the priest, and St Peter, the [?exorcist]; they worked many miracles in Rome and suffered a protracted martyrdom under the judge who was called Serenus. Ultimately he commanded them to be led far into the wood which is called *Silua Nigra*, 'the black wood', and in honour of these saints it is now called *Silua Candida*, 'the white wood'. He commanded that one should behead them there, and then they kissed each other, and then they were beheaded. And then the man, who beheaded them, told all the people that he could see their souls as they left the bodies, as if they were adorned with gems and gold, dressed in shining garments, and angels, rejoicing, were carrying them to heaven in their hands. The name of the man who beheaded them was Dorotheus, and he repented of that and received baptism and was converted to God.

2 June: Artemius, Candida and Virgo

99. On the same day St Artemius suffered martyrdom for Christ, who was first a prison-guard, but he nevertheless believed in God because of the miracles which he saw from these holy men, Marcellinus and Peter. And his wife believed with him, whose name was Candida, and their daughter, whose name was Virgo. Then the

dema ðone carcernweard slean mid sweorde for þæm[l] geleafan, ond þæt[m] wif ond þa dohtar[n] weorpan on seað[o] ond þær mid stanum offellan[p].

[l] þam C; [m] he het þæt C; [n] dohtor C; [o] anne seað C; [p] offyllan C.

9 June: Columba of Iona

100. On ðone nygeþan[a] dæg þæs monðes bið þæs halgan mæssepreostes tid[b] Sancte Columba[c], ðone nemnað [d]Sceottas Columchille[d]; se com of Scottum to Breotone[e], ond gelærde Peohtas to fullwihte, ond getimbrede him mynster on [f]þæm ealonde[f] þe is nemned Hii, ond he dyde monig[g] heofonlic wundor. His wundra [h]wæs sum[h] þæt tu[i] gesinhiwan[j] spræcon ymb[k] hine ealle niht, [l]oþ þæt[l] him[l] slæp ofereode[176]. Ða ongan se tun bernan[n] on þære nihte. Þa forburnen[o] [p]ealla þara monna[p] hus þe on þæm[q] tune wæron, [r]butan þara gesinhigna[r] þe ymb[s] hine spræcon. Ða on morgenne[t] het[u] þære ðeode biscop[v] ða gesinhiwan to[w] him, ond frægn [x]hi mid hwi hi[x] [y]gescildan heora hus[y] [177] wið þæs fyres frecennysse[z], ond cwæþ þæt hi[a] þæt hæfdon oþþe[b] to Gode geearnad[c] mid godum dædum, oþþe hi[d] þæt hæfdon gedon mid yflum[e] scinlacum[f]. Ða cwædon hi[g] þæt hi[h] naþer ne scinncræftas[i] cuþan[j], ne hi[k] mid nængum[l] godum weorcum þæt noht[m] swiðe to Gode geearnod[n] hæfdon[o], butan[p] þæt an, þæt hi[q] on þære nihte spræcon ymb þone halgan wer Sancte Columbe[r]. Ða ongeat[s] se biscop[t] þæt heora[u] hus þurh þæt wæron gescylde wið þæs fyres frecennisse[v], forþon[w] hi[x] [y]on ðæm husum dydon[y] ðæs halgan gemynd.

100. [a] nygoðan C; [b] gemynd C; [c] columban C; [d-d] scottas columcylle C; [e] brytene C; [f-f] þam ealande C; [g] mænig C; [h-h] sum ys C; [i] twa C; [j] gesynhywu C; [k] ymbe C; [l-l] oþþæt Ko; [m] hig C; [n] byrnan C; [o] forburnon C; [p-p] ealra þæra manna C; [q] þam C; [r-r] buton þæra gesynhyna C; [s] ymbe C; [t] mergenne C; [u] þa het C; [v] bysceop C; [w] cuman to C; [x-x] hig myd hwam hig C; [y-y] hyra huse gescyldon C; [z] frecednysse C; [a] hig C; [b] om. C; [c] geearnod C; [d] hig C; [e] yfelum C; [f] scyncræfte C; [g] hig C; [h] hig C; [i] scincræftas C; [j] ne cuðon C; [k] hig C; [l] nænegum C; [m] naht C; [n] gegearnod C; [o] næfdon C; [p] buton C; [q] hig C; [r] columban C; [s] onget C; [t] bysceop C; [u] hyra C; [v] frecednysse C; [w] forþam þe C; [x] hig C; [y-y] dydon on þam huse C.

10 June: Barnabas

101. On ðone[a] teogeþan[b] dæg[c] þæs monðes bið Sancte Barnabes tid; se wæs Cristes apostola discipul, forðæm[d] his noma[e] is gereaht[f] on Læden[g] filius consolationis, ðæt is on ure geþeode frofre sunu. He wæs acenned on [h]Cypro þæm ealonde[h], ond he wæs diacon æfter þære ealdan æ þeawe[i]. Ac he þa gelyfde on Crist ond bebohte[j] his lond[k], ond þæt wearð[l] gesealde [m]Hælendes ðegnum[m], ond ferde mid Pawle[n] [o]feorr ond wide geond middangeard[o], ond monige þeoda[p] gelærde to Godes geleafan. Ond on [q]þara anre[q] him mon sealde attor drincan, ond [r]him þæt hwæþre[r] ne eglede.

101. [a] þam C; [b] teoðan C; [c] dæge C; [d] om. C; [e] nama C; [f] gereht C; [g] lyden C; [h-h] cypra þam ealande C; [i] þeawum C; [j] he sealde C; [k] land C; [l] weorð C; [m-m] þæs hælendes þances C; [n] paule C; [o-o] wyde geond þysne myddaneard C; [p] þeode C; [q-q] þære anre þeode C; [r-r] hwæðre hym þæt nan þing C.

judge commanded the prison-guard to be killed with a sword, for his faith, and the wife and the daughter to be thrown into a pit and killed there by stoning.

9 June: Columba of Iona

100. On the ninth day of the month is the feast of the holy priest St Columba, whom the Gaels call Colum Cille; he came from the Gaels to Britain, and introduced the Picts to baptism, and constructed a monastery for them [or 'himself'] on the island which is called Hii [i.e. Iona], and he worked many heavenly miracles. One of his miracles was that a married couple were talking about him all night, until sleep overcame them. Then the village began to burn during the night. Then the houses of all people burnt down that were in that village, except for that of the couple who had been talking about him. Then in the morning the bishop of those people summoned the couple to him, and asked them by what means they had protected their house against the dangerous fire, and said that they had either merited it from God with good deeds, or that they had done it with nasty witchcraft. Then they said that they neither knew witchcraft, nor had they particularly earned it from God with any good deeds, except for the one thing, that they had been talking about the holy man St Columba during that night. Then the bishop realised that their house had been protected by that from the dangerous fire – because they had commemorated the saint in that house.

10 June: Barnabas

101. On the tenth day of the month is the feast of St Barnabas; he was a follower of Christ's apostles, which is why his name in Latin is *filius consolationis*, which in our language means 'the son of consolation'. He was born in the island of Cyprus, and he was a minister according to the custom of the old law [or 'Old Testament']. But he then believed in Christ and sold his land, and donated the proceeds to the followers of the Saviour, and he travelled with Paul far and wide throughout the world, and introduced many nations to God's faith. And in one of them one gave him poison to drink, but it did not harm him.

15 June: Vitus and Modestus

102. On þone fifteogþan[a] dæg þæs monðes bið Sancte Uites þrowung; he wæs seofon geara[b] cniht ða he campode for Criste. Ærest his fæder [c]mid medum hine wolde[c] [d]oncerran from[d] Cristes geleafan; ða ne mihte he. Da sealde he hine Ualerianum[e] þæm[f] gerefan, ond he hine swencte mid [g]witum, ond[g] he [h]hine ne mihte[h] oferswiðan. Ða ætywde[i] Drihtnes[j] engel ond hine gelædde to sumum[k] sæ, ond his festerfæder[l] mid hine[m]. [n]Þær hi[n] gemetton[o] scip, ond [p]on þæm se engel hi lædde[p] of Lucania[q] þære mægðe ofer þone[r] sæ on oþer land. Þær he gehælde Dioclitianus sunu ðæs caseres [s]from deofolseocnesse[s], ond se casere him bead gold ond seolfor ond deorwyrðe gerelan[t] ond half[u] his rice [v]wið þon[v] þe he forlete Cristes geleafan, ond he þon[w] wiðsoc. Þa het se casere meltan[x] [y]on hwere[y] lead ond scipteora[z] ond pic, ond he het þone cniht on þæs hweres [a]welm asetton[a], ond him þæt no[b] ne geeglde[c]. Ac[d] Godes engel hine þa gelædde ond his festerfæder[e] mid hine[f], Sanctum Modestum, on þæs flodes neaweste se is cweden Siler. Ðær [g]gesegon Cristne[g] men [h]heora sawle[h] fleogan[i] to heofonum[j] swa swa culfran, ond hi[k] wæron seofon siðum hwittran[l] þonne snaw. Ond earnas heoldon [m]ða lichoman[m] ðær þreo[n] dagas, [o]oþ þæt[o] þær com to sum arfæst[p] wif ofer þone flod, seo wæs on noman[q] Florentia. Ond hire þa ætywde þæs cildes gast on [r]þæm wættre[r] [s]þæm wife[s], ond het [t]hi bebyrgan heora lichoman[t], ond heo þa hi[u] bebyrgde[v] on þære stowe seo is cweden[w] Marianus.

102. [a] fifteoðan C; [b] geare C; [c-c] hyne wolde myd medum C; [d-d] oncyrran fram C; [e] ualeriane C; [f] þam C; [g-g] wytum ac C; [h-h] ne mihte hyne C; [i] ætywde hym C; [j] dryhtenes C; [k] sumre C; [l] fosterfæder C; [m] hym C; [n-n] Þær hyg C; [o] gemytton C; [p-p] se engel hig gelædde on þæt C; [q] luciana C; [r] þa C; [s-s] fram deofolseocnysse C; [t] gegyrlan C; [u] healf C; [v-v] wiðþon Ko; [w] þan C; [x] myltan C; [y-y] om. C; [z] pictyran C; [a-a] wylm asettan C; [b] na C; [c] eglede C; [d] ah B, ac se C; [e] fosterfæder C; [f] hym C; [g-g] gesawon crystene C; [h-h] hyra sawla C; [i] fleon C; [j] heofenum C; [k] hig C; [l] hwitran C; [m-m] heora lychaman C; [n] þry C; [o-o] oþþæt Ko; [p] arwyrðe C; [q] naman C; [r-r] þam wætere C; [s-s] om. C; [t-t] bebyrgean hyra lychaman C; [u] hig C; [v] gebyrigde C; [w] gecweden C.

16 June: Ferreolus and Ferrucio

103. On ðone sextegðan[a] dæg þæs monðes bið þara[b] eadigra weora[c] ðrowung Sancte Fereones[d] ðæs mæssepreostes ond Sancte Feruciones ðæs diacones, ða þrowedon martyrdom[e] for Criste on þære ceastre Bisoncensi[f] under [g]Claudium þæm[g] gerefan. Se wolde [h]hi mid[h] feo beswican þæt hi[i] Criste wiðsocan[j]; [k]ða hi[k] þæt ne geþafedon, þa het he him ða tungan forceorfan. Ac hi[l] spræcon butan tungan, swa hi[m] ær dydon, ond God heredon. Þa het he [n]hi slean[n] mid sweorde[o], ond hi[p] þa onsendon heora[q] gastas, ond þær [r]þa com[r] micel wynsum stenc. Ond Cristne[s] men bebyrgdon[t] [u]heora lichoman[u] on ðæm[v] ylcan scræfe þær hi[w] ær Gode[x] þeowedon[y].

103. [a] syxteoðan C; [b] þæra C; [c] wera C; [d] ferreones C; [e] om. C; [f] þe hatte bisoncensi and C; [g-g] claudia þam C; [h-h] hig myd C; [i] hig C; [j] wyðsocen C; [k-k] ac hig C; [l] hig C; [m] hig C; [n-n] hig ofslean C; [o] swurde C; [p] hig C; [q] hyra C; [r-r] com þa C; [s] crystene C; [t] bebyrigdon C; [u-u] hyra lychaman C; [v] þam C; [w] hig C; [x] on gode C; [y] þeowodon C.

15 June: Vitus and Modestus

102. On the fifteenth day of the month is the passion of St Vitus; he was a boy of seven years when he was martyred for Christ. First his father tried to convert him from Christianity with bribes, but he did not succeed. Then he handed him over to the reeve Valerianus, and he afflicted him with tortures, but he could not overcome him. Then an angel of the Lord appeared and led him to some sea, and his fosterfather with him. There they found a ship, and on that the angel led them from the province of Lucania across the sea to another country. There he cured the son of the emperor Diocletian from possession by the devil, and the emperor offered him gold and silver and precious garments and half his empire, provided that he would renounce Christianity, and he still refused. Then the emperor commanded lead and tar and pitch to be melted in a cauldron, and he commanded the boy to be put into the boiling cauldron, but it did not harm him at all. But God's angel then led him and his fosterfather, St Modestus, with him to the vicinity of the river which is called Siler [i.e. Sele]. There some Christians saw their souls fly to heaven like doves, and they were seven times whiter than snow. And eagles guarded the bodies there for three days, until an honourable woman arrived across the river, who was called Florentia. And the child's spirit appeared to her – to the woman – on the water, and commanded her to bury their bodies, and she buried them then in the place which is called Marianus.

16 June: Ferreolus and Ferrucio

103. On the sixteenth day of the month is the passion of the blessed men St Ferreolus, the priest, and St Ferrucio, the deacon, who suffered martyrdom for Christ in the city of Bisontium [i.e. Besançon] under Claudius the reeve. He wanted to beguile them with money to renounce Christ; when they refused, he commanded their tongues to be cut out. But they were able to speak without tongues in the same way as they had done before, and praised God. Then he commanded them to be killed with the sword, and they then gave up the ghost, and there came a powerful, pleasant smell then. And Christians buried their bodies in the same cave where they had previously served God.

17 June: Nicander

104. On ðone seofontegðan[a] dæg þæs monðes bið Sancte Nicandes tid þæs martyres, ðæs gemynd sceal beon mærsad[b] mid mæssesongum[c], ond his mæsse bið geseted on [d]ðæm eldran[d] mæssebocum.

104. [a] seofonteoðan C; [b] mærsod C; [c] mæssesangum C; [d-d] þam yldran C.

17 June: Blastus

105. Ond on þone ylcan dæg bið Sancte Blastes ðrowung[a] þæs martyres on Rome; se þrowade[b] fyres bryne for Criste, ond tu[c] hund[d] Cristenra monna[e] mid hine[f] [g]ond tu[g] ond syxtig.

105. [a] tyd and þrowung C; [b] þrowode C; [c] twa C; [d] hundred C; [e] manna C; [f] hym C; [g-g] and twa C

18 June: Mark and Marcellian

106. On ðone eahtategþan[a] dæg þæs monðes bið þara[b] æþelra wera ðrowung Sancte Marces[c] ond Sancte Marcellianes[d], þæt wæron gebroþra[e] ond hi[f] wæron begen Cristene. Þa bebead Dioclitianus se casere ðæt hi[g] guldon deofolgyld[h], oþþe hi[i] man beheafdade[j]. Ða hi[k] þa eodon to þære beheafdunga[l], þa com him ongean wepende[m] fæder ond modor[n] ond [o]hiora wif tu[o] mid monegum[p] cildum, ond halsedon [q]hi þæt hi[q] forletan[r] ðone Cristes geleafan. Ða oncierde[s] him [t]seo gehygd[t] to deofolgylde. Þa ongeat[u] þæt Sanctus Sebastianus se Cristna[v] wer, ða ongan he him[w] secgan hu lytel ond hu scomlic[x] ðæs monnes[y] lif bið her on worolde[z], ond hu long[a] ond hu ondrysnlic[b] þæt ece wite bið, ond hu wuldorlic[c] seo ece eadignes[d] bið, [e]oþ ðæt[e] him [f]seo heorte eft[f] to Criste gecerde[g]. Ond[h] hi[i] þa gecyston hi[j], ond ða[k] wæron for Criste gemartyrad[l].

106. [a] ehtateoðan C; [b] þæra C; [c] marce C; [d] marcelline C; [e] gebroðer C; [f] hig C; [g] hig C; [h] deofolgyldum C; [i] hig C; [j] beheafdode C; [k] hig C; [l] beheafdunge C; [m] om. C; [n] moder C; 5 [o-o] hyra twa wif C; [p] manegum C; [q-q] hig þæt hig C; [r] forleton C; [s] oncyrde C; [t-t] se hyht C; [u] onget C; [v] cristena C; [w] heom C; [x] sceort C; [y] mannes C; [z] worulde C; [a] lang C; [b] ondrysnlic C; [c] wundorlic C; [d] eadignys C; [e-e] oþðæt Ko; [f-f] eft seo heorte C; [g] gecyrde C; [h] om. C; [i] hig C; [j] hig C; [k] hig þa C; [l] gemartyrode C.

19 June: Gervase and Protase

107. On ðone nygentegðan[a] dæg ðæs monðes bið þara[b] haligra gebroðra tid Sancte[c] Geruasi ond Sancte[d] Protasi. Hie[e] wæron getwinnas ond heora[f] fæder noma[g] wæs Uitalis[h] ond heora[i] modor Ualeriae[j], ond hie[k] wæron [l]bu Gode[l] swiðe gecorene, ond æfter heora[m] geleornesse[n] Astachius[o] se gesið[p] [q]nedde hi[q] þæt hi[r] Criste wiðsocan[s]. Þa hit[t] þæt ne geþafedon, þa het he swingan þone Geruasi [u]oþ þæt[u] he his gast onsende,

107. [a] nigonteoðan C; [b] þæra C; [c] sancti C; [d] sancti C; [e] hig C; [f] hyra C; [g] nama C; [h] uitales C; [i] hyra C; [j] nama wæs ualeria C; [k] hig C; [l-l] gode butu C; [m] hyra C; [n] gewytennysse C; [o] astaccius C; [p] syð C; [q-q] nydde hig C; [r] hig C; [s] wyðsocon C; [t] hig C; [u-u] oþþæt Ko;

17 June: Nicander

104. On the seventeenth day of the month is the feast of the martyr St Nicander, whose commemoration shall be celebrated with masses, and his mass is included in the older massbooks.

17 June: Blastus

105. And on the same day is the passion of the martyr St Blastus in Rome; he suffered martyrdom by fire for Christ, and 262 Christians with him.

18 June: Mark and Marcellian

106. On the eighteenth day of the month is the passion of the noblemen St Mark and St Marcellian, who were brothers and they were both Christians. Then emperor Diocletian commanded that they worship pagan idols, or they would be beheaded. When they then went to the beheading, their weeping father and mother and their two wives with many children came towards them, and implored them to abandon Christianity. Then their thoughts turned to pagan devil-worship. When St Sebastian, the Christian man, saw that, he began to tell them how insignificant and how shameful man's life is here in the world, and how long and how terrible eternal torment is, and how glorious eternal bliss is, until their hearts turned back towards Christ. And then they kissed, and then suffered martyrdom for Christ.

19 June: Gervase and Protase

107. On the nineteenth day of the month is the feast of the holy brothers St Gervase and St Protase. They were twins and their father's name was Vitalis and their mother's Valeria, and they were both very acceptable to God, and after their death Astachius the governor forced them [i.e. Gervase and Protase] to renounce Christ. When they refused, he commanded Gervase to be beaten until he gave up the ghost, ond[v] þone Protasi beheafdian. Ond[w] æfter monegum[x] gearum heora[y] gastas æteawdon[z] Ambrosie [a]ðæm biscope[a], ond him getæht<on>[b] [178] [c]heora lichoman[c] on eorðan gehydde[d]. Ond he þa [e]hi hof up[e] ond getimbrede cyricean[f] on heora[g] naman, ond þa lichoman[h] on þa [i]gesette on[i] Mediolana þære ceastre.

[v] and he het C; [w] and þa C; [x] manegum C; [y] hyra C; [z] ætywdon C; [a-a] þam bysceope C; [b] getæhte B, getæhton C, getæht<on> He, Ko; [c-c] hyra lychaman C; [d] ahydde C; [e-e] hig up adyde C; [f] þar cyrcan C; [g] hyra C; [h] lychaman C; [i-i] asette in C.

22 June: James the Less

108. On ðone tu[a] ond twentegðan[b] dæg þæs monðes bið þæs apostoles ond þæs Godes ærendwracan[c] gemynd [d]þe on gewritum is[d] nemned Iacobus Alphei[e]; þæt[f] wæs Cristes modergan[g] sunu, Sancta Marian sweostorsunu[h], forþon he is cweden on gewritum frater Domini, Drihtnes broþor; ond æfter Drihtnes upastignesse[i] he wæs biscop[j] on Hierusalem. Ne æt he næfre flæsc, ne he win ne dranc, ne he wyllenra hrægla breac[k] ac linenra ealra[l] [179], ne he bæþes[m] gymde[n], ne he his loccas mid scearum wanode[o], ne his[p] beard mid seaxe scear[q]. Ac he a singallice him to Gode gebæd ðæt him [r]seo hyd aheardod wæs[r] on ðæm[s] cneowum, swa olfendan [t]cneo beoð[t]. Ðone Iacobum Iudaea[u] leorneras ofslogan[v] for Cristes læþþum mid webwyrhtan rode. Ac [w]seo his[w] unsynnige cwalu wæs swa gewrecen þæt sona coman[x] mid weorode[y] twegen caseras fram Rome ond towurpon ealle ða burh Hierusalem, ond [z]þa þe ðær oneardadan[180] slogan[z], ond mid hungre acwealdan[a], ond onweg bebohton[b].

108. [a] twa and twa C; [b] twentigoðan C; [c] ærendracan C; [d-d] se ys cweden on gewrytum and C; [e] alfei C; [f] se C; [g] modrian C; [h] swustersunu C; [i] upastigennysse C; [j] bysceop C; [k] ne breac C; [l] anra C; [m] baðes C; [n] ne gymde C; [o] ne wanode C; [p] he hys C; [q] ne scær C; [r-r] wæs seo hyd aheardod C; [s] þam C; [t-t] cneow byð C; [u] iudea C; [v] ofslogon C; [w-w] hys seo C; [x] comon C; [y] werode C; [z-z] ofslogon þa ðe þær onear eardedon C; [a] acwealdon C; [b] gesealdon C.

22 June: Alban

109. On ðone ilcan dæg bið Sancte Albanes ðrowung, se þrowade[a] on þisse Breotone[b] martyrdom for Criste. Ðurh sumne preost he wæs gelæred to Godes geleafan; þa bebead sum hæþen ealdormon[c] his cæmpum[d] þæt hi[e] sohton þone preost on Albanes huse. Ða[f] dyde Albanus on hine þæs preostes cæppan [g]ond eode ongean þæm cæmpan[g], ond hi[h] hine gebundon ond læddon to þæm[i] deman, ond se hine mid[j] miclum witum þreade þæt he Criste wiðsoce. Þa he þæt ne geþafode, þa het he hine lædan upp[k] on sume dune ond hine þær beheafdian. Þær Albanus abæd æt Gode þæt þær færinga com [l]upp wætres welle[l] beforan his fotum. Ond [m]þæm menn[m] ðe hine [n]beheafdade, þæm[n] sona afeollan[o] þa eagan [p]bu of þæm[p] heafde. Seo stow þær Albanus ðrowade[q] is neah ðære ceastre þe Bryttwalas[r] nemdon[s] Uerolamium[t], ond Ængla[u] þeod [v]nemnað nu Wætlingaceaster[v].

109. [a] þrowode C; [b] brytene C; [c] ealdorman C; [d] cempum C; [e] hig C; [f] and þa C; [g-g] om. C; [h] hig C; [i] þam C; [j] om. C; [k] up C; [l-l] up wæteres wylle C; [m-m] þam men C; [n-n] beheafdode C; [o] afeollon C; [p-p] buto of þam C; [q] geþrowode C; [r] brytwealas C; [s] nemnað C; [t] uerola imu C; [u] engla C; [v-v] hig nemnað wealyngaceaster C.

and St Protase to be beheaded. And after many years their ghosts appeared to Bishop Ambrose, and showed him their bodies hidden in the ground. And then he exhumed them and built a church in their names, and placed the bodies in it in the city of Mediolana [i.e. Milan].

22 June: James the Less

108. On the twenty-second day of the month is the commemoration of the apostle and God's messenger who in the literature is called Iacobus Alphei ['James son of Alpheus']; that was the son of Christ's maternal aunt, St Mary's nephew, wherefore he is called *frater Domini* in the literature, the Lord's brother; and after the Lord's ascension he was bishop in Jerusalem. He never ate meat, nor drank wine, nor wore woollen garments, but only linen ones, nor did he bother about bathing, nor cut his hair with scissors, nor trimmed his beard with a knife. But he constantly prayed to God, so that the skin on his knees had become hardened, like the knees of a camel are. Jewish scholars beat James to death with a fuller's pole, out of hatred towards Christ. But his unprovoked murder was avenged in that two emperors soon came with an army from Rome and destroyed the whole city of Jerusalem, and murdered those who lived there, and starved them to death, and sold them off into slavery.

22 June: Alban

109. On the same day is the passion of St Alban, who suffered martyrdom here in this Britain for Christ. He had been introduced to Christianity by a priest; then a pagan prefect commanded his soldiers that they should look for the priest in Alban's house. Then Alban put on the priest's cloak and went to meet the soldiers, and they tied him up and brought him before the judge and he forced him under great torments to renounce Christ. When he refused, he commanded him to be led up on a hill and to be beheaded there. Alban obtained from God that suddenly a surge of water came up there before his feet. Both the eyes soon fell out of the head of the man who had beheaded him. The place where Alban suffered is near the city which the Britons called Verolamium, and the English now call Wætlingaceaster [i.e. St Albans].

23 June: Æthelthryth

110. On ðone ðreo ond twentegþan[a] dæg þæs monðes bið þære halgan cwene geleornes[b] Sancte Æþeldryþe[c]; seo wæs twam werum gebrydod[d], ond hwæþre heo wæs clæne fæmne. Ærest heo wæs gebrydad[e] Tondberhte[f], Suðgerwa[g] ealdormen, ond æfter þæm[h] heo wæs seald[i] Ecgferðe [j]to cwene, Norðanhymbra[j] cyninge, forþon þe heo wæs Onnan[k] dohtor, Eastengla cyninges. Ond heo þa wæs twelf gear mid [l]Ecgferð þone cyning[l], ond he mid nængum[m] ðingum mihte[n] hire geþoht[o] oncerran[p]. Þa onfeng heo haligryfte on ðæm[q] mynstre ðe is nemned Colodesburh[r]. Þæs æfter anum geare heo timbrede fæmnena mynster on [s]ðæm londe[s] þe we nemn<a>ð[t 181] æt Elie. Ond heo wæs þær abbodysse[u], ond breac siððan wyllenra hrægla, ond seldon baðode[v] on hatum [w]bæþe butan[w] foran to eastrum[x], ond foran to þæm[y] [z]fiftigan dæge[z], ond foran to Cristes fullwihtes[a] dæge. Ond seldon on dæge heo eode oftor to gereordum þonne æne, ond fram uhtsanges tid[b 182] heo awunode[c 183] on cierecean[d] [e]on hire[e] gebede oð dæg. Ond þurh Godes gast heo self[f] ær foresægde[g] hwonne heo sceolde of middangearde[h] leoran[i], ond heo þa geleorde[j]; ond heo wæs sextene[k] gear on eorðan bebyrged. Ond þa mon[l] eft þone lichoman[m] [n]upp dyde[n], þa wæs he[o] swa ungebrosnad[p] gemeted, swa heo ðy ilcan dæge wære forðfered. Ond hire wæs micel wund open on [q]ðæm swyran[q] ða [r]heo mon[r] on byrgenne[s] dyde, ond þa hi[t] mon eft [u]up dyde[u] [v]of þære byrgenne[v], ða wæs hit gebatad[w] þæt þær næs butan[x] seo [y]swaðu on[y].

110. [a] twentigoðan C; [b] gewytennys C; [c] æðelþryðe C; [d] forgifen to bryde C; [e] forgifen C; [f] tondbyrhte C; [g] suðgyrwa C; [h] þam C; [i] geseald C; [j-j] norðhumbra C; [k] annan C; [l-l] ecgferðe þam cyninge C; [m] nænegum C; [n] ne myhte C; [o] geþanc C; [p] oncyrran C; [q] þam C; [r] coludesburh C; [s-s] þam lande C; [t] nemneð B, Ko, nemnað C; [u] abbudesse C; [v] heo baðode B with the he written on erasure Be and the o suprascript Ba, baðode C, <he>`o´ baðode Ko; [w-w] baðe buton C; [x] eastron C; [y] þam C; [z-z] fiftogoðan dæg C C; [a] fulwyhtes C; [b] tid B, tyde C, tide Herz, tid Ko; [c] a wunode Ko; [d] cyrcan C; [e-e] æt hyre C; [f] sylf C; [g] foresæde C; [h] myddanearde C; [i] gewitan C; [j] gewat C; [k] syxtyne C; [l] man C; [m] lichaman C; [n-n] uppdyde Ko; [o] heo C; [p] ungebrosnod C; [q-q] þam sweoran C; [r-r] hig man C; [s] byrgene C; [t] hig C; [u-u] updyde Ko; [v-v] om. C; [w] gehalod C; [x] buton C; [y-y] wundswaðu gesyne C.

24 June: The Birth of St John the Baptist

111. On ðone feower ond twentegðan[a] dæg þæs monðes bið Sancte Iohannes acennes[b] þæs fulweres[c]; se wæs acenned sex[d] monðum ær Crist, ond Gabrihel[e] se heahengel bodade[f] his acennesse[g] ond sægde[h] his fæder his noman[i] [j]ær þon[j] he acenned wære. Ðes Iohannes wæs mara[k] ðonne ænig oþer mon[l] buton Criste. Ealle heahfæderas ond Godes witgan[m] he [n]up oferhlifað[n], ond ealle þa[o] apostolas ond martyras he foregongeð[p], ond æghwelcne[q] þara[r] þe wæs of were ond of wife acenned. He com beforan Criste on middangeard[s], swa se morgensteorra cymð beforan þære sunnan, swa swa bydel[t] beforan deman cymð, and swa swa byme clypað beforan cyninge.

111. [a] twentigoðan C; [b] acennednys C; [c] fulluhtres C; [d] syx C; [e] gabriel C; [f] bodode C; [g] acennednysse C; [h] sæde C; [i] naman C; [j-j] ær þam þe C; [k] myd maria oftor C; [l] man C; [m] wytegan C; [n-n] upoferhlifað Ko; [o] om. C; [p] foregangeð C; [q] æghwylcne C; [r] þæra C; [s] B breaks off after middan; [t] fricca suprascript Ca.

23 June: Æthelthryth

110. On the twenty-third day of the month is the death of the holy queen St Æthelthryth; she was married to two men, and nevertheless she was a chaste virgin. First she was given in marriage to Tondberht, the ealdorman of the South Gyrwans, and later she was given to Ecgfrith as his queen, the king of the Northumbrians, because she was Anna's daughter, the king of the East Angles. And then she was with Ecgferth for twelve years, and he could by no means change her mind. She then took the veil in the monastery which is called Colodesburh [i.e. Coldingham]. And then after one year she established a community of virgins on the land which we call Ely. And there she was an abbess, and then used to wear woollen garments, and she rarely bathed in hot water except before Easter, and before the fiftieth day [i.e. Pentecost], and before the day of Christ's baptism [i.e. Epiphany]. And during the day, she rarely had a meal more than once a day, and from the time of matins she stayed in church, praying, until it was day. And through God's spirit she herself predicted when she would depart from the world, and she did then depart; and she was buried in the ground for sixteen years. And when her body was exhumed again, it was found to be as undecayed, as if she had died that same day. And a large wound had been open on her neck when she had been put in the grave, and when she was later exhumed from the grave, it had healed, so that there was nothing but a trace.

24 June: The Birth of St John the Baptist

111. On the twenty-fourth day of the month is the birth of St John the Baptist; he was born six months before Christ, and the archangel Gabriel foretold his birth and told his father his name before he was born. This John was greater than any other man except for Christ. He towers high above all patriarchs and God's prophets, and he ranks before all the apostles and martyrs and each one of those who was born of man and of woman. He came into the world before Christ, like the morning star appears before the sun, like a beadle walks before the judge, and like a trumpet sounds ahead of the king.

Iohannes wæs se engel se ðe eode beforan Gode, forþan ðe God wolde þa forð gangan[184] on menniscne lichaman. Þy syxtan monðe Iohannes fahnode on hys modor ynnoðe, þa Sancta Maria eode into hys meder Elizabethe; myd þy he getacnode Crist cumenne in þære clænan fæmnan ynnoð. Þæt wæs hræd ærendraca, se tylode to secganne hys ærndunge ær þon þe he lyfde. Ne genyhtsumað ænygum men to asecganne þæs acennedan engles mægen Iohannes.

24 June: Summer Solstice

111a. On þone ylcan dæg byð solstitia, þæt ys on ure geþeode sungihte, forþon ðe seo sunne standeð[185] on mydre lyfte. Swa Sanctus Arculfus sagað þæt he gesawe on Hierusalem ane syle on myddre þære ceastre, seo wæs aseted on þære stowe þær se deada man acwycode, þa hym man Dryhtnes rode ᵃofer setteᵃ. Þonne gelympeð þæt wundorlice[186] on þæs sumeres sungihte on mydne dæg, þonne seo sunne byð on þæs heofones mydle, þonne nafað seo syl nænige sceade. Þonne þæs sungihtes beoð þry dagas forð aurnen and se dæg byð hwene scyrtra, þonne hafað seo syl ærest lytle sceade, ond swa þa dagas forð onsceortiað, swa byð þære syle sceade lengra. Þeos syl cyþeð þæt Hierusalem seo ceaster ys geseted on myddre eorðan, and heo ys cweden umbilicus terre, þæt ys eorðan nafola, forþam on mydne sumor on mydne dæg scyneð seo sunne of myddum heofone gelyce on æghwylce healfe ymbe þa syle seo standeð on mydre eorðan.

111a. ᵃ⁻ᵃ ofersette Ko.

25 June: Luceia and Auceia

112. On þone fif and twentigoðan dæg þæs monðes byð Sancte Lucian tyd; þæt wæs haliges hades fæmne on Rome, ac heo wæs gehergod fram ælþeodegum cyninge, se wæs on naman Aceia. Heo wæs swyðe fæger fæmne. Þa wolde se cyning hig gewemman myd hys fyrenlustum, and þa cwæð heo to hym: 'Ic hæbbe mycelne brydguman, þæt ys Cryst, se gewrycðᵃ raðe mynne teonan on ðe.' Þa yrsode se cyning wyð hig ærest, ac þa ᵇæt nehstanᵇ he ongan hyre arian and het hyre getymbrian medomlic hus[187], on þæt nænig wer næfde ingang, and he hyre sealde seofon mædeno þæt hyre þenodon, and heo þær þeowode Gode on fæstenum and on gebedum. Þonne swa oft swa se cyning wolde feran to gefeohte wyð hys feondum, þonne ferde he ærest to þysse Crystes fæmnan and bæd hig þæt heo for hymᶜ gebæde to hyre Gode. Þonne dyde heo swa, þonne afylde he symle hys fynd, and he com eft ham symle gesund and gesygefæsted. Þa æfter twentigum gearum, þa ætywde þysse fæmnan heofonlicu gesyhð and hyre bebead þæt heo ferde eft to Rome; þa geþrowode heo þær martyrdom for Cryste. Þa eode se cyning to Romeburge gerefan, to þam ylcan þe hig ær gemartyrode, and bæd þæt he hete hyne beheafdian. Þa frægn se burhgerefa hyne hwæt he wære. 'Ic eom Aceia, mynre þeode cyning.' Þa cwæð se gerefa: 'Hu myht

112. ᵃ gewyrcð Ko, gewrycð Herz; ᵇ⁻ᵇ ætnehstan Ko; ᶜ e suprascript Ca.

John was the angel who walked before God, because God wanted to move into a human body. In the sixth month John kicked with joy in his mother's womb, when St Mary came to visit his mother Elizabeth; by that he marked that Christ had arrived in the womb of the chaste virgin. That was a speedy messenger, who wanted to tell his message before he had been born. It is impossible for any man to describe the virtue of the incarnate angel John.

24 June: Summer Solstice

111a. On the same day is solstitium, which in our language is 'solstice', because the sun stands in the middle of the sky. That is what St Arculf says – that he saw in Jerusalem a column in the middle of the city, which was situated in the place where the dead man was restored to life, when the Lord's cross was placed over him. Then, amazingly, it happens during the summer solstice at midday, that when the sun is in the middle of the sky, the column does not have any shadow. When three days have passed since the solstice and the day is a bit shorter, the column first has a little shadow, and as the days gradually become shorter, the column's shadow grows longer. This column demonstrates that the city of Jerusalem is positioned in the middle of the earth, and it is called *umbilicus terrae*, that is 'the navel of the earth', because in midsummer at midday the sun shines from the middle of the sky equally on all sides around the sundial which stands in the middle of the earth.

25 June: Luceia and Auceia

112. On the twenty-fifth day of the month is the feast of St Luceia; that was a virgin in holy orders in Rome, but she was captured by a foreign king, who was called Auceia. She was a very beautiful virgin. Then the king wanted to put her to shame with his sexual desires, and she then said to him: 'I have a great bridegroom, that is Christ, who will quickly avenge my abuse on you.' Then the king was first annoyed with her, but eventually began to show her some respect and commanded a small but worthy house to be built for her, to which no man had access, and he gave her seven girls to wait on her, and she served God there in fasting and prayer. Then whenever the king wanted to go into battle against his enemies, he first went to this virgin of Christ and asked her to pray to her God for him. When she did so, he always destroyed his enemies, and he always came home again, unharmed and victorious. Then after twenty years, a heavenly vision appeared to this virgin and told her to go back to Rome; then she suffered martyrdom there for Christ. Then the king went to the governor of the city of Rome, to the same one who had earlier martyred her, and asked him to have him beheaded. Then the governor asked him what he was. 'I am Auceia, the king of my people.' Then the governor said: 'How can you die for Christ;

þu for Cryste sweltan; nu ðu eart hæðen.' Þa cwæð se cyning: 'Ic gelyfe þæt mynes blodes agotenys me gelæde on Godes gesyhðe.' And þa on þære Godes andetnysse he geendode hys lyf.

26 June: John and Paul

113. On þone syx and twentigoðan dæg þæs monðes byð þæra æðelra wera gemynd Iohannes and Paules, þæra lychoma restað on Romebyrig. Hig wæron acennede of Constantines sidan[188] þæs myclan caseres, þæt ys of gestreonde, and hig wæron swyðe Crystene weras. Ac Iulianus se hæðena casere ongan hig nydan þæt hig deofolgyldum guldon and þam gelyfdon. Þa hig þæt ne geþafedon, þa sende he hig Terrentianum hys cempena ealdormen, and se het anne seað adelfan on nyht bynnan hyra huse. And he bebead þæt hig man on þam beheafdode, swa þæt ne wæs nænig tacen hyra cwale ofer eorðan gemeted. Þa sona forwearð Iulianus se casere; æfter þysum com an stræl of heofenum and hyne gewundode on hys oðer gewenge, and he þa swealt sona. And þæs mannes sunu awedde, þe hig ær beheafdode.

29 June: Peter and Paul

114. On þone nigon and twentigoðan dæg þæs monðes byð þæra eadigra apostola þrowung Petrus and Paulus, þa Neron se casere on Rome acwealde, Petrus on rode and Paulus myd sweorde.[189] Þas weras syndon þa twegen candelstafas þa lyhtað beforan Gode, and hig habbað swa mycele myhte þæt hig magon þone heofon belucan þam ðe hig wyllað, and eac in lætan þa ðe hig wyllað, forþam ðe hyra tungan syndon heofena rices cægan. Þas weras Petrus and Paulus wæron oft syððan æfter hyra þrowunge for mannum[190] gesewene on Crystenra manna geendunge, hwylum begen samod, hwylum hyra oðer onsundrum. And on þam cyrcum þe on hyra naman gehalgode syndon, ge æt Rome, ge feor ge wide geond myddaneard, ma heofonlicra wundra gewurdon þonne ænig deadlic man asecgan mæge.

29 June: Cassius

115. On þone ylcan dæg byð þæs bisceopes gewytennys se wæs nemned Sanctus Cassius. He wæs on þære byrig seo wæs haten Narmenti. Þæs bysceopes þeaw wæs þæt he sang æghwylce dæge mæssan Gode to lofe myd swyðe mycelre meagolmodnysse and myd wependum tearum, and he wæs swyðe ælmysgeorn. Þa ætywde ure Dryhten on nyht sumum mæssepreoste, and hyne het gangan and secgan þam bysceope þæt he ne geswyce na þæs þe he to Gode dyde, and he cwæð to hym: 'Saga hym þæt he cymð to me æt þæra apostola tyde Petrus and Paulus, and ic hym gylde hys mede.' Þa ne dorste se mæssepreost þæt þam bysceope secgan, forþam ðe hyt wæs þa þære tyde neah. Þa ætywde Drihten eft þam mæssepreoste, and hyne myd wordum þreade, and hyne het secgan þa ylcan word þe he hym ær bebead. And þa gyt agælde se mæssepreost hyt, and hyt hym ne sæde. Þa ætywde hym Dryhten þryddan syðe, and hyne þa þreade myd þearlwyslicere swingle for hys ungehyrsumnysse. Þa eode se mæssepreost to þam bysceope, and sæde þæt hym beboden wæs, and onfeold

you are still a pagan.' Then the king said: 'I believe that the shedding of my blood will lead me into the sight of God.' And then, professing God, he ended his life.

26 June: John and Paul

113. On the twenty-sixth day of the month is the commemoration of the noblemen John and Paul, whose bodies rest in the city of Rome. They were descended from the side, that is from the family, of the great emperor Constantine, and they were devout Christians. But the pagan emperor Julian began to force them to worship devils and to believe in them. When they refused, he sent them to Terentianus, the prefect of his soldiers, and he commanded a pit to be dug at night inside their house. And he commanded that one should behead them in that, so that there no trace of their murder could be found on earth. Then soon afterwards the emperor Julian perished; after that an arrow came from heaven and wounded him in one of his cheeks, and he died at once. And the son of the man who had beheaded them became insane.

29 June: Peter and Paul

114. On the twenty-ninth day of the month is the passion of the blessed apostles Peter and Paul, whom the emperor Nero executed in Rome, Peter on the cross and Paul with the sword. These men are the two candlesticks which shine before God, and they have such great influence that they can lock heaven for anyone they wish, and also let in anyone they wish, because their tongues are the keys of the kingdom of heaven. After their martyrdom, these men, Peter and Paul, were often seen by people at the death scenes of Christians, sometimes both together, sometimes one of them individually. And in the churches which are dedicated in their names, both in Rome and also far and wide throughout the world, more heavenly miracles have occurred than any mortal man can describe.

29 June: Cassius

115. On the same day is the death of the bishop called St Cassius. He lived in the city called Narnia [i.e. Narni]. The bishop's custom was that he sang mass every day in praise of God with great seriousness and weeping tears, and he was a very diligent giver of alms. Then our Lord appeared at night to a priest, and told him to go and tell the bishop to keep going with what he was doing for God, and he said to him: 'Tell him that he will come to me on the feast of the apostles Peter and Paul, and I will pay him his reward.' Then the priest did not dare tell the bishop that, because it was nearly the time [of the feast]. Then the Lord appeared again to the priest and forced him with words, and told him to report the same words which he had commanded him before. And still the priest was neglectful and did not tell him. Then the Lord appeared to him for a third time, and punished him with severe whipping for his disobedience. Then the priest went to the bishop, and reported what had been entrusted to him, and undid his clothes at his shoulders, and showed him the wounds

hys hrægl æt hys sceoldrum, and hym eowde þa læla þære swyngellan þe he from Dryhtne onfeng. Þa wæs se bysceop mycle þig reðran on godum weorcum, þe he ymbe[a] þa cuðlican mede gehyrde. Þa æfter seofen gearum se bysceop forðferde naht lange æfter þæm þe he hæfde mæssan gesungen æt þæra apostola tyde, swa hym ær gesæd wæs.

115. [a] suprascript Ca.

30 June: Martial

116. On þone þrytegoðan dæg þæs monðes byð þæs bysceopes gemynd Sancte Marcialis, þone Sanctus Petrus sylf gehalgode and gelærde, and hyne onsende myd twam mæssepreostum to Galwala mægðe, to þære ceastre þe ys nemned Limouex. Þa forðferde þæra mæssepreosta oðer on þam syðfate. Þa cyrde se bysceop eft to Rome and sæde Sancte Petre hu hys syðfæt wæs geletted. Ða cwæð Sanctus Petrus: 'Gang eft to þære byrgenne, and sege hym þæt he arise and fere myd þe to þære ylcan lare þe ic hym ær bebead.' Þa wæs hyt eal swa[191] geworden, and þa ceastergewaran þurh hyra lare onfengon sona Godes geleafan, þa ðe wæron ær swyðe heardes modes and swyðe torcyrres to Crystes geleafan. And on þære cyrcan gewurdon manege wundru, þe þyses bysceopes lychama on resteð. Þæt wæs þæra wundra sum þæt twegen men[192] on sumum ende þære cyrcan hig geþeoddon hig tosomne myd unryhtæmede. Þa wæron hig sona aworpene of þære cyrcan, swa hig sylfe nyston hu þæt gedon wæs; næs þær duru ontyned, ne weall toslyten, ne eahþyrl geopenod. And þa ne myhte hyra naðer fram oðrum beon aðyded, ær þam on morgen heora unryhtwysnys wæs geopenod[a] eallum folce, and myd þæs folces bene hig wæron gefreod fram þære sceandlican dæde.

116. [a] second o uncertain, letter is obscured by stitching.

The End of June

116a. Þonne se monoð byð geendod þe we nemnað se Ærra Lyða, þonne byð seo nyht syx[a] tyda lang, and se dæg eahtatyne[b] tyda lang.

116a. [a] .vi. C; [b] .xviii. C.

The Beginning of July

116b. On þone seofoðan monað on geare, þone we nemnað on Lyden Iulius, forþam ðe ealde men hæðene nemdon þone monoð þam naman on þæs caseres arweorðnysse þe Iulius wæs nemned, forþam ðe he wæs on þam monðe acenned. Þone monað we nemnað on ure geðeode se Æftera Lyða; on þam monðe byð [a]an and þritig[a] daga.

116b. [a-a] .xxxi. C.

of the whipping which he had received from the Lord. Then the bishop worked even harder on his good deeds, when he heard about the certain reward. Then after seven years the bishop died not long after he had sung mass on the feast of the apostles, as had been said to him earlier.

30 June: Martial

116. On the thirtieth day of the month is the commemoration of the bishop St Martial, whom St Peter himself consecrated and taught, and [he] sent him with two priests to Gaul, to the city which is called Lemouicum [i.e. Limoges]. Then one of the priests died during the journey. Then the bishop returned to Rome and told to St Peter how his journey had been cut short. Then St Peter said: 'Go back to the grave, and tell him to rise again and go with you for the same preaching with which I had entrusted him earlier.' That is also what happened then, and through their instruction the townspeople, who earlier had been of a very stubborn mind and very difficult to convert to the Christian religion, soon accepted the faith of God. And in the church, in which the bishop's body rests, many miracles have occurred. One of the miracles was that two people joined in illicit sex together somewhere inside the church. Then they were soon thrown out of the church, in such a way that they did not know how that had been done; the door had not been opened, nor the wall been torn down, nor the window been opened. And then neither could be separated from the other, before in the morning their wrongdoing had been revealed to all people, and through the crowd's prayers they were delivered from the shameful deed.

The End of June

116a. When the month is over which we call Ærra Lyða ['Earlier Mild (Month)'], the night is six hours long and the day eighteen.

The Beginning of July

116b. In the seventh month of the year, which in Latin we call *Julius*, because the ancient pagans called the month by that name in honour of the emperor who was called Julius, because he was born in that month. That month we call Æftera Lyða ['Later Mild (Month)'] in our language; in that month there are thirty-one days.

2 July: Processus and Martinianus

117. On þone æfteran dæg þæs monðes byð þæra martyra gemynd on Rome Sancti Processi and Sancti Martiniani; be þam sæde Sanctus Gregorius þæt sum æðele wif on Rome and swyðe æwfæst, heo sohte gelome þyssa martyra cyrcan. Þa gemette heo sume dæge þærute standan twegen Godes þeowas on ælþeodiglicum gegyrlan, and þa cwædon hig to hyre: 'Wif, gif þu secest unc, þonne sece[a] wit þe on domesdæge[b], ond þe gegearwiað[c] swa hwæt swa wit[d] magon.' Ond þa sona wæron hie[e] alædde[f] fram hira[g] eagum; ond þæt wif wæs a siððan þy[h] aredra[i] on hire bene, [j]forþon þe[j] heo onfeng swa cuþlicra[k] gehata.

117. [a] B resumes here; [b] domesdæg C; [c] gearwiað C; [d] we C; [e] hig C; [f] alæded C; [g] hyre C; [h] þe C; [i] anreddor C; [j-j] forþam þe C; [k] cuðra C.

[?4] July: Zoe

118. On ðone feorðan[a] [193] dæg þæs monðes bið þæs halgan wifes gemynd on Rome seo is nemned Soe[b]. Seo wæs sex[c] winter dumb[d] þurh sume mettrymnesse[e]; ða Sebastianus[f] gesegnade[g] hire muð mid Cristes rodetacne, ond þa mihte heo sona sprecan. Ond heo onfeng fullwihte[h] ond geþrowade[i] martyrdom for Criste.

118. [a] fiftan C; [b] sancta zoe C; [c] .vi. C; [d] dumba C; [e] mettrumnysse C; [f] sanctus sebastianus C; [g] gesenode C; [h] fulwyhte C; [i] geþrowode C.

6 July: Octave of Peter and Paul

119. On ðone sextan[a] dæg þæs monðes bið þara[b] apostola ea<h>tæþa[c] dæg Petres[d] ond Paules[e], se sceal beon mærsad[f] mid mæssesongum[g] ond mid godcundum gerynum.

119. [a] syxtan C; [b] þæra C; [c] eatæþa B, æ altered from a and final a altered from e in B, eahtoða C; [d] petrus C; [e] paulus C; [f] mærsod C; [g] mæssesangum C.

6 July: Tranquillinus

120. On ðone ilcan dæg bið þæs martyres ðrowung Sancti Tranquillini; ðæt wæs eald wer ond swiðe æþele on Rome, ond he wæs longe[a] ær swiðe earfaðcierre[b] to Godes geleafan. Ða geuntrumade[c] he mid þære mettrymnesse[d] podagre, ðæt is on ure geþeode fotadl, ond he ne mihte longe[e] tid owiht[f] gangan. Ða lærde[g] Sanctus Sebastianus hine ðæt [h]he onfenge[h] fullwihte[i], ond sona he mihte gan, ond he wæs swiðe anræd[j] geworden on Godes geleafan; ond he þrowade[k] wuldorlicne martyrdom for Criste.

120. [a] lange C; [b] earfoðcyrre C; [c] geuntrumode C; [d] mettrumnysse C; [e] langre C; [f] naht C; [g] gelærde C; [h-h] onfenge C; [i] fulwyhte C; [j] anræde C; [k] þrowode C.

2 July: Processus and Martinianus

117. On the second day of the month is the commemoration in Rome of the martyrs St Processus and St Martinianus; about those, St Gregory told that a noble and very devout woman in Rome – she often came to the church of these martyrs. Then one day she found two servants of God in foreign dress standing outside, and then they said to her: 'Woman, if you are looking for the two of us, then we will be looking for you on Doomsday, and will do for you whatever we can.' And then suddenly they were removed from her view; and, from then on, the woman was always even more active in her prayers, because she had received such a certain promise.

[?4] July: Zoe

118. On the [?fourth] day of the month is the commemoration in Rome of the holy woman who is called Zoe. She was mute for six years because of an illness; then Sebastian blessed her mouth with the sign of Christ's cross, and then suddenly she was able to speak. And she received baptism and suffered martyrdom for Christ.

6 July: Octave of Peter and Paul

119. On the sixth day of the month is the octave of the apostles Peter and Paul, which shall be celebrated with masses and with divine sacraments.

6 July: Tranquillinus

120. On the same day is the passion of the martyr St Tranquillinus; that was an old man and very noble in Rome, and he had for a long time before been very difficult to convert to God's faith. Then he suffered from the illness *podagra*, that is in our language 'foot-disease' [i.e. gout], and for a long time he could not at all walk. Then St Sebastianus preached to him so that he received baptism, and at once he was able to walk, and he became very resolute in God's faith; and he suffered a glorious martyrdom for Christ.

7 July: Procopius

121. On ðone seofoðan dæg þæs monðes bið þæs halgan weres gemynd Sancti Proconi; se wæs ᵃon Palestinaᵃ ðære mægþe, ond sona on his cnihthade he swencte his lichoman^b swa^c for Godes egsan ðæt him wæs hlaf an^{d 194} to gereordum ond wæter to drynce, ond ðis^{e f}ymb twegen^f dagas, hwilum ^gymb þry^g, hwilum æfter ealre^h wucan; acⁱ dæges ond nihtes he smeade a^j þone godcundan wisdom. Ond þa ^kæt nehston^k Flauianus se dema hine nedde^l on^m Cessaria ðære ceastre þæt he gulde ⁿðæm hæþnumⁿ godgyldum. Ða cwæþ he: 'Nis þæt god þæt þa monegan^o godas sien^p, ac^q an is ^rse soþa^r God.' Ond þa for ðeossum^s het se dema him þæt heafod ^tof aheawan^t, ond his se eadiga^u gast leorde^v on þæs heofonlican lifes ingong^w.

121. ᵃ⁻ᵃ in palesti C; ^b lychaman C; ^c swa swyðe C; ^d ana C; ^e þæt C; ^{f-f} ymbe twegen C; ^{g-g} ymbe þry C; ^h ealre þære C; ⁱ ah B, ac C; ^j om.C; ^{k-k} ætnehston Ko, æt nyhstan C; ^l nydde C; ^m in C; ⁿ⁻ⁿ þam hæðenum C; ^o manegan C; ^p syn C; ^q ah B, om. C; ^{r-r} soð C; ^s þysum C; ^{t-t} ofaheawan Ko; ^u æðe C; ^v gewende to heofenum and C; ^w ingang C.

7 July: Marina

122. On ðone ilcan dæg bið þære miclan fæmnan gemynd Sancta Marinan; ᵃseo wæs acenned on Antiochia ðære ceastre, ond hireᵃ fæder wæs hæþenra monna^b heahfæder. Ond heo wæs sona on hire cildhade befæsted^c Cristenum wife to fedanne, ond æt þære^d heo geleornode^e þæt heo on clænnesse^f God^g gelefde^h. Ða gelompⁱ þæt heo wæs fiftene^j geara^k, ða læswede^l heo hire festermodor^m sceapum^{n 195} ond heold mid oþrum mægdenum^o hire efnealdum^p. Þa ferde ðær Olibrius se gerefa to Antiochia ceastre, ða geseah he Marinan þæt mægden^q. Þa het he his þegnas hi^r geniman ond him ^sto gelædan^s, ond cwæð to hire: 'Ic þe onfo me to wife, ond þe bið ðonne well^t ofer ^ueall oþer^u wif.' Ða cwæð Marina: 'Ic þe þonne selle^v minne lichoman^w to deaðe, þæt ic on heofonum^x reste hæbbe mid þæm^y halgum fæmnum.' Ða het se gerefa hi^z swingan þæt þæt blod fleow of hire ᵃþæm merwan lichomanᵃ swa wæter of æspringe, ond ^bhet mid monige wite hi þreagan from^b Cristes geleafan, ond he mid ^cnænge ðara^c ne^d mihte hire ^egeþoht oncierran^e. Ða bead^f he þæt hi^g mon lædde to þære beheafdunga^h. Ða gebæd heo hiⁱ to Drihtne ond cwæð: 'Drihten, ic þe bidde þæt swa ^jhwelc mon^j swa ^kcierecean getimbre^k on minum naman, oþþe swa ^lhwelc mon^l swa ^mcondella onbærne^m on ciriceanⁿ of his gestreonum on minum noman^o, syn þæs monnes^p synna adilgade^q. Ond gif hwilc ^rmon sie^{r s}on ondyrstlecum wisum, ond he sy mines naman gemyndig, Drihten, gefriða þu hine from þæm brogan. Ond gif hwilc mon^s his synne^{t 196} geondette^u on minum naman, Drihten, forgif ^vþu him þa^v. Ond on^w swa

122. ᵃ⁻ᵃ þære C; ^b manna C; ^c befæst anum C; ^d hyre C; ^e leornode C; ^f clænnysse C; ^g gode C; ^h gelyfde C; ⁱ gelamp C; ^j fiftyne C; ^k wyntre C; ^l læswode C; ^m fostermoder C; ⁿ sceap C; ^o mædenum C; ^p efenealdum C; ^q mæden C; ^r hig C; ^{s-s} togelædan Ko; ^t wel C; ^{u-u} ealle oðre C; ^v sylle C; ^w lychaman C; ^x heofenum C; ^y þam C; ^z hig C; ᵃ⁻ᵃ þam mearwan lychaman C; ^{b-b} he het hyg myd manegum wytum þreatian fram C; ^{c-c} nan þæra wyta C; ^d ne ne C; ^{e-e} geþanc oncyrran C; ^f bebead C; ^g hig C; ^h beheafdunge C; ⁱ hig C; ^{j-j} hwylc man C; ^{k-k} cyrcan tymbrige C; ^{l-l} hwylc man C; ^{m-m} candele onæle C; ⁿ cyrcean C; ^o naman C; ^p mannes C; ^q adylgod C; ^{r-r} man sig C; ^{s-s} þæt he C; ^t synna C; ^u geandette C; ^{v-v} hym hys synna C; ^w om. C;

7 July: Procopius

121. On the seventh day of the month is the commemoration of the holy man St Procopius; he lived in the province of Palestine, and already in his youth he mortified his body for fear of God to such an extent that he had only bread for food and water for a drink, and that every two days, sometimes every three days, sometimes once a week; but day and night he was always studying divine wisdom. And then in the end the judge Flauianus forced him in the city of Caesarea to worship pagan idols. Then he said: 'It is not good that there should be so many gods, but only one is the true God.' And then because of this the judge commanded his head to be cut off, and his blessed spirit departed to enter the heavenly life.

7 July: Marina

122. On the same day is the commemoration of the great virgin St Marina; she was born in the city of Antioch, and her father was patriarch of the pagans. And early in her childhood she was handed over to a Christian woman for nurturing, and from her she learnt to believe in God in chastity. Then it happened that she was fifteen years old, then she was grazing her foster-mother's sheep and guarding [them] with other girls of the same age. When Olibrius the reeve came there to the city of Antioch, he saw the girl Marina. Then he ordered his men to take her and bring her to him, and said to her: 'I will take you as my wife, and then you will prosper above all other women.' Marina then said: 'Then I will give you my body to death, so that I can rest in heaven with the holy virgins.' Then the reeve ordered her to be beaten so that her blood flowed from her delicate body like water from a spring, and ordered her with many tortures to be forced away from Christ's faith, and with none of them could he change her mind. Then he commanded her to be led to her beheading. Then she prayed to the Lord and said: 'Lord, I ask you that whatever man build a church in my name, or whatever man light candles in church at his expense in my name, may the sins of that man be annulled. And if any man be in a terrible situation, and he remember my name, Lord, deliver him from his terror. And if any man confess his sins in my name, Lord, forgive him then. And in whatever place my martyrdom be

stowe swa min þrowung awriten sy[y], ond [z]man þa mærsige[z], afyr þu, Drihten, from[a] þære stowe blindnesse[b] ond helto[c] ond dumbnesse[d] ond deofolseocnesse[e], ac[f] cume on þa stowe blis[g] [h]ond sib[h] ond [i]soðlufu[i].'[197] Þa ondswarode[j] <hire>[k] stefn[l] of heofonum[m]: 'Þine bene[n] syndon gehered[o] beforan Godes gesihðe, ond swa hwær swa þin þrowung bið awriten, þonne[p][198] ne bið þær næfre yfel acenned, ah[q] þær bið [r]gefea ond blis[r]. Ond swa [s]hwelc mon[s] swa of ealre heortan mid tearum him[t] to Gode gebideð[u] on ðinum noman[v], he bið fram his synnum gefreod.' Þa wæs Sancta Marina for Criste beheafdad[w], ond se cwellere sona[x] hine [y]selfne ofslog[y] mid ðy[z] ilcan sweorde. Ond ða [a]ne wæs[a] hire [b]heafad no[b] on eorðan gemeted, ac is wen þæt englas [c]mid him hit[c] læddan[d] to Godes[e] neorxnawonge[f]; se lichoma[g] elles is geseted[h] on Antiochia ceastre.

[y] syg C; [z-z] men þa mærsion C; [a] fram C; [b] blyndnysse C; [c] hylto C; [d] dumnysse C; [e] deofolseocnysse C; [f] ah B, and C; [g] blyss C; [h-h] om. C; [i-i] soð lufu He; [j] andswarode C; [k] hire Herz, <hyre> Ko, him B, hyre C; [l] stefen C; [m] heofenum and cwæð C; [n] bena C; [o] gehyrede C; [p] om. C; [q] ac C; [r-r] blys and gefea C; [s-s] hwylc man C; [t] om. C; [u] gebyddeð C; [v] naman C; [w] beheafdod C; [x] om. C; [y-y] sylfne ofsloh C; [z]þig C; [a-a] næs C; [b-b] heafod na C; [c-c] hyt myd heom C; [d] læddon C; [e] om. C; [f] neorxnawange C; [g] lychama C; [h] gesett C.

10 July: The Seven Brothers

123. On ðone teogeþan[a] dæg þæs monðes bið seofon gebroðra ðrowung, þa þrowedon on Rome martyrdom for Criste on Antonius[b] dagum ðæs caseres. Hi[c] wæron ðære mæran wudewan[d] suna Sancta Felicitan. Ða gebroðor[e] [f]Publius, Romeburge gerefa, mid miclum witum wolde oncerran[f] fram Cristes geleafan, ah[g] hi[h] þæt ne geðafedon. Þa ofsloh he hi[i] mid misenlicum[j] witum, ond heora[k] gastas [l]somod flugan[l] to heofonum[m]. Ðyssa broðra[n] noman[o] seondon[p] Ianuarius[q] ond Felicis[r], Philippus ond Silanus[s], Alexander ond Uitalis[t] ond Martialis[u].

123. [a] teoðan C; [b] antonies C; [c] hig C; [d] wydewan C; [e] gebroðru C; [f-f] wolde paulicius romeburge gerefa myd myclum witum gecyrran C; [g] ac C; [h] hig C; [i] hig C; [j] myssenlicum C; [k] hyra C; [l-l] samod flugon C; [m] heofenum C; [n] gebroðra C; [o] naman C; [p] syndon þus gecweden C; [q] iunuarius C; [r] Felices B with i suprascript Ba; [s] gilanus C; [t] uitales C; [u] mersiales C.

10 July: Anatolia and Audax

124. On ðone ilcan dæg bið þære fæmnan tid, [a]þe hire noma wæs[a] [199] Sancta Anatolia[b]; seo wæs gelæded from[c] Rome on wræcsið on ða ceastre seo is nemned Piceno[d], [e]forþon þe[e] heo nolde on Rome onfon hæþnum[f] were ond Cristes geleafan forlætan. Ond þa dyde heo [g]monega wundur[g] on þære ceastre[200]; heo [h]hælde þær[h] bræcseoce[i] men ond deofolseoce mid hire wordum. Þeahhwæþre[j] sum hæþen dema het hi[k] belucan on stænenum cleofan, ond he het sumne wyrmgaldere micle næddran hire [l]into gelædan[l] þæt seo hi[m] abitan sceolde ond hire ban begnagan[n]. Ða stod seo

124. [a-a] om. C; [b] anatalia C; [c] fram C; [d] picino C; [e-e] forþam ðe C; [f] hæðenum C; [g-g] manege wundro C; [h-h] gehælde C; [i] bræceseoce C; [j] þeahhwæðere C; [k] hig C; [l-l] intogelædan Ko, in to gelædan Herz; [m] hig C; [n] begnoge C;

written down, and it be celebrated, Lord, turn away from that place blindness and lameness and dumbness and demonic obsession, but joy and peace and love may come to that place.' Then a voice from heaven answered her: 'Your prayers are heard before the sight of God, and wherever your martyrdom be written down, then no ill will ever arise there, but there will be joy and bliss. And whatever man prays to God, with all his heart, with tears, in your name, he will be released from his sins.' Then St Marina was beheaded for Christ, and the executioner straightaway killed himself with the same sword. And then her head was never found on earth, but the angels probably took it with them to God's paradise; apart from that, the body is located in the city of Antioch.

10 July: The Seven Brothers

123. On the tenth day of the month is the passion of the seven brothers, who suffered martyrdom for Christ in Rome in the days of the emperor Antoninus. They were the sons of the famous widow St Felicity. Publius, the reeve of the city of Rome, tried with many torments to turn them away from the Christian faith, but they did not accept that. Then he killed them with manifold tortures, and their souls flew together to heaven. The names of these brothers are Januarius and Felix, Philippus and Silanus, Alexander and Vitalis and Martialis.

10 July: Anatolia and Audax

124. On the same day is the feast of the virgin whose name was St Anatolia; she was led from Rome into exile to the city which is called Picenum, because in Rome she did not want to marry a pagan man and abandon her Christian faith. And then she worked many miracles in that city; she healed epileptics and obsessed people there with her words. Nevertheless a pagan judge ordered her to be locked into a stone cell, and he ordered a snake-charmer to put in a big snake along with her so that it would

fæmne forð[o] on hire gebede, ond [p]seo næddre stod[p] be hire; ðonne seo fæmne onleat[q], þonne onleat seo næddre[r]. [s]Ða gelyfde se wyrmgaldere[s] to Gode þurh þæt wundor, ond he sealde his feorh for Criste mid þære fæmnan, ond his noma[t] wæs Sanctus Audax[u].

[o] om. C; [p-p] stod seo nædre C; [q] om. C; [r] nædre C; [s-s] bi hyre and se wyrmgealdre gecyrde C; [t] nama C; [u] audux C.

10 July: Rufina and Secunda

125. On ðone ilcan dæg bið þara[a] haligra gesweostra ðrowung Sancta Rub<i>nae[b] ond Sancta Secundae[c], þara[d] lichoman[e] restað on Rome; þa þrowedon mærne martyrdom [f]for Criste[f] on Decies dagum þæs caseres. Sum [g]cæmpena ealdormon hi[g] het weorpan on Tibre[h] flod; þa ne [i]meahton hi[i] on ðæm[j] wætere gesincan þurh Cristes miht, [k]ah hi[k] sæton [l]ufan on[l] [m]ðæm swa swa[m] scipes byðme[n] [201] þonne hit[o] fleoteð on streame.

125. [a] þæra C; [b] Rubnae Ko, rubina C; [c] cunda C; [d] þæra C; [e] lychama C; [f-f] om. C; [g-g] cempena ealdorman hig C; [h] tyfre C; [i-i] myhton hig C; [j] þam C; [k-k] ac hig C; [l-l] onufan C; [m-m] þam wætre swa C; [n] bytme deð C; [o] heo C.

14 July: Phocas

126. On ðone feowertegðan[a] dæg þæs monðes bið þæs miclan martyres gemynd se is nemned Sanctus[b] Focas. He wæs biscop[c] on ðære mægðe ðe Pontus is nemned, ac[d] Traianus se casere hine ðreade mid unaseggendlicum[e] witum for[f] Cristes geleafan; [g]ond æt nehstan[g] he het hine sendan on byrnendne ofn[h], ond on ðæm[i] he onsende his gast. Ond ðrym dagum æfter þæm[j] he æteawde[k] beforan þæs caseres dura[l], ond cleopade[m] to þæm[n] casere, ond him sæde þæt him wære hell[o] ontyned ond hire[p] wite gegearwad[q], ond hine het efstan [r]to þæm[r]; ond þa sona æfter þæm[s] swealt se casere. [t]Þeosses biscopes[t] reliquias syndon [u]on Galwala mægðe on Mennia ðære ceastre, ond þa reliquias syndon swiðe mære geond middangeard[u].

126. [a] feowerteoðan C; [b] sancte C; [c] bisceop C; [d] and C; [e] unasecgendlicum C; [f] fram C; [g-g] ond ætnehstan Ko, and þa æt nyhstan C; [h] ofen C; [i] þam C; [j] þam C; [k] ætywde C; [l] healle dura C; [m] clypode C; [n] þam C; [o] hæl C; [p] þæt hym wære C; [q] gegearwod C; [r-r] to þam C; [s] þam C; [t-t] þyses bysceopes C; [u-u] swyðe mære C.

15 July: Cyricus and Julitta

127. On ðone fiftegðan[a] dæg þæs monðes bið Sancte Cyrices[b] tid þæs halgan cildes, ond Sancte Iulittan his modar[c]; [d]hi þrowedon[d] swiðe mærne martyrdom for Criste. Alexander se gerefa het [e]hi gefon[e] on ðære ceastre ðe is nemned Tharso, seo is on[f] Cilicia[g] þære mægðe, ond he ongan [h]hi þreagan[h] mid ondrystlicum[i] witum for Cristes geleafan; þa ne mihte he hi[j] hwæþre [k]mid nænge oferswiðan[k]. Sanctus Cyricus[l] ðæt cild hæfde læsse þonne þry monðas[m] þæs þriddan geares þa hit ærest ðone martyrdom

127. [a] fifteoðan C; [b] quirices C; [c] moder C; [d-d] heo þrowode C; [e-e] hyg befon C; [f] in C; [g] cilicio C; [h-h] hig þreagean C; [i] ondrysnlycum C; [j] hig C; [k-k] oferswyðan myd nænigum wite C; [l] quiricus C; [m] monað C;

bite her and gnaw at her bones. Then the virgin continued to stand and pray, and the snake stood next to her; when the virgin bowed, the snake bowed also. Then the snake-charmer believed in God on account of that miracle, and together with that virgin he gave up his life for Christ, and his name was St Audax.

10 July: Rufina and Secunda

125. On the same day is the passion of the holy sisters St Rufina and St Secunda, whose bodies rest in Rome; they suffered a famous martyrdom for Christ in the days of the emperor Decius. A military prefect ordered them to be thrown into the river Tiber; then, through the power of Christ, they could not sink under water, but they sat above it like the hull of a ship when it floats above the current.

14 July: Phocas

126. On the fourteenth day of the month is the commemoration of the famous martyr who is called St Phocas. He was a bishop in the province which is called Pontus, but the emperor Trajan tormented him with indescribable tortures for his Christian belief; and eventually he ordered him to be thrown into a burning oven, and in that he gave up the ghost. And three days after that he appeared before the emperor's gate and called to the emperor and told him that hell was opened up for him and its torments were ready, and told him to hurry up to get there; and soon after that the emperor died. The relics of this bishop are in Gaul in the city of Vienna [i.e. Vienne], and the relics are very famous throughout the world.

15 July: Cyricus and Julitta

127. On the fifteenth day of the month is the feast of the holy boy St Cyricus, and his mother St Julitta; they suffered a very famous martyrdom for Christ. The governor Alexander ordered them to be arrested in the city which is called Tarsus, which is in the country of Cilicia; and he began to torture them with terrible torments for their belief in Christ, but then he could not overcome them with any of them. The boy St Cyricus was less than three months away from his third birthday when he began his

ongonn[n]. Þa þæt halige cild ongeat þæt heora[o] lifes ende [p]to nealæhte[p], þa bæd hit Drihten ond þus cwæð: '[q]Drihten[202] God[q], beo þu gemedemad[r] me to geheranne[s]. Swa[t] hwilc mon[u] swa me timbreð[v] gebedhus, sele[w] þu [x]mede him[x] on heofonum[y]. Ond on swa hwelcre[z] stowe swa min gemynd [a]sy mærsad[a], gemicla þu, Drihten, ofer eorðan [b]þara monna[b] hwæte [c]ond heora win[c] ond [d]heora worldlice spede[d], ond ne [e]sy on heora[e] stowe gemeted [f]neata cwyld[f], ne adl, ne hlafes hungor, ne se unclæna gast [g]leore on ða stowe[g], ac þær [h]sy soðfæstnes[h] ond rihtwisnes[i] [203]. Ond gif [j]hwelc mon[j] fæste, oþþe nyhtewæccan[k] do, oþþe his [l]synne wepe[l] [204] on ðæm[m] dæge minre ðrowunge, sele[n] þu [o]ðæm monnum gode[o] mede. Drihten[p], gif hwilc [q]mon hæbbe micle scylde[q] ond he cyme[r] on cyrican[s], ond he þa andette on minum naman, adylga þu, Drihten, þæs mannes scylde[t], ond he[u] [v]sy hwittra[v] ðonne snaw[205]. Ond gif hwilc [w]mon wille[w] feran ofer sæs yþe, ond he þonne ne mæge, ond he wepende me gecige[x], gefultuma þu, [y]Drihten, him[y]. Ond gif hwilc [z]mon sy from[z] deofle geswenced, ond he cyme[a] to cyrican[b] ond him þær gebidde on minum noman[c], sele[d] þu, Dryhten, þæm[e] mildheortnesse[f]. Ond gif hwilc mon[g] owiht [h]bringe to ælmessan[h] to cirican[i] on minum noman[j], forgif þu þæm[k] mede on [l]worold worlda[l].' Þa com stefn[m] of heofonum[n] ðus cweþende: 'Ic selle minne fultum eallum þæm[o] þe me [p]gecegað þorh[p] ðinne noman[q].' Ond[r] þa onsende ðæt <c>ild[s] his gast to heofonum[t] mid micle[u] le<o>hte[v], ond his modor onsende hire gast [w]noht longe[w] [x]æfter þon[x], ond heo[y] wuniað nu a[z] on ecnesse[a] on Godes rice.

[n] ongan C; [o] hyra C; [p-p] tonealæhte Ko, nealæhte C; [q-q] domine deus C; [r] gemedemod C; [s] gehyranne C; [t] and swa C; [u] man C; [v] tymbrað C; [w] syle C; [x-x] hym mede C; [y] heofenum C; [z] hwylcere C; [a-a] gemærsod sig C; [b-b] þæra manna C; [c-c] om. C; [d-d] hyra woruldlican speda C; [e-e] sig on hyra C; [f-f] nytena cwealm C; [g-g] on þa stowe ne gewyte C; [h-h] sig soðfæstnys C; [i] ryhtwysnys C; [j-j] hwylc man C; [k] nyttewæccan B, with h suprascript Bf, nyhtwæccan C; [l-l] synna wepe C; [m] þam C; [n] syle C; [o-o] þam mannum C; [p] and dryhten C; [q-q] hæbbe C; [r] cume C; [s] cyrcan C; [t] synne C; [u] he B with o suprascript Ba, heo C, he`o´ Ko; [v-v] sig hwyttre C; [w-w] man sig þæt wylle C; [x] cige C; [y-y] hym Dryhten C; [z-z] man sig fram C; [a] cume C; [b] cyrcan C; [c] naman C; [d] syle C; [e] þam C; [f] myldheortnysse C; [g] om. C; [h-h] gesylle to ælmyssan and bringe C; [i] cyrcan C; [j] naman C; [k] þam C; [l-l] ealra worulda woruld C; [m] stefen C; [n] heofenum C; [o] þam C; [p-p] cigað þurh C; [q] naman C; [r] om. C; [s] tild B, cild C; [t] heofenum C; [u] mycele C; [v] lechte B, leohte C; [w-w] naht lange C; [x-x] æfter þam C; [y] hig C; [z] om. C; [a] ecnysse C.

17 July: Speratus and the Scillitan Martyrs

128. On ðone seofontegðan[a] dæg þæs monðes bið þæs biscopes[b] tid þæs noma[c] is Sperati[d]; se[e] þrowade[f] martyrdom for Criste on Cartagine þære miclan ceastre mid ealle his biscophirede[g], ge mid werum ge mid wifum.

128. [a] seofonteoðan C; [b] bysceopes C; [c] nama C; [d] sancte speratis C; [e] he C; [f] þrowode C; [g] bysceophyrede C.

martyrdom. When the holy boy realised that the end of their lives was drawing near, he invoked God and spoke thus: 'Lord God, deign to hear me. Whatever man build a house of prayer for me, reward him in heaven. And in whatever place my memory is celebrated, Lord, multiply on earth the people's wheat and their wine and their worldly wealth, and may in their area no cattle disease be found, nor illness, nor hunger for bread, nor may the unclean spirit pass through that place, but may there be justice and righteousness. And if any man should fast, or hold vigil for me, or weep over his sins on the day of my martyrdom, give that man a good reward. Lord, if any man is guilty of a great sin and he should come to church, and should confess it in my name, Lord, expunge the man's sin, and may he be whiter than snow. And if any man should want to travel across the sea, and he should not be able to, and weeping he should call on me, Lord, help him. And if any man should be plagued by the devil, and he should come to church and pray there in my name, Lord, grant him mercy. And if any man should bring anything as alms to church in my name, grant him a reward in the world to come.' Then a voice came from heaven speaking thus: 'I will give my help to all those who call on me in your name.' And then the child gave up the ghost to heaven with great light, and his mother gave up the ghost not long after that, and they now live in God's kingdom always and forever.

17 July: Speratus and the Scillitan Martyrs

128. On the seventeenth day of the month is the feast of the bishop whose name is Speratus; he suffered martyrdom for Christ in the great city of Carthage with his entire episcopal household, both men as well as women.

18 July: Symphorosa and her Seven Sons

129. On þone eahtategeþan[a] dæg þæs monðes bið þara[b 206] wudewan[c] tid [d]Sancte Simphorosan[d], seo þrowade[e] martyrdom for Criste mid hire seofon sunum. Þara[f] suna naman[g] wæron Crescentes ond Iolianus[h], Nemesius[i] ond Primitibus, Iustinus ond Sacsius[j] ond Eugenius; æt [k]þara lichoman[k] gewurdon monegu[l] heofonlico[m] wundru.

129. [a] ehtateoðan C; [b] þære C; [c] wydewan C; [d-d] sancta symphorosa C; [e] þrowode C; [f] þæra C; [g] nama C; [h] iulianus C; [i] nemesi C; [j] sactius C; [k-k] þæra lychaman C; [l] manyge C; [m] heofenlice C.

19 July: Christina

130. On ðone nigentegðan[a] dæg þæs monðes bið þære æþelan fæmnan gemynd þære noma[b] wæs Cristina[c], seo wæs on ðære ceastre ðe is nemned[d] Tyro. Ond sona swa[e] heo wæs ændlefen[f] geara[g 207], þa lufade[h] heo Crist ond [i]on hine gelyfde[i]. Ða het hire fæder Urbanus [j]hi bewyrcean[j 208] on anum torre mid twelf ðeowennum[k], þæt nænig wer [l]hi scolde[l] geseon butan[m] him anum. Ond he[n] het wyrcan [o]gyldeno godgeld[o] ond seolfrene[p], þæt hio[q] sceolde þa weorðian æfter hæþnum[r] þeawum. Ða abræc[s] þæt mægden[t] þæt gold ond þæt seolfor of [u]þæm godgeldum[u], ond [v]hit wearp[v] of ðæm[w] torre þearfendum monnum[x]. Ða yrsode se fæder swiðe forðon[y], ond he het gebindan [z]þæm mægdene[z] stan [a]on swiran[a] on æfenne[b 209], ond [c]hi sændan[c] on sæ. Þa onfengan[d] [e]Godes englas hire[e], ond heo eode mid him ofer þæt wæter. Þa on middeniht ætywde hire micel mon[f] ond [g]ondyrsnlic gongende[g] ofer þæs sæs yþe, ond he[h] wæs hæbbende [i]brunbasone gegyrelan[i], ond [j]wuldorlicne beag[j] on his heafde. Ond he cwæþ to hire: 'Ic eom Crist, þone ðu lufast.' Ond he þa dypte [k]hi þriwa[k] on ðære sæ ond cwæð: 'Cristina, ic þe fullwie[l 210] on minne God fæder, ond on mec[m], his efenecne[n] sunu, ond on þone halgan gast.' Ond he þa sealde hi[o] Sancte Michaele, ond he hi[p] lædde to þære eorðan. Ond on mergenne[q 211], þa hire fæder Urbanus eode to his gerefærne[r], ða geseah he þæt heo eode [s]bi þæm[s] sæ to þære ceastre. Ond hwæþre eft heo[t] þurh martyrdom hire gast onsende to Gode on heofona[u] rice.

130. [a] nygonteoðan C; [b] nama C; [c] sancta Cristina C; [d] genemned C; [e] þa C; [f] endlyfen C; [g] geare C; [h] lufede C; [i-i] gelyfde on hyne C; [j-j] hig belucan C; [k] þeowenum C; [l-l] hig ne sceolde C; [m] buton C; [n] om. C; [o-o] gyldene godas C; [p] sylfrene C; [q] heo C; [r] hæðenum C; [s] bræc C; [t] mæden C; [u-u] þam anlycnessum C; [v-v] wearp hyt C; [w] þam C; [x] mannum C; [y] forþam C; [z-z] þam mædene C; [a-a] to hyre sweoran C; [b] æfen C; [c-c] het hig sendan C; [d] onfengon C; [e-e] hyre godes englas C; [f] man C; [g-g] ondrysnlice gangende C; [h] se C; [i-i] brunbasune gegyrlan C, brun basone gegyrelan Ko; [j-j] wundorlicne beah C; [k-k] þrywa hig C; [l] fullie C; [m] me C; [n] efnecne C; [o] hig C; [p] hig C; [q] morgen C; [r] gereferne C; [s-s] be þære C; [t] om. C; [u] heofena C.

19 July: Arsenius

131. On þone ilcan dæg bið þæs fæder tid þe is nemned Sanctus Arsenius. Ðæs þeaw wæs ðæt he wacude[a] ealle niht, ond þonne he nede [b]sceolde slapan[b] on ærnemorgen for þære mænniscan[c] gecynde, þonne cwæþ he to þæm[d] slæpe: 'Cym[e], þu yfla[f]

131. [a] wacode C; [b-b] slapan sceolde C; [c] menniscan C; [d] þam C; [e] cum C; [f] yfela C;

18 July: Symphorosa and her Seven Sons

129. On the eighteenth day of the month is the feast of the widow St Symphorosa, who suffered martyrdom for Christ with her seven sons. The sons' names were Crescens and Julianus, Nemesius and Primitivus, Justinus and Stacteus and Eugenius; many miracles have happened at their bodies.

19 July: Christina

130. On the nineteenth day of the month is the commemoration of the noble virgin whose name was Christina, who lived in the city called Tyrus [i.e. Tyre]. And she was barely eleven years old, when she loved Christ and believed in him. Then her father Urbanus ordered her to be shut up in a tower with twelve maids, so that no man should see her except him alone. And he ordered golden pagan idols and silver ones to be made, so that she should worship them according to pagan custom. Then the girl broke the gold and the silver off the idols, and threw it from the tower to the poor people. Then the father became very angry because of that, and he ordered a stone to be tied to the girl's neck in the evening, and her to be thrown into the sea. Then the angels of God took her, and she went with them across the water. Then in the middle of the night a tall and terrifying man appeared to her, walking across the waves of the sea, and he was wearing a dark purple garment, and a glorious crown on his head. And he said to her: 'I am Christ, whom you love.' And he then immersed her into the sea three times and said: 'Christina, I baptise you in God the father and myself, his co-eternal son, and the Holy Spirit.' And he then handed her over to St Michael, and he took her onto dry land. And in the morning, when her father Urbanus went to his court-house, he saw that she was walking by the sea to the city. But later she gave up the ghost to God in the kingdom of heaven, through martyrdom.

19 July: Arsenius

131. On the same day is the feast of the father called St Arsenius. His custom was to stay awake all night, and when by necessity he had to sleep in the early hours because of human nature, then he said to the sleep: 'Come, you wicked servant.' Then sleep

ðeowᵍ.' Ðonne ofereode ʰse slæp hine hwonʰ þær he sæt, ond ⁱhe sona eftⁱ aras. Cwæþ sum halig biscopʲ, ða he wæs on sawlengaᵏ, be þeossumˡ fæder: 'Arseniusᵐ, þu wære eadig, forþonⁿ ðu hæfdest a þas tid beforan þinum eagum.'

ᵍ þeaw C; ʰ⁻ʰ hyne hwon se slæp C; ⁱ⁻ⁱ eftsona he C; ʲ bysceop C; ᵏ sawlunge C; ˡ þysum C; ᵐ arsemus C; ⁿ forþam C.

21 July: Victor of Marseilles etc.

132. <O>nᵃ þone an ond twentegþanᵇ dæg þæs monðes bið Sancte Uictores tid þæs martyres, ond þreora cempena mid hineᶜ. Þa gelyfdon ᵈhi Godeᵈ þurh þa wundraᵉ þe hiᶠ æt him gesegonᵍ, ʰond forðon hiʰ wæron ðrowiendeⁱ mid hineʲ martyrdom. Heoraᵏ naman ˡwæron Ðeoðeriusˡ, ond Felicianus, ond Alexandrus. Ðæs Uictores lichomaᵐ resteþ onⁿ Massiliaᵒ ðære ceastre.

132. ᵃ n B, initial missing; ᵇ twentygoðan C; ᶜ hym C; ᵈ⁻ᵈ hig on god C; ᵉ wundru C; ᶠ hig C; ᵍ gesawon C; ʰ⁻ʰ forðam hig C; ⁱ þrowigende C; ʲ hym C; ᵏ hyra C; ˡ⁻ˡ wær theodorius C; ᵐ lichama C; ⁿ in C; ᵒ messilia C.

22 July: Mary Magdalen

133. On ðone ᵃtu ond twentegðanᵃ dæg þæs monðes bið Sancta Marian tid þære Magdaleniscan, seo wæs ærest synnecgeᵇ, ond heo wæs midᶜ seofon deoflum full, þæt wæs mid eallum uncystum. Ac heo com to urum Drihtne þa he wæs monᵈ on eorðan, þær he wæs æt ᵉgereordum onᵉ sumes Iudiscesᶠ leorneres huse. Ond heo brohte hire alabastrum, þæt is hire glæsfæt, mid deorwyrðreᵍ smyrenisse, ond þa weop heoʰ on ðæs Hælendes fetⁱ, ond drigde mid hire loccum ond cyste, ond smyrede mid þære deorwyrðan smyrenisse. Þa cwæþ se Hælend to hire: 'Þe syndon þine synna forlætene, acʲ gang on sibbe.' Ond heo wæs siððan Criste swa gecoren ðæt he æfter his æriste ærest monnaᵏ hine hire æteawdeˡ, ond heo bodadeᵐ his æristⁿ his apostolum. Ond æfter Cristes upastignesseᵒ heo wæs on swa micelre longungeᵖ æfter him þæt heo nolde næfre siððan ᵍnænge monᵠ geseon. Ac heo gewat on westenneʳ ond ðær ˢgewunade þritigˢ geara, eallum monnumᵗ uncuð. Ne heo næfre ætᵘ mænniscneᵛ mete, ne heo ne dranc. Ac æt gehwelcreʷ gebedtide Godes englas comanˣ of heofonumʸ ond læddanᶻ hiᵃ on ða lyft, ond heo þær gehyrde²¹² ðære heofonlican wynsumnesseᵇ dæl, ond þonne ᶜgebrohtan hiᶜ eft on hire stanscræfe, ond forðon hiᵈ næfre hingredeᵉ ne ne þyrste. Ond þa æfter þrittegumᶠ geara gemette hiᵍ sum halig mæssepreost on ʰðæm westenneʰ, ond he hiⁱ gelædde on his cyricanʲ ond hire husl gesealde. Ond heo onsændeᵏ hire gast to Gode, ond se mæssepreost hiˡ bebyrgde, ond micele wundraᵐ wæron oft æt hire byrgenne.

133. ᵃ⁻ᵃ twa and twentygoðan C; ᵇ synycgge C; ᶜ om. C; ᵈ man C; ᵉ⁻ᵉ om. C; ᶠ om. C; ᵍ deorwyrðe Ko, deorwyrðre Herz; ʰ om. C; ⁱ fotas C; ʲ om. C; ᵏ manna C; ˡ ætywde C; ᵐ bodude C; ⁿ æryste C; ᵒ upastigennysse C; ᵖ langunge C; ᵠ⁻ᵠ nænigne man C; ʳ westen C; ˢ⁻ˢ wunode .xxx. C; ᵗ mannum C; ᵘ ne æt C; ᵛ menniscne C; ʷ æghwylcere C; ˣ comon C; ʸ heofenum C; ᶻ læddon C; ᵃ hig C; ᵇ wynsumnysse C; ᶜ⁻ᶜ gebrohton hig hig C; ᵈ hig C; ᵉ ne hyngrede C; ᶠ þryttygum C; ᵍ heo B with eo partly erased and i suprascript Ba, hig C; ʰ⁻ʰ þam westene C; ⁱ hig C; ʲ cyrcan C; ᵏ onsende C; ˡ hig C; ᵐ wundru C.

overcame him for a little while where he sat, and he then immediately got up again. A holy bishop, when he was on his death-bed, said about this father: 'Arsenius, you are blessed, because you always had this moment before your eyes.'

21 July: Victor of Marseilles etc.

132. On the twenty-first day of the month is the feast of the martyr St Victor, and of three soldiers with him. Then they believed in God because of the miracles which they saw from him, and they therefore suffered martyrdom with him. Their names were Theoderius, Felicianus, and Alexander. Victor's body rests in the city of Massilia [i.e. Marseilles].

22 July: Mary Magdalen

133. On the twenty-second day of the month is the feast of St Mary Magdalen, who was first a sinful woman, and she had seven devils inside her, that was all the vices. But she came to our Lord when he was a man on earth, where he was receiving hospitality in the house of a Jewish scholar. And she brought her *alabaster* [i.e. 'perfume bottle'], that is, her glass bottle, with precious ointment, and she then wept onto the Saviour's feet, and dried [them] with her hair and kissed [them] then and anointed them with the precious ointment. Then the Saviour said to her: 'Your sins are pardoned; go now in peace.' And she was afterwards so beloved by Christ that after his resurrection he appeared first to her among all men, and she announced his resurrection to his apostles. And after Christ's ascension her longing for him was so great that she never wanted to see another man again. And so she went into the desert and lived there for thirty years, unknown to all men. She never ate human food, or drank. But at every prayer-time God's angels came from heaven and lifted her up into the air, and there she heard some of the heavenly bliss, and then they carried her back to her cave, and for that reason she was never hungry or thirsty. And then after thirty years a holy priest came across her in the desert, and he led her to his church and gave her the Eucharist. And she gave up the ghost to God, and the priest buried her, and great miracles often happened at her tomb.

22 July: Apollinaris

134. On ðone ilcan dæg bið þæs biscopes[a] ðrowung þæs noma[b] wæs Sanctus[c] Apollinaris; ðone[d] Sanctus Petrus self[e] gelærde, ond hine to biscope[f] gehalgode, ond hine þa gecyste[g], ond hine onsænde[h] to þære byrig þe is nemned[i] Rafenna[j]. Ond he sona æt fruman gehælde [k]blindne mon[213] þæt he mihte[k] geseon, ond þurh þæt [l]micel folc he gecyrde[l] to fullwihte[m]. Ond he stefnde[n] Godes cyrican[o] ond Godes gesomnunga[p] on þære byrig eahta[q] ond twentig geara, ond þa geþrowade[r] martyrdom for Criste on ðæs caseres dagum þe wæs nemned Uespassianus.

134. [a] bysceopes C; [b] nama C; [c] om. C; [d] þæne C; [e] sylf C; [f] bysceope C; [g] ge suprascript Ba; [h] onsende C; [i] genemned C; [j] rauena C; [k-k] blynde men þæt hig myhton C; [l-l] he gecyrde mycel folc C; [m] fulluhte C; [n] sterde C; [o] cyrcan C; [p] gesomnunge C; [q] ehta C; [r] geþrowode C.

25 July: James the Greater

135. On ðone fif ond twentegðan[a] dæg þæs monðes bið þæs apostoles gemynd ond þæs Godes ærendwreocan[b] Sancte Iacobes[c], se ealra þara[d] apostola [e]ærest geþrowade[e] for Criste. Ðes Iacobus wæs þæs ealdan fæder sunu þe Zebedæg[f] wæs haten[g], ond he wæs Iohannes broðor þæs godspelleres, ond he wæs fiscere ærest. Ac he þa forlet þa nett ond his fæder mid scipe on sæ, þa [h]hine Crist[h] to him cegde[i] of sæs[j] ofre. Ond he wæs Criste se leofesta ðegn[k] to Sancte Petre ond[l] Iohanne his breþer. Þes Iacobus ærest monna[m] Hispanius[n], ða elreordegan[o] þeode ða syndon on middangeardes westdæle neah þære sunnan setlgonge[p], he hi[q] gelærde to Cristes geleafan.[214] Ðone Iacobum se wælgrimma Hyrde[r][215] acwealde mid sweorde, ac Crist gefremede[s][216] his gast to [t]þæm heofonlican heanessum[t].

135. [a] twentigoðan C; [b] ærendracan C; [c] iacobus C; [d] þæra C; [e-e] ærost geþrowode C; [f] zebedei C; [g] nemned C; [h-h] cryst hyne C; [i] gecigde C; [j] þæs sæs C; [k] þegen C; [l] and to C; [m] manna C; [n] yspania C; [o] ælreordygan C; [p] setlgange C; [q] hig C; [r] hyrde Ko; [s] geferede C; [t-t] þam heofenlicum heahnyssum C.

27 July: Simeon Stylites

136. On ðone seofon ond twentegþan[a] dæg þæs monðes bið þæs miclan muneces geleornes[b] Sancte Symeones[c]. Þa[d] he wæs [e]ðreottene geara[e] cniht, þa læswede[f] he <his>[g] fæder sceapum ond þa heold.[217] Ða geseah he sume Godes cyrican[h]. Þa forlet he þa sceap ond arn to þære Godes ciricean[i]. Þa geherde[j] he þær rædan Godes bec. Þa fregn[k] he ænne[l] ealdne mon[m] hwæt þæt wære. Þa cwæþ se ealda mann[n]: 'Hit is monna[o] sawla gestreon, ond þa þeawas ðe mon[p] sceal on mynstre healdan.' Ða eode <he>[q][218] sona of þære cirican[r] to sumes haliges abbodes[s] mynstre, se wæs on noman[t] Timotheus[u], ond læg fif dagas beforan ðæs mynstres geate, swa[219] he ne æt ne ne

136. [a] twentygoðan C; [b] gewytennys C; [c] simeonys C; [d] syððan C; [e-e] .xiii. geare C; [f] læswode C; [g] his C, mid his B, Ko; [h] cyrcan C; [i] cyrcan C; [j] gehyrde C; [k] frægn C; [l] anne C; [m] man C; [n] man C; [o] manna C; [p] man C; [q] om. B, Ko, he C, Herz; [r] cyrcan C; [s] abbudes C; [t] naman C; [u] timothei C;

22 July: Apollinaris

134. On the same day is the passion of the bishop whose name was St Apollinaris; St Peter himself taught him, and ordained him bishop, and kissed him then, and sent him to the city which is called Ravenna. And straightaway at the beginning he healed a blind man so that he could see, and with that he converted many people to baptism. And he presided over God's church and God's congregation in that city for twenty-eight years, and then suffered martyrdom for Christ in the days of the emperor who was called Vespasian.

25 July: James the Greater

135. On the twenty-fifth day of the month is the commemoration of the apostle and God's messenger St James, who first of all the apostles suffered for Christ. This James was the son of the old father who was called Zebedee, and he was the brother of John the Evangelist, and he was originally a fisherman. But he then abandoned his nets and his father with his ship in the lake [i.e. the Sea of Galilee], when Christ called to him from the lake's shore. And he was Christ's favourite follower after St Peter and his brother John. This James was the first man [to introduce] Spain, the barbarian nations who live in the west of the world near where the sun sets – he introduced them to the Christian faith. The cruel Herod killed James with a sword, but Christ [?expedited] his soul to heaven on high.

27 July: Simeon Stylites

136. On the twenty-seventh day of the months is the death of the great monk St Simeon. When he was a boy of thirteen years, he was grazing his father's sheep and guarding them. Then he saw a church of God. Then he abandoned the sheep and ran to that church of God. Then he heard God's books read there. Then he asked an old man what that was. Then the old man said: 'It is the treasure of human souls and the customs which are to be upheld in a monastery.' Then he soon went from the church to the monastery of a holy abbot, whose name was Timotheus, and lay in front of the monastery's gate for five days, without eating and drinking, asking for admission.

dranc, ac he bæd ingonges[v]. Þa underfeng se abbod[w] hine on þæt mynster. Ða geleornede[x] he his saltere on feower monðum, ond sona [y]he lifde[y] on swa heardum life for Gode þæt þa broðor[z] þæs mynstres cwædon to [a]þæm abbode[a]: 'Tohwon[b] gelæddest þu þysne mon[c] to us? Forðon[d] ne magon we aræfnan[e] his hearde[f] [220] þeawas.' Þa gewat he of þæm[g] mynstre deagollice[h] on sume dune, ond he stod þær on drygum stane[221] ðreo[i] gear; ealra geara he stod on [j]ðæm westenne[j] seofon ond feowertig. Sume[k] geare him [l]bærst micel[l] wund [m]on oþrum[m] þeo, ond he stod þurh eallne[n] þone gear on anum fet. Ond he dyde [o]monig heofonlic[o] wundor, ða sendon[p] ealle swiðe lange to[q] areccanne. Ond nu gyt eastdæles men swergiað[r] ðurh his noman[s], ond ne geþristlæcað [t]hi o þæt hi manswergen[t] on his noman[u].

[v] inganges C; [w] abbud C; [x] geleornode C; [y-y] lyfode C; [z] broðru C; [a-a] ðam abbude C; [b] tohwam C; [c] man C; [d] forþam C; [e] aðolian C; [f] heardan C; [g] þam C; [h] digollice C; [i] .iii. C; [j-j] þam westene C; [k] and sume C; [l-l] gebærst C; [m-m] on hys oðrum C; [n] ealne C; [o-o] mænig heofenlic C; [p] syndon C; [q] to to C; [r] sweriað C; [s] naman C; [t-t] hig na þæt hig æfre manswerion C; [u] naman C.

28 July: Nazarius and Celsus

137. On ðone [a]eahta ond twentigðan[a] dæg þæs monðes bið þæs martyres gemynd Sancte[b] Nazari ond his cnihtes, þæs noma[c] wæs [d]Sancte Celsi[d]. Ða sum dema het weorpan on sæ, [e]forþon þe hie[e] noldon forlætan Cristes geleafan. Þa eodon hi[f] ofer þæt wæter, swa [g]hi eodan[g] on dryge[h] eorðan. [i]Ond hi[i] deodan[j] [222] moni[k] oþer wundor, ond [l]heora lichoman[l] restað on þære byrig Mediolana.

137. [a-a] ehta and twentygoðan C; [b] sancti C; [c] nama C; [d-d] sancti celse C; [e-e] forþam ðe hig C; [f] hig C; [g-g] hig eodon C; [h] drigre C; [i-i] and hig C; [j] eodan B with d suprascript Ba, dydon C; [k] mænig C; [l-l] hyra lychaman C.

29 July: Lupus

138. On ðone [a]nigen ond twentegðan[a] dæg þæs monðes bið þæs biscopes[b] [c]gemynd ond his geleornis[c] þe is nemned Sanctus Lupus; se wæs ærest [d]on læwdum[d] hade geseted, ond he wæs seofan[e] gear on[f] [223] gesinscipe geseted ær his biscopdome[g]. Ond he wæs eft on his biscopdome[h] on swa micelre fullfremednesse[i], þæt he hælde laman mid his gebedum[j], ond dumbe mæn[k], ond sweltendum [l]monnum heora[l] lif geedneowade[m]. Ond he [n]self lifde[n] on [o]gneaðum woroldlife[o] for Gode: [p]An tunece wæs his gegerela[p], [q]ond þæt[q] wæs hæren, ond beren hlaf wæs his gereorde[r], ond þæt [s]hwilum ymb[s] [t]twa niht[t]. Ac he awunode[u] [224] on wependum gebedum, ond mid ælmessum[v] him[w] ceapode eces rices. [x]Ðæs biscopes lichoma[x] resteþ on[y] Trecassina[z] ðære byrig, þæt is on ure geþeode æt Triticum[a] [225].

138. [a-a] nygon and twentygoðan C; [b] bisceopes C; [c-c] gewitennes C; [d-d] lange on læwedum C; [e] .vii. C; [f] in Ko, on Herz; [g] bysceopdome C; [h] bisceopdome C; [i] fulfremednysse C; [j] gebede C; [k] men and deafe C; [l-l] mannum hyra C; [m] geednywode C; [n n] sylf leofode C; [o-o] gneðum woruldlyfe C; [p-p] and hys gegyrla wæs an tunece C; [q-q] seo C; [r] gereord C; [s-s] hwilon ymbe C; [t-t] twegen dagas C; [u] wunode a C, a wunode Ko; [v] ælmyssum C; [w] he C; [x-x] þyses lychama C; [y] in C; [z] tercassina C; [a] tricum C.

Then the abbot let him into the monastery. Then he learned his psalter within four months, and soon he lived such an austere life before God, that the brothers of the monastery said to the abbot: 'Why do you bring this man to us, given that we cannot bear his tough manners?' Then he secretly went from the monastery to a hill, and he stood there on a dry rock for three years; altogether he stood in the desert for forty-seven years. One year a large wound on one of his thighs burst open, and for the whole year he stood on one leg. And he performed many heavenly miracles, which are all too long to describe. And even now people in the East swear by his name, and they never dare to perjure themselves in his name.

28 July: Nazarius and Celsus

137. On the twenty-eighth day of the month is the commemoration of the martyr St Nazarius and that of his boy, whose name was St Celsus. A judge ordered them to be thrown into the sea, because they would not abandon the Christian faith. Then they walked across the water, as if they walked on dry land. And they performed many other miracles, and their bodies rest in the city of Mediolana [i.e. Milan].

29 July: Lupus

138. On the twenty-ninth day of the month is the commemoration and the death of the bishop called St Lupus; he first lived as a layman, and he was in a marriage for seven years before his episcopate. And later he conducted his episcopate with such great perfection, that he healed the lame with his prayers, and the mute, and to the dying restored their life. And he himself lived a frugal life before God: for clothing he had one tunic, and that was one made of hair, and barley bread was his food, and that only every other day. And he was always praying in tears, and with alms acquired for himself the eternal kingdom. The bishop's body rests in the city of Trecassium [i.e. Troyes], which in our language is 'æt Triticum'.

30 July: Abdon and Sennes

139. On ðone ðritegðan[a] dæg ðæs monðes bið þara[b] æþelra wera tid Abdo ond Sennes; þæt wæron twegen [c]Cristne ealdormenn[c] on Perscwara[d] mægðe. Þa het Decius se casere hi[e] gebindan, [f]forðon þe[f] hi[g] on Crist gelefdon[h], ond he het hi[i] lædan to Rome ond þær deoflum geldan[j]. Þa hi[k] þæt noldon, þa het he hi[l] nacode sendan on wildra deora geweald. Þa weop eall Romana dugoð for þære dæde, forþon[m] þa weras wæron wlitige ond [n]fægres lichoman[n]. Ða noldon þa wildan deor [o]him onhrinan[o] for Godes ege, ac þurh oþerne martyrdom hi[p] heora lif geendedon[q], ond hira lichoman[r] restað on Rome.

139. [a] þryttygoðan C; [b] þæra C; [c-c] cristene ealdormen C; [d] perswara C; [e] hig C; [f-f] forþam ðe C; [g] hig C; [h] gelyfdon C; [i] hig C; [j] gyldan C; [k] hig C; [l] hig C; [m] forþam C; [n-n] fægeres lychaman C; [o-o] hyra æthrynan C; [p] hig C; [q] geendodon C; [r] lychaman C.

The End of July

139a. Ðonne se monað[a] biþ geendo<d>[b] þe we nemnað se Æftera Liþa, þonne bið seo niht eahta[c] tida lang, ond se dæg sextene[d] tida.

139a. [a] monoð C; [b] geendon B, geendod C; [c] .viii. B, ehta C; [d] .xvi. B, syxtyne C.

The Beginning of August

139b. On ðam eahtoþan[a] monþe on geare biþ [b]an ond þritig[b] [226] daga; þone monaþ[c] mon nemneð on Leden Agustus monaþ[d]. Romana duguð[e] hine nemde [f]æryst þy noman[f], [g]forþon ðy[g] ærestan dæge þæs monþes he getrymede[h] Romana cynedom, ond oferswiþde þa þe ær ðæt[227] towurpon. Ond on ure geþeode we nemnaþ[i] þone [j]monaþ Weodmonaþ[j], [k]forþon þe[k] hi[l] on þam monþe mæst geweaxaþ.

139b. [a] ehtoðan C; [b-b] an and þritig C, an .xxxi. B, Ko, an ond þritig Herz; [c] om. C; [d] om. C; [e] dugoð C; [f-f] ærest þam naman C; [g-g] forþam on þam C; [h] getymbrede C; [i] ne suprascript Bb; [j-j] monoð weodmonoð C; [k-k] forþam ðe C; [l] hyg C.

1 August: The Machabees

140. On þone ærestan dæg þæs monþes biþ ðara[a] martyra tid þe we nemnaþ Machabeos[b]; þæt wæron seofon[c] gebroþor[d] ond [e]heora modor[e], ða geþrowedon deaþ for þære ealdan æ bebode ær Cristes acennednysse. Antiochus[f] se oferhydiga[g] cyning nydde [h]hi þæt hi[h] æten[i] swynen[j] flæsc; þæt wæs Godes folce forboden on þære ealdan æ, ac [k]hit Crist[k] eft geclænsode þurh his tocyme. Þa [l]hi þa[l] þæt ne geþafedon, þa het he æghwylcne æfter oþrum acwellan ondryslicum[m] witum. Þa hyra syxe[n] wæron acwealde beforan þære meder, ða cwæþ heo: 'Nat ic hu ge [o]ætywdon on[o] minum[p] innoþe. Ne forgeaf ic eow gast ne lif, ac middangeardes[q] Scyppend, se eow [r]agyfþ eft[r]

140. [a] þæra C; [b] machabeorum C; [c] .vii. B, C; [d] gebroþru C; [e-e] hyra moder C; [f] antiochius C; [g] ofermodega C; [h-h] hig þæt hig C; [i] æton C; [j] swynes C; [k-k] crist hyt C; [l-l] hig C; [m] myd ondrysenlicum C; [n] .vi. C; [o-o] ywdon C; [p] n suprascript Bb; [q] dyde myddaneardes C; [r-r] eft agyfð C;

30 July: Abdon and Sennes

139. On the thirtieth day of the month is the feast of the noblemen Abdon and Sennes; they were two Christian rulers in Persia. Then the emperor Decius ordered them to be arrested, because they believed in Christ, and he ordered them to be transported to Rome and to worship devils there. When they refused, he ordered them to be handed over into the power of wild animals, naked. Then the whole Roman senate wept because of that deed, because the men were handsome and beautiful of body. Then the wild animals would not touch them for fear of God, but they ended their lives through another martyrdom, and their bodies rest in Rome.

The End of July

139a. When the month is over which we call Æftera Liþa ['Later Mild (Month)'], the night is eight hours long and the day sixteen hours.

The Beginning of August

139b. There are thirty-one days in the eighth month of the year; that month is in Latin called Augustus's month. The Roman citizens first called it by that name, because on the first day of the month he established the Roman empire, and overcame those who had earlier overthrown it. And in our language we call that month Weodmonaþ ['Weed Month'], because in that month they grow most.

1 August: The Machabees

140. On the first day of the month is the feast of the martyrs whom we call the Machabees; they were seven brothers and their mother, who suffered death according to the precept of the old law before Christ's birth. The arrogant king Antiochus forced them to eat pork; that was forbidden to God's people under the old law, but Christ later made it clean with his arrival. When they refused to do that, he ordered one after the other to be killed under terrible tortures. When six of them had been killed in front of the mother, she said: 'I do not know how you appeared in my womb. I did not give you soul or life, but the Creator of the world did, who will later restore soul and

gast ond lif mid mildheortnesse^s on domesdæge^t.' Ða gyt wæs se gingesta^u to laue^v. Þa swor se cyning þæm^w þæt he ^{x}wolde hyne^x ^{y}weligne gedon, gyf he hyne wolde oncyrran^y ^{z}from Godes^z æ. Ða onhylde seo modor^a hig to þam, ^{b}to þæm cnihte$^{b\,228}$, ond cwæþ: 'Sunu min, myltsa me ond onfoh deaþe, þæt ðu ^{c}si efnmedome^c þinum broþrum.' Þa cwæþ se cniht to þam cyninge: 'Ic sylle mine sauwle^d ond minne lichoman^e for ussa^f fædera ðeodscipe, swa mine broþor^g dydon.' Ða het se cing^h þone hyra ealra grimlicost^i acwellan, ond þa modor ealra neahst^j. Ond þa sona æfter þon^k, ða gefeol$^{l\,229}$ hine se ofermodiga^m cyning of his scride^n. Þa^o afulode he sona, swa ðæt nænig mon^p ne meahte^q aræfnan^r þone stenc, ne furðon^s he sylua^t. Ac he ^{u}aweol eal^u wyrmum, ond earmlice swealt on elðeodigum^v muntum. Se wæs ær swa oferhydig þæt him wæs gesewen þæt he meahte^w on scipe liþan on eorðan, ond mid his fotum gangan on widsæ, ond mid his handum ^{x}geræcean heofenes^x tungol.

^{s} myldheortnysse C; ^{t} domesdæg C; ^{u} gingsta C; ^{v} lafe C; ^{w} þam C; $^{x-x}$ hyne wolde C; $^{y-y}$ gecyrran C; $^{z-z}$ fram cristes geleafan and fram godes C; ^{a} moder C; $^{b-b}$ om. C; $^{c-c}$ sig efnmedeme C; ^{d} sawle C; ^{e} lychaman C; ^{f} ure C; ^{g} broðro C; ^{h} cyning C; ^{i} wælgrymlicost C; ^{j} nehst C; ^{k} þam C; ^{l} gefeoll C; ^{m} oferhydiga C; ^{n} scryðe C; ^{o} and þa C; ^{p} man C; ^{q} myhte C; ^{r} aþolian C; ^{s} om. C; ^{t} sylf C; $^{u-u}$ aweoll eall C; ^{v} ælðeodigum C; ^{w} myhte C; $^{x-x}$ geræcan heofones C.

1 August: Germanus

141. On ðone ylcan dæg biþ Sancte Germanus geleornys^a þæs^b bisceopes, se com on ðas Bretene^c ofer sæ on Brytwala^d dagum. Ond he dyde her^e ^{f}monegu wundor^f, ge on sæ ge on eorþan, ond his dæda syndon awritene ealle mid endebyrdnysse on Ongelcynnes^g bocum.

141. ^{a} gewytennys C; ^{b} þæs halgan C; ^{c} brytene C; ^{d} brytweala C; ^{e} ær C; $^{f-f}$ manege wundru C; ^{g} angelcynnes C.

1 August: Eusebius of Vercelli

142. On ^{a}þam ylcan dæge$^{a\,230}$ byð þæs bisceopes tid ^{b}Sancti Eusebii^b. He wes^c þære burge bisceop Uercellensis^d, ond him wæs on swefne geywed^e hwylce dæge he sceolde to Criste geleoran^f. He seah^g on slæpe þæt he on flyhte wære on þam ^{h}kalendas dæge Augustus^h, þæt ys on þone dæg æt hlafsenunga^i, ond he þa gefleah on swiþe heage^j dune. Þæt swefn^k him tacnode^l þy ylcan dæge þæt hit sceolde beon his lifes ende þurh martyrdom, ond hys gast gefleogan$^{m\,231}$ to heofena heahnysse.

142. $^{a-a}$ þone ylcan dæg C; $^{b-b}$ sancte eusebi C; ^{c} wæs C; ^{d} þe ys nemned uercellensis C; ^{e} onywed C; ^{f} gewitan C; ^{g} geseah C; $^{h-h}$ dæge þe ys cweden kalendas agustus C; ^{i} hlafseninga C; ^{j} heahe C; ^{k} swefen C; ^{l} getacnode C; ^{m} gefleah C.

life to you in his mercy on Doomsday.' Then only the youngest was left. Then the king swore that he would make him wealthy, if he were willing to convert from God's law. Then the mother bent down to him, to the boy, and said: 'My son, have mercy on me and choose death, so that you may be just as worthy as your brothers.' Then the boy said to the king: 'I surrender my soul and my body for the law of our fathers, as my brothers have done.' Then the king ordered him to be killed in the most cruel way of them all, and his mother last of all. And then soon after that, the arrogant king caused himself to fall out of his chariot. And he became putrid straightaway, so that nobody could tolerate the stench, not even he himself. And he was crawling with worms all over, and died miserably in the mountains of a foreign land. He had previously been so arrogant that he seemed to be able to travel across land in a ship, and walk on the open sea with his feet, and touch the stars in the sky with his hands.

1 August: Germanus

141. On the same day is the death of the bishop St Germanus, who came to this Britain across the sea in the days of the Britons. And he performed many miracles both on sea and on dry land, and his deeds are all listed in the books about the English [i.e. the *Historia ecclesiastica*].

1 August: Eusebius of Vercelli

142. On the same day is the feast of the bishop St Eusebius. He was bishop of the town of Vercelli, and it was revealed to him in a dream on which day he should migrate to Christ. He saw in his sleep that he was flying through the air on the Kalends of August, that is on the day of the blessing of the bread [i.e. Lammas Day], and he then flew onto a very high mountain. That dream signified to him on the same day that his life should end through martyrdom, and his soul fly to heaven on high.

2 August: Pope Stephen I

143. On þone æfteran <dæg>[a] [232] ðæs monþes biþ Sancte Stefanus[b] ðrowung[c] þæs papan. He wæs gemartyrud[d] on Ualerianus tidum[e] þæs caseres, ond his lichoma[f] bebyrged in[g] Calestis[h] mynstre[233] æt Rome. Þes papa gesette þæt mæssepreostas ond diaconas ne sceoldon[i] brucan gehalgodra mæssehrægla to nænegum[j] woroldbroce[k], [l]ne no[l] buton on cyrcean[m] anre.

143. [a] om. B, Ko, dæg C, Herz; [b] stephanes C; [c] ðrowong B with v suprascript Bb; [d] gemartyrod C; [e] timan C; [f] lichama ys C; [g] on C; [h] calistes C; [i] sceal C; [j] nanum C; [k] woruldbryce C; [l-l] om. C; [m] cyrcan C.

2 August: Theodota and her Three Sons

144. On ðone ylcan dæg byþ ðære wydewan ðrowung mid hyre þrym[a] sunum þære nama ys Theodota[b], ond hyre yldesta sunu is[c] nem<n>ed[d] Sanctus Euodius[e]. Hi[f] wæron in[g] ðære mægþe Biþinia, ond in[h] ðære byrig seo is [i]nemned Necia[i]. Ðære burge ealdorman, [j]se wæs[j] on naman Nicetius[k], he het sumne scandfulne[l] man, se wæs on noman[m] Hirtacus, bysmrian ða halgan wydewan mid hys fyrenlustum. Ða he hyre nealæhte[n], þa stod hyre big [o]iong man fæger[o] mid gyldenum[p] hræglum gegyred; þæt wæs Godes engel, se hine sloh mid his[q] fyste on [r]þæt næsþyrl[r], þæt ðær [s]ut fleow[s] un[t]<geendod blod. And seo halige wydewe æfter þam þurh fyr>[t][234] geendode hyre lif mid hyre þrym sunum.

144. [a] r suprascript Bb; [b] sancte theotote C; [c] wæs C; [d] nemded B, nemned C; [e] efodus C; [f] and hig C; [g] on C; [h] on C; [i-i] genemned necie C; [j-j] wæs C; [k] necitius C; [l] sceandfulne C; [m] naman C; [n] genealæhte C; [o-o] sum fæger geong man C; [p] unidentified letter altered to l Bb; [q] hs B with i suprascript Bb, om. C; [r-r] þa næsþyrlo C; [s-s] utfleow Ko, He; [t-t] om. B, geendod blod and seo halige wydewe æfter þam þurh fyr C.

3 August: The Discovery of the Body of St Stephen

145. On ðone þryddan dæg þæs monþes byþ mærsod[a] Sancte[b] Stehpanes[c] [235] lichoman[d] gemetnes[e] ðæs ærestan martyres. Se wæs gemeted þurh sumne mæssepreost se wæs on naman Lucianus. Se wæs sume frigeniht [f]in ciricean[f], þa on þa þriddan tid ðære nihte ætywde him Gamalielus[g] gast healfslæpendum ond him þriwa onhran mid gyldynre[h] gyrde, ond [i]him to cwæþ[i]: 'Luciane, Luciane, Luciane, gang saga þisum bisceope [j]in Ierusalem[j] þæt he do [k]Stehpanus lichoman[k] up of eorþan. Saga him þæt he ys on twentigum[l] milum[m] from[n] Hierusalem, neah þam tune þe ys nemned Cafarcanialam[o] on þam londe[p] þe is cweden[q] Lagabra[r] [236].' Þa[s] sæde se mæssepreost þæt ðam bisceope; ða sende se bisceop hine ond oþre halige weras mid him. Þa dulfon [t]hi in[t] þære ylcan stowe. Ða [u]gemetton hi[u] stan mid eorðan bewrigenne; þa wæs on þam awriten 'Her ys se Godes Stehpanus[v] [237].' Þa [w]segdon hi[w]

145. [a] gemærsod C; [b] sanctus C; [c] stephanus C; [d] lychaman C; [e] myttynge C; [f-f] on cyrcan C; [g] gamalielis C; [h] gyldenre C; [i-i] cwæð hym to C, him tocwæþ Ko; [j-j] on hierusalem C; [k-k] stephanus lychaman C; [l] .xx.m B, twentigum C; [m] myla C; [n] fram C; [o] cafargamalan C; [p] lande C; [q] nemned C; [r] erasure before lagabra B, dalagabar C; [s] and þa C; [t-t] hig on C; [u-u] gemytton hig C; [v] stephanus C; [w-w] sædon hig C;

2 August: Pope Stephen I

143. On the second day of the month is the passion of Pope St Stephen. He was martyred in the time of the emperor Valerian, and his body buried in the church of Callistus in Rome. This pope decreed that priests and deacons should use dedicated liturgical vestments on no worldly occasion, but without exception in church only.

2 August: Theodota and her Three Sons

144. On the same day is the passion of the widow with her three sons whose name is Theodota, and her eldest son is called St Evodius. They lived in the country of Bithynia, and in the city which is called Nicaea. The governor of the city, whose name was Necitius, he ordered a vile man, whose name was Hyrtacus, to harass the holy widow for sex. When he came near her, a young handsome man in golden garments stood by her side; that was God's angel, who hit him on the nose with his fist, so that it began to bleed incessantly. And later the holy widow ended her life together with her three sons through fire.

3 August: The Discovery of the Body of Stephen

145. On the third day of the month the discovery of the body of St Stephen, the protomartyr, is celebrated. It was found by a priest whose name was Lucianus. He was in church in the early hours of one Friday, when at the third hour of the night the spirit of Gamaliel appeared to him who was half asleep, and touched him three times with a golden rod, and said to him: 'Lucianus, Lucianus, Lucianus, go tell this bishop in Jerusalem that he should exhume the body of Stephen from the earth. Tell him that it is twenty miles from Jerusalem, near the town that is called Caphargamala in the area called Delagabria.' Then the priest told the bishop that; then the bishop sent him and other holy men with him. Then they dug in the said place. Then they found a stone covered with soil; on it was written 'Here lies Stephen of God.' Then they told

þæt ðam bisceope; ða com he ðider mid oðrum halgum bisceopum. Þa ontyndon hi[x] þa þruh; ða com þær ut micelre[y] wynsumnysse stenc[z], ond monige[a] untrume men þær wæron sona hale gewordene[b]. Ða gelæddon hi ðone lichoman[c] in[d] Hierusalem. Hit wæs [e]ær þær singal druwunge[e], ond sona æfter þam com geþuhtsum[f] ren on eorþan.

[x] hig C; [y] milcelre B, mycel C; [z] n suprascript Bb; [a] mænige C; [b] geworden C;[c] lychaman C; [d] on C; [e-e] syngal druwung ær þam C; [f] genyhtsum C.

5 August: Oswald

146. On ðone fiftan[a] dæg þæs monþes biþ Sancti[b] Oswaldes[c] tid þæs [d]Cristinan kyninges[d]; se ricsode[e] nigon[f] gear [g]in Bretene[g], ond him sealde God mare rice þonne ænigum[h] hys forgengum[i]. Him wæron underðeodde[j] ða feowera[k] þeoda þe[l] syndon on Bretene[m], þæt syndon Brytwalas[n] ond Peohtas [o]ond Scottas[o 238] ond Ongle[p]. Oswald[q] endade[r] his lif [s]in gebedes wordum[s] ða hine mon[t] sloh, ond þa[u] he feol[v] on eorþan, þa cwæð he: 'Deus miserere animabus.' He cwæþ: 'God, miltsa þu saulum[w].' His handa siondan[x] ungebrosnode in[y] þære cynelican ceastre seo ys nemned Bebbanburh, ond his heafod wæs gelæded to Lindesfeare[z] ea, ond se lichoma[a] ys elles in[b] Lindesse mægþe æt Beardanegge[c]. Ond his wundor[d] wæron miclo[e], ge beheonan sæ ge begeondan[f].

146. [a] .v.an B, fiftan C; [b] sancte C; [c] oswoldes C; [d-d] crystenan cyninges C; [e] rixode C; [f] .viiii. B, nygon C; [g-g] on brytene C; [h] ænegum C; [i] foregengena C; [j] u altered from o B, underþeoded C; [k] .iiii. B, C; [l] þa ðe C; [m] brytene C; [n] brytwealas C; [o-o] sceottas C; [p] angle C; [q] oswold C; [r] geendode C; [s-s] on hys gebedwordum C; [t] n suprascript Bb, man C; [u] om. C; [v] feoll C; [w] sawlum C; [x] syndon C; [y] on C; [z] lyndesfarena C; [a] lychama C; [b] on C; [c] beardanige C; [d] wundra C; [e] mycele C; [f] beeondan C.

6 August: Pope Sixtus II

147. On þone sextan[a] dæg ðæs monþes bið Sancti[b] Sixtes þrowung[c] þæs papan in[d] Rome [e]mid his sex[f] deaconum[e]. Þone Syxtum nedde[g] Decius se casere [h]<to> Tiges[239] deofolgylde[h 240]; þa cwæð he to þam deofulgilde: 'Towyrpe[i] þe Crist.' Ða sona gefeol[j] þæs deofolgyldes[k] huses sum dæl. Ða het se casere hine gemartyrian[l] mid his deaconum. Ond his lichoma[m] [n]resteþ in[n] þam mynstre Calesti, ond his [o]deaconas in[o] þam myn<st>re[p 241] Pretextate[q].

147. [a] .vi.an B, syxtan C; [b] sancte C; [c] mæsse and þrowung C; [d] on C; [e-e] and hys syx diacona myd hym C; [f] .vi. B; [g] nydde C; [h-h] Tiges deofolgylde B, Ko, to Tiges deofolgilde Herz, þæt he gelyfde on hys deofolgyld C; [i] towurpe C; [j] tofeoll C; [k] deofolgyldes C; [l] ge suprascript Bc; [m] lychama C; [n-n] resteð on C; [o-o] diaconas on C; [p] mynþre B, Ko, mynstre C, Herz; [q] praete extate C.

7 August: Donatus and Hilarinus

148. On ðone seofoþan[a] dæg þæs monþes bið þæs bisceopes þreowung[b] Sancti Donati, ond þæs muneces mid him Sancti Hilarini. He wæs bisceop in[c] þære ceastre

148. [a] .vii. B, seofoðan C; [b] þrowung C; [c] on C;

the bishop that; then he came there with other holy bishops. Then they opened the coffin; then a very pleasant smell came out of there, and many sick men were healed there shortly afterwards. Then they transported the body to Jerusalem. There had earlier been a continual drought, but shortly afterwards abundant rain came down on earth.

5 August: Oswald

146. On the fifth day of the month is the feast of the Christian king St Oswald; he ruled for nine years in Britain, and God gave him greater authority than any of his predecessors. Subjected to him were the four nations which are in Britain, namely the Britons and the Picts and the Gaels and the English. Oswald ended his life in words of prayer when he was killed, and when he fell to the ground, he said: '*Deus miserere animabus.*' He said: 'God, have mercy on the souls.' His hands are undecayed in the royal city called Bamburgh, and his head was taken to the island of Lindisfarne, and the rest of the body is in the region of Lindsey at Bardney. And his miracles were many, both on this side of the sea and beyond.

6 August: Pope Sixtus II

147. On the sixth day of the month is the passion of St Sixtus the pope in Rome, together with his six deacons. The emperor Decius forced Sixtus to worship an idol of Tiu; then he said to the idol: 'May Christ destroy you.' Then immediately part of the idol's house collapsed. Then the emperor ordered him to be martyred with his deacons. And his body rests in the church of Callistus, and his deacons in the church of Praetextatus.

7 August: Donatus and Hilarinus

148. On the seventh day of the month is the passion of the bishop St Donatus, and also that of the monk St Hilarinus. He was bishop in the city of Arretium [i.e.

Awritensi[d], ond ða he ærestan siðe mæssan sang, þa eodon þa hæþenan weras [e]into þære ciricanˑ[e] ond toslogon his glæsenne[f] calic. Þa gesomnode[g] se bissceop[h] [i]þa brocu[i] ond him to Drihtne gebæd; ða wæs se calic eft swa gehal[j] swa he ær wæs. Ond þy[k] ilcan dæge [l]for þy[l] wundre þær onfeng fulwihte [m]twa hund monna ond fif ond feowertig monna[m].

[d] aritensi C; [e-e] on þa cyrcan C; [f] glæsena C; [g] gesamnode C; [h] bysceop C; [i-i] þæge brycas, but see Kotzor, II, 337; [j] gesund C; [k] þig C; [l-l] for þam ylcan C; [m-m] .cc. monna ond .xlv. monna B, twa hund manna and fif and feowertig C.

8 August: Afra, Hilaria, etc.

149. On þone eahtoþan[a] dæg þæs monþes bið Sancta Affran[b] þrowung ond hire mo<do>r[c] mid hire, þære noma[d] wæs Sancta Hilaia[e], ond hire þreo[f] ðeowena, þa wæron on naman Sancta Digna ond Sancta Eonomina[g] [242] ond Sancta Eotropia[h]. Sio[i] Affra wæs ærest forlegoswif[f] mid hire þeowenum; [k]hio ða eft þeah[k] gelyfde Gode[l] ond fulwihte[m] onfeng þurh ða wundor[n] [o]ðe ðe[o] heo geseah æt þam bisceope Sanctus[p] Narcisus[q]. Ac se deoma[r] Gaius mid witum [s]heo ongon[s] æft[t] nedan[u] to hæþenscipe, ond cwæð hire to: 'Þu eart meretrix', ðæt is forlegoswif[v], 'forðon[w] þu eart <fr>æmde[x] [y]from þara[y] Cristenra manna Gode.' Ða cwæþ Sancta Affra: 'Crist [z]self sægde[z] þæt he for ðam[a] synfullum monnum[b] astige of heofenum[c] on eorþan.' Ða het se dema hi[d] nacode[243] gebindan to anum stænge[e] ond hi[f] bærnan mid fyre, ond heo þæs dyde Gode þanccunga[g] ond hire gast onsende. Ond Cristene men gemitton hire lichoman gesundne[h] æfter þam fyre ond hine bebyrgdon[i] on þære æfteran mile fram þære ceastre þe is nemned Augusta[j].

149. [a] .viii.an B, ehtoðan C; [b] affan C; [c] mor B, modor C; [d] nama C; [e] hilaria C; [f] feower C; [g] eudomia and sancta theodote C; [h] eutropia C; [i] seo C; [j] forlegorwif Ko, forlegeswif C; [k-k] þeah heo þa C; [l] on god C; [m] fullwhyte C; [n] wundru C; [o-o] þe C; [p] se wæs nemned sanctus C; [q] narcissus C; [r] dema C; [s-s] hig ongan C; [t] om. C; [u] nydan C; [v] forlegeswif C; [w] forþam C; [x] æmde B, fremde C; [y-y] fram þæra C; [z-z] sylf sæde C; [a] om. C; [b] mannum C; [c] heofone C; [d] hig C; [e] stenge C; [f] hig C; [g] þancunge C; [h] ansund C; [i] bebyrigdon C; [j] agusta C.

9 August: Romanus

150. On ðone nigoþan[a] dæg þæs monþes bið þæs cempan tid[b] se is nemned Sanctus Romanus; se gelifde[c] [244] forþon ðe he geseah Godes engel stondan[d] ond drygan mid [e]sceatan Sancti[e] Laurentius limu, þa Decius se casere hine[245] het stingan[f] [246] mid irenum[g] gyrdum tyndehtum[h]. Ond he ða onfeng fulwihte ond geþrowode[i] martyrdom for Criste, ond his lichoma[j] is bebyrged æt Rome on ðam londe[k] Ueranum.

150. [a] .viiii.an B, nigoðan C; [b] om. C; [c] gelyfde on god C; [d] standan C; [e-e] scytan sancte C; [f] swingan C; [g] ysenum C; [h] tyn dagas C; [i] geþrowude C; [j] lychaman C; [k] lande C.

Arezzo], and when he sang mass for the first time, the pagan men came into the church and broke his glass chalice into pieces. Then the bishop picked up the pieces and prayed to the Lord; then the chalice was as whole again as it had been before. And on the same day, on account of that miracle, 245 men received baptism.

8 August: Afra, Hilaria, etc.

149. On the eighth day of the month is the passion of St Afra and also her mother, whose name was St Hilaria, and their three maids, who were called St Digna and St Eumenia and St Eutropia. This Afra was first a prostitute, together with her maids, but then again she came to believe in God and received baptism on account of the miracles which she had seen in the bishop St Narcissus. But the judge Gaius with torments subsequently began to force her to paganism, and said to her: 'You are a *meretrix*,' which means 'prostitute', 'because you are alien to the God of the Christians.' Then St Afra said: 'Christ himself said that he descended to earth from heaven for sinful people.' Then the judge ordered her to be tied to a pole, naked, and to be burned with fire, and she thanked God for that and gave up the ghost. And Christians found her body unharmed after the fire and buried it one or two miles outside the city called Augusta [i.e. Augsburg].

9 August: Romanus

150. On the ninth day of the month is the feast of the soldier who is called St Romanus; he believed because he saw God's angel stand and dry with a cloth the limbs of St Lawrence, when the emperor Decius ordered him to be pierced [or 'beaten'] with spiked iron clubs. And he then received baptism and suffered martyrdom for Christ, and his body is buried in Rome at the Ager Veranus.

10 August: Lawrence

151. On ðone teoþan[a] dæg þæs monþes bið Sancti[b] Laurentius <tid>[c] [d]þæs archidiacones[d,247]; se sealde monegum[e] blindum men[f] gesiðþe[g,248], ond he gedælde [h]eal ða[h] goldhord þa ðe wæron in[i] Godes [j]cyricum æt Rome[j] ðearfendum monnum[k] ond elðeodegum[l]; ond þa forþon[m] Decius se hæðena kasere[n] hine tintregode[o] mid unasecgendlicum witum. Ond [p]æt nehstan[p] he hine het aþenian on irenum[q] bedde, ond hine[r] cwicne hirstan ond brædan. Ond swa hine mon[s] ma[t] hirste, swa wæs he fægera[u] on ondwlitan[v]. Ond þa onhof[w] Laurentius his egan[x] up ond cwæð to þam kasere[y]: 'Geseoh[z] nu, þu earma, et nu þas sidan þe her gehirsted is, ond acer[a] me on þa oþre.' Ond þa dyde he Gode þoncunga[b] ond his gast onsende to heofnum[c]. Ond on æfentid Iustinus se mæssepreost ond Ypolitus se Cristena tungerefa, unrote ond wepende [d]hi byrgdon[d] his lichoman[e] on þan[f] lande Ueranum, on[g] þam wege þe hi[h] nemnað æt Rome Tiburtina.

151. [a] .x.an B, teoðan C; [b] sancte C; [c] om. B, Ko, tyd C; [d-d] þæs archidiacones æt rome C; [e] manegum C; [f] mannum C; [g] gesyhðe C; [h-h] eall þæt C; [i] on C; [j-j] cyrcan C; [k] mannum C; [l] ælþeodygum C; [m] forþam C; [n] casere C; [o] tyntergode C; [p-p] ætnehstan Ko; [q] ysenum C; [r] het hyne þa C; [s] man C; [t] swyðor C; [u] fægror C; [v] odwlitan B with suprascript n Bc, andwlytan C; [w] anhof C; [x] eagan C; [y] casere C; [z] beseoh ðe C; [a] wend C; [b] þancunge C; [c] heofenum C; [d-d] hig bebyrigdon C; [e] lychaman C; [f] þam C; [g] and on C; [h] suprascript Bc, hig C.

11 August: Tiburtius

152. On ðone endlyftan[a] dæg þæs monþes bið þæs halgan weres gemind Sancti Tiburtii[b], se wæs in[c] Rome ond swiþe late he wolde onfon Cristes gelefan[d] ond fulwihte, ond deofolgyld forlætan. Ac þurh[e] wundor[f] þe he seah[g] Sebastianum don he onfeng fulwihte, [h]ond Sebastianus him onfeng æt fulwihte[h]. Ond he wæs siðþan swa fulfremed[i] in[j] Godes geleafan ðæ<t>[k,249], gif he song[l] his credon[m] oððe[n] paternoster on untrumne mon[o], he wæs sona hal. Ac þa wæs sum swiðe [p]facenful mon[p] in[q] Rome, se wæs [r]in noman[r] Torquatris[s]; se geypte[t] hæþenum deman þæt [u]þæs Tiburtius[u] wæs Cristen, ond [v]he wæs[v] befangen [w]in ciricean[w,250] æt his gebede ond to martyrdome gelæded.

152. [a] .xi. an B, endlyftan C; [b] tyburti C; [c] on C; [d] geleafan C; [e] þa þurh þa C; [f] wundru C; [g] geseah C; [h-h] om. C; [i] fullfremed C; [j] on C; [k] ðæþ B, þæt C; [l] sang C; [m] credan C; [n] oððe hys C; [o] man C; [p-p] facenfull man C; [q] on C; [r-r] on naman C; [s] torquatius C; [t] geopenode þam C; [u-u] ðes tiburtinus C; [v-v] þæt he wæs on þam C; [w-w] om. C.

12 August: Euplius

153. On ðone twelftan[a] dæg þæs monþes bið Sancti[b] Euplis þrowung, se bær Cri<st>es[c,251] godspel in[d] fodre ofer his sculdrum[e] swa hwæder swa he eode. Ond he þa com in[f] þa ceastre þe is nemned Catinentia[g], ond he eode in[h] þæt domern [i]ðær, ðær[i]

153. [a] .xii.an B, twelftan C; [b] sancte C; [c] Criþes B, cristes C; [d] on C; [e] gescyldrum C; [f] on C; [g] continentia C; [h] on C; [i-i] þær C;

10 August: Lawrence

151. On the tenth day of the month is the [feast] of the archdeacon St Lawrence; he restored sight to many a blind man, and he distributed all the treasures which were in God's churches in Rome to the poor and the foreigners; and then because of that the pagan emperor Decius tortured him with unspeakable torments. And eventually he ordered him to be stretched out on an iron bed, and roasted and fried alive. And the more they roasted him, the more glorious he was to look at. And then Lawrence raised his eyes and said to the emperor: 'Look, you wretch, you can now eat this side which is cooked, here, and turn me over on the other.' And then he gave thanks to God and sent his spirit to heaven. And in the evening Justinus the priest and Hippolytus the Christian governor, sad and weeping, they buried his body on the Ager Veranus, on the road which in Rome is called [the Via] Tiburtina.

11 August: Tiburtius

152. On the eleventh day of the month is the commemoration of the holy man St Tiburtius, who lived in Rome and very late he decided to take up the Christian faith and baptism, and abandon devil-worship. But through a miracle which he saw Sebastian work, he received baptism, and Sebastian received him at baptism. And he was since then so perfect in God's faith that, whenever he recited his creed or the Lord's Prayer over a sick man, he was suddenly healed. But then there was a very deceitful man in Rome, whose name was Torquatus; he reported to the pagan judge that this Tiburtius was a Christian, and he was arrested in church during prayer, and taken away to his martyrdom.

12 August: Euplius

153. On the twelfth day of the month is the passion of St Euplius, who carried Christ's gospel in a case on his shoulders wherever he went. And he then came to the city which is called Catina [i.e. Catania], and he went to the court-house there, where

Caluisianus ʲwæs inʲ²⁵² miclum gemote mid hæðe<n>folceᵏ²⁵³. Þaˡ untyndeᵐ Epliusⁿ þæt Cristes godspel, ond sæde þam folce hwætᵒ þa halgan godspelleras feowere sægdonᵖ be ðam ondryslicanᑫ Godes dome. Ond ʳþa forþonʳ yrsode se dema ond het hine beheafdian. Ond þa he wæs lædedˢ to þære þrowunge, þa ontynde se heofon, ond he geseah urne Dryhten ᵗin his þrymmeᵗ.

ʲ⁻ʲ se dema wæs on C; ᵏ hæðefolce B, hæðenum folce C; ˡ and þa C; ᵐ ontynde C; ⁿ euplis C; ᵒ þæt C; ᵖ sædon C; ᑫ ondrysnlican C; ʳ⁻ʳ forþam C; ˢ gelæded C; ᵗ⁻ᵗ on godþrymme C.

13 August: Hippolytus

154. On ðone þreoteoþanᵃ dæg þæs monþes bið þæs þroweres gemynd Sancti Ypoliti; se wasᵇ tungerefa on Rome, ac he gelyfdeᶜ Godeᵈ þurhᵉ þa wundorᶠ þe he geseah æt Sanctiᵍ Laurentie þam deaconeʰ, ond he onfeng fulwihte ond ealle his þeowas gefreodeⁱ. Ða het Ualerianus, Deciusʲ prafestᵏ þæs caseres, gebindan ðysne Ypolitum on wildu hors²⁵⁴, þætˡ hyne drogonᵐ on gorstas ond on þornas. Ond þa gebæd he himⁿ to Drihtne ond onsende his gast, ond ða hors forleton ðone lichomanᵒ. Ond þa ymbe medmicelne fyrst æfter þam sweolt Ualerianus se prauost, ond ᵖær þanᵖ he swulte, he clypode ond cwæþ: 'Eala, Laurentius, þæt ðu me gebundenne mid fyrenum racenteagum tyhstᑫ in ece fyr.' Ond Decius se kasereʳ awedde, ond heˢ clypode ær he swulteᵗ: 'Eala, Yppolitusᵘ, þæt ðu meᵛ grimlice ʷlædest gebundenne inʷ forwyrd.'

154. ᵃ .xiii.an B, þrytteoðan C; ᵇ wæs C; ᶜ d suprascript Bc; ᵈ on god C; ᵉ inserted in margin; ᶠ wyndor B with v suprascript Bc, wundro C; ᵍ sancte C; ʰ diacone C; ⁱ he gefreode C; ʲ decius C; ᵏ prauost C; ˡ þæt ða C; ᵐ todrogon C; ⁿ hyne C; ᵒ lychaman C; ᵖ⁻ᵖ ær þam þe C; ᑫ on C; ʳ casere C; ˢ om. C; ᵗ swulte and cwæð C; ᵘ ypolitus C; ᵛ me swa C; ʷ⁻ʷ gebundenne lædest on C.

13 August: Cassian

155. On ðone ylcan dæg byþ þæs martyres tid Sanctiᵃ Casianiᵇ, se wæs lareow geongra manna inᶜ Godes æ. Ac þa com ᵈþær sum hæþen kasereᵈ; þa alyfdeᵉ se þam cnihtum þæt hiᶠ hyne ofslogenᵍ mid heoraʰ writbredumⁱ, ond hine ofsticodon mid hira writeyrenumʲ. Ond his þrowung wæs þe lengre ond þyᵏ heardre, þyˡ þe hyraᵐ handa wæro<n>ⁿ unstrange hine to acwellanne.

155. ᵃ sancte C; ᵇ cassiani C; ᶜ on C; ᵈ⁻ᵈ sumes hæðenes caseres rice C; ᵉ lyfde C; ᶠ hig C; ᵍ onslogon C; ʰ hyra C; ⁱ writebredum C; ʲ writingisenum C; ᵏ þe C; ˡ þig C; ᵐ heora C; ⁿ wæro B, wæron C.

15 August: The Assumption of the Virgin Mary

156. On þone fifteoþanᵃ dæg þæs monþysᵇ biþ seo tid ᶜþæt isᶜ Sancta ᵈMarian tidᵈ. On þone dæg heo geleordeᵉ of middangeardeᶠ to Criste, ond heo nu scineþ on þam heofonlican ᵍmægene betwyhᵍ ʰþa þreatasʰ²⁵⁵ haligra fæmnena, swa swa sunne scineþ on þisne middangeardⁱ. Englas þær blissiaþ, ond heahenglas þær wynsumiaþ, ond

156. ᵃ .xv.an B, fifteoðan C; ᵇ monðes C; ᶜ⁻ᶜ þe C; ᵈ⁻ᵈ maria C; ᵉ gewat C; ᶠ myddanearde C; ᵍ⁻ᵍ mægne betweoh C; ʰ⁻ʰ engla þreatas and C;

160

Calvisianus was there in a great assembly with a pagan crowd. Then Euplius opened the gospel of Christ, and told the people what the four holy evangelists said about the terrible judgement of God. And because of that the judge became angry and ordered him to be beheaded. And when he was led to his passion, heaven opened, and he saw our Lord in his glory.

13 August: Hippolytus

154. On the thirteenth day of the month is the commemoration of the martyr St Hippolytus; he was a governor in Rome, but he believed in God on account of the miracles which he saw from the deacon St Lawrence, and he received baptism and freed all his slaves. Then Valerianus, the prefect of the emperor Decius, ordered this Hippolytus to be tied to wild horses, so that they would drag him through the shrubs and thorny bushes. And then he prayed to the Lord and gave up the ghost, and the horses abandoned the body. And then a short time afterwards Valerianus the prefect died, and before he died he called out and said: 'Alas Lawrence, that you pull me into the eternal fire, tied with red-hot chains!' And the emperor Decius went insane, and before he died he shouted: 'Alas Hippolytus, that you cruelly lead me bound into perdition!'

13 August: Cassian

155. On the same day is the feast of the martyr St Cassian, who taught Christian religion to young boys. But then a pagan emperor came along; then he allowed the boys to beat him to death with their writing tablets, and to stab him with their pens. And his suffering was even more prolonged and more brutal, as their hands were hardly strong enough to kill him.

15 August: The Assumption of the Virgin Mary

156. On the fifteenth day of the month is the feast which is St Mary's feast. On that day she migrated from the world to Christ, and she now shines in the heavenly force among the hosts of holy virgins, as the sun shines onto this earth. Angels exult there,

ealle þa halgan þær gefeoþ in[j] Sancta Marian. Sancta Maria wæs on [k]feower ond sextigum[k 256] <[l]geara þa ða heo ferde to Criste[l]>. Sancta Maria is Godfæder snoru, ond Godes suna mo<d>ur[m], ond haligra sauwla[n] sweger, ond seo æþele cwen [o]þara uplica[o] cesterwara[p], seo stondeþ[q] [r]on þa[r] swyþran healfe ðæs [s]Heahfæder ond ðæs Heahkyninges[s].

[i] myddaneard C; [j] on C; [k-k] .lxiiii.um B, feower and syxtegum C; [l-l] om. B, geara þa ða heo ferde to criste C; [m] erasure in B, moder C; [n] sawla C; [o-o] þæra uplicra C; [p] ceastergewara C; [q] standeð C; [r-r] to ðære C; [s-s] heahan cyninges C.

17 August: Mamas

157. On ðone seofonteoþan[a] dæg þæs monðes biþ þæs[b] halgan cnihtes tid [c]Sancti Mommos[c], se wæs twelf[d] wintre[e] cniht ða he for Criste campode; he wæs in[f] Cesarea[g] ðære ceastre [h]in Capadocia[h] þære mægþe. Da he þær[i] geseah deofolgild begangan[j 257], þa gewat he in[k] þone þiccestan wudu; ond him com [l]unrim wildeora þær to[l] ond hine weorþodon, ond he lifde[m] be þara[n] wildeora meolcum. Ond þonne he his boc[o 258] rædde, ðonne sæton þa [p]wildeor ymutan[259] hine[p]. Ða [q]Alexander se gerefa het[q] hyne [r]him to gelædan[r], ond hi<ne>[s] ðreade mid[t] miclum witum from[u] Cristes geleafan. Ða he hine swiþost ðreade, ða com þær micel leo, se wæs ær mid þæm[v] cnihte on þam wuda, ond [w]se leo[w] cwæð: 'Eala[x] Mommos[y], þu eart ure hyrde. Ic eom nu genyded from[z] Godes englum þæt ic for ðe sprece from[a] minre gecynde.' Ond þa abat se [b]leo ðara[b] hæþenra [c]ond ðara[c] Iudea, þara[d] ðe hine bysmrodon, swa fela[e] ðæt þæt blod arn of[f] þære ylcan stowe swa flod. Ond þa bebead him[g] se cniht þæt se leo hwurfe[h] eft to his stowe. Ond þa het se dema hine stænan. Ða com stefn[i] of heofonum[j] ond seo cwæþ: 'Cum, Mommos[k], heofenas[l] ðe synt[m] mid gefean ontynede[n], ond Crist stondeð[o] æt þam ærestan gete[p], ond ðe gelædeþ in[q] his neorxnawang.' Ond ða onsende Sanctus Mommos[r] his gast to Gode.

157. [a] .xvii.an B, seofonteoðan C; [b] om. C; [c-c] sancte mommes C; [d] .xii. B, twelf C; [e] geare C; [f] on C; [g] cessaria C; [h-h] on Capadocia C; [i] þa ðær C; [j] began C; [k] on C; [l-l] to unrym wyldra deora C; [m] lyfode C; [n] þæra C; [o] bec C; [p-p] wyldan deor ymb hyne utan C; [q-q] Alexander se refa het with ge suprascript Bb, het alexander se gerefa C; [r-r] to hym gelædan C, him togelædan Ko; [s] hi B, hyne C; [t] myd myd C; [u] fram C; [v] þam C; [w-w] se C; [x] om. C; [y] mommes C; [z] fram C; [a] fram C; [b-b] leo þæra C; [c-c] and þæra C; [d] þæra C; [e] fæla C; [f] on C; [g] om. C; [h] hwurfe se leo C; [i] n suprascript Bb; [j] heofenum C; [k] mommes C; [l] heofnas C; [m] syndon C; [n] ontyned C; [o] standeð C; [p] geate C; [q] on C; [r] mommes C.

18 August: Agapitus

158. On ðone eahtateoþan[a] dæg þæs monðes biþ ðæs martyres tid on Rome [b]Sancti Agapites[b], ðæs mæssesang mæg[c] gemetan se þe secð[d] on þam niwran[e 260] sacramentorum[f 261], þæt ys on ðam[g] mæssebocum.

158. [a] .xviii. B, eahtateoðan C; [b-b] sancte agapiti C; [c] man mæg C; [d] seceð C; [e] nywan C; [f] B, C, sacramentorium Herz; [g] þam nywan C.

and archangels are joyful there, and all saints rejoice there in St Mary. St Mary was sixty-four years old when she went to Christ. St Mary is the daughter-in-law of God the Father, and the mother of God's Son, and the mother-in-law of holy souls, and the noble queen of the heavenly citizens, who stands on the right side of the Father on high and the King on high.

17 August: Mamas

157. On the seventeenth day of the month is the feast of the holy boy St Mamas, who was a boy of twelve years when he fought for Christ; he lived in the city of Caesarea in the country of Cappadocia. When he saw devils worshipped there, he went into the thickest forest; and innumerable wild animals came to him there and adored him, and he lived off the milk of the wild animals. And when he read his book, the wild animals sat in a circle around him. The Alexander the governor ordered him to be summoned, and tried to force him away from Christianity with severe torture. When he was torturing him the hardest, a great lion arrived who had earlier been in the forest with the boy, and the lion said: 'Look, Mamas, you are our shepherd. I am now compelled by God's angels that I speak for you, against my nature.' And then the lion savaged so many of the pagans and the Jews who had abused him, that the blood ran from that place like a river. And then the boy ordered the lion that it should go back to its place. And then the judge ordered him to be stoned. Then a voice came from heaven and it said: 'Come Mamas, the heavens are opened to you with joy, and Christ stands at the first gate, and will lead you into his paradise.' And then St Mamas gave up the ghost to God.

18 August: Agapitus

158. On the eighteenth day of the month is the feast of the martyr St Agapitus in Rome, whose mass anyone can find who looks for it in the more recent sacramentaries, that is in the massbooks.

19 August: Magnus

159. On ðone nigonteoþan[a] dæg þæs monðes biþ þæs martyres tid Sancti Magni, ðæs sang[b] [262] biþ gemeted on þam yldran mæssebocum.

159. [a] .xviiii.an B, nygonteoðan C; [b] erasure before sang B, mæssesang C.

22 August: Symphorian

160. On þone [a]twa ond twentigoþan[a] dæg ðæs monþes biþ ðæs weres[263] tid Sancti Symforiani[b], se wæs [c]in Galwala[c] mægðe in[d] þære ceastre Augustodonensi[e]; se onfeng fulwihte þa[f] he wæs þri[g] geare cniht. Ða he wæs in[h] werlicre giuguþe[i], þa nydde hine Heraclius hæþen[j] ealdorman[264] þæt he weorðode deofolgyld. Ða cwæþ he: 'Ne do ic þæt, [k]forðon þe[k] þeos mennisce tyddernes[l] biþ[m] swa slidende swa glæs[n] þonne hit scinþ[o] ond þonne[265] tobersteð, ac[p] Godes wuldor nafaþ nægnigne[q] ende.' Ða bebead se ealdorman þæt hine mon[r] lædde to cwale. Þa clypode his modor[s] of [t]þam cesterwealle[t] ond cwæþ: '[u]Cild, cild[u][266], Simforiane[v], beo nu arod[w][267], ond ne ondræd [x]þe no[x] þone dead [y]se þe[y] gelædeþ to[z] life. Loca to þam ðe on heofonum[a] ricsaþ; ne biþ þe no[b] todæg lif afyrred, ac biþ [c]gewenden in[c][268] þæt betere. [d]Þu cild, todæg þu leorest[d] to þære [e]upplican eþelnesse[e].' Ða wæs he beheafdud[f] butan þam wealle. Ond he wes[g] on þam felda[h] bebyrged in[i] lytylre[j] cytan, ond hwæþre mid [k]heofonlicum mægnum[k] swa[l] gecyþed þæt þa hæþenan selfe[m] hæfdon his wundor on þære mæstan are.

160. [a-a] .xxii.an B, twa and twentygoðan C; [b] symphoriani C; [c-c] in galmala B with suprascript w Be, on galwala C; [d] on C; [e] agustodonensi C; [f] þa ða C; [g] þreo C; [h] on C; [i] iugoðe C; [j] suprascript se and a Be to read se hæþena; [k-k] forþam ðe C; [l] tyddernys C; [m] ys C; [n] þæt glæs C; [o] scyneð C; [p] and C; [q] nænigne C; [r] man C; [s] moder C; [t-t] þære ceastre wealle C; [u-u] cun cun C, with horizontal abbreviation marks above un in both words; [v] symphoriane C; [w] anræde C; [x-x] þu ðe na C; [y-y] se þe ðe C; [z] to ecum C; [a] heofenum C; [b] na C; [c-c] onwended on C; [d-d] todæg þu cund gewitest C; [e-e] uplican æðelnysse C; [f] beheafdod C; [g] wæs C; [h] feldan C; [i] on C; [j] lytelre C; [k-k] heofenlicum mægenum C; [l] wearð swa C; [m] sylfe C.

22 August: Timothy

161. On ðone ylcan dæg byþ ðæs halgan weres gemynd in[a] Rome Sancti Timothei, se com from[b] Antiochia þære ceastre to Rome, ond he lærde þær ðæt folc[c][269] Godes geleafan. Ða [d]Tarquinus, ðære burge gerefa, for þisum hine het[d] beheafdian[e], ond his lichama is bebyrged neah Sanctæ[f] Paules ciricean[g] þæs apostoles. Ond se burhgerefa[h] hraþe[i] æfter þam swealt[j] mid arlease deaðe.

161. [a] on C; [b] fram C; [c] folc to C; [d-d] het torquinus þære burge gerefa hyne for þysum C; [e] e suprascript Bb; [f] sancte C; [g] cyrcan C; [h] burge gerefa C; [i] raðe C; [j] sweolt C.

19 August: Magnus

159. On the nineteenth day of the month is the feast of the martyr St Magnus, whose mass can be found in the older massbooks.

22 August: Symphorian

160. On the twenty-second day of the month is the feast of the man St Symphorian, who lived in Gaul in the city of Augustodunum [i.e. Autun]; he received baptism when he was a boy of three years. When he had reached male maturity, Heraclius the pagan governor forced him to into devil-worship. Then he said: 'I will not do that, because this human fragility is as perishable as glass when it shines and then breaks, but God's glory has no end.' Then the governor ordered him to be led away to his execution. Then his mother called from the city wall and said: 'Child, child, Symphorian, be strong now, and do not fear the death which will lead to life. Look to him who reigns in heaven; today life will not be taken from you, but will be turned into a better one. Today you, child, will migrate to the heavenly nobility.' Then he was beheaded outside the city wall. And he was buried in the field in a little chapel, and yet was made famous with heavenly miracles in such a way that even the pagans had the greatest admiration for his miraculous deeds.

22 August: Timothy

161. On the same day is the commemoration of the holy man St Timothy in Rome, who came from the city of Antioch to Rome, and there he taught people the Christian religion. Then Tarquinius, the city governor, ordered him to be beheaded for this, and his body is buried near the church of St Paul the apostle. And the city governor shortly afterwards died a dishonourable death.

25 August: Bartholomew

162. On ðone ᵃfif ond twentigoþanᵃ dæg þæs monþes biþ þæs apostoles tid ᵇSancte Bartholomeusᵇ; se wæs Cristes ᶜærendwreca inᶜ Indiaᵈ mægþe, seo is ealra eorðena seo ytemyste, ond on oþre healfe ysᵉ þystre land, on oþre healfe se sæ Oceanum, þæt is garsecg²⁷⁰. Inᶠ þisse mægþe he towerpᵍ deofolgild ða þe hiʰ ær beeodon. Ond þær him com to Godes engel ond ætywde þære ðeode hwæt hyraⁱ god wæs þe hiʲ ær beeodon. He him ætywde micelne Sigelhearwanᵏ ²⁷¹, ðæmˡ wæs seo onsyn sweartre þonne hrum, ond se beard ond þæt feax him ᵐwæron oþᵐ þa fet siden, ond ða eagan wæron swylce fyren ireno, ᵖond <him>²⁷² sprungonᵖ spearcan of þam muðe, ond ful recq him eode of ðæmʳ næsþyrlumˢ, ond he hæfde fiþru swylce þyrnen besma, ond ða handa wæron ᵗgebunden tosomneᵗ mid fyrenum racentumᵘ, ond he hrymde grimlicre stefneᵛ ond ladlicreʷ ond fleah awegˣ ond nahwær siþþanʸ ætywde. Þæt wæs þæt deofol, þætᶻ seo þeod ᵃhyre æraᵃ for god beeodon, ond ᵇhi nemdon þoneᵇ Astaroþ. Ða onfeng ðære þeode kyningᶜ fulwihte ond his cwen, ond ealᵈ ðæt folc þe to his rice belompᵉ. Þa foronᶠ ða hæþnanᵍ bisceopas ond ðæt wregdon to ðæs kyningesʰ breþer; se wæs on oþrum kynericeⁱ, ond he wæs yldra ðonne he. Þa het se forþon Bartholomeus ðone Cristes þegen cwicne beflean. Ða com se gelyfeda kyningʲ mid micle folce ond genomᵏ his lichaman ond hine þanon alædde mid micleˡ wuldre, ond hine gesette ᵐin wundorliceᵐ micleⁿ cyrceano. Ond se cyngᵖ awedde se þe hineq cwellan het, ond ealle ða hæþenan bisceopas aweddanʳ ond swulton þa ðe inˢ þære lare wæron.

162. ᵃ⁻ᵃ .xxv.an B, fif and twentygoðan C; ᵇ⁻ᵇ sancti bartholomei C; ᶜ⁻ᶜ ærendraca on C; ᵈ ndia B with i suprascript, iudea C; ᵉ heo þecceð C; ᶠ on C; ᵍ towearp þa C; ʰ hig C; ⁱ se C; ʲ hig C; ᵏ silhearwan C; ˡ þam C; ᵐ⁻ᵐ wæs æt C; ⁿ syd C; ᵒ ysen C; ᵖ⁻ᵖ and hym sprungon C, ond him sprungon Herz, ond sprungon Ko; q riec C; ʳ þam C; ˢ suprascript o above æ Be; ᵗ⁻ᵗ gebundene togædere C; ᵘ racenteagum C; ᵛ stemne C; ʷ laðlicre C; ˣ onweg C; ʸ ne C; ᶻ þe C; ᵃ⁻ᵃ ær hyre C; ᵇ⁻ᵇ hig nemnað hyne C; ᶜ cyning C; ᵈ eall C; ᵉ belamp C; ᶠ ferdon C; ᵍ hæðenan C; ʰ cyninges C; ⁱ cyneryce C; ʲ cyning C; ᵏ genam C; ˡ mycele C; ᵐ⁻ᵐ on wuldorlice C; ⁿ mycele C; ᵒ cyrcan C; ᵖ cyning C; q hene B with suprascript i Bb; ʳ aweddon C; ˢ on C.

25 August: Genesius the Comedian

163. On ðone ylcan dæg bið þæs martyres tid Sancti Genesi, se wæs ærest sumes kaseresᵃ mima²⁷³, þæt is leasere²⁷⁴, ondᵇ sang beforan him scandlicuᶜ leoþ ond plegode scandliceᵈ plegan. Ða ᵉæt nihstanᵉ ᶠða onganᶠ he rædan ða godcundan gewritu ond onfeng fulwihte. Ða ongan se casere hine eft ðreatian to hæðengylde. Ða cwæþ he: 'Ic geseah, ða ic fulwihte onfeng, ðæt Godes engel stod ond hæfde on gewrite ealle ða synna ðe ic æfre ærᵍ geworhte. Heʰ þa ⁱaþwoh ða ealle ond adwæscte inⁱ þæs fulwihtes bæþeʲ.' Ða het se kasereᵏ hine forþonˡ beheafdian.

163. ᵃ caseres C; ᵇ he C; ᶜ sceandlice C; ᵈsceandlicne C; ᵉ⁻ᵉ ætnihstan Ko, æt nehstan C; ᶠ⁻ᶠ ongan C; ᵍ om. C; ʰ and he C; ⁱ⁻ⁱ ealle adwæscte on C; ʲ baðe C; ᵏ casere C; ˡ forþam C.

25 August: Bartholomew

162. On the twenty-fifth day of the month is the feast of the apostle St Bartholomew; he was Christ's missionary in the country of India, which is the outermost of all regions, on whose one side lies the dark land, on whose other side lies the world ocean [or 'Oceanus'], that is Garsecg. In this country he cast out idols which they had previously worshipped there. And an angel of God came to them there and revealed to the people what their god was, whom they had worshipped previously. He showed them an enormous Egyptian whose face was blacker than soot, and his beard and hair reached down to his feet, and his eyes were like hot irons, and sparks came from his mouth, and a foul stench came out of his nostrils, and he had wings like a thorny broom, and his hands were tied together with fiery chains, and he cried out with a terrible and loathsome voice and fled away and never appeared again anywhere. That was the devil, whom the people had earlier worshipped for themselves as a god, and they called him Astaroth. Then the king of that people received baptism and his queen too, and all the people who belonged to his kingdom. Then the pagan bishops went and complained about that to the king's brother; he was in another kingdom, and he was older than he was. He therefore ordered Bartholomew, the servant of Christ, to be flayed alive. Then the believing king came with many people and took his body and transported it away with great splendour, and put it in a fantastically large church. And the king became insane, who wanted him killed, and all the pagan bishops became insane and died, who had reported him.

25 August: Genesius the Comedian

163. On the same day is the feast of the martyr St Genesius, who was first some emperor's *mimus*, that is an actor, and sang disgusting songs before him and played disgusting plays. Then eventually, he then started to read spiritual literature and received baptism. Then the emperor wanted to force him back into pagan worship. Then he said: 'When I received baptism, I saw that God's angel stood and had in writing all the sins which I had ever committed previously. He then washed them all away and erased them with the water of baptism.' Then the emperor ordered him to be beheaded for that.

26 August: Irenaeus and Abundius

164. On ðone ᵃsex ond twentigoþanᵃ dæg ðæs monþes biþ þaraᵇ martyra tid þeᶜ seondonᵈ nemned Sanctus Heremusᵉ ²⁷⁵, se wæs cægbora²⁷⁶ inᶠ Rome, ond Sanctus Habundiusᵍ. Hiʰ atugon sumes haliges wifes lichomanⁱ ofʲ anum adolseaðe ond þoneᵏ arwyrðliceˡ bebyrgdonᵐ; ða het Ualerianus se refaⁿ hiᵒ forþon acwellan inᵖ þam ylcan adolseaþeᑫ.

164. ᵃ⁻ᵃ .xxui.an B, syx and twentygoðan C; ᵇ þæra C; ᶜ þa C; ᵈ syndon C; ᵉ herenius C; ᶠ on C; ᵍ abundius C; ʰ hig C; ⁱ homan B with lic suprascript Bb, lychaman C; ʲ up of C; ᵏ hyne C; ˡ arwurðlice C; ᵐ bebyrigdon C; ⁿ gerefa C; ᵒ hig C; ᵖ on C; ᑫ adelseaðe C.

27 August: Rufus

165. On ðone ᵃseofon ond twentigoþanᵃ dæg þæs monðes biþ ðæs martyres tid Sancti Rufiᵇ ²⁷⁷, ðæs mæsse biþ gemetedᶜ on ðam yldran mæssebocum.

165. ᵃ⁻ᵃ .xxvii.an B, seofon and twentygoðan C; ᵇ rufini C; ᶜ geseted C.

28 August: Hermes

166. On ðone ᵃeahta ond twentigoþanᵃ dæg þæs monþes biþ <ðæs>ᵇ²⁷⁸ miclanᶜ weres tid Sancti Hermes, se wæs Romeburge gerefa; þaᵈ ²⁷⁹ he gelyfde Godeᵉ þurh ðæs papan lare Alexandresᶠ. Þætᵍ gelomp ʰ ⁱðy þe þæsⁱ Hermes sunu ongan sweltan; þa lædde se fæder ʲond seo modor hineʲ ²⁸⁰ to eallum heoraᵏ godgeldumˡ ond bædon his lifes; þa wæs he þeahhwæþreᵐ dead. Ða cwæð þæs cnihtes fostormodorⁿ to þam fæder: 'Gyf þu læddeᵒ þinne sunu to Sancte Petres ciriceanᵖ to Alexandre ðam papan, þonne hæfdest þu hineᑫ gesundne.' Ðaʳ genam heo þaneˢ deadan cniht ond arn mid to þanᵗ papan, ond he hine awehteᵘ of deaðe. Ond Hermes þa sona onfeng fulwihteᵛ þy ærestan easterdæge ond his ðeowasʷ mid him, ˣond ða eallexˣ ærest gefreode; þaraʸ þeowa wæs ðusend ond twa hundᶻ ond fiftiᵃ. Ond for ðisum ᵇTraianus se kasere sende Aurelianum ðone gesiþᵇ to Rome ond hetᶜ beheafdian þisne Hermen. ᵈOnd his swustor bebyrgdeᵈ his lichomanᵉ on þæmᶠ wege þe æt Rome is nemned Salariaᵍ.

166. ᵃ⁻ᵃ .xxviii.an B, ehta and twentigoðan C; ᵇ om. B, Ko, þæs C, ðæs Herz; ᶜ mycelan C; ᵈ and þeah C; ᵉ on god C; ᶠ se wæs nemned sanctus alexander C; ᵍ and þæt C; ʰ gelamp C; ⁱ⁻ⁱ þæt þyses C; ʲ⁻ʲ hyne and seo moder C; ᵏ hyra C; ˡ deofolgylde C; ᵐ sona C; ⁿ fæder moder C; ᵒ læddest C; ᵖ circean C; ᑫ ðynne sunu C; ʳ suprascript Bb; ˢ þone C; ᵗ þam C; ᵘ aweahte C; ᵛ fullwihte C; ʷ s suprascript Bb; ˣ⁻ˣ þa he C; ʸ þæra C; ᶻ hundred C; ᵃ fiftig C; ᵇ⁻ᵇ aurelianus se gesyð þone traianus se casere sende C; ᶜ he het C; ᵈ⁻ᵈ þa bebyrgdon hig C; ᵉ lychaman C; ᶠ þam C; ᵍ salarie C.

28 August: Augustine of Hippo

167. On ðone ylcan dæg biþ ᵃSanctus Agustinusᵃ tid ðæs bisceopes ond þæs æþelan leorneres; se wæs on ᵇAfrica londeᵇ, ond he þær his dagas geendode, ond ᶜhe wæsᶜ

167. ᵃ⁻ᵃ sancte agustines C; ᵇ⁻ᵇ affrica lande C; ᶜ⁻ᶜ wæs C;

26 August: Irenaeus and Abundius

164. On the twenty-sixth day of the month is the feast of the martyrs who are called St Irenaeus, who was a key-bearer in Rome, and St Abundius. They pulled the body of a holy woman from a sewer and buried it honourably; then Valerianus the governor ordered them to be executed for that in the same sewer.

27 August: Rufus

165. On the twenty-seventh day of the month is the feast of St Rufus, whose mass can be found in the older massbooks.

28 August: Hermes

166. On the twenty-eighth day of the month is the feast of the great man St Hermes, who was a governor of the city of Rome; then he came to believe in God through the teaching of Pope Alexander. Then it so happened that Hermes's son became terminally ill; then the father and the mother took him to all their idols and pleaded for his life, but he nevertheless died. Then the boy's nurse said to the father: 'If you could take your son to St Peter's church to Pope Alexander, then you might get him back alive.' Then she took the dead boy and ran with him to the pope, and he revived him from death. And then Hermes immediately received baptism on Easter Sunday, and his domestic staff with him, and first released them all from servitude; there were 1250 servants. And because of this the emperor Trajan sent Aurelianus the reeve to Rome and ordered this Hermes to be beheaded. And his sister buried his body on the road which in Rome is called the Via Salaria.

28 August: Augustine of Hippo

167. On the same day is the feast of the bishop and noble scholar St Augustine; he lived in the province of Africa, and he ended his days there, and he was buried with

arwyrðlice[d] bebyrged in[e] Sardinia[f] ðære byrig[281]. Ac þa hergodon þa hæþnan[g 282] Sarcinware on þa stowe. Đa forðon[h] Leodbrond[i], Longbearda[j] kyning[k], mid micle[l] feo gebohte Agustinus[m] lichoman[n], ond hine gelædde in[o] Ticinan ða burh, ond hine þær gesette mid gelimplicre are.

[d] arweorðlice C; [e] on C; [f] sardina C; [g] hæðenan C; [h] forþam C; [i] leodbrand C; [j] langbeardena C; [k] cyning C; [l] mycele C; [m] þæs agustinus C; [n] lychaman C; [o] on C.

29 August: The Death of St John the Baptist

168. On ðone [a]nigon ond twentigoþan[a] dæg þæs monþes biþ Sanctus[b] Iohannes þrowung þæs miclan fulwihteres[c], ðone het Herodes beheafdian, forðon þe he him loh[d] þæt he hæfde his broþor wif him[e] to cifese, ond þæt heafod het beran on disce ond sellan[f] anre sealticgan[g] hire plegan to mede; ðæt wæs þære his cifese dohtor, ond seo modor hi[h] þæt [i]ær gelærde[i]. Forhwon[j] wolde se ælmihtiga God þæt Sanctus Iohannes, se wæs ealra manna se mæsta ond se halgosta[k] to Criste seluum[l], ond he wæs heafde becorfen for scandfulra[m] wifa bene, ond for <geglisces>[n 283] mægdenes[o] plegan, ond scondfulles[p] gebeorscypes hleahtre, ond for [q]drucenes[284] kyninges[q] wordum, buton efne forþon[r] God hine[s] forlet in[t] þisse nyþerlican worulde swa <forsewenlicne>[u 285] ond swa orwyrþlicne[v] deð[w 286] þrowian, ðæt he[x] hine wolde in[y] ðære hean worulde gelædan to þam wuldre [z]þær ænig[z 287] mon[a] ne mæg monum[b] areccan[c]? Forþon[d] Herodes het beran þæt heafod on þam dissce[e], forðam þe[f] wæs [g]kyninga dohtro[g 288] þeaw, ðonne[h] [i]hi plegodon[i] mid gyldenum applum[j] on selfrenum[k] disce.

168. [a-a] .xxviiii.an B, nygon and twentigoðan C; [b] sancti C; [c] fulluhtres C; [d] beleade C; [e] om. C; [f] syllan C; [g] hleapestran C; [h] hig C; [i-i] æror lærde C; [j] forhwam C; [k] halgesta C; [l] sylfum C; [m] sceandfulra C; [n] geonlices B, geglisces C; [o] mædenes C; [p] sceandfulles C; [q-q] druncenes cyninges C; [r] om. C; [s] he ne C; [t] on C; [u] forslegenlice B, forsewenlicne C; [v] arwyrðlicne C; [w] deað C; [x] suprascript Bc; [y] on C; [z-z] þe nænig C; [a] man C; [b] mannum C; [c] asecgan C; [d] forþam C; [e] disce C; [f] þæt C; [g-g] cyninga dohtor C; [h] þa hwyle þe C; [i-i] hig plegedon C; [j] æpplum C; [k] sylfrenum C.

29 August: Sabina

169. On þone ilcan dæg bið þære fæmnan tid Sancta[a] Sabine in[b] Rome, þære mæsse bið gemeted on þam niwran[c] bocum[289].

169. [a] suprascript Bc; [b] on C; [c] nywan C.

30 August: Felix of Thibiuca etc.

170. On þone þritigþan[a] dæg þæs monðes bið þæs bisceopes gemynd Sancti Felicis[b]; <he>[c] wæs in[d] ðære ceastre þe is nemned Tubsocensi[e]. Þa het Dioclitianus se kasere[f] þære ceastre gerefa<n>[g 290] þæt he genam on þam biscope[h] ealle[i] Godes bec ond forbærnde[j]. Þa nolde se bisceop ða bec syllan, ac[k] cwæþ: 'Selre is ðæt [l]man me[l]

170. [a] .xxx.an B, þrytegoðan C; [b] felices C; [c] erasure in B, he C; [d] on C; [e] tubocensi C; [f] casere C; [g] gerefa B, C, Ko, gerefan Herz; [h] bisceope C; [i] ealle þa C; [j] forbærnde hig C; [k] ac he C; [l-l] me man C;

great honours in the city of Sardinia. But then the pagan Saracens occupied that place. Then Liutprand, king of the Lombards, therefore bought Augustine's body for a large price, and transported it to the city of Ticinum [i.e. Pavia], and deposited it there with appropriate honour.

29 August: The Death of St John the Baptist

168. On the twenty-ninth day of the month is the passion of St John the great baptist, whom Herod ordered to be beheaded, because he had criticised him that he kept his brother's wife as a concubine for himself, and ordered his head brought in on a dish and given to a dancer as a reward for her performance; that was his concubine's daughter, and the mother had taught her that previously. Why did the almighty God want that St John, who was of all men the greatest and holiest after Christ himself, and he was beheaded at the behest of scandalous women and for a lascivious girl's dance and for a laugh at a disgusting feast, and at the command of a drunken king, except for that reason that God allowed him in this world below to suffer such a despicable and disgraceful death, that he wanted to lead him in the world above to the glory which one cannot explain to men? Therefore Herod ordered the head brought in on a dish, because it was the king's daughters' custom, when they played with golden apples on a silver dish.

29 August: Sabina

169. On the same day is the feast of the virgin St Sabina in Rome, whose mass can be found in the more recent books.

30 August: Felix of Thibiuca etc.

170. On the thirtieth day of the month is the commemoration of the bishop St Felix; he lived in the city which is called Thibiuca. Then the emperor Diocletian instructed the governor of the city that he should confiscate from the bishop and burn all of God's books. Then the bishop did not want to surrender his books, but said: 'It is

selfne[m] bærne þonne ða godcundan gewritu.' Þa het[n] se dema hine[o] to oþrum reþran[p] deman mid his preostum. Swa he wæs onsended on monige[q] healfe to missenlicum demum, ond æghwylc hine þreatode æfter ðam[r] Godes bocum, [s]oþ þæt[s] he [t]becom in[t] þa ceastre þe is nemned Uenusio, sio[u] is on þam lande Apuliae[v]. Þa þreatode þære burge[w] gerefa æfter[x] þam bocum. Þa cwæþ he: 'Ic hi[y] hæbbe, ac ic hi[z] nelle syllan.' Þa het se hine lædan to þære[a] beheafdunga[b] mid his preostum. On æfænne[c] hine man beheafdode, ond[d] on ða ilcan tid wæs se mona in[e] blod becyrred. His mæssepreost þreowude[f] mid him, þæs nama wæs[g] Ianuarius, ond his leorneras twegen, ða wæron nemnede[h] Furtunatus ond Septimus.

[m] sylfne C; [n] sende C; [o] ne suprascript Bb; [p] om. C; [q] manege C; [r] om. C; [s-s] oþþæt Ko; [t-t] com on C; [u] seo C; [v] apulie C; [w] ceastre C; [x] hyne æfter C; [y] hig C; [z] hig C; [a] om. C; [b] c suprascript Bb, beheafdunge C, beheafdun`c´ga Ko; [c] æfen C; [d] om. C; [e] on C; [f] þrowode C; [g] wæs sanctus C; [h] nemned C.

31 August: Aidan

171. On ðone [a]an ond þritigþan[a] dæg þæs monðes biþ Sancte Aidanis[b] geleornis[c] ðæs bisceopes, þæs saule[d] [e]geseah Sancte Cuthberhtus[e] on middeniht englas læddan[f] micle[g] leohte to heofonum[h]. Se bisceop wæs Scyttisc, ond Sancte Oswald[i] se halga cyning hine begeat[j] on þas ðeode[k]. Ond he dyde fela wundra, ge lifgende[l] ge geleored[m], ond his ban syndon [n]healfe on Scottum, healfe[n] on [o]<Sancte Cuðberhtes>[o] [291] mynstre.

171. [a-a] .xxxi. B, an and þrytygoðan C; [b] aidanes C; [c] gewytennys C; [d] sawle C; [e-e] sanctus cuthberhtus geseah C; [f] lædan C; [g] myd mycele C; [h] heofenum C; [i] oswold C; [j] beget C; [k] brytene C; [l] lyfigende C; [m] þa ða he wæs forðfaren wæs C; [n-n] helf on sceottum helf C; [o-o] Glæstingabyrig on Sancta Marian B, Ko, sancte cuðberhtes C, Herzfeld, p. 234.

The End of August

171a. Ðonne se monaþ biþ geendod þe we nemnaþ Weodmonaþ, þonne bið seo niht tyn[a] tida lang, ond se dæg feowertyne[b] tida.

171a. [a] .x. B, C; [b] .xiiii. B, C.

The Beginning of September

171b. On [a]ðæm nigoþan[a] monþe on geare biþ þritig[b] daga. Se monaþ[c] hatte on Leden Septembris, ond on ure geþeode Haligmonaþ[d], forþon þe ure yldran, [e]þa þa hie[e] hæþene wæron, on þam monþe hi[f] guldon hiora[g] deofolgeldum[h].

171b. [a-a] þam nygeðan C; [b] .xxx. B, C; [c] monoð C; [d] haligmonoð C; [e-e] þa hwyle hig C; [f] hig C; [g] hyra C; [h] deofolgildum C.

better that I myself should be burned than the religious texts.' Then the judge assigned him, with his priests, to another, harsher, judge. Thus he was sent here and there, to all sorts of judges, and each one threatened him about the pious books, until he came into the city called Venusia [i.e. Venosa], which is in the province of Apulia. Then the city's governor made threats about the books. Then he said: 'I have them, but I will not hand them over.' Then he ordered him to be led to his execution with his priests. In the evening he was beheaded, and at the same time the moon was changed to blood. His priest suffered with him, whose name was Januarius, and his two pupils, who were called Fortunatus and Septimus.

31 August: Aidan

171. On the thirty-first day of the month is the death of the bishop St Aidan, whose soul St Cuthbert, at midnight, saw angels lead to heaven with a great light. That bishop was a Gael, and St Oswald the saintly king brought him to this country. And he performed many miracles, both whilst living and whilst deceased, and his bones are partly with the Gaels, partly in St Cuthbert's monastery.

The End of August

171a. When the month which we call 'Weodmonaþ' ['Weed Month'] comes to an end, the night is ten hours long and the day fourteen hours.

The Beginning of September

171b. There are thirty days in the ninth month of the year. In Latin the month is called September, and in our language Haligmonaþ ['Holy Month'], because our ancestors, when they were pagans, they practised their devil-worship in that month.

1 September: Priscus

172. On ðone ærestan dæg ðæs monþes biþ þæs martyris[a] tid Sancti Prisci[b], ðæs mæsse biþ gemeted on þam yldran mæssebocum.

172. [a] martyres C; [b] prisce C.

2 September: Antoninus

173. On ðone æfteran dæg þæs monþes biþ ðæs halgan weres gemynd þæs nama is Sanctus Antonius, se wæs in[a] Assiria mægþe on þære ceastre Apameno. He wæs Cristen[b] læce ond he eardode in[c] hæþenra midlene[d], swa swa rose sio[e] wyrt biþ on þorna midlynæ[f], ond he lærde men geornlice to Godes geleafan. Da feodon[g] hine þa hæþnan[h] forþon[i], ond hine ofslogon ðær[j] [k]<he eode feor to gebede to sumere cyrcan>[k], ond tocurfon þone lichaman on[l] [m]manugu sticceo[m], ond awurpon in[n] þæt wæter þe þær fleow in[o] þa burh Apamenam[p]. Þa gesomnodon[q] ða [r]sticceo hi in[r] þa þruh [s]þurh þa ðe þæt wæter fleow[s]. Da ne [t]meahte þæt[t] wæter flowan, ond hwæþere[u] [v]þeah ne meahte[v] nænig mon[w] ðone lichoman[x] findan, [y]ær þon þe[y] comon twa [z]wif geleaffulle[z] ond hine atugon of þam wætere. Ond hine þa sum mæssepreost bebyrgde[a], ond syþðan wæron æt þam lichoman[b] swa micle[c] <wundor>[d], þæt þa þe hine cwealdon for þam wundrum wæron gecyrred to Godes geleafan.

173. [a] on C; [b] crystes C; [c] on C; [d] mydle C; [e] seo C; [f] mydle C; [g] laðetton C; [h] hæðenan C; [i] forþam C; [j] þar C; [k-k] om. B, he eode feor to gebede to sumere cyrcan C; [l] [n] suprascript Bb; [m-m] manegu sticcu C; [n] on C; [o] on C; [p] apameno C; [q] gesamnodon C; [r-r] sticcu hig on C; [s-s] þar þæt wæter fleow þurh C; [t-t] myhte þæt C; [u] hwæðre C; [v-v] ne myhte C; [w] man C; [x] lychaman C; [y-y] ær þam ðe C; [z-z] geleaffulle wif C; [a] bebyrigde C; [b] lychaman C; [c] mycel C; [d] om. B, wundor C.

3 September: Aristion, Paternianus and Felicianus

174, 175. On ðone þryddan dæg þæs monþes biþ þæs bisceopes tid Sancti Aristome, ond þara[a] martyra Sanctæ[b] Paterniane[c] ond [d]Sancti Feliciani[d].

174, 175. [a] þæra C; [b] sancti C; [c] patermane C; [d-d] sancte feliciane C.

4 September: Marcellus

176. On ðone feorþan[a] dæg þæs monþes biþ þæs martyres tid Sancti Marcelli; se becom on wege to[b] [c-c]Prisce þam[c] hæþnan[d] gerefan þær[e] he deofolgeldum[f] geald. Þa laþode[g] he hine to his symble; ða sæde Marcellus him þæt he wære Cristen ond him nære alyfed þæt he birgde[h] þara[i] hæþenra symbles[j]. Þa yrsede[k] Priscus se gerefa ond het adelfan seaþ[l] oþ gyrdyls[m] deopne, ond he bebead [n]þone Godes wer þæt mon hine bebyrgde[292] in þam seaðe[n] oþ þone gyrdels, þæt him lifiendum[o] [p]wære þæt to wite[p].

176. [a] .iiii. B, feorðan C; [b] on C; [c-c] priscum þone C; [d] hæðenan C; [e] þar C; [f] deofolgyldum C; [g] gelaðode C; [h] abyrigde C; [i] þæra C; [j] metes C; [k] yrsode wyð C; [l] anne seað C; [m] hys gyrdel C; [n-n] þæt mon þone godes wer on þam seaðe bebyrigde C; [o] lyfigendum C; [p-p] wære B with þæt to wite suprascript and leofre expunged, þæt wære to wite gesceapen C;

174

1 September: Priscus

172. On the first day of the month is the feast of the martyr St Priscus, whose mass can be found in the older massbooks.

2 September: Antoninus

173. On the second day of the month is the commemoration of the holy man whose name is St Antoninus, who lived in the province of Assyria in the city of Apamea. He was a Christian doctor and he lived in the midst of pagans, as the rose, the plant, grows in the midst of thorns, and he eagerly educated people to God's religion. Then the pagans hated him therefore, and killed him while he was walking far to a church for prayer, and cut the body up into many pieces, and threw [them] into the water which flowed there into the city of Apamea. Then the pieces gathered themselves together in the pipe through which the water flowed. Then the water could not flow and, even so, nobody could find the body, before two believing women came and pulled it from the water. And a priest buried it then, and such great miracles happened near the body afterwards, that those who had killed him became converted to Christianity because of the miracles.

3 September: Aristion, Paternianus, Felicianus

174, 175. On the third day of the month is the feast of the bishop St Aristion and of the martyrs St Paternianus and St Felicianus.

4 September: Marcellus

176. On the fourth day of the month is the feast of the martyr St Marcellus; travelling along he came across Priscus the pagan governor while he was practising devil-worship. Then he invited him to his feast; then Marcellus told him that he was a Christian and he was not allowed to try the food of the pagans. Then Priscus the governor became angry and ordered a deep pit to be dug up to belt height, and he ordered that one should bury the man of God in the pit up to his belt, so that, alive,

þæt þam forþweardan[q] men biþ to reste[r]. Ond he þa þurhwunode[s] [t]swa in[t] þam seaðe ðry dagas lifgende[u] in[v] Godes lofsongum[w], ond þa ageaf ðone clænan gast, ond [x]þæs lichaman insmoh[x] forlet monnum[y] to mundbyrde.[293] Se resteþ in[z] þære byrig Cabilonenti[a].

[q] forðfarenum C; [r] reste gesceapen C; [s] forð wunode C; [t-t] swa on C; [u] lyfigende C; [v] on C; [w] lofsangum C; [x-x] þone lychoman hys man C; [y] mannum C; [z] on C; [a] cabilomenti C.

5 September: Quintus

177. <O>n[a] ðone fiftan[b] dæg þæs monðes biþ ðæs[c] Godes andetteres[d] tid Sancti Quinti, þæs mæsse bið gemeted on þam yldrum[e] mæssebocum.

177. [a] initial om. B, on C; [b] .v.an B, fiftan C; [c] om. C; [d] andeteres C; [e] yldran C.

5 September: Bertinus

178. On[a] ðone ylcan dæg byþ ðæs halgan abbodes[b] geleornes[c] Berhtinus[d], [e]<se dyde manege wundru. And>[e][294] he gesenode[f] an wines ful[g] ond onsende[h] sumum mærum[i] were, se afeol[j] of his horse ofer stænene[k] eorþan, ond him wæron þa limo[l] gecnyssed[m] ond þæt þeoh forod. Ond sona swa he þæs wines onbyrgde[n], he wæs hal geworden. Ðises [o]arwurþan abbodes[o] [p]lichoma is geseted in þam mynstre Sithio. Ðone[p] lichoman[q] gesohte sum deaf man ond feþeleas. Ofer þone[r] man becom færinga godcund wracu, [s]forþam þe[s] he ficsode[t] on sunnanniht[u][295], þæt he seþþan[v] ne meahte[w] ne gehyran ne gangan. Ac he gecreap in[x] þæs eadgan[y] Berhtinus[z] ciricean[a] sume sunnanuhtan, þa ðær man rædde þa nigoþan[b] rædinge[c] [d]on Cristes godspelle[d]. Þa meahte[e] he gehyran ond gangan, ond he ferde bliþe tu[f] his huse.

178. [a] and on C; [b] abbudes C; [c] gewytennys C; [d] sancti bertines C; [e-e] om. B, se dyde manege wundru and C; [f] senade C; [g] full C; [h] gesende to C; [i] mæran C; [j] afeoll C; [k] stænenne C; [l] lymu C; [m] gecnysede C; [n] onbyrigde C; [o-o] arweorðan abbudes C; [p-p] om. C; [q] lychaman C; [r] þæne C; [s-s] forþon C; [t] fiscode C; [u] sunnandæg B with l niht suprascript Bb; [v] syððan C; [w] myhte C; [x] on C; [y] eadegan C; [z] bertines C; [a] cyrcan C; [b] nygeðan C; [c] rædan C; [d-d] crystes godspelles C; [e] myhte C; [f] to C.

7 September: Sinotus

179. On ðone seofoþan[a] dæg ðæs monþes biþ þæs martyres tid Sancti Synoti, þæs mæsse biþ gemeted on þam yldrum[b] mæssebocum.

179. [a] .vii. B, seofoðan C; [b] yldran C.

8 September: The Birth of St Mary

180. On ðone eahtoþan[a] dæg þæs monþes byþ Sancta Marian acennednes[b]. Hyre fæder wæs nemned Ioachim ond hire modor Anna, ond hi[c] wæron twentig[d] geara[e]

180. [a] .viii.an B, ehtoðan C; [b] acennednis C; [c] hig C; [d] .xx. B, C; [e] Herz, C, geare Ko;

he would have that punishment which the deceased have in their rest. And he then lasted like that in that pit for three days, alive, singing God's praise, and then gave up his chaste spirit, and abandoned the slough of the body as a protection for people. He rests in the city of Cabillonum [i.e. Chalon].

5 September: Quintus

177. On the fifth day of the month is the feast of God's confessor St Quintus, whose mass can be found in the older massbooks.

5 September: Bertinus

178. On the same day is the death of the holy abbot Bertinus, who performed many miracles. And he blessed a cup of wine and sent it to a famous man, who had fallen off his horse onto hard ground, and his limbs were bruised and his thigh broken. And as soon as he drank from the wine, he was healed. The body of this honourable abbot is deposited in the monastery of Sithiu. A deaf man who could not walk came to visit that body. Divine punishment had suddenly come over the man, because he had been fishing on a Sunday night, so that afterwards he was unable to hear or walk. But he crept into the church of the blessed Bertinus one Sunday morning, when the ninth lesson of Christ's gospel was being read. Then he could hear and walk, and went back to his house, happy.

7 September: Sinotus

179. On the seventh day of the month is the feast of the martyr St Sinotus, whose mass can be found in the older massbooks.

8 September: The Birth of St Mary

180. On the eighth day of the month is the birth of St Mary. Her father was called Joachim and her mother Anna, and they were together for twenty years before they

[f]somod ær þon[f] hi[g] bearn hæfdon. Þa wæron [h]swiþe unrote; þa oþywde[h] Godes engel hiora[i] ægðrum onsundrum[j] hine[k], ond him sæde ðæt hi[l] sceoldon <habban>[m 296] swylc bearn swylce næfre ær in[n] worold[o] come[p], ne [q]ær ne eft[q].[297] Ða æfter twentigum[r] gearum[s] cende Anna <dohtor>[t], ond hieo[u] nemde þa Maria[v]. Ond þa hio[w] wæs þreo[x] geara eald, ða [y]læddon hi fæder ond modor[y] to Hierusalem, ond [z]sealdon hi[z] þær in[a] þara[b] fæmnena gemænnesse[c] [d]<þe ðær on Godes huse lofsang dydon dæges ond nihtes>[d 298]. Þa wæs þæt[e] cild sona snotor ond anræde, ond swa fulfremed þæt nænig æþelicor[f] ne sang þone Godes lofsang; ond hio[g] wæs swa beorht on ansyne ond wliti[h] þæt [i]mon hyre[i] meahte[j] uneaþe onlocyan. Ond on hyre [k]mægdenhade hio[k] dyde fela[l] wundra on webgeweorce[m] ond oþrum[o] cræftum ðæs þe[p] þa yldran don ne meahton.

[f-f] ætgædere ær þam þe C; [g] hig C; [h-h] hig swyðe unrote forþon ac hym ætywde C; [i] hyra C; [j] onsundron C; [k] om. C; [l] hig C; [m] om. B, habban C; [n] on C; [o] woruld C; [p] ne com C; [q-q] næfre eft ne cymð C; [r] .xx. B, twentygum C; [s] geara C; [t] om. B, dohtor C; [u] heo C; [v] þæt cild incised supra; [w] heo C; [x] þreora C; [y-y] lædde hyre fæder and hyre moder hyg C; [z-z] hig sealdon C; [a] on C; [b] þare B with e expunged and a suprascript Bb, þæra C; [c] gemænnysse C; [d-d] om. B, þe ðær on Godes huse lofsang dydon dæges ond nihtes C, <þe ðær on Godes huse lofsang dydon dæges ond nihtes> Ko; [e] þæt ðær C; [f] æðelucur C; [g] heo C; [h] swa wlitig C; [i-i] hyre man C; [j] myhte C; [k-k] mædenhade heo C; [l] fæla C; [m] webgeworce C; [o] on oðrum C; [p] om. C.

8 September: Audomarus

181. On ðone ylcan dæg byþ þæs bisceopes geleorudnes[a] Sancti Audomari, se dyde [b]monig heofonlic[b] wundor ge lybbende[c] ge[d] unlybbende[e]. Þa he his gast asende[f], þa wæs in[g] þam huse wynsum stenc, swa hit wære mid eallum deorweorþum[h] wyrtum gefylled, [i]ond his[i] lichama resteð in[j] Sithio[k] þam mynstre[l]. Ond his wundra wæs sum ðæt sum mon[m] sealde oþrum scilling seolfres to borge. Þa onsoc[n] se oþer eft ond cwæþ þæt he him nan[o] feoh ne sealde. Ða cwæþ se þe ðæt seolfor ahte: 'Uton gangan to Audomares ciricean[p], ond me[q] þær [r]gecyþ mid aþe[r] þæt þu me her wiðsæcest[s].' Þa eodon hi[t] [u]oþ þæt[u] [v]hi gesawon[v] þa ciricean[w]. Ða cwæð se, [x]se þæs[x] feos manode: 'God biþ æghwær[y] ondweard[z]; swere[a] me[b] her þær wit standaþ.' Þa wolde he swerian; þa feol[c] he sona niþerweard on þa[d] eorþan ond him toburston ða eagan, ond he lifde[e] twegen dagas ofer þæt, oþrum monnum[f] to brogan, ond þy þryddan dæge he swealt[g] mid earmlicum[h] deaþe.

181. [a] gewytennys C; [b-b] mænig heofonlic C; [c] lyfigende C; [d] e suprascript Bb; [e] syððan he forðfaren wæs C; [f] osende C; [g] on C; [h] deorwyrðum C; [i-i] hys C; [j] on C; [k] scythio C; [l] mynstræ C; [m] man C; [n] ætsoc C; [o] nænig C; [p] cyrcan C; [q] þu me C; [r-r] myd aðe gecyð C; [s] wiðsæcst C; [t] hig C; [u-u] oþþæt Ko; [v-v] hi sawon B with ge suprascript Bb, hig gesawon C; [w] cyrcan C; [x-x] þe ðæs C; [y] æghwar C; [z] andweard C; [a] swera C; [b] om. C; [c] feoll C; [d] om. C; [e] lyfede C; [f] mannum C; [g] sweolt C; [h] earmlice C.

11 September: Protus and Hyacinth

182. On ðone endlyftan[a] dæg þæs monþes biþ ðara[b] haligra wera tid Sancti Proti ond Sancti Iacinthi[c]; þæt wæron Eugenian þegenas[d] ðære æþelan fæmnan, ond hio[e]

182. [a] .xi. B, endlyftan C; [b] þæra C; [c] iacincti C; [d] þegnas C; [e] hig C;

had a child. They were very sad; then God's angel appeared to each of them individually, and told them that they should [have] such a child as had never come into the world before, neither before nor since. Then after twenty years Anna gave birth to a daughter, and she named her Mary. And when she was three years old, her father and mother took her to Jerusalem, and handed her over to a community of virgins there who sang praise in God's house day and night. Then the child soon became wise and resolute, and so perfect that nobody sang God's praise more beautifully; and she was so striking and beautiful in appearance that one could hardly look at her. And during her girlhood she worked many miracles in weaving and other skills, which those older than her were not able to perform.

8 September: Audomarus

181. On the same day is the migration of the bishop St Audomarus, who performed many heavenly miracles both whilst alive and whilst dead. When he gave up the ghost, there was a wonderful smell in the house, as if it had been filled with all precious spices, and his body rests in the monastery of Sithiu. One of his miracles was that a man gave a silver shilling to another man as a loan. Then the other disputed that and said that he had not given him any money. Then the one who owned the silver said: 'Let us go to the church of St Audomarus, and confirm for me with an oath there that you disagree with me here.' Then they walked until they saw the church. Then the one who was claiming the money back said: 'God is present everywhere; swear to me here where we are standing.' Then he tried to swear. Then he suddenly dropped to the ground and his eyes popped out, and he lived for two more days beyond that, to the horror of the other people, and on the third day he died a miserable death.

11 September: Protus and Hyacinth

182. On the eleventh day of the month is the feast of the holy men St Protus and St Hyacinth; they were servants of Eugenia, the noble virgin, and they received

onfengon fulwihte mid hire. Ond þa on Galienus[f] dagum þæs kaseres[g] het Necetius[h], Romeburge gerefa, hi[i] lædan to Þures[j][299] deofulgeldum[k], ond het hi[l] þæt weorðian. Ða dydon hi[m] gebed to Drihtne; þa feol[n] þæt deofolgild to hyra fotum [o]ond wearþ eal tobrocen[o]. Þa het se refa[p] [q]hi forðæm[q] beheafdian, ond hi[r] wæron Cristes martyras gefremede[s].

[f] gallianus C; [g] caseres C; [h] necitius C; [i] hig C; [j] hys C; [k] deofolgyldum C; [l] hig C; [m] hig C; [n] gefeoll C; [o-o] om. C; [p] gerefa C; [q-q] forðon hig C; [r] hig C; [s] gefremode C.

14 September: Pope Cornelius etc.

183. On ðone feowerteoþan[a] dæg þæs monþes biþ ðæs bisceopes ðrowung Sancti Corneli in[b] Rome; ðone [c]nydde Decius se kasere[c] deofolgeld[d] to begangenne. Þa he þæt ne geþafode, þa het he hine lædan to beheafdunga[e]. Ða he þa læded wæs, þa gehælde he sumes cempan wif mid his gebede; seo wæs ær [f]fif gear[f] loma[g]. Þæs [h]cempan noma[h] wæs Cerealis[i], ond þæs wifes nama wæs Salustia[j]. Ond he[k] geþrowode martirdom[l] mid [m]an <ond> twentigum[m] mannum, ond se cempa mid [n]his wife[n].

183. [a] .xiiii. B, feowerteoðan C; [b] on C; [c-c] decius se casere nydde C; [d] deofolgyld C; [e] beheafdunge C; [f-f] lange C; [g] lama C; [h-h] cempa nama C; [i] cereiles C; [j] salusta C; [k] seo C; [l] martyrdom for cryste C; [m-m] an and twentigum C, an twentigum B, Ko; [n-n] hym and his wif C.

14 September: Cyprian

184. On ðone ylcan dæg biþ Sancte Ciprianes[a] tid þæs bisceopes[b], [c]se wæs in[c] Kartagine[d] þære ceastre, ond he þrowode martyrdom on Ualerianus[e] dagum þæs kaseres[f]. Galerius se aldorman[g], beforan him [h]he het arædan[h] þæs kaseres[i] dom þæt he sceolde deofolgeldum[j] geldan[k] oððe sweordes dom þrowian. Þa se dom aræded wæs, ða andswarode him Ciprianus ond cwæþ: 'Gode[l] þanc.'[300] Þa hine man lædde to þære stowe þe[m] hine man beheafdude[n], [o]ða gesomnode he[301] miclo mænigiu broþra[o] ond sweostra[p], ond wacedon beforan þam durum ðær[q] he inne wæs. Ða bebead he þæt mon[r] heolde his mædenu clæne. Ne gemde[s] he na swa swyðe hu he on morgenne[t] [u]aræfnede ðæs unhyran cwelres hand[u],[302] swa he [v]þæs gymde[v] hu he Godes ywde[w] gescylde oþ þone ytemystan[x] dæg his lifes. Þa on morgenne[y] [z]ða aræfnode[z] he þa beheafdunga[a], ond he het ðæm[b] cwelre syllan [c]fif ond twentig[c] gyldenra myneta. Ða[d] æfter feaum[e] dagum swealt[f] se ealdorman þe hyne martyrode.

184. [a] cyprianus C; [b] biscopes C; [c-c] on C; [d] cartagine C; [e] ualerianes C; [f] caseres C; [g] ealdorman C; [h-h] gerædde C; [i] caseres C; [j] deofolgyldum C; [k] offrian C; [l] deo gratias gode C; [m] þar C; [n] beheafdode C; [o-o] þa gesomnode mycel mænigeo þær gebroðra C, þa gesomnode miclo menigiu broðra He; [p] swustra C; [q] þar C; [r] man C; [s] gymde C; [t] morgene C; [u-u] aþolode þa unhyran flæsccwelnysse C; [v-v] gymde þæs C; [w] eowde C; [x] ytemestan C; [y] morgene C; [z-z] aðolode C; [a] beheafdunge C; [b] þam C; [c-c] .xxv. B, fif and twentig C; [d] and C; [e] feawum C; [f] þa swealt C.

baptism with her. And then in the days of the emperor Gallienus, the governor of the city of Rome Necitius ordered them to be led to the idol of Thunor, and ordered them to worship that. Then they said a prayer to the Lord; then the idol fell down to their feet and got smashed to pieces. Then the governor ordered them to be beheaded because of that, and they became martyrs of Christ.

14 September: Pope Cornelius etc.

183. On the fourteenth day of the month is the passion of the bishop St Cornelius in Rome; the emperor Decius forced him to practise devil-worship. When he refused, he ordered him to be taken off to be beheaded. When he was then being taken along, he healed the wife of a soldier with his prayer; she had previously been lame for five years. The soldier's name was Cerealis, and the woman's name was Salustia. And he suffered martyrdom with twenty-one men, and so did the soldier with his wife.

14 September: Cyprian

184. On the same day is the feast of the bishop St Cyprian, who lived in the city of Carthage, and he suffered martyrdom in the days of the emperor Valerian. The governor Galerius, he ordered the emperor's decree to be read out in front of him, that he should either practise devil-worship or suffer punishment by the sword. When the decree had been read out, Cyprianus answered him and said: 'Thanks be to God.' When he was led to the place of his beheading, he assembled a large group of brothers and sisters, and they kept watch outside the doors of where he was inside. Then he asked that his girls should be kept chaste. He did not care so much at all about how in the morning he would suffer death at the hand of the grim executioner, as he cared about how he might protect God's flock until the last day of his life. Then in the morning he suffered beheading, and he asked for twenty-five golden coins to be given to the executioner. Then after a few days the governor, who had executed him, died.

15 September: Valerian

185. On ðone fifteoþan[a] dæg þæs monþes bið [b]Sancti Ualerianys[b] þrowung ðæs martyres, þone <Priscus>[c] se refa[d] nydde from[e] Cristes geleafan. Ða he þam[f] wiþsoc, ða het he [g]mid sweorde hine slean[g]. Þa hine man to þære cwale lædde, ða geseah he mid his eagum openne[h] heofon, ond he geseah Crist sylfne him bringan wuldorbeah[303] ongean, ond he þa þy[i] unforhtlicor ðone[j] deaþ aræfnode[k].

185. [a] .xv. B, fifteoðan C; [b-b] sancte ua ualerianus C; [c] om. B, priscus C, Herz; [d] gerefa C; [e] myd wytum from C; [f] þan C; [g-g] hyne myd sweorde ofslean C; [h] n suprascript Bb; [i] þe C; [j] om. C; [k] aþolode C.

15 September: Mamilian

186. On ðone ylcan dæg bið ðæs halgan munecys[a] geleornes[b] ond þæs ancran Sancti[c] Mamiliani; se dyde manega[d] wundru, ond he[e] hælde untrume[f] men mid his gebedum. Ond he wæs swa gistliþe[g] þæt he for Godes lufon eode to reordum[h] mid þam tocumendum mannum. Þa tælde hine an oferhydig bisceop forþon, ond sende[i] his [j]twegen cempan[j] þæt ða sceoldon ðone ancran him [k]to gelædan[k], þæt he ongeate[l] hwylce [m]his ðeawas wæron[m]. Ða bæd he þa cempan þæt hi[n] for Godes lufon onfengon gereorde[o] mid him; geþafode[p] þæt oþer[q], oðer ðam wiþsoc, se wæs yldra ond oferhydygra. Ða hi[r] þa eodon on þone weg, ða ongan ðone oferhydygan þyrstan [s]on deaþ[s]. Ða feol[t] he to ðæs Godes þeowes fotum ond him bæd miltse. Ða geseah se Godes þeow wilde[u] hinde[304] melce[v]; þa gesenode he hi[w]. Ða gestod[x] heo, ond se[y] geþyrsta mon[z] [a]meolcode[a] ða hinde ond dranc þa meolc[b], ond his ðurst wæs geliþad[c]. Ða [d]<forhtodon þa>[d] lattowas[e] swiðe[f] for ða<m>[g] wundrum. Þa he[h] com to þam oferhydigan bisceope, þa wæs ðær broht [i]to fulwihte niwan acenned cild[i]. Þa het se bisceop hine [j]fullian þæt cild[j]. Þa cwæþ he: 'Hwæs sunu is hit[j]?' Þa cwæþ se bisceop: 'Mines hereteman[k].' Þa locode Sanctus Mamilium[l] on þæt cild ond cwæþ: 'Saga me[m] hwa þin fæder sy[n].' Ða cwæþ þæt cild: 'Þes bisceop þe her stent[o].' Ða gerehte þæt cild beforan þam bisceope Sancti Mamiliani hu hit wæs gestryned ðurh ðæs bisceopes unrihtæmed. Ða gefullu<de he>[p] ðæt cild, ond þa demde he ðam bisceope[q] for his dyrnum geligrum[r], se ðohte ær þæt he sceolde him deman, [s]forþon þe[s] he for Godes lufon æt mid geswencedum[t] monnum[u].

186. [a] muneces C; [b] gewytennys C; [c] om. C; [d] manege C; [e] om. C; [f] manige untrume C; [g] cumlyðe C; [h] gereordum C; [i] onsende C; [j-j] ærendracan Ko; [k-k] togelædan Ko; [l] ongete C; [m-m] þeawa he hæfde C; [n] hig C; [o] gereorda C; [p] Ða geþafode C; [q] hyra oðer and se C; [r] hig C; [s-s] oð dead C; [t] feoll C; [u] an suprascript before wilde Bf, ane wylde C; [v] and seo wæs melc C; [w] hig C; [x] ætstod C; [y] suprascript Bb; [z] man C; [a] e suprascript Bb; [b-b] hig melcode and ondranc þære meoloce C; [c] gelyðegod C; [d-d] om. B, forhtodon þa C; [e] latteowas C; [f] followed by wundroda suprascript Bf; [g] ða B, þam C; [h] he þa C; [i-i] an cyld þæt wæs nywan acenned to fullianne C; [j-j] hyt fullian C; [k] heretyman C; [l] mamilius C; [m] om. C; [n] sig C; [o] bigstandeð C; [p] gefullue B, gefullode he C; [q] o suprascript Bc; [r] geligerum C; [s-s] forþam þe C; [t] geswenctum C; [u] mannum C.

15 September: Valerian

185. On the fifteenth day of the month is the passion of the martyr St Valerian, whom the governor Priscus tried to force away from Christ's faith. When he resisted him, he ordered him to be killed with the sword. When he was led to his execution, he saw with his eyes the open heaven, and he saw Christ himself bring him a crown of glory, and because of that he then suffered death even more fearlessly.

15 September: Mamilian

186. On the same day is the death of the holy monk and hermit St Mamilian; he performed many miracles, and he healed sick people with his prayers. And he was so hospitable that for the love of God he had his meals with any visitors who happened to be there. Then an arrogant bishop criticised him for that, and sent his two soldiers to escort the hermit to him, so that he might find out what he was doing. Then he asked the soldiers that they should for the love of God share a meal with him; one of them accepted, the other, who was older and more arrogant, declined. When they then set off on their way, the arrogant one began to die of thirst. He collapsed at the feet of the servant of God and begged him for mercy. Then the servant of God saw a wild hind who was in milk. Then he blessed her. Then she stood still, and the thirsty man milked the hind and drank the milk, and his thirst was quenched. Then the messengers were very afraid because of the miracle. When he came to the arrogant bishop, a newborn baby was brought in to be baptised. Then the bishop asked him to baptise the child. Then he said: 'Whose son is it?' Then the bishop said: 'My prefect's.' Then St Mamilian looked at the child and said: 'Tell me who your father is.' Then the child said: 'This bishop who is standing here.' Then in front of the bishop the child explained to St Mamilian how it had been conceived through the bishop's illicit sex. Then he baptised the child, and he condemned the bishop for his surreptitious fornications, who had earlier wanted to condemn him because he ate with troubled people for the love of God.

16 September: Euphemia

187. On ðone sexteoþan[a] dæg þæs monþes bið [b]<þære fæmnan>[b] ðrowung Sancta Eufemia, seo ðrowode[c] mærne martyrdom for Criste in[d] Calcidonia þære[e] ceastre on[f] Dioclitianus dagum þæs kaseres[g]. Priscus se [h]ealdormon geresde on[h] þa fæmnan [i]in cristenmonna[i] midle swa wullf[j] [k]geræsed[305] on[k] sceap on [l]miclum ewede[l], ond he nydde hi[m] þæt heo Criste wiðsoce. Þa heo þæt ne geþafode, ða het hi[n][306] weorpan in[o] byrnendne[p] ofen. Ða cwæþ þara[q] ðegna sum, se wæs on naman Sustenis: 'Ær ic me sylfne ofslea mid [r]mine sweorde[r], ær þon ic [s]sende mine hond[s] on þas fæmnan. Ic geseo [t]beort werod[t] mid hire.' Ða ongyrde[u] oþer þegn[v] þa fæmnan, se wæs on noman[w] Uictor. Ða cwæþ se: 'Eala[x], ealdormon[y], ðis me is hefi[z] to donne. Ic geseo [a]fægere weras[a] stondan[b] in[c] ðisses[d] ofnes muþe[e], þa tostre<d>að[f] þone lig þæt he ne mæg na sceðpan þisse fæmnan.' Þa genamon oþre twegen þa fæmnan ond wurpon[g] in[h] ðone ofn[i]; þa eode se lig of þam ofne ond forbærnde hi[j] begen, ond [k]hire he ne scepede[k]. Þisse fæmnan [l]lichoma restet[l] neah Calcidonia þære ceastre, ond[m] ure [n]fædras hi[n] nemdon þa sigefæstan fæmnan.

187. [a] .xvi.an B, syxteoðan C; [b-b] þara fæmnen with a erased after second n B, þære fæmnan C; [c] þrowude C; [d] on C; [e] om. C; [f] and on C; [g] caseres C; [h-h] ealdormon geresde B with on suprascript Bc, ealdorman geræsde C; [i-i] on cristenra manna C; [j] wulf C; [k-k] geræsed B with on suprascript Bc, geræseð C; [l-l] mycelre eowde C; [m] hig C; [n] he hig C; [o] byrnendne B, C, Herz, byrnende Ko; [q] þæra C; [r-r] mynum sweorde C; [s-s] myne hand sende C; [t-t] beorht wered C; [u] ungyrde C; [v] þegen C; [w] naman C; [x] om. C; [y] ealdorman C; [z] hefig C; [a-a] fæger werod C; [b] standan C; [c] on C; [d] þyses C; [e] dura C; [f] one letter erased after e in B, tostredað C; [g] weorpon C; [h] on C; [i] ofen C; [j] hig C; [k-k] he hyre na ne gesceðde C; [l-l] lichama resteð C; [m] iu C; [n-n] fæderas hig C.

19 September: Januarius etc.

188. On ðone nigonteoþan[a] dæg þæs monþes bið þæs bisceopes gemynd Sancti[b] Ianuari[c], se þrowode martyrdom for Criste in[d] ðære ceastre Beneuentum, ond his deaconas[e] mid him, þa wæron on noman[f] Sanctus Festus ond Sanctus Desiderius.

188. [a] .xviiii.an B, nygonteoðan C; [b] sancte C; [c] iunuarii C; [d] on C; [e] diaconas C; [f] naman C.

20 September: Fausta and Evilasius

189. On þone twentigoþan[a] dæg þæs monþes bið þære fæmnan gemynd Sancta Fausta ond Sancti Efilasi, þæt wæs se gerefa se þe <beheold>[b][307] þa witu [c]þa se[c] casere het don þære halgan fæmnan Faustan. Þa gelyfde he Gode[d] for þam wundrum [e]ða he þa[e] geseah æt hire[f], ond he ða geþrowode martyrdom mid hire.

189. [a] .xx. B, twentigoðan C; [b] gegeold B, with h suprascript above eo, beheold C, ge<he>old Ko, geheold Herz; [c-c] þa ðe se C; [d] on god C; [e-e] þe he C; [f] suprascript Bc.

184

16 September: Euphemia

187. On the sixteenth day of the month is the passion of the virgin St Euphemia, who suffered a famous martyrdom for Christ in the city of Chalcedon in the days of the emperor Diocletian. The governor Priscus pounced on the virgin in the midst of the Christians as a wolf pounces on a sheep in a large flock, and he threatened her so that she might renounce Christ. When she refused, he ordered her to be thrown into a hot furnace. Then one of the servants, who was called Sostenes, said: 'First I would kill myself with my sword, before I lay my hand on this virgin. I can see a shining host with her.' Then a second soldier, who was called Victor, ungirded the virgin. Then he said: 'O governor, this is difficult for me to do. I can see beautiful men standing at the door of this furnace, who are dispersing the flame so that it cannot harm this virgin.' Then two others took the virgin and threw her into the furnace; then the flame came from the oven and consumed both of them and it did not harm her. The body of this virgin rests near the city of Chalcedon, and our forefathers called her the victorious virgin.

19 September: Januarius etc.

188. On the nineteenth day of the month is the commemoration of the bishop St Januarius, who suffered martyrdom for Christ in the city of Beneuentum, and his deacons with him, who were called St Festus and St Desiderius.

20 September: Fausta and Evilasius

189. On the twentieth day of the month is the commemoration of the virgin St Fausta and St Evilasius; that was the governor who watched the tortures which the emperor ordered to be inflicted on the holy virgin Fausta. Then he believed in God because of the miracles which he saw in her, and he then suffered martyrdom with her.

21 September: Matthew

190. On ðone ᵃan ond twentigoþanᵃ dæg þæs monþes bið þæs apostoles tid Sanctus Matheus, se wæs ærest mid Iudeum theloniariusᵇ, þæt is gafoles moniendᶜ ondᵈ wicgerefa. Acᵉ Crist hine ceasᶠ him to þegeneᵍ, ond he wrat ealra mannaʰ ærest Cristes godspel mid Iudeum. Ond æfter Cristes upastignesseⁱ he gelærde twuaʲ mægþa to Godes geleafan, Macedonianᵏ þa mægðe ond Sigelwara mægðe. Ond of Sigalwar<um>ˡ he flymdeᵐ tw<e>genⁿ dryas ða þarᵒ worhton micel scinlac mid twam dracum. Ond he awehteᵖ hira cyninges sunu of deaþe, ond þone cyning gefulwadeq þæs nama wæs Eilippus, ond his quene r nomaˢ wæs Eufenisse. Ac hwæðretᵗ oþer kyningᵘ wæs æfter þam, se wæs on naman Hirtacus. He het þisne Matheum hindanᵛ mid sweorde þurstinganʷ, þærˣ he stod ætforan Godes weofode ʸin gebede, forðæm þeʸ he ᶻne moste ane Godes fæmnan, þæt wæs an nunne, him to wife onfonᶻ. Ac Matheus him sægdeᵃ þæt he wære swa synnig wið God, gif he ða gehalgodan fæmnan to legerteame onfenge, swa se ðeow wære se ðe fenge on ᵇkyninges queneᵇ to ᶜunryhtum hæmdeᶜ. Ond ða sona æfter Matheus þrowunge þa forbornᵈ ðæs cyninges heall mid eallum his spedum, ond his sunu awedde, ond he sylf ahreofode ᵉond tobærstᵉ mid wundum fromᶠ ðam heafde oð ða fet. Ond he asette his sweord upweard, ond ða hyne sylfne ofstangᵍ. Sanctus Matheus lichomaʰ resteð on Parthoraⁱ muntum ond bideð þære toweardan æriste.

190. ᵃ⁻ᵃ .xxi. B, an and twentigoðan C; ᵇ tweloniarius C; ᶜ maniend C; ᵈ and þæt ys C; ᵉ c suprascript Bc; ᶠ geceas C; ᵍ þegne C; ʰ n suprascript Bc; ⁱ upastigenysse C; ʲ twa C; ᵏ macedonia C; ˡ sigalwara B, first a altered from e, final a expunged with suprascript v, with abbreviation mark above, sigelwarum C; ᵐ aflymde C; ⁿ twgen B, twegen C; ᵒ ðær C; ᵖ aweahte C; q gefullode C; ʳ cwene C; ˢ hyre nama C; ᵗ om. C; ᵘ cyning C; ᵛ om. C; ʷ þurhstingan C; ˣ þar C; ʸ⁻ʸ forþon ðe C; ᶻ⁻ᶻ sceolde onfon anre godes fæmnan þæt wæs an nunne hym to wife C; ᵃ sæde C; ᵇ⁻ᵇ cyninges cwene C; ᶜ⁻ᶜ unrihthæmede C; ᵈ forbarn C; ᵉ⁻ᵉ om. C; ᶠ fram C; ᵍ myd ofstang C; ʰ lychama C; ⁱ parþora C.

22 September: Maurice and the Theban Legion

191. On ðone ᵃtwa ond twentigoþanᵃ dæg þæs monðes bið Sancti Maurices ðrowung ond ᵇsex þusyndoᵇ martyra mid him ond ᶜsex hundᶜ; þæt wæs cempena werod; þa comon of eastdæle of Campodociaᵈ ³⁰⁸ mægðe ðam casere to fultume Maximianeᵉ, ond hieᶠ wæron swiðe sigefæste weras inᵍ eallum gefeohtum. Ac ða onfandʰ se casere ⁱæt nehstanⁱ þæt hieʲ wæron Cristene; ða hetᵏ hyˡ ³⁰⁹ gemartyrian þæt heoraᵐ þæt haligeⁿ blod ornᵒ æfterᵖ eorðan swa swa flod. Nyton we qheora nomenaq naʳ ma þonne Sanctus Mauricius, se wæs ðæs werodes ealdormanˢ, ond Sanctus Exupriusᵗ ond Sanctus Candidus. Þaᵘ oðra nomanᵛ syndon awriteneʷ on heofenum on lifes bocum.

191. ᵃ⁻ᵃ .xxii. B, twa and twentygoðan C; ᵇ⁻ᵇ .vi. þusyndo B, syx þusenda C; ᶜ⁻ᶜ vi. hund B, eac syx hundred C; ᵈ cappadocia C; ᵉ sende se wæs maximianus haten C; ᶠ hig C; ᵍ on C; ʰ onfunde C; ⁱ⁻ⁱ ætnehstan Ko; ʲ hig C; ᵏ het he C; ˡ hig C; ᵐ hyra C; ⁿ gehalgode C; ᵒ arn C; ᵖ ofer C; q-q hyra namena C; ʳ om. C; ˢ ealdor C; ᵗ exsuperius C; ᵘ þæra C; ᵛ naman C; ʷ awriten C.

21 September: Matthew

190. On the twenty-first day of the month is the feast of the apostle St Matthew, who was first a *telonarius* among the Jews, that is a tax collector and town official. But Christ chose him as a follower, and he was the first of all men to write Christ's gospel among the Jews. And after Christ's resurrection he converted two nations to Christianity, the Macedonians and the Ethiopians. And he banished two sorcerers from Ethiopia who practised much witchcraft there with two dragons. And he revived their king's son from death, and baptised the king whose name was Eglippus, and his queen's name was Ephinissa. But another king came after him, whose name was Hyrtacus. He ordered this Matthew to be stabbed from behind with a sword, while he stood in front of God's altar in prayer, because he had not been allowed to marry one of God's virgins, who was a nun. But Matthew had told him that he would be as sinful towards God if he had a consecrated virgin in his bed, as the servant would be who gets involved with the king's consort for illicit sex. And then soon after Matthew's martyrdom the king's residence burnt down with all his riches, and his son became insane, and he himself became all scabby and burst out in sores from head to foot. And he turned his sword upwards, and then stabbed himself. St Matthew's body rests in the Parthian mountains and is waiting for the future resurrection.

22 September: Maurice and the Theban Legion

191. On the twenty-second day of the month is the passion of St Maurice and of 6600 martyrs with him; that was an army of soldiers; they came from the eastern parts of Cappadocia to the aid of the emperor Maximian, and they were very successful men in all battles. But then eventually the emperor noticed that they were Christians; then he ordered them to be martyred, so that their sacred blood flowed across the ground like a stream. We do not know their names except for that of St Maurice, who was the army's leader, and St Exsuperius and St Candidus. The other names are written down in heaven in the books of life.

23 September: Sosius

192. On ðone ᵃþreo ond twentigoþanᵃ dæg þæs monðes bið ðæs diacones gemynd ᵇse is nemnedᵇ Sancti Sossy. He wæs inᶜ ðære ceastre Meselana, ond sume dæge þa he rædde godspellᵈ æt mæssan, ða scanᵉ him heofonlic leoht ymb ðæt heafod. Ða cwæð se biscopᶠ se ðe his lareow wæs: 'Ne bið þes diacon ᵍnoht longeᵍ mid us, ac he sceal beon mid Criste.' Ond þaʰ æfter feawaⁱ dagum ða endodeʲ he his lif þurh martyrhad for Criste.

192. ᵃ⁻ᵃ .xxiii. B, þreo and twentygoðan C; ᵇ⁻ᵇ om. C; ᶜ on C; ᵈ godspel C; ᵉ scean C; ᶠ bysceop C; ᵍ⁻ᵍ naht lange C; ʰ þa ðæs C; ⁱ feawum C; ʲ geendode C.

23 September: Thecla

193. On ðone ilcan dæge bið Sancteᵃ Teclan tid þære halgan fæmnan, seo wæs inᵇ ðære ceastre Ioconioᶜ, ond heo wæs ðær beweddedoᵈ æðelum brydguman. Ða gehyrde heo Paules lare ðæs apostoles, ða gelyfde heo Godeᵉ ond awunode inᶠ hyre mægðhade, ond forðon heo arefndeᵍ moneguʰ witu. ⁱHy monⁱ wearp inʲ byrnende fyr, ond hioᵏ nolde byrnanˡ. Ond ᵐhy monᵐ sende ⁿin wildranⁿ deora menigoᵒ, ᵖin leonaᵖond ᑫin berenaᑫ, ond ða hieʳ noldon slitan. ˢHy monˢ wearp inᵗ sædeora seað, ond þa hyreᵘ ne sceðedonᵛ. ʷHy monʷ band on wilde fearras, ond ða hyre ne geegledonˣ. Ond ða ʸæt neahstanʸ heo scear hyre feax swa swa weras ᶻond gegyrede hy mid weres hrægleᶻ ond ferde mid Paulumᵃ þam Godes ærendracan. Tecle wæs swa myhtiguᵇ fæmne þæt heo geðingode to Gode sumreᶜ hæðenre fæmnan gæsteᵈ hwylcehweguᵉ ræsteᶠ inᵍ ðære æcanʰ worulde.

193. ᵃ sancta C; ᵇ on C; ᶜ iaconia C; ᵈ beweddod C; ᵉ on god C; ᶠ on C; ᵍ þolode C; ʰ manege C; ⁱ⁻ⁱ hig man C; ʲ on C; ᵏ þæt hig C; ˡ bærnan C; ᵐ⁻ᵐ hig man C; ⁿ⁻ⁿ on wyldra C; ᵒ mænigeo C; ᵖ⁻ᵖ on leon C; ᑫ⁻ᑫ on berena C; ʳ hig C; ˢ⁻ˢ hig man C; ᵗ on C; ᵘ hig C; ᵛ sceððedon C; ʷ⁻ʷ hig man C; ˣ eglodon C; ʸ⁻ʸ ætneahstan Ko, æt nyhstan C; ᶻ⁻ᶻ om. C; ᵃ paule C; ᵇ myhtig C; ᶜ sumere C; ᵈ gaste C; ᵉ healice C; ᶠ reste C; ᵍ on C; ʰ ecan C.

24 September: The Conception of St John the Baptist

194. On ðone ᵃfeower ond twentigoþanᵃ dæg þæs monðes bið Sancti Iohannis geeacnung þæs ᵇmiclan fulwihteresᵇ. Ðyᶜ dæge Gabriel se heahengel æteowdeᵈ Zacharie, Iohannisᵉ fæder, þær he stod æt ᶠðam weofodeᶠ ond ricels ᵍbærndeᵍ inᵍ Godes ansægdnesseʰ, ond him sægdeⁱ þæt him scoldeʲ beon ᵏ<sunu acenned, and þæs nama sceolde>ᵏ Iohannis gecigged ˡ.³¹⁰ Þa nolde Zacharias ðam engle gelyfan ᵐ<þæt hym>ᵐ ond his wife on ⁿheora yldo meahteⁿ beon sunu acenned. Þa cwæð se engel to him: 'Ðu bist dumbᵒ ᵖoð þone dæg ðe þis biðᵖ.'³¹¹ Ond hit ða wæs swa geworden.

194. ᵃ⁻ᵃ .xxiiii. B, feower and twentigoðan C; ᵇ⁻ᵇ mycelan fulluhteres C; ᶜ on þam C; ᵈ ætywde C; ᵉ iohannes C; ᶠ⁻ᶠ gebede C; ᵍ⁻ᵍ berende and C; ʰ onsægednysse C; ⁱ sæde C; ʲ sceolde C; ᵏ⁻ᵏ om. B, sunu acenned and þæs nama sceolde C; ˡ geciged C; ᵐ⁻ᵐ om. B, þæt hym C; ⁿ⁻ⁿ hyra ylde myhte C; ᵒ dum C; ᵖ⁻ᵖ oððæt ðe þis bið Ko, om. C.

23 September: Sosius

192. On the twenty-third day of the month is the commemoration of the deacon who is called St Sosius. He lived in the city of Misenum, and one day, when he was reading the gospel during mass, a heavenly light shone around his head. Then the bishop, who was his teacher, said: 'This deacon will not be with us for long, but he shall be with Christ.' And then after a few days he ended his life through martyrdom for Christ.

23 September: Thecla

193. On the same day is the feast of the holy virgin St Thecla, who lived in the city of Iconium, and she was there betrothed to a noble bridegroom. When she heard the teaching of Paul the apostle, she believed in God and remained in her virginity, and for that reason she suffered many torments. She was thrown into a burning fire, and she would not burn. And she was thrown to a horde of wild animals, to lions and to bears, and they would not tear her to pieces. She was thrown into a pit of sea animals, and they did not harm her. She was tied to wild bulls, and they did not harm her. And then eventually she cut her hair like men and dressed herself in man's clothing and went with Paul, God's messenger. Thecla was such an influential virgin that she interceded with God for some rest in the eternal world for a good pagan woman's soul.

24 September: The Conception of St John the Baptist

194. On the twenty-fourth day of the month is the conception of the great baptist St John. On that day the archangel Gabriel appeared to Zachary, John's father, while he stood at the altar and burned incense in an offering to God, and told him that a son would be born to him, and that his name should be John. Then Zachary did not want to believe the angel, that he and his wife would have a son at their old age. Then the angel said to him: 'You shall be dumb until the day when this will happen.' And that is how it turned out.

24 September: Andochius, Thyrsus and Felix

195. On ðone ilcan dæg bið þara[a] haligra wera tid Sancti Andochi [b]þæs mæssepreostes[b] ond Sancti Tirsi[c] þæs diacones; ða comon of eastdæle in[d] Galwala[e] mægðe ond þær [f]monige men[f] þur[g] fulwiht gelærdon to Cristes geleafan, ond ðær geþrowodon[h] martyrdom for Godes naman on Aurelianus dagum þæs caseres, ond sum [i]cepemon Cristen[i] mid him ðæs nama wæs Felix. Æryst[j] se casere him bead gold ond seolfor [k]wið ðon[k] ðe hy[l] forleton Cristes geleafan; ða noldon hy[m] ðæt. Ða het he [n]<hig weorpan on byrnende fyr, and hym þæt ne onhran. Þa het he>[n] mid stengum heora[o] sweoran forslean. Ða [p]leordon þa[p] gastas to ecum gefean, ond æt [q]heora lichoman[q] wæron monug[r] wundru gewordenu[s].

195. [a] þæra C; [b-b] om. C; [c] tirsi B with y suprascript Bd, tiersi C, T'y'rsi Ko; [d] on C; [e] gealwala C; [f-f] mænigne æðelne man C; [g] þurh C; [h] geþrowedon C; [i-i] cepman C; [j] ærest C; [k-k] wiððon Ko; [l] hig C; [m] hig C; [n-n] om. B, hig weorpan on byrnende fyr and hym þæt ne onhran þa het he> C; [o] hym þa C; [p-p] foron hyra C; [q-q] hyra lychaman C; [r] manege C; [s] om. C.

25 September: Ceolfrith

196. On ðone [a]fif ond twentigoþan[a] dæg þæs monðes bið ðæs [b]halgan weres gemind[b 312] se wæs on ðisse Brytene, ond he wæs nemned Ceolfrið[c]. He wæs sumes haliges mynstres abbod[d] be norðan gemære þæt wæs gehalgod Sancte Petre; ond ða on his yldo[e] ongan he feran to Rome. Ond þrim dagum [f]ær ðon þe[f] he ferde, he sægde[g] his siðfæt ðæs mynstres broðrum. Ond siððan he on siðe wæs, he asong[h] [i]ælce dæge[i] tuwa his saltere ond his mæssan butan[j] ðam[k] anum dæge ðe he on sæ wæs, ond þrim dagum ær his endedæge. He wæs on [l]feower ond hundseofontig[l] geara þa he forðferde. Æfter hundteontegum[m] daga[n] ond feowertynum[o] þæs ðe he of his mynstre ferde, he geleorde[p] on Burgenda[q] mægðe æt Linguna[r] ceastre. Ond he[s] wæs arwyrðlice[t] bebyrged in[u] ðære cirican[v] þe hy[w] nemnað Sanctos Geminos[313], æt ðam halgum getwinnum, mid micle wope [x]ge on[x] Angelcynnes monna[y] ge þiderleodiscra[z]. Þær his geferscipe hyne todælde on þreo; an dæl ferde forð[a] to Rome; oðer dæl[b] cyrde eft to Brytene ond þæt sægdon[c], ond se þridda dæl gesæt æt his byrgenne[d] for his lufan[e], betweoh ða men[f] þe heora[g] geþeodo[h] ne cuðon.

196. [a-a] .xxv. B, fif and twentygoðan C; [b-b] hal B with gan weres gemind suprascript Bf, halgan abbudes gewytennys C; [c] ceolferð C; [d] abbud C; [e] ylde þa C; [f-f] ær C; [g] gesæde C; [h] asang C; [i-i] om. C; [j] buton C; [k] þig C; [l-l] .lxxiiii. B, feower and hundseofentigum C; [m] hundteontigum C; [n] dagum C; [o] xiiii. B, feowertynum C; [p] gewat C; [q] burgundia C; [r] lyngwuna C; [s] om. C; [t] arweorðlice C; [u] on C; [v] cyrcan C; [w] hig C; [x-x] ægðer ge C; [y] manna C; [z] þæderlendiscra C; [a] om. C; [b] om. C; [c] sædon C; [d] byrgyne C; [e] lufon C; [f] mægðe C; [g] hig hyra C; [h] geþeode C.

24 September: Andochius, Thyrsus and Felix

195. On the same day is the feast of the holy men St Andochius the priest and St Thyrsus the deacon; they came from the eastern parts of Gaul and there converted many people through baptism to Christianity, and suffered martyrdom there for the name of God in the days of the emperor Aurelian, together with a Christian merchant whose name was Felix. First the emperor offered them gold and silver on condition that they would abandon Christianity; then they refused. Then he ordered them to be thrown into a burning fire, and that did not touch them. Then he ordered their necks to be broken with poles. Then their souls migrated to the eternal joy, and many miracles happened at their bodies.

25 September: Ceolfrith

196. On the twenty-fifth day of the month is the commemoration of the holy man who lived in this Britain, and he was called Ceolfrith. He was the abbot of a holy monastery consecrated to St Peter towards the northern end of the country; and then in his old age he set out to travel to Rome. And three days before he left, he explained his travel plans to the brothers of the monastery. And whilst he was travelling, he recited his psalter and his mass twice a day except for the one day when he was at sea, and three days before the day of his death. He was seventy-four years old when he died. One hundred and fourteen days after he left the monastery, he died in the province of Burgundy in the city of Lingones [i.e. Langres]. And he was honourably buried in the church which they call SS Gemini, 'the Holy Twins', with great lamentation both from the English and from the local population. There his company divided itself into three: one group continued to Rome; another group returned to Britain and reported it, and the third group stayed at his tomb for the sake of his love, amongst the people who did not know their language.

26 September: Justina and Cyprian

197. <O>nᵃ ðone ᵇsex ond twentigoþanᵇ dæg þæs monðes bið Sancta Iustinan tid þære fæmnan, ond ᶜþæs biscopes Sancti Cyprianusᶜ. Se Cyprianus wæs ærystᵈ ᵉealra dryᵉ se wyrstaᶠ, ond he wolde þære fæmnan mod onᵍ his scincræftum onwendan to hæðendomeʰ ond to unclænum hæmede. Ac ða gedwinon his drycræftas forⁱ hyre halignesseʲ swa swa recᵏ þonne he toglideð, oððe weax þonne hit for fyre gemelteðˡ. Þa forlet he þone drycræftᵐ, ond heⁿ wæs geworden halig biscopᵒ, ond mid þære ilcan fæmnan he þrowode eft martyrdom. Ond ᵖheora lichoma resteð³¹⁴ inᵖ ðære ceastre þe is nemned Antiochia.

197. ᵃ n B, on C; ᵇ⁻ᵇ .xxvi. B, C; ᶜ⁻ᶜ cyprianes C; ᵈ ærest C; ᵉ⁻ᵉ drya C; ᶠ wyrresta C; ᵍ myd C; ʰ hæðengylde C; ⁱ æt C; ʲ halignysse C; ᵏ ric B with e suprascript Bd; ˡ gemylteð C; ᵐ dreocræft C; ⁿ om. C; ᵒ bysceop C; ᵖ⁻ᵖ hyra lychaman restað on C.

27 September: Cosmas and Damian

198. On ðone ᵃseofon ond twentigoþanᵃ dæg þæs monðes bið þaraᵇ haligraᶜ gebroðra tid Sancti Cosme ond Sancti Damianiᵈ; þæt wæron heahlæcas and ᵉhy lacnodon æghwylceᵉ untrumnesseᶠ monnaᵍ, ond hyʰ ne onfengon ⁱnowiht æt nænigumⁱ men, ne æt weligumʲ ne æt heanum. Þa gehældonᵏ hieˡ sum wif of micelre medtrumnesseᵐ, ða brohte seo diogollicⁿ Sanctoᵒ Damiane medmicleᵖ gretinge; gewritu secgað þæt ðæt wæreᑫ þreo ægeroʳ;³¹⁵ ond heo hyne halsode þurh God þæt he ðam onfenge. ˢÐa onfeng he ðamˢ. Þa wæsᵗ broðor Cosmas³¹⁶ forðam swiðe unrot, ond forðamᵘ he bebead þæt monᵛ heora lichomanʷ ætsomne ne byrgdeˣ æt heoraʸ ende. Ða on ðære ilcan niht ætywde ureᶻ Dryhten Cosme ond cwæð: 'Forhwon spræceᵃ þu swa for ðære gretinge þe Damianus onfeng? Ne onfeng he ᵇðæt naᵇ to medsceatte, ac ᶜforðon þeᶜ he wæs þurᵈ me gehalsod.' Ðas ᵉgebroðor geþrowedonᵉ mærne martyrdomᶠ on Diaclitianusᵍ dagum ðæs caseres fromʰ Lissiaⁱ þam gerefan. Hyʲ wæron stæned, ond ða stanas wæron onbæcᵏ gecyrredˡ ond wundedon ða þe ða halgan stændon. Hyᵐ wæron mid strælum scotodeⁿ, ac ða strælas forcyrdonᵒ hyᵖ ond slogon ða hæðnanᑫ. ʳAc ðurhʳ beheafdunga hyˢ onsendon heoraᵗ gastᵘ to Gode. Ða ðohton ða men þaᵛ ðe heoraʷ lichomanˣ namon hwæðer ʸhy monʸ ætsomne byrgdeᶻ, ᵃforðon ðeᵃ Cosmas þæt ær forbead. Þa com ðær yrnan sum olbendaᵇ, ond se cwæð mid menniscre stefneᶜ: 'Ne todælaðᵈ ge ðaraᵉ haligra lichomanᶠ, ac byrgað hyᵍ ætsomne.' Ða dydon hyʰ swa him þæt dumbeⁱ neatʲ onwreah, ond þeahᵏ siððan³¹⁷ gelumpon heofonlicoˡ wundru þurh ðaraᵐ haligra mægen.

198. ᵃ⁻ᵃ .xxvii. B, C; ᵇ þæra C; ᶜ om. C; ᵈ damiane C; ᵉ⁻ᵉ hig lacnedon æghylce C; ᶠ mettrumnysse C; ᵍ manna C; ʰ hig C; ⁱ⁻ⁱ nan þing fram ænegum C; ʲ welegum C; ᵏ geheoldon B with æ suprascript Bd; ˡ hig C; ᵐ mettrumnysse C; ⁿ dygollice C; ᵒ sancte C; ᵖ medmycele C; ᑫ wæron C; ʳ ægru C; ˢ⁻ˢ om. C; ᵗ wæs hys C; ᵘ forþon C; ᵛ man C; ʷ lychaman C; ˣ byrigde C; ʸ hyra C; ᶻ urne C; ᵃ spricst C; ᵇ⁻ᵇ na þæt C; ᶜ⁻ᶜ forþan þe C; ᵈ on C; ᵉ⁻ᵉ broðro þrowedon C; ᶠ martyrdom for criste C; ᵍ dioclitianus C; ʰ fram C; ⁱ lisio C; ʲ hig C; ᵏ on bæc Ko; ˡ gehwyrfed C; ᵐ and hig C; ⁿ sceotode C; ᵒ oncyrdon C; ᵖ hig C; ᑫ hæðenan C; ʳ⁻ʳ æt þære C; ˢ and hig C; ᵗ hyra C; ᵘ gastas C; ᵛ om. C; ʷ hyra C; ˣ lychaman C; ʸ⁻ʸ hig man C; ᶻ byrigde C; ᵃ⁻ᵃ forþam þe C; ᵇ oluende C; ᶜ stemne C; ᵈ todæle C; ᵉ þæra C; ᶠ lychaman C; ᵍ hig C; ʰ hig C; ⁱ dume C; ʲ nyten C; ᵏ þær C; ˡ heofenlicu C; ᵐ þæra C.

26 September: Justina and Cyprian

197. On the twenty-sixth day of the month is the feast of the virgin St Justina, and the bishop St Cyprian. Cyprian was first the worst magician of all, and with his magic tricks he tried to change the virgin's mind to paganism and to dirty sex. But then because of her holiness his magic dwindled like smoke when it dissipates, or wax when it melts by the fire. Then he gave up sorcery, and he became a holy bishop, and with the same virgin he later suffered martyrdom. And [?]her body rests in the city called Antioch.

27 September: Cosmas and Damian

198. On the twenty-seventh day of the month is the feast of the holy brothers St Cosmas and St Damian; they were expert doctors and they cured any human illness, and they received nothing from anybody, neither from the wealthy nor from the poor. When they cured a woman of a great illness, she secretly brought St Damian a small gift; the texts say that it was three eggs. And she begged him for God's sake to accept them. He then took them. Then [his] brother Cosmas was very sad because of that, and therefore he asked that their bodies should not be buried together at the end of their lives. Then during the same night our Lord appeared to Cosmas and said: 'Why would you talk like that about the gift which Damian received? He did not receive it as payment, but because he was asked in my name.' These brothers suffered a great martyrdom in the days of the emperor Diocletian at the hands of the governor Lysias. They were stoned, and the stones turned back and hurt the ones who were stoning the saints. They were shot at with arrows, but the arrows turned around and killed the pagans. But through beheading they gave up the ghost to God. Then the men who collected their bodies were wondering whether they should be buried together, because Cosmas had earlier prohibited that. Then a camel came running there, and said in a human voice: 'Do not separate the saints' bodies, but bury them together.' Then they did as the dumb animal had told them, and yet heavenly miracles happened after that through the saints' power.

29 September: The Consecration of St Michael's Church

199. On ðone ᵃnigon ond twentigoþanᵃ dæg þæs monðes bið Sancte ᵇMichahelis ciricanᵇ ᶜgehalgung inᶜ Traclaᵈ þære ceastre ᵉin Eraclae³¹⁸ ðære mægðe. Feonda menigo com to þære ceastreᵉ ond hyᶠ ymbsæton. Þa ceasterwareᵍ þurh þreora daga fæsten anmodliceʰ bædon <God>ⁱ fultumes, ond bædon þæt he him þone ætywde þurh Sancteʲ Michahelᵏ. Ða ðy þriddan dæge stod Sanctus Michahelˡ ofer ðære ceastre geteᵐ ond hæfde fyren sweord inⁿ his hondaᵒ. Þa wæron ða fynd abregedeᵖ mid þyᵠ egesanʳ ond hyˢ gewiton onweg, ond þa ceasterwaraᵗ wunedonᵘ gesunde. Ond þær wæs getimbred ᵛSancte Michahelesᵛ ciriceʷ, ond seo wæs gehalgod on ðone dæg þe weˣ mærsiað ʸSancte Michahelesʸ gemynd.

199. ᵃ⁻ᵃ .xxviiii. B, nygon and twentigoðan C; ᵇ⁻ᵇ michaelis cyrcan C; ᶜ⁻ᶜ halgung on C; ᵈ traia C; ᵉ⁻ᵉ om. C; ᶠ hig C; ᵍ ceaster C; ʰ and anmodlice C; ⁱ om. B, god C; ʲ sanctus C; ᵏ michael C; ˡ michael C; ᵐ geate C; ⁿ on C; ᵒ handa C; ᵖ abregde C; ᵠ þam C; ʳ egsan C; ˢ hig C; ᵗ ceasterware C; ᵘ awunedon C; ᵛ⁻ᵛ sanctus michaeles C; ʷ cyrce C; ˣ we nu C; ʸ⁻ʸ sanctus michaeles C.

30 September: Jerome

200. On ᵃðone þritigþanᵃ dæg þæs monðes bið Hieronimisᵇ tid þæs mæssepreostes ond þæs æðelan leorneres, se wæs ᶜin Bethlem in ðære Iudiscan ceastreᶜ. ᵈBe ðam sagað Sanctus Arculfus þæt he gesawe medmicle cirican butan Bethlem þære ceastreᵈ, inᵉ ðære wæs geseted ᶠ<Heremmis lychama myd stane oferworht, and ofer þam wæs geseted>ᶠ byrnende leohtfæt ge dæges ge nihtes.

200. ᵃ⁻ᵃ ðone .xxx. B, þon þrytygoðan C; ᵇ sancte hieremis C; ᶜ⁻ᶜ on Bethlem þære ceastre C; ᵈ⁻ᵈ om. C; ᵉ on C; ᶠ⁻ᶠ om. B, heremmis lychama myd stane oferworht and ofer þam wæs geseted C.

The End of September

200a. Ðonne ᵃse mona<ð>³¹⁹ biðᵃ geendudᵇ ðe we nemnað Haligmonoðᶜ, þonne bið seo niht twelfᵈ tida longᵉ, ond se dæg biðᶠ þæt ilce.

200a. ᵃ⁻ᵃ byð se monoð C; ᵇ geendod C; ᶜ haligmonað C; ᵈ .xii. B, C; ᵉ om. C; ᶠ om. C.

The Beginning of October

200b. On ðam teoðan monðe ᵃon gearaᵃ bið ᵇan ond þritigᵇ daga; þone mon nemneð on Leden Octemberᶜ, ond on ure geðeode Winterfylleð.

200b. ᵃ⁻ᵃ om. C; ᵇ⁻ᵇ .xxxi. suprascript Bd, C; ᶜ October C.

29 September: The Consecration of St Michael's Church

199. On the twenty-ninth day of the month is the consecration of St Michael's church in the city of Thracia in the country of Heraclea. A multitude of enemies came to the city and besieged it. Through a fast of three days, the townspeople all together prayed to God for help, and prayed that he might reveal it to them through St Michael. Then on the third day St Michael stood above the city's gate and had a fiery sword in his hand. Then the enemies were petrified with fear and retreated back, and the townspeople remained unharmed. And St Michael's church was built there, and it was consecrated on the day on which we celebrate the commemoration of St Michael.

30 September: Jerome

200. On the thirtieth day of the month is the feast of the priest and noble scholar Jerome, who lived in the Jewish city of Bethlehem. St Arculf says about him that he saw a small church outside the city of Bethlehem, in which the body of Jerome was placed, covered with stone, and above that a lamp was placed which burned day and night.

The End of September

200a. When the month which we call Haligmonað ['Holy Month'] comes to an end, the night is twelve hours long and the day likewise.

The Beginning of October

200b. There are thirty-one days in the tenth month of the year. In Latin it is called *Octember*, and in our language Winterfylleð ['Winter Full Moon'].

3 October: The Two Hewalds

201. On ðone[a] ðriddan dæg þæs monðes bið þara[b] preosta[c] þrowung þa wæron begen [d]anes noman[d]; oðer wæs[e] se blaca Heawold, oðer se hwita Heawold. Ða[f] mæssepreostas ferdon[g] of ðisse Brytene east ofer sæ to Frysum ond ða[h] lærdon to Godes geleafan, ond ðær geðrowodon[i] martyrdom for Criste, ond heofonlic leoht wæs gesewen ofer heora lichoman[j]. Hyra[k] wundor synt[l] awriten on Angolcynnes[m] bocum, ðæt is on[n] Istoria Anglorum.

201. [a] ðone þone B, þone C; [b] þæra C; [c] haligra mæssepreosta C; [d-d] anum naman nemde C; [e] wæs nemned C; [f] þæs C; [g] gewendon C; [h] þær C; [i] geþrowedon C; [j] lychaman C; [k] heora C; [l] syndon C; [m] angelcynnes C; [n] om. C.

7 October: Pope Mark

202. On ðone seofoþan[a] dæg þæs monðes bið þæs papan tid þæs noma[b] wæs Sanctus Marcus; se wæs on Constan<tyn>us[c] dagum þæs caseres, ond his lichoma[d] wæs bebyrged [e]ond is in[e] ðam mynstre[320] þe hy[f] nemnað æt Rome Balbino[g].

202. [a] .vii. B, seofeðan C; [b] nama C; [c] constanus B with faded suprascript insertion, constantynes C; [d] lychama C; [e-e] on C; [f] hig C; [g] balbina C.

8 October: Dionysius, Rusticus and Eleutherius

203. On ðone eahtoþan[a] dæg þæs monðes bið ðæs biscopes[b] tid ond þæs halgan martires[c] Sancti Dionisi, ond his [d]diacona twega[d] [e]þara noman[e] wæron Rusticus ond Eleutherius; ða wæron in[f] ðære ceastre ðe [g]Parisius is nemned[g]. Þær [h]hy mon[h] nydde þæt hy[i] [j]deofulgyld weorðedon[j]. Da hy[k] þæt ne geðafedon, ða wæron for[l] Criste gemartyrod[m].[321] Ða woldon ða cwelleras sendan [n]heora lichoman[n] on deopne stream on ða ea þe hatte Secuana[o]. Ac ða sum cristenwif[p] hy[q] laðode to symble[r], [s]ond hy[s] ða hyre getæhton þara[t] haligra lichoman[u], ond hio[v] ða [w]het hyre men[w] on niht [x]þa lichoman forstelan[x] ond bebyrgan[y] on hyre æcere. Ond [z]se æcer þa[z] syððan gegreow[a] hundteontigum[b] siða selor[c] þonne he ær dyde. Þær [d]æfter ðon[d] Cristene men [e]timbredon cirican[e], ond ðær blinde men onfengon [f]heora gesyhðe[f], [g]ond healte heora gonge[g], ond deafe gehyrnesse[h].

203. [a] .viii. B, eahteðan C; [b] bisceopes C; [c] y suprascript Bd, martyres C, mart`y´res Ko; [d-d] twegra diacona C; [e-e] þæra nama C; [f] on C; [g-g] ys nemned parisius C; [h-h] hig mon C; [i] hig C; [j-j] deofolgyldum guldon and weorðodon C; [k] hig C; [l] hig for C; [m] gemartyrode C; [n-n] hyra lychaman C; [o] sequane C; [p] Cristen wif Ko; [q] hig C; [r] symle C; [s-s] and hig C; [t] þæra C; [u] lychaman C; [v] heo C; [w-w] hyre men het C; [x-x] forstelan þa lychaman C; [y] bebyrgean C; [z-z] he C; [a] greow C; [b] .c. B, hundteontigum C; [c] sel C; [d-d] eft C; [e-e] cyrcan tymbredon C; [f-f] hyra gesyhðe C; [g-g] om. C; [h] gehyrnysse C.

3 October: The Two Hewalds

201. On the third day of the month is the passion of the priests who both had the same name; one was the black Hewald, the other the white Hewald. Those priests travelled from this Britain eastwards across the sea to the Frisians and taught them God's faith, and there suffered martyrdom for Christ, and a heavenly light was seen above their bodies. Their miracles are described in the books of the English, that is in the *Historia anglorum*.

7 October: Pope Mark

202. On the seventh day of the month is the feast of the pope whose name was St Mark; he lived in the days of the emperor Constantine, and his body was buried and still lies in the church which in Rome they call [the church of] Balbina.

8 October: Dionysius, Rusticus and Eleutherius

203. On the eighth day of the month is the feast of the bishop and the holy martyr St Dionysius, and of his two deacons whose names were Rusticus and Eleutherius; they lived in the city which is called Parisius [i.e. Paris]. There they were forced to practise devil-worship. When they refused, they were martyred for Christ. Then the executioners planned to throw their bodies into a deep part of the river which was called Sequana [i.e. River Seine]. But then a Christian woman invited them to a meal, and they then informed her about the saints' bodies, and she then asked her men to steal the bodies at night and to bury them in her field. And since then the field flourished a hundred times better than it had done before. Later Christians built a church there, and blind men received their eyesight there, and lame men their ability to walk, and deaf men hearing.

11 October: Æthelburh

204. On ðone endlyftan dæg þæs monðes bið þære halgan[a] abbodissan[b] forðfor[c] ond ðære æðelan fæmnan þære noma[d] wæs Sancta Æðylburh[e]; sio[f] gestaðelode ðæt fæmna[g] mynster on Brytene þæt is nemned on Bercingum, ond on hyre dagum gelumpon [h]heofonlicu wundro[h] on ðam ilcan mynstre. Ond sum halig[i] fæmne geseah þære ilcan Æðylburge[j] gast mid gyldenum racenteagum beon getogen to heofenum. Hyre wundro[k] ond hyre mynstres[l] syndon awriten on Angolcynnes[m] bocum.

204. [a] om. C; [b] abbudyssan C; [c] gewytennys C; [d] nama C; [e] æðelburh C; [f] seo C; [g] femnena C; [h-h] heofenlicu wundru C; [i] haligu C; [j] æðelburge C; [k] wundor C; [l] mynster C; [m] angelcynnes C.

14 October: Pope Callistus I

205. On ðone feowerteoðan[a] dæg þæs monðes bið Sancti Calistis[b] gemynd þæs papan, se þrowode martyrdom for Criste on ðæs caseres dagum [c]se wæs nemned[c] Macrini, ond he is bebyrged in[d] ðam mynstre³²² Calepode[e], on ðam wege þe æt Rome is nemned Aurelia. Þes papa gesette [f]on Rome þreora sæternesdaga[f] fæsten on geare, ænne[g] for hwætes genihtsumnesse[h], oðerne for wines, þriddan for eles.

205. [a] .xiiii. B, feowerteoðan C; [b] calistes C; [c-c] om. C; [d] on C; [e] calepodi C; [f-f] þreor sæterdaga C; [g] anne C; [h] genyhtsumnysse C.

15 October: Lupulus

206. On ðone fifteoþan[a] dæg þæs monðes bið þæs martyres tid Sancti Lupul<i>[b], þæs mæsse bið gemeted on ðam yldran mæssebocum.

206. [a] .xv. B, fyfteoðan C; [b] lupulii B, lupili C.

18 October: Luke

207. On ðone eahtateoþan[a] dæg þæs monðes bið Sancte Lucas geleornes[b] ðæs godspelleres; [c]se wrat[c] ðone þriddan dæl Cristes boca³²³ in[d] Achaia ðære mægðe, ond [e]he wrat[e] ða maran[f] boc Actus Apostolorum. Lucas wæs acenned in[g] Siria mægðe, ond he wæs aryst[h] cræftig læce [i]in Antiochia[i] þære ceastre, ond he wæs eft Paulus gefera [j]in ælce[j] elðeodignesse[k], ond he wæs se clænosta[l] wer; næs he hæbbende wif[m] ne bearn. He gefor[n] þa he wæs on [o]seofon ond hundseofontigum[o] geara, ond he wæs æryst[p] [q]bebyrged in Bethania[q], ac his ban wæron eft alæded þanon on Constantines[r] dagum³²⁴ þæs caseres in[s] ða ceastre Constantinopili[t].

207. [a] .xviii. B, ehtateoðan C; [b] gewytennys C; [c-c] se awrat C; [d] on C; [e-e] he awrat C; [f] mæran C; [g] on C; [h] æryst Ko, ærest C; [i-i] on antiochia C; [j-j] on ælce C; [k] ælðeodignysse C; [l] clænesta C; [m] ne wyf C; [n] gewat C; [o-o] lxxvii. B, hundseofentigum C; [p] ærest C; [q-q] gebyrged on bethania þære stowe C; [r] constantinus C; [s] on C; [t] þe ys nemned constantinopolim C.

11 October: Æthelburh

204. On the eleventh day of the month is the death of the holy abbess and noble virgin whose name was St Æthelburh; she established the house of virgins in Britain which is called Barking, and in her days heavenly miracles happened in the same religious house. And a holy virgin saw the soul of the same Æthelburh being pulled up to heaven with golden chains. Her miracles and those of her monastery are written down in the books of the English.

14 October: Pope Callistus I

205. On the fourteenth day of the month is the commemoration of Pope St Callistus, who suffered martyrdom for Christ in the days of the emperor who was called Macrinus, and he is buried in the church of Calepodius, on the road which in Rome is called [Via] Aurelia. This pope established in Rome a fast on three Saturdays in the year, one for sufficiency of wheat, a second for wine, a third for oil.

15 October: Lupulus

206. On the fifteenth day of the month is the feast of the martyr St Lupulus, whose mass can be found in the older massbooks.

18 October: Luke

207. On the eighteenth day of the month is the death of St Luke the evangelist; he wrote the third part of the books of Christ in the province of Achaea, and he wrote the famous text *Actus Apostolorum* [i.e. Acts of the Apostles]. Luke was born in the province of Syria, and he was originally a skilled doctor in the city of Antioch, and he was later the companion of Paul during all his travels abroad, and he was a very chaste man; he had neither wife nor child. He died when he was seventy-seven years old, and he was first buried in Bithynia, but his bones were later taken away from there to the city of Constantinople, in the days of emperor [Constantius].

18 October: Tryphonia

208. On ðone ilcan dæg bið þære halgan cwene gemynd Sancta Trifonia; seo wæs Decies[a] cwen þæs caseres, ond heo wæs æryst[b] hæðen ond wælgrim. Ac heo geseah hu Decius se casere wedde ond hrymde dæges ond nihtes [c]ær ðon[c] he dead wære. Þa gelyfde heo on God ond [d]onfeng fulwihte[d]. Ond sume dæge ðær heo hy[e] gebæd, heo onsende hyre gast to Gode.

208. [a] decius C; [b] aryst Ko, ærest C; [c-c] ær þan C; [d-d] wearð gefullod C; [e] hyg C.

18 October: Justus

209. On ðone ilcan dæg bið þæs halgan cnihtes þrowung Sancti Iusti, se wæs [a]eahta wintre[a 325] þa he [b]martyrdom þrowode[b] for Criste; þone het beheafdian sum rice mon[c] se wæs on naman Ritsoalis. Ða woldon þa cwelleras niman þæt heafod ond lædan to ðam rican men. Þa aras se lichoma[d] ond genam þæt heafod him [e]on <hand>[e 326], ond seo tunge spræc of ðam heafde ond cwæð þus: 'Heofones[f] God ond eorðan, onfoh mine[g] sawle, forðon[h] ic wæs unsceððende[i] ond clænheort.' Þa gemette hine þær[j] his fæder ond his fædera swa beheafdodne. Ða cwædon hy[k]: 'Hwæt wille[l] wit don[327] be [m]ðissum lichoman[m]?' Ða spræc seo tunge eft of ðam heafde ond cwæð: 'Gongað[n] on ðis stanscræf ðæt[o] her neah is, ond git þær [p]metað weal se is[p] mid ifige bewrigen[q]. Bedelfað on ðam þone lichoman[r], ond sendað[s] min heafod [t]<on yncre teage>[t 328], ond bringað minre[u] meder þæt heo ðæt[v] cysse. Ond gif heo me geseon wylle, ðonne sece heo me in[w] Godes neorxnawonge[x].' Þa bedulfon hy[y] ðone lichoman[z] þær he ær bebead, ond brohton his heafod in[a] ða ceastre seo hatte Alticiotrum[b 329] to[c] his meder, þære [d]noma wæs Feliciæ[d], ond his [e]fæder noma[e] wæs Iustinus. Þa on niht scan[f] leoht [g]ofer ealle ða ceastre of ðam heafde[g]. Ða on mergen[h] com se biscop[i] þæder[j], ond þa ceasterwara[k] ealle mid leohtfatum ond mid candelum, ond bæron þæt heafod to[l] cirican[m] ond hit ðær asetton. Ond ðær [o]georn sextyne[n] wintre[o] mæden to ðære bære seo wæs blind acenned, ond heo meahte[p] sona geseon.

209. [a-a] .viii. wintre B, nygon geare C; [b-b] þrowode martyrdom C; [c] man C; [d] lychama C; [e-e] on B, Ko, on hand C, Herz; [f] heofena C; [g] minre C; [h] om. C; [i] unsceððend C; [j] om. C; [k] hig C; [l] wyllað C; [m-m] þysum lychaman C; [n] gangað C; [o] þe C; [p-p] gemetað weallhus C; [q] bewrogen C; [r] lychaman C; [s] wendað C; [t-t] an to gretinge B, on yncre teage C; [u] hyt mynre C; [v] hyt C; [w] on C; [x] neorxnawonge C; [y] hig C; [z] lychama C; [a] on C; [b] alticiorum C; [c] and to C; [d-d] nama wæs felicia C; [e-e] fæder nama C; [f] scean C; [g-g] of þam heafde ofer ealle þa ceastre and C; [h] morgen C; [i] bisceop C; [j] to þære ceastre C; [k] ceasterware C; [l] on C; [m] cyrcan C; [n] .xvi. B; [o-o] arn an syxtyne geare C; [p] myhte C.

19 October: Pelagia

210. On ðone nigonteoþan[a] dæg þæs monðes bið Sancta Pilagian[b] geleornes[c] þære Godes þeowenne; seo wæs æryst[d] mima in[e] Antiochia þære ceastre, þæt is scericge[f]

210. [a] .xviiii. B, nygonteoðan C; [b] pelagian C; [c] gewytennys C; [d] ærest C; [e] on C; [f] scearecge C;

18 October: Tryphonia

208. On the same day is the commemoration of the holy queen St Tryphonia; she was the wife of the emperor Decius, and she was originally a pagan and cruel. But she saw how the emperor Decius raged and shouted day and night before he was dead. Then she came to believe in God and received baptism. And one day while she was praying, she gave up the ghost to God.

18 October: Justus

209. On the same day is the passion of the holy boy St Justus, who was eight winters old when he suffered martyrdom for Christ; a powerful man whose name was Rizoalis ordered him to be beheaded. Then the executioners wanted to take the head and bring it to the powerful man. Then the body arose and took the head into its hand, and the tongue spoke from the head and spoke thus: 'God of heaven and earth, receive my soul, because I was innocent and pure of heart.' Then his father and his uncle found him there, thus beheaded. Then they said: 'What should we do about this body?' Then the tongue spoke again from the head and said: 'Go into this cave which is near here, and there you will find a wall which is covered with ivy. Bury the body next to that, and put my head into your bag, and take [it] to my mother so that she may kiss it. And if she wants to see me, she can find me in God's paradise.' Then they buried the body where he had indicated earlier, and took his head to the city which was called Alticiotrum to his mother, whose name was Felicia, and his father's name was Justinus. Then at night a light shone over the whole city from the head. Then in the morning the bishop went there, and all the townspeople with lamps and with candles, and carried the head to church and placed it there. And a girl of sixteen years, who had been born blind, ran to the bier, and she could suddenly see.

19 October: Pelagia

210. On the nineteenth day of the month is the death of God's handmaid St Pelagia; she was originally a *mima* in the city of Antioch, that is 'actress' in our language. She

on urum[g] geðeode[330]. Seo glengde hi[h] swa ⌈þætte noht næs on hyre gesewen⌉[i] buton gold ond gimmas, ond eall hyre ⌈gyrela stanc⌉[j] swa ælces cynnes ricels. Þa gecyrde heo æne into cirican[k] þær Nonnus[l] se ⌈biscop sægde⌉[m] godspel[n] be ðam toweardan Godes <dome>[o 331]. Ða weop heo sona swa[p] ðæt hyre fleowon þa tearas of ðam eagum swa swa flod. Ond ða ðy[q] ilcan dæge gesohte heo þone biscop[r] ond cwæð ⌈to him⌉[s]: 'Ic eom deofles ðinen; ic yðgode mid synnum swa[t] sæ mid yðum. Ic[u] wæs ⌈synna georn, ond in deaðlicum listum⌉[v] ic wæs beswicen, ond ic beswac monige[w] þurh me. Ac[x] gefulla me[332], þæt mine synna syn adilgode.' Þa gefullode ⌈se biscop hy⌉[y] ond hyre gesealde husl, ond æt ðam fulwihte[z] hyre onfeng sum Godes þeow<en>[a] þære noma[b] wæs[c] Romana. ⌈Þæs ða⌉[d] ymb[e] twegen dagas, þær heo slep æt ⌈ðære godmodor⌉[f] huse[g], þa com hyre deofol to ond hy[h] awehte ond cwæð ⌈to hyre⌉[i]: 'Min hlæfdige, gif ðe wæs gold[j] to lytel oððe seolfor[k] oððe deorwyrðra gimma oððe ænigra wor<ul>dwelena[l 333], ic ðæt sona gebete, ac ne forlæt me[m].' Ða cwæð heo: 'Ic ðe wiðsace, forðon[n] ic eom nu in[o] Cristes bure[p 334].' Þa on ðære ⌈eahtoðan nihte⌉[q] hyre fulwihtes[r], þa gegyrede heo hy[s] mid hærenre tunecan ond mid byrnan[335], þæt is mid lytelre hacelan, ond heo næs ⌈na leng⌉[t] ðær gesewen. Ac heo gewat on[u] Oliuetes dune ond hyre timbrede[v] lytle cytan in[w] ðære stowe þe[x] Crist him[y] gebæd þa he wæs mon[z] on eorðan; þær hio[a] wunode þreo gear; þær[b] nænig mon[c] wiste[d] hwæðer hio[e] wæs wer[f] ðe wif[336] ⌈ær ðon ðe⌉[g] heo forðfered[h] wæs. Ða onfand[i] se biscop[j] on Hierusalem, þær he hyre lichoman[k] gyrede, þæt heo wæs wif. Ða cwæð he: 'God, ⌈þe sy⌉[l] wuldor. Ðu hafast monigne[m] haligne ofer eorðan ahyded.'

[g] unrim C; [h] hig C; [i-i] þæt ne wæs aht C; [j-j] gegyrla wæs stincende C; [k] cyrcan C; [l] nonus C; [m-m] byscop sæde C; [n] om. C; [o] lombe B, Ko, lambe C; [p] swa swyðe C; [q] þig C; [r] bysceop C; [s-s] hym to C; [t] swa swa C; [u] and ic C; [v-v] swa leggeorn on deadlicum lustum and C; [w] manege C; [x] ac ic bydde þe C; [y-y] hig se bysceop C; [z] fulluhte C; [a] þeow B, þeowen C, Herz; [b] nama C; [c] om. C; [d-d] and þa þæs C; [e] ymbe C; [f-f] þare godmeder C; [g] om. C; [h] hig C; [i-i] hyre to C; [j] goldes C; [k] seolfres C; [l] wordwelena B, woruldwelena C; [m] þu me C; [n] forþon ðe C; [o] on C; [p] brydbure C; [q-q] ehtoðan nyht C; [r] fulluhtes C; [s] hig C; [t-t] næfre ma C; [u] to C; [v] getymbrede C; [w] on C; [x] þær C; [y] hyne C; [z] mann C; [a] heo C; [b] þæt C; [c] man C; [d] ne wyste C; [e] heo C; [f] þe wer C; [g-g] ær þan ðe C; [h] gewyten C; [i] onfunde C; [j] bisceop C; [k] lychaman C; [l-l] sig þe C; [m] mænigne C.

21 October: Hilarion

211. On ðone ⌈an ond twentigoþan⌉[a] dæg þæs monðes bið þæs halgan fæder geleornes[b] Sancti Hilariones, se wæs upcymen[c] ⌈in Palistina⌉[d] mægðe in[e] ðam tune ðe is nemned Ðabata. Ond he wæs sona on his cnihthade on gewritum gelæred, ond he gewat in[f] westen þa he wæs ⌈sextyne wintræ⌉[g 337], ond þær hyne dioflu[h] costodon ⌈in mislicum⌉[i] hywum. Hwilum hy[j] him raredon on swa ⌈hryðro, hwilum hy⌉[k] him lægon[l] big swilce nacode wifmen, ⌈hwilum hy⌉[m] ⌈æteowdon him swa swa þeotende wulf⌉[n], ⌈hwilum swa⌉[o] beorcende fox[p 338]. Ond[q] he ðæt eall oferswiðde þurh Cristes miht, ond[r] dyde unrim heofonlicra[s] wundra. Ðara[t] wæs sum þæt sum geong mon[u] bæd ⌈sume Gode<s>⌉[v 339]

211. [a-a] .xxi. B, an and twentigoðan C; [b] gewytennys C; [c] upcumen C; [d-d] on palestina C; [e] on C; [f] on C; [g-g] .xvi. wintræ B, .xv. geare C; [h] deoflu C; [i-i] on missenlicum C; [j] hig C; [k-k] hryðero hwylon hig C; [l] lagon C; [m-m] hwylon hig C; [n-n] þuton swa wulfas C; [o-o] hwilon swa C; [p] foxas C; [q] ac C; [r] and he C; [s] heofenlicra C; [t] þæra C; [u] man C; [v-v] sumre godes C, sume gode Ko;

adorned herself in such a way that absolutely nothing but gold and jewels was seen on her, and her whole attire smelled like perfume of every kind. Then once she went into a church where the bishop Nonnus was preaching the gospel about the coming [?judgement of God]. Then she suddenly wept so that her tears streamed from her eyes like rivers. And then on the same day she sought out the bishop and said to him: 'I am the devil's handmaid; I am flooded with sins, as the sea [is flooded] with waves. I was devoted to sins, and by deadly tricks I was deceived and I deceived many through me. But baptise me, so that my sins may be erased.' Then the bishop baptised her and gave her the Eucharist, and at the baptism a maid of God sponsored her, whose name was Romana. Two days later, when she slept at her godmother's house, the devil came to her and woke her and said to her: 'My lady, if you had too little gold or silver or of precious jewels or of any luxury, I could remedy that straightaway, but do not abandon me.' Then she said: 'I renounce you, because I am now in Christ's bridal chamber.' Then on the octave of her baptism, she dressed herself in a hair tunic and in a ?'birrus', that is in a short cloak, and she was no longer seen there. But she went on the Mount of Olives and built herself a small hut in the place where Christ had prayed when he was a man on earth; there she lived for three years; there nobody knew whether she was a man or a woman before she was dead. Then the bishop in Jerusalem, when he was preparing her body, discovered that she was a woman. Then he said: 'God, glory be to you. You have hidden many a saint on earth.'

21 October: Hilarion

211. On the twenty-first day of the month is the death of the holy father St Hilarion, who came from the province of Palestine from the town which is called Thabata. And even in his childhood he was learned in the scriptures, and he went into the desert when he was sixteen years old, and there devils tempted him in various shapes. Sometimes they bellowed at him like cattle, sometimes they laid themselves down next to him like naked women, sometimes they appeared to him like howling wolves, sometimes like barking foxes. And he overcame all that through Christ's power, and worked innumerable heavenly miracles. One of them was that a young man asked a

fæmnan unrihthæmedes; þa heo þæt ne geþafode, ða agrof se mon[w] on ærenum brede drycræftæs[x] word ond bedealf under þone þerscwold[y] þæs huses þær seo fæmne ineode. Ond þa sona swa heo ineode, þa [z]wæs heo[z] of hyre ryhtgewitte; ac[a] heo cleopode[b] to ðam geongan be his naman. Þa gelæddon[c] yldran[340] hy[d] to [e]Sancti Hilarione[e]. Þa hrymde ðæt deoful[f] in[g] ðære fæmnan, ond cwæð to him: 'Þu me nedest[h] [i]to utgonge[i], ond ic ne mæg, buton me se geonga læte se me under ðam þerscwolde[j] geband.' Þa cwæð se Godes wer to ðam deofle: 'Tohwon eodest ðu in[k] ðis Godes mægden[l]? Forhwon[m] noldest ðu [n]gongan in ðone mon[n] þe ðe [o]in hy[o] sende?' Þa cwæð ðæt deoful[p]: 'He hæfde[q] minne [r]geferan in[r] him, ðæt deofol ðe[s] hyne lærde ða unclænan lufan.' Ða geclænsode se Godes wer ða fæmnan [t]for ðon[t] [341] scindlacum[u]. Ða Sanctus Hilarion[v] wæs on hundeahtatigum[w] wintrum[x] þa [y]he forðferde[y]; ond þy[z] dæge þe he geleorde[a], he cwæð to him sylfum: 'Gong[b] ut, sawl, hwæt drædest[c] ðu ðe? Gong[d] ut, hwæt tweost [e]ðu ðe nu[e]? Hundseofontig[f] geara[g] þu þeowodest[h] Gode[i] [342], ond nu[j] gyt þone deað þe ondrædest?' Ond æt [k]ðissum worde[k] he onsende his[l] gast, ond his lichoma[m] is [n]in Palestina[n] mægðe, [o]in ðære[o] stowe þa[p] [343] hatte Maiuma[q].

[w] man C; [x] dreocræftes C; [y] þersceold C; [z-z] wæs heo sona C; [a] and C; [b] clypode C; [c] gebædon hyra C; [d] om. C; [e-e] sancte hilarionem C; [f] deofol C; [g] on C; [h] nydest C; [i-i] ut to ganne C; [j] þersceolde C; [k] on C; [l] mæden C; [m] forhwam C; [n-n] gan on þone C; [o-o] on hig C; [p] deofol to hym C; [q] hæfð C; [r-r] geferan on C; [s] þæt C; [t-t] fram þam C; [u] scinlacum C; [v] hilarionus C; [w] .lxxx.m B, hundeahtatigum C; [x] geara C; [y-y] forðferde he C; [z] þig C; [a] gewat C; [b] gang C; [c] ondrædest C; [d] gang C; [e-e] ðu nu C; [f] hundseofentig C; [g] gear C; [h] þeowedest C; [i] criste C; [j] þu nu C; [k-k] þysum wordum C; [l] þone C; [m] lichama C; [n-n] on palistina C; [o-o] on þære C; [p] þe C; [q] maioma C.

24 October: Genesius

212. On ðone [a]feower ond twentigoþan[a] dæg þæs monðes bið ðæs martyres tid[b] [344] Sancti Genesi; ðone mon[c] acwealde, [d]forðon ðe[d] he nolde deofulgild[e] weorðian. Þæs gemynd is mycel on twam burgum [f]on twa[f] healfa þæs flodes ðe hatte Rodanum, þæt is on ure geðeode Rodena[g] mere[345]. In[h] [i]oðre birg[i] is seo stow þe he mid his blode gehalgode þa hyne mon[j] martyrode; [k]in ðære[k] birg[l] is his lichoma[m] geseted.

212. [a-a] .xxiiii. B, C; [b] tid þrowung B, þrowung C, Herz; [c] man C; [d-d] forþam þe C; [e] deofolgyld C; [f-f] and on twa C; [g] rodenan C; [h] on C; [i-i] oðere byrig C; [j] man C; [k-k] and on oðere C; [l] byrig C; [m] lychama C.

24 October: Sixteen Soldiers

213. On ðone ilcan dæg bið sextyna[a] [346] cempena tid[b] [347], ða het Claudius se casere heafde beceorfan in[c] ðære ceastre Figligna[d], [e]forðon ðe hy[e] fulwihte onfengon, ond hie[f] wæron bliðran to ðam deaðe þonne hy[g] her on hæðengilde lifdon[h]. Þara[i] cempena feowra[j] wæron nemned[k] Þiosius[l] ond Lucius ond Marcus ond Petrus.

213. [a] .xvi. B, C; [b] tyd and hyra wifa C; [c] on C; [d] figlina C; [e-e] forþan ðe hig C; [f] hig C; [g] hig C; [h] lyfedon C; [i] þæra C; [j] .iiii. B, feower C; [k] þus genemned C; [l] þeodosius C.

virgin of God for illicit sex; when she refused, the man inscribed a magic charm on a bronze tablet and buried [it] under the threshold of the house where the virgin entered. And as soon as she went inside, she was out of her mind, and she also cried out to the young man with his name. Then the parents took her to St Hilarion. Then the devil roared inside the virgin, and said to him: 'You are trying to force me out, and I cannot [leave], unless the young man, who banished me under the threshold, lets me.' Then the man of God said to the devil: 'Why did you enter this maiden of God? Why did you not want to enter the man who sent you into her?' Then the devil said: 'He had my companion inside him, the devil who taught him unchaste love.' Then the man of God cleansed the virgin of that magic. Then St Hilarion was eighty years old when he died, and on the day when he died, he said to himself: 'Leave, soul, why are you afraid? Leave, why do you hesitate? You have served God for seventy years, and you are still afraid of death?' And with these words he gave up the ghost, and his body lies in the country of Palestine, in the place called Maiuma.

24 October: Genesius

212. On the twenty-fourth day of the month is the passion of the martyr St Genesius; he was killed, because he refused to practise devil-worship. This commemoration is famous in two cities on the two sides of the river which is called Rhodanum, which in our language is 'Rodena Mere'. In the one city is the place which he consecrated with his blood when he was martyred; in that city his body is located.

24 October: Sixteen Soldiers

213. On the same day is the feast of the sixteen soldiers whom the emperor Claudius ordered to be beheaded in the city of Figlina, because they had received baptism, and they were happier in death than if they had survived in the pagan religion. Four of the soldiers were called Theodosius and Lucius and Marcus and Petrus.

26 October: Cedd

214. On ðone ᵃsex ond twentigoþanᵃ dæg þæs monðes bið Sancte ᵇCeadweallan³⁴⁸ geleornesᵇ þæs biscopesᶜ. He wæs Ceaddan broðor, ond sum halig monᵈ geseah þæt he lædde Ceaddan sawle mid englum to heofenum. Ceaddeᵉ wæs biscopᶠ ᵍin Eastseaxumᵍ, ond hwæðereʰ his lichomaⁱ resteð be norðan gemære inʲ ðam mynstre Læstinga ea. Ond his dæda wæronᵏ awritene on Angolcynnesˡ bocum.

214. ᵃ⁻ᵃ .xxvi. B, syx and twentigoðan C; ᵇ⁻ᵇ ceddes gewytennys C; ᶜ bisceopes C; ᵈ man C; ᵉ ceadda C; ᶠ bisceop C; ᵍ⁻ᵍ on eastsexum C; ʰ hwæðre C; ⁱ lychama C; ʲ on C; ᵏ syndon C; ˡ angelcynnes C.

28 October: Simon and Thaddeus

215. On ðone ᵃeahta ond twentigoþanᵃ dæg þæs monðes ᵇ<bið> þaraᵇ apostola tid Simonisᶜ ond Thaddeosᵈ. Simonisᵉ wæs Sancta Marian swystorsunuᶠ, Cristes modrian sunu, ᵍseo wæsᵍ nemned on Cristes bocum³⁴⁹ Maria <Cleophe>ʰ. Þonne wæs Thaddeosⁱ oðer nomaʲ Iudas. Ðas apostolas æfter Cristes upastigenesseᵏ gewiton on Persidaˡ mægðe ondᵐ bodedon Cristes geleafan, ond dydon unrimⁿ wundra on ðæs cyninges ᵒdagum seᵒ wæs nemned Exerses; þær hyᵖ gedydon ðæt cild sprecende ᑫþæt neᑫ ³⁵⁰ wæs anre nihte eald. Simones lichomaʳ resteð ˢon ðam londe Bosfore, ond Thaddeos lichomaˢ in Armeniaᵗ mægðe inᵘ ðære ceastre Nerita.

215. ᵃ⁻ᵃ xxviii. B, ehta and twentigoðan C; ᵇ⁻ᵇ þara B, Ko, byð þæra C, bið þara Herz; ᶜ symones C; ᵈ taddeus C; ᵉ se symon C; ᶠ swustorsunu C; ᵍ⁻ᵍ seo ys C; ʰ cleopode B, cleophe C; ⁱ taddeus C; ʲ nama C; ᵏ upastigennysse C; ˡ persia C; ᵐ and þær C; ⁿ ungerym C; ᵒ⁻ᵒ ryce þe C; ᵖ hig C; ᑫ⁻ᑫ þe C; ʳ lychama C; ˢ⁻ˢ om. C; ᵗ ariroenia C; ᵘ on C.

28 October: Cyrilla

216. On ðone ilcan dæg bið Sancta Cyrillan þrowung þære fæmnan; seo wæs Decies dohtor þæs caseres, ᵃa<c> Claudiusᵃ se casere hyᵇ nydde þæt heo ᶜdeofolgild heredeᶜ. Þa heo ðonᵈ wiðsoc, ða het he hyᵉ mid sweorde ofstingan ond hyre lichomanᶠ weorpan hundum. Ða Iustinus se mæssepreost genomᵍ þone lichomanʰ ⁱon niht ondⁱ bebyrigde mid oðrum halgum monnumʲ.

216. ᵃ⁻ᵃ aclaudius B, ac claudius C; ᵇ hig C; ᶜ⁻ᶜ deofolgyldum hyrde C; ᵈ þam C; ᵉ hig C; ᶠ lichaman C; ᵍ genam C; ʰ lichaman C; ⁱ⁻ⁱ and hyne C; ʲ mannum C.

31 October: Quentin

217. On ðone ᵃan ond þritigþanᵃ dæg ᵇþæs <monðes>ᵇ bið Sancti Quintinesᶜ ðrowung þæs martyres, se com of Rome ᵈin Galwalasᵈ ᵉin ðaᵉ ceastre Ambeanis. Ðær ᶠRiciouarus se gerefa mid miclum witum hyne nyddeᶠ to hæðengylde. Ða he ðæt ne geðafode, ða het he hyne beheafdian. ᵍ<Þa sona> fleahᵍ <of>ʰ ³⁵¹ ðam lichomanⁱ

217. ᵃ⁻ᵃ .xxxi.an B, .xxxi. C; ᵇ⁻ᵇ þæs B, þæs monðes C; ᶜ quintinis C; ᵈ⁻ᵈ on galwalas C; ᵉ⁻ᵉ on þa C; ᶠ⁻ᶠ wæs an gerefa on þære ceastre se wæs haten riciouarus se hyne nydde myd myclum wytum C; ᵍ⁻ᵍ fleah B, þa sona fleah C; ʰ on B, Ko, of C, Herz; ⁱ lychaman C;

26 October: Cedd

214. On the twenty-sixth day of the month is the death of the bishop St Cedd. He was the brother of Chad, and a holy man saw that he led Chad's soul to heaven with angels. Cedd was bishop in Essex, but his body, however, rests in the northern region in the monastery of Lastingham. And his deeds were written down in the books of the English.

28 October: Simon and Thaddeus

215. On the twenty-eighth day of the month is the feast of the apostles Simon and Thaddeus. Simon was St Mary's nephew, the son of Christ's aunt, who was in the gospels called Mary of Cleophas. And Thaddeus also had a second name, Judas. After Christ's ascension these apostles went to the country of Persia and preached Christ's religion, and worked innumerable miracles in the days of the king who was called Xerxes; there they made the child speak who was not one night old. The body of Simon rests in the region of Bosphorus, and the body of Thaddeus rests in the province of Armenia in the city of Nerito.

28 October: Cyrilla

216. On the same day is the passion of the virgin St Cyrilla; she was the daughter of the emperor Decius, but the emperor Claudius forced her to worship pagan idols. When she rejected that, he ordered her to be stabbed to death with a sword and her body to be thrown to the dogs. Then the priest Justinus collected the body at night and buried it with other holy men.

31 October: Quentin

217. On the thirty-first day of the month is the passion of the martyr St Quentin, who came from Rome to the city of Ambeanis [i.e. Amiens] in Gaul. There the governor Riciouarus forced him with severe tortures into paganism. When he refused, he ordered him to be beheaded. Just then a dove as white as snow flew from the body,

culfre[j] swa hwit swa snaw, ond seo fleah to heofenum. Ða het se gerefa weorpan his lichoman[k] in[l] ða ea ðe [m]Sumena is nemned[m], ond þæt heafod þærto. Ond[n] æfter [o]fif ond fiftigum[o] geara[p] Godes engel getæhte sumum [q]geleaffullan wife[q], [r]seo wæs nemned Eusebia, ða stowe hwær se lichoma wæs[r]. Ond ða gebæd [s]heo hyre[s] on ðam ofre, ða [t]ahleop se lichoma[t] sona up of ðam wætere ond þæt heafod on oðre stowe, ond se lichoma [u]stanc ond þæt heafod[u] swa swote swa rosan blostma ond lilian. Ond þæt[v] wif heo ða arwyrðlice[w] bebyrgde[x],[352] ond ealle ða untruman men [y]þa ðe þyder comon to[y], hy[z] wæron sona hale.

[j] an culfre seo wæs C; [k] lychaman C; [l] on C; [m-m] ys nemned sumena C; [n] and þa C; [o-o] .lv.m B, fif and fiftegum C; [p] gearum C; [q-q] geleaffullum wifmen C; [r-r] þa stowe þær se lychama wæs seo wæs nemned eusebia C; [s-s] eusebia hig C; [t-t] hleop se lychama C; [u-u] and þæt heafod stanc C; [v] eusebia þæt C; [w] arweorðlice C; [x] bebyrigde þone lychaman C; [y-y] þe ðær to comon C; [z] hig C.

The End of October

217a. Þonne se mona<ð>[a][353] bið geendod ðe we nemnað Winterfylleð, þonne bið seo niht feowertyne[b] tida long[c], ond se dæg tyna[d].

217a. [a] monoð C; [b] .xiiii. B, feowertyne C; [c] lang C; [d] tyn tyda C.

The Beginning of November

217b. On ðam endlyftan[a] monðe on geare bið þritig[b] daga. Se monoð[c] is nemned on [d]Læden Nouembres[d], ond on ure geðeode Blodmonað[354], forðon[e] ure yldran, [f]ða hy[f] hæðenne[g] wæron, on ðam monðe [h]hy bleoton a[h], þæt is [i]þæt hy betæhton[i] ond benæmdon[j] hyra deofolgyldum ða neat þa ðe hy[k] woldon syllan[l][355].

217b. [a] t suprascript Bd; [b] xxx. B, C; [c] monað C; [d-d] leden nouembris C; [e] forþan ðe C; [f-f] þa hwyle hig C; [g] hæðene C; [h-h] hig a bleoton C; [i-i] acendon C; [j] benemndon C; [k] hig C; [l] slean C.

1 November: All Saints

218. On ðone ærystan[a] dæg [b]þæs <monðes>[b] bið ealra haligra[c] tid. [d]<Þa tyd> æryst[d] gesette Bonefacius[e] se papa on Rome, [f]myd þy þe he[f] on ðone dæg gehalgode to cirican[g] Sancta Marian ond eallum Cristes martyrum ðæt deofolgylda hus þæt [h]hy nemnað[h] Pantheon[i]; [j]in ðam[j] Romane guldon, [k]ða hy[k] hæðene wæron, eallum heora[l] deofolgyldum. Ond siððan hy[m] Cristene wæron, hy[n] ðær weorðedon[o] eallra[p] haligra gemynd. Ond se papa ða bebead[q] þæt æghwylce geare se dæg [r]in Godes ciricum in Cristenum folcum wære[r] on [s]swylcre arwyrðnesse[s] swylce se ærysta[t] dæg In Natale Domini, ðæt is ærysta[u] geohheldæg[v].

218. [a] ærestan C; [b-b] þæs B, þæs monðes C; [c] halgena C; [d-d] æryst B, þa tyd ærest C; [e] bonefatius C; [f-f] and myd þyg þe hig C, mydþy þe he Ko; [g] cyrcan C; [h-h] hig nemndon C; [i] pantatheon C; [j-j] on þam huse C; [k-k] þa hwyle hig C; [l] hyra C; [m] hig C; [n] hig C; [o] weorðodon C; [p] ealra C; [q] bead C; [r-r] wære on godes cyrcan and on crystenum folce C; [s-s] swylcere arweorðnysse C; [t] se æresta C; [u] se æresta C; [v] giehheldæg C.

and it flew to heaven. Then the governor ordered his body to be thrown into the river which is called Somena [i.e. Somme], and the head too. And after fifty-five years God's angel revealed to a believing woman, who was called Eusebia, the place where the body was. And when she prayed on the river bank, the body jumped straight out of the water and the head in second place, and the body and the head smelled as sweetly as the blossoms of the rose and the lily. And the woman buried them honourably, and all the sick people who visited there, they were healed immediately.

The End of October

217a. When the month which we call Winterfylleð ['Winter Full Moon'] comes to an end, the night is fourteen hours long and the day ten.

The Beginning of November

217b. There are thirty days in the eleventh month of the year. In Latin that month is called *November*, and in our language Blodmonað ['Sacrifice Month'], because our ancestors, when they were pagans, always made sacrifices during that month, that is, that they presented and declared to their devil-idols the cattle which they wanted to give.

1 November: All Saints

218. On the first day of the month is the feast of All Saints. Pope Boniface in Rome first established that feast, when on that day he consecrated the house of pagan idols which they call Pantheon as a church to St Mary and all the Christian martyrs. In that [house], the Romans, when they were pagans, had worshipped all their pagan idols. And since they were Christians, they worshipped the commemoration of all saints there. And the pope then decreed that each year that day should be granted the same honour in God's churches among Christians as the first day *In Natale Domini*, that is the first day of Christmas.

1 November: Caesarius

219. On ðon<e>[a] ilcan[b] dæg bið þæs diacones tid Sancti Cesari[c], se ðrowode martyrdom on[d] Aurelianus dagum þæs caseres. Ðone Leontinus[e][356] se ealdormon[f] het adrencan in[g] strongum[h] streame for Cristes geleafan, ond þæt wæs gewrecen on ðone ilcan dæg. Se ealdormon[i] rad þurh sumne wudu; þa ræsde an næddre of holum treowe æt ðam healsetan[j][357], him on ðone bosm, ond hyne toslat þæt he wæs sona dead.

219. [a] þone C; [b] ærestan C; [c] cessari C; [d] for criste on C; [e] leontius C; [f] ealdorman C; [g] on C; [h] strangum C; [i] ealdorman C; [j] heafodsmæle and C.

1 November: Benignus

220. On ðone ilcan dæg bið þæs mæssepreostes ðrowung[a] Sancti Benigni; se com from[b] eastdæle on Galwala mægðe ond [c]eardode in[c] ðam tune þe hatte Spaniaca[d]. Ða het Aurelianus se casere hyne mid witum þreatian from[e] Cristes geleafan. Ða he þæt ne geþafode, þa het he hyne belucan [f]in carcerne[f] sex[g] dagas ond sex[h] niht, ond twelf[i] gehyngrede[j] hundas mid him, þæt he wære from[k] ðam tobroden. Ða wæron him ða hundas milde for Godes egesan[l] ond [m]his na ne onhrinon[m]. Ða [n]ðy sextan[n] dæge het se casere him forslean þone sweoran. Ða sona com fleogan [o]of ðam carcerne[o] snawhwit culfre, ond seo fleah to heofenum. Ond ðær com to ðam lichoman[p] swyðe wynsum stenc, ond eac fyrhto mid.[358] Ond sum[q] cristenwif[r] [s]on niht genam ðone lichoman[s] ond hyne [t]arwyrðlice bebyrgde[t], ond æt ðam wæron [u]siððan oft[u] heofonlico[v] mægen.

220. [a] gemynd and hys þrowung C; [b] of C; [c-c] he eardode on C; [d] spamaca C; [e] fram C; [f-f] on cwearterne C; [g] .vi. B, syx C; [h] vi. B, syx C; [i] xii. B, C; [j] gehyngrode C; [k] fram C; [l] egsan C; [m-m] hym ne æthrynon and C; [n-n] .vi.an B, þig syxtan C; [o-o] om. C; [p] lychaman C; [q] þa sum C; [r] Cristen wif Ko; [s-s] genam þone lychaman on nyht C; [t-t] arweorðlice bebyrigde C; [u-u] oft syððan C; [v] heofonlicu C.

6 November: Winnoc

221. On ðone sextan[a] dæg þæs monðes bið þæs abbodes[b] geleornes[c] Sancti[d] Wynnoci[e]. He wæs ðæs mynstres hlaford ðe be suðan sæ is[f] nemned Wurmhol[g], ond he wæs [h]hwæðere <swa eaðmod>[h] þæt he wolde wyrcan æghwylc ðara[i] weorca þe ðam oðrum broðrum wæs heard ond hefig. Ond [j]æt nehstan[j] þa ha ealdode and he ne myhte ute wyrcan,[359] þa wolde he grindan mid his halgum hondum[k] þam broðrum to mete[l] Cristes þam þearfendum[m].[360] Ða sona þa[n] he þære cweorna nealæhte[o] ond þæt corn þær [p]on lægde[p], þa orn[q] seo cweorn ðurh godcunde miht, ond se abbod[r] beleac ða duru ond stod be ðære cweorna ond song[s] his gebedu. Ða [t]æt nehstan[t] wæs ðær

221. [a] .vi. B, syxtan C; [b] abbudes C; [c] gewytennys C; [d] sancte C; [e] wynnoci B with v suprascript Bd, wynnoco C, W<u>nnoci Ko; [f] se ys C; [g] wurmholt C; [h-h] hwæðere B, hwæðre swa eaðmod C; [i] þæra C; [j-j] þa æt nyhstan C, ætnehstan Ko; [k] handum C; [l] hlafe and C; [m] þearfiendum C; [n] swa C; [o] genealæhte C; [p-p] on lede C, onlægde Ko; [q] grand C; [r] abbud C; [s] sang C; [t-t] æt nyhstan C, ætnehstan Ko;

210

1 November: Caesarius

219. On the same day is the feast of the deacon St Caesarius, who suffered martyrdom in the days of the emperor Aurelian. The governor Leontius ordered him to be drowned in a torrential river for his Christian belief, and that was avenged on the same day. The governor rode through a forest; then a snake pounced from a hollow tree at his neckline, into his shirt, and bit him so that he died on the spot.

1 November: Benignus

220. On the same day is the passion of the priest St Benignus; he came from the east to Gaul and lived in the town which is called Spaniacum [i.e. Épagny]. Then the emperor Aurelianus ordered him to be forced away under tortures from his Christian belief. When he refused, he ordered him to be locked into a prison for six days and six nights, together with twelve starved dogs, so that he might be torn apart by them. And for the fear of God the dogs were friendly to him then and would not touch him. Then on the sixth day the emperor ordered his neck to be broken. Then suddenly a snow-white dove came flying from the prison, and it flew to heaven. And there came a very pleasant smell over the dead body, and also awe. And during the night a Christian woman collected the body and buried it reverently, and heavenly miracles took place near it afterwards.

6 November: Winnoc

221. On the sixth day of the month is the death of the abbot St Winnoc. He was the head of the monastery which across the English Channel is called Wormhout, and he was yet so humble that he would do all the tasks which for the other brothers were hard and strenuous. And eventually when he grew old and he could work no longer outside, he would do the grinding with his holy hands for the brothers [and] Christ's paupers, for their food. Then soon, when he went near the mill and put the grain in there, the mill ran by divine power, and the abbot closed the door and stood by the mill and chanted his prayers. Then in the end there was such an abundance of flour

swylc^u genihtsumnes meluwes^v ðæt ^why ðæt^w ealle wundredon hwonon^x þæt come. Ða sume dæge^y an ðara^z broðra locode in^a ðæt hus þurh ^ban lytel ðyrel^b. Þa gestod seo cweorn sona ond se mon^c ablindode, ond hyne ða oðre^d swiðe afyrhte þanon læddon, ond he sægde^e ^fþam broðrum þæs mynstres^f ðæt wundor þæt he ðær geseah. Ond ða oðre dæge onleat^g he wepende to ðæs abbodes^h fotum ond him bæd forgifnesseⁱ. Ond ða gebletsode^j se abbod^k his eagan on^l Dryhtnes naman, ond he myhte sona^m geseon.

^u swyðlic C; ^v melewes C; ^{w-w} hig þæs C; ^x hwanon C; ^y dæg C; ^z þæra C; ^a on C; ^{b-b} lytel þyrl C; ^c man C; ^d oðre men C; ^e sæde C; ^{f-f} þæs mynstres broðrum C; ^g aleat C; ^h abbudes C; ⁱ forgyfennysse C; ^j gesenode C; ^k abbud C; ^l þurh C; ^m eftsona C.

7 November: The Beginning of Winter

221a. On ðone seofoþan^a dæg þæs monðes bið ^bwintres <fruma>^b. Se winter^c hafað tu^d ond hundnigontig^e ^fdaga, ond^f ðonne gongað^{g 361} þa seofon^h steorran upⁱ on æfen, ond on dægered^j on setl^k.

221a. ^a .vii. B, seofeðan C; ^{b-b} wintres B, wyntres fruma C; ^c F starts here; ^d twa C, F; ^e hundnigantig F; ^{f-f} daga F; ^g gongeð B with a suprascript Bd, gangað C, F; ^h .vii. B, seofon C, F; ⁱ upp F; ^j dægred C, F; ^k F breaks off after setl.

8 November: The Four Crowned Ones

222. On ðone eahtoðan^a dæg þæs monðes bið ðara^b martyra þrowung þe we nemnað on gewritum Quattuor Coronatorum^c, þæt is þara^d gesigefæstan³⁶² weras feowere^e.³⁶³ Þara^f naman wæron Claudius, Castorius^g, Simfonianus^h, Nicostratus. Ðæt wæron feowereⁱ stancræftigan in^j Rome. Þær wæs samod^k sex^l hund^m cræftigenaⁿ ond ^otwa ond twentig^o, ond ^pnæron nane^p oðre him gelice. ^qHy gesenedon^q ælce morgen heora^r iserngeloman^s, ond^t ðonne næron hy^u na tobrocene, ac hy^v grofon^w æghwylcne^x stan swa se casere geðohte. Ða wæs ^yðara cræftigena^y ^zon naman an^z Simplicus^a; ða lyfde^b se God<e>^{c 364} ond fulwihte^d onfeng, ond ða siððan dyde he eall ðæt ða oðre dydon. Þa sealde ^eGod³⁶⁵ þissum^e ^ffif cræftegum^f maran gyfa^g þonne ðam oðrum. Ða wregdon ða oðre ^hcræftigan hy^h to ðam casere ond sægdonⁱ him þæt hy^j wæron Cristene, ond þæt hy^k þurh drycræft^l dydon ða cræftlican weorc, ^mfor ðe hy^m þa ⁿweorc senodonⁿ mid Cristes rodetacne. Þa yrsode se casere^o ond het hy^p cwice^{q 366} ^rbelucan in^r leadenum^s cistum, ond ða weorpan ^tin flod^t. Ond ða æfter ^utwam ond feowertigum^u daga^v, sum cristenmon^w ateah ða cista^x up ^ymid þam lichoman^{y 367} ond ^zasette in^z his hus, ond siððan wæron ^amonegu wundru^a ðurh ðas halgan weras geworden^b.

222. ^a ehtoðan C; ^b þæra haligra C; ^c coronatores C; ^d þa C; ^e feowere C; ^f þæra C; ^g and castorisus C; ^h and symphonianus and C; ⁱ .iiii. B, feowere C; ^j on C; ^k samod ætgædere C; ^l .vi. B, syx C; ^m hundred C; ⁿ cræftgana C; ^{o-o} xxii. B, twa and hundteontig C; ^{p-p} ne wæron nænige C; ^{q-q} hig gesenodon C; ^r hyra C; ^s yrenan tol C; ^t om. C; ^u hig C; ^v hig C; ^w grofon B, He, C, grofen Ko; ^x æghilcne C; ^{y-y} þæra cræftgana C; ^{z-z} an on naman C; ^a symplicius C; ^b gelyfde C; ^c goda B, Ko, gode Herz, on god C; ^d fulluhte C; ^{e-e} se casere þam C; ^{f-f} .v. cræftegum B, fif cræftgan C; ^g gyfe C; ^{h-h} cræftgan hig C; ⁱ sædon C; ^j hig C; ^k hig C; ^l þæt dreocræf C; ^{m-m} forþon ðe hig C; ⁿ⁻ⁿ tol and þa weorc gesenodon C; ^o casere wyð hig C; ^p hig C; ^q om. C; ^{r-r} belucan on C; ^s ledenum C; ^{t-t} on flod C; ^{u-u} xlii.m B, twam and feowertygum C; ^v dagum C; ^w cristenman C, Cristen mon Ko; ^x cyste C; ^{y-y} om. C; ^{z-z} sette on C; ^{a-a} manege wundor C; ^b gewordene C.

that they were all wondering from where that came. Then one day one of the brothers peered into the building through a little hole. Then the mill suddenly stood still and the man became blind, and the others led him away, very afraid, and he reported to the brothers of the monastery the miracle which he had seen there. And on the next day he bowed down weeping to the feet of the abbot and asked him for forgiveness. And then the abbot blessed his eyes in the name of the Lord, and suddenly he could see again.

7 November: The Beginning of Winter

221a. On the seventh day of the month is the beginning of winter. Winter is ninety-two days long, and at that time the Seven Stars [i.e. Pleiades] rise in the evening and set at dawn.

8 November: The Four Crowned Ones

222. On the eighth day of the month is the passion of the martyrs whom in literature we call *Quattuor Coronati*, that is the four crowned men. Their names were Claudius, Castorius, Symphorianus and Nicostratus. They were four stonemasons in Rome. Altogether there were 622 craftsmen, and nobody else was equal to them. Every morning they blessed their metal tools, and then they were never damaged, but they sculpted each stone as the emperor desired. Then one of the craftsmen was called Simplicius; then he believed in God and received baptism, and then afterwards he did everything which the others did. Then God gave these five craftsmen greater gifts than the others. Then the other craftsmen complained about them to the emperor and told him that they were Christians, and that they did the skilful jobs through witchcraft, because they blessed their work with the sign of Christ's cross. Then the emperor became annoyed and ordered them to be locked into leaden boxes, alive, and to be thrown into the river. And then after forty-two days, a Christian man pulled the boxes with the bodies out and took [them] home, and afterwards many miracles happened on account of these holy men.

11 November: Martin of Tours

223. On ðone endlyftan[a] dæg þæs monðes bið[b] Sancti Martines gewytennys þæs halgan bysceopes, þæs lychama resteð on þære mægðe þe ys nemned Gallea, and on þære ceastre Toronice þa we nemnað Turnum. Sancti Martynes æryste wundor wæs þæt hym com ongean an þearfende man nacod on cealdum wyntra. Þa tocearf he hys scyccel on twa and þa hyne gesealde healfne þam þearfendum men, and myd healfum he hyne sylfne eft gegyrede. And þa þære ylcan nyht ætywde ure Dryhten hyne hym on þam ylcan gegyrlan þe he þam þearfendum men ær gesealde and cwæð: 'Ongit nu þysne gegyrlan.' And Sanctus Martinus aweahte þry men of deaðe þurh Crystes fultum, and he gecyste þone man þe wæs egeslice hreof, and he wæs sona hal. And an scyp wæs syncende on sæ for anum myclum storme; þa genemde þæra scypmanna an Sanctus Martynus and hyne bæd hylpes. Þa stylde se storm sona, and seo sæ wearð eft smylte, and hig comon gesunde to hyðe.

223. [a] .xi.n B, endlyftan C; [b] B breaks off after bið.

11 November: Mennas and Heliodorus

224. On þone ylcan dæg byð twegra haligra wera tyd þa wæron nemnede Sanctus Minas and Sanctus Eliodorus; þa wæron ærest caseres cempan, and hig gelyfdon eft on Cryst and for hym martyrdom þrowedon on Dioclitianus dagum þæs caseres. And se heretoga wæs nemned Pyrrus; he het hig beheafdian for Cristes geleafan.

15 November: Milus and Senneus

225. On þone fifteoþan[a] dæg þæs monðes byð þæs bysceopes tyd se wæs nemned Sanctus Mynus, and his diacones nama wæs Senneus. Þes bysceop wæs acenned on þære ceastre þe ys nemned Drasythio, and on þære ceastre[368] þe ys nemned Leila, and he gedyde mænig heofenlic wunder. He eode dryum[b] fotum ofer wæter, and he geþrowode martyrdom for Cryste on þære ceastre þe ys nemned Malhþar. Þær twegen arlease gebroðro hyne nyddon þæt he weorðode sunnan deofulgyld. Þa he þæt nolde, þa stycodon hig hyne myd hyra sperum, oðer foran oðer hyndan. Þa cwæð he to þam broðrum: 'Tomorgen to þysse tyde yncer ægðer ofslyhð oðerne on þysse ylcan stowe, and hundas licciað eowre blod, and fugelas fretað incer flæsc, and yncer wif beoð on anum dæge wudewan.' Þa gelamp þæt hig huntedon on mergen on þære ylcan stowe. Þa gearn sum hynd betweox þam gebroðrum, and hig sceoton hyra strælas to þære hynde on twa healfa tosomne, and þa becom þæs yldran stræl on þæs gingran ynnoð, and þæs gyngran stræl on þæs yldran breost, and hig wæron sona deade on þære ylcan stowe þe hig ær þone Godes man slogon. And Sanctus Mylas ys bebyrged on þam tune þe ys nemned Malchan, and þær beoð mycele tacnu æt hys byrgenne.

225. [a] .xv. C; [b] g suprascript Ca, dry`g´um Ko.

11 November: Martin of Tours

223. On the eleventh day of the month is the death of the holy bishop St Martin, whose body rests in the country which is called Gaul, and in the city of Turonica [i.e. Tours] which we call Turnum. St Martin's first miracle was that he came across a naked pauper in the cold winter. He then cut up his cloak in two and gave one half to the poor man, and with the other half he clothed himself again. And then in the same night our Lord appeared to him in the same coat which he had earlier given to the poor man and said: 'Recognise this coat now.' And St Martin revived three men from death with the help of Christ, and he kissed the man who had terrible leprosy, and he was healed on the spot. And a ship was sinking on the sea in a big storm; then one of the sailors invoked St Martin and asked him for help. Then the storm suddenly abated, and the sea was made calm again, and they returned safely to harbour.

11 November: Mennas and Heliodorus

224. On the same day is the feast of the two holy men who were called St Mennas and St Heliodorus; they were initially soldiers of the emperor, and later they believed in Christ and suffered martyrdom for him in the days of emperor Diocletian. And the officer was called Pyrrhus; he ordered them to be beheaded for Christ's faith.

15 November: Milus and Senneus

225. On the fifteenth day of the month is the feast of the bishop who was called St Milus, and his deacon's name was Senneus. This bishop was born in the city which is called Razichitae, and in the city called Ila, and he performed many heavenly miracles. He walked over water with dry feet, and he suffered martyrdom for Christ in the city called Maheldagdar. Two evil brothers forced him there to worship an idol of the sun. When he refused, they stabbed him with their spears, one from the front and one from behind. Then he said to the brothers: 'At this time tomorrow each one of you will kill the other in this same place, and dogs will lap your blood, and birds will pick at your flesh, and your wives will become widows in a single day.' Then it happened that they were hunting in the morning in the same area. Then a hind ran between the brothers, and they shot their arrows at the hind from both sides at the same time, and the arrow of the older brother went into the younger one's stomach, and the arrow of the younger brother went into older one's chest, and they died immediately in the same place where they had earlier killed the man of God. And St Milus is buried in the town which is called Malchan, and there great miracles happen at his grave.

17 November: Hild

226. On þone seofenteoðan dæg þæs monðes byð þære halgan abbudessan gewytennys on Brytene þære nama wæs Sancta Hylda; heo wæs seo æryste tymbrend þæs mynstres þe ys nemned Steorneshealh. Hyre fæder nama wæs Hereric and hyre moder nama wæs Bregoswyð; and þære meder wæs on slæpe ætywed, þa heo myd þam bearne wæs, þæt hyre man stunge ane syle on þone bosum and seo ongunne scynan ofer ealle Brytene; þæt tacnode þone hlysan þære fæmnan halignysse. And Sancta Hylda wæs ªþry and þrytigª geara on læwedum hade and þry and þrytig geara under haligryfte[b], and heo þa gewat to Cryste. And hyre Godes þeowa sum geseah hu en<g>las[c 369] hyre gast to heofenum læddon, and heo glytenode on þæra engla mydle swa scynende sunne oððe nigslycod hrægel. And seo ylce Godes þeowen gehyrde, on þa ylcan tyd þa heo gewat, wundorlicre bellan sweg on þære lyfte, and heo geseah eac þæt englas hofon up ongean hyre gast swyðe mycle and wundorlice Crystes rode, and seo scean swa heofenes tungol. And myd swylcere blysse Sancta Hyldan gast wæs gelæded on heofenas cyneþrym, þær heo nu a butan ende gesyhð urne Dryhten, þæs wyllan heo ær fremede þa hwyle heo on lyfe wunode on hyre lychaman.

226. ª⁻ª .xxxiii. C; [b] halig ryfte Ko; [c] enlas C, en<g>las Co, Ko, englas He.

22 November: Cecilia

227. On þone ªtwa and twentigoþanª dæg þæs monðes byð Sancta Cecilian þrowung þære halgan fæmnan; seo wæs on hyre geogoðe æðelum were beweddod, and se wæs hæðen and heo wæs Cristen. Heo wæs gegyred myd hæran æt hyre lychaman, and onufan þære hæran heo wæs gegyred myd [b]golde awefenum[b] hrægelum. And on þære nyhte þa heo wæs ingelæded on þone brydbur, þa sæde heo þam[c] brydguman þæt heo gesawe engel of heofenum and se wolde hyne slean myd færdeaðe, gif he hyre æfre onhryne myd unclænre lufon. Þa gelærde heo þone brydguman þæt he onfeng fullwyhte and on God gelyfde. Þa he gefullod wæs and yneode on þone brydbur, þa stod se engel big hyre myd scynendum fyðerum and hæfde twegen beagas on hys handa þa glysnodon hwylum swa rosan blosman, hwylum swa lilian blostman. And þa sealde he oðerne þæra beaga þære fæmnan and oðerne þam brydguman and cwæð: 'Healdað ge þas beagas myd clænlicum dædum, forþam ðe ic hig brohte ync of Godes neorxnawange.' Þeos fæmne geþrowode martyrdom for Cryste. Almatheus[370] hatte Romeburge gerefa, he nydde hig þæt heo Cryste wyðsoce. Þa heo þæt ne geþafode, þa het he hig belucan on byrnendum baðe, on þam heo wæs dæg and nyht, swa[371] heo na ne geswætte. Þa eode hyre se cwellere to myd sweorde, and he hig sloh þrywa myd þam sweorde, and he ne myhte hyre þæt heafod [d]of aslean[d], ac heo gebæd hig to þam papan se wæs haten Urbanus,[372] and þa beforan þam papan heo todælde eall þæt hyre wæs and him gesealde and cwæð to hym: 'Þyssa þreora daga fæc ic me abæd æt Dryhtne þæt ic þe þys sealde, þæt ðu gehalgie myn hus to cyrcan.' And heo þa onsende hyre gast to Gode.

227. ª⁻ª .xxii. C; [b⁻b] goldeawefenum Ko, golde awefenum He; [c] suprascript Ca; [d⁻d] ofaslean Ko, of aslean He.

17 November: Hild

226. On the seventeenth day of the month is the death of the holy abbess in Britain whose name was St Hild; she was the first constructor of the monastery which is called Streoneshealh [i.e. Whitby]. Her father's name was Hereric and her mother's name was Bregoswith; and it had been revealed to the mother in her sleep, when she was with child, that a piece of jewellery would be pinned to her chest and it would begin to shine over the whole of Britain; that signified the fame of the virgin's sanctity. And St Hild lived for thirty-three years as a laywoman, and for thirty-three years after taking the veil, and she then migrated to Christ. And one of her servants of God saw how angels took her soul to heaven, and it shone amid the angels like the bright sun or a new dress. And the same maid of God heard, at the same time as she died, the noise of a beautiful bell in the air, and she also saw that angels lifted up towards her soul a very large and marvellous Christian cross, and it shone like a star in the sky. And with such honour St Hild's soul was led into the royal majesty of heaven, where she can now look at our Lord always without end, whose will she had accomplished previously while she was alive in her body.

22 November: Cecilia

227. On the twenty-second day of the month is the passion of the holy virgin St Cecilia; in her youth she was betrothed to a nobleman, and he was a pagan; she was a Christian. She was dressed in haircloth next to her body, and over the haircloth she was dressed in clothes of woven gold. And on the night when she was brought into the marital bedroom, she told her husband that she could see an angel from heaven, and he would kill him on the spot, if he were ever to touch her for unchaste love. She then taught her husband so that he received baptism and believed in God. When he had been baptised and walked into the bedroom, the angel stood by her with shiny wings and had two crowns in his hand which glistened sometimes like the blossoms of the rose, sometimes like the blossoms of the lily. And he gave one of the crowns to the virgin and the other to the husband and said: 'Preserve these crowns with chaste behaviour, because I brought them to you both from God's paradise.' This virgin suffered martyrdom for Christ. Almatheus was the name of the governor of the city of Rome; he forced her to renounce Christ. When she refused, he ordered her to be locked into a scalding bath, in which she was one day and one night, and she never even sweated. Then the executioner came at her with a sword, and he hit her three times with the sword, and could not cut her head off, but she appealed to the pope who was called Urban, and in front of the pope she handed out all that she owned and gave it to him and said to him: 'The reprieve of the last three days I obtained by praying to the Lord so that I might give you this, so that you might consecrate my house as a church.' And she then sent her spirit to God.

23 November: Pope Clement I

228. On ðone þreo and twentigoðan dæg þæs monðes byð Sancti Clementis tyd þæs papan, þone Sanctus Petrus sylf gehalgode to papan and hym sealde þa ylcan myhte þe Dryhten Cryst hym sealde, þæt h<e>[a] heofna rices cægan and helle geweald ahte. Þar þes Clementes gedyde þurh hys gebed þæt of þære eorðan wæter [b]upp arn[b] þær ær nænig wylm ne wæs. And Traianus se casere onsende hys heretogan, se wæs on naman Aufidianus, and se nydde þysne Clementem þæt he Cryste wiðsoce; þa ne myhte he hyne oncyrran. Þa het he hym gebyndan anne ancran on hys sweoran and hyne forsendan on sæ. Þa stodon Crystene men on þam waroðe and weopon, and þa adruwode seo sæ þrytig[c] [373] mila. Þa eode þæt Crystene folc on þa sæ, and hig gemytton þær stænen hus fram Dryhtne gegearwod, on þam wæs geseted Clementes lychama on stænenre earce, and se ancra þær wæs [d]big geseted[d], myd þam he wæs ær on þa <sæ>[e] [374] sended. And æghwylce geare syððan æt hys tyde se sæ gearwode drigne syðfæt seofen dagas tocumendum mannum to hys cyrcan[f]. Seo cyrce ys on þrym mylum fram þære eorðan on þære sæ, and heo ys on easteweardre Ralia[375] mægðe. Þær hwylon sum wyf on þære cyrcan ofergeat hyre cyld slæpende, and seo sæ fleow ymbe þa cyrcan. Þa æfter geares fæce, þa þæt folc eft þyder com to Clementes tyde, þa gemetton hig þæt cyld lyfigende and slapende on þære cyrcan, and hyt ferde myd hys meder.

228. [a] h C, h<e> Co, Ko, englas Herz; [b-b] upparn Ko, upp arn Herz; [c] .xxx. C; [d-d] biggeseted Ko, big geseted Herz; [e] om. C; [f] r suprascript Ca.

23 November: Felicity

229. On þone ylcan dæg byð þære halgan wudewan gemynd þære nama ys Felicita, seo þrowode for Cryste myd hyre seofon sunum. Heo gelærde þa hyre suna to Godes geleafan, and heo acende hyg Gode myd gaste, þa ðe heo myd lychaman on myddangearde gebær. Þeos wyduwe ys mare þonne martyre;[376] heo onsende hyre seofen suna to heofena rice; swa oft heo wæs dead beforan hyre sylfre. Heo ondred þæt gif þa suna ofer hig lyfedon, and heo wæs fægnigende þa hig swulton. Heo wyscte þæt heo nanne æfter hyre ne forlete, þe læs[377] gif hyra hwylc wære hyre oferstealla, þæt se ne myhte on heofenum beon hyre efngemæcca.

24 November: Chrysogonus

230. On þone feower and twentygoðan dæg þæs monðes byð Sancti Crissogones tyd and þrowung, se wæs beorht myd eorðlicere æðelnysse and wundorlicra on godcundre snytro. Þam Crissogone Deoclitianus se casere gehet ealdordomes medomnysse, gif he wolde forlætan Crystes geleafan. Þa cwæð he to þam casere: 'Ic aworpe þa myht fram me þe me fram þe gehaten ys, swa þæt lam þe ic myd mynum fotum [a]on trede[a].' Ða het se casere hyne beheafdian, and weorpan þone lychaman and þæt heafod on sæ. And þa sum halig mæssepreost feng to þam lychaman þe þar

230. [a-a] ontrede Ko, on trede Herz;

23 November: Pope Clement I

228. On the twenty-third day of the month is the feast of the pope St Clement, whom St Peter himself consecrated as pope and whom he gave the same power that the Lord Christ had given him, so that he might have the keys of the heavenly kingdom and power over hell. Through his prayer this Clement caused water to well up from the earth where before there had been no spring. And the emperor Trajan sent his general, who was called Aufidianus, and he forced this Clement to renounce Christ; then he could not change his mind. Then he ordered an anchor to be tied to his neck and him to be thrown into the sea. Then Christians stood on the shore and wept, and then the sea dried up for thirty miles. Then the Christians walked out into the sea, and there they found a stone house made ready by the Lord, in which Clement's body had been placed in a stone sarcophagus, and the anchor, with which he had earlier been thrown into it [i.e. the sea], was placed nearby. And each year since then on his feastday the sea has allowed dry passage for seven days for visitors coming to his church. The church is three miles into the sea from the land, and it is in the eastern part of the country of [?Italy]. Once a woman forgot her sleeping child in the church, and the sea flowed around the church. Then after a year had passed, when the people arrived there on Clement's feastday, they found the child alive and sleeping in the church, and it went away with its mother.

23 November: Felicity

229. On the same day is the commemoration of the holy widow whose name is Felicity, who suffered for Christ with her seven sons. She brought up her sons in God's faith, and she brought them forth to God in spirit when she gave birth to them in body on earth. This widow is greater than a martyr; she sent her seven sons to the kingdom of heaven; she died as many times, before [she died] herself. She feared that her sons might survive her, and was glad when they died. She wished that she would leave none behind her, so as to avoid a situation where, if one of them was to survive her, he would not be her equal in heaven.

24 November: Chrysogonus

230. On the twenty-fourth day of the month is the feast and passion of St Chrysogonus, who shone with his secular nobility and was even more amazing in his religious wisdom. The emperor Diocletian promised the dignity of a high office to Chrysogonus, if he was to renounce the Christian faith. Then he said to the emperor: 'I cast off the power from me which you have promised me, like the mud on which I walk with my feet.' Then the emperor ordered him to be beheaded, and the body and the head to be thrown into the sea. And a holy priest then got hold of the

aworpen wæs to þam waroðe, and he hyne arweorðlice bebyrigde. And eft þurh Godes ætywednesse he funde þæt heafod þær hyt seo sæ [b]up wearp[b], and he þæt ða bær and alede hyt to þam lychaman.

[b-b] upwearp Ko, He.

28 November: Saturninus

231. On þone ehta and twentygoðan dæg þæs monðes byð þæs bysceopes þrowung Sancti Saturnini; se wæs on þære ceastre þe ys nemned Þolosane, and þa for þæs bysceopes halignysse geswigdon eall þa deofolgyld þe hig ær [a]<on> þære ceastre[a] [378] beeodon. And þa syððan forþam yrsodon þa hæðenan ceastergewaran[b] wyð hyne, and gebundon þone halgan bysceop be þam fotum on sumne fearr, and þone gegremedon þæt he hleop on unsmeðe eorðan and þam bysceope þæt heafod tobeot, and ealle hys lymu wæron toslytene. And he þa Criste hys sawle ageaf, and twa Crystene wyf ahyddon þone lychaman under myclum stangefealle, [c]oð þæt[c] ðæra bysceopa sum, þe hys æfterfyligend wæs, getymbrede fægere cyrcan and on þa þone lychaman gesette.

231. [a-a] þære ceastre B, Ko, <on> þære ceastre Herz; [b] ceaster suprascript Ca; [c-c] oðþæt Ko.

28 November: Chrysanthus and Daria

232. On þone ylcan dæg byð Sancti Crisantes tyd þæs æðelan weres; þone hys yldran befæston on hys cnyhthade to Alexandrea ceastre sumum woruldwysan men þæt he æt þam leornode þa seofon cræftas on þam beoð gemeted ealle weoruldwysdomas, þæt ys ærest arythimetica, þæt ys þonne rymcræft, and astraloia, þæt ys þonne tungolcræft, and astronomia, þæt ys tungla gang, and geometrica, þæt ys eorðgemet, and musica, þæt ys dreamcræft, and m<ech>anica[a], þæt y<s>[b] weoruldweorces cræft, and medicina, þæt ys læcedomes cræft. Þa he þas cræftas ealle hæfde þurhsmeade, þa com he to sumum mæssepreoste; þa lærde se hyne godcunde gewrytu. Þa forlet he þa woruldgewrytu and lufode þa godcundan gewritu and onfeng fulwyhte and Gode þeowode on clænnysse. Þa he þa wæs on þære iugoðe, þa ongunnon hys yldran hyne laþian to brydþyngum. Þa wyðsoc he þam. Þa het se fæder gefrætewian sum hus myd mycelum fægernyssum, and het beran on þæt hus manegra cynna symbel, and het þone cnyht lædan on þæt hus, and het fif mædenu swyðe geglengede gangan on þæt hus. Þa onhylde se halga cnyht hys ansyne ondune and nolde hig na geseon þe ma ðe fif[c] næddran crupon on þæt hus. And þa sona eode slæp on þa mædenu, and hig slepon dæg and nyht, swa lange swa hig on þam huse wæron. Þa het se fæder hym gelædan to swyðe gleawe[379], seo wæs gefrætwod myd golde and myd gymmum, þæt seo sceolde hys geþoht oncyrran; þære nama wæs Darie. Þa gelærde he þa to Crystes geleafan, and hig lyfedon hym þa samod on clænnysse, and samod hyra lyf geendodon on martyrdome, and samod restað on anre byrgenne and þa gastas samod gefeoð on anum wuldre, and God dyde þurh hig manege wundru, ge þurh lifigende ge þurh forðfarene.

232. [a] mthanica C; [b] y C; [c] .v. C.

body which had been washed up ashore there, and he buried him honourably. And later through a revelation from God he found the head where the sea had washed it up, and he then took it and put it next to the body.

28 November: Saturninus

231. On the twenty-eighth day of the month is the passion of the bishop St Saturninus; he lived in the city which is called Tolosa [i.e. Toulouse], and then because of the bishop's sanctity all the pagan idols which they had previously worshipped in that city became silent. And then for that reason the pagan townspeople became annoyed with him, and tied the holy bishop to a bull by his feet, and made it wild so that it ran over hard ground and smashed the bishop's skull, and all his limbs were torn to pieces. And he then gave up the ghost to Christ, and two Christian women hid the body under a pile of rubble, until one of the bishops, who was his successor, built an attractive church and placed the body in it.

28 November: Chrysanthus and Daria

232. On the same day is the feast of the nobleman St Chrysanthus; his parents handed him over in his childhood to the city of Alexandria to a scholar so that he might learn from him the seven arts in which all the worldly knowledge can be found, that is first arithmetic (that is the science of numbers), and astrology (that is the science of the stars), and astronomy (that is the movement of the stars), and geometry (that is land measurement), and music (that is the science of harmony), and mechanics (that is the science of physical processes), and medicine (that is the science of healing). When he studied all these subjects thoroughly, he came to a priest; then he taught him Christian scripture. Then he abandoned the secular books and came to love spiritual literature and received baptism and served God in celibacy. When he became a young man, his parents tried to get him interested in marriage. Then he resisted. Then his father ordered a house to be done up with many luxuries, and ordered all sorts of delicacies to be brought into the house and ordered the boy to be brought into the house, and ordered five very dressed-up girls to go into the house. Then the holy boy turned his face down, and wanted to look at them no more than as if five snakes had crept into the house. And then straightaway the girls went to sleep, and they slept day and night, for as long as they were in the house. Then his father ordered him to be taken to a very wise [woman], who was dressed up with gold and with jewels, so that she might change his mind; her name was Daria. Then he educated her about the Christian faith, and then they lived together in celibacy, and ended their life together, and rest together in one tomb and the souls rejoice together in one glory, and God performed many miracles through them, both when they were alive and when they were dead.

30 November: Andrew

233. On þone þryttygoðan dæg þæs monðes byð Sancte Andreas tyd þæs apostoles. He wæs Sancte Petres broðer, and he wæs se æresta Dryhtnes þegen, and he ys cweden se wlytega Dryhtnes þegen, forþam ðe he wæs wlitig on lychaman and he wæs wlitig on mode. And æfter Cristes upastigennysse he gecyrde twa mægða to Godes geleafan, þa wæron þus genemned: Scyððiam þa mægðe and Achaiam þa mægðe. And on Patria þære ceastre he wæs ahangen on rode, and myd mycele leohte he onsende hys gast to Gode. And Egeas se ealdorman se þe hyne het ahon, þyg ylcan dæge he wæs fram deofle forbroden and he sweolt. And þæs Egeas broðor, se wæs on naman Stratohles, and Egeas wif, þære nama wæs Maximille, hig bebyrigdon Andreas lichaman myd wyrtgemengnyssum and myd swetum stencum. And on Constantinus dagum[380] þæs caseres, Andreas lic wæs þanon alæd on þa ceastre þe ys nemned Constantinopolim.

The End of November

233a. Þonne se monað byð geendod þe we nemnað Blodmonað[381], þonne byð seo nyht syxtyne[a] tyda lang, and se dæg ehta[b] tyda.

233a. [a] .xvi. C; [b] .viii. C.

The Beginning of December

233b. On þam twelftan monðe on geare byð an and þrytig[a] daga. Se monað ys nemned on Leden Decembris, and on ure geþeode se Ærra Geola. Forþam þa monðas twegen syndon nemde anum naman, oðer se Ærra Geola, oðer se Æftera, forþan ðe hyra oðer gangeð beforan þæra sunnan ær þon ðe heo cyrre hig to þæs dæges lenge, oðer æfter.

233b. [a] .xxx. C.

10 December: Eulalia

234. On þone teoðan dæg þæs monðes byð Sancta Eulalian þrowung þære fæmnan, seo wæs on þære mægðe þe ys nemned Hisponia[a], and on þære ceastre þe ys nemned Barcilona. Seo fæmne wæs þrytyne[b] geare þa Datianus[382] se gerefa ferde on þa ceastre Crystene men to nydanne fram Crystes geleafan. Þa eode þæt mæden hym ongean and cwæð: 'Þu Godes feond, tohwan gangest þu on þas burh? And tohwan ehtst þu Crystenra manna? And tohwon tylast þu þæt ðu forleose Godes fæmnan?' Þa yrsode he and gebealh hyne, and het hig aðenian on yren bed and hig begeotan myd weallende leade, and hyre þæt ne geeglode. Þa het he hig don on fyrenne ofen, þa ne gederede hyre þæt. Þa het he hys leasere hig behamelian, and hig þa nacode geunarian, þa cwæð heo: 'Ic wat for hwæne ic þys þrowige, efne for Cryst.' Þa het he hig lædan to beheafdinge, þa cwæð heo to hym: 'Ic cume eft on domesdæg and þe þonne wrege beforan Crystes þrymsetle, and þu þonne ongitst þu myne ansyne.' And sona swa hig man heafdode, þa com þær fæger culfre of þam lichaman and fleah

30 November: Andrew

233. On the thirtieth day of the month is the feast of the apostle St Andrew. He was the brother of St Peter, and he was the first of the Lord's disciples, and he is called the beautiful disciple of the Lord, because he was handsome in his physique and had a beautiful mind. And after Christ's ascension he converted two provinces to God's religion, which were called as follows: the province of Scythia and the province of Achaea. And in the city of Patras he was hanged on the cross, and with much light he gave up the ghost to God. And the governor Egeas, who had ordered him to be hanged, on the same day he was torn to pieces by a devil and he died. And the brother of Egeas, who was called Stratocles, and the wife of Egeas, whose name was Maximilla – they buried Andrew's body with various spices and sweet perfumes. And in the days of the emperor [Constantius], Andrew's body was taken from there into the city called Constantinople.

The End of November

233a. When the month which we call Blodmonað ['Sacrifice Month'] comes to an end, the night is sixteen hours long and the day eight hours.

The Beginning of December

233b. There are thirty-one days in the twelfth month of the year. In Latin that month is called *December*, and in our language 'Ærra Geola' [The First Month of Yule]. The reason why the two months are called by one name, 'Ærra Geola' the one and 'Æftera Geola' the other, is because the one precedes the point where the sun turns to lenghtening the day again, the other one follows it.

10 December: Eulalia

234. On the tenth day of the month is the passion of the virgin St Eulalia, who lived in the country which is called Spain, and in the city which is called Barcelona. The virgin was thirteen years old when the governor Datianus came to the city to force the Christians away from Christianity. Then the girl walked up to him and said: 'You enemy of God, why do you come into this city? And why do you persecute Christian men? And why do you try to destroy God's virgins?' Then he became angry and lost his temper, and ordered her to be tied to an iron rack and [ordered] her to be covered with boiling lead, and it did not torment her. When he ordered her to be put into a hot oven, that did not harm her. When he commanded his guard to mutilate her and to dishonour her naked, she said: 'I know for whom I suffer this, namely for Christ.' When he ordered her to be led to her beheading, she said to him: 'I will come back on Doomsday and will then accuse you in front of Christ's throne of glory, and then you will see my face.' And as soon as she had been beheaded, a beautiful dove came

ymbe þone lychaman and hyne freode[383], and þa fleah to heofenum. And hyre lychama resteð on Barcilonia ceastre.

234. [a] i suprascript in later hand; [b] .xiii. C.

13 December: Lucy

235. On þone þryteoþan[a] dæg þæs monðes byð Sancta Lucian tyd þære æðelan fæmnan, seo wæs on þære mægðe þe ys nemned Sicilia mægðe, and on þære ceastre þe ys nemned Siracusana. Þa þreatode hig þære mægðe ealdorman, se wæs on naman Fascassius, myd myclum wytum to deofolgyldum and cwæð hyre to: 'Gif þu nelt forlætan þone Crystes geleafan, ic þe hate lædan to forlegeswifa huse and þe ðær bysmrian.' Þa cwæð heo: 'Nys me þynes weales hæmed næfre þe leofre þe me nædre toslyte.' Þa gesealde he þa fæmnan his leaserum and cwæð: 'Bysmriað hig, [b]oð þæt[b] heo dead sig.' Þa hig þa woldon hig lædan, þa ne myhton hig nahwyder hig onstyrian. Þa eodon heora manege of þæs ealdormannes þenungwerode; sume sceufon, sume tugon and swyðe swætton, [c]oð þæt[c] hig geteorode wæron, and seo Godes fæmne hwæðre stod. Þa brudon hig rapas on hyre handa and on hyre fet, and hig tugon myd þam, and hig ne myhton hig þa git anne fotlast furður ateon. Þa het se wælgrymma[d] ealdorman hig myd sweorde wundian on þone ynnoð, and þa cwæð heo to þam Crystenan mannum þe hyre ymbestodon: 'Þære tyde ys neah þæt Godes cyrce hafað sybbe on eorðan and Crystene men. And Dioclitianus, se hæðena casere þe nu rixað, byð of hys rice aworpen, and Maximianus his gerefa byð todæge dead. And ic beo eower þyngere to Gode, gif ge habbað Godes geleafan and hys wyllan doð.' And se ealdorman þe hig wundian het beforan hyre eagum wæs gebunden myd ysenum racenteagum and wæs gelæded to Rome, and eall Romana dugoð hyne gedemde to deaðe. And he wæs þær heafde beheawen, and hys þæt synnige blod wæs agoten on þa wrace hyre þæs unsceððian blodes. And Sancta Lucian ær ne gewat, ær hyre com to Godes sacerd and hyre gesealde husl, and heo þa hyre to Gode gebæd and hyre gast ageaf.

235. [a] .xiii. C; [b-b] oðþæt Ko; [c-c] oðþæt Ko; [d] wæl suprascript Ca.

13 December: Ursicinus

236. On þone ylcan dæg byð þæs læces tyd Sancti Ursicine, se wæs on Rauenna þære ceastre. Þa nydde Paulinus se dema hyne þæt he sceolde Crystes geleafan forlætan oððe beon beheafdod. Þa hyne man lædde to þære beheafdinge, þa getweode hyne on hys mode, and wolde gecyrran to þam deofolgyldum. Þa clypode sum Crysten man and cwæð: 'Ursicine, ær þu hældest oðre men, and nu þu wundast þe sylfne.' And þa gehreow hym þæt hyne æfre swa on hys geþohte getweode, and he geþrowode martyrdom for Cryste, and Gode ageaf þone deorwyrðan gym þone þe deofol wolde gereafian, þæt ys seo halige sawl.

from the body and flew around the body and touched it gently and then flew to heaven. And her body rests in the city of Barcelona.

13 December: Lucy

235. On the thirteenth day of the month is the feast of the noble virgin St Lucy, who lived in the province which is called Sicily, and in the city which is called Syracuse. Then the country's governor, whose name was Paschasius, forced her with severe torments into devil-worship and said to her: 'If you do not want to abandon the Christian faith, I will order you to be taken to a house of prostitutes and [order] you to be dishonoured there.' Then she said: 'Sex with your slave is no more attractive to me than that a snake should bite me.' Then he gave the virgin to his guards and said: 'Dishonour her, until she is dead.' When they wanted to take her away, they could not move her in any direction. Then many of them from the governor's household came; some pushed, some pulled and tried very hard, until they were tired, and the virgin of God stood still. Then they tied ropes to her hands and her feet, and they pulled with those, and still they could not move her one foot further. Then the bloodthirsty governor ordered her to be stabbed in the stomach with a sword, and she said to the Christians who stood near her: 'It is time for God's church and Christians to have peace on earth. And Diocletian, the pagan emperor who now rules, will be thrown out of his empire, and Maximian his governor will die today. And I will be your intercessor with God, if you have God's faith and perform his will.' And the governor who had ordered her to be stabbed was tied up before her eyes with iron chains and was led to Rome, and the whole Roman senate sentenced him to death. And he then was beheaded, and his sinful blood was shed in punishment for her innocent blood. And St Lucy did not pass away before God's priest came to her and gave her the Eucharist, and she then prayed to God and gave up the ghost.

13 December: Ursicinus

236. On the same day is the feast of the doctor St Ursicinus, who lived in the city of Ravenna. Then the judge Paulinus forced him to abandon Christ's faith or to be beheaded. When they led him to the execution, he hesitated in his mind, and wanted to revert to devil-worship. Then a Christian shouted and said: 'Ursicinus, previously you healed others, and now you hurt yourself.' And then he regretted that he had ever doubted in his mind like that, and he suffered martyrdom for Christ, and gave the precious jewel to God which the devil had wanted to steal, that is the holy soul.

14 December: Higebald

237. On þone feowerteoðan dæg þæs monðes byð Sancte Hygebaldes gewytennys þæs halgan abbudes, þæs lychama resteð on Lyndesse mægðe. Be þam wrat Beda se leornere on Angelcynnes bocum þæt he wære haliges lyfes and swiðe clænes.

21 December: Thomas

238. On þone [a]an and twentygoþan[a] dæg þæs monðes byð Sancte Thomas tyd þæs apostoles, se wæs on Grecisc nemned Didimus and on Romanisc Geminus, þæt ys on ure geþeode getwyn. Forþam he wæs swa geciged, forþam ðe he wæs urum Hælende gelic on menniscre onsyne. And æfter Crystes upastigennysse he gelærde monige þeode to Crystes geleafan: Parðwara[b] and Medware and Persware and Hyrcanas and Bactrianas and twa Indea mægðe. And he þurhferde hæðenre þeode eorð<an>[c 384] and myddangeardes eastdæl, and myd Indeum he getymbrede hyra cyninges healle on heofenum, se wæs on naman Gundaforus. And þæt geseah þæs cyninges broðor, þæs sawl wæs on heofenas gelæded myd Godes englum, þæt seo heall wæs getymbred ynnan and utan myd grenum and myd hæwenum and myd hwytum,[385] and se wæs eft lyfigende on eorðan, se ðe sæde þæt hyt wære þus getymbred on heofenum. Ac on oðre Indea mægðe Mygdæg se cyning and hys ealdorman, se wæs on naman Caritius, he nydde þysne Thomum þæt he weorðode sunnan deofolgyld. Þær wæs þære sunnan anlycnys geworht of golde, and heo wæs on gyldenum scryðe[d 386], and æt þam wæron gyldene hors, and on þam wæron þa wealdleðer swa [e]up getiged[e] [387] swa swa hig urnon to heofenum up. Þa Þome þæder ineode, þa eode þær egeslic deoful ut of þam goldgeweorce and stod beforan hym, and þæt goldgeworc eall todreas, swa swa weax gemylt æt fyre. Þa þæra hæðenra bysceopa sum ofsloh þone Crystes þegen, and gewrytu secgað hwylum þæt he wære myd sweorde þurhstungen, hwylum hig secgað þæt he wære myd sperum ofsticod. He þrowode in Calamina on Indea ceastre, and hys lychama wæs alæded of Indeum on þa ceastre þe ys nemned Edyssa. Þær he[388] ys geseted on sylfrene cyste, and seo hangað on sylfrenum racenteagum. Ne mæg þær nænig gedwolman lyfian on þære ceastre, ne nænig þæra þe deofolgyld begangað, ne næfre syððan ne myhton ælreorde þeode hergian on þa ceastre.

238. [a-a] .xxi. C; [b] Warðwara Ko, Parðwara Herz, difference between þ and w slight in this hand, but still discernible; [c] eorð C, Ko, eard Herz; [d] scryð Ko, scryde He; [e-e] upgetiged Ko.

14 December: Higebald

237. On the fourteenth day of the month is the departure of the holy abbot St Higebald, whose body rests in the province of Lindsey. Bede the scholar wrote about him in the books about the English that he led a holy and very chaste life.

21 December: Thomas

238. On the twenty-first day of the month is the feast of the apostle St Thomas, who in Greek was called Didymus and in Latin Geminus, that is 'twin' in our language. The reason why he was called that is that he was similar in physical appearance to our Saviour. And after Christ's ascension he instructed many nations in Christ's faith: the Parthians and the Medes and the Persians and Hyrcanians and Bactrians and two Indian nations. And he travelled through the lands of pagan people and the eastern part of the world, and in India he built their king's hall in heaven, whose name was Gundaphorus. And the king's brother saw that, whose soul was led to heaven with God's angels, that the hall was built inside and outside with green [stones] and purple ones and white ones, and he was alive again on earth, who said that it was built like that in heaven. And in another Indian country King Mygdeus and his governor, whose name was Caritius, he forced this Thomas to worship the devil-idol of the sun. There was a sun's image made of gold, and it was in a golden chariot, and there were golden horses in front of it, and their reins were tied up in such a way, as if they were going to run up to heaven. When Thomas went in there, a horrible devil came out from the golden structure there and stood before him, and the golden structure completely disintegrated, just as wax melts near a fire. One of the pagan bishops then killed the servant of Christ, and the texts sometimes say that he was stabbed with a sword, sometimes they say that he was stabbed with spears. He suffered in the city of Calamina in India, and his body was transported from India to the city which is called Edessa. There it is placed in a silver reliquary, and that hangs from silver chains. No heretic can live in that city there, nor any of those who practise devil-worship, nor could ever since then any foreign nations sack the city.

Commentary

Each of the entries below comments on a particular text section, and consists of three parts. The first aims to summarise the sources of each section and comment on the presumed composition; the second provides notes on specific passages and points of difficulty; the third gives a summary bibliography. Within the bibliography, items are ordered according to the extent to which they comment on the entire text section: more wide-ranging items are listed first, and are followed by items commenting on more detailed aspects. The term 'source' is used to refer to texts which the martyrologist could have accessed directly or indirectly (in the latter case as an antecedent source, that is, excerpted or quoted from an otherwise unidentified intermediary text).

The notes below are not intended to provide comprehensive biographical information on the saints themselves; this can be found in the standard dictionaries of saints, for example Farmer, *The Oxford Dictionary of Saints*, John and Attwater, *The Penguin Dictionary of Saints*, Kelly, *The Oxford Dictionary of Popes*, or easily accessible electronic tools, such as the *Catholic Encyclopedia*. More detailed biographical, literary and historical information on each saint can also be found in Whatley, 'Acta Sanctorum', Blair, 'A Handlist of Anglo-Saxon Saints', and Caraffa, ed., *Bibliotheca Sanctorum*. Overlap between the feasts of the *Old English Martyrology* and other martyrologies and Anglo-Saxon calendars is presented in user-friendly tables in Kotzor, I, 290–300 and 302–11, together with the relevant bibliographical details of such comparative material. I have here followed Kotzor's classification of overlapping commemorations in Bede, *Martyrologium* as B (narrative entry), B I (short entry, manuscripts of group I), or B II (short entry, manuscripts of group II), for which see Kotzor, I, 290.

1. The Birth of Christ: 25 December; commemorated in the *Calendar of Willibrord* and Bede, *Martyrologium* (B II). The details of the birth and the angel's appearance to the shepherds are probably derived from Adomnán, *De locis sanctis*, 2.2.2–5, and 2.6.8–12, and Luke 2.8–14. The specified age of the world has several parallels, e.g. Bede, *De temporibus*, 22.3–4, or Orosius, *Historiae aduersum paganos*, 1.1.5–6. The ultimate (but not direct) source for the portents described is Livy; a number of later collectors of Livian prodigies provide analogues: Iulius Obsequens, *De prodigiis*, 14, 26, 32, 54, Orosius, *Historiae aduersum paganos*, 4.5.2, 5.6.3, 5.18.3–5, and Patrick of Dublin, *De signis et prodigiis*, 11–16. Several of these and other analogues are historiographic or annalistic in type and assign the portents to given years in world history, but, as Hall shows, the connection of Livian portents with the Nativity also has parallels in the homiletic genre, namely in a number of Christmas sermons. The martyrologist probably drew on an (unknown) list of portents similar to the analogues, perhaps most likely contained in a homiletic text. The link which is made between the portents and the virgin's purity has not been sourced in detail, but could be derived from a further Christmas sermon, Pseudo-Augustine, Sermo 127, 1997. The detail of Christ's bath water is probably derived from Adomnán, *De locis sanctis*, 2.3.4–13, which refers to a miraculous spring in the rocks.

COMMENTARY

1. *Beth<l>em*. Bethem D, Beth<leh>em Ko, beth<l>em Co; the prevalent spellings for this place-name in Old English texts are 'Bethlem' or 'Bethleem'. 'Bethlehem' seems to be unattested in an Old English context; see also Note 18.

2. *siðan*. Unusual spelling of 'siððan', possibly triggered by the instances of 'sið' which follow, but see Sisam, Review of Kotzor, p. 68.

3. *swa*. See Schleburg, *Altenglisch swa*, §627.

4. *Eall þis...butan fæder*. This passage emphasises that Christ was, paradoxically, inside a virgin, without violating her virginity. (A later section, **56**, shows that the conception was thought to have occurred through the ear). Although the passage seems to be based on Augustine, it now resembles a riddle, exploiting the impossibilium of Christ's combined human and divine origin. Condie, 'Representations of the Nativity', p. 141, doubts the textual veracity of these lines, pointing out that the passage as it stands could be misinterpreted as suggesting that the adult Christ had sex with his mother. Condie therefore suggest emendation of the text by repunctuating before 'ac' to start a new sentence, and by deleting the 'and' which precedes 'hæfde þa modur' in D. But emendation seems unnecessary here, as the martyrologist may not have shrunk back from referring explicitly to the fact that the unborn baby Christ was touching the virgin's inside; see Hall, 'Christ's Birth' for general background, and Coleman, *Love, Sex, and Marriage*, pp. 70, 148 and 158, for 'gehrinan' and its sexual connotations.

Bibliography: Cross, 'De signis et prodigiis'; T. N. Hall, 'The Portents at Christ's Birth in Vercelli Homilies V and VI'; Cross, 'Portents and Events', pp. 215–20; Hughes, Review of Gwynn; Condie, 'Representations of the Nativity', pp. 136–49; Rauer, *Fontes*; Cross, 'The Influence of Irish Texts and Traditions', p. 185; Kotzor, II, 277; Cook, *Biblical Quotations*, p. 19; Rauer, 'Usage', p. 126n; Clayton, 'Feasts of the Virgin', pp. 222–3; Hall, 'Christ's Birth'.

2. Anastasia: 25 December; d. Palmaria, ?304, under Diocletian; not commemorated in the *Calendar of Willibrord*; commemorated in Bede, *Martyrologium* (B). Based on the *Passio S. Anastasiae* (*BHL* 401), 32–6.

5. *gereua<n>*. gereuas D, Ko, gerefan Herz; cp. **170** for a similar case. The singular form here also explains the correct singular form of the verb, 'sceolde', which Kotzor, II, 277 sees as erroneous.

6. *þa wæs hire ansin swa reod*. Cross posits an unknown additional source for the saint's red face. It seems, however, that this is derived from a confusion and mistranslation of *robur* and *rubor* in the cited Latin source.

Bibliography: Rauer, 'The Sources of the *Old English Martyrology*', p. 96n; Rauer, *Fontes*; Whatley, s. v. 'Anastasia'; Moretti, La *Passio Anastasiae*; Lanéry, 'Hagiographie d'Italie', pp. 45–60; Cross, 'A Lost Life of Hilda of Whitby', pp. 32–3; Kotzor, II, 277; Rauer, 'Female Hagiography'.

3. Eugenia: 25 December; third century, martyred under Valerian; not commemorated in the *Calendar of Willibrord*; commemorated in Bede, *Martyrologium* (B II). Gretsch rightly points out that this feastday is unattested for Eugenia in Anglo-Saxon calendars; it is, however, the same as in the martyrologies of Usuard and Hrabanus Maurus, and is, like the bulk of this section, likely to have been derived from the Latin source text, the *Passio S. Eugeniae* (*BHL* 2666), 605–12, 615–16 and 619–20. Not all details have parallels in the printed versions of this Latin source, however, and Cross and Whatley suggest that the source text used by the martyrologist probably combined characteristics of more than one surviving Latin variant; see Whatley, 'Textual Hybrids', for the complexity of this textual tradition.

7.   *Eu<g>e<n>ian*. eufemian D; probably scribal error caused by confusion with Euphemia, **187**.

8.   *sealde blindum mannum gesihðe and deofulseoce gehælde*. The cluster of insertion and abbreviations is difficult to interpret, but, to judge from the Latin text, both the blind and the possessed are in the pl. (*daemones ex obsessis corporibus pelleret, et caecorum oculos aperiret*).

9.   *æfter hire fæder <deaðe>*. The passage is defective; a reference to the father's death is missing here; see also Sisam, Review of Kotzor, p. 68, and Leinbaugh, Review of Kotzor, p. 173. Herz and Marsden emend to 'æfter hire fæder deaðe', and this emendation is followed here. The Latin texts explain in greater detail how her father Philippus (introduced by name also in the Old English text) suffers an illustrious persecution and martyrdom himself, and the question remains whether the martyrologist would have elaborated on his death with a more complex reference than is suggested here.

10.   *het he bindan hire stan to þam swuran*. Possibly corrupt, but cp. **130** for similar phrasing and syntax. Whatley (pers. comm.) explains that the detail of the saint's neck is lacking in *BHL* 2666, which merely refers to the saint being tied (*ligari, colligari*) to a rock. *BHL* 2667 by contrast specifies involvement of the saint's shoulders. Whatley suggests (pers. comm.) that influence from this tradition which refers to the shoulders, or an erroneous reading of *collo ligato*, from *colligato*, could explain the details of the attempted drowning here.

11.   *tobærs<t>*. tobærs D, Ko, tobærst Herz; see Frankis, Review of Kotzor, p. 314.

12.   *het hi...het hie*. Non-expression (or non-repetition) of subject not exactly typical of this text, but not ungrammatical; see Mitchell, *Old English Syntax*, §§1503–1514.

13.   *Þi illcan...eorþan com*. Clearly garbled; Christ's speech was probably meant to emphasise that Christ was taking Eugenia to heaven on that day of the year on which he himself was born. See also Sisam, Review of Kotzor, p. 68, and Herzfeld, p. 225, and the equivalent speech in the Latin text, *eodem die te in coelis recipiam, quo ego descendi ad terram*.

14.   *ma<n>*. ma D, ma<n> Herz, but see the comments in Sisam, Review of Kotzor, p. 68.

Bibliography: Cross, '*Passio S. Eugeniae*'; Whatley, s. v. 'Eugenia'; Whatley, 'Textual Hybrids'; Rauer, *Fontes*; Sisam, Review of Kotzor, p. 68; Herzfeld, pp. 6 and 225; Leinbaugh, Review of Kotzor, p. 173; Frankis, Review of Kotzor, p. 314; Marsden, *The Cambridge Old English Reader*, pp. 178–80; Gretsch, *Ælfric and the Cult of Saints*, p. 7; Whatley, 'Eugenia before Ælfric'; Rauer, 'Female Hagiography'; Stodnick, 'Bodies of Land'; Magennis, 'Occurrences of Nuptial Imagery'.

4. Stephen: 26 December; d. ?35; commemorated in the *Calendar of Willibrord* and Bede, *Martyrologium* (B II). The details up to Stephen's stoning are probably derived from Acts 6–7 and Pseudo-Isidore, *De ortu et obitu patrum*, 64.1–3. The burial and exhumation are probably inspired by the *Reuelatio Stephani*, of which two relevant versions survive; see *Reuelatio Stephani* (*BHL* 7851), 194, 196 and 214, and *Reuelatio Stephani* (*BHL* 7855), 195, 197 and 215. No direct source is known for the anecdote concerning the child killed in the traffic accident, which ultimately goes back to Augustine, *De ciuitate Dei*, 22.8.311–15. Cross suspects involvement of a homiliary of Paul the Deacon for this detail.

15.   *Þa hine...to Hierusalem*. The change from singular to plural in 'updide' and 'læddon' is uncharacteristic for this text, and may indicate missing material between the two clauses.

16.   *cild<es>*. See Frankis, Review of Kotzor, p. 314.

Bibliography: Cross, 'Saints' Lives in Old English', pp. 40–5; Cross, 'The Use of Patristic Homilies', p. 125; Rauer, 'Errors and Textual Problems'; Rauer, *Fontes*; Cross, 'On the Library', p. 237; Frankis, Review of Kotzor, p. 314; Cook, *Biblical Quotations*, p. 20; Godden, *Ælfric's Catholic Homilies: Introduction, Commentary and Glossary*, p. 357.

5. John the Evangelist: 27 December; first century; commemorated in the *Calendar of Willibrord* and Bede, *Martyrologium* (B II). This section seems to be a complex interweaving of any or all of the following: John 13.23–5, Aldhelm, *De uirginitate* (prose), 254.8–255.15, Aldhelm, *Carmen de uirginitate*, 460–78, Pseudo-Abdias, *Passio S. Iohannis* (*BHL* 4316), 531.13–589.12, Pseudo-Isidore, *De ortu et obitu patrum*, 48.1–5, and Isidore, *De ortu et obitu patrum*, 71.1–4.

17.   *<niddon>*. snidon D. Herz and later also Sisam plausibly suggest that the word is a corruption of a form of the verb '(ge)nidan' ('to compel'), which would also be supported by the Latin sources of this passage. For parallel constructions, cp. **225**, for example.

Bibliography: Cross, 'The Apostles', pp. 34–7; Kotzor, I, 250n and II, 278; Rusche, 'The *Old English Martyrology* and the Canterbury Aldhelm Scholia'; Rauer, *Fontes*; Biggs, *The Apocrypha*, p. 39; Cross, 'On the Library', pp. 230 and 243; Cross, 'The Influence of Irish Texts and Traditions', p. 187; Cross, 'Two Saints', p. 106n; Sisam, Review of Kotzor, p. 68; Mitchell, *Old English Syntax*, §3840; Stodnick, 'Bodies of Land'.

6. The Holy Innocents: 28 December; first century before Christ; commemorated in the *Calendar of Willibrord* and Bede, *Martyrologium* (B II). Petrus Chrysologus, Sermo 152, 950.14–955.85 was probably used as a source for the milk and blood imagery. The opening has parallels in Matthew 2.6–18, and Rufinus, *Historia ecclesiastica*, 71.5–6, presents an analogue for the closing lines.

18.   *Bethlem*. l corrected from e D, Bethlehem Ko; see also Note 1.

19.   *tu hund and feowertig and feower mille*. The number of children killed, 244,000, seems to be a corruption of the 144,000 mentioned, for example, in Apocalypse 14.1, although it is not clear whether the scribe, the author or another

source is reponsible for the discrepancy. If the error is scribal, 'tu' may be a redundant anticipation of 'cc'; cp. also **139b** below for a similar case. Two Anglo-Saxon calendars also refer to 144,000 children; see Rushforth, *Saints in English Kalendars*.
Bibliography: Cross, 'The Use of Patristic Homilies', pp. 109–11; Cross, 'The Latinity', pp. 281–2; Hall, 'Petrus Chrysologus'; Cross, 'On the Library', p. 237; Kotzor, II, 278; Rauer, *Fontes*; Cook, *Biblical Quotations*, pp. 18–19.

7. Pope Silvester I: 31 December; *s.* 314–35; commemorated in the *Calendar of Willibrord* and Bede, *Martyrologium* (B II). Whatley suggests that the B-Text of the *Gesta S. Siluestri* (*BHL* 7739), which remains unedited, was the source for the bulk of this section. For a similar passage, cp. *Gesta S. Siluestri* (*BHL* 7725–32), 508.42–509.1 and 531.39–41. (The relevant passage in the *Gesta S. Siluestri* in turn alludes to Luke 12.20). Cross argues that the reference to the pope's many miracles could be derived from Aldhelm, *De uirginitate* (prose), 258.1, or his *Carmen de uirginitate*, 543–4.
20.   *On þone vii dæg*. On þone vii dæg þæs monþes D, Ko; 'þæs monþes' is underlined in D. Scribal error, based on a confusion of the days of Christmas with the days of the month which are used in the openings of subsequent entries. Silvester's feast is on the seventh day of Christmas, or of the year, but not of the month. The error demonstrates that a scribe knew at an early stage of the copying process what format the rest of the text would be taking.
Bibliography: Whatley, s. v. 'Silvester'; Cross, 'Popes of Rome', pp. 199 and 201–4; Gioanni, 'Hagiographie d'Italie', pp. 390–2; Cross, 'The Latinity', pp. 281–2; Rauer, 'Usage', p. 140; Cook, *Biblical Quotations*, p. 19.

8. Columba: 31 December; third century; commemorated in the *Calendar of Willibrord* (as a later addition to the Calendar) and Bede, *Martyrologium* (B). Probably based on a *passio* of this saint, although there remains some doubt about the precise variant; see, for example, *Passio S. Columbae* (*BHL* 1892), 370.51–371.14.
21.   *hwæþer heo sceolde hine cucene þe deadne*. Cross, 'Columba of Sens', takes 'heo' to refer to the saint ('she would have him alive or dead'), although the implied usage of 'sculan' seems to be rare; cp. **180** and **194** below. The alternative would equate 'heo' with the bear.
Bibliography: Cross, 'Columba of Sens'; Cross, 'Old English *leasere*', p. 485; Cross, Review of Kotzor, p. 520; Swaen, 'Contributions to Anglo-Saxon Lexicography', p. 176; Rauer, 'Female Hagiography'.

8a. The Beginning of January: 1. The source for the sections on the beginnings of the months could have been Bede, *De temporum ratione*, 12 and 15, although it is not clear in all cases whether this represents an antecedent or direct source. Kotzor signals relevant information in a number of liturgical calendars and martyrologies which could also have served as sources. Given the common nature of the details presented in this section, a literary source may not have been involved at all.

Bibliography: Kotzor, I, 268 and II, 278–9; Anderson, 'The Seasons of the Year', p. 252; Rauer, 'Usage', pp. 143–4.

9. Octave of Christ and Mary (Circumcision of Christ): 1 January; commemorated in the *Calendar of Willibrord* and Bede, *Martyrologium* (B I/II). Cross discusses a number of biblical passages and biblical commentaries as sources for this passage; Pseudo-Isidore, *De ortu et obitu patrum*, 42.1, may have been used for the Greek, Latin and Hebrew linguistic detail.

22.   *Ihesus...Hælend*. The interpretation of Jesus's name is the same as that given in **35**.

Bibliography: Cross, 'The Influence of Irish Texts and Traditions', pp. 190–1; Cross, 'On the Library', p. 243; Cross, 'The Use of a Patristic Homilies', pp. 120–1; Herzfeld, p. 225; Cook, *Biblical Quotations*, p. 19; Rauer, 'Usage', p. 129n.

10. Pope Anteros: 3 January; *s*. 235–6; not commemorated in the *Calendar of Willibrord*; commemorated in Bede, *Martyrologium* (B). Probably based exclusively on the *Liber pontificalis*, I.147.1–3.

23.   *Calistes mynster*. The martyrologist refers on eight occasions to popes resting in early Christian cemeteries, or catacombs (here translated as 'church'): **10, 20, 28, 91, 143, 147, 202, 205**. All eight references go back to the *Liber pontificalis*, which in all cases presents *cymiterium* (more conventionally L. *coemeterium*), which the martyrologist consistently translates as 'mynster'. Anglo-Saxon glossators tend to refer to a *cymiterium* in a more narrow sense as a burial place: cp. Cleopatra Glosses (Stryker) 1227, 'byrgenstowe'; Second Corpus Glossary (Hessels) C.433, 'licburg' and C.978, 'locus ubi requiescunt corpora'; Antwerp-London Alphabetical Glossary (Porter) 345, 'halig legen'; Occ. Glosses (Gough) 5, 'licrest'. The author of the Old English Bede, 388.5, emphasises more widely the location of a cymiterium in a place of worship, translating it as 'gebaedhus ond ciricean' (for which see Bede, *Historia ecclesiastica*, ed. Colgrave and Mynors, p. 456n; I am grateful to Michael Lapidge for referring me to this passage). But what comes closest to the martyrologist's translation of *cymiterium* as 'mynster' is a gloss to Aldhelm's prose *De uirginitate* containing a reference to a surrounding monastic environment, 'in cimiterio, s. in monasterio, on licreste, lictune', Aldhelm Glosses 13.1 (Napier), 4355. The word Catacumbe, by contrast, occurs only once in the *Old English Martyrology*, **27**, where it seems to be understood as a place-name. For general background on the martyrologist's knowledge of Rome, see Roberts, '*Fela martyra*', pp. 158–60 and Lapidge, 'Roman Martyrs'; see also Izzi, 'Representing Rome' and 'Anglo-Saxons Underground' for Anglo-Saxon contacts with the catacombs.

Bibliography: Cross, 'Popes of Rome', pp. 191–2; Cross, 'On the Library', p. 243; Gioanni, 'Hagiographie d'Italie', pp. 389–90; Kotzor, I, 269 and II, 280; Herzfeld, p. xxxvii.

11. Emiliana: 5 January; sixth century; not commemorated in the *Calendar of Willibrord*, nor in Bede, *Martyrologium*. For this section, the martyrologist seems to have drawn on Gregory, *Homiliae in Euangelia* 38, 374.367–375.412.

Bibliography: Cross, 'On the Library', pp. 232 and 234; Kotzor, I, 255n and II, 280; Cross, 'The Use of Patristic Homilies', p. 107; Cross, 'The Latinity', pp. 281–2; Rauer, 'Female Hagiography'; Tupper, 'Anglo-Saxon Dæg-Mæl', pp. 212–13; Thijs, 'Wærferth's Translation', p. 48.

12. Epiphany, Baptism of Christ, etc.: 6 January; commemorated in the *Calendar of Willibrord* and in Bede, *Martyrologium* (B I/II). For this section, the martyrologist seems to have drawn on homiletic traditions (which in turn rely on biblical passages), although the precise source remains unidentified. Cross adduces a number of interesting analogues, including Petrus Chrysologus, Sermo 160, 990.23–993.86.

24.   *myrran þa wyrt*. Myrrh is technically a resin, not a plant. It is not clear whether its interpretation as a plant was already in the source, or whether the martyrologist added it; other Anglo-Saxon texts in any case present the same misunderstanding.

25.   *twegen mittan oþþe ðreo*. A 'mitta' is an early English measure, here used to translate Latin *metreta*; the source for the statement that the pots held two or three smaller units is ultimately John 2.6, *capientes singulae metretas binas uel ternas*, although it is not clear whether this was used directly, or was embedded in a homiletic source, such as Haymo of Auxerre, Sermo 18, 135. (I am grateful to Michael Lapidge for pointing out this homily).

Bibliography: Cross, 'The Use of Patristic Homilies', pp. 111–13; Rauer, *Fontes*; Hall, 'Petrus Chrysologus'; Cook, *Biblical Quotations*, pp. 18–19; Hagan, *Anglo-Saxon Food*, p. 322.

13. Julian and Basilissa: 6 January; fourth century, under Diocletian; not commemorated in the *Calendar of Willibrord*, nor in Bede, *Martyrologium*. Cross has argued that this section is based on a version of the saints' *passio*; cp. for example *Passio S. Iuliani* (*BHL* 4529), 27.6–33.14 and 46.11–47.12. Michael Lapidge suggests (pers. comm.) that the source could alternatively be Aldhelm, *De uirginitate* (prose), 280.8–284.17, which is in turn based on a *passio* of these saints. Ælfric's treatment of these saints shows that several divergent traditions of Julian and Basilissa were available in Anglo-Saxon England, and the precise route of transmission of this material to the martyrologist remains uncertain.

Bibliography: Cross, 'Identification: Towards Criticism', pp. 232–4; Rauer, *Fontes*; Whatley, s. v. 'Iulianus et Basilissa'; Upchurch, 'Virgin Spouses'; Upchurch, *Ælfric's Lives of the Virgin Spouses*, pp. 13–15.

14. Pope Telesphorus: 6 January; *s*. ?125–?36; not commemorated in the *Calendar of Willibrord*, nor in Bede, *Martyrologium*. Based on the *Liber pontificalis*, I.129.1–3.

26.   *casere*. casere B, Ko, casera Herz; form unattested as a gen. pl. of 'casere'; perhaps emend to 'caser<a>, following He.

27.   *Antonius ond Marcus*. The intended emperors are Antoninus Pius and Marcus Aurelius.

Bibliography: Cross, 'Popes of Rome', pp. 191–2 and 202; Cross, 'On the Library', p. 243; Kotzor, I, 269 and II, 281; Gioanni, 'Hagiographie d'Italie', pp. 389–90.

15. Pega: 9 January; d. ?719; not commemorated in the *Calendar of Willibrord*, nor in Bede, *Martyrologium*. Cockayne identified Felix, *Vita S. Guthlaci* (*BHL* 3723), 168.6–170.10 as the source for this section.

28.   *Gutlaces*. Probably a misspelling which does not seem to be attested elsewhere and perhaps an error for 'Guthlaces', the spelling which this scribe (Ba) uses for the same name further below, **63**.

Bibliography: Cockayne, *The Shrine*, p. 50; Kotzor, I, 14n, 268 and II, 282; Cross, 'On the Library', p. 246; *PASE*, Pega 1; Rauer, 'Female Hagiography'.

16. Paul the Hermit: 10 January; d. ?345; not commemorated in the *Calendar of Willibrord*; commemorated in Bede, *Martyrologium* (B). Cross discussed Jerome, *Vita S. Pauli* (*BHL* 6596), as the main source for this section, although Aldhelm, *De uirginitate* (prose), 265.8–11, and *Carmen de uirginitate*, 780–5 were perhaps also used, especially for the details of the animals and the food found in the desert, which have no close parallels elsewhere.

29.   *naht opres...wulfa gerar*. The curious and illogical reference to the seeing and hearing of the animals' noises may be incomplete or otherwise defective, and seems to be unattested in the Latin tradition (Harvey, pers. comm.).

30.   *westenes æppla*. The source makes clear that the 'fruit of the desert' are dates, but it is not certain whether this was understood by the martyrologist or his audience.

31.   *ðæt wæter dranc of his holre hand*. The reference of the saint drinking water from his hand, for which there seems to be no parallel in any possible source text, could be based on a misunderstanding of Latin *palma*, 'palm tree' (referred to by Aldhelm), which can also denote the 'palm of the hand'.

Bibliography: Cross, 'On the Library', pp. 227–8 and 231; Cross, 'A Lost Life of Hilda of Whitby', pp. 33–4; Rauer, *Fontes*; Hagan, *Anglo-Saxon Food*, p. 60; Bierbaumer, *Der botanische Wortschatz*, III, 182–3.

17. Benedict Biscop: 12 January; d. 689; not commemorated in the *Calendar of Willibrord*, nor in Bede, *Martyrologium*. This section is based on Bede, *Historia abbatum*, 1–4, 6 and 14, as 'an over-simplified outline of Bede's detailed narrative' (Kotzor). Unlike Bede, the martyrologist refers to only one of the saint's six visits to Rome.

32.   *mynster*. mynstre Herz; perhaps emend to 'mynstere' or 'mynstre' with Herz, since the usage of 'on' or 'in' with dat. of place is otherwise fairly regular in this text, but B on three occasions presents nouns with anomalous endings following 'on', all with intervening gen. phrases, which may indicate an authorial or scribal pattern; cp. **28** and **49**, and Kotzor, II, 295.

33.   *freo*. Apparently translating *libera*, hence adjectival rather than adverbial.

Bibliography: Kotzor, I, 267, 280n and II, 283; Cross, 'The Latinity', pp. 281–2; Cross, 'Source, Lexis, and Edition', pp. 27 and 32; Cross, 'On the Library', pp. 238–9; Rauer, *Fontes*; *PASE*, Biscop 2; Bately, 'The Place Which is Called'.

18. Hilary of Poitiers: 13 January; ?315–68; commemorated in the *Calendar of Willibrord* and in Bede, *Martyrologium* (B). The shortness of this section makes it difficult to identify a source for its details. Bede, *Martyrologium*, 108, has been considered in this context, but cannot represent the sole source.

34.   *ðreotte<oþ>an*. þreottegðan Herz; ðreottegan B. The form in B lacks the expected second dental fricative and is clearly corrupt; the emendation is one of several possible ones.

Bibliography: Whatley, s. v. 'Hilarius Pictavensis, vita'; Kotzor, I, 209; Cross, 'On the Library', p. 241n.

19. Felix: 14 January; commemorated in the *Calendar of Willibrord* and Bede, *Martyrologium* (B). This problematic section reflects a confusion of Felix of Rome (martyred in Monte Pincio, to whom the first few lines of this section relate) and Felix of Nola (d. 260, to whom the martyrdom and the closing lines relate), caused either by the martyrologist or his source. The tortures described, together with the feastday, belong to Felix of Nola; Bede, *Vita S. Felicis* (*BHL* 2873), 790–1, 798, and his *Martyrologium*, 106–7, have been discussed as possible sources for these details. The parallels are, however, not always close, and the Old English appears to be textually defective (the fact that the saint was tied up, for example, may originally have been included in the account of the martyrdom which seem somewhat garbled). Whatley suspects the use of further, so far unidentified source material, possibly of a liturgical sort.

35.   *tid mæssepreostes*. tid þæs mæssepreostes Herz; possibly emend following Herzfeld; normal usage of this opening formula in the text does include the 'þæs'. No emendation here, however, as the phrase is grammatical as it stands, and the section may have other textual defects.

36.   *nacod ond*. nacod Herz; perhaps delete redundant 'ond' following Herzfeld, but see the point above regarding the details of the saint's martyrdom which could be defective.

Bibliography: Cross, 'On the Library', p. 241; Whatley, s. vv. 'Felix Nolanus presbyter' and 'Felix Romaus presbyter'; Kotzor, I, 209 and 224; Rauer, *Fontes*.

20. Pope Marcellus: 16 January; *s.* 306–8; commemorated in the *Calendar of Willibrord* and Bede, *Martyrologium* (B). The *Liber pontificalis*, I.164.1–6, appears to be the sole source for this section.

37.   *blancan*. The crux 'blancan' would seem to be a mistranslation of Latin *plancas* 'planks' on the part of the martyrologist, despite Cross's reservations.

38.   *mynstre*. See Note 23.

Bibliography: Kotzor, I, 209, 218, 269 and II, 284; Herzfeld, pp. xxxvi–xxxvii, 225; Cross, 'Popes of Rome', pp. 191–2, 202; Gioanni, 'Hagiographie d'Italie', pp. 389–90; Cross, 'On the Library', p. 241n and 243; Cross, 'The Latinity', p. 285; Whatley, s. v. 'Marcellus papa'; Rauer, 'Old English *blanca*'; Swaen, 'Contributions to Anglo-Saxon Lexicography', p. 176.

21. Fursa: 16 January; d. 650; not commemorated in the *Calendar of Willibrord*, nor in Bede, *Martyrologium*. This section is probably a conflation of two sources, Bede, *Historia ecclesiastica*, 274.26–9, and possibly also 268–276, and the anonymous *Vita S. Fursei* (*BHL* 3213a), 5 and 29.12–14, and possibly also 26–30.3.

39.   *ondry<sn>lices*. See also Kotzor, II, 284.

40.   *Þes Fursing*. There seems to be no explanation for this version of the name, which looks like a patronymic form. The lettering in B comes across as cramped and irregular, and it may be that the form hides a copying error. Herz and Cross, 'The Influence of Irish Texts and Traditions' emend to 'Furseus'.

41.   *Cnofesburh*. In Bede, *Historia ecclesiastica*, 270.10, referred to as Cnobheresburg; on the identification of the modern site, see Pestell, *Landscapes of Monastic Foundation*, pp. 56–7.

42.   *Clodfeo*. Frankis interprets the spelling of 'Clodfeo' as typically English, but it also closely reflects the dative or ablative form of one of the most conventional Latin spellings of the king's name, 'Clodoveus'.

43.   *Ferano*. Place-name probably corrupt; in Latin conventionally *Peronna*.

Bibliography: Cross, 'The Influence of Irish Texts and Traditions', pp. 178–80; Cross, 'A Lost Life of Hilda of Whitby', pp. 25–30; Cross, 'On the Library', pp. 230 and 235; Kotzor, I, 254n and II, 284; Frankis, Review of Kotzor, p. 314; Cross, 'Identification: Towards Criticism', p. 234; Cross, 'Pelagia in Mediaeval England', p. 286; Whatley, s. v. 'Furseus'; Pestell, *Landscapes of Monastic Foundation*, pp. 56–7; *PASE*, Fursa 1 and Sigeberht 3; *ODNB*, s. v. 'Fursa'; Bately, 'Old English Prose', pp. 114–18; Rauer, 'Usage', p. 126n; Klaeber, 'Notes on Old English Prose Texts', p. 247.

22. Antony the Hermit: 17 January; 251–356; commemorated in the *Calendar of Willibrord* and Bede, *Martyrologium* (BI/II). The main source seems to have been the *Vita S. Antonii* in Evagrius's translation (*BHL* 609; see Rauer, *Fontes* or Cross, 'On the Library' for specific passages); Bede, *Chronica maiora*, 66.1714–16, may have supplied the detail of Antony's burial place.

44.   *swa*. Syntactically difficult to interpret; see Mitchell, *Old English Syntax*, §3477, and Schleburg, *Altenglisch swa*, §623; the source text in any case presents no concessive construction.

45.   *deofla*. Unproblematic as a nom. pl., but contrasts with nom. pl. 'deofol' a few lines further on, perhaps indicating a missing collective noun or other lacuna, in that case with 'deofla' as a gen. pl., but cp. also **211** for similar phrasing.

46.   *þæt deofol*. The curious switch between one or more devils in this section can be explained by the martyrologist's inconsistent use of his source material which refers to encounters with both groups of devils and individuals.

Bibliography: Cross, 'On the Library', pp. 240 and 246; Rauer, *Fontes*; Cross, 'The Use of a *Passio S. Sebastiani*', p. 50n; Kotzor, II, 285.

23. Speusippus, Eleusippus and Meleusippus: 17 January; second century; not commemorated in the *Calendar of Willibrord* and Bede, *Martyrologium* (B). The source seems to be a particular variant of the *Passio S. Speusippi* (*BHL* 7828), 1–16.

47.   *byran*. Kotzor remarks on the curious and otherwise unattested spelling of 'byran' (for 'beran'). Alternatively, the spelling could hide a corruption of 'byrnan', or a similar verb, which would fit the context better; cp. also **149** for remarkably similar phrasing.

48.   *Sanctos Geminos*. Named after the triplet saints (rather than twins), in Latin conventionally known as *tergemini*; cp. also **196**.

Bibliography: Whatley, s. v. 'Speusippus'; Cross, 'The Latinity', pp. 285–7; Cross, 'On the Library', p. 229n; Cross, 'Source, Lexis, and Edition', pp. 32–3; Kotzor, I, 273–4n and II, 285; Herzfeld, pp. xxxvii and 226; Bately, 'The Place Which is Called'.

24. Prisca: 18 January; Rome, third century, under Claudius; not commemorated in the *Calendar of Willibrord*; commemorated in Bede, *Martyrologium* (B II). Kotzor suspects the use of a sacramentary in the composition of this section.

49.   *bið ðære halgan fæmnan Sancte Prisce*. The opening formula is clearly defective here, lacking a reference to a feast ('tid', 'geleornes', 'gemynd', or similar) and the expected 'þæs monðes'; see also Kotzor, I, 409–10.

Bibliography: Kotzor, I, 209, 259 and 264; Cross, 'On the Library', p. 241n.

25. The Consecration of St Peter's Church: 18 January; commemorated in the *Calendar of Willibrord*; not in Bede, *Martyrologium*. No precise source has been established for this minimal section, but analogues can be found in a number of other martyrologies, for example that by Usuard (18 January).

50.   *On<d> ðy ilcan dæge*. In B, this section follows on directly at the end of the previous section, without being given a new line. The opening also deviates from the normal formula in B of 'on' with acc.; cp. also **77** and **88**.

Bibliography: Kotzor, I, 221; Lendinara, 'Pietro, apostolo, vescovo e santo'.

26. Ananias, Petrus etc.: 19 January; Bithynia, third or fourth century, under Diocletian; not commemorated in the *Calendar of Willibrord*, nor in Bede, *Martyrologium*. The *Passio S. Ananiae* (*BHL* 397), 492B–495D, seems to be the source; *pace* Cross, the edited *passio* does refer to the soldiers' drowning with leaden weights around their necks. Elsewhere the saints' feast is variously given as 26 or 27 January or 25 February.

51.   *On ðone...in Biðinie ðære mægðe*. The opening formula of this section deviates from the normal patterns and may be defective, since the saint's feast was obviously not restricted to Bithynia under Diocletian.

52.   *spræc<an>*. spræc B, Ko; emendation also reflects similar construction in Latin source. Alternatively one could understand the change from non-finite to finite construction and back again as a further example of the martyrologist's anacoluthic style.

53.   *sændon*. The final vowel could be anticipating the finite 'onsendon' two manuscript lines further down, but see also Campbell, *Old English Grammar*, §377.

Bibliography: Cross, '*Passio S. Eugeniae*', p. 395; Whatley, 'Ananias et Petrus et Septem Milites'; Rauer, *Fontes*; Stodnick, 'Bodies of Land'.

27. Sebastian: 20 January; d. Rome, ?300, under Diocletian; commemorated in the *Calendar of Willibrord* and Bede, *Martyrologium* (B). This section is based on Pseudo-Ambrose, *Passio S. Sebastiani* (*BHL* 7543), 278.85–9.

54.   *Ðone Dioclitianus...mid strælum ofscotian*. The confused syntax of this passage, in which the author changes construction twice, is unusual even by the standards of this text, where anacoluthon is not infrequent. If not authorial, the disjointedness may alternatively also indicate missing material originally included (for example on the geographical location or the saint's rejection of the pagan religion, which remain unmentioned).

55.   *Ond mid ðy...swa acwellan*. Ambiguous syntax; 'mid ðy' is here intrepreted in the function of a conjunction, 'when'; see also Schleburg, *Altenglisch swa*, §64. By contrast, Ko punctuates differently, linking this phrase with the previous sentence, presumably interpreting 'mid ðy' as 'with that [i.e. these tortures]', although the 'swa' then seems redundant.

Bibliography: Cross, 'The Use of a *Passio S. Sebastiani*', p. 41; Whatley, 'Sebastianus'; Lanéry, *Ambroise de Milan*, esp. pp. 503–7; Lanéry, 'Hagiographie d'Italie', pp. 68–80; Kotzor, I, 209–10, 273n and II, 286; Cross, 'On the Library', pp. 236n and 241n.

28. Pope Fabian: 20 January; *s.* 236–50; not commemorated in the *Calendar of Willibrord*; commemorated in Bede, *Martyrologium* (B). The *Liber pontificalis*, I.148.1–5 can probably be regarded as one of the sources used for this section; but the anecdote of the dove which settles on Fabian's head remains unaccounted for in the transmitted version of the *Liber pontificalis*. This passage probably goes back to Rufinus, *Historia ecclesiastica*, 583.13–585.5, but Cross suggested that this miracle account might have been attached to the pope's entry in the *Liber pontificalis* which the martyrologist used.

56.   *Calistes mynster*. See Notes 23 and 32.

Bibliography: Cross, 'Popes of Rome', pp. 191, 194–5 and 203; Cross, 'On the Library', pp. 243 and 248; Gioanni, 'Hagiographie d'Italie', pp. 389–90.

29. Marius, Martha, Audifax and Abacuc: 20 January; Rome, third century, under Claudius; not commemorated in the *Calendar of Willibrord*; commemorated in Bede, *Martyrologium* (B). This short and somewhat minimal section is difficult to source; similar information occurs in a number of other martyrologies, one or more of which may have served as a source. On the basis of **105**, Whatley suggests that the martyrologist also knew the *Passio SS. Marii et Marthae* (*BHL* 5543), which seems to be the source for both entries.

Bibliography: Whatley, 'Marius et Martha'; Lanéry, 'Hagiographie d'Italie', pp. 250–7; Kotzor, I, 210 and 214n; Cross, 'On the Library', p. 241n; Frere, *Studies in Early Roman Liturgy*, p. 46; Pfaff, 'The Hagiographical Peculiarity'.

30. Agnes: 21 January; d. Rome, third or fourth century; commemorated in the *Calendar of Willibrord* and in Bede, *Martyrologium* (B). As Phillips has recently shown, the main source is probably Pseudo-Ambrose, *Passio S. Agnetis* (*BHL* 156),

735–41, although the martyrologist may also have been influenced by Aldhelm, *De uirginitate* (prose), 298.12–299.17, and Aldhelm, *Carmen de uirginitate*, 1925–74. The reference to the saint's garment is faintly reminiscent of Mark 9.2, but could have been more directly derived from Pseudo-Ambrose Sermo 48 (*BHL* 158a), 703, as Phillips has suggested. Lanéry, *Ambroise de Milan*, pp. 81–8 and 414–26, provides extensive information on the saint's hagiographical dossier in general; for *BHL* 156 in particular, see Lanéry, *Ambroise de Milan*, pp. 347–83; for *BHL* 158a, see Lanéry, *Ambroise de Milan*, pp. 414–15.

57   <*aswalt*>. aslat B, Ko, Herz. The reading in B ('he tore apart'), in an otherwise unattested intransitive usage, seems doubtful, as the breaking up of the assailant's body is absent from the various source texts. The source apparently presented *exspirauit*, and 'aslat' is therefore perhaps a corruption of 'aswalt', from 'asweltan', 'to die'. The parallel with **233**, 'he wæs fram deofle forbroden and he sweolt', and its Latin source is striking. An alternative interpretation can be found in the *DOE*, s. v. 'aslidan', 4. a, where 'aslat' is interpreted as a form of 'aslidan', 'slip away, perish'.

Bibliography: Phillips, 'St Agnes of Rome'; Phillips, 'Materials for the Study', esp. pp. 158–66; Lanéry, *Ambroise de Milan*; Lanéry, 'Hagiographie d'Italie', pp. 192–203; Cross, 'A Lost Life of Hilda of Whitby', pp. 31–2; Cross, 'On the Library', p. 230; Kotzor, I, 250n and II, 286; Whatley, s. v. 'Agnes'; Herzfeld, pp. xxxvii and 226; Stodnick, 'Bodies of Land'; Magennis, 'Occurrences of Nuptial Imagery'.

31. Vincent: 22 January; d. Valencia, 304, under Diocletian; not commemorated in the *Calendar of Willibrord*; commemorated in Bede, *Martyrologium* (B II). Probably based on the *Passio S. Vincentii* (*BHL* 8631), 2–15, although much remains open regarding the relationships between the various versions of this *passio*.

58.   *Datianus se casere*. The martyrologist, possibly inspired by his sources for the entries on George (23 April) and Alexandria (27 April), errs in making Datianus an emperor; the *passio* describes him as a more minor official; see also Introduction, p. 16.

59.   *blæc fugel...þa oþre fuglas*. Cross shows that manuscript copies of the *passio* are confused in variously assigning the swiftness to the raven's wings or those of the other birds, and the syntax here also seems somewhat awkward, as if the martyrologist was similarly struggling with the Latin passage. Alternatively one could repunctuate and emend to 'hæfde micele feðra ond swift<e>'; it is interesting to note that that phrase (understood as a split-up heavy group, 'great and swift wings') would then be an exact word-for-word translation (and misinterpretation) of *magnificas pennisque pernices* (12), and may have been the martyrologist's original intention.

Bibliography: Whatley, s. v. 'Vincentius Caesaraugustanus'; Cross, 'Saints' Lives in Old English', pp. 51–8; Saxer, *Saint Vincent diacre et martyr*, pp. 151–226.

32. Anastasius: 22 January; d. 628; not commemorated in the *Calendar of Willibrord*; commemorated in Bede, *Martyrologium* (B). The bulk of this section is probably derived from Bede, *Chronica maiora*, 66.1792–1809. The idea that

COMMENTARY

Heraclius brought the saint's body to Rome seems to be a mistranslation on the martyrologist's part, as Franklin suggests. The only relevant literary parallel for the reference to the Roman procession involving the saint's head can be found in the *Miraculum Romae ad Aquas Saluias* (*BHL* 412), 57–60, which may have served as a source here, although Franklin is right in suggesting that an oral rather than literary source could have been responsible for this detail; the Roman cult of this saint was in any case well known in Anglo-Saxon England. Pseudo-Jerome, *Martyrologium*, XI Kal. Feb., does not seem to refer to the saint's head, and is therefore less likely to have been the source here; moreover, as Kotzor shows, there is also no evidence that this text was used as a source by the martyrologist.

60.   *Anastas<i>*. See also Note 74.

Bibliography: Cross, 'On the Library', p. 239; Cross, 'The Use of a *Passio S. Sebastiani*', p. 50n; Franklin, *The Latin Dossier of Anastasius*, pp. 224–8; Kotzor, I, 178–80, 268n and II, 287; Bischoff and Lapidge, *Biblical Commentaries*, pp. 68–9; Whatley, s. v. 'Anastasius'.

33. Emerentiana: 23 January; d. Rome, ?304; not commemorated in the *Calendar of Willibrord*; commemorated in Bede, *Martyrologium* (B). The source seems to be the Pseudo-Ambrosian *Passio S. Agnetis* (*BHL* 156), 741.

Bibliography: Whatley, s. v. 'Emerentiana'; Kotzor, I, 210 and II, 287; Lanéry, 'Hagiographie d'Italie', pp. 192–203; Cross, 'On the Library', p. 241n.

34. Babylas etc.: 24 January; third century, under Numerian; commemorated in the *Calendar of Willibrord* and in Bede, *Martyrologium* (B I/II). Probably based on the *Passio S. Babylae* (*BHL* 890), 127.35–53, 128.51–3 and 129.54–130.3. The detail of the boys' names (not mentioned in the *passio*) occurs in a number of analogues, one or more of which could have served as a source; cp. for example Bede, *Martyrologium*, 49.

61.   *duru <Numeriane>*. duru a Numer<i> B, letters partially erased after Numer-, remainder left to serve as i B. The passage has suffered several erasures and corrections in B, and remains problematic. The 'a' could be what remains of '-ano', an annotation originally perhaps above 'Numeri', correcting the emperor's name, which should properly read Numerianus, dat. Numeriane; it is noteworthy that two letters seem to have been erased following the 'a', perhaps pointing to an original form '-ane' or '-ano'. Alternatively, the otherwise unexplained 'a' could go back to an attempt to correct 'duru' to 'dura'; cp. **63** duru B, dura C. As a third possibility, the 'a' could be the remainder of an erased preposition; Herz suggests emendation to 'agean Numeriano', although 'forstandan' usually takes an indirect object in the dative, without preposition; see *DOE*, s. v. 'forstandan' 3. c. The 'a' now carries an accent in B, which may indicate that it was interpreted as the adverb 'a' ('always') at least by this latest scribe.

Bibliography: Cross, 'On the Library', p. 242; Herzfeld, p. 226; Whatley, s. v. 'Babylas'; Rauer, *Fontes*; *DOE*, s. v. 'forstandan' 3. c.

35. The Conversion of St Paul: 25 January; commemorated in the *Calendar of Willibrord*; not commemorated in Bede, *Martyrologium*. Most of this section is based on Acts 22.4–16. The reference to Paul's status among Christians is attested in a variety of possible sources, including Aldhelm, *Carmen de uirginitate*, Isidore, *De ortu et obitu patrum*, and Pseudo-Isidore, *De ortu et obitu patrum*.

62. *Ic eom Ihesus (ðæt is Hælend)*. The interpretation of Jesus's name is the same as that given in **9**.

Bibliography: Cross, 'The Apostles', pp. 39–40; Rauer, *Fontes*; Cook, *Biblical Quotations*, p. 20.

36. The Discovery of the Head of St John the Baptist: February; not commemorated in the *Calendar of Willibrord*; commemorated in Bede, *Martyrologium* (B I/II, for 24 February). The opening of this section is lost and thus lacks the formula which elsewhere identifies the feast day; attestations in a wide range of analogues demonstrate that 24 or 27 February are the most plausible options. The precise source remains unidentified; Cross discusses a number of analogues, among them Dionysius Exiguus, *De inuentione capitis Joannis baptistae* (*BHL* 4290–1), 421–3.

63. ...*Sanctus Iohannes*. Herzfeld plausibly speculates that the acephalous opening sentence once explained that the saint 'revealed himself to that man' ('<Þa ætywde> Sanctus Iohannes hine þæm men').

Bibliography: Cross, 'Blickling Homily XIV', pp. 154 and 158–60; Cross, 'On the Library', p. 241n; Kotzor, I, 210, 224 and II, 288; Herzfeld, pp. 32–3; Lapidge, 'Acca of Hexham', pp. 34 and 70–1.

36a. The End of February. The name of the month could have been derived from Bede, *De temporum ratione*, 15.8. The information on the daylight hours has parallels in a number of liturgical calendars; see Kotzor, I, 302–11 for a comprehensive table of Anglo-Saxon liturgical calendars and their entries for the beginnings and ends of the months which present such information; see also Rauer, 'Usage', pp. 132–3 for the example of the calendar in Oxford, Bodleian Library, Digby 63 ('nox horas .xiiii. dies x', end of February). Like the *Old English Martyrology*, this calendar, for example, also presents parallels for the birth of Adam, astronomical and cosmological events, feasts of the Easter cycle and the beginning of summer and winter.

Bibliography: Kotzor, II, 288; Tupper, 'Anglo-Saxon Dæg-Mæl', p. 120; Blackburn and Holford-Strevens, *The Oxford Companion to the Year*, pp. 661–2; Borst, *Kalenderreform*, pp. 61–9, and 431–46; Borst, *Der karolingische Reichskalender*, I, 25; and Rauer, 'Usage', pp. 132–3 and the literature cited there.

36b. The Beginning of March: 1 March. The source for the sections on the beginnings of the months could have been Bede, *De temporum ratione*, 12 and 15, although it is not in all cases clear whether this represents an antecedent or direct source. Kotzor signals relevant information in a number of liturgical calendars and martyrologies which could also have served as sources. Given the common nature of

the details presented in this section, a literary source may not have been involved at all.
Bibliography: Kotzor, I, 268 and II, 278–9, 288.

37. Chad: 2 March; d. 672; commemorated in the *Calendar of Willibrord*; not commemorated in Bede, *Martyrologium*. The martyrologist himself refers to Bede, *Historia Ecclesiastica*, as his source; the relevant passages are 336.10–23, 336.28–9, 338.31–342.11, 344.19–25 and 344.28.
64. *ðyder*. Syntactically unusual and also oddly redundant as it stands, perhaps pointing to a lost indication of place in one of the preceding clauses, or reflecting a corruption of 'ðy dæge'.
65. *his Godes þeow sum*. Cp. the identical phrase in **51**, where Herz emends to part. gen. 'þeowa'; C presents 'þeowa sum' in **51** and **226**. Given the ambiguity which often surrounds constructions with 'sum', the pattern found in B may be authorial or scribal; see also Mitchell, *Old English Syntax*, §405.
Bibliography: Rauer, *Fontes*; Kotzor, I, 252 and II, 289–90; Cross, 'On the Library', pp. 230 and 235; Cross, 'A Lost Life of Hilda of Whitby', p. 24; *PASE*, Chad 1, Cedd 1, Owine1, Hygebald 2 and Ecgberht 2.

38. Adrian and Natalia: 4 March; d. Nicomedia ?304 under Maximian; not commemorated in the *Calendar of Willibrord*; commemorated in Bede, *Martyrologium* (B II, for 8 September). The source is a *passio* such as the *Passio S. Hadriani et sociorum* (*BHL* 3744), 23.47–24.3, 24.35–56, 25.51–3, 27.29–30 and 28.57–30.3, although not all narrative details, such as the length of time spent together by the saints, have exact parallels in the text variant cited here. The translations 'godwebbe' (*purpura*) and 'medmiclum scipe' (*carabus modica navis*) also have parallels in glosses.
66. *heo begeat...godwebbe*. What Natalia does with the saint's hand is put more specifically in the Latin (*inuoluit purpura, infundens in myrro*) and again points to a misunderstanding of myrrh as a plant (see also **12**).
67. *Wel þu come*. The phrase translates 'bene uenisti', here functioning as a conventional greeting, but also alluding to the fact that the saint had just arrived safely after danger, and also linking to the following clause.
Bibliography: Cross, 'The Latinity', pp. 281–2 and 296; Whatley, s. v. 'Hadrianus et Natalia'; Cross, 'Source, Lexis, and Edition', pp. 29 and 32; Kotzor, I, 342–3 and II, 290; *DOEC*, s. v. 'carabus', 'purpura'.

39. Perpetua and Felicity: 7 March; d. Carthage, 203; commemorated in the *Calendar of Willibrord* and in Bede, *Martyrologium* (B). Cross identifies Bede, *Chronica maiora*, 66.1203–4 and a *passio* of this saint as probable sources; cp. *Passio SS. Perpetuae et Felicitatis* (*BHL* 6633), 10.15–32 and 15.1–19. One phraseological detail ('mid werlice geðohte') has parallels in Augustinian sermons and the saint's acta (*animus uirilis, uirilis uirtus*), perhaps pointing to an additional source, see, for example, Augustine, Sermo 281, 1284 or Sermo 282, 6; on gendered vocabulary, see also Williams, 'Perpetua's Gender'.

68. *ðara lichoma resteþ*. Switch to sg. unexplained; cp. **125** for the expected phrase. The error is either scribal, or may have been caused by the original omission of St Felicity, who could have been introduced into this section at a later point during transmission; see also next note.

69. *Đonne wæs...cristenwif*. The connection between the two saints is not explained in this section as preserved, and this passage may be corrupt.

Bibliography: Cross, 'The Latinity', pp. 284 and 288; Cross, 'On the Library', pp. 237 and 240; Kotzor, I, 207 and II, 290; Herzfeld, p. 226; Rauer, *Fontes*; Whatley, s. v. 'Perpetua et Felicitas'; Frere, *Studies in Early Roman Liturgy*, p. 46.

40. Eastorwine: 7 March; d. 686; not commemorated in the *Calendar of Willibrord*, nor in Bede, *Martyrologium*. Based on Bede, *Historia abbatum*, 7–8.

70. *Ond þa...twentigum geara*. As Herzfeld first pointed out, the martyrologist here misunderstands his source which makes the saint twenty-four years of age on entering the monastery.

Bibliography: Kotzor, I, 14n, 267 and II, 291; Cross, 'On the Library', p. 238; Herzfeld, p. 37; Rauer, *Fontes*; *PASE*, Eosterwine 1 and Ecgfrith 4.

41. Forty Soldiers of Sebastea: 9 March; d. 320, under Licinius; commemorated in the *Calendar of Willibrord* and Bede, *Martyrologium* (B). Probably based on the *Passio SS. Sebastenorum* (*BHL* 7539), 20–1.

71. *Lyssiarchus*. Cross suggested that the otherwise unattested form 'Lyssiarchus' may hide, by metathesis, 'Siliarchus', an attested manuscript variant (according to Cross), or the variant Chiliarchus (according to Patricia Karlin-Hayter, pers. comm.). Alternatively, the form could have been influenced by the name of one of the soldiers, 'Lysimachus', or could preserve 'Lysias archos', a Greek version of 'Lysias dux', or 'Lysias praeses', as he is referred to in the *passio*.

72. *neddon*. See Kotzor, II, 291 and Note 53 above.

73. *wuldorbeaga*. Hofstetter, *Winchester und der spätaltenglische Sprachgebrauch*, p. 410, suggests that 'wuldorbeah' here and in **185** is a late scribal substitution of a different original word, but Kotzor, I, 332, and Kirschner, 'Die Bezeichnungen', pp. 159–62, are more cautious in their interpretations. The fact that 'wuldorbeah' occurs in both branches of transmission (B, C) suggests that the word does constitute an original reading. That the word becomes part of standard late West Saxon vocabulary does not preclude usage in earlier Anglian texts; the word also occurs in the Old English translation of Gregory, *Dialogi*, 26.232.6. The cited Latin texts for the passage here and for **185** both present *corona*.

Bibliography: Kotzor, II, 291; Cross, 'Identification: Towards Criticism', pp. 234–6; Whatley, s. v. 'Sebasteni'; Rauer, *Fontes*; Karlin-Hayter, 'Passio of the XL Martyrs'; Stodnick, 'Bodies of Land'.

42. Pope Gregory the Great: 12 March; *s*. 590–604; commemorated in the *Calendar of Willibrord* and Bede, *Martyrologium* (B I/II). The precise source remains unidentified, but various analogues have been identified, including the interpolated version of Paul the Deacon's *Vita S. Gregorii* (*BHL* 3648), 56–8 and the Whitby *Vita*

S. Gregorii (*BHL* 3637), 120–2 and 126–8. Kotzor shows that the translations of *altor* and *alumni* could have been derived from a gloss.

74. *Gregori<u>s*. Gregories B with v suprascript above second e Ba, Gregori<u>s Ko. The handling of name endings is highly inconsistent in the text, and seems to be at least partly determined by scribal preferences. See Kotzor, I, 426–34, for an outline of the various patterns.

75. *culfran of heofonum*. A verb in the infinitive seems to be missing here; Herz suggests 'cuman'.

Bibliography: Whatley, s. v. 'Gregorius Magnus'; Kotzor, I, 250 and II, 292; Cross, 'A Lost Life of Hilda of Whitby', pp. 24–5; Herzfeld, p. xxxvii; Thijs, 'Wærferth's Translation', p. 48.

43. Macedonius, Patricia and Modesta: 13 March; dates unknown; d. Nicomedia; not commemorated in the *Calendar of Willibrord*; commemorated in Bede, *Martyrologium* (B I/II). Manuscript B breaks off after a few lines of this section, and it is not clear whether the entire section is preserved. The information given could have been derived from a martyrology, but is too minimal to allow a precise sourcing.

Bibliography: Kotzor, I, 211 and 214; Cross, 'On the Library', p. 241.

44. Patrick: 17 March; ?385–?461; commemorated in the *Calendar of Willibrord* and in Bede, *Martyrologium* (B II). The origin of most of this section remains mysterious; Cross concludes that the 'martyrologist had access to rare information about St Patrick'. See also Introduction, p. 21, for the unusual transmission of this text section.

76. *Contablata*. This name is not attested elsewhere as the name of Patrick's mother, but is not entirely implausible; Patrick Sims-Williams points out (pers. comm.) that the name consists of two well-attested Celtic name elements.

Bibliography: Cross, 'The Influence of Irish Texts and Traditions', pp. 173–6 and 181n; Kotzor, 'St Patrick'; Cross, 'On the Library', p. 247; Dumville, *Saint Patrick*, pp. 89–92; Rauer, 'Usage', pp. 126n and 131; Rauer, *Fontes*; *ODNB*, s. v. 'Patrick'; Bately, 'Old English Prose', pp. 114–18.

45. The First Day of Creation: 18 March. Incomplete section, lacking the opening formula which elsewhere identifies the feast day. The dates of the following days of Creation are probably derived from Bede, *De temporum ratione*, 6.78–82. The minimal detail given here is based on Gen. 1.4–5 or on one of its derivatives. Anderson suggests that an entry for Lent could also have been included under 18 March, before the text was fragemented at this point of the year. It is important to note that the notion of Lent is briefly referred to in the section on Eadberht, **80**.

Bibliography: Cross, '*De ordine creaturarum*', p. 133; Kotzor, II, 292; Rauer, 'Usage', 132n; Anderson, 'The Seasons of the Year', p. 241n.

46. The Second Day of Creation: 19 March. This section is probably derived from Genesis 1.7 and Pseudo-Isidore, *De ordine creaturarum*, 921. The date is probably based on Bede, *De temporum ratione*, 6.78–82. Anlezark suggests that the passage may have served as a source for the *Meters of Boethius*.

77.   <*þæs*>. om. B, Ko, <þæs> Herz; not ungrammatical without a definite article, but normal usage in this text overwhelmingly favours the article.

Bibliography: Cross, '*De ordine creaturarum*', pp. 133–4; Cross, 'The Influence of Irish Texts and Traditions', p. 186; Cross, 'On the Library', p. 242; Cross, 'The Latinity', pp. 281–2; Anlezark, 'Three Notes', pp. 13–14; Rauer, 'Usage', pp. 132n and 135–6; Kotzor, II, 292; Herzfeld, pp. 226–7; Godden and Irvine, ed., *The Old English Boethius*, II, 511–12.

47. Gregory Nazianzen: 19 March; 329–89; not commemorated in the *Calendar of Willibrord*; commemorated in Bede, *Martyrologium* (B I/II, for different date). Cross has identified Aldhelm, *De uirginitate* (prose), 262.8–263.3 and his *Carmen de uirginitate*, 710–29 as the probable sources for this section.

78.   *æteawdon...nihtlice gesihð<e>*. The variant readings indicate the possibility of an earlier construction in which 'nihtlice gesihþ', nom. sg., was the subject of the verb.

79.   *fægre fæmnan*. twa fægre fæmnan C; 'twa' possibly authorial, with close parallels in the source texts.

80.   *þenden*. þa hwile C; see Kotzor, I, 363.

Bibliography: Cross, 'On the Library', pp. 231–2; Kotzor, II, 293; Rauer, *Fontes*; Whatley, s. v. 'Gregorius Nazianzenus'; Leinbaugh, Review of Kotzor, p. 173.

48. The Third Day of Creation: 20 March. Most of this section is probably derived from Genesis 1.9–10 and Pseudo-Isidore, *De ordine creaturarum*, 930 and 936–7. Cross and Sayers show that the information on the spring- and neap-tides given here has parallels in a number of other Latin texts; in Old English the only parallels can be found in the glosses discussed by Kotzor and Rusche, which may be linked to the martyrologist's environment. The date is probably based on Bede, *De temporum ratione*, 6.78–82.

81.   *fersc<e>*. fersc B, Ko, hig fersce C, Herz p. 227; qualifies the rains as fresh, not salty, water, with 'heo' probably nom. pl. masc., but cp. Note 82 below.

Bibliography: Cross, '*De ordine creaturarum*', pp. 134–5; Sayers, 'The Etymology of Late Latin *malina*'; Kotzor, I, 250 and II, 293; Rauer, 'Usage', p. 132n; Cross, 'On the Library', p. 242; Cross, 'The Influence of Irish Texts and Traditions', p. 186; Cook, *Biblical Quotations*, p. 17; Herzfeld, p. 227; Rusche, 'The *Old English Martyrology* and the Canterbury Aldhelm Scholia'.

49. Cuthbert: 20 March; d. 687; commemorated in the *Calendar of Willibrord* and Bede, *Martyrologium* (B I/II). A number of passages in Bede, prose *Vita S. Cuthberti* (*BHL* 2021), seem to have served as sources for this section, among them 178.13–16 (contact with angels), 208.29–210.2 (healing miracles) and 264.14–266.11 (the miracle of water tasting like wine). Further, minor, parallels can be found in Bede, *Historia ecclesiastica*, 430.19–448.31 (his office, his feastsdays, his area of activity) and Bede, *Martyrologium*, 50 (office, feastday), but as Kotzor points out, the prose *Vita* is likely to have served as the main source.

82. *heo*. hig C; 'heo' is probably nom. pl. fem., but Kotzor, II, 295, offers an alternative explanation; cp. also Note 81 above.

83. *mynster*. mynstre C; see Note 32 above, and Kotzor, II, 295.

84. *ðæs mynstres profoste*. The reference to the provost ('profoste' B, 'prauast' C) of this monastery is unparalleled in literary sources, and may arise from the preceding description of the man as 'standing by' (*proxime astabat*, 'ætstod'), which may have been interpreted by the martyrologist not in terms of physical proximity at the time of drinking the water, but as referring to the man's office as a deputy, i.e. a provost, as this man seems to assist the most senior man in a female house. Alternatively, the martyrologist may have had rare additional information concerning the brother, who in marginal glosses of the *vita*, 266, is also identified as Frithumund.

Bibliography: Kotzor, I, 267 and II, 294–5; Cross, 'On the Library', p. 238; Rauer, *Fontes*; *PASE*, Cuthbert 1; *ODNB*, s. v. 'Cuthbert'; Mitchell, *Old English Syntax*, §2924; Gretsch, *Ælfric and the Cult of Saints*, p. 74.

50. The Fourth Day of Creation: 21 March. This section is probably based on Pseudo-Isidore, *De ordine creaturarum*, 923–5; the date is probably taken from Bede, *De temporum ratione*, 6.78–82, and Cross further highlights scriptural echoes. Ælfric seems to have borrowed from this section for his *De falsis diis* (but see Cross, Review of Pope, who suggests that Ælfric may have drawn on the *De ordine creaturarum* directly). Irvine Homily 6 is possibly also based on this section.

85. *dæg*. dæg þæs monðes C, Herz; the variant could be authorial.

86. *seofoðan*. þryddan C; the variant reading of 'one third' for 'one seventh' remains unexplained.

87. *beorhtre*. beorhtre B, Ko, beorhtor C, Herz; reading in B possibly erroneous, but could also be authorial; see Kotzor, II, 295.

88. <*ac he...hys leoht*>. As preserved in B, this section lacks two important phrases which can, however, be supplied from C; the phrases are both present also in the source material (*in suo ordine semper stabit*, 924, and *quoties autem solem antecedit, detrimenta sui splendoris agit*, 925).

89. *swa...swa...swa...swa*. see Schleburg, *Altenglisch swa*, §494.

Bibliography: Cross, '*De ordine creaturarum*', pp. 135–6; Rauer, 'Usage', pp. 132n, 135 and 136; Irvine, *Old English Homilies*, pp. 152–3; Frankis, Review of Kotzor, p. 314; Kotzor, II, 295; Cross, 'On the Library', p. 242; Cross, 'The Influence of Irish Texts and Traditions', p. 186; Flood, *Representations of Eve*, pp. 49–64; Herzfeld, p. 227; Cook, *Biblical Quotations*, p. 17; Cross, Review of Pope.

51. Benedict of Nursia: 21 March; ?480–550; commemorated in the *Calendar of Willibrord* and in Bede, *Martyrologium* (B I/II). This section is based on Gregory, *Dialogi*, 2.prol.1–15, 2.3.12–37, 2.4.1–32, and 2.37.15–26.

90. *Nursia ðære mægðe*. The martyrologist's designation of Nursia as a region follows his source, *prouincia Nursiae*, 2.prol.6.

91. *Godes þeow sum*. Godes þeowa sum C; see Note 65.

92.   *mid hwitum ryftum*. Cross suspects a misunderstanding behind the reference to the white vestments, whose colour is not directly specified in the source.

93.   *Drihtnes*. Herzfeld's emendation to Drihtnes <þegn> is unnecessary in view of the parallel phrasing in the source passage, *Haec est uia, qua dilectus Domino* [with variant readings *Domini* and *Dei*] *caelum Benedictus ascendit*, 2.37.22–3.

Bibliography: Kotzor, I, 270 and II, 296–7; Cross, 'On the Library', pp. 228n and 245; Rauer, *Fontes*; Mitchell, *Old English Syntax*, §1313n.

52. The Fifth Day of Creation: 22 March. This section is based on Genesis 1.21 and Pseudo-Isidore, *De ordine creaturarum*, 937–8, and the date is probably taken from Bede, *De temporum ratione*, 6.78–82.

94.   *dæg worolde*. worulde dæg C; the word order in C represents the normal pattern for the other days of creation also in B.

95.   *swimmaþ nu <a on> sealtum yþum*. swimmaþ nu sealtum yþum B, Ko, swymmað nu a on sealtum yðum C, swimmað nu a on sealtum yðum Herz; the emendation is based on C and a corresponding phrasing in the source, *in salsis undis semper supernatent*, 937.

96.   *geworht*. geworhte C; cp. also earlier gesceapen B, gesceapene C; C's concord is more consistent in this section.

Bibliography: Cross, '*De ordine creaturarum*', pp. 136–7; Cross, 'On the Library', p. 242; Cross, 'The Influence of Irish Texts and Traditions', p. 186; Rauer, *Fontes*; Cook, *Biblical Quotations*, p. 17; Rauer, 'Usage', p. 132n.

53. The Sixth Day of Creation, Adam and Eve: 23 March. The section is based on Pseudo-Isidore, *De ordine creaturarum*, 940, Genesis 2.22 and 5.4–5, and Adomnán's *De locis sanctis*, 2.9.3–31; the date is probably from Bede, *De temporum ratione*, 6.78–82. Ælfric seems to have borrowed from this section for his *De falsis diis* (but see Cross, Review of Pope, who suggests that Ælfric may have drawn on Pseudo-Isidore, *De ordine creaturarum* directly).

97.   *him is ðæt heafod suð gewend ond þa fet norð*. Herzfeld pointed out that the martyrologist seems to misunderstand the details of Adam's burial given by Adomnán and turns him the wrong way around.

Bibliography: Cross, '*De ordine creaturarum*', pp. 137–8; Kotzor, II, 297; Cross, 'On the Library', pp. 232 and 242; Cross, 'The Influence of Irish Texts and Traditions', p. 186; Herzfeld, p. 228; Flood, *Representations of Eve*, pp. 49–64; Rauer, *Fontes*; Rauer, 'Usage', pp. 132n and 136; Cook, *Biblical Quotations*, p. 17; Cross, Review of Pope.

54. Theodoret: 23 March; d. 362; not commemorated in the *Calendar of Willibrord*, nor in Bede, *Martyrologium*. A *passio* of this saint, such as the *Passio S. Theodoreti* (*BHL* 8074), 43–4, probably served as the source for this section. The hagiographical tradition of this saint is characterised by frequent disagreement on his name and feast day. The details given in this section have parallels in the *passio* and in other early texts and do not indicate any error on the martyrologist's part.

98.   *swa.* see Schleburg, *Altenglisch swa*, §762.
Bibliography: Whatley, s. v. 'Theodoretus'; Rauer, *Fontes*; Galuzzi, 'Teodoreto'.

55. The Seventh Day of Creation: 24 March. This section is based on Genesis 2.2–3; the date is probably from Bede, *De temporum ratione*, 6.78–82.
Bibliography: Kotzor, II, 298; Cook, *Biblical Quotations*, p. 17.

56, 56a. Annunciation Day, The Crucifixion: 25 March; Annunciation not commemorated in the *Calendar of Willibrord*, but in Bede, *Martyrologium* (B I/II); Crucifixion commemorated in the *Calendar of Willibrord*, but not in Bede, *Martyrologium*. This section is based on Adomnán's *De locis sanctis*, 2.26.14–17 and 3.3.3–53, Pseudo-Isidore, *De ortu et obitu patrum*, 42.11, and scriptural sources such as Luke 1.26–38, 23.44–5, and Matthew 27.45–53. For the technicalities of the conception, Cross signalled an analogue in a Hiberno-Latin gospel commentary (*BCLL* 772, meanwhile edited by Forte), and Wright a further parallel in the Linz Homily collection. The reference to the creation could be derived from Gregory, *Homiliae in Euangelia* 10, 66.20–67.47.
99.   *of þæm ostum*. The knots referred to are the points where the original tree (from which the cross was made, and whose fragments are preserved in the box), sprouted branches.
100. *wæte*. The fem. noun 'wæte' seems to be supported by both branches of transmission, although the masc. 'wæta', which is preferred by Ba, could also present the original reading.
Bibliography: Cross, 'The Use of Patristic Homilies', pp. 121–2; Cross, 'The Influence of Irish Texts and Traditions', pp. 182–4; Cross, 'On the Library', p. 232; Wright, 'Vienna Commentary on Matthew'; Clayton, 'Feasts of the Virgin'; Clayton, *The Cult of the Virgin Mary*, pp. 213–14; Rauer, *Fontes*, s. vv. 'Annunciation Day' and 'Crucifixion'; Forte, 'A Critical Edition of a Hiberno-Latin Commentary', p. 36; Kotzor, II, 298; Hall, 'The Ages of Christ and Mary'; Bately, 'The Place Which is Called'; Rauer, 'Usage', pp. 128 and 132; Cook, *Biblical Quotations*, pp. 18–19; Tupper, 'Anglo-Saxon Dæg-Mæl', p. 223.

57. Christ's Descent into Hell: 26 March; not commemorated in the *Calendar of Willibrord*, nor in Bede, *Martyrologium*. This seems to be the earliest surviving English vernacular description of Christ's Harrowing of Hell. The precise source of this complex section remains unidentified, although Cross and others have identified a number of Latin and vernacular analogues, including Blickling Homily 7, 85.3–89.34, *De descensu Christi ad inferos*, 1–206, and Pseudo-Augustine, Sermo 160, 2059–61; see Cross, 'The Use of Patristic Homilies' for the voluminous secondary literature on this topic.
101. *On ðone...þær geband*. The somewhat breathless opening sentence may be corrupt; a reference to Christ's transition from grave to hell could have dropped out. Any possible textual problem must in any case have occurred early during transmission, since both B and C, and an early reader Bf all seem to have struggled with this opening passage; Herzfeld similarly suspects textual error.

102. *þis*. þus C; 'þus' appears in similar contexts in the analogues for this passage and is better attested generally; 'þus' is perhaps the original reading.
103. *genere nu*. genera C; see Kotzor, II, 298.
104. *ban...flæsce*. flæsc of mynum flæsce and ban of mynum banum C; see Cross, 'The Use of Patristic Homilies', p. 117n.
105. *gesigefæsted*. see Kirschner, 'Die Bezeichnungen', pp. 161–2.
Bibliography: Cross, 'The Use of Patristic Homilies', pp. 117–20; Glaeske, 'Eve in Anglo-Saxon Retellings'; Morey, 'Gospel of Nicodemus', p. 47; Cross, 'On the Library', p. 237; Biggs and Morey, 'The Gospel of Nicodemus'; Clayton, *The Cult of the Virgin Mary*, p. 256; Karkov, 'Exiles from the Kingdom', pp. 194 and 196; Kotzor, II, 298; Campbell, 'To Hell and Back', pp. 142–3; Flood, *Representations of Eve*, pp. 49–64; Dumville, 'Liturgical Drama', pp. 386 and 406; Cook, *Biblical Quotations*, p. 17; Tupper, 'Anglo-Saxon Dæg-Mæl', p. 224.

58. Resurrection: 27 March; commemorated in the *Calendar of Willibrord*; not commemorated in Bede, *Martyrologium*. This section seems to be based on scriptural passages (probably including Luke 20.27 and 24.42 and John 24.39) and on Adomnán, *De locis sanctis*, 1.2.15–60. For the reference to Christ's ten posthumous appearances, Cross highlighted a number of analogues, including the *Catachesis celtica* and Augustinian material, but its precise source (possibly a homily or Bible commentary) remains unidentified.
106. *mannes*. medemum men C; variant in C closer to the Latin *alicuius non breuis staturae stantis hominis* and thus possibly authorial.
107. *hierr<e>*. hierra B, Ko, hierre C, Herz; see Kotzor, II, 299.
Bibliography: Cross, 'The Influence of Irish Texts and Traditions', p. 184; Cross, 'The Use of Patristic Homilies', p. 121; Cross, 'On the Library', pp. 232–3; Kotzor, I, 257 and II, 298–9.

58a. The End of March: Monthly information on the length of day and night can be found in liturgical calendars; see also **36a**. Bede, *De temporum ratione*, 15 represents an analogue for the English names of the months.
Bibliography: Kotzor, I, 305 and II, 299; Tupper, 'Anglo-Saxon Dæg-Mæl', p. 120.

58b. The Beginning of April: 1 April. The source for the sections on the beginnings of the months could have been Bede, *De temporum ratione*, 12 and 15, although it is not in all cases clear whether this represents an antecedent or direct source. Kotzor signals relevant information in a number of liturgical calendars and martyrologies which could also have served as sources.
Bibliography: Kotzor, I, 268 and II, 278–9, 299.

59. Agape, Chionia and Irene: 3 April; d. Thessalonica, 304, under Diocletian; not commemorated in the *Calendar of Willibrord*; commemorated in Bede, *Martyrologium* (B, for 1 April). This section is a conflation of passages from Aldhelm, *De uirginitate* (prose), 305.13–306.6, his *Carmen de uirginitate*, 2222–44, and the anonymous *Passio S. Anastasiae* (*BHL* 118), 12, 16 and 18. The translation of *larua* as 'egesgrima' has parallels in various glosses which could also have been used. The hagiographical tradition of these saints sometimes assigns one feastday to all three of them (for which see Rauer, 'Female Hagiography') as happens here in the opening lines, but the *passio* clearly states that Irene was martyred a few days later than her sisters, which accounts for the specific reference to only two of the saints at the end of the section and the separate section **61** for Irene.

108. *ond behrumig*. om. C; the phrasing in B is closer to that of the source.

Bibliography: Kotzor, I, 250n, 256–7, 273n and II, 299–300; Rauer, 'Female Hagiography'; Cross, 'On the Library', pp. 230–1; Cross, 'The Use of Patristic Homilies', pp. 281–2; Lanéry, 'Hagiographie d'Italie', pp. 45–60; Cross, 'Source, Lexis, and Edition', pp. 29 and 33; Rusche, 'The *Old English Martyrology* and the Canterbury Aldhelm Scholia'; Whatley, s. v. 'Agape, Chionia, et Irene'; Lapidge, 'Acca of Hexham', p. 54; Stodnick, 'Bodies of Land'.

60. Ambrose of Milan: 5 April; 339–97; commemorated in the *Calendar of Willibrord* (under a different date), and in Bede, *Martyrologium* (B II, different date). Paulinus of Milan, *Vita S. Ambrosii* (*BHL* 377), 47 and 51, presents parallels for some, if not all, details. Current editions of this *vita* are not entirely reliable, however, and it is difficult to envisage at this stage what text variant of the *vita* the martyrologist could have used. Orosius, *Historiae aduersum paganos*, 7.36.7–13, also presents parallels, but is unlikely to represent the main source.

109. *ðæm swylcne hyll swa*. þam felda swylce hylle swylce C; Herz and Schleburg, *Altenglisch swa*, §48, follow C in retaining 'felda', which may be authorial, but is not strictly necessary.

110. *sona he wæs, se reða here*. þa sona wæs se reða here C; reading in C possibly authorial and in any case more elegant, but parenthetic construction in B not uncharacteristic of the text.

Bibliography: Cross, 'On the Library', p. 248; Rauer, *Fontes*; Whatley, s. v. 'Ambrosius'; Gioanni, 'Hagiographie d'Italie', pp. 392–4.

61. Irene: 5 April; d. Thessalonica, 304, under Diocletian; not commemorated in the *Calendar of Willibrord*; commemorated in Bede, *Martyrologium* (B). Based on the *Passio S. Anastasiae* (*BHL* 118), 18, which, however, deviates in some respect. For the saint's feastday, see section **59** for Agape, Chionia, Irene.

111. *twegen Godes englas*. In the Latin text, Irene's helpers are not explicitly characterised as angels.

112. *hi gelæddan on swa heanne munt...to genealæcean*. The somewhat odd correlative construction seems to point to the height of the mountain as the reason why no persecutor can touch the saint, whereas the Latin has her magically protected, as her persecutor is confined to moving in circles (*gyrans*) for an entire day. This latter reference may have not have been understood by the martyrologist, or could have been absent from his Latin source (as at least one text variant of the *passio* omits the phrase).

113. *heo þær hire gast onsænde*. The Old English account gives no specific details of the saint's death, which in the Latin is brought about with bow and arrow.

Bibliography: Kotzor, I, 273n; Cross, 'The Latinity', p. 284; Rauer, 'Female Hagiography'; Stodnick, 'Bodies of Land'; Lanéry, 'Hagiographie d'Italie', pp. 45–60; Schleburg, *Altenglisch swa*, §298.

62. Seven Women at Sirmium: 9 April; ?fourth century; not commemorated in the *Calendar of Willibrord*; commemorated in Bede, *Martyrologium* (B). The information given here has parallels in various other martyrological and liturgical texts, but the section is too short to allow a more precise sourcing.
114.   *on Syria mægðe*. The martyrologist (or his source before him) erroneously locates these saints in Syria rather than Sirmium.
Bibliography: Kotzor, II, 300; Herzfeld, p. xxxviii; Delehaye, *Étude sur le légendier*, p. 62; Rauer, 'Female Hagiography'.

63. Guthlac: 11 April; d. 714; not commemorated in the *Calendar of Willibrord*, nor in Bede, *Martyrologium*. Ultimately based on Felix, *Vita S. Guthlaci* (*BHL* 3723), 74.20–76.4, 78.3–4, 156.14–21, 160.10–11, although there is disagreement among commentators on the direct or indirect nature of this borrowing. The martyrologist is unusual among authors in omitting any reference to Guthlac's demonic encounters.
115.   *His nama is on Læden belli munus*. From 'guþ', f. ('battle', 'war', 'combat') and 'lac', n. ('offering', 'gift', 'present', 'sacrifice'). The translation is taken from the Latin source, 78.3–4; a third instance of this translation appears in the Old English prose Life of Guthlac, 107, 'Guðlac se nama ys on romanisc belli munus'. For the spiritual connotations of 'lac' and *munus*, which are also explained in the texts, see Bolton, 'The Background and Meaning of *Guthlac*' and Robinson, 'The Significance of Names', pp. 43–50.
Bibliography: Roberts, 'An Inventory', pp. 203–4; Rauer, *Fontes*; Kotzor, I, 268 and II, 301; Whatley, s. v. 'Guthlacus'; Cross, 'English Vernacular Saints' Lives'; Cross, 'On the Library', p. 246; Dendle, *Satan Unbound*, pp. 162–3; *PASE*, Guthlac 2; *ODNB*, s. v. 'Guthlac'.

64. Valerianus, Tiburtius and Maximus: 14 April; d. Rome, third century; commemorated in the *Calendar of Willibrord* and in Bede, *Martyrologium* (B). Probably based on the *Passio S. Caeciliae* (*BHL* 1495), 22–4; Upchurch's Latin text is closer to the Old English than previous editions. With its anacoluthon, translationese ('mid heora feþera flihte', *remigio alarum suarum*), acculturation of virginal imagery, and compression of information, this section is a classic example of the martyrologist's stylistic methods.
116.   *Allmachius*. almatheus C; Kotzor, I, 162 regards the reading in B as the better variant, but interestingly, the Latin tradition knows the same wide range of spelling variants for this name. Given the common mixing of c and t in Latin, it could be that, starting from a single spelling in the original *Old English Martyrology*, the divergence arose within the Old English tradition through varying scribal practice. Alternatively, the scribes of both the B and C tradition may have been familiar with the Latin narrative and its details and may have preferred different spellings. The same figure is also mentioned at **227** (C only), in a passage which is based on the

same Latin tradition. It could therefore also be that sections **64** and **227** of an original *Old English Martyrology* differed in its spellings of the name, which could also account for the divergence between B and C here.

117.   *fægre gefretwade*. Tyler comments on the traditional collocation 'fægre gefretwade' (apparently translating *quasi ornatas uirgines*) which, together with the continuing alliteration, could indicate poetic or homiletic influence, as well as possible contacts with an Old English Phoenix tradition.

Bibliography: Whatley, s. v. 'Caecilia'; Kotzor, II, 301; Tyler, *Old English Poetics*, pp. 93–7; Upchurch, 'Homiletic Contexts'; Lanéry, 'Hagiographie d'Italie', pp. 80–8; Delehaye, *Étude sur le légendier romain*, pp. 73–96.

65. Eleutherius and Antia: 18 April; Rome, second century, under Hadrian; not commemorated in the *Calendar of Willibrord*, nor in Bede, *Martyrologium*. Based on the *Passio S. Eleutherii* (*BHL* 2451), 445.47–446.48.

118.   *Mechania*. Mæchania A, Mecherie C; the city's name is clearly corrupt, and the corruption already seems to characterise the Latin tradition.

119.   *ðonne hofan ða deor heora fet upp*. The Latin source specifies that the animals raise only their right paws.

120.   *his huntan*. om. C; the Latin source specifies that hunters (*uenatores*) only *discover* the saint in the wilderness, reporting him to the emperor, whereupon Hadrian dispatches *comites suos et milites armatos* who then seize the saint: this may account for C's omitting the reference to the hunters altogether, perhaps in view of the narrative error.

Bibliography: Whatley, s. v. 'Eleutherius, Antia'; Quentin, *Les martyrologes historiques*, pp. 256–7; Kotzor, II, 302; Rauer, *Fontes*; Siegmund, *Die Überlieferung der griechischen christlichen Literatur*, p. 234; Frere, *Studies in Early Roman Literature*, p. 47.

66. Æthelwald: 21 April; d. 699; commemorated in the *Calendar of Willibrord*; not commemorated in Bede, *Martyrologium*. The opening lines are probably based on Bede, *Vita S. Cuthberti* (prose) (*BHL* 2021), 302.9–11 and 302.27–9; Whatley furthermore identifies Bede, *Vita metrica S. Cuthberti* (*BHL* 2020), 918–28, as the source for the saint's miracle. The saint's feastday has a parallel in the Calendar of Willibrord (which presents other interesting feasts which overlap with the *Old English Martyrology*, as Rushforth shows).

121.   *ðære ecean eadignesse*. The collocation of 'ece' and 'eadignes' is traditional and particularly well attested in homiletic texts; here it seems to have been chosen as an idiomatic rather than close translation of Bede's *supernae beatitudinis*.

Bibliography: Whatley, s. v. 'Oethelwaldus'; Cross, 'On the Library', pp. 238 and 248; Rushforth, *Saints in English Kalendars*, p. 18 and Table IV; *PASE*, Æthelwald 8.

67. George: 23 April; biographical dates unclear; d. ?Nicomedia, ?303, under Diocletian; not commemorated in the *Calendar of Willibrord*; commemorated in Bede, *Martyrologium* (B II). The last three lines of this entry abbreviate two much longer episodes in Adomnán, *De locis sanctis*, 3.4.2–134. Parallels for the preceding parts can be found in the texts now distinguished as the *Passio S. Georgii* (*BHL* 3363), 70.8–9 and 49.1–68.15 and the *Passio S. Georgii* (*BHL* 3379), 529.25–34. But it is not clear if the martyrologist conflated two differing versions of the *passio*, or was familiar with a 'mixed' version of that text, now lost.

122. *ðone...hine.* Anacoluthon; attempts a combination of two different quasi-formulaic constructions; cp. Note 54.

123. *Datianus.* See Introduction, p. 16.

124. *næfre.* næfre A, C, Herz, no hwæþre B, nohwæþre Ko; reading in AC preferred, as it occurs in both branches of transmission, but the reading in B, perhaps to be translated as 'not at all, however', could alternatively be original.

125. *Hælende...mildheortnesse.* See Rauer, 'Direct Speech, Intercession, and Prayer', and Introduction, pp. 17–18.

126. *Swa hwelc.* and swa hwylc man C, swa hwelc mon Herz; 'man' or 'mon' possibly authorial, but not strictly necessary.

127. *se geunarade.* se ðe geunarode C, se þe geunarade Herz. The reading in C could be original, but that in B is not ungrammatical.

128. *geþingung.* geþingu with abbreviation mark B, þyngunge C (with paraphrase); from '(ge-)þingung', 'intercession', which gives better meaning than 'geþingum', as it is expanded in Ko. Cp. also Note 136 for the same difficulty.

Bibliography: Cross, 'Saints' Lives in Old English', pp. 45–51; Cross, 'The Influence of Irish Texts and Traditions', pp. 180–1; Cross, 'On the Library', pp. 229n, 232 and 236; Hill, 'Saint George before the Conquest'; Kotzor, I, 254–5 and II, 302; Hill, 'Georgius'; Herzfeld, pp. 228–9; Rauer, 'Direct Speech, Intercession, and Prayer'; Haubrichs, *Georgslied und Georgslegende*, pp. 329–30, 355–7 and 464; particularly for the later medieval development, see also Good, *The Cult of Saint George in Medieval England*.

68. Wilfrid: 24 April; d. 709x710; not commemorated in the *Calendar of Willibrord*, nor in Bede, *Martyrologium*. Probably based on passages in Stephen of Ripon, *Vita S. Wilfridi* (*BHL* 8889), including 4.8–22, 120.26–122.13, 140.26–8, although not all details have very close parallels there.

Bibliography: Kotzor, I, 268 and II, 303–4; Cross, 'On the Library', pp. 235 and 246; Whatley, s. v. Wilfridus; *PASE*, Wilfrid 2; *ODNB*, s. v. 'Wilfrid'.

69. Rogation Day: 25 April; not commemorated in the *Calendar of Willibrord*, nor in Bede, *Martyrologium*. The precise source for this section remains unidentified; Cross and Hill discuss a number of analogues. Cross points out that 'zymologesin' (*exomologesin*) is also used by a number of patristic authors and Hrabanus Maurus. But it is noteworthy that it also occurs twice in the Second Corpus Glossary, s. v. 'exomologesin'.

Bibliography: Cross, 'The Use of Patristic Homilies', pp. 115 and 123–4; Cross, 'On the Library', p. 247; Kotzor, II, 304; Hill, 'The *Litaniae maiores*'; Rauer, 'Usage', p. 132; *DOEC*, s. v. 'exomologesin'.

70. Mark: 25 April; first century; commemorated in the *Calendar of Willibrord* (under different date) and in Bede, *Martyrologium* (B). The opening lines are probably based on Pseudo-Isidore, *De ortu et obitu patrum*, 59.1–2; the remainder seems to be derived from the *Passio S. Marci* (*BHL* 5276), 347–9.

129. *æfter*. See Swaen, 'Contributions to Anglo-Saxon Lexicography', p. 177.

Bibliography: Cross, 'The Influence of Irish Texts and Traditions', pp. 188–9; Cross, 'On the Library', pp. 241n and 243; Kotzor, I, 211, 224 and II, 304.

71. Alexandria: 27 April; fourth century, under Diocletian; not commemorated in the *Calendar of Willibrord*, nor in Bede, *Martyrologium*. As with **67. George**, parallels for this section can be found in various versions of the *Passio S. Georgii*; see, for example, the *Passio S. Georgii* (*BHL* 3379), 527.30–528.8. Again it is not clear whether two differing versions were conflated by the martyrologist, or whether a 'mixed' variant, now lost, was used.

130. *Datianus cwen ðæs hæðnan caseres*. For Datianus, see also Introduction, p. 16.

131. *þin neorxnawong*. þynne neorxnawang C, þinne neorxnawong Herz. 'þin' seems to point to 'neorxnawong' as an unusual neuter, or else represents a copying error triggered by an original '-ne ne-'; in that case perhaps emend to 'þinne', as Herz does.

Bibliography: Cross, 'Saints' Lives in Old English', pp. 45–51; Whatley, s. v. 'Georgius'; Kotzor, II, 304; Rauer, 'Female Hagiography'; Stodnick, 'Bodies of Land'.

72. Vitalis: 28 April; d. Ravenna, first or second century; not commemorated in the *Calendar of Willibrord*; commemorated in Bede, *Martyrologium* (B II). Probably based on Pseudo-Ambrose, *Passio S. Geruasii* (*BHL* 3514), 744–5.

132. *deofolgylde*. deofolgylda C; reading in B represents a copying error or rare interpretation of 'deofolgyld' as fem.; perhaps emend to -a or -es; see Kotzor, II, 305.

Bibliography: Whatley, s. v. 'Gervasius et Protasius'; Lanéry, *Ambroise de Milan*, esp. pp. 305–47; Lanéry, 'Hagiographie d'Italie', pp. 61–8; Rauer, *Fontes*; Kotzor, II, 305; Stodnick, 'Bodies of Land'.

73. Christopher: 28 April; Lycia, ?third century, under Decius; not commemorated in the *Calendar of Willibrord*; commemorated in Bede, *Martyrologium* (B II). Based on a version of the saint's *passio*; cp. for example *Passio S. Christophori* (*BHL* 1764), 3–34; the precise text variant used remains to be located.

133. *Ða...worldwisena*. See Rauer, 'Direct Speech, Intercession, and Prayer', and Introduction, pp. 17–18.

134. *hwæ<te>s gneað<n>es*. See also Leinbaugh, 'St Christopher and the *Old English Martyrology*'.

135. *þæt he næfre...oþerra worldwisena*. The list of misfortunes from which relic owners are spared remains problematic, despite the emendation of Herzfeld and Leinbaugh; the Latin passage (as transmitted) refers to hail storms, crop damage and infertility of vines or vineyards (*sterilitas vinearum*), none of which seem to have

very close parallels in the rather collective 'woruldwelena' ('worldly goods', C), nor in 'worldwisena' ('fashions of the world', B), although the variant in C seems the more plausible reading. One suspects that the passage is now garbled in both manuscripts, and that a more difficult phrase, possibly involving words like OE 'wise', f. ('plant'), OE 'weod', f. ('weed'), or OE 'win', n. ('wine'), has been rationalised.

136.   *geþingung*. geþingu with abbreviation mark B, C; see Note 128.

Bibliography: Leinbaugh, 'St Christopher and the *Old English Martyrology*'; Whatley, s. v. 'Christophorus'; Kotzor, II, 305; Cross, 'On the Library', p. 235n; Herzfeld, pp. 229–30; Orchard, *Pride and Prodigies*, pp. 12–18; Lionarons, 'From Monster to Martyr'; Rauer, 'Direct Speech, Intercession, and Prayer'; Mitchell, *Old English Syntax*, §2924; Bierbaumer, *Der botanische Wortschatz*, I, 143.

73a. The End of April: Monthly information on the length of day and night can be found in liturgical calendars; see the note above for **36a**. Bede, *De temporum ratione*, 15, represents an analogue for the English names of the months.

Bibliography: Kotzor, I, 306 and II, 305; Tupper, 'Anglo-Saxon Dæg-Mæl', p. 120.

73b. The Beginning of May: 1 May. The source for the sections on the beginnings of the months could have been Bede, *De temporum ratione*, 12 and 15; it is not in all cases clear whether this represents an antecedent or direct source, although the section on the beginning of May seems to be unusually close to Bede. Kotzor signals relevant information in a number of liturgical calendars and martyrologies which could also have served as sources.

Bibliography: Kotzor, I, 268 and II, 278–9, 305; Herzfeld, p. 230; Rauer, 'Usage', p. 127.

74. Philip: 1 May; first century; commemorated in the *Calendar of Willibrord* and in Bede, *Martyrologium* (B I/II). The latter part of this section is probably based on Pseudo-Abdias, *Passio S. Philippi* (*BHL* 6814), 385.1–48. The etymological information could have been derived from a number of possible sources, as discussed by Cross.

Bibliography: Cross, 'The Apostles', pp. 28–9; Biggs, *The Apocrypha*, p. 54; Kotzor, II, 306; Robinson, 'The Significance of Names', p. 42n; Herzfeld, pp. xxxviii and 230.

75. Athanasius: 2 May; ?296–373; not commemorated in the *Calendar of Willibrord*; commemorated in Bede, *Martyrologium* (B I/II). Aldhelm, *De uirginitate* (prose), 272.13–273.13, Aldhelm, *Carmen de uirginitate*, 971–93, and Rufinus, *Historia ecclesiastica*, 980.11–981.22 (which represents Aldhelm's source) could have been used individually or together as sources for this section.

Bibliography: Whatley, s. v. 'Athanasius'; Rauer, *Fontes*; Cross, 'On the Library', p. 231.

76. Pope Alexander I, Eventius and Theodolus: 3 May; Alexander *s.* ?109–?16; not commemorated in the *Calendar of Willibrord*; commemorated in Bede, *Martyrologium* (B). The source seems to be the *Passio S. Alexandri* (*BHL* 266), 374–5.
Bibliography: Cross, 'Popes of Rome', pp. 199–200 and 202–4; Whatley, s. v. 'Alexander papa'; Lanéry, 'Hagiographie d'Italie', pp. 301–3; Kotzor, II, 306.

77. Discovery of the Holy Cross: 3 May; not commemorated in the *Calendar of Willibrord*; commemorated in Bede, *Martyrologium* (B II). The source seems to be the *Inuentio S. Crucis* (*BHL* 4169), 378.33–47 and 379.31–4; the martyrologist himself refers to 'holy writings'.
137. *Ðær...gemeted.* The Latin text makes it clear that the smell emanated from the ground before the Cross was found. Various possibilities exist for punctuating this passage, see Mitchell, *Old English Syntax*, §§2519–2525.
138. *wæs gemeted...wæs gemeted.* Only B has this sequence of two similar sounding phrases; C omits the first and E omits the second phrase. The reading in B appears to be the correct one, as the most explicit version; the versions in C and E may go back to erroneous deletion of what might have looked like a redundant phrase.
139. *lichoman.* B refers to a body, whereas C and E for unclear reasons refer to a body and a grave ('byrgenne'). There is no grave mentioned in the Latin, and for the miracle to make sense the dead man needs to be carried around in the open air. The branch of transmission to which C and E belong may have been influenced by a misunderstanding of 'þæt treow wæs geseted' as referring to a planting of the cross (or tree) in the ground, which the martyrologist may have intended as a metaphorical, but not literal, reading.
Bibliography: Biggs, 'Inventio Sanctae Crucis'; Cross, 'On the Library', p. 234n; Harbus, *Helena of Britain*, p. 31; Whatley, s. v. 'Iesus Christus, Inventio Sanctae Crucis'; Kotzor, I, 258.

78. Rogation Days: Not commemorated in the *Calendar of Willibrord*, nor in Bede, *Martyrologium*. The second half of this section seems to be a conflation of two sermons by Caesarius of Arles, Sermo 207, 828.56 and 830.17–21, and Sermo 208, 833.5–21 and 833.25–6. The information given in the first half is of a more general nature for which Cross has identified a number of analogues. Godden has shown that an anonymous Winchester homily borrows from this section.
140. *ciric<an>*. ciricum B, cyrcan C, ciercean E; cp. also **2**, **4**, and Kotzor, II, 307.
141. *<cl>æsnungdrenceas*. a æsnungdreceas B, clænsung in the margin Be, clæsnungdrencas C, E, a <cl>æsnungdrenceas Ko; see Kotzor, I, 137n.
Bibliography: Cross, 'The Use of Patristic Homilies', pp. 113–16; Hill, 'The *Litaniae maiores*'; Trahern, 'Caesarius of Arles'; Kotzor, II, 307; Rauer, 'Usage', pp. 128, 132 and 134; Godden, 'Old English Composite Homilies'; Cross, 'On the Library', p. 237; Tupper, 'Anglo-Saxon Dæg-Mæl', pp. 122, 161, and 172.

79. Ascension: 5 May; commemorated in the *Calendar of Willibrord*; not commemorated in Bede, *Martyrologium*. This section is largely derived from Adomnán, *De locis sanctis*, 1.23.1–99; the opening lines are loosely based on Luke 24.51 (Zwiep, pers. comm.) and Acts 1.1–12. Cross, 'The Use of Patristic Homilies' suspected a homily or commentary behind the reference to the earth moving to heaven, pointing to Pseudo-Augustine, Sermo 395, 1717 and Sermo 176, 2081 from which the image could have been derived; Zwiep (pers. comm.) identifies Augustine, Sermo 130, 727 as a further possible source. Man's exaltation over the hosts of angels generally mirrors information given in 1 Pe 3.22; in terms of phrasing one suspects a connection with the phrase *super choros angelorum*, which frequently refers to the Assumption of the Virgin Mary and which Zwiep (pers. comm.) also traces to a number of later medieval references to the Ascension of Christ; Old English equivalents, such as 'ofer ealle engla þretas' or 'bufon engla ðrymme', also occur. This section shares some of its imagery and analogues with Blickling Homily 11.

142. <*nolde seo eorðe him onfon*>. Herz, seo eorðe him onufan scealde B, Ko, nolde seo eorðe hym onfon C, nolde sio eorðe him onfon E; see Kotzor, II, 309.
143. *þe*. B, þe hig C, þe ða E; relative clause possibly defective in B.
144. *on sæton*. onsæton Ko, on asetton C; see also Kotzor, II, 309.
145. *ðære*. þara C; see Kotzor, II, 309.
146. *Drihtne*<*s*>. drihtne B, Drihtne<s> Ko, Herz, dryhtnes C; see Kotzor, II, 309.
147. *swaða*. swaðe C; see Kotzor, II, 309.
148. *ondry*<*sn*>*lice*. ondrynslice B, Ko, ondryslice C; see Kotzor, II, 309.

Bibliography: Cross, 'On the Blickling Homily for Ascension Day'; Cross, 'The Use of Patristic Homilies', p. 122; Cross, 'The Influence of Irish Texts and Traditions', pp. 180–1; Clayton, *The Cult of the Virgin Mary*, p. 243; Oetgen, 'Common Motifs', p. 442; Cross, 'On the Library', p. 232; Kotzor, I, 254–5 and II, 307–9; Rauer, 'Usage', p. 128; Ó Broin, '*Rex Christus Ascendens*', pp. 198–259.

80. Eadberht: 6 May; d. 698; not commemorated in the *Calendar of Willibrord*, nor in Bede, *Martyrologium*. The source for this section is Bede, prose *Vita S. Cuthberti* (*BHL* 2021), 286.19–20, 292.1–12, 292.23–8, 292.30–294.1, 294.3–7, 294.9–28, and 296.1–8.

149. *clænre*. mycelre C, E; variant perhaps closer to source, *miro affectu*.
150. *þæt...restep*. on þære stowe reste and *C*, on ðære stowe ræste E; phrase in B probably defective.

Bibliography: Kotzor, I, 267 and II, 310–11; Rauer, *Fontes*; Whatley, s. v. 'Eadberht'; Cross, 'On the Library', p. 238; *PASE*, Eadberht 3; *ODNB*, s. v. 'Eadberht'.

81. John of Beverley: 7 May; d. 721; not commemorated in the *Calendar of Willibrord*, nor in Bede, *Martyrologium*. Largely based on Bede, *Historia ecclesiastica*, 456.12–468.34.

151. *Sancte Iohannes geleornes*. The death of this saint in 721 seems to be the latest datable event mentioned in the *Old English Martyrology* (but cp. also Note 291).
Bibliography: Kotzor, I, 252–3 and II, 311–12; Cross, 'A Lost Life of Hilda of Whitby', pp. 24 and 36n; Cross, 'On the Library', p. 230; Lapidge, 'Acca of Hexham', p. 40; Wilson, *The Life and After-Life*, pp. 29–30; *PASE*, John 18; *ODNB*, s. v. 'John of Beverley'; Rauer, 'Female Hagiography'.

82. Discovery of St Michael's Church: 8 May; not commemorated in the *Calendar of Willibrord*, nor in Bede, *Martyrologium*. Probably based on the *Apparitio S. Michaelis* (*BHL* 5948), 541.24–31.
Bibliography: Whatley, s. v. 'Michaelis archangelus'; Johnson, *Saint Michael the Archangel*, pp. 50–63; Cross, 'An Unrecorded Tradition', p. 12n.

83. Victor Maurus: 8 May; d. Milan, 303, under Maximian; not commemorated in the *Calendar of Willibrord*, nor in Bede, *Martyrologium*. Probably derived from the *Passio S. Victoris* (*BHL* 8580), 288–90.
152. *heafdum*. See Campbell, *Old English Grammar*, §574.4, Swanton, ed., *The Dream of the Rood*, p. 126, and diPaolo Healey, 'Old English *heafod* "head": A Lofty Place?', p. 34.
Bibliography: Cross, 'Old English *leasere*', p. 485; Whatley, s. v. 'Victor Maurus'; Cross, 'The Latinity', pp. 281–2; Lanéry, 'Hagiographie d'Italie', pp. 261–4; Kotzor, II, 312; Roberts, '*Fela martyra*', p. 170.

83a. The Beginning of Summer: 9 May. The date and the information on the Pleiades are possibly derived from Bede, *De temporum ratione*, 35.41–51, and more or less reflect astronomical reality (pers. comm. Cameron). Only two of the four implied seasons are mentioned in the *Old English Martyrology*: summer (ninety days long, beginning 9 May) and winter (ninety-two days, beginning 7 November; cp. **221a**), which raises questions regarding the length of the entire year. The Anglo-Saxon calendrical tradition knows similar entries for the beginnings of the seasons, and it is probable that a calendar served as a source here; see, for example, the calendar in Oxford, Bodleian Library, Digby 63, fols. 40–45, 9 May, *Æstas inicium habet dies xc* and 7 November, *Hiems habet dies inicium xci*; that particular calendar also has an entry for the beginning of spring, 7 February, *Verus* (sic) *inicium habet dies xci*. As the section for early February is missing from the *Old English Martyrology*, it is hard to say whether a similar entry for the beginning of spring also appeared there. Several calendars put the beginning of autumn on 7 August, but the *Old English Martyrology* does not list this event against that date, for unknown reasons. It is therefore possible that the martyrologist aimed at presenting a four-seasons system, without, however, finalising it. Alternatively, it may be that the author intended to follow the older two-season system, without, however adjusting the length of the two seasons to make up a full year.
153. *æfen*. There seems to be no explanation for the variant 'undern' C.

Bibliography: Anderson, 'The Seasons of the Year', pp. 231–2 and 238–40; Rauer, 'Usage', pp. 127, 132, 134 and 139; Kotzor, I, 306 and II, 312; Wormald, *English Kalendars before A.D. 1100*, pp. 1–13; Tupper, 'Anglo-Saxon Dæg-Mæl', pp. 149 and 203.

84. Gordianus: 10 May; Rome, fourth century, under Julian; not commemorated in the *Calendar of Willibrord*; commemorated in Bede, *Martyrologium* (B II). Possibly based on information derived from a sacramentary.
Bibliography: Kotzor, I, 211, 218, 225, 259, 264 and II, 312; Whatley, s. v. 'Gordianus et Epimachus'; Cross, 'On the Library', pp. 234 and 241n.

85. Calepodius: 10 May; Rome, third century; not commemorated in the *Calendar of Willibrord*; commemorated in Bede, *Martyrologium* (B). Possibly derived from Bede, *Martyrologium*, 66.
Bibliography: Kotzor, I, 211, 214n, 225, and II, 313; Cross, 'On the Library', p. 241n; Whatley, s. v. 'Callistus'.

86. Pancras: 12 May; commemorated in the *Calendar of Willibrord* and in Bede, *Martyrologium* (B). Most of this section is based on the *Passio S. Pancratii* (*BHL* 6421), 16.4–6, 17.5–7 and 17.19–18.9; the detail concerning the saint's burial place may or may not have been derived from the *Liber pontificalis*, I.324.5. The chronology of the events described, including references to the saint's baptism by Pope Cornelius (251–3), persecution by Diocletian (*c.* 244–*c.* 312) and martyrdom at a young age (*c.* 304), is implausible, but is already present in the Latin tradition. On the chronological problems in particular, see Drobner, *Der heilige Pankratius*, pp. 12–15.
154.   *Frigia*. Phrygia is a region rather than a city; the misunderstanding in the Old English text seems to have been caused by a variant reading in the *passio*, 'ciuitate frigia'.
Bibliography: Cross, 'Identification: Towards Criticism', pp. 231–2; Whatley, s. v. 'Pancratius'; Gioanni, 'Hagiographie d'Italie', pp. 389–90; Drobner, *Der heilige Pankratius*; Cross, 'On the Library', p. 243 n; Kotzor, II, 313.

87. Victor and Corona: 14 May; Egypt, second century, under Antoninus; not commemorated in the *Calendar of Willibrord*; commemorated in Bede, *Martyrologium* (B). The source seems to be the *Passio S. Victoris* (*BHL* 8559), 266–8.
155.   *Antoninus*. The emperor referred to is Antoninus Pius.
Bibliography: Whatley, s. v. 'Victor & Corona'.

88. Pentecost: 15 May; commemorated in the *Calendar of Willibrord*; not commemorated in Bede, *Martyrologium*. The sources for this section have not conclusively been established. Acts 1.15, 2.2–4 and 2.43 represent antecedent sources; for the association of Pentecost with the giving of the law to Moses, see the analogues adduced by Cross, 'The Use of Patristic Homilies'. Dekker discusses dove imagery in a pentecostal context.

156.   *forþon ðe.* forþon on þone dæg C, forðon þe on þone dæg Herz; reading in C gives better sense and is possibly authorial.

157.   *Hælend<e>s.* hælendas B, hælendes C, hælend<e>s Ko, Herz; reading in B possibly a spelling variant, but here more likely to be an error triggered by the ending of the following word.

Bibliography: Cross, 'The Use of Patristic Homilies', pp. 122–3; Cross, 'On the Library', p. 247; Kotzor, II, 313; Rauer, 'Usage', pp. 128 and 132; Dekker, 'Pentecost and Linguistic Self-Consciousness'; Cook, *Biblical Quotations*, pp. 17 and 19–20.

89. Pope John I: 18 May; *s.* 523–6; not commemorated in the *Calendar of Willibrord*; commemorated in Bede, *Martyrologium* (B, under different date). Apparently based on the *Liber pontificalis*, I.276.6, and Gregory, *Dialogi*, 3.2.22–6 and 4.31.9–31.

158.   *Þeodoric<us> Gotona cyning.* Þeodoricost gotona cyning B, Þeodoric ostgotona cyning Ko; 'Ost-' is extremely rare in Old English and is probably not the authorial reading. Herzfeld suspected a garbled -us ending for the preceding name behind the -ost; see the subsequent references to 'Ðeodoricus' further on in this section. It is noteworthy that the C tradition clearly also had problems with this element, as did the B scribe who attaches 'ost' to the preceding word.

159.   *lædon.* lædan C, Herz; for the infinitive ending, see Campbell, *Old English Grammar*, §377.

160.   *ond ungyred.* ungyrd C, Herz; omission of conjunction in C is perhaps preferable, but B seems to reflect the complex series of participles of the Latin source.

Bibliography: Cross, 'Popes of Rome', pp. 194–5 and 202–3; Cross, 'On the Library', pp. 235n, 243 and 245; Kotzor, I, 269n and 270n; Gioanni, 'Hagiographie d'Italie', pp. 389–90; Herzfeld, p. 230.

90. Basilla: 20 May; Rome, third century, under Gallienus; not commemorated in the *Calendar of Willibrord*, nor in Bede, *Martyrologium*. Based on a text variant similar to the *Passio S. Eugeniae* (*BHL* 2666), 616–19.

161.   *forbead ðæm duruweardum þæt heo hine hire gesægde.* Pompeius's arrival at Basilla's house contains several textual difficulties which cannot be entirely resolved, although C appears to present a somewhat better text here. Both B and C agree on the verb 'forbeodan'; this verb seems to be used here, unusually, in a positive sense, 'to command', translating *imperare*, without a negative injunction in the dependent clause. Whatley (pers. comm.) confirms that in the Latin manuscript tradition no significant variant readings have been found that could have triggered this rare usage, of which, he adds, one or two additional instances are cited in a semantic study of OE 'bebeodan' 'and forbeodan' by Haessler. The Latin tradition properly has the *ianitores* in the plural (whilst B and C disagree on the number of the verb); 'heo' may hide an original nom. masc. pl., subsequently misunderstood as nom. fem. sg.

162. *onheldon*. onhyldan *C*; for the infinitive ending, see Campbell, *Old English Grammar*, §377.
Bibliography: Cross, '*Passio S. Eugeniae*'; Whatley, s. v. 'Eugenia'; Whatley, 'Eugenia before Ælfric'; Haessler, 'Old English *Bebeodan*'; Kotzor, I, 273n and II, 314; Rauer, 'Female Hagiography'; Stodnick, 'Bodies of Land'; Magennis, 'Occurrences of Nuptial Imagery'.

91. Pope Urban I: 25 May; *s.* 222–30; not commemorated in the *Calendar of Willibrord*; commemorated in Bede, *Martyrologium* (B). The *Liber pontificalis*, I.143.1–4 seems to be the sole source for this section; the length of the saint's pontificate is probably derived from an (as yet untraced) variant reading in the *Liber pontificalis* which differs from that in the edited text.
163. *mynstre*. See Note 23.
Bibliography: Cross, 'Popes of Rome', pp. 191–2 and 202–3; Cross, 'On the Library', p. 243; Kotzor, I, 269 and II, 314; Gioanni, 'Hagiographie d'Italie', pp. 389–90.

92. Augustine of Canterbury: 26 May; d. 604x609; not commemorated in the *Calendar of Willibrord*; commemorated in Bede, *Martyrologium* (B I/II). As acknowledged by the martyrologist, this section is based on various passages in Bede, *Historia ecclesiastica*, among them probably 136.13–21 and 144.8–14.
Bibliography: Cross, 'A Lost Life of Hilda of Whitby', pp. 24–5; Cross, 'On the Library', p. 230; Kotzor, I, 252–3 and II, 315; Whatley, s. v. 'Augustinus Cantuariensis'; *PASE*, Augustine 1; *ODNB*, s. v. 'Augustine'.

93. Sisinnius, Martyrius and Alexander: 29 May; d. 397; not commemorated in the *Calendar of Willibrord*, nor in Bede, *Martyrologium*. The minimal information given (feast, name, general martyrdom) could have been derived from another martyrology or calendar (although no surviving Anglo-Saxon calendar presents an entry for this feast).
Bibliography: Kotzor, I, 294, 306 and II, 315; Quentin, *Les martyrologes historiques*, p. 574; Frere, *Studies in Early Roman Liturgy*, pp. 46–7.

94. Petronilla: 31 May; first century, Rome; not commemorated in the *Calendar of Willibrord*; commemorated in Bede, *Martyrologium* (B II). Probably based on the *Vita S. Petronillae* (*BHL* 6061), 10.
164. *all*. ealle *C*; see Kotzor, II, 315.
165. *eall*. ealle *C*; see Kotzor, II, 315.
Bibliography: Whatley, s. v. 'Petronilla & Felicula'; Kotzor, II, 315; Lendinara, 'Pietro, apostolo, vescovo e santo'; Stodnick, 'Bodies of Land'.

94a. The End of May: Monthly information on the length of day and night can be found in liturgical calendars; see the note above for **36a**. Bede, *De temporum ratione*, 15 represents an analogue for the English names of the months.
Bibliography: Kotzor, I, 306 and II, 315; Tupper, 'Anglo-Saxon Dæg-Mæl', p. 120.

94b. The Beginning of June: 1 June. The source for the sections on the beginnings of the months could have been Bede, *De temporum ratione* 12 and 15; it is not in all cases clear whether this represents an antecedent or direct source, although the section on the beginning of June seems to be unusually close to Bede. Kotzor signals relevant information in a number of liturgical calendars and martyrologies which could also have served as sources.

166. *Ærra Liða...liðað*. Notwithstanding the pun in this section, 'liþan' ('to travel') and 'liþe' ('mild') are etymologically not related.

Bibliography: Kotzor, I, 268 and II, 278–9, 316; Anderson, 'The Seasons of the Year', pp. 251–2.

95, 96. Priscus and Nicomedes: 1 June; Priscus d. ?272; Nicomedes d. Rome, first century; Priscus is commemorated in the *Calendar of Willibrord*, but not in Bede, *Martyrologium*. Nicomedes is not commemorated in the *Calendar of Willibrord*, but in Bede, *Martyrologium* (B II). The source for these entries was probably a liturgical book from Capua or more generally the region of Campania, most likely brought to Anglo-Saxon England by Hadrian.

167. *sacramentorium*. sacramentorum C; cp. also **158** and Gneuss, 'Liturgical Books', p. 100.

168. *niwran*. The text contains three references to new sacramentaries, **96**, **158** and **169**; in all cases B presents a comparative form, 'niwran', 'newer, more recent' sacramentaries, whereas C refers to 'nywan', 'new' sacramentaries. It is difficult to say which of these represents the original reading, or what the significance of this difference might be. According to Bischoff and Lapidge, *Biblical Commentaries*, p. 162n, this 'new' sacramentary was probably a copy of the *Gregorianum*. For the distinction between different types of sacramentary (in this context the *Gelasianum* and the *Gregorianum*), see the seminal studies and handlists by Gamber, *Sakramentartypen* and *Codices liturgici latini antiquiores*, I, 233–7; for a detailed discussion of this and further secondary literature by Gamber and others, and the classification of the 'old' and 'new' sacramentary into a particular type, see Kotzor, I, 258–66.

Bibliography: Hohler, 'Theodore and the Liturgy', pp. 226–8; Bischoff and Lapidge, *Biblical Commentaries*, pp. 161–7; Kotzor, I, 258–66 and II, 316; Frere, *Studies in Early Roman Liturgy*, p. 45; Cross, 'On the Library', p. 234; Gneuss, 'Liturgical Books', pp. 99–101; Ambrasi, 'Prisco da Capua'; Ambrasi, 'Prisco vescovo di Capua'.

97. Erasmus: 2 June; d. ?300, under Diocletian; commemorated in the *Calendar of Willibrord*; not commemorated in Bede, *Martyrologium*. This section seems to be based entirely on a variant of the saint's *passio*; cp. *Passio S. Erasmi* (*BHL* 2582), 485.1–7, 485.15–17, 486.16–19, 486.30–47, 487.17–30 and 488.25–46. The Latin tradion conflates two saints of the same name, which also results in a confusion of the chronology and localities in the martyrologist's source.

169. *<engellic>*. ænlic B, Ko, Herz, engellic C. Cross suggested an authorial reading of '<engellic>', which would mirror the source's phrasing 'angelico' closely,

although the possibility remains that B's 'ænlic' which is elsewhere attested to have an angelic connotation, represents the authorial reading. If 'ænlic' had been the original reading, it would be hard to see how a subsequent C-tradition could have emended to 'engellic' without further consultation of the Latin source.

170.   *sunnan leoma.* sunnan leoman C; Cross argued that the plural in C 'is closer to the plural of "radii solis"' than the singular variant in B. Either could theoretically be the original reading.

171.   *Ludican.* lucridam C; equally garbled in the Latin tradition where forms similar to *Lucrida* appear, as well as forms similar to *Sidugridum*. Cross shows that the martyrologist was working with a Latin text (possibly resembling *BHL* 2585 in some details) which presented a place-name similar to *Lucida* or *Lucrida*; Bratož suspects the place-name of Singidunum (modern Belgrade) as the original reading in the Latin tradition, although that cannot be said to be located in 'Italia'. See also Breeze, 'Locating *Ludica*'.

172.   *hæðnan.* om. C; the reading in C seems closer to the presumptive source, as presented in the cited edition.

Bibliography: Cross, 'A Lost Life of Hilda of Whitby', p. 31; Whatley, s. v. 'Erasmus'; Luongo, 'Erasmo di Formia'; Cross, 'Source, Lexis, and Edition', pp. 28–9 and 34–6; Rauer, *Fontes*; Johnson, *Saint Michael the Archangel*, pp. 75–6; Rauer, 'Direct Speech, Intercession, and Prayer'; *DOE*, s. v. 'ænlic' 3. c.; Bratož, 'Die diokletianische Christenverfolgung', p. 131.

98. Marcellinus and Peter: 2 June; d. Rome, 304, under Diocletian; not commemorated in the *Calendar of Willibrord*; commemorated in Bede, *Martyrologium* (B). Probably based on a variant of the *passio*; cp. *Passio S. Marcellini* (*BHL* 5231), 173.

173.   *cristneres*. Cross identified 'cristnere' as a hapax legomenon which seems to translate the source's *exorcista*. The *DOE* interprets 'cristnere' as an office more associated with antebaptismal rites (catechism). The C variant ('crystenan weres') seems to be a total reinterpretation in ignorance of the Latin source, and shows what an impenetrable coinage 'cristnere' must have represented.

174.   *heo.* heo B, Herz, hig C, Ko; 'heo' can here be interpreted as nom. pl. fem.; emendation is probably unnecessary. Cp. also **90** for what may be a similar textual problem.

175.   *mid gimmum gefretwade ond mid golde, beorhtum hreglum gegerede.* Assuming the Latin source to read *ornatas gemmis et auro et splendidis uestibus indutas*, Cross suggested emendation of 'goldebeorhtum' in Herz to 'golde ond beorhtum', although emendation to 'golde ond mid beorhtum' would reflect the source as cited by Cross even better ('mid gimmum gefrætwade ond mid golde <ond mid> beorhtum hreglum gegerede'), with the middle element apo koinou. However, it is important to note that the source edition cited here omits the *et* before *splendidis*, inserting a comma in the same place; most economically, the Old English reading of B is therefore retained here by inserting a comma between the two phrases in apposition. The variant in *C* demonstrates incomprehension of what must have been an unexpected construction, and moves further from the source by omitting the

reference to 'hreglum', *uestibus*. See also *DOE*, s. v. goldbeorht, which has only two attestations, one of them the passage under discussion here.

Bibliography: Cross, 'A Virgo in the *Old English Martyrology*', pp. 104–5; Cross, 'A Lost Life of Hilda of Whitby', pp. 33–4; Whatley, s. v. 'Marcellinus et Petrus'; Lanéry, 'Hagiographie d'Italie', pp. 291–2; Rauer, *Fontes*; Kotzor, II, 316; Cross, Review of Kotzor, pp. 519–20; *DOE*, s. vv. 'cristnere' and 'goldbeorht'.

99. Artemius, Candida and Virgo: 2 June; Rome, fourth century, under Diocletian; not commemorated in the *Calendar of Willibrord*, nor in Bede, *Martyrologium*. Based on the same *passio* as the previous section, the *Passio S. Marcellini* (*BHL* 5231), 171–3. For the daughter's alternative name, Paulina, see Cross, 'A Virgo in the *Old English Martyrology*'.

Bibliography: Cross, 'A Virgo in the *Old English Martyrology*'; Whatley, s. v. 'Marcellinus et Petrus'; Lanéry, 'Hagiographie d'Italie', pp. 291–2; Cross, 'The Latinity', pp. 286–8; Cross, 'Popes of Rome', p. 193.

100. Columba of Iona: 9 June; ?521–97; commemorated in the *Calendar of Willibrord*; not commemorated in Bede, *Martyrologium*. Probably derived from Bede, *Historia ecclesiastica*, 220.30–1, 222.1–2, 222.15–17 and 478.2–6. The miracle of the couple who save their home from fire by discussing Columba all night remains unsourced, and may be connected to an early life of Columba, now lost.

176. *hi slæp ofereode*. The collocation of 'slæp' and 'ofergan' is not particularly well attested, and parallels seem to occur mainly in poetry; cp. also **131**.

177. *heora hus*. The reference to the couple's house is ambiguous in number; the reference further below ('þæt heora hus þurh þæt wæron') is itself ambiguous in number, but is given a plural verb ('wæron') in both B and C; the reference at the end of the section ('ðæm husum') is plural in B and singular in C. It is difficult to account for this variety, and one suspects consistent singular usage in the original text.

Bibliography: Cross, 'The Influence of Irish Texts and Traditions', pp. 177–8; Cross, 'A Lost Life of Hilda of Whitby', pp. 25 and 29–30; Whatley, s. v. 'Columba Hiensis'; Rauer, *Fontes*; Kotzor, II, 317; Cross, 'On the Library', pp. 230 and 248; Herzfeld, p. 231; Rauer, 'Usage', p. 126n; Thacker, 'Lindisfarne and the Origin of the Cult of St Cuthbert', p. 112; *PASE*, Columba 1; *ODNB*, s. v. 'Columba'; Bately, 'Old English Prose', pp. 114–18.

101. Barnabas: 10 June; first century; commemorated in the *Calendar of Willibrord* (under different date) and in Bede, *Martyrologium* (B I/II, also under different date). The information of the opening lines is derived from Acts 4.36–37 and 13.1–15.41; for the poisoning episode, a parallel can be found in Rufinus, *Historia ecclesiastica*, 289.16–291.2, although that is attached to a different person, Barsabas.

Bibliography: Cross, 'The Apostles', pp. 37–8 and 40–1; Cross, 'On the Library', p. 235n; Rauer, *Fontes*; Kotzor, II, 317–18; Cook, *Biblical Quotations*, p. 20; Cross, 'Mary Magdalen', p. 16n.

102. Vitus and Modestus: 15 June; d. ? Rome, ?303, under Diocletian; commemorated in the *Calendar of Willibrord* and in Bede, *Martyrologium* (B II). Based on the *Passio S. Viti*. The text variant used by the martyrologist (*BHL* 8712) is as yet unedited and a more detailed source analysis remains to be undertaken, but a number of parallels can be found for example in the *Passio S. Viti* (*BHL* 8714), 634.29–638.26.
Bibliography: Cross, 'Saints' Lives in Old English', pp. 58–62; Whatley, s. v. 'Vitus, Modestus, and Crescentia'; Cross, 'A Lost Life of Hilda of Whitby', p. 30; Frere, *Studies in Early Roman Liturgy*, p. 46; Kotzor, II, 318.

103. Ferreolus and Ferrucio: 16 June; third century, under Aurelian; not commemorated in the *Calendar of Willibrord*; commemorated in Bede, *Martyrologium* (B). The source seems to be a *Passio S. Ferreoli*, although some doubt remains about the precise variant. For parallels, cp. *Passio S. Ferreoli* (*BHL* 2903), 7–8.
Bibliography: Whatley, s. v. 'Ferreolus et Ferrucio'; Cross, 'On the Library', p. 241n; Kotzor, I, 212, 216 and II, 318.

104. Nicander: 17 June; second century; commemorated in the *Calendar of Willibrord*; not commemorated in Bede, *Martyrologium*. The source was probably a liturgical book from the region of Campania, most likely brought to Anglo-Saxon England by Hadrian.
Bibliography: Hohler, 'Theodore and the Liturgy', pp. 226–8; Bischoff and Lapidge, *Biblical Commentaries*, pp. 161–2; Kotzor, I, 258, 262, 263n and II, 319; Frere, *Studies in Early Roman Liturgy*, p. 46; Gneuss, 'Liturgical Books', pp. 99–101.

105. Blastus: 17 June; third century; not commemorated in the *Calendar of Willibrord*, nor in Bede, *Martyrologium*. Probably based on the *Passio SS. Marii et Marthae* (*BHL* 5543), 216; cp. also **29** above.
Bibliography: Whatley, s. v. 'Marius et Martha'; Lanéry, 'Hagiographie d'Italie', pp. 250–7.

106. Mark and Marcellian: 18 June; d. Rome, ?286, under Diocletian; not commemorated in the *Calendar of Willibrord*; commemorated in Bede, *Martyrologium* (B II). Based on Pseudo-Ambrose, *Passio S. Sebastiani* (*BHL* 7543), 265.3–4, 265.6–266.8, 266.9–268.22 and 277.84–278.84.
Bibliography: Cross, 'The Use of a *Passio S. Sebastiani*', pp. 41–3; Lanéry, *Ambroise de Milan*, esp. pp. 503–7; Lanéry, 'Hagiographie d'Italie', pp. 68–80; Cross, 'On the Library', p. 236n; Kotzor, I, 273n and II, 319; Rauer, *Fontes*; Whatley, s. v. 'Sebastianus'.

107. Gervase and Protase: 19 June; d. Milan, second century, under Nero; commemorated in the *Calendar of Willibrord* and in Bede, *Martyrologium* (B). Probably derived from Pseudo-Ambrose, *Passio S. Geruasii* (*BHL* 3514), 743–6. Cross (pers. comm., see Whatley) suspected use also of Ambrose, *Epistola* 22 (*BHL*

3513), although it is difficult to see which details should have been derived from this text. For general information on *BHL* 3513, see also Lanéry, *Ambroise de Milan*, pp. 29–41.

178.   *getæht<on>*. The plural form found in C seems preferable to the sg. in B, if the narrative in this passage is correct as it stands. Alternatively, sg. 'getæhte' could be the original reading, if the passage once followed its Latin source in describing not just two spirits appearing to Ambrose, but in a separate vision also a figure reminiscent of St Paul, who instructs him (*docuerat*, 743) regarding the location of the bodies.

Bibliography: Whatley, s. v. 'Gervasius et Protasius'; Lanéry, *Ambroise de Milan*, esp. pp. 305–47; Lanéry, 'Hagiographie d'Italie', pp. 61–8.

108. James the Less: 22 June; first century; commemorated in the *Calendar of Willibrord* and Bede, *Martyrologium* (B I, under different date in BII). Parallels can be found in Rufinus, *Historia ecclesiastica*, Pseudo-Isidore, *De ortu et obitu patrum*, 51.1–3, Isidore, *De ortu et obitu patrum*, 76, and several versions of the saint's *passio*, including *Passio S. Iacobi minoris* (*BHL* 4093), 136–7, and Pseudo-Abdias, *Passio S. Iacobi minoris* (*BHL* 4089), 591.1–607.7, but the precise scenario of composition remains somewhat unclear. Like many other authors, the martyrologist conflates James the Less with James Alphaei.

179.   *ealra*. ealra B, anra C; probably translates *tantum* 'only'; the variant in C seems more idiomatic and may be authorial. See also *DOE*, s. v. an, A.4.c.i.d and 121.3 below for similar usage.

180.   *ðær oneardadan*. Ko; word division chosen to reflect a presumptive close translation of *inhabitare*, but alternatives 'ðær on eardadan' and 'ðæron eardadan' are also plausible.

Bibliography: Cross, 'The Apostles', pp. 29–31; Cross, 'On the Library', p. 234n; Rauer, *Fontes*; Biggs, *The Apocrypha*, pp. 46–7; Kotzor, I, 257–8 and II, 320; Clayton, *The Cult of the Virgin Mary*, pp. 216–17.

109. Alban: 22 June; Verolamium, third century, under Diocletian; not commemorated in the *Calendar of Willibrord*; commemorated in Bede, *Martyrologium* (B). The source is Bede, *Historia ecclesiastica*, 28.16–30.13, 32.14–33 and 34.8–11.

Bibliography: Kotzor, I, 254n and II, 320–1; Cross, 'A Lost Life of Hilda of Whitby', pp. 25–6; Cross, 'On the Library', p. 230; Stodnick, 'Bodies of Land'.

110. Æthelthryth: 23 June; d. 679; not commemorated in the *Calendar of Willibrord*; commemorated in Bede, *Martyrologium* (B). Largely based on Bede, *Historia ecclesiastica*, 390.25–394.2 and 394.12–35.

181.   *nemn<a>ð*. nemneð B, Ko, nemnað C; Kotzor, II, 323 suspects scribal error in B, but does not emend.

182.   *tid*. tid B, tyde C, tide Herz, tid Ko; Kotzor, II, 323 suspects scribal error in B, but reading in B perhaps authorial; *DOE*, s. v. fram I.B.2 also presents usage of 'fram' with acc. in biblical glosses.

183. *awunode*. See *DOE*, s. v. awunian 1.a., here translates *persteterit*; cp. also **138**.

Bibliography: Kotzor, I, 254n and II, 322–3; Cross, 'A Lost Life of Hilda of Whitby', pp. 25–7; Cross, 'On the Library', p. 230; Whatley, s. v. 'Ætheldrytha'; Foot, 'Anglo-Saxon Minsters', p. 222; Rauer, 'Female Hagiography'; Gretsch, *Ælfric and the Cult of Saints*, pp. 202–3; Bately, 'The Place Which is Called'; Blanton, *Signs of Devotion*; *PASE*, Æthelthryth 2 and Ecgfrith 4; *ODNB*, s. v. 'Æthelthryth'; Incitti, 'Modelli agiografici'.

111. The Birth of St John the Baptist: 24 June; commemorated in the *Calendar of Willibrord* and in Bede, *Martyrologium* (B I/II). The section seems to combine details from Petrus Chrysologus, Sermo 91, 566.72–568.106 and Caesarius of Arles, Sermo 216, 858.12–860.6; these sermons are themselves indebted to biblical material, which could additionally have influenced the martyrologist directly. Hall discusses variant versions of the cited homiletic material, which could also have been known to the martyrologist.

184. *forð gangan*. Could alternatively be divided as 'forðgangan' (apparently translates *processurus*), see *DOE*, s. v. forþ, A.6.a.ii and *DOE*, s. v. forþgangan.

Bibliography: Cross, 'Blickling Homily XIV', pp. 154–6; Cross, 'The Use of Patristic Homilies', pp. 108 and 125; Cross, 'The Latinity', pp. 281–2; Cross, 'On the Library', p. 237; Hall, 'Petrus Chrysologus'; Hall, 'The Armaments of John the Baptist', pp. 289–91; Trahern, 'Caesarius of Arles'; Cook, *Biblical Quotations*, pp. 18–19.

111a. Summer Solstice: 24 June. Not commemorated in the *Calendar of Willibrord*. Based on Adomnán, *De locis sanctis*, 1.11.4–21.

185. *standeð*. The reference to the sun *standing* in the sky seems to gloss the etymology of *solstitium*, from *sistere*, 'to stand'.

186. *wundorlice*. Here understood as the adv.; *mirum in modum* in the Latin text also has an adverbial function. Alternatively, 'wundorlice' could be seen as a weak adj. here used as a noun, although this seems less likely; see Mitchell, *Old English Syntax*, §§132–4.

Bibliography: Cross, 'The Influence of Irish Texts and Traditions', p. 180; Kotzor, I, 254–5, 280n and II, 323; Cross, 'On the Library', p. 232; Rauer, 'Usage', p. 132; Tupper, 'Anglo-Saxon Dæg-Mæl', pp. 203–4.

112. Luceia and Auceia: 25 June; Rome, third or fourth century, under Diocletian; not commemorated in the *Calendar of Willibrord*, nor in Bede, *Martyrologium*. The source is the *Passio S. Luciae* (*BHL* 4980), 13–14.

187. *medomlic hus*. *Cubiculum condignum* in the Latin text.

Bibliography: Cross, 'Identification: Towards Criticism', p. 238; Whatley, s. v. 'Luceiae Romae'; Rauer, 'Female Hagiography'; Stodnick, 'Bodies of Land'; Magennis, 'Occurrences of Nuptial Imagery'.

113. John and Paul: 26 June; fourth century, under Julian; commemorated in the *Calendar of Willibrord* and Bede, *Martyrologium* (B). Probably based on a *passio* of these saints, although the precise variant remains to be further specified; for some parallels, cp. *Passio SS. Gallicani, Iohannis et Pauli* (*BHL* 3236, 3238), 569.40–572.46.

188. *acennede of Constantines sidan*. The notion of the saints' imperial descent seems to be based on the Latin source, although in the published version of the Latin text, the saints are described as connected to the empress or emperor's daughter (*ex latere auguste*), rather than the emperor himself. To what extent the martyrologist interpreted or misunderstood his Latin source could be better determined with the help of a more comprehensive edition of the Latin source. The issue is further complicated by the fact that the Latin tradition itself lacks historical accuracy.

Bibliography: Whatley, s. v. 'Iohannes & Paulus'; Cross, 'The Latinity', p. 288; Cross, 'Popes of Rome', p. 193; Lanéry, 'Hagiographie d'Italie', pp. 204–15; Herzfeld, p. 231; Leyser, 'A Church in the House of Saints', pp. 147–52.

114. Peter and Paul: 29 June; first century; commemorated in the *Calendar of Willibrord* and Bede, *Martyrologium* (B I/II). Conceivably based on Isidore, *De ortu et obitu patrum*, 67.5 and 68.5, or Pseudo-Isidore, *De ortu et obitu patrum*, 44.5 and 45.5, or on both these authors. The section also echoes Apc. 11.4, 11.6 and Matthew 16.19 which are likely to represent indirect sources and were possibly part of a homiletic or liturgical text used by the martyrologist; in support of this scenario, Cross adduces an interesting analogue in the Hyde Breviary. Cross also shows that references to the saints' posthumous miracles can be found in a number of analogues.

189. *þa Neron...sweorde*. Ambiguous syntax; punctuation here follows similar patterns involving relative clauses in the opening formulae of entries. Ko punctuates differently, taking 'þa' as an adverb and the beginning of a new and independent clause.

190. *for mannum*. Syntactically ambiguous; here understood to qualify 'gesewene'; cp. for example the Old English translation of Gregory, *Dialogi*, 10.77.8, 'þæt for mannum gesewen wære', but could, less plausibly, also refer to the preceding 'þrowunge', as 'for mannum' represents a traditional collocation in references to Christ's self-sacrifice.

Bibliography: Cross, 'The Apostles', pp. 38–9; Cross, 'The Use of Patristic Homilies', p. 108n; Lendinara, 'Pietro, apostolo, vescovo e santo'.

115. Cassius: 29 June; d. 558; not commemorated in the *Calendar of Willibrord*, nor in Bede, *Martyrologium*. The source is Gregory, *Homiliae in Euangelia* 37, 355.195–357.268.

Bibliography: Kotzor, I, 255n and II, 324–5; Whatley, s. v. 'Cassius Narniensis'; Cross, 'On the Library', pp. 232 and 234; Cross, 'The Use of Patristic Homilies', p. 107; Frere, *Studies on Early Roman Liturgy*, p. 47.

116. Martial: 30 June; date unknown; not commemorated in the *Calendar of Willibrord*, nor in Bede, *Martyrologium*. The earlier parts of this section are apparently based on the *Vita S. Martialis* (*BHL* 5551), 239.20–242.13. The miracle of the illicit lovers seems to be derived from the *Miracula S. Martialis* (*BHL* 5561), 245.7–19.

191.   *eal swa*. ealswa Ko; ambiguous construction; an alternative word division and interpretation is possible; see Schleburg, *Altenglisch swa*, §§30 and 104.

192.   *twegen men*. Herzfeld's translation refers to two men, but he and Whatley also draw attention to the fact that, in the edited Latin versions of the *miraculum*, the lovers are a man and a woman. The text here seems to use 'mann' in the sense of gender-neutral 'person', and there is therefore no divergence from the source.

Bibliography: Whatley, s. v. 'Martialis'; Herzfeld, pp. 111 and 231.

116a. The End of June: Monthly information on the length of day and night can be found in liturgical calendars; see **36a** above. Bede, *De temporum ratione*, 15, represents an analogue for the English names of the months.

Bibliography: Kotzor, I, 307 and II, 325; Tupper, 'Anglo-Saxon Dæg-Mæl', p. 120.

116b. The Beginning of July: 1 July. The source for the sections on the beginnings of the months could have been Bede, *De temporum ratione* 12 and 15, although it is not in all cases clear whether this represents an antecedent or direct source. Kotzor signals relevant information in a number of liturgical calendars and martyrologies which could also have served as sources.

Bibliography: Kotzor, I, 268 and II, 278–9, 326; Anderson, 'The Seasons of the Year', p. 252.

117. Processus and Martinianus: 2 July; Rome, first century, under Nero; not commemorated in the *Calendar of Willibrord*; commemorated in Bede, *Martyrologium* (B I/II). Probably based on Gregory, *Homiliae in Euangelia* 32, 285.212–24.

Bibliography: Kotzor, I, 255–6 and II, 326; Cross, 'The Use of Patristic Homilies', p. 107; Cross, 'On the Library', p. 232; Stodnick, 'Bodies of Land'; Thijs, 'Wærferth's Translation', pp. 48–9.

118. Zoe: ?4 July; d. Rome, third century, under Diocletian; not commemorated in the *Calendar of Willibrord*, nor in Bede, *Martyrologium*. Probably based on Pseudo-Ambrose, *Passio S. Sebastiani* (*BHL* 7543), 268.24 and 276.74.

193.   *feorðan*. fiftan C; the two manuscripts disagree on the feastday of this saint; either 4 or 5 July could be the martyrologist's original reading. Cross shows that the ambiguity arises from the relative timing of a series of martyrdoms in the *Passio S. Sebastiani*, and that discrepant variants already occur in the Latin tradition. Lapidge, 'Acca of Hexham', pp. 59 and 62, points out that the commemoration does not occur in Pseudo-Jerome, *Martyrologium*, and also suggests that it was derived from the *Passio S. Sebastiani*.

Bibliography: Cross, 'The Use of a *Passio S. Sebastiani*', pp. 41 and 43–4; Lanéry, *Ambroise de Milan*, esp. pp. 503–7; Lanéry, 'Hagiographie d'Italie', pp. 68–80;

Cross, 'On the Library', pp. 235n and 236n; Kotzor, I, 273n and II, 327; Whatley, s. v. 'Sebastianus'; Rauer, 'Female Hagiography'.

119. Octave of Peter and Paul: 6 July; not commemorated in the *Calendar of Willibrord*; commemorated in Bede, *Martyrologium* (B II). The minimal information presented in this section is probably derived from a liturgical text.
Bibliography: Kotzor, I, 259 and 264; Cross, 'On the Library', p. 234; Lendinara, 'Pietro, apostolo, vescovo e santo'.

120. Tranquillinus: 6 July; d. Rome, third century, under Diocletian; not commemorated in the *Calendar of Willibrord*, nor in Bede, *Martyrologium*. Probably based on Pseudo-Ambrose, *Passio S. Sebastiani* (*BHL* 7543), 265.7, 271.36, 272.45–7 and 276.75.
Bibliography: Cross, 'The Use of a *Passio S. Sebastiani*', pp. 41 and 44; Lanéry, *Ambroise de Milan*, esp. pp. 503–7; Lanéry, 'Hagiographie d'Italie', pp. 68–80; Cross, 'On the Library', p. 236n; Kotzor, I, 273n and II, 327; Whatley, s. v. 'Sebastianus'; Rauer, 'Usage', p. 128.

121. Procopius: 7 July; d. Palestine, 303; not commemorated in the *Calendar of Willibrord*; commemorated in Bede, *Martyrologium* (B under a different date). Probably based on the *Passio S. Procopii* (*BHL* 6949), 50.1–51.15, which, like several other texts, also gives the saint's feastday as 7 July.
194.   *hlaf an*. See Kotzor, II, 327; *DOE*, s. v. an, A.4.c.i.f.
Bibliography: Whatley, s. v. 'Procopius Caesareae'; Kotzor, II, 327; Sauget, 'Procopio', cols. 1164–5; Lapidge, 'Acca of Hexham', p. 36.

122. Marina: 7 July; d. Antioch, date unknown; not commemorated in the *Calendar of Willibrord*, nor in Bede, *Martyrologium*. Clearly based on a *Passio S. Margaretae*, although the precise variant used by the martyrologist remains unidentified and is probably lost; for some parallels, cp. Pseudo-Theotimus, *Passio S. Margaretae* (*BHL* 5303), 3–10, 19–20 and 22–4.
195.   *sceapum*. sceap C; cp. also the very similar passage at **136** and Note 217.
196.   *synne*. synna C; see Kotzor, II, 328.
197.   *Drihten...lufu*. See Rauer, 'Direct Speech, Intercession, and Prayer', and Introduction, pp. 17–18.
198.   *swa hwær...þonne*. See Schleburg, *Altenglisch swa*, §805.
Bibliography: Clayton and Magennis, *The Old English Lives*, pp. 51–6; Cross, 'The Notice on Marina'; Whatley, s. v. 'Margareta'; Kotzor, II, 328; Rauer, 'Female Hagiography'; Stodnick, 'Bodies of Land'; Rauer, 'Direct Speech, Intercession, and Prayer'.

123. The Seven Brothers: 10 July; second century; commemorated in the *Calendar of Willibrord* and Bede, *Martyrologium* (B). The source is probably the *Passio S. Felicitatis* (*BHL* 2853), 3–90; the intended emperor is Antoninus Pius. The separation of this feast from that of the saints' mother Felicity (see **229**) is already attested in the

Latin tradition which the martyrologist seems to have followed here, and is explained by the fact that the sons are not martyred on the same day as their mother.
Bibliography: Cross, 'The Use of Patristic Sources', p. 107n; Lanéry, 'Hagiographie d'Italie', pp. 35–45; Cross, 'On the Library', p. 241n; Whatley, s. v. 'Felicitas & Septem Fillis'; Rauer, 'Female Hagiography'; Lapidge, 'Acca of Hexham', p. 56; Kotzor, I, 212 and II, 328.

124. Anatolia, Audax: 10 July; third century, under Decius; not commemorated in the *Calendar of Willibrord*; commemorated in Bede, *Martyrologium* (B, under a different date). Cross suggested that three different sources were conflated in the composition of this section, the *Passio S. Anatholiae et Audacis* (*BHL* 418), 672–3, Aldhelm, *De uirginitate* (prose), 309.25–310.9 and Aldhelm, *Carmen de uirginitate*, 2426–45. But much remains unclear regarding the early development of the Latin tradition for this saint, and the martyrologist may have known a text which was very different from surviving versions.
199.   *þe...wæs*. om. C; unusual opening formula in B, possibly defective.
200.   *ða ceastre seo is nemned Piceno...ceastre*. Picenum is a region rather than a city.
Bibliography: Whatley, s. v. 'Anatolia et Audax'; Cross, 'On the Library', p. 231; Franklin, 'Theodore and the *Passio S. Anastasii*', p. 186; Frere, *Studies in Early Roman Liturgy*, p. 47; Mara, *I martiri della Via Salaria*, pp. 151–201; Rauer, 'Female Hagiography'.

125. Rufina and Secunda: 10 July; d. Rome, third century; not commemorated in the *Calendar of Willibrord*, nor in Bede, *Martyrologium*. Probably based on Aldhelm, *Carmen de uirginitate*, 2331–7, although this text fails to account for the saints' feastday, the detail of the Roman emperor, and the saints' burial place.
201.   *byðme*. An unusual spelling variant of 'bytme', a word only rarely attested. The word may have been derived from a gloss, and reflects a similar spelling of the word in the Corpus Glossary, 'bythne'.
Bibliography: Cross, 'On the Library', p. 231; Kotzor, I, 250n and 257n; Cross, 'A Lost Life of Hilda of Whitby', p. 31; *DOE*, s. v. bytme, 1; Rauer, 'Female Hagiography'.

126. Phocas: 14 July; ?fourth century, under Diocletian; not commemorated in the *Calendar of Willibrord*; commemorated in Bede, *Martyrologium* (B). Most of this section is probably based on the *Passio S. Phocae* (*BHL* 6838), 420.34–40, 421.29–45 and 421.52–422.4. The reference to the saint's relics in Vienne (B only, with a lacuna in C, probably caused by eyeskip) has parallels in a number of martyrologies and other texts, including, for example, the martyrology by Hrabanus Maurus (14 July).
Bibliography: Whatley, s. v. 'Phocas Sinope'.

127. Cyricus and Julitta: 15 July; d. Tarsus, ?304, under Diocletian; not commemorated in the *Calendar of Willibrord*; commemorated in Bede,

Martyrologium (B I/II). Clearly based on a *Passio S. Cyrici*, although the precise variant used by the martyrologist remains unidentified; for some parallels, cp. the *Passio S. Cyrici* (*BHL* 1802–8), 29 and 33.

202. *Drihten...worlda*. See Rauer, 'Direct Speech, Intercession, and Prayer', and Introduction, pp. 17–18.

203. *soðfæstnes ond rihtwisnes*. Although the saint's prayer does have some parallels in the relevant Latin text, this phrase is one of several in the prayer for which no close parallel has been identified in printed Latin sources. Questions remain open regarding its translation; see Kotzor, I, 364, and Bately, 'Did King Alfred', pp. 199–200.

204. *synne wepe*. synna wepe C; see Kotzor, II, 329.

205. *he sy hwittra ðonne snaw*. B and C disagree on whether it is the sin (C, with fem. pronoun 'heo' and adj. 'hwyttre') or the man (B, with masc. pronoun 'he' and masc. adj. 'hwittra') which is whiter than snow after being cleansed; Ba corrects the pronoun but not the adj. to fem. endings; Ko sides with C, whereas the reading in B is preferred here. The image does not seem to appear in versions of the saint's *passio*, and either version could be original. The image is utterly conventional, however, and in Christian literature ultimately goes back to Ps 50 (51). 9 (7), where it refers to the sinner rather than the sin, which perhaps also represents the more plausible reading here. See also Kotzor, II, 329, and Cross, 'A Lost Life of Hilda of Whitby', pp. 33 and 43.

Bibliography: Whatley, s. v. 'Cirycus & Julitta'; Cross, 'A Lost Life of Hilda of Whitby', pp. 32–3; Kotzor, I, 364 and II, 329; Hohler, 'Theodore and the Liturgy', pp. 223–4; Rauer, 'Direct Speech, Intercession, and Prayer'.

128. Speratus and the Scillitan Martyrs: 17 July; d. Carthage, 180; not commemorated in the *Calendar of Willibrord*; commemorated in Bede, *Martyrologium* (B). The *Passio SS. Scillitanorum* (*BHL* 7531), 214, has been considered as a possible source for this section, but Whatley points out that not all details have parallels in that text.

Bibliography: Whatley, s. v. 'Scillitani'.

129. Symphorosa and her Seven Sons: 18 July; second century, under Hadrian; commemorated in the *Calendar of Willibrord* and Bede, *Martyrologium* (B, under a different date). Cross suggested that this very brief section is based on the *Passio S. Symphorosae* (*BHL* 7971), 358–9, although all of the details, with the exception of the saint's widowhood, could also have been derived from elsewhere.

206. *þara*. þære C; see Kotzor, II, 330.

Bibliography: Whatley, s. v. 'Symphorosa & Filiis'; Kotzor, I, 212, 225 and II, 330; Lanéry, 'Hagiographie d'Italie', pp. 233–8; Cross, 'On the Library', p. 241n; Rauer, 'Female Hagiography'.

130. Christina: 19 July; ?fourth century, under Diocletian; not commemorated in the *Calendar of Willibrord*; commemorated in Bede, *Martyrologium* (B II, under a different date). The martyrologist seems to have made use of Aldhelm, *De uirginitate* (prose), 300.24–301.20 and a still elusive variant of the saint's *passio*; for parallels, cp. *Passio S. Christinae* (*BHL* 1748b), 173.1–181.17. The feastday of 19 July (as opposed to the more widely attested 24 July) also appears in several Anglo-Saxon calendars.

207.   *geara*. geare C; see Kotzor, II, 330.
208.   *hi bewyrcean*. hig belucan C; see *DOE*, s. v. bewyrcan, 5, *pace* Swaen, 'Contributions to Anglo-Saxon Lexicography', p. 178n, but notice that the redactor in the C tradition must also have felt that 'bewyrcan' might lead to confusion.
209.   *æfenne*. æfen C; see Kotzor, II, 330.
210.   *fullwie*. fullie C; see *DOE*, s. v. fullian, 1 and 2a.
211.   *mergenne*. morgen C; see Kotzor, II, 330.

Bibliography: Cross and Tuplin, 'An Unrecorded Variant'; Whatley, s. v. 'Christina'; Cross, 'On the Library', p. 230; Cross, '*Passio S. Eugeniae*', p. 395; Johnson, *Saint Michael the Archangel*, pp. 75–6; Rauer, *Fontes*; Rushforth, *Saints in English Kalendars*.

131. Arsenius: 19 July; fifth century; not commemorated in the *Calendar of Willibrord*; commemorated in Bede, *Martyrologium* (B). Peter Jackson (pers. comm.) argues that the source for both anecdotes is the anonymous *Vitae patrum* (*BHL* 6527–9), 861 and 865.

Bibliography: Whatley, s. v. 'Arsenius'; Cross, 'On the Library', pp. 244–5; Cross, 'The Latinity', p. 283; Rauer, *Fontes*; Stodnick, 'Bodies of Land'.

132. Victor of Marseilles etc.: 21 July; d. Marseilles, third century, under Maximian; not commemorated in the *Calendar of Willibrord*, nor in Bede, *Martyrologium*. The source seems to be the *Passio S. Victoris* (*BHL* 8570), 4.

Bibliography: Whatley, s. v. 'Victor Massiliensis'.

133. Mary Magdalen: 22 July; first century; not commemorated in the *Calendar of Willibrord*; commemorated in Bede, *Martyrologium* (B I/II). The details in the opening lines have parallels in Mark 16.9, Luke 7.37–8 and 8.2, Gregory, *Homiliae in Euangelia* 25, 205.1–10 and *Homiliae in Euangelia* 33, 288.1–13, and Bede, *In Lucae euangelium expositio*, 172.263–77 and *In Marci euangelium expositio*, 643.1859–77, any or all of which could have been used by the martyrologist. The second half of this section is probably based on the *Vita S. Mariae Magdalenae* (*BHL* 5453), 21.1–22.22.

212.   *gehyrde*. Cross commented on the saint's aural experience in heaven as having no parallel in the *Vita*, where the context seems to be more one of eating (*ostendunt partem suauitatis celestis et tam iocunda suauitate satiatam perducunt me iterum ad speluncam meam*), and he suggested that an unidentified source text could have contained a variant reference to aural bliss in the form of heavenly music. But one wonders whether the textual problem lies in the Old English rather than the Latin text; emending 'gehyrde' to 'gebyrgde' ('tasted') would perhaps fit the context of eating food, which can be found in both texts, better.

Bibliography: Cross, 'Mary Magdalen'; Whatley, s. v. Maria Magdalena; Chenard, 'Narratives of the Saintly Body', pp. 133–55; Ortenberg, 'Le culte de sainte Marie Madeleine'; Kotzor, II, 330–1; Cross, 'On the Library', p. 235; Lapidge, 'Acca of Hexham', p. 71; Hohler, 'Theodore and the Liturgy', pp. 224–5; Rauer, *Fontes*; Rauer, 'Female Hagiography'; Stodnick, 'Bodies of Land'.

134. Apollinaris: 22 July; first century; commemorated in the *Calendar of Willibrord* and Bede, *Martyrologium* (B, under a different date). This section seems to be based on the *Passio S. Apollinaris* (*BHL* 623), 344–5 and 350.

213.   *blindne mon.* blynde men C; the two manuscripts disagree on the number of blind men healed; the variant in C would seem closer to the source in some respects, as the *passio* in its edited format does refer to several episodes of blindness being healed, although only one of them is described as occurring at the beginning of the saint's career, which is implied in B.

Bibliography: Whatley, s. v. 'Apollinaris Ravennae'; Rauer, *Fontes*.

135. James the Greater: 25 July; d. 44; commemorated in the *Calendar of Willibrord* and Bede, *Martyrologium* (B I/II). Cross shows that most of this section is, directly or indirectly, derived from scriptural passages, among them Mark 1.20, 5.37, 9.1, 14.33, Matthew 4.21, 17.1, 26.37, Luke 5.10, 8.51, 9.28, and Acts 12.2. The reference to the saint's missionary activity in Spain has parallels in a number possible sources, among them Pseudo-Isidore, *De ortu et obitu patrum*, 47.2, and Isidore, *De ortu et obitu patrum*, 70; Aldhelm, *Carmina ecclesiastica*, 4.4, also echoes details concerning James's mission and his death.

214.   *Þes...geleafan.* The syntax here is clearly unusual and represents either an example of the frequent anacoluthic constructions in this text, or a textually defective passage, or both.

215.   *Hyrde.* hyrde Ko; see Sisam, 'An Early Fragment', pp. 212 and 216–17, and Kotzor, I, 27n.

216.   *gefremede.* geferede C; passage perhaps defective; see *DOE*, s. v. gefremman 7.

Bibliography: Cross, 'The Apostles', pp. 32–4; Biggs, The *Apocrypha*, p. 44; Cross, 'Mary Magdalen', p. 16n; Kotzor, II, 331; Cook, *Biblical Quotations*, pp. 18 and 20.

136. Simeon Stylites: 27 July; 390–459; commemorated in the *Calendar of Willibrord* and Bede, *Martyrologium* (B II). Probably based on a *vita* of this saint, although the precise variant remains to be determined; Whatley suggests that a mixed variant, combining features of several edited versions, was possibly used. For parallels, cp. *Vita S. Symeonis stylitae* (*BHL* 7957, 7958), 325–6 and 328.

217.   *þa læswede he <his> fæder sceapum ond þa heold.* An almost exact repetition of **122** 'ða læswede heo hire festermodor sceapum ond heold'. That 'mid his' (B) for 'his' (C) is likely to be an error is confirmed by the source's *pascebat oues patris sui*; 'læswian' with dative seems unusual, but is also attested in the Old English translation of Gregory, *Dialogi*, 17.215.5. See also Note 195.

218. *<he>*. om. B, Ko, he C; the non-expression of the the subject could be authorial; see Mitchell, *Old English Syntax*, §1514, but textual error in B seems more likely here and the reading in C is preferable.
219. *swa*. See Mitchell, *Old English Syntax*, §2862, and Schleburg, *Altenglisch swa*, §627.
220. *hearde*. heardan C; see Mitchell, *Old English Syntax*, §121.
221. *on drygum stane*. The reference to the saint's habitation seems to be based on the Latin source; the Latin variant cited here presents *clausuram ex lapide sicco*, for example.
Bibliography: Whatley, s. v. 'Symeon Stylites'; Rauer, *Fontes*; Kotzor, II, 331–2.

137. Nazarius and Celsus: 28 July; d. Milan, first century, under Nero; not commemorated in the *Calendar of Willibrord*, nor in Bede, *Martyrologium*. Probably based on a *passio* of the saint, but, as Whatley suggests, many questions remain open regarding the precise variant used by the martyrologist. For some parallels, cp. *Passio S. Nazarii* (*BHL* 6039), 331.24–332.6 and 334.32–3. Pseudo-Ambrose, Sermo 55, 716–17, could also have played a role, and further parallels can also be found in Ennodius, *Carmina* 254.1.18.
222. *deodan*. dydon C; see Kotzor, II, 332.
Bibliography: Whatley, s. v. 'Nazarius et Celsus'; Cross, 'A Lost Life of Hilda of Whitby', p. 32; Lanéry, 'Hagiographie d'Italie', pp. 264–72; Rauer, *Fontes*; Zanetti, 'Les passions'.

138. Lupus: 29 July; d. 478; commemorated in the *Calendar of Willibrord* and Bede, *Martyrologium* (B). The source is probably the *Vita S. Lupi* (*BHL* 5087), 296.3–10 and 299.3–300.17.
223. *on*. in Ko, on Herz; see Leinbaugh, Review of Kotzor, p. 173.
224. *awunode*. wunode a C, a wunode Ko; see *DOE*, s. v. 'awunian' 1.a.; here translates *perdurabat*; cp. also **110**.
225. *Triticum*. tricum C; the Latin name for Troyes survives in a wide variety of spellings (*Trices-*, *Tricas-*, *Treces-*), but an Old English version of the name seems to be attested only here, and its origin and link with the Latin form are unclear. It may be that the Latin placename *Trices-* was linked, by way of folk-etymology, with the Latin numeral for thirty, *trices-*, whose Old English equivalent would be 'þritig-', and could conceivably have led to Tritic- (B). But Bately also points out an interesting and similarly odd translation of a placename in the Old English Bede, 422.7–8, 'Galleas nemnað Traiectum [i.e. Utrecht]; we cueðað æt Treocum', which, Bately suggests, could have involved a possible 'misrepresentation of an ancestor of the first syllable of the name Utrecht' in the Old English Bede. The variant which C presents here, 'Tricum', could in that case also point to a confusion with this name for Utrecht, rather than Troyes.
Bibliography: Cross, 'A Lost Life of Hilda of Whitby', pp. 25–6; Rauer, *Fontes*; Bately, 'The Place Which is Called', p. 348; Kotzor, II, 332; Whatley, s. v. 'Lupus Trecensis'.

139. Abdon and Sennes: 30 July; d. Rome ?250 under Decius or ?303 under Diocletian; commemorated in the *Calendar of Willibrord* and Bede, *Martyrologium* (B). Derived from the *Passio SS. Abdon et Sennen* (*BHL* 6), 76.3–15, 77.29–30, 78.12–14, 78.18–19, 78.23–79.6, 79.24–30 and 80.1–15. (The *passio* forms part of the composite *Passio S. Laurentii*.)
Bibliography: Cross, 'The *Passio S. Laurentii*', pp. 203–5; Rauer, *Fontes*; Whatley, s. v. 'Abdon et Sennen'; Kotzor, I, 274n.

139a. The End of July: Monthly information on the length of day and night can be found in liturgical calendars; see the note above for **36a**. Bede, *De temporum ratione*, 15, represents an analogue for the English names of the months.
Bibliography: Kotzor, I, 308 and II, 333; Tupper, 'Anglo-Saxon Dæg-Mæl', p. 120.

139b. The Beginning of August: 1 August. The source for the beginnings of the months could have been Bede, *De temporum ratione*, 12 and 15, although it is not in all cases clear whether this represents an antecedent or direct source. Kotzor signals relevant information in a number of liturgical calendars and martyrologies which could also have served as sources.
226. *an ond þritig.* an .xxxi.. B. The month's length is clearly intended to be thirty-one days, which elsewhere in the text is written out in words; the B scribe in question elsewhere uses numerals for the length of months and here gets the two systems muddled; cp. also **6** above for a similar case.
227. *ðæt*. OE 'cynedom' is normally masculine, and the usage of 'ðæt', if intended to refer back to the word, seems anomalous.
Bibliography: Kotzor, I, 268 and II, 278–9, 333; Stodnick, 'Bodies of Land'.

140. The Machabees: 1 August; d. ?168; commemorated in the *Calendar of Willibrord* and Bede, *Martyrologium* (B II). Probably based on 2 Mcc. 7.1–42 and 9.1–28.
228. *to þæm cnihte.* om. C; it is hard to say whether this recapitulation is authorial (and in line with similar recapitulatory phrases elsewhere in the text) or represents a later addition, inserted to clarify whom the mother is addressing.
229. *gefeol*. See Swaen, 'Contributions to Anglo-Saxon Lexicography', p. 177.
Bibliography: Cross, 'The Use of Patristic Homilies', pp. 127–8; Cross, 'On the Library', p. 234; Whatley, s. v. 'Machabei'; Rauer, *Fontes*; Frere, *Studies in Early Roman Liturgy*, p. 46; Kotzor, II, 333; Cook, *Biblical Quotations*, p. 17.

141. Germanus: 1 August; ?378–448, d. Ravenna; not commemorated in the *Calendar of Willibrord*; commemorated in Bede, *Martyrologium* (B). The martyrologist himself refers to Bede, *Historia ecclesiastica*, which probably served as a source, cp. 55.10–67.26.
Bibliography: Cross, 'A Lost Life of Hilda of Whitby', p. 24 and p. 36n; Kotzor, I, 252–3 and II, 334; Cross, 'On the Library', p. 230.

142. Eusebius of Vercelli: 1 August; d. 371; not commemorated in the *Calendar of Willibrord*; commemorated in Bede, *Martyrologium* (B). Two sources may have been combined for this section, the *Passio S. Eusebii* (*BHL* 2748–9), 160.20–161.1 and Pseudo-Maximus, Sermo 8 (*BHL* 2752d), 28.2–3.

230. *On þam ylcan dæge*. þone ylcan dæg C; the opening formula in B here uses dative rather than the accusative normally used in the text to indicate days, but is similar to the normal opening formula which the text uses to indicate months, e.g. 'on ðæm syxtan monðe', **94b**.

231. *gefleogan*. gefleah C; 'gefleogan' in B in apposition to the preceding 'beon', both dependent on 'sceolde', but it is interesting that the C-tradition prefers to switch to a finite construction.

Bibliography: Cross, 'Two Saints', pp. 101–3; Cross, 'On the Library', pp. 235 and 237; Cross, 'The Use of Patristic Homilies', p. 108; Whatley, s. v. 'Eusebius Vercellensis'.

143. Pope Stephen I: 2 August; *s.* 254–7; not commemorated in the *Calendar of Willibrord*; commemorated in Bede, *Martyrologium* (B). The *Liber pontificalis*, I.154.1–4, seems to be the sole source for this section.

232. <*dæg*>. om. B; word and spelling taken from C.

233. *mynstre*. See Note 23.

Bibliography: Cross, 'Popes of Rome', pp. 191 and 202; Cross, 'On the Library', p. 243; Whatley, s. v. 'Stephanus papa'; Kotzor, I, 269 and II, 334–5; Gioanni, 'Hagiographie d'Italie', pp. 389–90.

144. Theodota and her Three Sons: 2 August; d. Nicaea, ?304, under Diocletian; not commemorated in the *Calendar of Willibrord*; commemorated in Bede, *Martyrologium* (B). Based on the *Passio S. Anastasiae* (*BHL* 8093), 29–31.

234. <*geendod...fyr*>. om. B; phrase and spelling taken from C.

Bibliography: Whatley, s. v. 'Theodota'; Cross, 'Source, Lexis, and Edition', pp. 29–30, 33; Lanéry, 'Hagiographie d'Italie', pp. 45–60; Kotzor, I, 273n and II, 335; Rauer, 'Female Hagiography'.

145. Discovery of the Body of St Stephen: 3 August; not commemorated in the *Calendar of Willibrord*, nor in Bede, *Martyrologium*. Probably based on the *Reuelatio S. Stephani*; cp. the two surviving recensions, *BHL* 7851, 191.1–217.11 and *BHL* 7855, 190.1–216.6. It is not clear whether the martyrologist conflated two text variants or used a mixed version now lost.

235. *Stehpanes*. stephanus C; unusual spelling probably scribal.

236. *Cafarcanialam on þam londe þe is cweden Lagabra*. The first place-name roughly agrees with forms found in the Latin and Greek traditions. The second place-name seems less garbled in C which is likely to preserve the original Old English reading (Lagabra B, Dalagabar C), as the Latin tradition has *De-*. It is interesting to note that *B* presents an erasure before 'Lagabra', which may well hide an original 'Da-', or 'De-', as in C. Since the identification of the equivalent modern localities

237.   *Godes Stehpanus*. Kotzor acknowledges Cockayne's emendation of 'Godes' to 'Godes þeow', but no emendation is required as the text is complete as it is, reflecting the wordplay on the meaning of 'Stephanus' found in the Latin source, 'Celihel, quod interpretatur stephanus Dei', 'Celihel, that is the crown of God'.
Bibliography: Cross, 'Saints' Lives in Old English', pp. 40–5; Whatley, s. v. 'Stephanus diaconus protomartyr'; Cross, 'On the Library', p. 236; Cross, 'The Use of Patristic Homilies', p. 125; Kotzor, II, 335; Abel, 'Mélanges'.

146. Oswald: 5 August; d. 642; commemorated in the *Calendar of Willibrord*; not commemorated in Bede, *Martyrologium*. Based on Bede, *Historia ecclesiastica*, 230.3–7, 240.21–2, 240.27–242.4, 246.5–29, 250.25–30, 252.3–4 and 252.5–7.
238.   *Scottas*. In line with other ninth-century texts, the martyrologist consistently uses 'Scottas' (translating Latin *Scotti*) to refer to both the Irish living in Ireland and those of Dál Riata which extended from Ireland to modern Scotland. Intended here are the inhabitants of Dál Riata; see Stancliffe, 'Oswald: Most Holy and Most Victorious King', pp. 58–60, and Woolf, 'Reporting Scotland' for political background, and Bately, 'Old English Prose', pp. 114–18, for vocabulary.
Bibliography: Cross, 'A Lost Life of Hilda of Whitby', pp. 25–7; Rauer, *Fontes*; Kotzor, I, 254n and II, 336–7; Whatley, s. v. 'Oswaldus Rex'; Cross, 'On the Library', p. 230; *PASE*, Oswald 1; *ODNB*, s. v. 'Oswald'.

147. Pope Sixtus II: 6 August; *s.* 257–8; commemorated in the *Calendar of Willibrord* and in Bede, *Martyrologium* (B). The section is a conflation of material from the *Liber pontificalis*, I.55.2 and the *Passio S. Sixti* (*BHL* 7801), 85.21–23 and 84.24–85.28. (The *Passio S. Sixti* forms part of the composite *Passio S. Laurentii*.)
239.   *Tiges.* hys C. As Shaw explains, the reference to the god of war matches references to Mars in the source, and is therefore likely to be original, but it is important to note that the alternative reading in *C* could be older than its appearance in that manuscript. See also a very similar reference to Þur (Þunor) in **182**, also supported by its source.
240.   *nedde Decius se casere <to>...deofolgylde*. The construction involving 'nidan' and 'deofolgyld' seems ungrammatical and defective; references to forced devil-worship frequently occur elsewhere in the text, where 'nidan' is usually followed by a dependent clause, or an infinitive construction, or a prepositional phrase. Any of these could have formed the original reading here; Herzfeld's prepositional construction perhaps represents the most economical emendation.
241.   *myn<st>re*. mynþre B, Ko, mynstre C, Herz; see Kotzor, II, 337, and Note 23.
Bibliography: Cross, 'The *Passio S. Laurentii*', pp. 203 and 205; Rauer, *Fontes*; Cross, 'Popes of Rome', pp. 194–6 and 202–4; Cross, 'On the Library', p. 243; Shaw, 'Uses of Wodan', pp. 141–2; North, *Heathen Gods*, pp. 230–2; Gioanni, 'Hagiographie d'Italie', pp. 389–90; Kotzor, I, 269n, 274n and II, 337.

148. Donatus and Hilarinus: 7 August; fourth century, under Julian; commemorated in the *Calendar of Willibrord* and in Bede, *Martyrologium* (B). One possible source for this section is the *Passio S. Donati* (*BHL* 2289–92), 120.1–121.17, but Bede, *Martyrologium*, 102. and Gregory, *Dialogi*, 1.7.31–42, were perhaps also used. See the comments on **83a** above for calendrical entries regarding the beginning of autumn on 7 August, which is not marked in the *Old English Martyrology*.

Bibliography: Whatley, s. v. 'Donatus Aretii'; Rauer, *Fontes*; Cross, 'On the Library', p. 241n; Kotzor, I, 213, 225, 270n and II, 337; Quentin, *Les martyrologes historiques*, p. 102; Frere, *Studies in Early Roman Liturgy*, p. 46; Lanéry, 'Hagiographie d'Italie', pp. 307–8.

149. Afra, Hilaria, etc.: 8 August; d. Augsburg ?304 under Diocletian; not commemorated in the *Calendar of Willibrord*, nor in Bede, *Martyrologium*. Probably based on the *Passio S. Afrae* (*BHL* 108–9), 55.3–56.3, 61.17–62.2 and 63.1–24, rather than the earliest *passio* (*BHL* 107b). Only the later *passio* has the information regarding the miracles of bishop Narcissus and Afra's resulting conversion, and references to her unblemished dead body (*inuenerunt Afrae corpus integrum*, 'gemitton hire lichoman gesundne') and her burial place (*tulit corpus eius et posuit secundo milariorio a ciuitate Augusta*, 'hine bebyrgdon on þære æfteran mile fram þære ceastre þe is nemned Augusta').

242.   *Eonomina*. eudomia and sancta theodote C. An associate called Theodota is otherwise not associated with Afra, and it is unclear why this name appears in C.

243.   *nacode*. The saint's nakedness was not introduced by the martyrologist; this detail is in both the older *passio* (*BHL* 107b, *expoliantes eam*) and in the later *passio*, the presumed source (*BHL* 109, *eam expoliantes*).

Bibliography: Whatley, s. v. 'Afra'; Rauer, 'Female Hagiography'; Stodnick, 'Bodies of Land'; Rauer, 'Usage', p. 137; Chenard, 'Narratives of the Saintly Body', p. 156n.

150. Romanus: 9 August; d. 258; not commemorated in the *Calendar of Willibrord*; commemorated in Bede, *Martyrologium* (B). Based on the composite *Passio S. Laurentii* (*BHL* 4753), 90.15–16, 90. 22–6 and 90.32–91.8.

244.   *gelifde*. gelyfde on god C; the reading in C seems closer to the probable source's *credidit domino Iesu Christo* and could be the original reading.

245.   *hine*. The saint referred to is Lawrence, not Romanus.

246.   *stingan*. swingan C; the reading in C seems closer to the source's *affligite* and could be the original reading.

Bibliography: Cross, 'The *Passio S. Laurentii*', pp. 203 and 206; Rauer, *Fontes*; Whatley, s. v. 'Romanus miles'; Kotzor, I, 274n and II, 338; Cross, 'Source, Lexis, and Edition', pp. 31 and 33.

151. Lawrence: 10 August; d. Rome, 258; commemorated in the *Calendar of Willibrord* and in Bede, *Martyrologium* (B). Based on the composite *Passio S. Laurentii* (*BHL* 4753), 81.31, 83.4–7, 83.29–84.7, 86.12–87.10 and 92.6–93.23.

247. *þæs archidiacones*. þæs archidiacones æt rome C; 'æt rome' could also have been part of the original opening formula which is clearly defective in B.

248. *gesiðþe*. gesyhðe C; unusual spelling in B perhaps characteristic for scribe Bc, see Kotzor, II, 337, but the spelling is attested elsewhere.

Bibliography: Cross, 'The *Passio S. Laurentii*', pp. 203 and 206–8; Rauer, *Fontes*; Whatley, s. v. 'Laurentius'; Kotzor, I, 274n and II, 338–9; Cross, 'The Latinity', pp. 283–4.

152. Tiburtius: 11 August; Rome, third century, under Diocletian; not commemorated in the *Calendar of Willibrord*; commemorated in Bede, *Martyrologium* (B II). Derived from Pseudo-Ambrose, *Passio S. Sebastiani* (*BHL* 7543), 274.59, 275.62, 276.71, 277.77 and 277.82.

249. *ðæ<t>*. ðæþ B, þæt C; see Kotzor, II, 337.

250. *in ciricean*. om. C; the presumptive source merely refers to the saint's praying, not specifying the location as a church; the reading in C is closer to the source and may have been the original one.

Bibliography: Cross, 'The Use of a *Passio S. Sebastiani*', pp. 41 and 44–5; Lanéry, *Ambroise de Milan*, esp. pp. 503–7; Lanéry, 'Hagiographie d'Italie', pp. 68–80; Rauer, *Fontes*; Whatley, s. v. 'Sebastianus'; Cross, 'On the Library', p. 236n; Kotzor, I, 273n and II, 339.

153. Euplius: 12 August; d. Catania, fourth century, under Diocletian; not commemorated in the *Calendar of Willibrord*; commemorated in Bede, *Martyrologium* (B). Based on the *Passio S. Eupli* (*BHL* 2729), 448.30–449.31.

251. *Cri<st>es*. Criþes B, cristes C; see Kotzor, II, 337.

252. *wæs in*. se dema wæs on C; 'se dema' possibly authorial, as a judge is then referred to later in this section.

253. *hæðe<n>folce*. hæðefolce B, hæðenum folce C; see Kotzor, II, 339.

Bibliography: Cross, 'The Influence of Irish Texts and Traditions', pp. 191–2; Whatley, s. v. 'Euplus'; Frere, *Studies in Early Roman Liturgy*, p. 47.

154. Hippolytus: 13 August; d. ?236; commemorated in the *Calendar of Willibrord* and in Bede, *Martyrologium* (B). Based on a part (*BHL* 3961) of the composite *Passio S. Laurentii* (*BHL* 4753), 86.9–11, 87.11–24, 93.24–6, 95.17–20 and 97.1–12.

254. *gebindan...hors*. þysne ypolytum on untame hors gebyndan C; Cross points out that C 'untame' seems to be closer to the source's *indomitorum* than the reading in B and may thus be authorial.

Bibliography: Cross, 'The *Passio S. Laurentii*', pp. 203 and 208–10; Whatley, s. v. 'Hippolytus'; Rauer, *Fontes*; Kotzor, II, 339.

155. Cassian: 13 August; d. Imola, ?363; commemorated in the *Calendar of Willibrord* and in Bede, *Martyrologium* (B). The precise source for this section remains unidentified; close analogues can, however, be found in Bede, *Martyrologium*, 68, and the *Passio S. Cassiani* (*BHL* 1626), 280.15–44.

Bibliography: Cross, 'On the Library', pp. 241–2; Whatley, s. v. 'Cassianus Ludimagister'; Kotzor, I, 213 and II, 340; Lanéry, 'Hagiographie d'Italie', p. 321.

156. Assumption of the Virgin Mary: 15 August; commemorated in the *Calendar of Willibrord* (under a different date) and in Bede, *Martyrologium* (B II). Clayton and Cross have identified a number of parallels in Pseudo-Gregory, *Liber responsalis*, 798. The list of Mary's various roles seems to have been derived from Aldhelm, *De uirginitate* (prose), 292.6–8. Clayton, *The Apocryphal Gospels*, p. 107, notes the lack of explicit detail regarding Mary's death.

255. *þa þreatas*. engla þreatas and C; reading in B closer to what seems to have been the wording of the Latin source, 'inter choros uirginum'.

256. *feower ond sextigum*. The information regarding Mary's age at the time of death seems to have no parallel, but could perhaps be explained as a copying error or confusion of a cardinal and ordinal number in an unidentified source or antecedent source ('in the sixty-fourth year [i.e. 63 years old], changing to 'sixty-four years old').

Bibliography: Clayton, *The Cult of the Virgin Mary*, pp. 214–15; Clayton, *The Apocryphal Gospels*, p. 107; Cross, 'The Use of Patristic Homilies', pp. 125–7; Cross, 'The Latinity', p. 282; Cross, 'On the Library', pp. 230 and 247; Kotzor, II, 340; Hall, 'The Ages of Christ and Mary'; Clayton, 'Feasts of the Virgin', p. 223.

157. Mamas: 17 August; Caesarea, third century, under Aurelian; not commemorated in the *Calendar of Willibrord*, nor in Bede, *Martyrologium*. The *Passio S. Mammetis* (*BHL* 5194), 126.2–29 and 128.46–129.26 seems to be the source.

257. *begangan*. Either intended as a past participle, or else as an infinitive, perhaps influenced by the the infinitives in the Latin source (*uideret impleri...et...fieri*); 'began' C is similarly ambiguous.

258. *boc*. bec C; reading in B closer to probable source reading 'librum' than C.

259. *ymutan*. Unusual spelling of this word with assimilated 'b'; see Campbell, *Old English Grammar*, §484.

Bibliography: Cross, 'Identification: Towards Criticism', pp. 238–40; Whatley, s. v. 'Mamas'.

158. Agapitus: 18 August; Praeneste, third century, under Aurelian; not commemorated in the *Calendar of Willibrord*; commemorated in Bede, *Martyrologium* (B II). The source for this section was probably a Roman massbook, possibly a *Gregorianum*.

260. *niwran*. The *Old English Martyrology* contains three references to new sacramentaries, **96**, **158** and **169**; in all cases B presents a comparative form, 'niwran', 'newer, more recent' sacramentaries, whereas C refers to 'nywan', 'new' sacramentaries. It is difficult to say which of these represents the original reading, or what the significance of this difference might be. See Note 168 above for further secondary literature on the 'new' sacramentary.

261. *sacramentorum*. B, C, sacramentorium Herz; cp. also **95** and Gneuss, 'Liturgical Books', p. 100.

Bibliography: Bischoff and Lapidge, *Biblical Commentaries*, p. 162n; Kotzor, I, 258–66 and II, 340; Whatley, s. v. 'Agapitus Praeneste'; Cross, 'On the Library', p. 234; Frere, *Studies in Early Roman Liturgy*, p. 46; Gneuss, 'Liturgical Books', pp. 99–101.

159. Magnus: 19 August; third century; not commemorated in the *Calendar of Willibrord*; commemorated in Bede, *Martyrologium* (B II). The source was probably a sacramentary from Capua or more generally the region of Campania, most likely brought to Anglo-Saxon England by Hadrian.

262.   *sang*. The erasure before 'sang' in B perhaps points to C's 'mæssesang' as the earliest Old English reading.

Bibliography: Hohler, 'Theodore and the Liturgy', pp. 226–8; Bischoff and Lapidge, *Biblical Commentaries*, pp. 160–7; Kotzor, I, 258–66 and II, 341; Cross, 'On the Library', p. 234; Frere, *Studies in Early Roman Liturgy*, p. 46; Gneuss, 'Liturgical Books', pp. 99–101.

160. Symphorian: 22 August; d. Autun, ?200; not commemorated in the *Calendar of Willibrord*; commemorated in Bede, *Martyrologium* (B II). The information regarding the saint's baptism at the age of three has a parallel in the *Passio S. Andochii* (*BHL* 424), 461.4–11. The remainder of the section seems to be derived from a *passio* of the saint, such as the *Passio S. Symphoriani* (*BHL* 7967–8), 497. Cross demonstrated that no surviving text seems to present parallels for the entire section, and concluded that the martyrologist may have drawn on more than one source or on a lost source.

263.   *weres*. In the opening formula normally accompanied by an adj., e.g. halgan; the phrase here is perhaps defective; see Herzfeld, p. 151.

264.   *Heraclius hæþen ealdorman*. Not ungrammatical without an article, but uncharacteristic usage for this text and possibly defective. Perhaps emend to 'sum hæþen ealdorman', or 'se hæþena ealdorman'. For the adj. 'hæþen', the text presents four examples of the former construction and four of the latter (**26**, **109**, **124**, **155** and **2**, **113**, **235**, **151**). Be corrects to 'se hæþena ealdorman'.

265.   *þonne...þonne*. Ko and Herz punctuate differently.

266.   *Cild cild*. cun cun C, with horizontal abbreviation marks above 'un' in both words. The reading in C is intriguingly close to the presumptive source's *natus* and may represent the original reading, with unusual usage of 'cynd'; see *DOE* s. v. 'cynd' 3 and Cross, '*Passio Symphoriani*'.

267.   *arod*. anræde C, the reading in C seems somewhat closer to the presumptive source's *resume constantiam*; see Cross, '*Passio Symphoriani*'.

268.   *gewenden in*. onwended on C, Kotzor, II, 341 suspects that the reading in B is an error for 'gewended', but see 'God on midle hise ne bið onwenden', *deus in medio eius non commovebitur*, PsGlE (Harsley), C7.3.

Bibliography: Cross, '*Passio Symphoriani*'; Cross, 'The Latinity', p. 282; Cross, 'Source, Lexis, and Edition', pp. 30 and 33; Whatley, s. v. 'Symphorianus Augustoduni'; Klaeber, 'Notes on Old English Prose Texts', p. 247.

161. Timothy: 22 August; d. Rome, fourth century; commemorated in the *Calendar of Willibrord* (under a different date) and in Bede, *Martyrologium* (B). The source seems to have been a version of the *Gesta S. Siluestri*, namely, as Whatley suggests, the so-called B-text (unedited, *BHL* 7739); for some parallels in an edited text, cp. the C-text of the *Gesta S. Siluestri* (*BHL* 7725–32), 508.27–37.

269. *folc*. folc to C, reading in C possibly authorial, as the collocation 'læran' with 'Godes geleafan' occurs many times elsewhere in the text and invariably with to, but cp. for example **75** for 'læran' with acc. of object taught.

Bibliography: Whatley, s. v. 'Silvester'; Gioanni, 'Hagiographie d'Italie', pp. 390–2; Kotzor, I, 214n.

162. Bartholomew: 25 August; first century; commemorated in the *Calendar of Willibrord* and in Bede, *Martyrologium* (B II, under a different date). Probably based on a *passio* of the saint; for some parallels, cp. for example the *Passio S. Bartholomaei* (*BHL* 1002), 140.33–5, 143.26–35 and 143.52–144.37. Cross, 'The Apostles', pp. 19–20, discusses a number of motifs which indicate the type of *passio* used by the martyrologist; these motifs include the features of the monster, the geographical location of the king's brother, and the flaying of the saint.

270. *garsecg*. See *DOE*, s. v. 'garsecg', and North, *Heathen Gods*, pp. 217–19.

271. *Sigelhearwan*. Here apparently translating *Aegyptium*; elsewhere in Old English also applied to Ethiopians, Africans or black people generally.

272. *ond <him> sprungon*. and hym sprungon C, ond him sprungon Herz, ond sprungon B, Ko; reading in C perhaps more compatible with the word order of this phrase, although the wording in B could be original.

Bibliography: Cross, 'The Apostles', pp. 19–20; Cross, 'A Lost Life of Hilda of Whitby', pp. 30–1; O'Leary, 'Apostolic *Passiones*'; Biggs, *The Apocrypha*, p. 43; Cross, 'The Latinity', p. 286; Cross, 'Popes of Rome', p. 193; Thacker, 'In Search of Saints', pp. 272–3; Scarfe Beckett, *Anglo-Saxon Perceptions*, p. 171.

163. Genesius the Comedian: 25 August; Rome, ?third century, under Diocletian; not commemorated in the *Calendar of Willibrord*, nor in Bede, *Martyrologium*. Based on a *passio* of the saint, identified by Whatley and Cross as a so-called A-text of the *Passio S. Genesii* (*BHL* 3320), 1–12, which also gives the saint's feastday as 25 August ('octavo Kalendas Septembris').

273. *mima*. Since Latin *mima* is normally of fem. gender and only refers to female persons, this form here has been seen by Cross, 'Old English *leasere*', as a scribal corruption for Latin *mimus*, but could also be an error on the author's part; alternatively it could be that *mima* here is intended not as a Latin word but a hybrid Latin-Old English coinage, with an Old English ending of the weak masc. noun declension. The word also occurs in **210** where the referent is female. The words intended to explain its meaning, 'leasere', 'scericge' (**163** and **210**), similarly seem to be new coinages or rare forms.

274. *leasere*. See previous note and Cross, 'Old English *leasere*'.

Bibliography: Whatley, s. v. 'Genesius mimus Romae'; Cross, 'Genesius of Rome'; Cross, 'Old English *leasere*', p. 484; Lapidge, 'Acca of Hexham', p. 55; *DMLBS*, s. v. 'mimus, -a'.

164. Irenaeus, Abundius: 26 August; Rome, third century under Valerian; not commemorated in the *Calendar of Willibrord*; commemorated in Bede, *Martyrologium* (B). Based on part of the composite *Passio S. Laurentii*, the *Passio SS. Irenaei et Abundii* (*BHL* 4464), 95.21–96.26.

275. *Heremus*. A corruption of Herenius, preserved in C, but the spellings of this name also vary widely in the Latin source.

276. *cægbora*. Cross, 'The *Passio S. Laurentii*' suspects a confusion of Latin *cloacarius* ('sewer-worker'), the saint's occupation in the source text, and *clauicularius* ('key-bearer'). The word 'adelseaþ' is, however, translated correctly from Latin *cloaca*, which makes the martyrologist's misinterpretation of *cloacarius* even more curious, and points to a corrupt spelling of *cloacarius* in the Latin source; the Old English account, as it stands, raises the question as to what a key-bearer is doing in a sewer.

Bibliography: Cross, 'The *Passio S. Laurentii*', pp. 203 and 210; Whatley, s. v. 'Irenaeus et Abundius'; Cross, 'On the Library', p. 228n; Cross, 'The Latinity', p. 286; Kotzor, I, 274n.

165. Rufus: 27 August; first century; not commemorated in the *Calendar of Willibrord*, nor in Bede, *Martyrologium*. The source was probably a sacramentary from Capua or more generally the region of Campania, most likely brought to Anglo-Saxon England by Hadrian.

277. *Rufi*. Rufi B, Rufini C; Kotzor, II, 342, suspects a confusion between Rufus (*BHL* 7376–7) and Rufinus (*BHL* 7371–2), both with connections to Capua, although they may also be the same person under two different names.

Bibliography: Kotzor, I, 258–66 and II, 342; Hohler, 'Theodore and the Liturgy', pp. 226–8; Bischoff and Lapidge, *Biblical Commentaries*, pp. 160–7; Cross, 'On the Library', p. 234; Gneuss, 'Liturgical Books', pp. 99–101; Frere, *Studies in Early Roman Liturgy*, p. 46; Ambrasi, 'Rufo'; Ambrasi, 'Rufo e Carpoforo'.

166. Hermes: 28 August; Rome, dates unclear; not commemorated in the *Calendar of Willibrord*; commemorated in Bede, *Martyrologium* (B II). The *Passio S. Alexandri* (*BHL* 266), 371–3, seems to be the source for this section.

278. <ðæs>. om. B, þæs C; reading in B not ungrammatical, but C more in line with formulaic phrasing at the beginning of other sections; 'miclan weres tid Sancti Hermes' B is copied on the remaining blank space of the previous line, and 'ðæs' would have been the first word of this part of the text, which may have contributed to its omission in B.

279. *þa*. and þeah C; reading in C perhaps authorial.

280. *ond...hine*. hyne and seo moder C; reading in C perhaps authorial, which would also account for the change from singular to plural in 'lædde' and 'bædon'.

Bibliography: Cross, 'Popes of Rome', pp. 200–1 and 203; Cross, 'The *Passio S. Laurentii*', p. 210n; Whatley, s. v. 'Alexander papa'; Lanéry, 'Hagiographie d'Italie', pp. 301–3; Rauer, *Fontes*.

167. Augustine of Hippo: 28 August; 354–430; commemorated in the *Calendar of Willibrord* and in Bede, *Martyrologium* (B). The source seems to be Bede, *Chronica maiora*, 66.2061–5.

281. *in Sardinia ðære byrig*. The misidentification of Sardinia as a city is not evident in the Latin source, and may have been caused by a misunderstanding of a martyrological entry; several martyrologies present near-identical phrasing which could have been misconstrued in such a way, e.g. Usuard, *Martyrologium*, 28 August *qui primo de sua ciuitate propter barbaros Sardiniam translatus*.

282. *hæþnan*. Scarfe Beckett points out that the word does not occur in the source and seems to have been added by the martyrologist to emphasise the Saracens' religious status.

Bibliography: Cross, 'On the Library', pp. 239–40; Kotzor, I, 214n, 268n and II, 342–3; Whatley, s. v. 'Augustinus Hipponensis'; Scarfe Beckett, *Anglo-Saxon Perceptions*, pp. 180–1.

168. The Death of St John the Baptist: 29 August; commemorated in the *Calendar of Willibrord* and in Bede, *Martyrologium* (B). Probably a complex conflation of scriptural passages, including Mark 6.17–29 and Matthew 14.1–12 and several passages from Gregory, *Moralia in Iob*, including 3.7.54–60.

283. *<geglisces>*. geonlices B, geglisces C; as Herzfeld had already recognised, the reading in B is clearly garbled, whereas C retains the correct adjective; see *DOE*, s. v. 'gagolisc, geaglisc, geglesc'.

284. *drucenes*. See Kotzor, II, 343.

285. *<forsewenlicne>*. forslegenlice B, forsewenlicne C; it is highly likely that B is defective here and that C retains the correct adjective; see *DOE*, s. vv. 'forslegenlic' and 'forsewenlic'.

286. *deð*. Otherwise unattested spelling.

287. *þær ænig*. þe nænig C, which is certainly better than the reading in B, but B is possibly hiding an original 'þæt nænig'.

288. *dohtro*. See Kotzor, II, 343.

Bibliography: Cross, 'Blickling Homily XIV', pp. 151, 154 and 156–8; Rauer, *Fontes*; Whatley, s. v. 'Iohannes Baptista'; Cross, 'On the Library', p. 246; Cross, 'The Use of Patristic Homilies', p. 121; Kotzor, II, 343; Herzfeld, p. 234; Cook, *Biblical Quotations*, pp. 18–19.

169. Sabina: 29 August; d. ?Rome, first century; not commemorated in the *Calendar of Willibrord*; commemorated in Bede, *Martyrologium* (B II). The source for this section was probably a Roman massbook, possibly a *Gregorianum*.

289. *niwran bocum*. 'more recent books', i.e. sacramentaries, referred to more explicitly in other entries; see Kotzor, I, 258–66. The text contains three references to new sacramentaries, **96, 158** and **169**; in all cases B presents a comparative form,

'niwran', 'newer, more recent' sacramentaries, whereas C refers to 'nywan', new' sacramentaries. It is difficult to say which of these represents the original reading, or what the significance of this difference might be. See also Note 168 above for further secondary literature on the 'new' sacramentary.
Bibliography: Whatley, s. v. 'Sabina Romae'; Bischoff and Lapidge, *Biblical Commentaries*, p. 162n; Kotzor, I, 229, 258–66 and II, 343; Cross, 'On the Library', p. 234; Frere, *Studies in Early Roman Liturgy*, p. 46; Gneuss, 'Liturgical Books', pp. 99–101.

170. Felix of Thibiuca: 30 August; 247–303, d. under Diocletian; not commemorated in the *Calendar of Willibrord*; commemorated in Bede, *Martyrologium* (B). Kotzor and Whatley have suggested the *Passio S. Felicis Tubzocensis* (*BHL* 2895b), 526.1–527.8 as the source for this section. Like the martyrologist's account, this *passio* also gives the feastday as 30 August (*die III Kl. septembris*).
290.   *gerefa<n>*. But cp. **2** for the same form, in a near-identical phrase.
Bibliography: Whatley, s. v. 'Felix Tubzacensis'; Kotzor, II, 343–4; Lapidge, 'Acca of Hexham'.

171. Aidan: 31 August; d. 651; commemorated in the *Calendar of Willibrord*; not commemorated in Bede, *Martyrologium*. Probably based on two works by Bede, *Historia ecclesiastica*, 218.10–20, 260.4–264.33, and 308.32–5, and the prose *Vita S. Cuthberti* (*BHL* 2021), 164.17–166.24 although the use of a further anonymous *vita* of this saint cannot quite be ruled out.
291.   *<Sancte Cuðberhtes>*. C, Glæstingabyrig on Sancta Marian B; the two main manuscripts differ regarding the saint's burial place. The attribution of some of St Aidan's relics to Glastonbury occurs only in B and is thought to be a tenth- or eleventh-century addition to the text.
Bibliography: Cross, 'A Lost Life of Hilda of Whitby', pp. 25, 27–8 and 30; Kotzor, I, 254n, 267n and II, 344–5; Rauer, *Fontes*; Cross, 'On the Library', p. 238; Cross, 'The Latinity', p. 276; Herzfeld, p. 234; Rauer, 'Usage', p. 130; Sisam, Review of Kotzor, p. 68; Blair, 'A Handlist of Anglo-Saxon Saints', p. 510; *PASE*, Aidan 1; *ODNB*, s. v. 'Áedán'; Bately, 'Old English Prose', pp. 114–18.

171a. The End of August: Monthly information on the length of day and night can be found in liturgical calendars; see the note above for **36a**. Bede, *De temporum ratione*, 15, represents an analogue for the English names of the months.
Bibliography: Kotzor, I, 308 and II, 345; Tupper, 'Anglo-Saxon Dæg-Mæl', p. 120.

171b. The Beginning of September: 1 September. The source for the beginnings of the months could have been Bede, *De temporum ratione*, 12 and 15, although it is not in all cases clear whether this represents an antecedent or direct source. Kotzor signals relevant information in a number of liturgical calendars and martyrologies which could also have served as sources.
Bibliography: Kotzor, I, 268 and II, 278–9, 345.

172. Priscus: 1 September; third century; commemorated in the *Calendar of Willibrord*; not commemorated in Bede, *Martyrologium*. The source was probably a sacramentary from Capua or more generally the region of Campania, most likely brought to Anglo-Saxon England by Hadrian.
Bibliography: Kotzor, I, 258–66 and II, 345; Hohler, 'Theodore and the Liturgy', pp. 226–8; Bischoff and Lapidge, *Biblical Commentaries*, pp. 160–7; Cross, 'On the Library', p. 234; Frere, *Studies in Early Roman Liturgy*, p. 46; Gneuss, 'Liturgical Books', pp. 99–101; Ambrasi, 'Prisco da Capua'; Ambrasi, 'Prisco vescovo di Capua'.

173. Antoninus: 2 September; Apamea, date unknown; not commemorated in the *Calendar of Willibrord*, nor in Bede, *Martyrologium*. A *passio* of this saint probably served as the source, although the precise text variant used remains to be identified. For some parallels, cp. *Passio S. Antonini* (*BHL* 568), 21–2. The image of the rose amongst thorns in this context ultimately appears in Jerome, *Vita S. Hilarionis* (*BHL* 3879), 29, but also in Aldhelm, *De uirginitate* (prose), 266.1–3, either or both of which could have served as a source. The notion that nobody was able to find the dismembered body (contradicted in the following clause by the statement that two women did find the body) is not attested elsewhere and may be based on a misunderstanding of a sentence in the Latin source; *non exiguus quidam cumulus est repertus*. Cross, 'Antoninus of Apamea', suggested that the negation *non* could have been misconstrued as relating to the finding of the body, rather than to the mass of body parts found, which was 'not small'.
Bibliography: Cross, 'Antoninus of Apamea'; Whatley, s. v. 'Antoninus Apameae'; Cross, 'On the Library', pp. 230–1, 236; Cross, 'A Lost Life of Hilda of Whitby', p. 32; Stodnick, 'Bodies of Land'.

174, 175. Aristion, Paternianus and Felicianus: 3 September; first century; not commemorated in the *Calendar of Willibrord*, nor in Bede, *Martyrologium*. Because of the minimal amount of detail given, which also occurs in several other texts, precise sources are difficult to establish. The feast for Aristion occurs in a number of martyrologies, including those of Ado (3 September) and Hrabanus Maurus (3 September). It is interesting to see that at least some texts associate Aristion with Capua; this association seems to be based on an error, however, and information about the saint need not have reached the martyrologist in the same way as that concerning other Capuan saints. The tenth-century Anglo-Saxon calendar contained in Salisbury Cathedral Library 150 refers to Paternus (*sic*) and Felicianus for 3 September.
Bibliography: Kotzor, II, 346; Salsano, 'Aristione'; Frere, *Studies in Early Roman Liturgy*, p. 47.

176. Marcellus: 4 September; second century; not commemorated in the *Calendar of Willibrord*, nor in Bede, *Martyrologium*. Based on the *Passio S. Marcelli* (*BHL* 5245), 197.

292. *he bebead þone Godes wer þæt mon hine bebyrgde*. he bebead þæt mon þone godes wer on þam seaðe bebyrigde C; reading in B seems defective, and may hide an original reading similar to that found in C.

293. *þæs lichaman insmoh forlet monnum to mundbyrde*. The translation of 'insmoh' remains uncertain. The Latin has *sancti corporis nobis exuuias ad patrocinium*, which the Old English translates almost word for word. Both the Latin and the Old English metaphorically refer to the soul leaving its useless shell, the body, behind. The literal image used, however, is ambiguous in both texts, and could be either that of clothing stripped off, or the image of a snake or other animal leaving its skin behind (with the 'mundbyrd' then being the saintly body which protects its worshippers as a relic) or that of the spoils of war staying behind on fallen soldiers on the battlefield, which could very well still be regarded as *patrocinium* or 'mundbyrd' for other, later users. The issue is complicated by the fact that 'insmoh' is a hapax legomenon, and is related to another hapax legomenon, 'æsmogu', which very clearly refers to a shed snakeskin.

Bibliography: Whatley, s. v. 'Marcellus Cabillonensis'; Rauer, *Fontes*; *DOE*, s. v. 'æsmogu'; Stodnick, 'Bodies of Land'.

177. Quintus: 5 September; date unknown; commemorated in the *Calendar of Willibrord*; not commemorated in Bede, *Martyrologium*. The source was probably a sacramentary from Capua or more generally the region of Campania, most likely brought to Anglo-Saxon England by Hadrian.

Bibliography: Kotzor, I, 258–66 and II, 346; Hohler, 'Theodore and the Liturgy', pp. 226–8; Bischoff and Lapidge, *Biblical Commentaries*, pp. 160–7; Cross, 'On the Library', p. 234; Frere, *Studies in Early Roman Liturgy*, p. 46; Gneuss, 'Liturgical Books', pp. 99–101.

178. Bertinus: 5 September; d. 698; not commemorated in the *Calendar of Willibrord*, nor in Bede, *Martyrologium*. Based on the *Vita S. Bertini* (*BHL* 763), 766.15–767.14 and 768.6–769.11.

294. *<se dyde manege wundru. And>*. om. B; phrase and spelling taken from C.

295. *sunnanniht*. In the Latin text *nocte dominica*, which can refer to either Saturday or Sunday night. The logic of the story probably points to the early hours of Sunday or Sunday evening.

Bibliography: Kotzor, I, 274, 452 and II, 347–8; Whatley, s. v. 'Bertinus'; Rauer, *Fontes*; Rauer, 'Female Hagiography'; Tupper, 'Anglo-Saxon Dæg-Mæl', pp. 132–5; Russcher and Bremmer, 'Fracture Treatment'.

179. Sinotus: 7 September; date unknown; commemorated in the *Calendar of Willibrord*; not commemorated in Bede, *Martyrologium*. The source was probably a sacramentary from Capua or more generally the region of Campania, most likely brought to Anglo-Saxon England by Hadrian.

Bibliography: Kotzor, I, 258–66 and II, 348; Hohler, 'Theodore and the Liturgy', pp. 226–8; Bischoff and Lapidge, *Biblical Commentaries*, pp. 160–7; Cross, 'On the

Library', p. 234; Frere, *Studies in Early Roman Liturgy*, p. 46; Gneuss, 'Liturgical Books', pp. 99–101.

180. The Birth of St Mary: 8 September; commemorated in the *Calendar of Willibrord*, but at slightly different date. Is in Bede, *Martyrologium* (B II). This section seems to be based solely on the *Euangelium Pseudo-Matthei* (*BHL* 5334–42), although it is not clear which precise variant was used; for parallels, cp. *Euangelium Pseudo-Matthei*, 1.1–2, 3.1–2, 4, and 6.1.

296.   *sceoldon <habban>*. 'habban' supplied from C, following Kotzor and Herzfeld, but cp. **8** for a similar use of 'sculan', and also **194** and Swaen, 'Contributions to Anglo-Saxon Lexicography'.

297.   *swylc bearn swylce næfre ær in worold come, ne ær ne eft.* The reiteration of 'ær' seems redundant and even illogical, and C significantly has a different construction, 'næfre eft ne cymð'. The second half of the relevant Latin phrase seems to have been something like *sed postea numquam erit ei similis uentura*, in which *numquam* and *uentura* would perhaps also suggest that a reading like that in C may have been the original one. For similar constructions, cp. also **1** and **13**.

298.   *<þe ðær on Godes huse lofsang dydon dæges ond nihtes>*. om. B; phrase and spelling taken from C.

Bibliography: Kotzor, I, 278n and II, 348–9; Clayton, *The Apocryphal Gospels*, pp. 107–8 and 138; Clayton, *The Cult of the Virgin Mary*, pp. 213 and 216; Hall, 'Gospel of Pseudo-Matthew'; Cross, 'The Use of Patristic Homilies', pp. 125–6; Cross, 'On the Library', p. 248.

181. Audomarus: 8 September; d. ?690; not commemorated in the *Calendar of Willibrord*, nor in Bede, *Martyrologium*. Based on the *Vita S. Audomari* (*BHL* 763), 762.20–763.3 and 763.16–764.18.

Bibliography: Kotzor, I, 274, 452 and II, 350; Whatley, s. v. 'Audomarus'; Rauer, *Fontes*; Rauer, 'Female Hagiography'.

182. Protus and Hyacinth: 11 September; Rome, third century, under Gallienus; not commemorated in the *Calendar of Willibrord*; commemorated in Bede, *Martyrologium* (B). From the *Passio S. Eugeniae* (*BHL* 2666), 610 and 619.

299.   *Þures.* hys C. As Shaw explains, the reference to the pagan god matches references to Jupiter in the source, and is therefore likely to be original, but it is important to note that the alternative reading in C could be older than its appearance in that manuscript. Cp. also a very similar reference to Tiu in **147**, also supported by its source.

Bibliography: Cross, '*Passio S. Eugeniae*', pp. 392 and 397; Whatley, s. v. 'Protus et Hyacinthus'; Kotzor, I, 273n and II, 351; Shaw, 'Uses of Wodan', pp. 141–2; Whatley, 'Eugenia before Ælfric', p. 350n.

183. Pope Cornelius etc.: 14 September; Cornelius *s.* 251–3; commemorated in the *Calendar of Willibrord* and in Bede, *Martyrologium* (B). This section seems to abbreviate the *Passio S. Cornelii* (*BHL* 1958), 373.1–51.

Bibliography: Cross, 'Popes of Rome', pp. 199 and 201–4; Whatley, s. v. 'Cornelius'; Lanéry, 'Hagiographie d'Italie', pp. 108–12.

184. Cyprian: 14 September; third or fourth century, under Diocletian; commemorated in the *Calendar of Willibrord* and in Bede, *Martyrologium* (B). Most of this section seems to be based on a text similar to the *Acta S. Cypriani* (*BHL* 2038), 15.15–16.18 and 17.4–14. The saint's concerns during his execution have close parallels in Augustine, Sermo 309, 1411 and Pseudo-Fulgentius, Sermo 6, 741.
300.   *Gode þanc.* deo gratias gode þanc C. The variant in C, which may represent the orginal reading, mirrors the wording of the *Acta* which does present 'deo gratias', and also fits the pattern of sporadic Latin quotations with Old English translation which punctuate the text. The Latin phrase could, however, also have been guessed at during later transmission.
301.   *he.* om. C. The reading in C presents 'mænigeo' as a subject instead, with an intransitive verb, which is very close to the wording of Augustine's sermon *atque illuc se multitudo fratrum ac sororum congregans*, and may represent the original reading, as Herzfeld's text assumes. The switch from a singular to a plural verb ('gesomnode', 'wacedon') need not speak against such a scenario; see Mitchell, *Old English Syntax*, §§367 and 433.
302.   *ðæs unhyran cwelres hand.* C presents the hapax legomenon 'flæsccwelnysse' instead of 'cwelres'; Augustine's sermon presents *manus iam proxima cruenti carnificis.* As it is unusual that C preserves a reading which is in some way closer to the source, it may be that neither the wording in C nor that in B is original. The OE word which would come closest to the source's *carnifex* is 'flæsccwellere', a gloss word attested only twice, which may have something to do with the passage here.
Bibliography: Cross, 'The Use of Patristic Homilies', pp. 107–8; Whatley, s. v. 'Cyprianus Carthaginensis'; Rauer, *Fontes*; Cross, 'On the Library', p. 237; Cross, 'A Lost Life of Hilda of Whitby', p. 31.

185. Valerian: 15 September; second century; not commemorated in the *Calendar of Willibrord*, nor in Bede, *Martyrologium*. A full discussion of the source for this section remains to be presented, but Cross (pers. comm.) and Whatley have signalled the *Passio S. Valeriani* (*BHL* 8488), 21–2, as a probable source.
303.   *wuldorbeah.* See Note 73.
Bibliography: Whatley, s. v. 'Valerianus Trenorchii'; Kotzor, I, 217n and II, 351.

186. Mamilian: 15 September; not commemorated in the *Calendar of Willibrord*, nor in Bede, *Martyrologium*. No source has been established for this section; close analogues for the precise sequence of events (the feeding of strangers, the milking of the hind, and the talking baby) can, however, be found in the *Vita S. Pamphili* (*BHL* 6418), 1–4, and the *Vita S. Goaris* (*BHL* 3565), 2–7. As Canart shows, the motif of the talking baby in particular seems to occur in many hagiographical traditions (including that of Aldhelm). The constellation of materials in this section seems to point to at least some level of confusion between the traditions of Mamilianus (Bishop of Palermo, feastday 15 September, who can be grouped with other rare

Italian saints mentioned in the *Old English Martyrology*, but whose hagiography presents no narrative overlap), and either Pamphilus (bishop of Sulmona, of a different feastday, but whose hagiography has close narrative parallels and who has tended to be confused with a bishop of Capua of the same name), or Goar (hermit in Trier, also with narrative parallels, but no other apparent links). The corrupt name in **186** ('Mamilium' B, C), the oddly military vocabulary used for the bishop's personnel, and the fact that no place-names are mentioned in this section perhaps support the idea that the martyrologist was dealing with several contradictory traditions, on which further research is needed. Mamilianus and Pamphilus are otherwise unattested in Anglo-Saxon England; a (now lost) life of Goar, possibly of a Worcester provenance, seems to have been seen by Joscelyn; see Sanders Gale, 'John Joscelyn's Notebook', pp. 264–5.

304.   *wilde hinde*. ane wylde hynde C, 'an' suprascript before 'wilde' Bf; article possibly authorial.

Bibliography: Whatley, s. v. 'Mamilianus'; Kotzor, II, 352; Canart, 'Le nouveau-né qui dénonce son père'; Rauer, 'The Sources of the *Old English Martyrology*', p. 95n; Cross, 'On the Library', p. 248; Stiene, ed., *Wandelbert of Prüm*, pp. 103–5; Frere, *Studies in Early Roman Liturgy*, p. 47; Amore, 'Goar'; Amore, 'Mamiliano'; Caraffa, 'Panfilo'; Ambrasi, 'Panfilo'.

187. Euphemia: 16 September; d. Chalcedon, early fourth century, under Diocletian; commemorated in the *Calendar of Willibrord* and in Bede, *Martyrologium* (B). Most of this section seems to be based on the *Passio S. Euphemiae* (*BHL* 2708), 454.31–2, 455.46–53, 456.21–44 and 458.54–5. Cross demonstrated that the designation of Euphemia as 'victorious', probably *triumphatrix* before translation, has parallels in liturgical material; several texts related to the Council of Chalcedon also designate Euphemia as *triumphatrix*.

305.   *geresde on* and *geræsed on*. In both cases in B 'on' is originally omitted and only inserted by a later hand Bc; C also omits 'on' in both cases. Transitive usage of 'geræsan' does not seem to be attested elsewhere, but may have been the original reading here.

306.   *ða het hi.* þa het he hig C; B seems to be lacking a pron., unless 'hi' is understood as a masc. form, in which case the dir. obj. is not expressed. Cp. also **191**.

Bibliography: Cross, 'Euphemia and the Ambrosian Missal'; Whatley, s. v. 'Euphemia'; Cross, 'Popes of Rome', p. 193; Kotzor, II, 352; Cross, 'On the Library', p. 247; ePL, s. v. 'triumphatri-'; Stodnick, 'Bodies of Land'.

188. Januarius etc.: 19 September; d. ?305, under Diocletian; commemorated in the *Calendar of Willibrord* and in Bede, *Martyrologium* (B). Some of the information given in this section can be found in the *Passio S. Ianuarii* (*BHL* 4132), 258.1–2, but the minimal detail supplied could also have been derived from other sources, including Bede, *Martyrologium*, 75–7, and a Campanian sacramentary.

Bibliography: Cross, 'Identification: Towards Criticism', pp. 236–7; Cross, 'On the Library', p. 241n; Whatley, s. v. 'Ianuarius et Sosius'; Bischoff and Lapidge, *Biblical*

Commentaries, pp. 98–9, 110–11 and 160–7; Kotzor, I, 213, 214n and II, 352; Frere, *Studies in Early Roman Liturgy*, p. 47.

189. Fausta and Evilasius: 20 September; d. fourth century, under Diocletian or Maximian; not commemorated in the *Calendar of Willibrord*; commemorated in Bede, *Martyrologium* (B). The precise source remains unidentified; Bede, *Martyrologium*, 72–3, and the *Passio SS. Faustae et Evilasii* (*BHL* 2833), 144–6, could have served as sources.

307.   <*beheold*>. gegeold B with h suprascript above eo, beheold C, ge<he>old Ko, geheold Herz; the reading of C is preferred here because Evilasius's visual impression is highlighted several times in the *passio*, and because 'behealdan' also carries connotations of causing things to get done ('to take care of'); cp. also the very similar construction and context in **64**. But the conjecture of Herzfeld and Kotzor, that 'geheold' ('controlled') was intended in B and represents the authorial reading is also plausible. Hrabanus Maurus, *Martyrologium*, has *tradi ad turpitudinem*, which could alternatively point to an original form of 'gyldan', 'to hand over', although that would then require an indirect object. All sources make it clear in any case that Evilasius is responsible for Fausta's torture, and is not just a spectator.

Bibliography: Cross, 'On the Library', p. 241n; Whatley, s. v. 'Fausta et Evilasius'; Kotzor, I, 213 and 214n.

190. Matthew: 21 September; first century; commemorated in the *Calendar of Willibrord* and in Bede, *Martyrologium* (B II). The more generally available information given in the opening lines can be found in a number of texts and is therefore more difficult to source. The remainder is mainly based on a *passio* of the saint similar to the *Passio S. Matthei* (*BHL* 5690), 637.7–667.7. The detail concerning the saint's burial may have been derived from Isidore, *De ortu et obitu patrum*, 75, or Pseudo-Isidore, *De ortu et obitu patrum*, 53.3, and the reference to Macedonia may similarly have been derived from one or both of these texts.

Bibliography: Cross, 'The Apostles', pp. 23–5; O'Leary, 'Apostolic *Passiones*'; Cross, 'Mary Magdalen', p. 16n; Kotzor, I, 250n and II, 353; Rauer, 'Female Hagiography'; Rauer, *Fontes*; Biggs, *The Apocrypha*, pp. 49–50; Cook, *Biblical Quotations*, p. 18.

191. Maurice and the Theban Legion: 22 September; d. Agaunum, ?287, under Diocletian; commemorated in the *Calendar of Willibrord* and in Bede, *Martyrologium* (B II). Probably derived from Eucherius, *Passio S. Mauricii* (*BHL* 5737), 33.16–34.9, 37.6–19 and 38.7–9, although Whatley points to problems in the classification of the variants of this text.

308.   *Campodocia*. Cappadocia C; the saint seems to be associated with Cappadocia in no other text, and the form found in C may therefore be a rationalisation of the form 'Campodocia' found in B (or a similar form), whose origin remains unexplained, however. The source text makes reference to Exsuperius's office as a *campidoctor* ('drill-master', 35.17), a rare military term which could have been misunderstood. It is interesting to note that many manuscripts of the source texts

suppress the place-name *Agaunum*, which may have aided a misunderstanding of *campidoctor* as a place-name. (It is also noteworthy that no placenames are given at the opening of this section). Alternatively, the location of Thebes could have been misinterpreted as being in Cappadocia.

309.   *ða het hy.* þa het he hig C; B seems to be lacking a pron., unless 'hy' is understood as a masc. form, in which case the dir. obj. is not expressed. Cp. also Note 306.

Bibliography: Whatley, s. v. 'Mauritius'; Kotzor, I, 228 and II, 353; Rauer, *Fontes*; Speidel, 'Die thebäische Legion', p. 43; Zelzer, 'Zur Überlieferung', pp. 328–9; Dekker, 'Eucherius of Lyons in Anglo-Saxon England'.

192. Sosius: 23 September; fourth century; commemorated in the *Calendar of Willibrord* and in Bede, *Martyrologium* (B). Cross discusses the *Passio S. Ianuarii* (*BHL* 4132), 253.4–5, 254.8–15 and 258.1–2, as a possible source for this section, although some problems remain. Bede, *Martyrologium*, 75–7, and a Campanian sacramentary could also have played a role in the composition of this section.

Bibliography: Cross, 'Identification: Towards Criticism', pp. 236–7; Cross, 'On the Library', p. 241n; Whatley, s. v. 'Ianuarius et Sosius'; Bischoff and Lapidge, *Biblical Commentaries*, pp. 95, 98–9 and 160–7; Frere, *Studies in Early Roman Liturgy*, p. 47; Kotzor, II, 354.

193. Thecla: 23 September; first century; not commemorated in the *Calendar of Willibrord*; commemorated in Bede, *Martyrologium* (B). Whatley has identified the *Passio S. Theclae* (*BHL* 8020n, Gebhardt's version Cd), 3.13–127.8, as the probable source for this section.

Bibliography: Whatley, s. v. 'Thecla'; Rauer, *Fontes*; Kotzor, II, 354; Stodnick, 'Bodies of Land'.

194. The Conception of St John the Baptist: 24 September; commemorated in the *Calendar of Willibrord* and in Bede, *Martyrologium* (B II). This section seems to be based exclusively on Luke 1.5–20.

310.   *þæs nama sceolde> Iohannis gecigged.* Perhaps still defective, with an infinitive such as 'beon' missing, but cp. **8** and **180** for similar constructions with 'sculan'.

311.   *oð þone dæg ðe þis bið.* oð þone dæg oð ðæt ðe þis bið B; cp. Luke 1.20, *usque in diem quo haec fiant.* B seems odd, presenting an otherwise unattested correlative construction; see Mitchell, *Old English Syntax*, §2759 for attested patterns. C solves the problem by omitting the entire phrase.

Bibliography: Cross, 'Blickling Homily XIV', p. 154; Kotzor, II, 354; Rauer, *Fontes*; Cook, *Biblical Quotations*, pp. 18–19.

195. Andochius, Thyrsus and Felix: 24 September; third century, under Aurelian; not commemorated in the *Calendar of Willibrord*; commemorated in Bede, *Martyrologium* (B). This section is based on the *Passio S. Andochii* (*BHL* 424), 459.16–464.27.

Bibliography: Whatley, s. v. 'Andochius'; Kotzor, I, 213, 273–4n and II, 354–5; Cross, 'On the Library', p. 241n; Cross, '*Passio Symphoriani*', p. 274.

196. Ceolfrith: 25 September; d. 716; not commemorated in the *Calendar of Willibrord*, nor in Bede, *Martyrologium*. Most of this section seems to have been derived from Bede, *Historia abbatum*, 15–17, 21–3. The reference to Burgundy only seems to have a parallel in the *Vita S. Ceolfridi* (*BHL* 1726), 400.28 (whose author may or may not be Bede), although the precise relationship with that work remains unclear.

312. *halgan weres gemind*. hal B, with gan weres gemind suprascript by Bf, halgan abbudes gewytennys C; the variant of 'gewytennys' for 'gemind' is part of a systematic preference for this word in C. The manuscripts also disagree on the status of the saint, and either 'weres' or 'abbudes' could be the original reading, as the origin of the later insertion in B is unclear.

313. *Sanctos Geminos*. Named after the triplets (rather than twins) Speusippus, Eleusippus and Meleusippus, in Latin conventionally known as *tergemini*; cp. also **23**.

Bibliography: Kotzor, I, 267 and II, 355–6; Whatley, s. v. 'Ceolfridus'; Rauer, *Fontes*; Cross, 'On the Library', p. 239; Blair, 'A Handlist of Anglo-Saxon Saints', p. 520; Bately, 'The Place which is Called'; *PASE*, Ceolfrith 1; *ODNB*, s. v. 'Ceolfrith'.

197. Justina and Cyprian: 26 September; d. ?300; not commemorated in the *Calendar of Willibrord*; commemorated in Bede, *Martyrologium* (B). Both the *Passio S. Iustinae* (*BHL* 2047, 2050), 71.18–73.30 and 74.53 and Aldhelm, *De uirginitate* (prose), 295.5–20 and 296.11–14 (itself based on the *passio*) qualify as possible sources. Because of the relatively general nature of the details given by the martyrologist, it is difficult to rule out the one or the other source; even the most specific image, the comparison of magic with smoke and wax, occurs in both potential sources. Given the level of detail in both the *passio* and Aldhelm's account, it is not clear why the martyrologist restricted himself to a more general summary.

314. *heora lichoma resteð*. hyra lychaman restað C. The reading in C refers to bodies in the pl., whereas B seems to refer to a single body, perhaps with 'heora' as a rare sg. fem. form (see Campbell, *Old English Grammar*, §703, for a similar form 'hiora' in the Kentish Glosses); but C seems less complicated textually, and could also present the original reading. Moreover, no source has been identified which would indicate Antioch as the burial place for either saint; elsewhere the saints' bodies are said to have been left exposed for six days, before being taken to Rome.

Bibliography: Whatley, s. v. 'Cyprianus et Iustina'.

198. Cosmas and Damian: 27 September; third century, under Diocletian; commemorated in the *Calendar of Willibrord* and in Bede, *Martyrologium* (B). The main source for this section seems to be the *Passio S. Cosmae* (*BHL* 1970), 474–7, which does seem to account for all details presented. Cross suggested that the designation of the two saints as 'heahlæcas' could have been influenced by

Aldhelm's account, with the Latin term *archiatros* at *De uirginitate* (prose), 275.9, which is indeed possible. But it is interesting to note that *archiatros* is also translated as 'heahlæcas' in a wide range of glosses, some of which have already been associated with the martyrologist: cp. for example Aldhelm Glosses 13.1 (Napier), 3034, 'heage læcas'; Cleopatra Glosses (Stryker) 77, 'heahlæcas oððe cræfgan' and 376, 'heahlæcas'; Second Corpus Glossary (Hessels) A.773, 'healecas'.

315.   *ða brohte seo diogollice Sancti Damiane medmicle gretinge; gewritu secgað þæt ðæt wære þreo ægero*. Some, but not all, manuscripts of the *passio* specify the woman's gift as three eggs; see, for example Zurich, Zentralbibliothek, C 10i, fol. 192v, *occulte obtulit sancto Damiano oua tria*; other manuscripts present the more general *occulte obtulit sancto Damiano quoddam munus*. It may be that the martyrologist was working with copies from both manuscript traditions, which would explain his (characteristically literal) translation which accommodates both wordings. Zurich, Zentralbibliothek, C 10i, a ninth-century legendary from St Gall, is now available in digitised format at http://www.e-codices.unifr.ch.

316.   *Þa wæs broðor Cosmas*. Þa wæs hys broðor Cosmas C. Possible textual defect in B.

317.   *ond þeah siððan*. and þær syððan C; reading in C seems to give better sense and may be original.

Bibliography: Cross, 'Cosmas and Damian'; Cross, 'On the Library', pp. 230 and 236; Whatley, s. v. 'Cosmas et Damianus'; Kotzor, I, 250n; *DOEC*, s. v. 'archiatros'; Rauer, 'Usage', p. 137.

199. The Consecration of St Michael's Church: 29 September; commemorated in the *Calendar of Willibrord* and in Bede, *Martyrologium* (B II). The source was probably a single unidentified text concerning St Michael similar to the material in Tristram Homily 2, 131–42.

318.   *in Tracla þære ceastre in Eraclae*. The geographical reference, which is badly garbled and has originally nothing to do with the tradition of St Michael, is likely to go back to a conflation of two martyrological entries, probably the one for Michael and the one following. See for example, the correct entry in Pseudo-Jerome, *Martyrologium* (29 September), *In Tracia ciuitate Eraclea Eutici et Plauti et dedicatio basilicae sancti Michaelis. Eracla ciuitate Placidi Ambodi*, or the correct entry in Hrabanus Maurus, *Martyrologium* (29 September): *Dedicatio aeclesiae sancti angeli Michahelis in Monte Gargano. In Tratia ciuitate Aeraclea natale Eutici, Plauti*. The author of Tristram Homily 2 and the martyrologist both conflate the location of Michael's commemoration and the location of the one following. Since the homily and the entry in the *Old English Martyrology* are thought to have been independently derived from the same Latin source text, it is likely that that text (based on an unidentified martyrology) already contained the error which led to the garbled geographical detail.

Bibliography: Cross, 'An Unrecorded Tradition'; Johnson, *Saint Michael the Archangel*, pp. 51–3; Cross, 'The Latinity', p. 284; Whatley, s. v. 'Michael archangelus'; Ruggerini, 'Saint Michael'; Grant, *Three Homilies*, pp. 47–8 and 62–3; Amore, 'Eutichio, Plauto ed Eraclea'.

200. Jerome: 30 September; ?341–420; commemorated in the *Calendar of Willibrord* and in Bede, *Martyrologium* (B). This section conflates two passages from Adomnán, *De locis sanctis*, 2.4.6–9 and 2.5.3–10.
Bibliography: Cross, 'The Influence of Irish Texts and Traditions', p. 180; Rauer, *Fontes*; Kotzor, I, 254–5 and II, 358; Cross, 'On the Library', p. 232.

200a. The End of September: Monthly information on the length of day and night can be found in liturgical calendars; see the note above for **36a**. Bede, *De temporum ratione*, 15, represents an analogue for the English names of the months.
319.   *mona<ð>*. Cp. also the same form in B in **217a**, 'mona'; otherwise regular usage of 'monaþ' in similar contexts throughout the text.
Bibliography: Kotzor, I, 309 and II, 358; Tupper, 'Anglo-Saxon Dæg-Mæl', p. 120.

200b. The Beginning of October: 1 October. The source for the beginnings of the months could have been Bede, *De temporum ratione*, 12 and 15, although it is not in all cases clear whether this represents an antecedent or direct source. Kotzor signals relevant information in a number of liturgical calendars and martyrologies which could also have served as sources.
Bibliography: Kotzor, I, 268 and II, 278–9, 358.

201. The Two Hewalds: 3 October; seventh century; commemorated in the *Calendar of Willibrord* (under a different date) and in Bede, *Martyrologium* (B). The source is Bede, *Historia ecclesiastica*, 480.19–22, 480.23–6, 482.20–1 and 482.22–9.
Bibliography: Kotzor, I, 252, 280n, and II, 359; Cross, 'A Lost Life of Hilda of Whitby', pp. 24–5; Rauer, *Fontes*; Whatley, s. v. 'Hewaldi Duo'; Cross, 'On the Library', p. 230; *PASE*, Hewald 1 and Hewald 2.

202. Pope Mark: 7 October; *s.* 336; not commemorated in the *Calendar of Willibrord*; commemorated in Bede, *Martyrologium* (B II). Based solely on the corresponding entry in the *Liber pontificalis*, I.202.1–5.
320.   *mynstre*. See Note 23.
Bibliography: Cross, 'Popes of Rome', pp. 191, 203; Cross, 'On the Library', p. 243; Kotzor, I, 269 and II, 360; Gioanni, 'Hagiographie d'Italie', pp. 389–90.

203. Dionysius, Rusticus and Eleutherius: 8 October; d. ?250; not commemorated in the *Calendar of Willibrord*; commemorated in Bede, *Martyrologium* (B II, under a different date). This section seems to be based on a *passio* of this saint, and possibly on a lost version, as Whatley suggests. For some parallels, cp. *Passio S. Dionysii* (*BHL* 2171), 581–3. The saints' feastday is in other texts given as 9 October; the origin of the earlier date given here remains unclear, and could be an error; see Lapidge.
321.   *ða wæron for Criste gemartyrod*. C presents an explicit pronoun 'hig'; variant in B either defective, or a case of non-expression of subject; see Mitchell, *Old English Syntax*, §1510.
Bibliography: Whatley, s. v. 'Dionisius'; Lapidge, 'Acca of Hexham', p. 38n.

204. Æthelburh: 11 October; d. 675; not commemorated in the *Calendar of Willibrord*, nor in Bede, *Martyrologium*. The source for this section is Bede, *Historia ecclesiastica*, 354.23–356.2 and 360.1–19. Bede's account, however, describes Erkenwald (and not directly his sister Æthelburh) as the founder of Barking. Since Bede's knowledge of the saint seems to be based on some lost material, it cannot be ruled out that the martyrologist was also familiar with that material.
Bibliography: Cross, 'A Lost Life of Hilda of Whitby', pp. 24–5; Cross, 'On the Library', p. 230; Rauer, *Fontes*; Whatley, s. v. 'Æthelburga'; Kotzor, I, 252–3 and II, 361; Foot, 'Anglo-Saxon Minsters', p. 222; Bately, 'The Place which is Called'; Rauer, 'Female Hagiography'; *PASE*, Æthelburg 3; *ODNB*, s. v. 'Æthelburh'; Incitti, 'Modelli agiografici'.

205. Pope Callistus I: 14 October; *s.* 217–22; not commemorated in the *Calendar of Willibrord*; commemorated in Bede, *Martyrologium* (B). The *Liber pontificalis*, I.141.1–4, seems to have been the sole source for this section.
322.   *mynstre*. See Note 23.
Bibliography: Cross, 'Popes of Rome', pp. 191 and 202; Cross, 'On the Library', p. 243; Gioanni, 'Hagiographie d'Italie', pp. 389–90; Kotzor, I, 269 and II, 361; Whatley, s. v. 'Callistus'.

206. Lupulus: 15 October; d. Capua, date unknown; commemorated in the *Calendar of Willibrord*; not commemorated in Bede, *Martyrologium*. The source was probably a sacramentary from Capua or more generally the region of Campania, most likely brought to Anglo-Saxon England by Hadrian.
Bibliography: Kotzor, I, 258–66 and II, 362; Hohler, 'Theodore and the Liturgy', pp. 226–8; Bischoff and Lapidge, *Biblical Commentaries*, pp. 160–7; Cross, 'On the Library', p. 234; Frere, *Studies in Early Roman Liturgy*, p. 46; Gneuss, 'Liturgical Books', pp. 99–101.

207. Luke: 18 October; first century; commemorated in the *Calendar of Willibrord* and in Bede, *Martyrologium* (B). Either Isidore, *De ortu et obitu patrum*, 81, or Pseudo-Isidore, *De ortu et obitu patrum*, 60, or both, were used by the martyrologist as sources here.
323.   *ðone þriddan dæl Cristes boca*. Refers to the idea that Luke was the third of the four evangelists; cp. Pseudo-Isidore, *evangelista tertius*. Cross suggested that the precise wording ('þriddan dæl') could have been influenced by similar Latin phrasing, e.g. Aldhelm, *De uirginitate* (prose), 254.8.
324.   *on Constantines dagum*. The translation of the saint's relics is in the Latin tradition variously assigned to the time of Constantine or (more accurately) to Constantius II; the reference to the former here is perhaps more likely to be authorial than scribal, as the same reference is given regarding the relics of Andrew (**233**).
Bibliography: Cross, 'The Influence of Irish Texts and Traditions', pp. 189–90; Cross, 'On the Library', pp. 233 and 243; Cook, *Biblical Quotations*, p. 20; Cross, 'The Latinity', p. 285.

208. Tryphonia: 18 October; third century; commemorated in the *Calendar of Willibrord* and in Bede, *Martyrologium* (B). Based on the *Passio S. Laurentii* (*BHL* 4753), 96.7–97.20.

Bibliography: Cross, 'The *Passio S. Laurentii*', pp. 204 and 211; Whatley, s. v. 'Tryphonia'; Kotzor, I, 274n and II, 362; Rauer, 'Female Hagiography'.

209. Justus: 18 October; third century; not commemorated in the *Calendar of Willibrord*, nor in Bede, *Martyrologium*. The source is probably the *Passio S. Iusti* (*BHL* 4590), 1–69.

325. *eahta wintre*. nygon geare C. The Latin tradition presents *novem annorum*, indicating that C may preserve the original reading here; it is not clear where the detail of the eight-year-old boy originated, whether in a Latin text variant, during the composition of the Old English text, or during its later transmission.

326. *on <hand>*. on hand C; cp. the relevant Latin reading, *in manibus suis*.

327. *Hwæt wille wit don*. sg. verb unusual with dual pronoun and possibly defective; perhaps emend to 'willen' (subj. after interr. pronoun, as e.g. in **198**), or cp. 'willað' in C.

328. *<on yncre teage>*. Cp. the relevant Latin reading, *in montegam uestram* (postcl. *mantega* < L. *mantica*, f., cloak bag, portmanteau). The Latin word and its Old English translation also occur in Anglo-Saxon glosses, Cleopatra Glosses (Stryker) 3915, '*mantega* tig'; Second Corpus Glossary (Hessels) M.118, '*mantega* taeg'. On this word, see also Coens, 'Un fragment retrouvé', pp. 104–5; 'Kotzor, II, 362–3, and *DMLBS*, s. vv. 'mantega', 'mantica'.

329. *Alticiotrum*. See Zechiel-Eckes, 'Unbekannte Bruchstücke', pp. 6–7.

Bibliography: Cross, 'Two Saints'; Cross, 'The Latinity', pp. 282–3; Whatley, s. v. 'Iustus Bellovacensis'; Kotzor, I, 271–2 and II, 362–3; Coens, 'Nouvelles recherches', esp. pp. 14–19; Coens, 'Un fragment retrouvé'; Zechiel-Eckes, 'Unbekannte Bruchstücke'; Wasyliw, *Martyrdom, Murder, and Magic*.

210. Pelagia: 19 October; ?fifth century; not commemorated in the *Calendar of Willibrord*, nor in Bede, *Martyrologium*. Probably based on material from Eustochius, *Vita S. Pelagiae*, although it is not clear if more than one version of this text was used, and which version or versions were involved. For parallels, cp. *Vita S. Pelagiae* (*BHL* 6605, version A1), 4, 17–18, 20, 24, 30, 34–5, 41–3 and 49 and *Vita S. Pelagiae* (*BHL* 6609, version B), 4–5, 16–18, 20, 24, 30, 34–5, 40–1, 43 and 49.

330. *scericge*. scearecge C. A rare word, possibly corrupt; see Williamson, *The Old English Riddles*, p. 158, for some background; alternatively, a female form of 'sceawere'?

331. *Godes <dome>*. The transmitted phrase (Godes lombe B and Godes lambe C) is probably defective, despite occurring in both manuscript traditions; Cockayne was the first to suggest that the phrase is a corruption of 'Godes dome' or a similar phrase, which would represent an accurate translation of the relevant phrase in the source (*futuro iudicio*, A1, 17 and *futurum iudicium*, B, 17); see also Kotzor, I, 27n. The possibility remains that the transmitted phrase is original, in which case it represents a major, fairly idiosyncratic, departure from the identified source.

332. *Ac gefulla me.* Ac ic bydde þe gefulla me C. Variant in C is closer to the Latin versions (*peto me baptizari* A1, 24, *obsecro baptizari* B, 24) and may represent the original phrasing.

333. *wor<ul>dwelena.* wordwelena B, woruldwelena C; the Latin text has *cunctis diuitiis* (B, 34).

334. *Cristes bure.* Cristes brydbure C. Either variant could be the original reading, as both 'bur' and 'brydbur' are attested in other texts as translations of *thalamus*, the noun presented by the Latin texts in the relevant passage (A1, 35 and B, 35).

335. *byrnan.* The Latin texts present *birrum* (A1, 41, with variant readings *bisrum*, *byrro*, *birram*) and *byrrum* (B, 41, with variant readings *byrro*, *byssum*); see Rauer, 'Pelagia's Cloak'.

336. *wer ðe wif.* Despite the reservations expressed by Chenard, 'Narratives of the Saintly Body', pp. 161 and 163, this seems to conform to the conventional construction 'hwæþer (...) (þe)...þe'; see Mitchell, *Old English Syntax*, §2086.

Bibliography: Cross, 'Pelagia in Mediaeval England'; Whatley, s. v. 'Pelagia'; Cross, 'Source, Lexis, and Edition', pp. 31 and 33; Chenard, 'Narratives of the Saintly Body', pp. 155–68; Kotzor, II, 363; Rauer, 'Female Hagiography'; Cockayne, *The Shrine*, p. 140; Rauer, 'Pelagia's Cloak'.

211. Hilarion: 21 October; ?291–371; not commemorated in the *Calendar of Willibrord*; commemorated in Bede, *Martyrologium* (B). Derived from Jerome, *Vita S. Hilarionis* (*BHL* 3879), 29–31, 38–9 and 52.

337. *sextyne wintræ.* .xvi. wintræ. B, .xv. geare C; the reading in C may be the correct one, since most manuscripts of the *Vita S. Hilarionis* present the same information, *annorum quindecim.* However, the variant of sixteen also occurs in one of the Latin manuscripts (Harvey, pers. comm.); the error perhaps most likely arose independently in both traditions, unless a more complicated scenario, namely correction with recourse to the source text, applies.

338. *hy æteowdon him swa swa þeotende wulf, hwilum swa beorcende fox.* The clause seems anomalous with its mixture of pl. adjectives ('þeotende', 'beorcende') and what look like sg. nouns ('wulf', 'fox'). It is interesting to see that C has the more conventional pl. nouns, which would point to textual error, or at least idiosyncratic usage, in B. The textual problem could perhaps be resolved by relocating 'swa swa' and 'swa' ('hy æteowdon him þeotende swa swa wulf, hwilum beorcende swa fox'). Alternatively, but less plausibly, the readings in B could perhaps be interpreted as early collective forms for animal types. It is also interesting to see that neither foxes nor wolves are mentioned in the Latin text, where the noises instead emanate from sheep, cattle and lions. Did the martyrologist add European wildlife for local colour?

339. *sume Gode<s>.* sumre godes C, sume gode Ko. The presumptive source consistently presents *virginem Dei* in its manuscripts (Harvey, pers. comm.) and C's 'godes' therefore seems preferable. The same woman is also referred to as 'Godes mægden' in **211**, and the phrase 'Godes fæmne' is a common one with five further attestations in the text. (The switch in C from acc. 'sume' to dat. 'sumre' is less significant, as 'biddan' can take either acc. or dat.; see *DOE*, s. v. 'biddan' I.b.i).

340.   *yldran*. Normally accompanied by an article or possessive, both in this text and elsewhere in Old English; C similarly supplies 'hyra'. The passage may be defective in *B*, and the difference between B and C is interesting here. The source has *perducta ergo a parentibus ad monasterium*, which would indicate that the verb found in *B* is the correct one (B gelæddon, C gebædon). It may be that the lack of a possessive in the Latin influenced the Old English.

341.   *for ðon*. fram þam C; the reading in C seems preferable and may be the original one; one wonders whether the reading in B goes back to a wrongly expanded abbreviation; see also Kotzor II, 363.

342.   *þeowodest Gode*. þeowedest Criste C; the vast majority of manuscripts of the Latin text present *servisti Christo*, and the reading in C may therefore be the original one. However, the variant *Deo* does occur in some of the Latin witnesses (Harvey, pers. comm.), and it is possible that B reflects that reading. The variants may have arisen independently in the Old English and Latin traditions.

343.   *þa*. Elsewhere in the text 'þe', as in C; cp. **203**, 'on ða ea þe hatte Secuana'.
Bibliography: Rauer, *Fontes*; Whatley, s. v. Hilarion; Cross, 'Antoninus of Apamea'; Kotzor, II, 363.

212. Genesius: 24 October; fourth century; not commemorated in the *Calendar of Willibrord*, nor in Bede, *Martyrologium*. Probably based on a variant of the saint's *passio*; cp. *Passio S. Genesii* (*BHL* 3304), 163.2–164.4.

344.   *tid*. tid þrowung B, þrowung C. The reading in B is clearly defective and probably presents an automatic insertion of 'tid' on the part of a scribe at some point during transmission; the most likely original reading is probably preserved in C. However, Kotzor suggests the original reading 'tid ond þrowung', which is also possible, although the opening formula usually restricts itself to one term only.

345.   *Rodena mere*. rodenan mere C. This Old English term seems to be otherwise unattested. Intended is probably the Rhone delta, the Camargue, with its many lakes.
Bibliography: Cross, 'Genesius of Rome'; Whatley, s. v. 'Genesius Arelatensis'; Kotzor, II, 364.

213. Sixteen Soldiers: 24 October; third century, under Claudius; not commemorated in the *Calendar of Willibrord*; commemorated in Bede, *Martyrologium* (B, under a different date). Based on the *Passio S. Laurentii* (*BHL* 4753), 97.22–98.32.

346.   *sextyna*. .xvi. B, C. Both manuscripts give the number as sixteen, although the number should really be forty-six. The error may have been present in the Latin source, or was introduced by the martyrologist through a misreading of *xlvi* as *xvi*; it is less likely that the error arose through scribal error in two separate branches of transmission of the Old English text.

347.   *cempena tid*. cempena tyd and hyra wifa C. The source does refer to wives, and C may present the original reading here; see also Whatley for Ælfric's adapation of the same material which also makes mention of the wives.
Bibliography: Cross, 'The *Passio S. Laurentii*', pp. 204 and 211–12; Whatley, s. v. 'Quadraginta Sex Milites'; Kotzor, I, 274n and II, 364.

214. Cedd: 26 October; d. 664; not commemorated in the *Calendar of Willibrord*, nor in Bede, *Martyrologium*. Derived from Bede, *Historia ecclesiastica*, 286.1–2, 288.8–14 and 344.19–25.

348.   *Ceadweallan.* ceddes C. The saint is referred to by two different names in B, Ceadwealla and Ceadde. The most likely explanation for this discrepancy is scribal error in the case of the first name, where the saint was confused with the king of the West Saxons Cædwalla, as suspected by Kotzor; in that case the original reading in the opening line would have to be Ceddes (or similar) as recorded in C. However, various complications arise: Cedd and Chad may be hypocoristic forms of fuller names which remain undetermined, but could plausibly include Cædwalla, and the hagiographical traditions of the two brothers may also have been interwoven to some extent, because of their similar names (if two saints really ever existed and do not represent a literary doublet of a single historical figure).

Bibliography: Rauer, *Fontes*; Kotzor, I, 252–3 and II, 364–5; Whatley, s. v. 'Ceadda'; Frankis, Review of Kotzor; Cross, 'A Lost Life of Hilda of Whitby', p. 24; Cross, 'On the Library', p. 230; Lapidge, 'Acca of Hexham', p. 50n; Blair, 'A Handlist of Anglo-Saxon Saints', p. 520; *PASE*, Cedd 1; *ODNB*, s. v. 'Cedd'.

215. Simon and Thaddeus: 28 October; Persia, first century; commemorated in the *Calendar of Willibrord* and in Bede, *Martyrologium* (B II). This section seems to be a conflation of a *Passio SS. Simonis et Iudae* (*BHL* 7749–50), 591.1–592.9 and 625.17–626.24, Isidore, *De ortu et obitu patrum*, 77 and 79, and Pseudo-Isidore, *De ortu et obitu patrum*, 54.1–2 and 55.

349.   *Cristes bocum.* See Gneuss, 'Liturgical Books', p. 107.

350.   *þæt ne.* þe C. Either reading, that the child was or was not one night old, could be the original reading, as the Latin source variants also disagree on this point; see Cross, 'The Apostles', pp. 26 and 49.

Bibliography: Cross, 'The Apostles', pp. 25–7; Rauer, *Fontes*; O'Leary, 'Apostolic *Passiones*'; Biggs, *The Apocrypha*, pp. 54–5; Cross, 'The Influence of Irish Texts and Traditions', p. 187; Cross, 'On the Library', pp. 233 and 243; Clayton, *The Cult of the Virgin Mary*, p. 217; Kotzor, I, 258 and II, 365; Cook, *Biblical Quotations*, p. 19.

216. Cyrilla: 28 October; third century; not commemorated in the *Calendar of Willibrord*; commemorated in Bede, *Martyrologium* (B). Based on the *Passio S. Laurentii* (*BHL* 4753), 97.12–98.17.

Bibliography: Cross, 'The *Passio S. Laurentii*', pp. 204 and 212–13; Whatley, s. v. 'Cyrilla'; Kotzor, I, 214, 274n and II, 365; Rauer, 'Female Hagiography'.

217. Quentin: 31 October; third or fourth century, under Maximian; commemorated in the *Calendar of Willibrord* and in Bede, *Martyrologium* (B). The source is probably the *Passio et Inuentio S. Quintini* (*BHL* 6999–7000), 781–3 and 785–6.

351.   <*of*>. on B, of C, Herz. The wording of the presumptive source is *statim exiit de collo eius columba candida tamquam nix*; see also Kotzor, II, 365.

352.   *Ond þæt wif heo ða arwyrðlice bebyrgde.* And Eusebia þæt wyf heo þa arweorðlice bebyrigde þone lychaman C. In B, 'heo' is here understood to be a

recapitulatory nom. sg. fem. pron., with 'ða' as the direct object in the pl.. Alternatively, 'heo' could be taken as the dir. obj., with 'ða' as an adv.. C presents an altogether more explicit version, which looks like a rephrasing of an originally ambiguous construction.
Bibliography: Whatley, s. v. 'Quintinus'; Rauer, *Fontes*; Kotzor, II, 365; Förster, Zur altenglischen Quintinus-Legende', pp. 260–1; Stodnick, 'Bodies of Land'.

217a. The End of October: Monthly information on the length of day and night can be found in liturgical calendars; see the note above for **36a**. Bede, *De temporum ratione*, 15 represents an analogue for the English names of the months.
353. *mona<ð>*. Cp. also the same form in B in **200a**, 'mona'; both are copied by scribe Bd. Otherwise regular usage of 'monaþ' in similar contexts throughout text.
Bibliography: Kotzor, I, 310 and II, 288 and 366; Tupper, 'Anglo-Saxon Dæg-Mæl', p. 120.

217b. The Beginning of November: 1 November. The source for the beginnings of the months could have been Bede, *De temporum ratione*, 12 and 15, although it is not in all cases clear whether this represents an antecedent or direct source. Kotzor signals relevant information in a number of liturgical calendars and martyrologies which could also have served as sources.
354. *Blodmonað*. As a translation of *mensis immolationum*, probably a variant spelling of 'blotmonaþ' ('month of sacrifice') rather than blodmonaþ ('blood month').
355. *syllan*. slean C. The reading in C seems to be closer to the wording of the probable source (*quae occisuri erant*) and may be the original phrasing.
Bibliography: Kotzor, I, 268, and II, 278–9, 366; *DOE*, s. vv. 'blotmonaþ', 'blodmonaþ', and 'blotan'.

218. All Saints: 1 November; not commemorated in the *Calendar of Willibrord*; commemorated in Bede, *Martyrologium* (B II). Probably a conflation of two sources, Bede, *Chronica maiora*, 66.1780–4, and the sermon 'Legimus in ecclesiasticis historiis' (*BHL* 6332d), 5–14; Bede, *Historia ecclesiastica*, 148.8–14, could also have played a role. As Cross pointed out, the 'Legimus' sermon seems to be the only text to present a parallel (both in terms of content and phrasing) for the statement that the feast of All Saints was to be accorded the same importance as Christmas.
Bibliography: Cross, 'Legimus in ecclesiasticis historiis', pp. 131–4; Rauer, *Fontes*; Cross, 'On the Library', pp. 237 and 240; Hall, 'The Development of the Common of Saints', pp. 40–6; Kotzor, I, 34–5, 222, 227, 268n, 272–3 and 278n and 451; Lapidge, 'Acca of Hexham', pp. 42–3; Cross, 'The Use of Patristic Homilies', p. 108; Bischoff and Lapidge, *Biblical Commentaries*, p. 161; Clayton, Review of Kotzor, p. 348; Rauer, 'Usage', p. 128; Rauer, 'Female Hagiography'; Falmagne, *Die Handschriften*, I, 193–4; Huglo, 'Trois livres manuscrits'.

219. Caesarius: 1 November; dates disputed, possibly ?second century, under Trajan; not commemorated in the *Calendar of Willibrord*; commemorated in Bede, *Martyrologium* (B). A *passio* of this saint seems to have served as a source, but, as Whatley points out, the precise variant used remains unidentified; for parallels see, for example, *Passio S. Caesarii* (*BHL* 1511), 114–15.

356. *Leontinus*. Leontius C. The account mixes up two figures, Luxurius and Leontius, from the *passio*, where Luxurius is said to be the one who orders the execution. It is not clear whether the error is that of the martyrologist or is already present in the Latin tradition.

357. *healsetan*. heafodsmæle C. The suggestion is that the snake gets into the man's clothes via the opening for the neck and head (*capitium*), and then bites him in the chest.

Bibliography: Whatley, s. v. 'Caesarius'; Kotzor, II, 366; Lanéry, 'Hagiographie d'Italie', pp. 192–246; Herzfeld, p. 238.

220. Benignus: 1 November; third century, under Aurelian; not commemorated in the *Calendar of Willibrord*; commemorated in Bede, *Martyrologium* (B). Probably based on *passio* of the saint, but the precise variant remains unidentified; for parallels, cp. the *Passio S. Benigni* (*BHL* 1153), 465.22–468.9.

358. *swyðe wynsum stenc, ond eac fyrhto mid*. Herzfeld suspected a textual omission here, but the Latin presents *tantusque odor suavitatis et metus*, and no assumption of further text seems to be necessary.

Bibliography: Whatley, s. v. 'Benignus'; Kotzor, I, 273–4 and II, 367; Herzfeld, pp. 201 and 238.

221. Winnoc: 6 November; d. ?717; not commemorated in the *Calendar of Willibrord*, nor in Bede, *Martyrologium*. Probably derived from the *Vita S. Winnoci* (*BHL* 8952), 770.14–17 and 771.22–772.30.

359. *he ne myhte ute wyrcan*. It is unclear whether work under the open sky is referred to, or more generally mundane work outside the monastery; there seems to be no corresponding content in the source, except perhaps for a reference to work taking place *cottidie* ('daily').

360. *þa wolde he grindan mid his halgum hondum þam broðrum to mete Cristes þam þearfendum*. Possibly defective (cp. the insertion in C of an extra 'and', which is also present in the Latin); alternatively reflexive of the complex Latin phrasing (771.27–772.1); the Latin *pauperibus Christi* demonstrates that 'Cristes' is likely to qualify 'þam þearfendum'.

Bibliography: Kotzor, I, 274, 452 and II, 367–9; Cross, 'The Influence of Irish Texts and Traditions', p. 192; Rauer, 'Female Hagiography'.

221a. The Beginning of Winter: 7 November. The date and the information on the Pleiades are possibly derived from Bede, *De temporum ratione*, 35.41–51, and more or less reflect astronomical reality (pers. comm. Cameron). See Commentary on **83a** above for calendrical entries regarding the beginning of winter, one of which may have served as a source here.

361. *gongað*. The B scribe uses a sg. verb, presumably thinking of the Pleiades as a constellation, wheras Bd, C and F opt for the grammatically more correct pl., emphasising the multiplicity of the seven stars. It is interesting to compare modern English usage, which is equally flexible in this type of case.
Bibliography: Anderson, 'The Seasons of the Year', pp. 235–8; Rauer, 'Usage', pp. 127, 132, 134 and 139; Kotzor, I, 310 and II, 369; Tupper, 'Anglo-Saxon Dæg-Mæl', p. 203.

222. The Four Crowned Ones: 8 November; early fourth century, under Diocletian; not commemorated in the *Calendar of Willibrord*; commemorated in Bede, *Martyrologium* (B II). Probably based on the *Passio S. Claudii et sociorum* (*BHL* 1836), 765–73 and 778.
362. *gesigefæstan*. See Kirschner, 'Die Bezeichnungen', pp. 161–2.
363. *Quattuor Coronatorum, þæt is þara gesigefæstan weras feower*. Scribal error or deliberate authorial change of construction from genitive to nominative; C has more consistent phrasing, which may or may not be authorial.
364. *God<e>*. goda B, Ko, gode Herz, on god C; see also Kotzor, I, 149, and II, 369, and **132, 189** and **193**, for similar phrasing; in all three of these examples C presents 'on God' for B 'Gode'. The relevant Latin passage is not very close here, presenting *ego credo quia vere ipse est deus verus Christus Iesus*.
365. *God*. se casere C; although narrative logic implies that it is God who helps the stonemasons, C may still preserve the original and correct reading here, as the corresponding Latin passage describes how the emperor rewards the men, *et dona multiplicauit*, which reflects the Old English wording almost verbatim.
366. *cwice*. om. C; C misses the point that the saints go into the boxes alive (*vivos*), but come out dead ('ateah ða cista up mid þam lichoman', *levavit loculos cum corpora*).
367. *mid þam lichoman*. om. C; see previous note.
Bibliography: Whatley, s. v. 'Claudius et soc.'; Rauer, *Fontes*; Kotzor, II, 369; Lanéry, 'Hagiographie d'Italie', pp. 290–1.

223. Martin of Tours: 11 November; ?316–97; commemorated in the *Calendar of Willibrord* and in Bede, *Martyrologium* (B II). Probably conflated from Sulpicius Severus, *Vita S. Martini* (*BHL* 5610), 3.1–5, 7.1–8.1 and 18.3, and Sulpicius Severus, *Dialogi* (*BHL* 5614–16), 212.3–8.
Bibliography: Rauer, *Fontes*; Szarmach, 'Sulpicius Severus'; Hewish, 'Living on the Edge', pp. 135–6; Kotzor, I, 270n and II, 370.

224. Mennas, Heliodorus: 11 November; d. ?300, under Diocletian; not commemorated in the *Calendar of Willibrord*; commemorated in Bede, *Martyrologium* (B II). Herzfeld suggested a link with the *Passio S. Mennae* (*BHL* 5921), 118.15–16, but Whatley remains sceptical.
Bibliography: Whatley, s. v. 'Mennas'; Rauer, *Fontes*; Kotzor, II, 370; Herzfeld, p. xlii.

225. Milus and Senneus: 15 November; date unknown; not commemorated in the *Calendar of Willibrord*, nor in Bede, *Martyrologium*. Parallels for the narrative details survive in the Syriac tradition, but no Latin version is known to have existed, and it is not clear how the martyrologist would have had access to this material. Kotzor suggests that a Latin version (now lost) may have been used. It is likely that the hagiographical tradition of these saints entered Anglo-Saxon England under the influence of Archbishop Theodore, as outlined by Hohler.

368.   *on þære ceastre...on þære ceastre*. Two cities are referred to, instead of a combination of country and city as is perhaps expected (and seems to be the case in the Syriac tradition). It may be that the martyrologist misunderstood a reference in his source; subsequent scribal error is another possibility.

Bibliography: Whatley, s. v. 'Milus et Senneus'; Hohler, 'Theodore and the Liturgy', pp. 225–6; Kotzor, II, 370.

226. Hild: 17 November; d. 680; commemorated in the *Calendar of Willibrord*; not commemoratated in Bede, *Martyrologium*. Bede, *Historia ecclesiastica*, 404.32–406.1, 406.4–8, 408.4–7, 410.20–31 and 414.11–15, probably served as a source for this section, although, as Cross suggested, further source material (now lost) could also have been involved, particularly for the details of the second vision which has no exact parallels in Bede.

369.   *en<g>las*. enlas C; emendation accepted by Ko, Herz and Co; all other occurrences of the word 'engel' in the text do present -g-. But see Kalbhen, ed., *Kentische Glossen*, p. 271, for elision of g in Kentish, and the Kentish Hymn, 5, for a similar form, 'ænlum'. In view of other features which have been interpreted as Kentish by other commentators (see Introduction above, pp. 5–6, 11, 19 and 22), the spelling here seems noteworthy.

Bibliography: Cross, 'A Lost Life of Hilda of Whitby'; Whatley, s. v. 'Hilda'; Kotzor, I, 254n, 272n and II, 371; Cockayne, *The Shrine*, p. 149; Cross, 'On the Library', pp. 230 and 248; Rauer, 'Female Hagiography'; *PASE*, Hild 1, Hereric 1 and Bregoswith 1; *ODNB*, s. v. 'Hild'; Incitti, 'Modelli agiografici'.

227. Cecilia: 22 November; third century; commemorated in the *Calendar of Willibrord* and in Bede, *Martyrologium* (B). The source seems to be the *Passio S. Caeciliae* (*BHL* 1495), 3–9 and 31.

370.   *Almatheus*. See Note 116.

371.   *swa*. See Mitchell, *Old English Syntax*, §3477.

372.   *heo gebæd hig to þam papan se wæs haten Urbanus*. The connection between Cecilia and Pope Urban (222–30) already appears in the Latin tradition, although there is no historical foundation for such an association; see Delehaye, *Étude sur le légendier romain*, pp. 80–88.

Bibliography: Rauer, *Fontes*; Whatley, s. v. 'Caecilia'; Lanéry, 'Hagiographie d'Italie', pp. 80–8; Delehaye, *Étude sur le légendier romain*, pp. 73–96; Upchurch, *Ælfric's Lives of the Virgin Spouses*, pp. 13–15 and 30; Upchurch, 'Homiletic Contexts'; Kotzor, II, 371; Rauer, 'Female Hagiography'.

228. Pope Clement I: 23 November; s. ?91–?101; commemorated in the *Calendar of Willibrord* and in Bede, *Martyrologium* (B). Probably a conflation of several sources, including the *Liber pontificalis*, I.118.5 and I.123.3, and the *Passio S. Clementis* (*BHL* 1848), 344.4–6 and 344.21–38; two further passages, Gregory of Tours, *Miraculum S. Clementis* (*BHL* 1855), 345.13–42, and Matthew 16.19 could have been used as direct or indirect sources. Cross points to relevant variants which are not present in the edited texts of the sources.

373. *þrytig mila*. .xxx. mila C. Only three miles, *tria fere milia*, in the source, which also fits better with the statement regarding the location of the church later on in this section.

374. *þa <sǣ>*. Not ungrammatical without the noun, but usage is uncommon in the *Old English Martyrology*.

375. *Ralia*. See Cross, 'Popes of Rome', p. 198.

Bibliography: Cross, 'Popes of Rome', pp. 194, 196–9 and 202–4; Rauer, *Fontes*; Whatley, s. v. 'Clemens'; Lanéry, 'Hagiographie d'Italie', pp. 88–96; Gioanni, 'Hagiographie d'Italie', pp. 389–90; Cross, 'On the Library', p. 243; Kotzor, II, 371; Cross, '*Passio S. Eugeniae*', p. 395; Lapidge, 'The Saintly Life', pp. 251–2.

229. Felicity: 23 November; Rome, second century, under Antoninus; not commemorated in the *Calendar of Willibrord*; commemorated in Bede, *Martyrologium* (B). Probably based on Gregory, *Homiliae in Euangelia* 3, 21.26–23.78, although additional homiletic material could have influenced the image of the suffering mother (see note below). This section is dedicated to the female saint; because of their staggered martyrdom, her sons are commemorated on a different day and in a separate section, **123**.

376. *mare þonne martyre*. The source cited presents a similar idea (*recte ergo hanc feminam ultra martyram dixerim*), but even closer parallels occur in the homiletic sources of Ælfric's Catholic Homily I. 9 on the Purification of Mary (C.B.1.1.10), lines 174–5 ('heo wæs mare þonne martyr', *plus quam martyr fuit*), where the image is applied to Mary, who, like Felicity, suffers by seeing her offspring murdered (although Mary, unlike Felicity, is ultimately not martyred herself); see Godden, *Ælfric's Catholic Homilies: Introduction, Commentary and Glossary*, p. 75.

377. *þe læs*. See Mitchell, *Old English Syntax*, §2928.

Bibliography: Whatley, s. v. 'Felicitas cum septem filiis'; Rauer, *Fontes*; Herzfeld, p. 239; Cross, 'On the Library', pp. 232–3; Lapidge, 'Acca of Hexham', p. 56; Rauer, 'Female Hagiography'.

230. Chrysogonus: 24 November; d. Aquileia, ?304, under Diocletian; commemorated in the *Calendar of Willibrord* and in Bede, *Martyrologium* (B). Derived from the *Passio S. Chrysogoni* (*BHL* 1795), 8–9, which forms part of the composite *Passio S. Anastasiae*.

Bibliography: Whatley, s. v. 'Chrysogonus'; Lanéry, 'Hagiographie d'Italie', pp. 45–60; Kotzor, I, 273n.

231. Saturninus: 28 November; third century; not commemorated in the *Calendar of Willibrord*, nor in Bede, *Martyrologium*. Probably based on a *passio* of this saint, although the precise variant remains unidentified; for some parallels, cp. the *Passio S. Saturnini* (*BHL* 7495–6), 1–6. As Whatley points out, several details have no close parallels in the printed version of the *passio*, and may relate to variant readings which remain to be traced.

378.   <on> þære ceastre. þære ceastre B, Ko, <on> þære ceastre Herz; see also Kotzor, II, 372.

Bibliography: Whatley, s. v. 'Saturninus Tolosanus'; Rauer, *Fontes*; Lapidge, 'Acca of Hexham', pp. 39 and 56.

232. Chrysanthus and Daria: 28 November; third century, under Numerian; not commemorated in the *Calendar of Willibrord*, nor in Bede, *Martyrologium*. At least partially based on Aldhelm, *De uirginitate* (prose), 276.24–278.23 and 280.5–7, which does, however, not specify the Christian teacher of the saint as a priest, nor the number of girls as five; these and other details could have been derived from the *Passio SS. Chrysanthi et Dariae* (*BHL* 1787), 2–27.

379.   swyðe gleawe. Possibly defective; Herzfeld emends to swyðe gleawe <fæmnan>; see Kotzor, II, 372.

Bibliography: Kotzor, I, 257n and II, 372; Cross, 'On the Library', p. 231; Upchurch, *Ælfric's Lives of the Virgin Spouses*, pp. 13–15; Upchurch, 'The Legend of Chrysanthus and Daria'; Lanéry, 'Hagiographie d'Italie', pp. 138–48; Corona, *Ælfric's Life of Saint Basil*, p. 104n; Mitchell, *Old English Syntax*, §3243; Frere, *Studies in Early Roman Liturgy*, p. 46.

233. Andrew: 30 November; d. Patras, ?60; commemorated in the *Calendar of Willibrord* and in Bede, *Martyrologium* (B II). The *Passio S. Andreae* (*BHL* 428), 107.37–45, and the *Passio S. Andreae* (*BHL* 430), 514.21–515.7, Isidore, *De ortu et obitu patrum*, 69, and Pseudo-Isidore, *De ortu et obitu patrum*, 60, have been discussed as possible sources. Cross also points to further scriptural and Hiberno-Latin analogues for the opening lines and the detail concerning the saint's beauty.

380.   on Constantinus dagum. The translation of the saint's relics is in the Latin tradition variously assigned to the time of Constantine or (more accurately) to Constantius II; the reference to the former here is perhaps more likely to be authorial than scribal, as the same reference is given regarding the relics of Luke, **207**.

Bibliography: Cross, 'Popes of Rome', pp. 27–8; Rauer, *Fontes*; Biggs, *The Apocrypha*, pp. 39 and 42; Cross, 'The Influence of Irish Texts and Traditions', p. 187; Cross, 'On the Library', p. 243; Kotzor, II, 372; Conner, 'On Dating Cynewulf', p. 38.

233a. The End of November: Monthly information on the length of day and night can be found in liturgical calendars; see the note above for **36a**. Bede, *De temporum ratione*, 15, represents an analogue for the English names of the months.

381.   Blodmonað. See Note 354.

Bibliography: Kotzor, I, 311 and II, 288, 373; *DOE*, s. vv. 'blotmonaþ', 'blodmonaþ', and 'blotan'; Tupper, 'Anglo-Saxon Dæg-Mæl', p. 120.

233b. The Beginning of December: 1 December. The source for the beginnings of the months could have been Bede, *De temporum ratione*, 12 and 15, although it is not in all cases clear whether this represents an antecedent or direct source. Kotzor signals relevant information in a number of liturgical calendars and martyrologies which could also have served as sources.
Bibliography: Kotzor, I, 268 and II, 278–9, 373; Anderson, 'The Seasons of the Year', p. 252.

234. Eulalia: 10 December; d. ?304, under Diocletian; commemorated in the *Calendar of Willibrord* and in Bede, *Martyrologium* (B). Probably based on a variant of the saint's *passio*; cp. *Passio S. Eulaliae* (*BHL* 2696), 1–4.
382.   *Datianus*. See Introduction, p. 16.
383.   *freode*. Use of 'freogan' here not entirely implausible, but, as Cross suggested, the correct reading here could alternatively be something like 'frefrode' (cp. *consolabatur* in the Latin text).
Bibliography: Cross, 'Eulalia of Barcelona'; Whatley, s. v. 'Eulalia Barcinone'; Cross, 'Old English *leasere*'; Cross, 'Source, Lexis and Edition', pp. 30–1, 33; Kotzor, II, 373; *DOE*, s. vv. 'freogan' 2.a.ii and 'frefran'; Stodnick, 'Bodies of Land'.

235. Lucy: 13 December; d. Syracuse, ?304, under Diocletian; not commemorated in the *Calendar of Willibrord*; commemorated in Bede, *Martyrologium* (B). Mainly based on the *Passio S. Luciae* (*BHL* 4992), 108.6–109.28, except for the image of the saint's blood avenged with her tormentor's blood, which was probably taken from Aldhelm, *Carmen de uirginitate*, 1840–1, and perhaps some overlap with Bede, *Martyrologium*, 81, for the saint's immobility.
Bibliography: Cross, 'The Latinity', pp. 277–80; Whatley, s. v. 'Lucia Syracusis'; Cross, 'On the Library', p. 231; Cross, 'Old English *leasere*', p. 485; Cross, 'Source, Lexis and Edition', pp. 30–1 and 33; Rauer, 'Female Hagiography'; Stodnick, 'Bodies of Land'.

236. Ursicinus: 13 December; d. Ravenna, first century, under Nero; not commemorated in the *Calendar of Willibrord*, nor in Bede, *Martyrologium*. Probably based on Pseudo-Ambrose, *Passio S. Geruasii* (*BHL* 3514), 744–5.
Bibliography: Whatley, s. v. 'Gervasius et Protasius'; Lanéry, *Ambroise de Milan*, esp. pp. 305–47; Lanéry, 'Hagiographie d'Italie', pp. 61–8; Kotzor, II, 374; Rauer, *Fontes*.

237. Higebald: 14 December; seventh century; not commemorated in the *Calendar of Willibrord*, nor in Bede, *Martyrologium*. Derived from Bede, *Historia ecclesiastica*, 344.16–27, with the exception of the references concerning the saint's resting place, which, as Rollason points out, resemble phrasing in the *Secgan*, a list of saints' resting places.

Bibliography: Cross, 'A Lost Life of Hilda of Whitby', pp. 24–5; Cross, 'On the Library', p. 230; Rollason, 'Lists of Saints' Resting Places', p. 74; Kotzor, I, 252–3 and II, 374–5; Blair, 'A Handlist of Anglo-Saxon Saints', pp. 539–40; *PASE*, Hygebald 2.

238. Thomas: 21 December; first century; commemorated in the *Calendar of Willibrord* and in Bede, *Martyrologium* (B II). Probably a conflation of more than one source, including the *Passio S. Thomae* (*BHL* 8136), 14.5–15.12, 16.9–17.10, 37.5–40.11 and 41.7–12, and possibly also Isidore, *De ortu et obitu patrum*, 73, and Pseudo-Isidore, *De ortu et obitu patrum*, 49.3.

384.   *eorð<an>*. eorð C, Ko, eard Herz. The word is the last word in the topmost line of the last manuscript page; the text adjacent to the right margin of this page is damaged in many places or even made illegible through wear. The ungrammatical form 'eorð' is otherwise only attested as a truncated form in glosses; see *DOE*, s. v. 'eorþe'. The most probable scenarios are that the text either read 'eorðan' (with the -an subsequently erased through wear), or that through lack of space the truncated form 'eorð' was copied, either with or without abbreviation mark, with the intended meaning of acc. sg. or pl. 'eorðan'. Herz's suggestion that 'eard' was intended can be ruled out, as a letter 'ð' is still legible.

385.   *myd grenum and myd hæwenum and myd hwytum*. The Latin account suggests precious stones; the Old English passage could also imply stones (and could possibly have contained a word denoting stones, which dropped out), or may alternatively suggest colours, as Cross suspects.

386.   *scryðe*. scryð Ko, scryde Herz; e only very faint in the margin; cp. also **65** and **140** for acc. and dat. usage of this word.

387.   *wealdleðer swa up getiged*. Cross shows that the Latin account is likely to have presented *habenis effuis*, 'with loose reins', which clarifies the image somewhat; cp. also Vergil, *Aeneid*, V.818.

388.   *he*. Refers either to 'lychama' (which is masc. in gender) or the saint in more general terms.

Bibliography: Cross, 'The Apostles in the *Old English Martyrology*', pp. 21–3; Cross, 'The Influence of Irish Texts and Traditions', p. 187; O'Leary, 'Apostolic *Passiones*'; Cross, 'On the Library', pp. 234n, 236 and 243; Biggs, *The Apocrypha*, p. 56; Rauer, *Fontes*; Kotzor, I, 258 and II, 375; Cross, 'Euphemia and the Ambrosian Missal', p. 18; Cross, 'Cosmas and Damian', pp. 17–18; Cross, 'Pelagia in Mediaeval England', p. 286; Cook, *Biblical Quotations*, p. 19; Casiday, 'Thomas Didymus from India to England'.

Appendix 1: Manuscript A, London, British Library, Add. 23211, fol. 2

A is a damaged fragment of the *Old English Martyrology* which contains only a short sequence of text; for further details, see p. 19 above. This Appendix presents a separate edition of manuscript A. The editorial principles are the same as outlined for the main text (see above, pp. 25–30); the layout of this edition follows that found in the manuscript. Lost lettering is indicated by three dots enclosed in parentheses (...); I have not attempted to calculate the number of missing letters. Uncertain readings appear in parentheses.

APPENDIX 1

MS A: *OLD ENGLISH MARTYROLOGY*, LONDON, BRITISH LIBRARY, ADD. 23211, FOL. 2

14 April: Valerianus, Tiburtius, Maximus

64. mid[a] hiora fiðra flyhte. Ond se mon ða gele(...)
Gode, ond he wæs sungen[b] on dead for Criste, ond h(..)
noma wæs Maximus.

64. [a] MS A starts here; this entry is acephalous; [b] see Sisam, 'An Early Fragment', p. 211; [c] n suprascript Aa.

18 April: Eleutherius, Antia

65. On ðone eahtategðan dæg ðæs monðes (...)
ðæs halgan biscepes tid Sancte Eleutheri, (...)
modor ðære noma wæs Sancte Anthiæ. He wæs (...)
burge biscep ðe is nemned Mæchania, in Ap(...)
ðære mægðe, ah he geðrowade eft in Rom(...)
martyrdom for Criste. Adrianus se caser(...)
ðreatade ðæt he Criste wiðsoce. Ða he ðæt (...)
walde, ða heht se casere gesponnan fiow(...)
wildo hors to scride ond hine gebundenne in ð(...)
asetton, ðæt ða wildan hors scealden iornan (...)
hearde wegas in westenne ond him ða limo all (...)
brecan. Ða cwom Godes engel of hiofonum (...)
stillde ðæm horssum, ond hio gelæddon ðæt scrid (...)
hea dune; ðær him cwom to monigra cynn(...)
deor ond wunedon mid hine. Ond ðonne he hof (...)
hond upp to hiofonum, ðonne hofon ða de(...)
ra fotas upp ond heredon God mid hine. Ð(...)
se casere his huntan hine ðær gefecca(...)
hine mid sueorde ofslean. Ða cwom stef(...)
hiofonum[c] ond cwæð: 'Cym, min ðeow Eleuthe(...),
mine englas ðec lædað in ða hiofonlican (...)
lem.' Ða feoll his modor ufan on his lic(h...)
ond cwæð: 'Min sunu, gemyne ðu mec on ðære (...)
(reste).' Ond se casere hio heht gemartyria(...)

21 April: Æthelwald

66. ðon ðe tuelf gear ðær wunode, ða eode he in
ðone gefean ðære ecan eadinesse. Ðæs Æðelwaldes wunder wæs ðæt he spræc to his
liornæra sumum, ond ða feringa oðsuigde he
suæ he hwæshwegu hercnade. Ða frægn se his
ðegn hine, forhwon he suæ dede. Ða cuæð he:
'Hu meahte ic bu somod ge in heofon geheran
ge her spræcan?'

23 April: George

67. On ðone ðrio[a] ond tuentegðan dæg ðæs monðes bið
Sancte Iorius tid ðæs æðelan weres; ðone
Datianus se casere seofon gear mid una-
sæcgendlicum witum hine ðreade ðæt he Crist(...)
wi<ð>soce[b], ond he næfre hine ofersuiðan meahte;
ond ða æfter sefan gearum heht he hine beheafdian. Ða he ða wæs læded to ðære beheafdunga,
ða cuom fyr of heofonum ond forbærnde ðone
hæðnan casere ond alle ða ðe mid hine ær tinter-
gedon ðone halgan wer. Ond he, Sanctus Georgius,
(...)im to Dryhtne gebæd ond ðus cuæð: 'Hælende
(...)rist, onfoh minum[c] gaste. Ond ic ðec biddo ðæt suæ
(...)welc mon ðe mine gemynd on eorðan doe,
(ð)onne afierr ðu from ðæs monnes husum
(...)lce untrymnesse; ne him fiond sceððe, ne
(...)ungor, ne monncwild. Ond gif monn minne
(...)oman nemneð in ænigre frecennisse, oððe
(...)n sæ oððe on siðfæte, ðonne ge(fylge se ðin[d])

---

67. [a] i suprascript Aa; [b] Ko, widsoce A, Sw, see Kotzor, I, 47 for the close similarity of the letter forms d and ð in this manuscript; [c] n suprascript Aa; [d] MS A breaks off here – this entry is incomplete.

Appendix 2: Manuscript E,
London, British Library, Add. 40165 A.2, fols 6–7

What follows below is an edition of Manuscript E, a damaged text fragment of the *Old English Martyrology*; for further details, see p. 22 above. Because the manuscript is so badly damaged, examination with modern technology is crucial; Celia Sisam was the first to investigate the manuscript under ultraviolet light.[1] For the edition below, a new set of ultraviolet images was produced which turned out to be of higher quality than the images at Sisam's disposal and which have been used to re-examine her readings. Uncertain readings are given in parentheses. Capitalisation, punctuation and subdivision into paragraphs are modern; tironian notes have been expanded throughout ('ond'). The number of dots are intended to represent the number of missing letters, but in cases of longer passages which now appear illegible because of surface damage or truncation of the page, I have not attempted to calculate the number of lost letters. Such passages are here signalled with square brackets and a reference indicating illegibility or missing text. The text contains annotations by what seem to be two hands, here designated Ea and Eb; their contributions are signalled in the apparatus.

---

[1] Sisam, 'An Early Fragment', p. 217; Kotzor, I, 110n.

MS E: *OLD ENGLISH MARTYROLOGY*, LONDON, BRITISH LIBRARY, ADD. 40165 A.2, FOLS 6–7

2 May: Athanasius

75. On[a] ðone æfterran dæg þæs monðes (biþ ðæs hal)g [text missing] Sancte Athanasi; he uuæs biscop in ðære miclan ceast(r)e[b] Alexand(ria); his hal(i)gnes uuæs foretacnad on his cneahthade. Þære burge biscop (.)r him wæs nemned Alexandre; se sæt sume symbeldæge in ðære c(ier)cean, (.) (ð)a geseah he ðurh ð(a) eagduru plegean micel cneahta we(r)od bi sæs waroðe; þara uuæs an Aþanasias. Þa ongon he fulwian ða oþere cneahtas on þæs sæs yþum, ond hie eodan him under hond, sua he biscop wære. Ond ða son(a) heht se biscop þone cneht him to gelædan, ond hine lærde gastlicne wisdom. Ond he uuæs all mid Godes snyttro gefylled.

75. [a] MS E starts here; [b] suprascript r?

3 May: Pope Alexander I, Eventius, Theodolus

76. On ðone þriddan dæg ðæs monðes bið Sancte Alexandres þrowung þæs iungan papan in (.)ome, ond tuegra mæssepreosta mid hine þa wæran nemnede Sanctus (E)u(......) ond Sanctus Þeodolus. (Ð)a Aurelia(n.)s se gesi(ð), se ðær cualde Cr(i)stene menn, þa ongon he (.)ie nædan ðæt hie Criste wiþsocen. Ða hie ðæt ne geðafodan, þa heht he send(..) hie alle þrie in bernendne ofn; þa nolde hie ðæt fyr no bæ(.)nan. Ða (h...) he ða (mæ.s)epreostas beheafdian, ond þone papan ofstician. Þa sona cu(o)m stefn (o.) heofon(.)m ond seo cuæð: 'Aurelianus, ðeossum monnum þe ðu her (.)ismerodes(.)[a], (.)im is Godes neorxnawong ontyned, ond þe siendan helletin(.)ergu ontyned.' Ða sua(..) he sona ðære ilcan neaht mid egeslice deaðe. Ond his w(i)if, sio (.)æs on (.)oman S(...)riane, hio bebyrgde ðæs papan lichoman ond ðæran mæssep(.)eosta arweorðli(..) on ðære seofoðan mile from Romebyrg on ðam wege þe (.)atte Numen(t...). Ðes Sanctus Alexandre uuæs se fifta papa æfter Sancte Petre.

76. [a] faint trace of final letter visible under ultraviolet light, (.)ismerodes Ko, Si, bismrodest B, bysmrodest C.

3 May: Discovery of the Holy Cross

77. On ðone ilcan dæg biþ sio ti(i)d ðæt Cristes rod uuæs gem(et.)d ærest, s(.)a (..) ða halg(.)n gewrioto secgaþ, on ðone dæg þe we nemn(a)ð Qui(n)ta Nonas M(..... ...) cuom u(..) of ðære eorðan wynsumes stences rec, þær [a]sio rod uuæs geme(te.)[a]. (...)ow uuæs (a)seted ofer deades monnes byrgenne[b] ond lichoman[c], ond se sona (....). (... ....) ðæt wundor uuæs gecyþed þæt (.)æt uuæs soðlice Cristes[d] (.)od.

77. [a–a] see Commentary; [b] see Commentary; [c] n suprascript Ea; [d] s suprascript Ea.

APPENDIX 2

Rogation Days

78. Ymb þas d(.... ....), hwilum (.)r, hwilum æfter, bioð ða þrie dagas on ðam (G)odes ciercean (. ....) folc mæ(r)siað Letanias, þæt is þonne bene ond relicgo(.)gas for(.)n to (.....) upas(.)ignesse [illegible] [missing text] (..)s g(elic) agot(e)n fore allum monnum. On ðam þrim dagum Cristene menn sceolon alætan hiera þa worldlican weorc on ða þriddan tid dæges, þæt is on undern, ond forð gonge<n>[a] mid þara haligra reliquium oþ ða niogoðan tid, þæt is ðonne non. Þa dagas siendan ryhtlice to gefæstanne, ond ðara metta to brucanne þe menn brucaþ on ðæt fiowertiges neah(.)a fæsten ær eastrum. Ond ne bið alefed on ðissuum dagum ðæt monn him blod læte oþðe clæsnungdrencas drince oðþe oht feor gewite fore worldrices bisigung from ðære stowe þe he sceal Gode ætþiowian. Ðas þrie dagas siendan monnes saule læcedom ond gastlic wyrtdrenc; forþon hie siendon to haldonne mid heortan onbryrdnesse, ðæt is mid wependum gebedum ond mid rumedlicum ælmessum ond fulre blisse allra menniscra fionda, forðon þe God us forgifeð[b] his eorre, gief we ure monnum forgifað.

78. [a] forðgonge Ko, emendation suggested by Si; [b] f suprascript Ea.

5 May: Ascension of Christ

79. On ðone fiftan dæg þæs monðes bið se dæg þe ure Dryhten on to hiofonum astag. Þy dæge hine gesegon nest his þegnas on Oliuetes dune; ðær he bletsade hie ond ða gewat mid þy lichoman on hiofon. Þy dæge eode sio eorðe in heofon, þæt is se monn[a] ofer ængla ðrym. Ond on Oliuetes dune siendan nu get ða suaþu Dryhnes fotlæsta. Ymb þa Dryhtnes fotlæstas timbredon Cristene menn sionowalte ciercean wundorlice. Ond ne me(.)hte sio his suaþu næfre mid nænigre oðerre wisan bion þam oðerum flore geonlicad ond gelice gehiowad. Gif ðær monn hwæt mennisces on asette[b], þonne nolde sio eorðe him onfon, ðeah hit wære marmanstanas, þa aswengede on ðære onsion[c] þe ða þær[d] [e]on setton[e]. Ðæt dust þæt (.)od þær [f]on træd[f], ond ða his suaþe þe ðær on aðrycced siondon, wæron[g] monnum[h] (.. ....)e lare; ond dæghwamlice geleaffulle menn ðær niomaþ þæt sond, ond ðær hwæðere ne biþ nænegu wonung on ðam sonde ðære Dryhtnes fota suaþe. Sancte Arculuos sægde[i] þæt ðær ne meahte nænig h(.)of bion on ðære ciercean in þære stowe þe ure Dryhten on stod, he ða to hiofonum astag, ah þæt se weg þær wære a to hiofonum open [missing text] (..)annes wære oð monnes suioran, ond ðæt þær wære ðyrel onm(..... ...) hweole, þurh ðæt menn meahten ufan beorhtlice sceawian (........) fota suaþu, ond ðæt hie meahten mid hiera hondum ræcan ond (n.... ...) halgan dustes dæl. Ond Sanctus Arculuos sægde þæ<t>[j] ðær hongad(. ......) leohtfæt, ond ðæt wære biernende a dæges ond neahtes ofer þære Dr(y.....) (....) suaðe; ond he sægde ðæt

79. [a] second n on erasure; [b] Si, onasette Ko; [c] e suprascript Eb; [d] on erasure; [e-e] Si, onsetton Ko; [f-f] Si, ontræd Ko; [g] suprascript Eb; [h] n suprascript Ea; [i] s and cauda inserted on erasure; [j] emendation suggested by Si.

316

æghwelce geare ðy dæge æt Cristes uppas(.........) on middes dæges tiid, æfter ðon þe mæssesongas wæron geendode in (ð... ....) ciercean, ðæt ðær ᵏto cuomeᵏ stronggestan windes ystæ, ond ðæt se sua st(.........) hrure on ða ciercean, ðæt þær ne meahte nænig monn ænige gemette (.. ....)cean beon oðþe on hire neahstowe meahte gestondan oþðe gesittan, ah (... ....) menn ðe ðær þonne wæran, lægon aðenede on ðære iorðan mid ofdu(......)dum ondwlitan, ˡoþ ðætˡ sio ondrysnlice yst forþgeleoreð. Se ondrys(..... ....) ðæt deð þæt se dæl þære ciercean ne mæg habban ðone hrof þær ðæs H(.......) fotlastas under siondon. Sancte Arculuos sægde þæt he seolf þær (w...) (...)weard æt ðære ilcan ciercean þy dæge æt Cristes uppastignesse, þ(. .. ..) ond se forhtlica wind onræsde.

ᵏ⁻ᵏ Si, tocuome Ko; ˡ⁻ˡ oþðæt Ko.

6 May: Eadberht

80. On ðone sextan dæg þæs monðes bið Sancte Eadbrehtes geleorne(. ... ..)wyrðan (......), se uuæs biscop on Breotone æfter Sancte Cuþbrehte on ðæm hal(g.. ...)stre ðe is nemned Lindesfarene ea. Ðam Eadbrehte uuæs gewunel(..) (... ..) symle feowertig daga ær eastran ond eac feowertig daga ær Cristes (.......)se, ðæt is ær geolum, he wunode on dægelre stowe on his gebeodum (... ....)licum weorcumᵃ; ond sio stow uuæs utan ymburnen mid sæs stre(a.)um. Þa o(. ... .)tenfæsten, on ðam þæsᵇ mynstres broðor dydon Sancte Cuþbreh(t)es lic of e(......), ond hie ðæt gemettan sua gesun(d) suelce he ða get lifde, (... .æ)t uuæs (..... ....) gearum þæs ðe he uuæs bebyrged. Ða bæran hie ðæs lichrægles d(æ. .. ..)hte þam biscope, ond he ðæt cyste mid micelreᶜ lufan, ond he weop (... .. ...)hte uneaðe ænig word cueðan, ond he cuæð: 'Hwylc mon mæg arecea(n.....)nes giefe? He ðæt seleð þam ðe hiene lufiað ðæt þa saula lifiað a (.. ....) ond in ðære hiofonlican heannesse, ond he haldeð ða deadan lichoman (............) [missing text] (...t)t(.g)u þe (.. ....) C(..)brehtes licho(m)a in r(.....) [text missing] Dryhten for(..)feð on ðære stowe ræsteᵈ.' Ond þa noht longe æf(.)er þ(e..... .. .. r)umode Godes se leofa Eadbreht biscop, ond ð(æ)s þa æf(.e)r seofon ond (......... .aga) he onsende his gast to Gode, ond his (....)oma uuæs geseted in þa il(...) (..... .æ)r (.)ancte Cuðbrehtes lichoma ær on resteð.

80. ᵃ r suprascript Ea; ᵇ suprascript thorn Ea with expansion suggested by Si; ᶜ see Commentary; ᵈ see Commentary.

7 May: John of Beverley

81. (.. .... s)eofoþan dæg þæs monðes bið Sancte Ioha(.)es geleorn(.)s, se uuæs (......) (.. .r)etone on Norþhymbra þeode; se gedyde dumbum menn spræce, (... ... .) (sien)dan awriten on Istoria Anglorum on ð(æ)re bec, ond his li(c)homa (... ....)n ðære stowe ðe is nemned Derewuda.

APPENDIX 2

8 May: Discovery of St Michael's Church

82. (.. ....)h(...a)n dæg þæs monðes biþ ðæt Sancte Mic(..)h(e.e)s (.)ierce (..)est fun [illegible] e Gargano, ðær[a] se monn uuæs of(s)ceoten mid his (..e)ne [illegible] (he) walde þone fear sceotan se stod on þæs scræfes[b] (.)ura.

82. [a] æ on erasure; [b] s suprascript Ea.

8 May: Victor Maurus

83. [illegible] biþ Sancte Uictores þrowung ðæs martyres, (þæ)s licho(m.) [illegible] ðære ceastre. Se Uictores he uuæs M(..)ra cynnes, [illegible] (es) cempa þæs hæðnan caseres, ah he uuæs Criste(s) þegen. [illegible] (ine) ðæt he forlete Cristes geleafan. Þa he þ(æt) ne geðafode [illegible] mid (.)itum. (He) heht hine begeotan mid wallende lead(.), [illegible] ð(e) m(a) ðe cald wæter. Ða heht he his leaseras h(...) [illegible] s(e..) ge(.....) Dulmis ond hiene ðær beheafdian. Þa cu(.. ..) [illegible]: 'Secgað ge Maximiane þæm casere þ(.)t he bið [illegible] (h)im beoð ða sco(n)can forb(ro)ce(.)ne ær ðon þe he (...) b(...)r(...).' [illegible] (ad se caser. ...) n(....) mo(..) hi(s) licho(m..) be(..)rgde [illegible] ene (sc...)den forsu(.....) wildu dior [illegible] þone lich(.)man, oðer æt þ(am) [illegible] ð(am fo..m .)þ ðæt [illegible] ternus se biscop [illegible] ðlice be(.......).

9 May: The Beginning of Summer

83a. [illegible] n dæg þ(..) m(..)ðes b(..) (.)umeres fruma. Se sumor hafað hundniogon [illegible] (.onne) (go.... .. ..o)fon steor(.a)n on (uh)tan u(.)p, ond on (..)en on s(e)tl.

10 May: Gordianus

84. [illegible] mon(...) biþ þæs martyres tiid Sancti Gordi(.)ni[a]

84. [a] MS E breaks off here; this entry is incomplete.

Appendix 3: Manuscript F,
London, British Library, Harley 3271, fol. 92v

The text fragment edited below constitutes Manuscript F of the *Old English Martyrology*.[1] The two text sections have been edited separately before by Heinrich Henel, and were also known to the last editor of the *Old English Martyrology*, Günter Kotzor, although the latter did not designate the text fragment in Harley 3271 as a distinct manuscript of the *Old English Martyrology*, probably because the text in Harley 3271 can indeed be interpreted as very faithful quotations from the *Old English Martyrology*, rather than a witness in its own right.[2] It is, however, noteworthy that in Harley 3271 the two entries are not embedded in another text, but form two items in a longer list of short notes concerned with the topic of chronology, some of which were possibly copied by the same scribe Fa.[3]

The possibility remains that the two short notes on the Beginning of Summer and Winter in Harley 3271 are not excerpts from the *Old English Martyrology*, but represent one of its sources: in theory, the martyrologist could have derived the information and wording of these entries from a set of Old English notes contained in an earlier encyclopaedic manuscript. A more plausible scenario, however, is that the martyrologist derived the information found in these entries from Bede, *De temporum ratione*, 35.41–51, a text which he is otherwise thought to have used for other sections concerned with chronology and cosmology; it is also important to note that no further vernacular source texts seem to have been used in the composition of the *Old English Martyrology*. If the text sections below are unlikely to have served as a source, therefore, they would have to be derivative of the *Old English Martyrology*; they should be seen as representing quotations of, or excerpts from, the text, and could be considered to constitute a separate witness of the text.

Recent research has concentrated on the contents and composition of Harley 3271 as an outstanding example of late Anglo-Saxon encyclopaedic book production.[4] Further work needs to be done to explore the nature of the short notes which bookend the two *Martyrology* excerpts in the manuscripts and which may shed further light on the possible readership of the *Old English Martyrology* and its literary and scientific interests.

---

[1] For further reading, see Rauer, 'An Annotated Bibliography', s. v. 'Manuscripts', and pp. 22–3 above.
[2] Henel, 'Altenglischer Mönchsaberglaube', pp. 347–8; Kotzor I, 3n.
[3] See Ker, pp. 309–12 and Chardonnens, 'London, British Library, Harley 3271' for the codicological and paleographical context.
[4] Chardonnens, 'London, British Library, Harley 3271' and Rauer, 'Usage of the *Old English Martyrology*'.

APPENDIX 3

MS F: *OLD ENGLISH MARTYROLOGY*, LONDON, BRITISH LIBRARY, HARLEY 3271, FOL. 92V

TEXT

83a. Sumor hafað hundnigantig daga; þonne gangað þa seofan steorran on uhtan upp, and on æfen on setl.

221a. Winter hafað twa ond hundnigantig daga; þonne gangað þa seofon steorran upp on æfen, and on dægred on setl.

TRANSLATION

83a. Summer is ninety days long; at that time the Seven Stars [i.e. Pleiades] rise at dawn and set in the evening.

221a. Winter is ninety-two days long; at that time the Seven Stars rise in the evening and set at dawn.

Glossary

This glossary consists of two parts, one for Old English vocabulary and one for Latin and Greek vocabulary. Apart from definite articles, demonstrative, personal, and possessive pronouns, and relative particles, all words used in the *Old English Martyrology* are listed, and all occurrences of a given word are listed, except in the case of high-frequency words, where omissions are indicated. The prefix *-ge* is ignored in the alphabetical ordering. The numbering refers to text sections containing the relevant word; 'ap' indicates that a word appears in the apparatus, and not in the main text of a given text section. R = rarely attested vocabulary, form or usage; Hp = Hapax legomenon. The words are in alphabetic order, with æ listed to follow a; þ is made to follow t; ð is not used.

Old English vocabulary

a, adv., always, 13, 31, 47, 50, 51, 52, 57, 79, 80, 108, 117, 121, 127, 131, 136, 217b, 226

abbod, noun, m., abbot, 3, 17, 37, 40, 51, 136, 178, 196, 221, 237

abbodesse, noun, f., abbess, 49, 110 204, 226

abiddan, st. vb. V, to ask for, pray, 109, 227

abifian, wk. vb. II, to tremble, 21, 56a ap [R]

abitan, st. vb. I, to eat, 1, 97, 124, 157

ablacian, wk. vb. II, to turn pale, 5, 21 [R]

ablindian, wk. vb. II, to become blind, 221 [R]

abrecan, st. vb. IV, to break apart, 130

abregan, wk. vb. I, to terrify, 199

abyrgan, wk. vb. I, to taste, 176ap

abysgung, noun, f., activity, 78ap [R]

ac, conj., but, yet, 1, 4, 5, 11, 16, 23, 26, 30, 31, 38, 40, 50, 53, 57, 65, 68ap, 70, 71, 72, 73, 79, 83, 86, 87, 90, 99, 101, 102, 103, 108, 112, 113, 121, 122, 123, 125, 126, 127, 133, 135, 136, 138, 139, 140, 149, 152, 154, 155, 160, 167, 170, 178, 190, 191, 192, 197, 198, 203, 207, 208, 210, 211, 216, 222, 227, 238

acennan, wk. vb. I, to give birth, to declare, 1, 21, 39, 51, 63, 68, 86, 101, 111, 113, 116b, 122, 186, 194, 207, 209, 217b ap, 225, 229

acennednes, noun, f., birth, 1, 2, 63ap, 68ap, 80ap, 111ap, 140, 180

acennes, noun, f., birth, 3, 9, 11, 63, 68, 80, 111

aceorfan, st. vb. III, to cut out, 9, 38, 58

acolian, wk. vb. II, to cool down, 3

acwellan, wk. vb. I, to kill, 6, 27, 31, 108, 114, 135, 140, 155, 164, 212

acwician, wk. vb. II, to revive, 111a

acyrran, wk. vb. I, to turn, 151

adelfan, st. vb. III, to dig, 16, 72, 113, 176

adelseaþ, noun, m., sewer, 164 [R]

adiligian, wk. vb. II, to destroy, 122, 127, 210

adl, noun, f., ailment, 127

adon, anom. vb., to take away, to exhume, 39, 107ap

adrencan, wk. vb. I, to drown, 219

adrifan, st. vb. I, to drive away, 31

adrugian, wk. vb. II, to dry up, 228

adwæscan, wk. vb. I, to extinguish, 57, 163

afeallan, st. vb. VII, to fall off, 26, 73ap, 109, 178

afedan, wk. vb. I, to bring up, 33

aflyman, wk. vb. I, to put to flight, 51ap, 190ap

afulian, wk. vb. II, to become foul, 140

afyllan, wk. vb. I, to cut down, 112

afyrhtan, wk. vb. I, to frighten, 221

afyrran, wk. vb. I, to take away, 7, 67, 122, 160

agan, pret. pres. vb., to own, 181, 228

agan, anom. vb., to pass, 58a

agangan, st. vb. VII, to pass, 1, 58a

agælan, wk. vb. I, to neglect, 115

agen, adj., own, 6, 21, 26, 58, 59, 82

ageotan, st. vb. II, to pour, 78, 235

GLOSSARY

agotennes, noun, f., pouring out, 112
agrafan, st. vb. VI, to inscribe, 211
agyfan, st. vb. V, to give, 44, 60, 65, 68, 140, 176, 231, 235, 236
aheardian, wk. vb. II, to harden, 108
aheawan, st. vb. VII, to cut off, 121
ahleapan, st. vb. VII, to jump up, 217 [R]
ahon, st. vb. VII, to hang, to suspend, 23, 32, 56a, 71, 233
ahreofian, wk. vb. II, to become afflicted with a skin disease, 190 [Hp]
aht, pron., adv., anything, 73, 78, 210ap
ahydan, wk. vb. I, to hide, 107ap, 210, 231
alædan, wk. vb. I, to lead, 19, 21, 97, 117, 162, 207, 233, 238
alætan, st. vb. VII, to abandon, 78
alecgan, wk. vb. I, to deposit, to lay down, 230
alyfan, wk. vb. I, to allow, 78, 155, 176
alysan, wk. vb. I, to release, 57
amearcian, wk. vb. II, to mark, 89ap
an, adj., pron., one, a, an, 1, 4, 6, 8, 8a, 12, 16, 23, 26, 30 34, 36b, 38, 41, 44, 48, 50, 51, 56, 56a, 58, 63, 66, 71ap, 73, 73b, 75, 87, 88, 94, 99ap, 100, 101, 108ap, 110, 111a, 113, 116b, 121, 122ap, 130, 132, 136, 138, 139b, 143, 149, 164, 168, 171, 176ap, 178, 183, 186, 190, 196, 200b, 201, 205, 211, 215, 217, 219, 221, 222, 223, 225, 226, 228, 232, 233b, 235, 238
geanbidian, wk. vb. II, to await, 71
ancor, ancra, noun, m. anchor, 228
ancor, ancra, noun, m. hermit, 15, 16, 37, 63, 66, 186
ancorsetl, noun, n., hermitage, 63, 66 [R]
and, conj., and, 1, 2, 3, 4, 5, *etc.*
andetnes, noun, f., confession, 112
andettan, wk. vb. I, to confess, 49, 127
geandettan, wk. vb. I, to confess, 122
andettere, noun, m., confessor, 177
andfenge, adj., acceptable, 68
andswarian, wk. vb. II, to answer, 122, 184
andweard, adj., present, 2, 79, 86, 181
andwlita, noun, m., face, 79, 151
anforlætan, st. vb. VII, to let go, 90
geanlician, wk. vb. II, made similar to, 79 [R]

anlicnes, noun, f., likeness, 56a, 67, 97, 130ap, 238
anmodlice, adv., unanimously, 199
anræde, anræd, adj., resolute, 38, 117ap, 120, 160ap, 180
anrædlice, adv., resolutely, 33
ansund, adj., whole, 149ap
ansyn, noun, f. (occ. m. or n.), face, 2, 73, 79, 97, 162, 180, 232, 234, 238
anweald, noun, m., authority, 51
apostol, noun, m., apostle, 74, 94, 101, 108, 111, 114, 115, 119, 133, 135, 161, 162, 190, 193, 215, 233, 238
ar, are, noun, f., reverence, 26, 98, 160, 167
arædan, wk. vb. I, to read out, 184
aræfnan, aræfnian, both wk. vb. I and wk. vb. II forms occur in the *Old English Martyrology*, to suffer, 136, 140, 184, 185, 193
arcebisceop, noun, m., archbishop, 37
arcediacon, noun, m., archdeacon, 151
areccan, wk. vb. I, to narrate, 80, 136, 168
arfæst, adj., pious, 102
arian, wk. vb. II, to honour, 31, 112
arisan, st. vb. I, to stand up, to arise, 16, 38, 49, 50, 56a, 58, 77, 80, 116, 131, 209
arleas, adj., dishonourable, 161, 225
arod, adj., strenuous, 117, 160
arwurþe, adj., respectable, 22, 80, 102ap, 178
arwurþian, wk. vb. II, to celebrate, 2, 4
arwurþlice, adv., with dignity, 20, 41, 76, 83, 164, 167, 168ap, 196, 217, 220, 230
arwurþnes, noun, f., reverence, 116b, 218
asecgan, wk. vb. III, to relate, 21, 111, 114, 168ap
asendan, wk. vb. I, to send, 37, 181
asettan, wk. vb. I, to put, 38, 65, 77ap (see also Appendix 2), 79, 102, 107ap, 111a, 190, 209, 222
asingan, st. vb. III, to chant, 196
aslean, st. vb. VI, to cut off, 227
asmorian, wk. vb. II, to smother, 57 [R]
asteorfan, st. vb. III, to die 70 [R]
astigan, st. vb. I, to board (a ship), to ascend, 3, 38, 51, 79, 97, 149

GLOSSARY

astyrian, wk. vb. I, to move, 22

aswætan, wk. vb. I, to begin to sweat, to break out into a sweat, 21 [Hp]

asweartian, wk. vb. II, to grow dark, 56a [R]

asweltan, st. vb. III, to die, 30

aswengan, wk. vb. I, to fling, 79 [R]

ateon, st. vb. II, to pull, 164, 173, 222, 235

attor, ator, noun, n., poison, 5, 51, 87, 101

aþ, noun, m., oath, 181

aþennan, aþenian, both wk. vb. I and wk. vb. II forms occur in the *Old English Martyrology*, to stretch out, 79, 90, 151, 234

aþeostrian, aþystrian, wk. vb. II, to grow dark, 56a ap

aþolian, wk. vb. II, to suffer, 136ap, 140ap, 184ap, 185ap

aþryccan, wk. vb. I, press, 79ap [R]

aþwean, st. vb. VI, to wash, 163

aþydan, wk. vb. I, to separate, 116 [R]

aweallan, st. vb. VII, to swarm, 140

aweccan, wk. vb. I, to revive, resuscitate, 5, 13, 18, 70, 74, 97, 166, 190, 210, 223

awedan, wk. vb. I, to become mad, 113, 154, 162, 190

awefan, st. vb. V, to weave, 227 [R]

aweg, awege, adv., away, 3ap, 162

aweorpan, st. vb. III, to throw, 8, 41, 89, 116, 173, 230, 235

awiht, pron., adv., anything, at all, 120, 127

awreccan, wk. vb. I, to arouse, 74ap

awritan, st. vb. I, to write, 58, 81, 88, 92, 122, 141, 145, 191, 201, 204, 207ap, 214

awunian, wk. vb. III, to remain, 110, 138, 193

ayrnan, st. vb. III, to elapse 111a

æ, noun, f., law, 88, 101, 140, 155

æcer, noun, m., field, 203

æfen, noun, m., evening, 41, 63, 70, 83a, 130, 170, 221a

æfentid, noun, f., evening, 151

æfest, adj., pious, 70, 117

æfest, noun, m., envy, 89

æfestigian, wk. vb. II, to envy, 70 [R]

æfre, adv., ever, 38, 50ap, 57, 136ap, 163, 227, 236

æfter, adv., prep., after, afterwards, 2, 3, 4, 6, 9, 13, 15, 17, 26, 30, 32, 35, 38, 40, 50, 56a, 57, 58, 66, 67, 68, 70, 74, 76, 78, 79, 80, 88, 94, 101, 107, 108, 110, 112, 113, 114, 115, 121, 126, 127, 130, 133, 140, 144, 145, 149, 154, 161, 170, 180, 184, 190, 191, 192, 196, 203, 215, 217, 222, 228, 229, 233, 233b, 238

æfterfylgend, noun, m., successor, 231

æfterra, adj., latter, second, 4, 8a, 37, 46, 75, 97, 116b, 117, 139a, 143, 149, 173, 233b

æg, noun, n., egg, 46, 198

æghwær, adv., everywhere, 36, 181

æghwilc, adj., pron., each, every, 9, 12, 16, 52, 63, 73, 79, 88, 97, 111, 111a, 115, 133ap, 140, 170, 198, 218, 221, 222, 228

ægþer, pron., each, 49, 180, 196ap, 225

ælc, adj., pron., each, every, 2, 5, 26, 48, 67, 88, 196, 207, 210, 222

ælmesgeorn, adj., charitable, 115 [R]

ælmesse, noun, f., alms, 78, 127, 138

æmtig, adj., empty, 80

æne, adv., once, 110, 210

ænig, adj., pron., any, some, 8, 52, 67, 79, 80, 111, 114, 146, 168, 198ap, 205, 210

ænlic, adj., handsome, 38, 97ap

æppel, noun, m., fruit, apple, 16, 168

ær, adv., prep., conj., earlier, before, 1, 3, 6, 7, 9, 13, 14, 15, 16, 30, 35, 44, 49, 57, 60, 67, 70, 73, 75, 78, 80, 83, 88, 89, 90, 99, 103, 110, 111, 112, 113, 115, 116, 120, 138, 139b, 140, 141ap, 145, 148, 154, 157, 162, 163, 168, 173, 180, 183, 186, 187, 196, 198, 203, 208, 209, 210, 223, 225, 226, 228, 231, 233b, 235, 236

æren, adj., made of brass, 79, 211

ærende, noun, n., message, 56

ærendung, noun, f., message, 111 [R]

ærendwreca, ærendraca, noun, m., messenger, 74, 108, 111, 135, 162, 186ap, 193

ærest, adv., first, 13, 14, 16, 25, 32, 56, 66, 70, 72, 76, 77, 82, 92, 102, 110, 111a, 112, 127,

323

GLOSSARY

133, 135, 138, 139b, 149, 163, 166, 190, 195, 197, 207, 208, 210, 218, 224, 232

ærist, noun, m. or f., resurrection, 58, 133, 190

ærnemergen, noun, m., early morning, 63, 131

ærra, ærest, adj., early, previous, first, 1, 4, 8a, 9, 12, 53, 56, 66, 70, 74, 94b, 95, 116a, 139b, 140, 145, 148, 157, 166, 172, 218, 223, 226, 232, 233, 233b

æspring, noun, m. or n., spring, 122

æt, adv., prep., at, near, 1, 3, 5, 6, 11, 12, 16, 17, 22, 23, 27, 28, 30, 32, 37, 38, 40, 49, 51, 54, 56a, 58, 63, 68, 70, 73, 79, 83, 84, 86, 97, 98, 99, 109, 110, 112, 114, 115, 121, 122, 126, 129, 132, 133, 134, 138, 142, 143, 146, 149, 150, 151, 152, 154, 157, 163, 166, 173, 189, 191, 192, 193, 194, 195, 196, 198, 202, 205, 210, 211, 219, 220, 221, 225, 227, 228, 232, 238

æteowan, ætywan, wk. vb. I, to show, to appear, 1, 3, 11, 13, 22, 30, 38, 47, 58, 60, 61, 68, 70, 89, 97, 102, 107, 112, 115, 126, 130, 133, 140, 145, 162, 180ap, 194, 198, 199, 211, 223, 226

æteowednes, ætywednes, noun, f., showing, appearance, 11, 12, 230

ætforan, prep., in front of, 190

ætgædere, adv., together, 180ap, 222ap

æthrinan, st. vb. I, to touch, 139ap, 220ap

ætsacan, st. vb. VI, to deny, 181ap

ætsomne, adv., together, 198

ætstandan, st. vb. VI, to stand by, 49, 186ap

ætswigan, wk. vb. I, to be silent, 66ap [R]

geættrian, wk. vb. II, to poison, 87

ætþeowian, wk. vb. II, to serve, 78 [R]

ætwitan, st. vb. I, to criticise, 33

æþele, adj., noble, famous, 2, 3, 5, 13, 17, 27, 29, 35, 38, 40, 49, 67, 86, 90, 91, 94, 106, 113, 117, 120, 130, 139, 156, 167, 182, 193, 195ap, 200, 204, 227, 232, 235

æþellice, æþelice, adv., splendidly, 17, 180 [R]

æþelnes, noun, f., glory, 160, 230 [R]

ban, noun, n., bone, 5, 26, 53, 57, 124, 171, 207

gebaswod, past part. of *gebaswian, stained crimson, 70 [Hp]

batian, wk. vb. II, to heal, 110 [R]

baþian, wk. vb. II, to bathe, 1, 88, 110

bær, noun, f., bed, 209

bærnan, wk. vb. I, to burn, 23, 46, 53, 76, 100, 149, 170, 193ap, 194

bæþ, noun, n., bath(-water), 1, 26, 41, 108, 110, 163, 227

be, big, prep., conj., adv., by, near, 1, 2, 32, 37, 41, 51, 53, 56a, 70, 71, 75, 89, 117, 124, 130, 131, 144, 153, 157, 196, 200, 209, 210, 211, 214, 221, 227, 228, 231, 237

beag, noun, m., ring, crown, 87, 130, 227

bealdnes, noun, f., boldness, courage, 4 [Hp]

beard, noun, m., beard, 108, 162

bearm, noun, m., bosom, 5

bearn, noun, n., child, 39, 180, 207, 226

bebeodan, st. vb. II, to command, decree, 8, 31, 73, 83, 97, 98, 106, 109, 112, 113, 115, 116, 122ap, 157, 160, 176, 184, 198, 209, 218

bebicgan, wk. vb. I, to sell, 101, 108

bebod, noun, n., command, 53, 88, 140

bebrædan, wk. vb. I, to spread, cover, 51 [Hp]

bebyrgan, wk. vb. I, to bury, 4, 10, 26, 53, 70, 74, 76, 80, 83, 86, 91, 102, 103, 110, 133, 143, 149, 150, 151ap, 160, 161, 164, 166, 167, 173, 176, 196, 202, 203, 205, 207, 216, 217, 220, 225, 230, 233

beceorfan, st. vb. III, to cut off (the head), 168, 213

becuman, st. vb. IV, to reach, 13, 170, 176, 178, 225

becyrran, wk. vb. I, to turn, 170

gebed, noun, n., prayer, 23, 42, 49, 51, 78, 80, 94, 110, 112, 124, 138, 146, 152, 173, 182, 183, 186, 190, 194ap, 221, 228

bedd, noun, n., bed, 58, 151, 234

bedelfan, st. vb. III, to bury, 209, 211

gebedhus, noun, n., prayer-house, oratory, 127

gebedtid, noun, f., prayer-time 51, 133 [R]

gebedword, noun, n., word of prayer, 146ap [Hp]

GLOSSARY

befæstan, wk. vb. I, to commit, 122, 232
beflean, st. vb. VI, to flay, 87, 162 [R]
befon, st. vb. VII, to seize, 127ap, 152
beforan, adv., prep., before, 1, 38, 50, 57, 90, 97, 109, 111, 114, 122, 126, 131, 136, 140, 163, 184, 186, 227, 229, 233b, 234, 235, 238
began, anom. vb., to practise, to worship, 157ap, 162, 231
begangan, st. vb. VII, to practise, to worship, 8, 51, 72, 157, 183, 238
begen, adj., both 26, 49, 57, 66, 87, 106, 107, 109, 114, 187, 201
begeondan, prep., beyond, 146
begeotan, st. vb. II, to cover, 38, 83, 234
begnagan, st. vb. VI, to gnaw at, 124 [Hp]
begytan, st. vb. V, to receive, 171
behamelian, wk. vb. II, to mutilate, 234 [R]
beheafdian, wk. vb. II, to behead, decapitate, 32, 34, 54, 64, 67, 71, 76, 83, 86, 98, 106, 107, 109, 112, 113, 122, 153, 160, 161, 163, 166, 168, 170, 182, 184, 209, 217, 224, 230, 236
beheafdung, noun, f., beheading, 67, 71ap, 73, 106, 122, 170, 183, 184, 198, 234, 236 [R]
behealdan, st. vb. VII, to behold, 64, 189
beheawan, st. vb. VII, to cut, 235
beheonan, prep., on this side, 146
behrumig, adj., sooty, 59 [Hp]
behydelice, adv., carefully, 89 [R]
belean, in other texts st. vb. VI, but here wk., to criticise, to reproach, to blame, 168ap [R]
gebelgan, st. vb. III, to become angry, 234
belimpan, st. vb. III, to belong to, 95, 162
belle, noun, f., bell, 226
belucan, st. vb. II, to lock up, 2, 26, 56a, 114, 124, 130ap, 220, 221, 222, 227
ben, noun, f., prayer, 69, 78, 116, 117, 122, 168
bend, noun, m., bond, 26
benemnan, wk. vb. I, to designate, 217b
beobread, noun, n., honeycomb, 58
beod, noun, m., table, 23
beodan, st. vb. II, to offer, to command, 73, 98, 102, 122, 195, 218ap

beon, anom. vb., to be, not to be (with neg.) 1, 2, 3, 4, 5, *etc.*
beorcan, st. vb. III, to bark, 31, 211 [R]
beorg, noun, m., pile, 5
beorht, adj., bright, glorious, 50, 51, 57, 98, 180, 187, 230
beorhte, adv., gloriously, 21
beorhtlice, adv., clearly, 79 [R]
beorhtnes, noun, f., brightness, 50
gebeorscipe, noun, m., feast, 168
beorðor, noun, n., pregnancy, 39
beot, noun, n., peril, 57ap [R]
gebeot, noun, n., peril, 57 [R]
bera, noun, m., bear, 193
beran, st. vb. IV, to bring, carry around, 22, 23, 32, 49, 64, 80, 97, 98, 153, 168, 209, 230, 232
geberan, st. vb. IV, to bear a child, 6, 229
beren, adj., of barley, 138
berstan, st. vb. III, to burst, 56a, 136
geberstan, st. vb. III, to burst, 136ap [R]
besciran, st. vb. IV, to cut (hair), 3
beseon, st. vb. V, to look, 151ap
besma, noun, m., broom, 162
besmitan, st. vb. I, to pollute, 34
bestandan, st. vb. VI, to stand nearby, 186ap
bestingan, st. vb. III, to thrust, 30 [R]
beswican, st. vb. I, to deceive, 71, 103, 210
beswicennes, noun, f., deception, 38 [R]
gebetan, wk. vb. I, to correct, amend, 210
betæcan, wk. vb. I, to commit, dedicate, 217b
betera, compar. adj., better, 2, 160
betst, superl. adj., best, 12, 49
betweoh, prep., adv., between, 16, 46, 67, 89, 156, 196, 225
beweddian, wk. vb. II, to betroth, 90, 193, 227
bewindan, st. vb. III, to wrap, 38, 58
bewreon, st. vb. I, to cover, 16, 53, 145, 209
bewyrcan, wk. vb. I, to surround, to shut up, 79, 130
gebicgan, wk. vb. I, to buy, 73, 167
bidan, st. vb. I, to await, 190
biddan, st. vb. V, to ask, 22, 38, 58, 60, 67, 69, 71, 73, 94, 97, 112, 122, 127, 136, 166, 186, 199, 210ap, 211, 221, 223

325

GLOSSARY

gebiddan, st. vb. V, to pray, to beseech, 58, 59, 60, 67, 73, 79, 97, 108, 112, 122, 127, 148, 154, 208, 210, 211ap, 217, 227, 235

bifian, wk. vb. II, to tremble, 56a, 80

bindan, st. vb. III, to tie, 3, 193, 235

gebindan, st. vb. III, to tie, tie up, 7, 26, 57, 65, 89, 109, 130, 139, 149, 154, 162, 211, 228, 231, 235

binn, binne, noun, f., basket, 12 [R]

binnan, adv., prep., within, 3, 113

bisceop, noun, m., bishop, 18, 23, 31, 34, 37, 44, 47, 49, 60, 65, 66, 68, 70, 73, 75, 80, 81, 83, 88, 92, 97, 100, 107, 108, 115, 116, 126, 128, 131, 134, 138, 141, 142, 145, 148, 149, 162, 167, 170, 171, 174, 181, 183, 184, 186, 188, 192, 197, 203, 209, 210, 214, 223, 225, 231, 238

bisceopdom, noun, m., bishopric, 28, 138

bisceophired, noun, m., episcopal household, 128 [R]

bisceopsetl, noun, n., episcopal see, 92

blæc, blac, adj., black, dark, 31, 201

blæd, noun, m., blowing, blast, 56, 79ap

blanca, blance, noun, (white) horse, 20 [R]

bletsian, wk. vb. II, to bless, 49, 79

gebletsian, wk. vb. II, to bless, 67, 221

blind, adj., blind, 3, 15, 89, 92, 134, 151, 203, 209

blindnes, noun, f., blindness, 122

bliss, bliþs, noun, f., bliss, joy, 31, 78, 122, 226

blissian, wk. vb. II, to rejoice, 156

bliþe, adj., happy, 51, 57, 213

bliþe, adv., happily, 178

blod, noun, n., blood, 1, 5, 6, 23, 70, 78, 112, 122, 144, 157, 170, 191, 212, 225, 235

bloma, noun, m., mass or lump of metal, 26 [R]

blostm, noun, m., blossom, 56a, 217, 227

blostmian, wk. vb. II, to blossom, 56 [R]

blotan, st. vb. VII, to sacrifice, 217b [R]

blotmonaþ, noun, m., sacrifice month, 217b, 233a

boc, noun, f., book, 37, 42, 59, 67, 81, 92ap, 96, 136, 141, 157, 169, 170, 191, 201, 204, 207, 214, 215, 237

bodian, wk. vb. II, to announce, 74, 111, 133, 215

borg, noun, m., loan, 181

bosm, noun, m., bosom, 6, 219, 226

bræcseoc, adj., epileptic, 124 [R]

brædan, wk. vb. I, to cook, 40, 151 [R]

gebrædan, wk. vb. I, to cook, 58

brecan, st. vb. IV, to break, 1, 23, 130ap

bred, noun, n., plank, 88, 211

bregan, wk. vb. I, to terrorise, 2

bregdan, st. vb. III, to tie, 70, 235 [R]

brengan, wk. vb. I, to bring, 2, 12, 16, 21, 30, 73, 92, 133, 186, 198, 209, 227

gebrengan, wk. vb. I, to bring, 133

breost, noun, n., breast, 5, 6, 225

bringan, st. vb. III, to bring, 127, 185

brocu, noun, n., fragment, pieces, 148

broga, noun, m., terror, 122, 181

broþor, noun, m., brother, 3, 37, 40, 49, 51, 64ap, 80, 108, 123, 135, 136, 140, 162, 168, 184, 196, 198, 214, 221, 225, 233, 238

gebroþor, noun., m., brothers, 64, 106, 107, 123, 140, 184ap, 198, 225

brucan, st. vb. II, to use, 78, 108, 110, 143

brunbasu, adj., purple, 130

bryd, noun, f., bride, 3, 13, 38, 90, 110ap

brydbur, noun, m., bridal chamber, 13, 210ap, 227

brydguma, noun, m., bridegroom, husband, 90, 112, 193, 227

brydniht, noun, f., wedding-night, 13 [Hp]

gebrydian, wk. vb. II, to marry, 87, 110 [R]

brydrest, noun, f., marriage bed, 38 [R]

brydþing, noun, n., marriage ceremony, 12, 94, 232 [R]

brymm, noun, m., sea, 94b [R]

bryne, noun, m., fire, 68, 105

bufan, prep., above, 58

gebugan, st. vb. II, to move across, 41

bur, noun, m., bridal chamber, 210

burh, noun, f., fortress, town, city, 3, 23, 28, 36, 41, 53, 56a, 60, 65, 75, 94, 108, 115, 134, 137, 138, 142, 144, 161, 167, 170, 173,

GLOSSARY

176, 212, 234
burhgerefa, noun, m., reeve, 30, 112, 161 [R]
butan, adv., prep., conj., without, except, 1, 3, 4, 8, 11, 16, 26, 50, 100, 103, 110, 111, 130, 143, 160, 168, 196, 200, 210, 211, 226
bydel, noun, m., herald, 111
bylgan, wk. vb. I, to bellow, 22 [Hp]
byme, noun, f., trumpet, 80, 111
gebyrd, noun, f., birth, 2
byren, byrene, noun, f., female bear, 8, [R]
byrgan, wk. vb. I, to taste, 23, 176
byrgan, wk. vb. I, to bury, 83ap, 151, 198
gebyrgan, wk. vb. I, to bury, 27, 53ap, 102ap, 207ap
byrgen, noun, f., grave, tomb, 5, 16, 30, 53, 56a, 57, 58, 77ap (see also Appendix 2), 94, 110, 116, 133, 196, 225, 232
byrnan, st. vb. III, to burn, 3, 68, 76, 79, 89, 100ap, 126, 187, 193, 195, 200, 227
byrst, f., spine, 27 [R]
byrþen, noun, f., burden, bundle, 5
bysgung, noun, f., activity, 78
bysmorian, wk. vb. II, to rape, 30, 61, 76, 144, 157, 235
gebysmorian, wk. vb. II, to rape, 59
bytme, noun, f., keel, 125 [R]

calic, noun, m., chalice, 148
campian, wk. vb. II, to fight, 102, 157
candel, noun, f., candle, 122, 209
candelstæf, noun, m., candlestick, 114 [R]
carcern, noun, n., prison, 2, 3, 7, 8, 19, 26, 39, 70, 97, 220
carcernweard, noun, m., prison-guard, 26, 99 [R]
casere, noun, m., emperor, 2, 3, 10, 14, 23, 26, 27, 28, 31, 32, 34, 38, 42, 54, 59, 65, 67, 71, 72, 73, 83, 86, 87, 90, 97, 102, 106, 108, 113, 114, 116b, 123, 125, 126, 134, 139, 143, 147, 150, 151, 154, 155, 163, 166, 170, 182, 183, 184, 187, 189, 191, 195, 198, 202, 205, 207, 208, 213, 216, 219, 220, 222, 224, 228, 230, 233, 235
cæg, noun, f., key, 114, 228
cægbora, noun, m., key-bearer 164 [R]

cæppe, noun, f., hood, cloak, 109
ceald, adj., cold, 41, 83, 223
cealf, noun, n., calf, 40
ceapian, wk. vb. II, to buy, 138
ceapmann, noun, m., merchant, 195
ceaster, noun, f., fortified settlement, city, town, 1, 4, 5, 6, 8, 13, 18, 22, 31, 34, 38, 39, 41, 47, 54, 56, 61, 70, 72, 73, 74, 75, 83, 86, 89, 92, 97, 103, 107, 109, 111a, 116, 121, 122, 124, 126, 127, 128, 130, 132, 146, 148, 149, 153, 157, 160, 161, 170, 173, 184, 187, 188, 192, 193, 196, 197, 199, 200, 203, 207, 209, 210, 213, 215, 217, 223, 225, 231, 232, 233, 234, 235, 236, 238
ceasterwara, noun, m., inhabitant of a city, 156, 199, 209
ceastergewara, noun, m., inhabitant of a city, 116, 156ap, 231
ceasterweall, noun, m., city-wall, 160 [Hp]
celan, wk. vb. I, to cool down, 46
cempa, noun, m., warrior, soldier, 26, 41, 61, 72, 73, 83, 87, 109, 113, 125, 132, 150, 183, 186, 191, 213, 224
cennan, wk. vb. I, to bear (a child), 1, 180
ceosan, st. vb. II, to choose, 190
geceosan, st. vb. II, to choose, 74, 107, 133, 190ap
cifes, noun, f., concubine, 168
cigan, wk. vb. I, to call, to summon, 67ap, 73ap, 97, 127ap, 135
gecigan, wk. vb. I, to call, 21, 35, 67, 73, 83, 127, 135ap, 194, 238
cild, noun, n., child, 1, 4, 6, 12, 44, 102, 106, 127, 160, 180, 186, 215, 228
cildhad, noun, m., childhood, 122
cist, noun, f., box, reliquary, 56a, 222, 238
clæne, adj., clean, pure, chaste, 1, 13, 34, 47, 49, 80, 88, 110, 111, 176, 184, 207, 237
clænheort, adj., pure of heart, 209
clænlic, adj., virtuous, 227
clænnes, noun, f., chastity, purity, 13, 34, 47, 122, 232
geclænsian, wk. vb. II, to cleanse, 140, 211
clænsung, noun, f., cleansing, atonement, chastity, 9

GLOSSARY

clænsungdrenc, noun, m., purgative drink, 78 [R]
cleofa, noun, m., chamber, 124
clifian, wk. vb. II, to cling, to stick, 70
clipian, wk. vb. II, to call, 8, 31, 35, 38, 44, 111, 126, 154, 160, 211, 215ap, 236
clyppan, wk. vb. I, to embrace, 59
clywen, noun, n., ball, 1
cneow, noun, n., knee, 108
cniht, noun, m., boy, 3, 22, 23, 24, 34, 42, 51, 75, 86, 102, 136, 137, 140, 155, 157, 160, 166, 209, 232
cnihtcild, noun, n., boy, 6, 9 [R]
cnihthad, noun, m., boyhood, youth, 13, 51, 75, 121, 211, 232
gecnyssan, wk. vb. I, to beat, knock, 178
corn, noun, n., grain, 40, 221
coss, noun, m., kiss, 40
costian, wk. vb. II, to tempt, 22, 211
cræft, noun, m., skill, 180, 232
cræftig, adj., skilled, 207
cræftiga, noun, m., craftsman, 222
cræftlic, adj., skilled, 222 [R]
creda, noun, m., creed, 152
creopan, st. vb. II, to creep, 232
gecreopan, st. vb. II, to creep, 178 [Hp]
Crist, noun, m., Christ, 1, 2, 3, 4, 5, 6, 8, 9, 10, 12, 13, 14, 19, 23, 28, 29, 30, 31, 32, 35, 38, 39, 41, 42, 47, 54, 56a, 57, 59, 60, 62, 64, 65, 67, 70, 71, 72, 73, 74, 76, 77, 78, 79, 80, 83, 86, 87, 88, 90, 91, 93, 99, 101, 102, 103, 105, 106, 107, 108, 109, 110, 111, 112, 116, 118, 120, 122, 123, 124, 125, 126, 127, 128, 129, 130, 133, 134, 135, 137, 139, 140, 142, 147, 149, 150, 152, 153, 156, 157, 162, 168, 178, 182, 183ap, 185, 187, 188, 190, 192, 195, 198ap, 201, 203, 205, 207, 209, 210, 211, 215, 218, 219, 220, 221, 222, 223, 224, 225, 226, 227, 228, 229, 230, 231, 232, 233, 234, 235, 236, 238
Cristen, adj., Christian, 1, 23, 26, 31, 32, 34, 35, 38, 56, 70, 76, 78, 79, 83, 90, 97, 98ap, 102, 103, 105, 106, 113, 114, 122, 139, 146, 149, 151, 152, 173, 176, 187ap, 191, 195, 203, 218, 220ap, 222, 227, 228, 231, 234, 235, 236
cristenmann, noun, m., Christian man, 187, 222
cristenwif, noun, n., Christian woman, 39, 203, 220
cristnere, noun, m., exorcist, 98 [Hp]
cruma, noun, m., crumb, 23
crycc, noun, f., staff, 60
cu, noun, f., cow, 40
culfre, noun, f., dove, pigeon, 26, 28, 42, 88, 102, 217, 220, 234
cuman, st. vb. IV, to come, 2, 3, 4, 8, 12, 13, 16, 26, 28, 29, 31, 33, 35, 37, 38, 41, 44, 48, 56, 56a, 57, 60, 63, 65, 67, 68, 70, 73, 73b, 76, 77, 78, 79, 83, 87, 94, 97, 100, 102, 103, 106, 108, 109, 111, 112, 113, 115, 122, 127, 131, 133, 141, 145, 153, 155, 157, 161, 162, 173, 180, 186, 191, 195, 198, 199, 209, 210, 217, 220, 221, 223, 228, 232, 234, 235
cumliþe, adj., hospitable, 186ap
cunnan, pret. pres. vb., to know, 100, 117ap, 196
cuþlic, adj., certain, 115, 117 [R]
cuþlice, adv., certainly, 80
cwalu, noun, f., violent death, 108, 113, 160, 185
cwealm, noun, m., massacre, 6, 127ap
cweartern, noun, n., prison, 220ap
cwellan, wk. vb. I, to kill, 6, 26, 54, 76, 162, 173
cwellere, noun, m., killer, murderer, 35, 71, 83ap, 122, 184, 203, 209, 227
cwen, noun, f., queen, 71, 110, 156, 162, 190, 208
cweorn, noun, f., mill, 221
cweþan, st. vb. V, to speak, to say, 1, 3, 7, 8, 11, 17, 22, 23, 30, 31, 34, 35, 38, 44, 47, 51, 57, 60, 63, 65, 66, 67, 70, 71, 73, 76, 80, 83, 86, 87, 89, 90, 97, 100, 102, 108, 111a, 112, 115, 116, 117, 121, 122, 123ap, 127, 130, 131, 133, 136, 140, 142ap, 145, 146, 147, 149, 151, 154, 157, 160, 163, 166, 170, 181, 184, 186, 187, 192, 194, 198, 209, 210, 211, 223, 225, 227, 230, 233, 234, 235, 236

GLOSSARY

gecweþan, st. vb. V, to speak, to say, 80, 102ap, 123ap

cwic, adj., living, alive, 5, 8, 57, 72, 80, 87, 151, 162, 222

cwyld, noun, pestilence, 127

cyle, noun, m., cold, 21

cyme, noun, m., arrival, 57, 88

cynd, noun, n., child, 160ap [R]

gecynd, noun, f., manner, 1, 48, 131, 157

cynedom, noun, m., empire, kingship, 139b

cynelic, adj., royal, 70ap, 90, 146

cynerice, noun, n., kingdom, 162

cyneþrym, noun, m., royal majesty, 226 [R]

cyning, noun, m., king, 12, 21, 23, 32, 40, 41, 89, 90, 110, 111, 112, 140, 146, 156ap, 162, 167, 168, 171, 190, 215, 238

cynn, noun, n., kind, family, 5, 10, 14, 50, 52, 53, 65, 83, 86, 210, 232

cyrice, noun, f., church, 2, 4, 17, 20, 23, 24, 25, 33, 34, 51, 56, 56a, 69, 70, 74, 75, 78, 79, 82, 84, 86, 107, 110, 114, 116, 117, 122, 127, 133, 134, 136, 143, 145, 148, 151, 152, 161, 162, 166, 173, 178, 181, 196, 199, 200, 203, 209, 210, 218, 227, 228, 231, 235

cyrran, wk. vb. I, to turn, 89, 116, 196, 233b

gecyrran, wk. vb. I, to turn, 12, 41, 56a, 60, 70, 91, 98, 106, 123ap, 124ap, 134, 140ap, 173, 198, 210, 233, 236

cyssan, wk. vb. I, to kiss, 59, 80, 133, 209

gecyssan, wk. vb. I, to kiss, 98, 106, 134, 223

cyte, noun, f., cell, 160, 210

cyþan, wk. vb. I, to tell, 4, 111a

gecyþan, wk. vb. I, to reveal, 4, 12, 21, 57, 60, 67, 68, 77, 160, 181

dæd, noun, f., deed, 9, 68, 100, 116, 139, 141, 214, 227

dædbot, noun, f., penance, 69

dæg, noun, m., day, 1, 2, 3, 4, 5, 6, 7, 8a, 9, 10, 11, 12, 13, 14, 15, 16, 17, 18, 19, 20, 21, 22, 23, 24, 25, 26, 27, 28, 29, 30, 31, 32, 33, 34, 35, 36a, 36b, 37, 38, 39, 40, 41, 42, 43, 44, 45, 46, 47, 48, 49, 50, 51, 52, 53, 54, 55, 56, 56a, 57, 58, 58a, 58b, 59, 60, 61, 62, 63, 64, 65, 66, 67, 68, 69, 70, 71, 72, 73, 73a, 73b, 74, 75, 76, 77, 78, 79, 80, 81, 82, 83, 83a, 84, 85, 86, 87, 88, 89, 90, 91, 92, 93, 94, 94a, 94b, 95, 97, 98, 99, 100, 101, 102, 103, 104, 105, 106, 107, 108, 109, 110, 111, 111a, 112, 113, 114, 115, 116, 116a, 116b, 117, 118, 119, 120, 121, 122, 123, 124, 125, 126, 127, 128, 129, 130, 131, 132, 133, 134, 135, 136, 137, 138, 139, 139a, 139b, 140, 141, 142, 143, 144, 145, 146, 147, 148, 149, 150, 151, 152, 153, 154, 155, 156, 157, 158, 159, 160, 161, 162, 163, 164, 165, 166, 167, 168, 169, 170, 171, 171a, 171b, 172, 173, 174, 176, 177, 178, 179, 180, 181, 182, 183, 184, 185, 186, 187, 188, 189, 190, 191, 192, 193, 194, 195, 196, 197, 198, 199, 200, 200a, 200b, 201, 202, 203, 204, 205, 206, 207, 208, 209, 210, 211, 212, 213, 214, 215, 216, 217, 217a, 217b, 218, 219, 220, 221, 221a, 222, 223, 224, 225, 226, 227, 228, 229, 230, 231, 232, 233, 233a, 233b, 234, 235, 236, 237, 238

dæghwamlice, adv., daily, 79

dægred, noun, n., dawn, daybreak, 221a

dæl, noun, m., part, 4, 33, 50, 79, 80, 97, 133, 147, 196, 207

gedælan, wk. vb. I, to divide, 151

dead, adj., dead, 4, 5, 8, 18, 30, 41, 53, 56a, 57, 58, 70, 77, 80, 83, 89, 97, 111a, 166, 208, 219, 225, 229, 235

deadlic, adj., mortal, 12, 50, 114, 210

deaf, adj., deaf, 138ap, 178, 203

deaþ, noun, m., death, 3, 5, 12, 13, 18, 53, 57, 58, 64, 70, 74, 76, 86, 97, 122, 140, 160, 161, 166, 168, 181, 185, 186, 190, 211, 213, 223, 235

deaw, noun, m., dew, 52

delfan, st. vb. III, to dig, 145

dema, noun, m., judge, magistrate, 23, 54, 72, 98, 99, 109, 111, 121, 124, 137, 149, 152, 153, 157, 170, 236

deman, wk. vb. I, to judge, 186

gedeman, wk. vb. I, to judge, 90, 235

deofol, noun, n., devil, 22, 30, 31, 34, 38, 39, 127, 133, 139, 162, 210, 211, 233, 236, 238

329

deofolgyld, noun, n., pagan religion, idolatry, 3, 20, 70, 72, 87, 97, 106, 113, 147, 152, 157, 160, 162, 166ap, 171b, 176, 182, 183, 184, 203, 212, 216, 217b, 218, 225, 231, 235, 236, 238

deofolseoc, adj., possessed by devils, 3, 124

deofolseocnes, noun, f., possession, 102, 122

deop, adj., deep, 41, 57, 72, 176, 203

deor, noun, n., animal, beast, 8, 27, 31, 65, 83, 97ap, 139, 157ap, 193

derian, wk. vb. I, to hurt, to harm, 83, 87ap

gederian, wk. vb. I, to hurt, to harm, 234

diacon, noun, m., deacon, 4, 31, 101, 103, 143, 147, 154, 188, 192, 195, 203, 219, 225

digol, adj., secret, 80

digollice, adv., secretly, 136, 198

dimm, adj., dark, 53

disc, noun, m., dish, 168

discipul, noun, m., disciple, 101

dohtor, noun, f., daughter, 3, 43, 74, 94, 99, 110, 168, 180, 216

dom, noun, m., judgement, 153, 184, 210

domern, noun, n., court chamber, law-court, 153

domesdæg, noun, m., doomsday, 16, 50, 117, 140, 234

don, anom. vb., to do, 1, 3, 4, 7, 11, 15, 21, 30, 50, 57, 66, 67, 70, 73ap, 79, 80, 88, 94, 97, 98, 100, 103, 109, 110, 112, 115, 124, 125ap, 127, 136, 137, 140, 141, 145, 149, 151, 152, 160, 171, 178, 180, 181, 182, 186, 187, 189, 198, 203, 209, 211, 215, 222, 232, 234, 235

gedon, anom. vb., to give, to make, 81, 86, 89, 100, 116, 140, 215, 225, 228

draca, noun, m., dragon, 97, 190

dragan, st. vb. VI, to drag, 70, 154

drædan, st. vb. VII, to dread, 211

dreamcræft, noun, m., art of music, 232 [R]

gedrefed, past part. of gedrefan, disturbed, 90

drencan, wk. vb. I, to drown

drifan, st. vb. I, to drive, 57

drincan, st. vb. III, to drink, 5, 16, 49, 51, 78, 101, 108, 133, 136, 168, 186

dropa, noun, m., drop, 52, 56a

drugung, noun, f., drought, 145 [R]

dry, noun, m., magician, sorcerer, 32, 190, 197

drycræft, noun, m., magic, sorcery, 197, 211, 222

drygan, wk. vb. I, to dry, 133, 150

dryge, adj., dry, 136, 137, 225, 228

dryhten, noun, m., lord, 3, 11, 12, 38, 50, 51, 57, 58, 67, 71, 73, 79, 80, 102, 108, 111a, 115, 122, 127, 133, 148, 153, 154, 182, 198, 221, 223, 226, 227, 228, 233

dryicge, noun, f., witch, sorceress, 30 [R]

drync, noun, m., drink, 22, 121

duguþ, noun, f., citizens, senate, 139, 139b, 235

dumb, adj., dumb, mute, 81, 118, 138, 194, 198

dumbnes, noun, f., dumbness, speechlessness, 122 [R]

dun, noun, f., hill, 65, 79, 88, 109, 136, 142, 210

durran, pret. pres. vb., to dare, 73, 115

duru, noun, f., door, gate, entrance, 8, 19, 34, 63, 82, 116, 126, 184, 187ap, 221

duruweard, noun, m., gatekeeper, 90

dust, noun, n., dust, 16, 79

dwæscan, wk. vb. I, to extinguish, 68 [R]

gedwinan, st. vb. I, to dwindle, 197 [R]

gedwolmann, noun, m., heretic, 238

dypan, wk. vb. I, to dip, 130

dyrne, adj., secret, 22, 186

dyrwurþe, adj., precious, 38, 102, 133, 181, 210, 236

dysig, adj., foolish, 7

dysignes, noun, f., foolishness, 33

ea, noun, f., river, 80ap, 146, 203, 214, 217

eac, adv., prep., also, moreover, 12, 21, 22, 44, 49, 57, 73b, 80ap, 89ap, 114, 220, 226

eacen, adj., pregnant, 56

geeacnian, wk. vb. II, to conceive, become pregnant, 9

geeacnung, noun, f., conception, 194

eadig, adj., blessed, happy, 59, 80, 87, 98, 103, 114, 121, 131, 178

eadignes, noun, f., happiness, 66, 106

330

GLOSSARY

eagduru, noun, f., window, 22, 26, 75 [R]
eage, noun, n., eye, 15, 71, 73, 79, 97, 109, 117, 131, 151, 162, 181, 185, 210, 221, 235
eagþyrel, noun, n., window, 75ap, 116
eahta, numeral, eight, 38, 72, 94a, 134, 137, 139a, 166, 209, 215, 231, 233a
eahtateoþa, numeral, eighteenth, 24, 65, 89, 106, 129, 158
eahtatyne, numeral eighteenth, 116a
eahteoþa, numeral, eighth, 8a, 9, 82, 119, 139b, 149, 180, 203, 207, 210, 222
eala, interj., oh, 154, 157, 187
ealand, noun, n., island, 17, 66, 89, 100, 101
eald, adj., old, parent (used as a noun), 6, 9, 13, 23, 30, 78, 85, 88, 95, 101, 104, 116b, 120, 135, 136, 140, 144, 159, 162, 165, 171b, 172, 177, 179, 180, 186, 206, 211, 215, 217b, 225, 232
ealdian, wk. vb. II, to grow old, 221
ealdor, noun, m., leader, 94, 191ap
ealdordom, noun, m., authority, power, 230
ealdormann, noun, m., chief, ruler, 20, 38, 41, 71, 89, 109, 110, 113, 125, 139, 144, 160, 184, 187, 191, 219, 233, 235, 238
eall, adj., all, 1, 3, 5, 6, 8, 12, 23, 24, 31, 35, 39, 40, 41, 49, 50, 52, 53, 56a, 57, 59, 67, 68, 69, 71, 76, 78, 79, 84, 88, 92, 94, 97, 98, 100, 108, 111, 116, 121, 122, 127, 128, 131, 133, 135, 136, 139, 140, 141, 151, 154, 156, 162, 163, 166, 168, 170, 181, 190, 191, 197, 209, 210, 211, 217, 218, 221, 222, 226, 227, 231, 232, 235
eall, adv., completely, 21, 59, 65, 75, 116, 140, 182, 238
eallmihtig, ælmihtig, adj., almighty, 168
eallswa, adv., like, also, likewise, 22
ear, noun, n., ear (of grain), 1
earc, noun, f., ark, chest, 228 [R]
eardian, wk. vb. II, to dwell, 97, 108ap, 173, 220
eardung, noun, f., dwelling, 97
eare, ear, noun, n., ear, 56
earfoþcyrre, adj., difficult to convert to Christianity, 120 [Hp]
earm, adj., miserable, 151

earmlic, adj., miserable, 181
earmlice, adv., miserably, 140
earn, noun, m., eagle, 102
geearnian, wk. vb. II, to earn, 63, 100
geearnung, noun, f., desert, merit, 21
eastan, adv., from the east, 1, 51, 53, 58, 201
eastdæl, noun, m., east, 12, 136, 191, 195, 220, 238
easterdæg, noun, m., Easter-day, 70, 166
easteweard, adj., lying towards the east, 228
eastormonaþ, noun, m., Easter-month, 58b, 73a [R]
eastre, noun, f., Easter, 14, 60, 78, 80, 110
eaþmod, adj., humble, 40, 69ap, 221
eaþmodlic, adj., humble, 69
ece, adj., eternal, 12, 38, 56a, 65, 66, 70, 79, 89, 97, 106, 138, 154, 160ap, 193, 195
ecnes, noun, f., eternity, 80ap, 127
edniwian, wk. vb. II, to renew, 50
geedniwian, wk. vb. II, to renew, 138
efenbliþe, adj., equally joyful, 30 [Hp]
efeneald, adj., of the same age, 122 [R]
efenece, adj., co-eternal, 130
efengemæcca, noun, m., an equal, 229 [R]
efenmedeme, adj., equally worth, 140 [Hp]
efestan, wk. vb. I, to hasten, 126
efne, adv., equally, just, 22, 54, 168, 234
eft, adv., again, later, 2, 3, 4, 14, 17, 21, 26, 28, 39, 50, 51, 56a, 57, 63, 65, 80, 87, 88, 89, 97, 106, 110, 112, 115, 116, 130, 131, 133, 138, 140, 148, 149, 157, 163, 180, 181, 196, 197, 207, 209, 223, 224, 228, 230, 234, 238
eftsona, adv., straightaway, 131ap, 221ap
ege, noun, m., fear, 139
egesa, noun, m., terror, 121, 199, 220
egesgrima, noun, m., ghost, 59 [R]
egeslic, adj., terrible, 22, 76, 238
egeslice, adv., terribly, 223
eglan, both wk. vb. I and wk. vb. II forms occur in the *Old English Martyrology*, to torment, 101, 102ap, 193ap
geeglan, both wk. vb. I and wk. vb. II forms occur in the *Old English Martyrology*, to torment, 102, 193, 234 [R]

ehtan, wk. vb. I, to persecute, 35, 234
ehtere, noun, m., persecutor, 35, 39
ele, noun, m., oil, 56a, 205
elles, adv., else, 122, 146
eln, noun, f., ell, 97
elreord, adj., foreign, 238 [R]
elreordig, adj., foreign, 135 [R]
elþeodiglic, adj., foreign, 117 [Hp]
elþeodignes, noun, f., exile, travel, 207
elþeodig, adj., foreign, 112, 140, 151
ende, noun, m., end, 16, 22, 60, 116, 127, 142, 160, 198, 226
endebyrdnes, noun, f., order, 50, 141
endedæg, noun, m., last day of one's life, 196
endian, wk. vb. II, to end, 146, 192
geendian, wk. vb. II, to end, 20, 21, 22, 36a, 73, 73a, 79, 94, 94a, 112, 116a, 139, 139a, 144, 146ap, 167, 171a, 192ap, 200a, 217a, 232, 233a
endleofan, numeral, eleven, 14, 28, 80, 130
endlyfta, numeral, eleventh, 63, 152, 182, 204, 217b, 223
geendung, noun, f., conclusion, 114
engel, noun, m., angel, 1, 9, 13, 16, 19, 21, 22, 30, 37, 49, 56, 61, 63, 64, 65, 68, 70, 79, 80, 97, 98, 102, 111, 122, 130, 133, 144, 150, 156, 157, 162, 163, 171, 180, 194, 214, 217, 226, 227, 238
engellic, adj., angelic, 97
eofor, noun, m., wild boar, 73
eorþcyning, noun, m., earthly king, 71 [R]
eorþe, noun, f., earth, 1, 3, 4, 8, 22, 23, 26, 30, 46, 48, 52, 56a, 57, 60, 67, 70, 72, 73, 77, 79, 80, 107, 110, 111a, 113, 122, 127, 130, 133, 137, 140, 141, 145, 146, 149, 162, 178, 181, 191, 209, 210, 228, 231, 235, 238
eorþlic, adj., earthly, 2, 40, 230
eorþgemet, noun, n., geometry, 232 [R]
eowan, wk. vb. I, to show, 58ap, 115, 140ap
geeowan, wk. vb. I, to show, 142
eowde, noun, n., flock, herd, 184, 187
eowu, noun, f., ewe, 40 [R]
erian, wk. vb. I, to plough, 1 [R]
etan, st. vb. V, to eat, 16, 70, 73, 87, 108, 133, 136, 140, 151, 186

eþel, noun, m., home, homeland, 17
eþian, wk. vb. II, to breathe, 5, 42, 73

facenfull, adj., deceitful, 152
faran, st. vb. VI, to go, 162, 195ap
gefaran, st. vb. VI, to die, 207
faþu, noun, f., aunt, 11 [R]
fæc, noun, n., period, 227, 228
fæder, noun, m., father, 1, 3, 23, 42, 44, 80, 86, 102, 106, 107, 111, 122, 130, 131, 135, 136, 140, 166, 180, 186, 187, 194, 209, 211, 226, 232
fædera, noun, m., paternal uncle, 209
fæger, adj., beautiful, 2, 21, 47, 63, 97, 112, 139, 144, 151, 187, 231, 234
fægere, adv., beautifully, 64
fægernes, noun, f., beauty, 2, 13, 232
fægnian, wk. vb. II, to rejoice, 98ap, 111, 229
fæmne, noun, f., virgin, woman, 1, 2, 3, 8, 11, 13, 15, 24, 30, 33, 47, 59, 61, 62, 74, 90, 94, 110, 111, 112, 122, 124, 130, 156, 169, 180, 182, 187, 189, 190, 193, 197, 204, 211, 216, 226, 227, 234, 235
færdeaþ, noun, m., sudden death, 227 [R]
færinga, færunga, adv., suddenly, 35, 66, 88, 109, 178
fæstan, wk. vb. I, to fast, 14, 22, 78, 80ap, 127
gefæstan, wk. vb. I, to fast, 78ap (see also Appendix 2)
fæsten, noun, n., fast, 78, 112, 199, 205
fæt, noun, n., vessel, 12, 51
feallan, st. vb. VII, to fall, 1, 23, 65, 73, 146, 181, 182, 186
gefeallan, st. vb. VII, to fall, 140, 147, 182ap
gefea, noun, m., joy, 66, 122, 157, 195
fearr, noun, m., bull, ox, 22, 82, 193, 231
feawa, adj., few, 184, 192
feax, noun, n., hair, 3, 59, 162, 193
fedan, wk. vb. I, to feed, 16, 48, 122
fela, quasi-noun, adj., adv., much, many, 7, 157, 171, 180
gefelan, wk. vb. I, to notice, 49
feld, noun, m., field, 52, 60, 160
fenn, noun, n., marsh, 52
feogan, wk. vb. II, to hate, 173

GLOSSARY

feoh, noun, n., money, 73, 103, 167, 181
gefeoht, noun, n., fighting, war, 60, 112, 191
feohtan, st. vb. III, to fight, 39
gefeon, st. vb. V, to rejoice, 38, 88, 98, 156, 232
feond, noun, m., enemy, 51, 57, 67, 78, 90, 112, 199, 234
feorh, noun, n., life, spirit, soul, 7, 124
feorr, adv., far, 50, 53, 78, 98, 101, 114, 173
feorþa, numeral, fourth, 6, 38, 50, 58b, 118, 176
feower, numeral, four, 6, 12, 34, 40, 48, 55, 65, 68, 87, 91, 111, 136, 146, 149ap, 153, 156, 194, 196, 212, 213, 222, 230
feowerteoþa, numeral, fourteenth, 19, 64, 87, 126, 183, 205, 237
feowertig, numeral, forty, 6, 41, 78, 80, 136, 148, 222
feowertyne, numeral, fourteen, 36a, 73a, 171a, 196, 217a
gefera, noun, m., companion, 59ap, 207, 211
feran, wk. vb. I, to go, travel, 2, 17, 36, 38, 51, 60, 73, 90, 94, 101, 112, 116, 122, 127, 156, 162ap, 178, 193, 196, 201, 228, 234
ferian, wk. vb. I, to carry, to transport, 31, 135ap
geferian, wk. vb. I, to carry, to transport, 135ap
fersc, adj., fresh, 48, 52
geferscipe, noun, m., fellowship, 196
festerbearn, noun, n., foster-child, 42 [Hp]
festerfæder, noun, m., foster-father, 42, 102 [R]
festermodor, noun, f., foster-mother, 122 [R]
fetian, wk. vb. II, to fetch, 37
gefetian, wk. vb. II, to fetch, 65
feþeleas, adj., lame, 178 [R]
feþer, noun, f., feather, wing, 31, 64, 162, 227
fif, numeral, five, 1, 12, 17, 22, 35, 56, 69, 91, 112, 135, 136, 148, 162, 183, 196, 217, 222, 232
fifta, numeral, fifth, 11, 52, 60, 73b, 76, 79, 118ap, 146, 177
fifteoþa, numeral, fifteenth, 88, 102, 127, 156, 185, 206, 225
fiftig, numeral, fifty, 52, 110, 166, 217
fiftigoþa, numeral, fiftieth, 110ap
fiftyne, numeral, fifteen, 3, 86, 122
findan, st. vb. III, to find, 82, 173, 230
firenlust, noun, m., sin, extravagance, 112, 144
fisc, noun, m., fish, 12, 48, 52, 58
fiscere, noun, m., fisherman, 135
fiscian, wk. vb. II, to fish, 178
flæsc, noun, n., flesh, 57, 70, 87, 108, 140, 225
flæsccwellnes, noun, n., execution, 184ap [Hp]
fleam, noun, m., flight, 60
fleogan, st. vb. II, to fly, 17, 26, 28, 52, 70, 102, 123, 162, 217, 220, 234 [see also **fleon**]
gefleogan, st. vb. II, to fly [R], 142
fleon, st. vb. II, to flee, 59, 102ap [see also **fleogan**]
fleotan, st. vb. II, to float, to swim, 3, 52, 125
flod, noun, both m. and n. forms occur in the *Old English Martyrology*, flood, river, 3, 48, 52, 73, 102, 125, 157, 191, 210, 212, 222
flor, noun, f., floor, 58, 79
flowan, st. vb. VII, to flow, 1, 56a, 73, 122, 144, 173, 210, 228
flyht, noun, m., flight, 64, 68, 142
flyman, wk. vb. I, to put to flight, 190
geflyman, wk. vb. I, put to flight, 51
fodder, noun, n., case, container, bag, 153 [R]
folc, noun, n., people, 1, 9, 33, 34, 57, 69, 70, 78, 88, 97, 98, 116, 134, 140, 153, 161, 162, 218, 228
fon, st. vb. VII, to receive, 190, 230
gefon, st. vb. VII, to seize, 127
for, prep., conj., for, before, 2, 3, 6, 10, 13, 17, 23, 26, 28, 29, 30, 38, 39, 40, 51, 54, 57, 58, 59, 62, 64, 65, 71, 78, 86, 87, 89, 90, 93, 98, 99, 102, 103, 105, 106, 108, 109, 112, 114, 115, 118, 120, 121, 122, 123, 124, 125, 126, 127, 128, 129, 131, 134, 135, 136, 138, 139, 140, 148, 149, 150, 157, 161, 162, 166, 168, 173, 183ap, 186, 187, 188, 189, 192, 195, 196, 197, 198, 201, 203, 205, 209, 211, 219, 220, 222, 223, 224, 225, 227, 229, 231, 234, 236

333

GLOSSARY

foran, forn, adv., prep., in front, before, 14, 78, 110, 225
forbærnan, wk. vb. I, to burn up, 59, 67, 70, 170, 187
forbeodan, st. vb. II, to forbid, 90, 140, 198
forbrecan, st. vb. IV, to break up, 83
forbregdan, st. vb. III, to drag someone, 30, 233 [R]
forbyrnan, st. vb. III, to burn up, 100, 190
forceorfan, st. vb. III, to cut up, 103
forcyrran, wk. vb. I, to turn around, 198
fordeman, wk. vb. I, to condemn, 73
forealdian, wk. vb. II, to age, 53
foregangan, st. vb. VII, to precede, 111 [R]
foregenga, noun, m., predecessor, 146
foresecgan, wk. vb. III, to predict, 110
foretacnian, wk. vb. II, to prefigure, 75 [R]
foreweard, adj., early, 41 [R]
forgyfan, st. vb. V, to forgive, 69, 78, 80, 110ap, 122, 127, 140
forgyfenes, noun, f., forgiveness, 221
forhtian, wk. vb. II, to fear, to be afraid, 186
forhtlic, adj., inspiring fear, 79 [R]
forhwon, adv., conj., why, 66, 71, 168, 198, 211
forlætan, st. vb. VII, to let, abandon, 2, 17, 31, 38, 39, 40, 51, 71, 83, 89ap, 90ap, 102, 106, 124, 133, 135, 136, 137, 152, 154, 168, 176, 195, 197, 210, 229, 230, 232, 235, 236
forlegiswif, noun, n., prostitute, 149, 235 [R]
forleosan, st. vb. II, to destroy, 234
forma, fyrmest, adj., numeral, first, 1, 3, 13
forod, adj., broken, 178
forsendan, wk. vb. I, to send away, 228 [R]
forsewenlic, adj., despicable, 168
forslean, st. vb. VI, to strike, to break, 195, 220
forstandan, st. vb. VI, to stop, to prevent, 34
forstelan, st. vb. IV, to steal, 203
forswelgan, st. vb. III, to swallow, 26, 31, 83
forþ, adv., forwards, further, 26, 57, 78, 111, 111a, 124, 176ap, 196, 235
forþæm, forþon, forþy, adv., conj., because, therefore, 4, 5, 6, 9, 23, 30, 35, 38, 39, 48, 51, 57, 70, 72, 73b, 78, 88, 94b, 100, 101, 108, 110, 111, 111a, 114, 115, 116b, 117, 124, 130, 131, 132, 133, 136, 137, 139, 139b, 149, 150, 151, 153, 160, 162, 163, 164, 167, 168, 171b, 173, 178, 182, 186, 190, 193, 198, 209, 210, 212, 213, 217b, 227, 231, 233, 233b, 238
forþfaran, st. vb. VI, to go forth, to depart, 171ap, 176ap, 181ap, 232
forþferan, wk. vb. I, to go by, to pass, to depart, 110, 115, 116, 196, 210, 211
forþfor, noun, f., death, 204
forþgeleoran, wk. vb. I, to go away, to die, 79 [R]
forþgewitan, st. vb. I, to depart, 79ap
forþweard, adj., dead, 176
forweorþan, st. vb. III, to perish, die, 6, 90, 113
forwyrd, noun, f., death, 154
fostorfæder, noun, m., fosterfather, 102ap
fostormodor, noun, f., fostermother, 122ap, 166
fot, noun, m., foot, 53, 57, 58, 65, 79, 83, 109, 133, 136, 140, 162, 182, 186, 190, 221, 225, 230, 231, 235
fotadl, noun, f., footdisease, 120
fotlæst, noun, m., footprint, 79, 235
fotswæþ, noun, n., footprint, 79
fox, noun, m., fox, 211
fram, prep., adv., from, away, 1, 3, 9, 12, 13, 23, 30, 31, 33, 39, 51, 55, 56a, 59, 60, 67, 73, 74, 76, 78, 86, 87, 89, 102, 108, 110, 112, 115, 116, 117, 122, 123, 124, 126ap, 127, 140, 145, 149, 157, 161, 185, 190, 198, 220, 228, 230, 233, 234
frætwe, frætwa, noun, f., treasure, 17
gefrætwian, wk. vb. II, to adorn, 17, 64, 98, 232
frecennes, noun, f., danger, 67, 100
frecne, adj., dangerous, 60
fremde, adj., foreign, 149
fremman, wk. vb. I, to make, to perform, 226
gefremman, wk. vb. I, to perform, to make, 73, 135, 182
freo, frig, adj., free, 17
freogan, wk. vb. II, to touch gently, 234

GLOSSARY

gefreogan, wk. vb. II, to free, liberate, 12, 42, 116, 122, 154, 166

fretan, st. vb. V, to eat, 225

fricca, noun, m., herald, 111ap [R]

frigeniht, noun, f., night before Friday, Thursday night, 145 [R]

frignan, st. vb. III, to ask, 66, 100, 112, 136

gefriþian, wk. vb. II, to save, 122

frofor, noun, f., consolation, 101

fruma, noun, m., beginning, fruman 1, 8a, 22, 83a, 134, 221a

fugel, noun, m., bird, 4, 31, 52, 68, 225

fugelcynn, noun, n., family of birds, 52ap

ful, adj., foul, 22, 162, 178

full, adj., full, 12, 27, 78, 133

full, noun, n., cup, 178

fullfremed, adj., perfect, 152, 180

fullfremednes, noun, f., perfection, 138

fullian, fullwian, wk. vb. II, to baptise, 23, 75, 130, 186

gefullian, gefullwian, wk. vb. II, to baptise, to cleanse, 3, 6, 13, 23, 86, 88, 186, 190, 208ap, 210, 227

fulluht, fulwiht, noun, n. or f., baptism, 3, 9, 11, 12, 20, 23, 35, 42, 70, 92, 97, 98, 100, 110, 118, 120, 134, 148, 149, 150, 152, 154, 160, 162, 163, 166, 182, 186, 195, 208, 210, 213, 222, 227, 232

fultum, noun, m., help, 127, 191, 199, 223

fultuman, fultumian, wk. vb. I, to help, 90

gefultuman, gefultumian, wk. vb. II, to help, 38, 127

fullwere, noun, m., baptist, 12, 111 [R]

fulwa, noun, m., fuller, 30 [Hp]

fulwihtere, noun, m., baptist, 111ap, 168, 194

furþum, adv., even, 140

fylgan, wk. vb. I, to obtain, 67ap

gefylgan, wk. vb. I, to obtain, to perform, 51, 67

gefyllan, wk. vb. I, to fill, to perform, to fulfil, 39, 71, 72, 75, 88, 181

fylleþflod, noun, m., spring tide, 48 [R]

fyr, noun, n., fire, 23, 53, 59, 67, 76, 88, 89, 100, 105, 144, 149, 154, 193, 195, 197, 238

fyren, adj., fiery, 1, 26, 154, 162, 199, 234

fyrhtu, noun, f., dread, fear, 220

fyrst, noun, m., period of time, 154

fyst, noun, f., fist, 144

gafol, noun, n., tribute, 190 [R]

gagolisc, geaglisc, geglesc, adj., lascivious, 168 [R]

gan, anom. vb., to go, walk, 2, 3, 22, 26, 40, 41, 56a, 59, 66, 70, 71, 75, 79, 97, 98, 106, 109, 110, 111, 112, 115, 120, 130, 136, 137, 148, 153, 162, 173, 181, 186, 187, 211, 225, 227, 228, 232, 234, 235, 238

gang, noun, m., course, ability to walk, 203, 232

gangan, st. vb. VII, to go, walk, 8, 34, 50, 51, 64, 78, 83a, 111, 115, 116, 120, 130, 133, 140, 145, 178, 181, 209, 211, 221a, 232, 233b, 234

garsecg, noun, m., ocean, 162

gast, gæst, noun, m., breath, spirit, ghost, 2, 3, 11, 17, 21, 22, 23, 26, 27, 28, 30, 31, 33, 38, 40, 41, 44, 56a, 60, 61, 65, 67, 68, 70, 72, 80, 88, 94, 97, 102, 103, 107, 110, 121, 123, 126, 127, 130, 133, 135, 140, 142, 145, 149, 151, 154, 157, 176, 181, 193, 195, 198, 204, 208, 211, 226, 227, 229, 232, 233, 235

gastlic, gæstlic, adj., spiritual, pious, 17, 74, 75, 78, 80, 92

ge, conj., and, **ge ... ge**, both ... and, 17, 56a, 66, 70, 78, 114, 128, 141, 146, 171, 181, 196, 200, 232

gear, noun, n., year, 1, 3, 4, 6, 8a, 10, 12, 14, 16, 17, 22, 28, 30, 34, 36b, 38, 40, 44, 48, 53, 56a, 58b, 63, 66, 67, 69, 73b, 79, 80, 86, 87, 91, 94b, 97, 102, 107, 110, 112, 115, 116b, 122, 127, 130, 133, 134, 136, 138, 139b, 146, 156, 157ap, 160, 171b, 180, 183, 196, 200b, 205, 207, 209ap, 210, 211, 217, 217b, 218, 226, 228, 233b, 234

gearwian, wk. vb. II, to prepare, 117ap, 228

gegearwian, wk. vb. II, to prepare, 117, 126, 228

geat, noun, n., gate, 136, 157, 199

geo, adv., long ago, 73b

geoguþ, noun, f., youth, 13, 47, 160, 227, 232

335

geohhol, Gehhol, Geol, noun, n., Christmas, 8a, 80, 233b [R]

geohholdæg, noun, m., Christmas day, 1, 8a, 218 [R]

geond, prep., adv., 22, 56a, 57, 101, 114, 126

geong, adj., young, 38, 76, 78, 87, 140, 144, 155, 211, 225

geonglic, adj., youthful, 168ap [R]

georn, adj., eager for, 210

geornlice, adv., eagerly, 173

gif, conj., if, 9, 21, 41, 53, 56a, 67, 73, 78, 79, 90, 117, 122, 127, 140, 152, 166, 190, 209, 210, 227, 229, 230, 235

gimm, noun, m., gem, 5, 98, 210, 232, 236

glæs, noun, n., glass, 160

glæsen, adj., made of glass, 148

glæsfæt, noun, n., glass, 133 [R]

gleaw, adj., wise, 232

glengan, wk. vb. I, to adorn, 210

geglengan, wk. vb. I, to adorn, 22, 232

glidan, st. vb. I, to glide, 22

glisnian, wk. vb. II, to glitter, 227 [R]

glitenian, wk. vb. II, to glitter, 226

gneaþ, adj., austere, 138 [R]

gnornian, wk. vb. II, to mourn, 40

gnyþnes, noun, f., scarcity, 73 [R]

god, adj., good, 1, 88, 100, 115, 121, 127, 211ap, 222ap

God, noun, god, 1, 2, 3, 4, 8, 9, 12, 13, 17, 19, 21, 23, 26, 30, 31, 32, 34, 37, 38, 39, 40, 41, 42, 46, 48, 50, 51, 52, 53, 55, 56, 56a, 59, 61, 63, 64, 65, 68ap, 69, 70, 71, 72ap, 73, 74, 75, 76, 78, 79, 80, 88, 89, 90, 94, 97, 98, 99, 100, 101, 102, 103, 107, 108, 109, 110, 111, 112, 114, 115, 116, 117, 120, 121, 122, 124, 127, 130, 132, 133, 134, 135, 136, 138, 139, 140, 144, 145, 146, 149, 150, 151, 152, 153, 154, 155, 156, 157, 160, 161, 162, 163, 166, 168, 170, 173, 176, 177, 180, 181, 184, 186, 189, 190, 193, 194, 195, 198, 199, 201, 208, 209, 210, 211, 217, 218, 220, 222, 225, 226, 227, 229, 230, 232, 233, 234, 235, 236, 238

godcund, adj., spiritual, 17, 36, 42, 47, 57, 119, 121, 163, 170, 178, 221, 230, 232

Godfæder, noun, m., God the Father, 156

godgyld, noun, n., image of a pagan god, idol, 121, 130, 166 [R]

godmodor, noun, f., godmother, 210 [R]

godspell, noun, n., gospel, 58, 70, 74, 153, 178, 190, 192, 210

godspellere, noun, m., evangelist, 5, 70, 135, 153, 207

godsunu, noun, m., godson, 70 [R]

godþrymm, noun, m., divine majesty, 4, 153ap [R]

godwebb, noun, n., expensive fabric, 38

godwræc, godwrece, adj., exiled from God, impious, 70 [R]

gold, noun, n., gold, 5, 12, 22, 73, 98, 102, 130, 195, 210, 227, 232, 238

goldhord, noun, m., treasure, 71, 151

goldgeweorc, noun, n., object made of gold, 238 [Hp]

gorst, noun, m., gorse, 154

gærs, græs, noun, n., grass, 52

grafan, st. vb. VI, to carve, 222

Grecisc, adj., Greek, 9, 10, 14, 238

gegremman, wk. vb. I, to irritate, 231

grene, adj., green, 238

gretan, wk. vb. I, to visit, 90ap

gegretan, wk. vb. I, to visit, 90

greting, noun, f., greeting, 198, 209

grimlic, adj., terrible, 162

grimlice, adv., cruelly, 140, 154

grindan, st. vb. III, to grind, 221

growan, st. vb. VII, to grow, 203ap

gegrowan, st. vb. VII, to grow, 203 [R]

grund, noun, m., bottom 26

grymettung, noun, f., roaring, 16 [R]

gyfu, gifu, noun, f., gift, 12, 80, 222

gyldan, st. vb. III, to pay, worship, 2, 70, 97, 106, 113, 115, 121, 139, 171b, 176, 184, 203ap, 218

gylden, adj., golden, 1, 97, 130, 144, 145, 168, 184, 204, 238

gyman, wk. vb. I, to pay attention to, 108, 184

gyrd, noun, f., stick, 5, 51, 145, 150

gyrdels, noun, m., belt, 176

gyrela, noun, m., dress, 210

GLOSSARY

gegyrela, noun, m., dress, clothing, 3, 73, 102ap, 117, 130, 138, 210ap, 223

gyrstandæg, noun, m., yesterday, 89

gyrwan, wk. vb. I, to dress, 210

gegyrwan, wk. vb. I, to dress, 98, 144, 193, 210, 223, 227

gystliþe, adj., hospitable, 186 [R]

gyt, adv., yet, still, 79, 80, 115, 136, 140, 211, 235

habban, wk. vb. III, to have, not to have (with neg.), 1, 4, 9, 16, 23, 28, 31, 34, 36, 38, 39, 49, 50, 56a, 60, 73, 79, 83a, 90, 97, 100, 111a, 112, 114, 115, 122, 127, 130, 131, 160, 162, 163, 166, 168, 170, 180, 186ap, 199, 207, 210, 211, 221a, 227, 232, 235

hacele, noun, f., cloak, 210

had, noun, m., office, order, 112, 138, 226

hal, adj., whole, 145, 152, 178, 217, 223

gehal, adj., whole, 16, 148

gehalgian, wk. vb. II, to consecrate, to ordain, 4, 15, 17, 25, 55, 114, 116, 134, 143, 190, 191ap, 196, 199, 212, 218, 227, 228

halgung, noun, f., consecration, 199ap

gehalgung, noun, f., consecration, 199

gehalian, wk. vb. II, to heal, 110ap

halig, adj., holy, Saint (used as a noun), 2, 4, 6, 7, 9, 10, 11, 15, 16, 17, 18, 22, 23, 24, 26, 28, 29, 30, 32, 33, 34, 39, 40, 41, 44, 47ap, 49, 51, 54, 56a, 59, 60, 61, 64, 65, 66, 67, 68, 71, 74, 75, 77, 78, 79, 80, 87, 88, 90, 93, 98, 99, 100, 107, 110, 112, 116, 118, 121, 122, 125, 127, 130, 131, 133, 136, 141ap, 144, 145, 152, 153, 156, 157, 161, 164, 168, 171, 173, 178, 182, 186, 189, 191, 193, 195, 196, 197, 198, 203, 204, 208, 209, 210, 211, 212, 214, 216, 218, 221, 222, 223, 224, 226, 227, 229, 230, 231, 232, 236, 237

haligmonaþ, noun, m., holy month, 171b, 200a [R]

halignes, noun, f., holiness, 63, 68, 75, 197, 226, 231

haligrift, noun, f., holy garment, 110, 226 [R]

halsian, wk. vb. II, to beseech, exorcise, 57, 106, 198

gehalsian, wk. vb. II, to beseech, 198

ham, adv., home, 112

hanasang, noun, m., cock-crow, 2 [R]

hand, noun, f., hand, 6, 16, 31, 32, 34, 38, 39, 58, 60, 63, 65, 75, 79, 88, 89, 98, 140, 146, 155, 162, 184, 187, 199, 209, 221, 227, 235

hangian, wk. vb. II, to hang, 79, 238

hat, adj., hot, 41, 110

gehat, noun, n., promise, 117

hatan, st. vb. VII, to call, to command, 2, 3, 4, 5, 6, 7, 20, 23, 26, 27, 30, 31, 32, 34, 36, 41, 47, 49, 54, 59, 60ap, 64, 65, 67, 71, 72, 73, 75, 76, 76ap, 83, 86, 87, 91, 97, 98, 99, 100, 102, 103, 107, 109, 112, 113, 115, 121, 122, 124, 125, 126, 127, 130, 135, 137, 139, 140, 144, 147, 149, 150, 151, 153, 154, 157, 161, 162, 163, 164, 166, 168, 170, 171b, 176, 182, 183, 184, 185, 186, 187, 189, 190, 191, 195, 203, 203, 209, 211, 212, 213, 216, 217, 219, 220, 222, 224, 227, 228, 230, 232, 233, 234, 235

gehatan, st. vb. VII, to promise, 230

hælan, wk. vb. I, to heal, 49, 70, 124, 138, 186, 236

gehælan, wk. vb. I, to heal, 1, 3, 44, 49ap, 102, 124ap, 134, 183, 198

Hælend, noun, m., saviour, 1, 4, 5, 9, 12, 35, 57, 67, 71, 74, 79, 88, 101, 133, 238

hælu, noun, f., health, 4

hæmed, noun, n., sex, 190, 197, 235

hære, noun, f., haircloth, 227

hæren, adj., made of hair, 138, 210

hæte, noun, f., heat, 21, 46

hæþen, adj., pagan, 2, 5, 13, 19, 23, 26, 27, 33, 34, 38, 39, 42, 54, 67, 70, 71, 83, 86, 87, 90, 97, 109, 112, 113, 116b, 121, 122, 124, 130, 148, 151, 152, 153ap, 155, 157, 160, 162, 167, 171b, 173, 176, 193, 198, 208, 217b, 218, 227, 231, 235, 238

hæþendom, noun, m., paganism, 197

hæþenfolc, noun, n., pagan crowd, 153 [R]

hæþengild, noun, n., pagan worship, 2, 19, 163, 197ap, 213, 217

hæþenscipe, noun, m., paganism, 7, 31, 149

hæwen, adj., purple, 238

GLOSSARY

heafdian, wk. vb. II, to behead, 234

heafod, noun, n., head, 28, 32, 36, 38, 42, 53, 58, 73, 83, 109, 121, 122, 130, 146, 168, 190, 192, 209, 213, 217, 227, 230, 231, 235

heafodsmæl, noun, n., hole for the head, 219ap

heah, adj., high, 58, 61, 65, 97, 142, 156ap, 168

heahcyning, noun, m., chief, overlord, king on high, 156

heahengel, noun, m., archangel, 97, 111, 156, 194

heahfæder, noun, m., patriarch, father on high, 111, 122, 156

heahlæce, noun, m., great physician, 198 [R]

heahlic, adj., distinguished, 193ap

healdan, st. vb. VII, to hold, to keep, 40, 78, 79, 80, 83, 102, 122, 136, 184, 227

gehealdan, st. vb. VII, to hold, to keep, 53, 73

healf, adj., half, 16, 58, 102, 111a, 156, 162, 170, 171, 212, 223, 225

healf, noun, f., side, 74

healfslæpende, adj., half asleep, 145 [R]

heall, noun, f., hall, 71, 126ap, 190, 238

healseta, noun, m., hole for the head, neckline, 219 [R]

healt, adj., lame, 203

hean, adj., poor, 198

heanes, noun, f., highness, 79, 80, 135, 142

heard, adj., hard, 65, 116, 136, 155, 221

hebban, st. vb. VI, to raise up, 65, 107, 226

hefig, adj., difficult, 187, 221

helan, st. vb. IV, to hide, 70

hell, noun, f., hell, 13, 42, 57, 126, 228

hellegrund, noun, m., deepest hell, 57

helletintreg, noun, n., torment of hell, 76

help, noun, m., help, 223

helpan, st. vb. III, to help, 57

gehelpan, st. vb. III, to help, 57ap

helto, noun, f., lameness, 122

heofon, noun, m., heaven, 1, 2, 3, 4, 16, 22, 26, 28, 30, 35, 37, 41, 42, 46, 50, 51, 63, 64, 65, 66, 67, 68, 71, 73, 76, 79, 87, 88, 97, 98, 102, 111a, 113, 114, 121ap, 122, 123, 127, 130, 133, 140, 142, 149, 151, 153, 157, 160, 171, 185, 191, 204, 209, 214, 217, 220, 226, 227, 228, 229, 234, 238

heofonlic, adj., heavenly, 1, 2, 4, 13, 23, 40, 49, 63, 65, 72, 80, 88, 100, 112, 114, 121, 129, 133, 135, 136, 156, 160, 181, 192, 198, 201, 204, 211, 220, 225

heonu, interj., oh, *ecce*, 38

heorcnian, wk. vb. II, to listen, 66

heorte, noun, f., heart, 9, 73, 78, 88, 106, 122

her, adv., here, 23, 40, 53, 60, 66, 76, 89ap, 106, 141, 145, 151, 181, 186, 209, 213

here, noun, m., army, 32, 60

heretema, noun, m., general, 186 [R]

heretoga, noun, m., general, 60, 224, 228

hergian, wk. vb. II, to ravage, 57, 167, 238

gehergian, wk. vb. II, to capture, 112

herian, wk. vb. I, to praise, 41, 65, 103, 216

herigendlic, adj., praiseworthy, 70

hider, adv., hither, 57

hind, noun, f., hind, 186, 225

hindan, adv., from behind, 190, 225

hirde, noun, m., shepherd, 1, 157

hiw, noun, n., shape, colour, 3, 22, 26, 39, 61, 211

gehiwian, wk. vb. II, to shape, 52, 79

hlaf, noun, m., bread, 1, 2, 12, 16, 22, 23, 40, 121, 127, 138, 221ap

hlafgebroc, noun, n., fragments of bread, 12 [R]

hlaford, noun, m., lord, 38, 221

hlafsenung, noun, f., blessing of bread, 142 [R]

hlæfdige, noun, f., lady, 210

hleahtor, noun, m., laughter, 168

hleapan, st. vb. VII, to leap, 41, 217ap, 231

hleapestre, noun, f., female dancer, 168ap [R]

hliehhan, st. vb. VI, to laugh, 60

hlinian, wk. vb. II, to lean, 5

hlisa, noun, m., renown, 226

hluttor, adj., clear, 88

hlystan, wk. vb. I, to listen, 66ap

hol, adj., hollow, 1, 16, 219

hors, noun, n., horse, 65, 154, 178, 238

hrace, noun, f., throat, 30 [R]

hraþe, adv., quickly, 4, 112, 161

338

GLOSSARY

hræd, adj., quick, prompt, 111
hræfn, noun, m., raven, 16, 97
hrægel, noun, n., garment, 41, 51, 59, 98, 108, 110, 115, 144, 193, 226, 227
hræw, noun, m., corpse, 21
hredmonaþ, noun, m., March, 36b, 58a
hreof, adj., leprous, 70, 223
gehreowan, st. vb. II, to repent, 236
hreran, wk. vb. I, to stir, 79
gehreran, wk. vb. I, to stir, 79ap
hreowsung, noun, f., repentance, 69, 98
gehrinan, st. vb. I, to touch, 1
hrof, noun, m., roof, 79
hrum, noun, m., soot, 162
hryman, wk. vb. I, to cry out, 162, 208, 211
hryþer, noun, n., ox, 211
hu, adv., how, 38, 66, 68, 106, 112, 116, 140, 184, 186, 208, 226
hulic, pron., of what sort, 73
hund, noun, m., dog, 31, 73, 216, 220, 225
hund, numeral, hundred, 1, 6, 53, 73, 105, 148, 166, 191, 222
hundeahtatig, numeral, eighty, 211
hundendlefontig, numeral, one hundred and ten, 16
hundnigontig, numeral, ninety, 83a, 221a
hundseofontig, numeral, seventy, 196, 207, 211
hundteontig, numeral, hundred, 22, 44, 52, 88, 196, 203, 222ap
hungor, noun, m., hunger, 67, 108, 127
hunig, noun, m., honey, 58
hunta, noun, m., hunter, 65, 74
huntian, wk. vb. II, to hunt, 225
hus, noun, n., 34, 56, 58, 59, 63, 67, 68, 74, 88, 90, 100, 109, 112, 113, 133, 147, 178, 180, 181, 210, 211, 218, 221, 222, 227, 228, 232, 235
husel, noun, n., Eucharist, 94, 133, 210, 235
hwa, pron., who, 186, 234
hwanne, adv., when, 110
hwanon, adv., whence, 221
hwæder, adv., where, 153
hwær, adv., where, 122, 217
hwæs, pron., whose, 186

hwæt, pron., what, 35, 52, 79, 112, 117, 136, 153, 162, 209, 211
hwæte, noun, m., wheat, 1, 73, 127, 205
hwæthwega, pron., something, 66
hwæþer, conj., whether, 5, 8, 198, 210
hwæþere, adv., conj., however, but, 22, 23, 40, 41, 50, 52, 73, 79, 99, 101, 110, 127, 130, 160, 173, 190, 214, 221, 235
hwelc, pron., adj., which, 41, 67, 73, 80, 90, 122, 127, 142, 186, 229
gehwelc, pron., adj., each, 133
hwene, adv., a bit, a little, 16, 60, 111a
hweorfan, st. vb. III, to turn, to go, 17, 157
gehweorfan, st. vb. III, to turn, to overturn, 60ap, 73, 198ap
hweowol, noun, n., wheel, 4, 79
hwer, noun, m., pot, 59, 102
hwil, noun, f., time, while, 5, 22, 36, 47ap, 50ap, 71, 78, 114, 121, 138, 168ap, 171b ap, 211, 217b ap, 226, 227, 228, 238
hwilchwega, pron., some, 193
hwit, adj., white, 16, 42, 51, 73, 98, 102, 127, 201, 217, 238
hwon, adj., little, 38, 131
hwy, pron., through what, 100
gehwyrfedness, **gehwyrfenes**, noun, f., conversion, 35
hyd, noun, f., skin, 108
gehydan, wk. vb. I, to hide, 107
gehygd, noun, f., intention, 106
hyht, noun, m., joy, 38, 106ap
gehyhtan, wk. vb. I, to hope, 57
hyll, noun, m., hill
hyngran, wk. vb. I, to be hungry, 133
gehyngran, wk. vb. I, to be hungry, 220
hyran, wk. vb. I, to obey, 3
gehyran, wk. vb. I, to hear, 1, 5, 13, 16, 37, 66, 67, 88, 89, 90, 115, 122, 127, 133, 136, 178, 193, 226
gehyrnes, noun, f., hearing, 56, 203
hyrstan, wk. vb. I, to roast, 151
gehyrstan, wk. vb. I, to roast, 151
hyþ, noun, f., harbour, 223

ifig, noun, n., ivy, 209

ig, noun, f., island, 37, 80
igil, noun, m., hedgehog, 26
ilca, pron., adj., same, 2, 3, 12, 13, 14, 19, 21, 23, 25, 28, 29, 31, 32, 33, 39, 40, 47, 49, 51, 54, 56, 56a, 58a, 60, 61, 70, 73, 76, 77, 79, 80, 83, 85, 88, 89, 97, 98, 99, 103, 105, 109, 110, 111a, 112, 115, 116, 120, 122, 124, 125, 131, 134, 141, 142, 144, 145, 148, 155, 157, 161, 163, 164, 167, 169, 170, 178, 181, 184, 186, 193, 195, 197, 198, 200a, 204, 208, 209, 210, 213, 216, 219, 220, 223, 224, 225, 226, 228, 229, 232, 233, 236
in, prep., in, on, 2, 8, 13, 21, 22, 26, 28, 31, 32, 34, 38, 58, 65, 66 (see Appendix 1), 67 (see Appendix 1), 70ap, 72ap, 73ap, 88ap, 97ap, 107ap, 114, 121ap, 127ap, 132ap, 138ap, 143, 144, 145, 146, 147, 148, 151, 152, 153, 154, 155, 156, 157, 160, 161, 162, 163, 164, 167, 168, 169, 170, 173, 176, 178, 180, 181, 183, 184, 187, 188, 190, 191, 192, 193, 194, 195, 196, 197, 199, 200, 202, 203, 205, 207, 209, 210, 211, 212, 213, 214, 215, 217, 218, 219, 220, 221, 222
ingan, anom. vb., to go in, 8, 211, 227, 238
ingang, noun, m., entrance, 58, 112, 121, 136
ingelædan, wk. vb. I, to introduce, 227
inne, adv., inside, 4, 59, 68, 88ap, 184, 238
innoþ, noun, m., entrails, stomach, bowels, 54, 111, 140, 225, 235
ingesamnian, wk. vb. II, to gather in, 56a ap
insmoh, noun, m., slough, 176 [Hp]
intinga, noun, m., cause 90
into, prep., into, 111, 124, 148, 210
iren, adj., iron, 150, 151, 222ap, 234
iren, noun, n., iron, 40, 162
irre, noun, n., anger, 73, 78
irsian, wk. vb. II, to be angry, to rage, 72, 112, 130, 153, 176, 222, 231, 234
is, noun, n., ice, 41
isen, adj., iron, 150ap, 151ap, 235
isen, noun, n., iron, 162ap
iserngeloman, noun, m., tools, 222 [R]
Iudisc, adj., Jewish, Hebrew (language), 9, 133, 200
la, interj., oh, 38, 57

lacnian, wk. vb. II, to heal, 198
ladlic, adj., horrible, 162
ladteow, noun, m., leader, 186
laf, noun, f., rest, remains, 12, 140
lam, noun, n., mud, 230
lama, adj., lame, 138, 183
lamb, noun, n., lamb, 1, 23, 210ap
land, noun, n., land, 1, 3, 21, 73b, 97, 101, 102, 110, 145, 150, 151, 162, 167, 170, 215
lang, adj., long, 36a, 57, 58, 58a, 68, 72, 73a, 94a, 106, 111a, 116a, 120, 136, 139a, 155, 171a, 200a, 217a, 233a
lange, adv., long, 26, 30, 80, 115, 120, 127, 138ap, 183ap, 192, 210, 232
langung, noun, f., longing, 133
lar, noun, f., teaching, 23, 71, 79, 90, 92, 116, 162, 166, 193
lareow, noun, m., teacher, 18, 35, 74, 155, 192
late, adv., late, 57, 152
laþettan, wk. vb. I, to hate, 173ap
laþian, wk. vb. II, to invite, 38, 176, 203, 232
gelaþian, wk. vb. II, to invite, 176ap
læce, noun, m., doctor, 173, 207, 236
læcedom, noun, m., medicine, 78, 232
lædan, wk. vb. I, to lead, 4, 7, 22, 30, 32, 37, 38, 40, 42, 61, 65, 67, 68, 71, 73, 83, 89, 94, 97, 98, 102, 109, 122, 130, 133, 139, 153, 154, 160, 166, 170, 171, 180, 182, 183, 184, 185, 209, 214, 221, 226, 232, 234, 235, 236
gelædan, wk. vb. I, to lead, to take, 23, 38, 61, 65, 67ap, 73, 75, 89, 102, 112, 122, 124, 133, 136, 145, 146, 152, 153ap, 157, 160, 167, 168, 186, 211, 226, 232, 235, 238
Læden, noun, n., Latin, 9, 36b, 48, 58b, 63, 73b, 74, 94b, 101, 116b, 139b, 171b, 200b, 217b, 233b
læl, noun, f., bruise, 115
læmen, adj., made of clay, 17
læran, wk. vb. I, to teach, 8, 22, 38, 44, 72, 75, 83, 86, 120, 161, 168ap, 173, 201, 211, 232
gelæran, wk. vb. I, to teach, 100, 101, 109, 116, 120, 134, 135, 168, 190, 195, 211, 227, 229, 232, 238
læs, adv., less, lest, 1, 41, 46, 229
læssa, adj., comp. of **lytel**, less, 50, 87, 127

læswian, wk. vb. II, to put out to grass, 122, 136

lætan, st. vb. VII, to let, 4, 8, 78, 114, 211

læþþu, noun, f., hatred, 108

læwede, adj., lay, 138, 226

leac, noun, m., vegetables, 40

lead, noun, n., lead, 26, 83, 102, 234

leaden, adj., leaden, 222

geleafan, noun, m., belief, 23, 32, 38, 41, 44, 70, 71, 72, 73, 83, 86, 90, 91, 99, 101, 102, 106, 109, 116, 120, 122, 123, 124, 126, 127, 135, 137, 140ap, 152, 157, 161, 173, 185, 190, 195, 201, 215, 219, 220, 224, 229, 230, 232, 233, 234, 235, 236, 238

geleafful, adj., faithful, 4, 12, 36, 73, 79, 173, 217

lean, st. vb. VI, to blame, to criticise, 168

leasere, noun, m., thug, 8, 83, 163, 234, 235

leasung, noun, f., deception, 22

lecgan, wk. vb. I, to lay, 221

legergeorn, adj., keen on sex, 210ap

legerteam, noun, m., sex, 190 [R]

lenctenfæsten, noun, n., fast of Lent, 80

leng, noun, f., length, 233b

leo, noun, m., lion, 16, 157, 193

leof, adj., dear, 5, 51, 80, 135, 235

leoht, noun, n., light, 1, 13, 35, 41, 50, 57, 127, 171, 192, 201, 209, 233

leohte, adv., brightly, 73

leohtfæt, noun, n., lamp, 51, 74, 79, 200, 209

leoma, noun, m., light, 97

leoran, wk. vb. I, to depart, to pass away, to move, 49, 70, 110, 121, 127, 160, 195

geleoran, wk. vb. I, to go to, to join, to die, 51, 59, 110, 142, 156, 171, 196, 211

geleoredness, noun, f., death, 181

leornere, noun, m., disciple, scholar, 37, 46, 66, 108, 133, 167, 170, 200, 237

geleornes, noun, f., death, feast, 15, 21, 22, 24, 37, 40, 42, 49, 51, 60, 63, 66, 68, 80, 81, 107, 110, 138, 141, 171, 178, 186, 207, 210, 211, 214, 221

leornian, wk. vb. II, to learn, to study, 17, 56a, 70, 122ap, 232

geleornian, wk. vb. II, to learn, 122, 136

leoþ, noun, n., song, 163

gelettan, wk. vb. I, to delay, to interrupt, 116

libban, wk. vb. III, to live, 4, 5, 26, 47, 53, 80, 89, 111, 136, 138, 157, 171, 176, 181, 213, 228, 229, 232, 238

lic, noun, n., body, 60, 80, 233

gelic, adj., equal, 222, 238

liccian, wk. vb. II, to lick, 225

gelice, adv., also, equally, similarly, 78, 79, 111a

licgan, st. vb. V, to lie, 4, 8, 79, 136, 211

lichama, noun, m., body, 1, 2, 3, 4, 5, 7, 9, 10, 13, 14, 16, 17, 20, 21, 22, 23, 24, 26, 27, 28, 30, 31, 32, 33, 37, 38, 39, 41, 49, 56a, 57, 58, 59, 60, 61, 63, 64, 65, 69, 70, 73, 74, 76, 77, 79, 80, 81, 83, 84, 86, 98, 102, 103, 107, 110, 111, 113, 116, 121, 122, 125, 129, 132, 137, 138, 139, 140, 143, 145, 146, 147, 149, 150, 151, 154, 161, 162, 164, 166, 167, 173, 176, 178, 181, 187, 190, 195, 197, 198, 200, 201, 202, 203, 209, 210, 211, 212, 214, 215, 216, 217, 220, 222, 223, 226, 227, 228, 229, 230, 231, 233, 234, 237, 238

lichrægel, noun, n., shroud, 80 [R]

lician, wk. vb. II, to please, 51

licþegnung, noun, f., funeral, 94 [R]

geliefan, wk. vb. I, to believe, 3, 8, 19, 20, 23, 26, 32, 38, 56a, 57, 64, 71, 72, 87, 99, 101, 112, 113, 122, 124, 130, 132, 139, 147ap, 149, 150, 154, 166, 181, 189, 193, 194, 208, 222ap, 224, 227

liefan, wk. vb. I, to believe, 222

lif, noun, n., life, 2, 9, 20, 37, 68, 89, 94, 106, 112, 121, 127, 136, 138, 139, 140, 142, 144, 146, 160, 166, 184, 191, 192, 226, 232, 237

lig, noun, m., fire, flame, 68, 187

geliger, noun, n., fornication, 22, 186 [R]

ligetsliht, noun, f., flash of lightning, 33 [R]

lihtan, wk. vb. I, to shine, 50, 114

lilie, noun, f., lily, 217, 227

lim, noun, n., limb, 9, 40, 41, 65, 150, 178, 231

gelimpan, st. vb. III, to happen, 7, 60, 111a, 122, 166, 198, 204, 225

gelimplic, adj., suitable, 167

linen, adj., linen, 108

GLOSSARY

list, noun, m., skill, trick, 210
liþan, st. vb. I, to sail, 38, 94b, 140
liþe, adj., gentle, 94b, 116a, 116b, 139a
geliþian, wk. vb. II, to relieve, 186
locc, noun, m., lock, hair, 71, 73, 108, 133
locian, wk. vb. II, to look, 4, 8, 21, 160, 186, 221
lof, noun, n., praise, 115
lofsang, noun, m., song of praise, 4, 14, 176, 180
gelome, adv., frequently, 117
lufian, wk. vb. II, to love, 3, 30, 80, 130, 232
lufu, noun, f., love, 80, 122, 186, 196, 211, 227
lust, noun, m., desire, 22, 59
lutan, st. vb. II, to bow, 57
lyfan, wk. vb. I, to allow, 155ap
gelyfed, adj., believing, faithful, 162
lyft, noun, m., air, 48, 68, 94b, 111a, 133, 226
lytel, adj., little, 5, 22, 51, 56a, 60, 106, 111a, 160, 210, 221

ma, adj., adv., more, 21, 50, 83, 114, 151, 191, 210ap, 232
magan, pret. pres. vb., to be able to, 3, 4, 12, 15, 21, 22, 27, 30, 31, 38, 49, 52, 53, 58, 61, 66, 67, 71, 73, 79, 80, 88, 90, 94, 102, 110, 114, 116, 117, 118, 120, 122, 125, 127, 134, 136, 140, 158, 168, 173, 178, 180, 187, 194, 209, 211, 221, 227, 228, 229, 235, 238
gemang, noun, n., crowd, 6
manian, wk. vb. II, to claim back, 181
maniend, noun, m., collector, 190 [R]
manig, adj., pron., many, 1, 3, 4, 17, 20, 26, 54ap, 56a, 65, 70, 91, 98, 100, 101, 106, 107, 116, 121, 122, 124, 129, 136, 137, 141, 145, 151, 170, 173, 178, 181, 186, 193, 195, 210, 222, 225, 232, 235, 238
manigfeald, adj., various, 54, 98
mann, noun, m., man, 1, 3, 4, 5, 9, 10, 12, 13, 14, 15, 16, 17, 18, 19, 21, 22, 26, 31, 32, 35, 36, 38, 49, 52, 53, 56, 56a, 57, 58, 59, 61, 63, 64, 67, 68, 70, 72, 73, 74, 76, 77, 78, 79, 80, 81, 82, 83, 88, 89, 90, 91, 92, 94b, 97, 98, 100, 102, 103, 105, 106, 109, 111, 111a, 113, 114, 116, 116b, 122, 124, 127, 130, 133, 134, 135, 136, 138, 140, 144, 145, 148, 149, 151, 152, 155, 168, 173, 176, 178, 181, 183, 186, 190, 195, 196, 198, 203, 209, 210, 211, 214, 216, 217, 221, 223, 225, 228, 232, 234, 235, 236
manncwealm, noun, m., death, pestilence, 67ap
manncwild, noun, f., death, pestilence, 67
manswerian, st. vb. VI. to swear falsely, to commit perjury, 136
marmanstan, noun, m., marble, 79ap
marmarstan, noun, m., marble, 79 [R]
martyr, noun, m., martyr, 4, 14, 27, 38, 67ap, 71, 72, 73, 83, 84, 87, 89, 93, 95, 96, 104, 105, 111, 117, 120, 126, 132, 137, 140, 145, 155, 158, 159, 163, 164, 165, 172, 175, 176, 179, 182, 185, 191, 203, 206, 212, 217, 218, 222, 229
martyrdom, noun, m., martyrdom, 2, 3, 10, 23, 28, 29, 30, 38, 39, 41, 54, 59, 62, 65, 71, 73, 93, 98, 99, 103, 109, 112, 118, 120, 123, 125, 127, 128, 129, 130, 132, 134, 139, 142, 150, 152, 183, 184, 187, 188, 189, 195, 197, 198, 201, 205, 209, 219, 224, 225, 227, 232, 236
martyrhad, noun, m., martyrdom, 192
martyrian, wk. vb. II, to martyr, 87ap, 184, 212
gemartyrian, wk. vb. II, to martyr, 65, 87, 106, 112, 143, 147, 191, 203
mægden, noun, n., girl, 3, 112, 122, 130, 168, 184, 209, 211, 232, 234
mægdenhad, noun, m., girlhood, virginity, 39, 180
mægen, noun, n., strength, force, miracle, 48, 111, 156, 160, 198, 220
mægsibb, noun, f., kinship, 57
mægþ, noun, f., country, region, nation, tribe, 1, 12, 21, 26, 29, 31, 32, 36, 39, 44, 49, 51, 62, 65, 70, 74, 87, 89, 97, 102, 116, 121, 126, 127, 139, 144, 146, 157, 160, 162, 173, 190, 191, 195, 196, 199, 207, 211, 215, 220, 223, 228, 233, 234, 235, 237, 238
mægþhad, noun, m., girlhood, virginity, 94, 193

342

GLOSSARY

gemænnes, noun, f., community, 180
mære, adj., famous, distinguished, 3, 12, 22, 34, 59, 70, 88, 123, 125, 126, 127, 178, 187, 198, 207
gemære, noun, n., end, limit, region, 37, 196, 214
mærsian, wk. vb. II, proclaim, 24, 78, 84, 104, 119, 122, 127, 145, 199
gemærsian, wk. vb. II, proclaim, 127ap, 145ap
mæsse, noun, f., mass, 14, 70, 104, 115, 147ap, 148, 165, 169, 172, 177, 179, 192, 196, 206
mæsseboc, noun, f., missal, 95, 104, 158, 159, 165, 172, 177, 179, 206
mæssehrægel, noun, n., vestment, 143
mæssepreost, noun, m., priest, 19, 21, 23, 26, 40, 43, 49, 54, 76, 85, 94, 98, 100, 103, 115, 116, 133, 143, 145, 151, 170, 173, 195, 200, 201, 216, 220, 230, 232
mæssesang, noun, m., sung mass, service, 79, 84, 95, 104, 119, 158
mæst, adj., most, greatest, 12, 33, 160, 168
mæst, adv., most, 139b
mætan, wk. vb. I, to dream, 39
meagolmodnes, noun, f., earnestness, seriousness, 115
mearcian, wk. vb. II, to note, 89
mearu, adj., delicate, 122
med, noun, f., reward, 97, 102, 115, 127, 168
gemedemian, wk. vb. II, to deign, to deem worthy, 127
medmicel, adj., moderate, little, 38, 71, 154, 198, 200
medsceatt, noun, m., payment, 198
medtrumnes, noun, f., illness, 118, 120, 198
medume, adj., average, worthy, 58ap, 73
medumlic, adj., worthy, 112
medumnes, noun, f., worthiness, dignity, 230
melc, adj., in milk, giving milk, 186
melcan, st. vb. III, to milk, 40
meltan, st. vb. III, to melt, 102
gemeltan, st. vb. III, to melt, 41, 59, 197, 238
melu, noun, n., flour, 221
menigu, noun, f., crowd, 184, 193, 199
mennisc, adj., human, 1, 17, 50, 53, 73ap, 78, 79, 111, 131, 133, 160, 198, 238

meolc, noun, f., milk, 1, 6, 157, 186
meolcian, wk. vb. II, to milk, 73b, 186
mere, noun, m., lake, 41, 52, 73, 212
merigen, noun, m., morning, 63ap, 70, 100ap, 130, 209, 225
met, noun, n., measure, 79ap
gemet, noun, n., measure, 58, 73, 79
metan, wk. vb. I, to find, 209
gemetan, wk. vb. I, to find, 5, 56, 60ap, 77, 80, 89, 97, 102, 110, 113, 117, 122, 127, 133, 145, 158, 159, 165, 169, 172, 177, 179, 206, 209, 228, 232
mete, noun, m., food, 1, 2, 3, 22, 23, 26, 78, 97, 133, 176, 221
gemetnes, noun, f., discovery, 145
micel, adj., great, 1, 4, 5, 12, 21, 22, 23, 26, 31, 38, 39, 41, 50, 56, 67, 68, 69, 70, 73, 75, 80ap (see also Appendix 2), 87, 88, 97, 103, 109, 110, 111, 112, 113, 114, 115, 122, 123, 124, 126, 127, 128, 130, 133, 134, 136, 138, 145, 146, 153, 157, 162, 166, 167, 168, 171, 173, 184, 187, 190, 194, 196, 198, 212, 217, 222, 223, 225, 226, 229, 231, 232, 233, 235
micle, adv., much, 2, 4, 17, 40, 115
gemiclian, wk. vb. II, to multiply, 127
mid, prep., with, among, 1, 2, 3, 4, 5, 6, 8a, 9, 11, 12, 13, 16, 17, 19, 22, 23, 26, 27, 29, 31, 32, 33, 34, 36, 37, 38, 39, 41, 42, 47, 49, 51, 53, 54, 56, 56a, 57, 58, 59, 60, 63, 64, 65, 67, 68, 69, 70, 71, 72, 73, 75, 76, 78, 79, 80, 82, 83, 84, 87, 88, 90, 94, 97, 98, 99, 100, 101, 102, 103, 104, 105, 106, 108, 109, 110, 111, 111ap, 112, 114, 115, 116, 118, 119, 120, 122, 123, 124, 126, 127, 128, 129, 130, 132, 133, 135, 138, 140, 141, 144, 145, 147, 148, 149, 150, 151, 153, 154, 155, 157, 160, 161, 162, 166, 167, 168, 170, 181, 182, 183, 185, 186, 187, 188, 189, 190, 191, 192, 193, 195, 196, 197, 198, 199, 200, 204, 209, 210, 212, 214, 216, 217, 218, 220, 221, 222, 223, 225, 226, 227, 228, 229, 230, 232, 233, 234, 235, 238
midd, adj., middle, mid-, 35, 56a, 79, 97, 111a
middangeard, noun, m., earth, world, 1, 5, 22, 80, 101, 110, 111, 114, 126, 135, 140, 156,

GLOSSARY

229, 238

middel, noun, m., middle, 41, 111a, 173ap, 187, 226

middeneaht, noun, f., midnight, 30, 38, 97ap, 130, 171

midlen, noun, n., middle, 173

miht, noun, f., power, 49, 59, 67, 89, 114, 125, 211, 221, 228, 230

mihtig, adj., mighty, 3, 60, 193

mil, noun, f., mile, 1, 76, 145, 149, 228

milde, adj., friendly, 220

mildheortnes, noun, f., mercy, compassion, 67, 127, 140

milts, noun, f., mercy, favour, 186

miltsian, wk. vb. II, to show mercy, to be merciful, 57, 140, 146

missenlic, adj., various, 71, 73, 97, 123, 170, 211

mitta, noun, m., mitta, measure, 12

mittan, wk. vb. I, to find, 4

gemittan, wk. vb. I, to find, 60, 68, 102ap, 145ap, 149, 228

mitting, noun, f., discovery, 145ap

mod, noun, n., mind, heart, spririt, 41, 51, 116, 197, 233, 236

modor, noun, f., mother, 1, 3, 4, 6, 23, 44, 65, 86, 106, 107, 111, 127, 140, 149, 156, 160, 166, 168, 180, 209, 226, 228

modrige, noun, f., aunt, 108, 215

mona, noun, m., moon, 1, 50, 170

monaþ, noun, m., month, 7ap, 8a, 9, 10, 11, 12, 14, 15, 16, 17, 18, 19, 20, 22, 24, 26, 27, 28, 31, 34, 35, 36b, 37, 38, 39, 41, 42, 43, 44, 46, 48, 50ap, 52, 53, 54, 56, 56a, 57, 58, 58b, 59, 60, 62, 63, 64, 65, 66, 67, 68, 69, 71, 72, 73a, 73b, 74, 75, 76, 79, 80, 81, 82, 83a, 84, 86, 87, 88, 89, 90, 91, 92, 93, 94, 94a, 94b, 95, 97, 100, 101, 102, 103, 104, 106, 107, 108, 110, 111, 112, 113, 114, 116, 116a, 116b, 117, 118, 119, 121, 123, 126, 127, 128, 129, 130, 132, 133, 135, 136, 137, 138, 139, 139a, 139b, 140, 143, 145, 146, 147, 148, 149, 150, 151, 152, 153, 154, 156, 157, 158, 159, 160, 162, 164, 165, 166, 168, 170, 171, 171a, 171b, 172, 173, 174, 176, 177, 179, 180, 182, 183, 185, 187, 188, 189, 190, 191, 192, 194, 196, 197, 198, 199, 200, 200a, 200b, 201, 202, 203, 204, 205, 206, 207, 210, 211, 212, 214, 215, 217, 217a, 217b, 218, 221, 221a, 222, 223, 225, 226, 227, 228, 230, 231, 233, 233a, 233b, 234, 235, 237, 238

morgen, noun, m., morning, 100, 116, 130ap, 184, 222

morgensteorra, noun, m., morning-star, 73, 111 [R]

gemot, noun, n., meeting, 153

motan, pret. pres. vb., to be allowed to, 23, 51, 97, 190

gemunan, pret. pres. vb., to remember, 21

mund, noun, f., hand, 58

mundbyrd, noun, f., protection, 176

munt, noun, m., hill, 61, 82, 140, 190

munuc, noun, m., monk, 22, 136, 148, 186

muþ, noun, m., mouth, 42, 54, 73, 74, 118, 162, 187

gemynd, noun, n., feast, memory, 4, 18, 21, 24, 26, 39, 59, 67, 75, 84, 91, 92, 95, 96, 100, 104, 108, 113, 116, 117, 118, 121, 122, 126, 127, 130, 135, 137, 138, 152, 154, 161, 170, 173, 188, 189, 192, 196, 199, 205, 208, 212, 218, 220ap, 229

gemyndig, adj., mindful, 23, 73, 122

gemynegian, wk. vb. II, to remember, 57, 65

mynet, noun, n., coin, 184

mynster, noun, n., monastery, 3, 10, 17, 20, 21, 28, 32, 37, 40, 49, 51, 80, 91, 100, 110, 136, 143, 147, 171, 178, 181, 196, 202, 204, 205, 214, 221, 226

myrre, noun, f., myrrh, 12

na, adv., not at all, 23, 30, 34, 50, 73, 76ap (see also Appendix 2), 83, 102, 115, 122, 136ap, 143, 160, 184, 187, 191, 198, 210, 220, 222, 227, 232

nacod, adj., naked, 19, 30, 139, 149, 211, 223, 234

nafela, noun, m., navel, 111a

nahwær, adv., nowhere, 162

nahwider, adv., to no place, 235

nama, noun, m., name, 9, 13, 22, 29, 34, 35, 37, 38, 41, 43, 44, 59, 62, 63, 64, 65, 67, 71, 73, 74, 76, 86, 87, 90, 94, 98, 99, 101, 102, 107, 111, 112, 114, 116b, 122, 123, 124, 127, 128, 129, 130, 132, 134, 136, 137, 139b, 144, 145, 149, 152, 170, 173, 183, 187, 188, 190, 191, 194, 195, 201, 202, 203, 204, 209, 210, 211, 215, 221, 222, 225, 226, 228, 229, 232, 233, 233b, 235, 238

nan, pron., adj., no one, none, no, 2, 3, 5, 51ap, 61ap, 68ap, 83ap, 101ap, 122ap, 143ap, 181, 222, 229

nanwuht, pron., nothing, 13, 16, 22, 30, 51, 80, 115, 120ap, 127, 192, 198, 210

nanwuht, adv., not at all, 53, 83ap, 100

naþor, adj., pron., adv., neither, 100, 116

næddre, noun, f., snake, serpent, 124, 219, 232, 235

næfre, adv., never, 1, 13, 16, 21, 30, 38, 49, 50, 53, 67, 73, 79, 108, 122, 133, 180, 210ap, 235, 238

nænig, pron., none, no one, 5, 22, 30, 31, 38, 51, 61, 68, 79, 83, 90, 100, 110, 111a, 112, 113, 122, 127, 130, 133, 140, 143, 160, 173, 180, 198, 210, 222ap, 228, 238

næsþyrel, noun, n., nostril, 144, 162

ne, adv., conj., not, nor, 1, 2, 3, 5, 13, 16, 21, 22, 26, 30, 31, 34, 41, 49, 50, 53, 64, 65, 67ap, 68, 73, 76, 78, 79, 80, 83, 90, 100, 101, 102, 103, 108, 110ap, 111, 113, 115, 116, 120, 122, 127, 133, 136, 140, 143, 160, 168, 173, 178, 180, 181, 184, 187, 192, 193, 195, 196, 198, 203, 207, 210, 211, 215, 217, 220, 221, 227, 228, 229, 234, 235, 238

neah, adv., near, 14, 16, 23, 30, 50, 54, 68ap, 70, 79, 98, 109, 112, 115, 121, 126, 135, 140, 145, 151, 161, 163, 187, 191, 193, 209, 221, 235

neahealand, noun, n., neighbouring island, 89 [R]

neahmann, noun, m., neighbour, 68 [R]

neahstow, noun, f., neighbouring place, 79 [R]

nealæcan, wk. vb. I, to approach, 144, 221

genealæcan, wk. vb. I, to approach, 8, 61, 73, 127, 144ap, 221ap

neat, noun, n., cattle, 20, 73b, 127, 198, 217b

neawest, noun, f., neighbourhood, 102

nemnan, wk. vb. I, to name, to call, 3, 8a, 10, 12, 13, 14, 17, 19, 21, 23, 26, 30, 32, 35, 36b, 38, 40, 43, 48, 49, 53, 54, 58b, 65, 67, 69, 73, 73a, 73b, 75, 76, 77, 80, 81, 86, 88, 89, 91, 94b, 97, 98, 100, 108, 109, 110, 115, 116, 116a, 116b, 118, 124, 126, 127, 130, 131, 134, 135ap, 138, 139a, 139b, 140, 142ap, 144, 145, 146, 149, 150, 151, 153, 162, 164, 166, 170, 171a, 180, 187, 192, 196, 197, 200a, 200b, 202, 203, 204, 205, 207ap, 211, 213, 215, 217, 217a, 217b, 218, 221, 222, 223, 224, 225, 226, 231, 233a, 233b, 234, 235, 238

genemnan, wk. vb. I, to name, 98, 130, 134ap, 213ap, 233

neorxenawang, noun, m. paradise, 50, 71, 76, 122, 157, 209, 227

nepflod, noun, m., neap tide, 48 [R]

generian, wk. vb. I, to save, to deliver, to set free, 57

nett, noun, n., net, 135

nidan, wk. vb. I, to force, 3, 5, 20, 23, 31, 32, 41, 64, 72, 76, 87, 90, 107, 113, 121, 140, 147, 149, 160, 183, 185, 187, 203, 211, 216, 217, 225, 227, 228, 234, 236, 238

genidan, wk. vb. I, to force, 13, 31, 59, 90ap, 157

nide, adv., necessarily, 21, 131

nidþearfnes, noun, f., necessity, need, 73

nieten, noun, n., cattle, 127ap, 198ap

nigon, numeral, nine, 34, 53, 58, 93, 114, 138, 146, 168, 199

nigonteoþa, numeral, nineteenth, 26, 46, 107, 130, 159, 188, 210

nigoþa, numeral, ninth, 15, 41, 62, 78, 83a, 89, 100, 150, 171b, 178

niht, noun, f., night, 1, 2, 3, 6, 7, 19, 22, 26, 36, 36a, 39, 40, 41, 45, 54, 56a, 58a, 60, 70, 73a, 76, 78, 79, 94a, 97, 100, 113, 115, 116a, 121, 131, 138, 139a, 145, 171a, 180, 198, 200, 200a, 203, 208, 209, 210, 215, 216, 217a, 220, 223, 227, 232, 233a

nihterne, adv., for a night, 21

nihtlic, adj., nightly, nocturnal, 11, 47, 59
genihtsum, adj., abundant, 69, 145ap
genihtsumian, wk. vb. II, to suffice, 111
genihtsumnes, noun, f., abundance, 73b, 205, 221
nihtwæcce, noun, f., vigil, 127 [R]
niman, st. vb. IV, to take, 3, 4, 37, 79, 198, 209
geniman, st. vb. IV, to take, 32, 38, 61, 122, 162, 166, 170, 187, 209, 216, 220
niþerlic, adj., low, 46, 168
niþerweard, adv., down, 181
niwan, adv., newly, 186
niwe, adj., new, 96, 158, 169
niwslicod, adj., newly glossed, 226 [R]
non, noun, n., ninth hour, noon, 56a, 78, 89
norþ, adv., north, in a northerly direction, 53
norþan, adv., from the north, 37, 196, 214
norþhealf, noun, f., north, 58
nu, adv., now, 2, 23, 38, 50, 52, 57, 71, 74, 79, 88, 98, 109, 112, 127, 136, 151, 156, 157, 160, 210, 211, 223, 226, 236
nunne, noun, f., nun, 190

of, prep., from, of, 1, 2, 3, 4, 5, 6, 8, 13, 16, 18, 21, 23, 26, 28, 29, 35, 37, 38, 41, 42, 48, 49, 51, 52, 53, 56a, 57, 58, 63, 64, 65, 67, 68, 70, 73, 73b, 74, 76, 77, 80, 86, 87, 88, 97, 98, 100, 109, 110, 111, 111a, 113, 116, 121, 122, 127, 130, 133, 135, 136, 140, 145, 149, 156, 157, 160, 162, 164, 166, 173, 178, 190, 191, 195, 196, 198, 201, 209, 210, 217, 219, 220, 223, 227, 228, 234, 235, 238
ofdune, adv., down, 79
ofen, noun, m., oven, 3, 17, 76, 126, 187, 234
ofer, noun, m., river bank, 135, 217
ofer, prep., adv., over, after, 1, 3, 5, 21, 28, 35, 38, 41, 48, 52, 73, 77, 79, 88, 102, 111a, 113, 122, 127, 130, 137, 141, 153, 178, 181, 199, 201, 209, 210, 225, 226, 229
oferfaran, st. vb. VI, to cross, to pass through, 97ap
ofergan, anom. vb., to overcome, 100, 131
ofergytan, st. vb. V, to forget, 228
oferhlifian, wk. vb. II, to tower above, 111
oferhydig, adj., proud, arrogant, 140, 186
oferliþan, st. vb. I, to cross, 97
ofermæte, adj., excessive, 22
ofermodig, adj., proud, arrogant, 140
ofersæwisc, adj., from beyond the sea, 17
ofergesettan, wk. vb. I, to put in charge, 51
oferstealla, noun, m., survivor, 229 [R]
oferswiþan, wk. vb. I, to overcome, 39, 67, 71, 73, 102, 127, 139b, 211
oferwyrcan, wk. vb. I, to cover, 200
offrian, wk. vb. II, to worship, 184ap
offyllan, wk. vb. I, to kill off, 99
ofscotian, wk. vb. II, to shoot, 27, 82
ofslean, st. vb. VI, to kill, to beat to death, 23, 33, 65, 70, 73, 89, 90, 103ap, 108, 122, 123, 155, 173, 185ap, 187, 225, 238
ofstician, wk. vb. II, to stab to death, 76, 155, 238
ofstingan, st. vb. III, to stab to death, 6, 190, 216 [R]
ofswingan, st. vb. III, to scourge to death, 64 [R]
oft, adv., often, 13, 48, 49, 67, 72, 110, 111ap, 112, 114, 133, 220, 229
oftorfian, wk. vb. II, to stone to death, 4
ofweorpan, st. vb. III, to stone to death, 4
olfend, noun, m., camel, 108, 198
on, prep., on, in, 1, 2, 3, 4, 5, *etc.*
onælan, wk. vb. I, to light, to kindle, 122ap
onbæc, adv., backwards, 198
onbærnan, wk. vb. I, to light, to kindle, 23, 122
onbeodan, st. vb. II, to order, to ask, 90, 94
onbryrdnes, noun, f., compunction, 78
onbyrgan, wk. vb. I, to taste, 49, 178
oncyrran, wk. vb. I, to turn, 38, 59, 71, 73, 102, 106, 110, 122, 123, 140, 198ap, 228, 232
ondrædan, st. vb. VII, to fear, 160, 211, 229
ondrincan, st. vb. III, to drink of, 49, 186ap
ondryslic, adj., terrible, 122, 127, 140, 153
ondrysnlic, adj., terrible, 21, 79, 106, 130, 140ap, 153ap
ondune, adv., down, 232
oneardian, wk. vb. II, to inhabit, 108

GLOSSARY

oneowan, wk. vb. I, to show, to reveal, 142ap
onfealdan, st. vb. VII, to open, to unwrap, 115 [R]
onfindan, st. vb. III, to find out, to discover, 3, 191, 210
onfon, st. vb. VII, to take, to receive, 3, 4, 9, 12, 13, 17, 23, 28, 35, 67, 79, 88, 90, 97, 98, 110, 115, 116, 117, 118, 120, 122, 124, 130, 140, 148, 149, 150, 152, 154, 160, 162, 163, 166, 182, 186, 190, 198, 203, 208, 209, 210, 213, 222, 227, 232
ongean, prep., adv., against, towards, back, 31, 60, 106, 109, 185, 223, 226, 234
onginnan, st. vb. III, to begin, 8, 30, 38, 41, 75, 76, 86, 87, 94, 100, 106, 112, 113, 127, 149, 163, 166, 186, 196, 226, 232
ongyrwan, wk. vb. I, to undress, 187
ongytan, st. vb. V, to perceive, to find out, 3, 22, 41, 57, 58, 67, 71, 90, 100, 106, 127, 186, 223, 234
onhebban, st. vb. VI, to lift up, to raise, 71, 151
onhon, st. vb. VII, to hang up, 4
onhrinan, st. vb. I, to touch, 23, 139, 145, 195, 220, 227
onhyldan, wk. vb. I, to bend down, 90, 140, 232
onlihtan, wk. vb. I, to cause to shine, 50
onlucan, st. vb. II, to open, to unlock, 56a, 180
onlutan, st. vb. II, to bend down, 124, 221
onmiddan, prep., in the middle of, 79
onræsan, wk. vb. I, to rush, to rage, 79
onsacan, st. vb. VI, to deny, 181
onsægednes, noun, f., sacrifice, offering, 194
onsceortian, wk. vb. II, to grow short, 111a [R]
onsendan, wk. vb. I, to send, 3, 11, 19, 23, 26, 27, 30, 31, 33, 38, 39, 40, 41, 42, 56a, 57, 60ap, 61, 68ap, 70, 72, 80, 88, 94, 97, 103, 107, 116, 126, 127, 130, 133, 134, 149, 151, 154, 157, 170, 178, 186ap, 198, 208, 211, 227, 228, 229, 233
onsetenes, noun, f., laying on, 88 [R]
onslapan, st. vb. VII, to fall asleep, 38 [R]
onstyrian, wk. vb. I, to move, to excite, 59, 235
onsund, adj., separate, individual, 88
onsundrum, adv., separately, 68, 114, 180
ontynan, wk. vb. I, to open, 71, 76, 116, 126, 145, 153, 157
onþwean, st. vb. VI, to wash, 23
onufan, prep., on, upon, 65ap, 72ap, 79ap, 125ap, 227
onweg, adv., away, off, 70, 108, 162ap, 199
onwendan, wk. vb. I, to turn, to change, 160ap, 197
onwreon, wk. vb. I, to disclose, 198
open, adj., open, 56a, 71, 79, 110, 185
geopenian, wk. vb. II, to open, to reveal, 116, 152
openlice, adv., in public, openly, 22, 37
orsorg, adj., free from sorrow, relaxed, 23
orwirþlic, adj., disgraceful, 168
ost, noun, m., knot, 56a
oþ, prep., up to, until, 2, 16, 51ap, 56a, 78, 79, 86, 110, 162, 176, 184, 186ap, 190, 194
oþer, adj., pron., other, another, next, 1, 5, 8, 12, 16, 17, 20, 22, 31, 32, 34, 35, 38, 47, 49, 51, 58, 70, 72, 73, 75, 79, 83, 87, 96, 97, 102, 111, 113, 114, 116, 122, 136, 137, 139, 140, 145, 151, 162, 170, 180, 181, 186, 187, 190, 191, 196, 201, 205, 212, 215, 216, 217, 221, 222, 225, 227, 233b, 236, 238
oþeowan, wk. vb. I, to show, 180
oþswigan, wk. vb. I, to become silent, 66 [R]
oþ þæt, conj., until, 16, 22, 27, 33, 56a, 70, 72, 79, 80, 83, 100, 102, 106, 107, 170, 181, 231, 235
oþþe, conj., or, either, 5, 6, 12, 21, 67, 71, 78, 79, 90, 100, 106, 122, 127, 152, 184, 197, 210, 226, 236
oxa, noun, m., ox, 1

panne, noun, f., pan, 59
papa, noun, m., pope, 7, 10, 14, 20, 28, 76, 86, 89, 91, 143, 147, 166, 202, 205, 218, 227, 228
papsetl, noun, n., papal throne, 14 [R]

GLOSSARY

paternoster, noun, n., Lord's prayer, 152
Pentecosten, noun, m., Pentecost, 88
pic, noun, n., pitch, 102
pictirwa, noun, m., pitch, tar, 102ap [R]
plega, noun, m., game, 163
plegan, both wk. vb. I and wk. vb. II forms occur in the *Old English Martyrology*, to play, 4, 75, 163, 168
prafost, noun, m., officer, 49, 154
preost, noun, m., priest, 109, 170, 201
preosthad, noun, m., priesthood, 17

racentteah, noun, f., chain, 154, 162, 204, 235, 238
rap, noun, m., rope, 70, 235
gerar, noun, n., roaring, 16 [R]
rarian, wk. vb. II, to roar, 211
ræcan, wk. vb. I, to reach, 79
geræcan, wk. vb. I, to reach, 140
rædan, wk. vb. I, to read, 67, 136, 157, 163, 178, 192
gerædan, wk. vb. I, to read, 184ap
ræding, noun, f., reading, 178
ræsan, wk. vb. I, to rush, 30, 57, 219
geræsan, wk. vb. I, to rush, to pounce, 187
reaf, noun, n., vestment, 51ap
gereafian, wk. vb. II, to steal, 236
rec, noun, m., smoke, 77, 162, 197
gereccan, wk. vb. I, to explain, translate, 74, 101, 186
recels, noun, n., incense, perfume, 12, 194, 210
refa, noun, f., prefect, 157ap, 164, 182, 185 [R]
gerefa, noun, m., prefect, magistrate, 2, 3, 7, 26, 30, 41, 59, 64, 94, 102, 103, 112, 122, 123, 127, 157, 161, 164ap, 166, 170, 176, 182, 185ap, 189, 198, 217, 227, 234, 235
gerefærn, noun, n., court-house, 130 [R]
regn, noun, m., rain, 48, 70, 145
gerela, noun, m., clothing, clothes, 30, 102
relicgang, noun, m., procession, 69, 78 [R]
reliquias, m., relics, 4, 32, 73, 78, 126
reod, adj., red, 2
reord, noun, f., meal, 186

gereord, noun, n., food, meal, 2, 5, 23, 49, 110, 121, 133, 138, 186
gereordan, wk. vb. I, to feed, 12
rest, noun, f., rest, bed, 38, 42, 65, 70, 97, 122, 176, 193
restan, wk. vb. I, to rest, 2, 3, 7, 13, 14, 16, 20, 21, 22, 23, 24, 28, 30, 32, 33, 37, 39, 57, 58, 60, 61, 63, 72, 74, 80, 81, 83, 84, 113, 116, 125, 132, 137, 138, 139, 147, 176, 181, 187, 190, 197, 214, 215, 223, 232, 234, 237
gerestan, wk. vb. I, to rest, 55, 79
reþe, adj., cruel, fierce, 4, 60, 115, 170
ribb, noun, n., rib, 53
rice, noun, n., kingdom, power, authority, 3, 40, 71, 102, 114, 127, 130, 138, 146, 155ap, 162, 215ap, 228, 229, 235
rice, adj., powerful, 5, 19, 38, 209
ricsian, wk. vb. II, to reign, 146, 160, 235
ridan, st. vb. I, to ride, 219
rift, noun, n., veil, cloak, vestment, 51
riht, adj., fitting, right, 89
rihte, adv., in the direction of, due, 51
rihtlice, adv., rightly, 78
rihtwisnes, noun, f., righteousness, 127
rihtgewitt, noun, n., right mind, sanity, 211
rimcræft, noun, m., science of numbers, 232 [R]
rod, noun, f., cross, rod, 4, 56a, 57, 77, 108, 111a, 114, 226, 233
rodetacn, noun, n., sign of the cross, 118, 222
rodor, noun, m., sky, heaven, 46, 50
romanisc, adj., Roman, 238
rose, noun, f., rose, 173, 217, 227
rumedlic, adj., generous, 78
geryne, noun, n., sacraments, 63, 119

sacerd, noun, m., priest, 235
saltere, noun, m., psalter, 136, 196
gesamnian, wk. vb. II, to collect, 56a, 148, 173, 184
gesamnung, noun, f., congregation, 134
samod, adv., together, 38, 57, 66, 114, 123, 180, 222, 232
Sancta, noun, f., (female) saint, St, 1, 2, 3, 9, 11, 15, 24, 30, 33, 39, 56, 57, 59, 61, 65, 71,

348

87, 90, 94, 108, 110, 111, 112, 118ap, 122, 123, 124, 125, 127, 129, 130ap, 133, 144ap, 149, 156, 169, 180, 187, 189, 193, 196, 204, 208, 210, 215, 216, 218, 226, 227, 234, 235

Sanctus, noun, m., (male) saint, St, 4, 5, 7, 10, 13, 14, 15, 16, 17, 18, 19, 20, 21, 22, 23, 25, 26, 27, 28, 31, 32, 32, 34, 35, 36, 37, 38, 40, 42, 43, 44, 47, 49, 51, 60, 63, 64, 65, 66, 67, 68, 70, 71, 72, 73, 74, 75, 76, 79, 80, 81, 82, 83, 84, 85, 86, 87, 89, 91, 92, 93, 94, 95, 96, 97, 98, 99, 100, 101, 102, 103, 104, 105, 106, 107, 109, 111, 111a, 115, 116, 117, 118ap, 120, 121, 124, 126, 127, 128ap, 130, 131, 132, 134, 135, 136, 137, 138, 141, 142, 143, 144, 145, 146, 147, 148, 149, 150, 151, 152, 153, 154, 155, 157, 158, 159, 160, 161, 162, 163, 164, 165, 166, 167, 168, 170, 171, 172, 173, 174, 175, 176, 177, 179, 181, 182, 183, 184, 185, 186, 188, 189, 190, 191, 192, 194, 195, 196, 197, 198, 199, 200, 202, 203, 205, 206, 207, 209, 211, 212, 214, 217, 219, 220, 221, 223, 224, 225, 228, 230, 231, 232, 233, 236, 237, 238

sand, noun, n., sand, 16, 79
sang, noun, m., song, singing, 1, 37, 159
sar, noun, n., suffering, 6, 26, 53, 54
sarspell, noun, n., horror story, 13 [R]
sawlung, noun, f., final hours, death-bed, 131 [R]
sawol, noun, f., soul, 16, 37, 42, 49, 56a, 57, 64, 78, 80, 89, 98, 102, 136, 140, 146, 156, 171, 209, 211, 214, 231, 236, 238
sæ, noun, both f. and m. forms occur in the *Old English Martyrology*, sea, 21, 26, 38, 46, 48, 52, 67, 75, 80, 94b, 102, 127, 130, 135, 137, 141, 146, 162, 196, 201, 210, 221, 223, 228, 230
sædeor, noun, m., sea-beast, 26, 193 [R]
sæflod, noun, m., sea, sea water, flood, 48ap
sæscill, noun, f., sea-shells, shellfish, 19 [R]
sæstream, noun, m., sea water, 80ap
Sæterndæg, noun, m., Saturday, 60, 97, 205
scead, noun, n., shadow, shade, 111a
gesceaft, noun, n., creation, 46, 50, 56a
sceamlic, adj., shameful, 106

sceanc, noun, m., leg, 83
sceandful, adj., shameful, 144, 168
sceandhus, noun, n., brothel, 30
sceandlic, adj., disgraceful, disgusting, vile, 116, 163
sceap, noun, n., sheep, 122, 136, 187
sceaphirde, noun, m., shepherd, 1
scear, noun, f., scissors, 108
scearp, adj., sharp, 19, 73
scearu, noun, f., tonsure, 17
sceat, noun, m., sheet, cloth, 58, 150
sceawian, wk. vb. II, to look, 5, 79
sceotan, st. vb. II, to shoot, 82, 198, 225
sceran, st. vb. IV, to cut, to shave, 108, 193
gescerian, wk. vb. I, to set up, 48ap
scericge, noun, f., actress, 210 [R]
sceþþan, st. vb. VI, but wk. forms occur in the *Old English Martyrology*, to harm, 67, 87, 187, 193
gesceþþan, st. vb. VI, but wk. in the *Old English Martyrology*, to harm, 187ap
sciccel, noun, m., cloak, 223
gescildan, wk. vb. I, to protect, 67, 100, 184
gescildnes, noun, f., protection, 60
scill, noun, f., shell, 46
scilling, noun, m., shilling, 181
scinan, st. vb. I, to shine, 1, 36, 50, 51, 64, 73, 111a, 156, 160, 192, 209, 226, 227
scincræft, noun, m., witchcraft, magic, 100ap, 197
scinlæca, noun, m., magician, witch, 30, 71, 87, 100, 190, 211
scip, noun, n., ship, 38, 97, 102, 125, 135, 140, 223
sciplibend, adj., seafaring, 89
scipmann, noun, m., sailor, 223
scippan, st. vb. VI, to create, 9
gescippan, st. vb. VI, to create, 46, 52, 53, 176ap
Scippend, noun, m., the Creator, 140
scipteora, noun, m., pitch, 102 [R]
scondlic, adj., shameful, 59, 61
scort, adj., short, 106ap, 111a
scræf, noun, n., cave, 82, 103
scrid, noun, n., chariot, 65, 140, 238

349

GLOSSARY

scufan, st. vb. II, to push, 235
sculan, pret. pres. vb., to have to, 2, 8, 9, 21, 24, 47, 48, 59ap, 64, 65, 68, 69, 70, 78, 83, 84, 104, 110, 119, 124, 130, 131, 136, 142, 143, 180, 184, 186, 192, 194, 232, 236
sculdor, noun, m., shoulder, 115, 153
scyld, noun, f., guilt, sin, 127
gescyldru, noun, n., shoulders, 153ap
Scyttisc, adj., Gaelic (relating to the inhabitants of both Ireland and of Dál Riata), 171
sealt, noun, n., salt, 15, 22
sealt, adj., salty, 48, 52
sealticge, noun, f., dancer, 168 [R]
seaþ, noun, m., pit, 72, 89, 99, 113, 176, 193
seax, noun, n., knife, 108
secan, wk. vb. I, to seek, 49, 67, 109, 117, 158, 209
gesecan, wk. vb. I, to seek, 40, 67ap, 178, 210
secgan, wk. vb. III, to say, 1, 2, 4, 9, 13, 22, 37, 46, 49, 52, 60, 63, 64, 68, 70, 73, 77, 79, 83, 89, 98, 106, 111, 111a, 115, 116, 117, 126, 145, 149, 153, 176, 180, 186, 190, 194, 196, 198, 200, 210, 221, 222, 227, 238
gesecgan, wk. vb. III, to announce, 90, 115, 196ap
segl, noun, n., sail, 38
segnian, wk. vb. II, to bless, to make the sign of the cross, 22, 23, 51, 178ap, 222
gesegnian, wk. vb. II, to bless, 5, 51ap, 63, 118, 178, 186, 221ap, 222
seldan, adv., rarely, 110
self, pron., adj., self, 3, 4, 6, 13, 22, 44, 53, 60, 70, 73, 79, 110, 116, 122, 134, 138, 140, 149, 160, 168, 170, 185, 187, 190, 211, 223, 228, 229, 236
sellan, wk. vb. I, to give, to sell, 2, 3, 40, 49, 51, 56a, 59, 61, 73, 80, 87, 88, 92, 94, 101, 102, 110, 112, 122, 124, 127, 130, 140, 146, 151, 168, 170, 180, 181, 184, 217b, 222, 227, 228
gesellan, wk. vb. I, to give, 59ap, 94ap, 101, 108ap, 110ap, 127ap, 133, 210, 223, 227, 235
selor, adv., better, 203

selra, adj., better, 49, 56a, 170
sendan, wk. vb. I, to send, to throw, 3, 26, 47, 48, 59, 73, 76, 78, 89, 113, 126, 130, 136, 139, 145, 166, 186, 187, 191ap, 193, 203, 209, 211, 228
gesendan, wk. vb. I, to send, 178ap
seofon, numeral, seven, 14, 26, 34, 50, 58, 62, 67, 71, 80, 83a, 94, 97, 102, 112, 115, 123, 129, 133, 136, 138, 140, 165, 198, 207, 221a, 228, 229, 232
seofonteoþa, numeral, seventeenth, 22, 44, 104, 128, 157, 226
seofoþa, numeral, seventh, 7, 39, 50, 55, 76, 81, 94, 116b, 121, 148, 179, 202, 221a
seolfor, noun, n., silver, 22, 73, 102, 130, 181, 195, 210
seolfren, adj., made of silver, 130, 168, 238
seon, st. vb. V, to see, 142, 152, 181
geseon, st. vb. V, to see, 1, 4, 5, 6, 13, 15, 16, 21, 22, 26, 38, 41, 42, 49, 51, 56a, 57, 59, 60, 63, 64, 68, 71, 73, 75, 79, 87, 89, 90, 98, 99, 102, 110ap, 111a, 114, 122, 130, 132, 133, 134, 136, 140, 142ap, 149, 150, 151ap, 153, 154, 157, 163, 171, 181, 185, 186, 187, 189, 200, 201, 204, 208, 209, 210, 214, 221, 226, 227, 232, 238
seonuwealt, adj., round, 58, 79
setl, noun, m., seat, 10, 50, 83a, 221a
setlgang, noun, m., setting, 135
settan, wk. vb. I, to set, 40, 79, 111a, 222ap
gesettan, wk. vb. I, to set (down), establish, 14, 28, 38, 46, 48, 50, 59, 66, 68, 73, 77, 80, 104, 107, 111a, 122, 138, 143, 162, 165ap, 167, 178, 200, 205, 212, 218, 228, 231, 238
sibb, noun, f., peace, 40, 70, 122, 133, 235
siblic, adj., peaceful, 69
side, noun, f., side, 58, 73, 113, 151, 162
sigefæst, adj., victorious, successful, 31, 41, 97, 187, 191
gesigefæst, adj., victorious, successful, 222
sigle, noun, f., necklace, 226
gesigefæstan, wk. vb. I, to triumph, 57, 112
gesihþ, noun, f., sight, vision, 3, 11, 13, 21, 47, 87, 89, 92, 112, 122, 151, 203
sincan, st. vb. III, to sink, 223

GLOSSARY

gesincan, st. vb. III, to sink, 125
singal, adj., continual, 145
singallice, adv., constantly, 108
singan, st. vb. III, to sing, 14, 70, 80, 115, 148, 152, 163, 180, 221
gesingan, st. vb. III, to sing, 115
gesinhiwan, noun, m., couple, married people, spouses, 29, 100
gesinscipe, noun, m., marriage, 38, 138
sittan, st. vb. V, to sit, 10, 14, 26, 38, 40, 42, 52, 75, 88, 125, 131, 157
gesittan, st. vb. V, to sit, 79, 196
siþ, noun, m., journey, time, 1, 48, 50, 58, 102, 115, 148, 196, 203
siþ, noun, m., governor, 59ap
gesiþ, noun, m., governor, 59, 61, 76, 87, 107, 166
siþfæt, noun, m., journey, 13, 21, 38, 67, 92, 116, 196, 228
siþian, wk. vb. II, to travel, 57
siþþan, conj., adv., after, afterwards, later, 1, 3, 13, 26, 31, 50, 51, 67, 72, 73, 83, 88, 110, 114, 117, 133, 136ap, 152, 162, 173, 178, 196, 198, 203, 218, 220, 222, 228, 231, 238
gesiþwif, noun, n., noblewoman, 2, 94 [R]
six, numeral, six, 12, 57, 92, 111, 113, 116a, 118, 140, 147, 164, 191, 197, 214, 220, 222
sixta, numeral, sixth, 12, 53, 80, 94b, 111, 119, 147, 220, 221
sixteoþa, numeral, sixteenth, 19, 103, 187
sixtig, numeral, sixty, 2, 16, 105, 156
sixtyne, numeral, sixteen, 16, 17, 38, 94a, 110, 139a, 209, 211, 213, 233a
slæp, noun, m., sleep, 38, 100, 131, 142, 226, 232
slæpan, st. vb. VII, to sleep, 5, 131, 210, 228, 232
slean, st. vb. VI, to hit, kill, 40, 51, 57, 60, 68, 99, 103, 108, 144, 146, 185, 198, 217b ap, 225, 227
slidan, st. vb. I, to slip, 160
slitan, st. vb. I, to tear, 53, 193
smæte, adj., refined, 5
smeagan, wk. vb. I, to study, 121
smic, noun, m., smoke, 22

smirenes, noun, f., ointment, 133
smirwan, wk. vb. I, to anoint, to smear, 133
smylte, adj., mild, 88, 94b, 223
smyltelic, adj., mild, 69
snaw, noun, m., snow, 16, 102, 127, 217
snawhwit, adj., snow-white, 220
sniþan, st. vb. I, to cut, 41
snoru, noun, f., daughter-in-law, 156
snotor, adj., wise, 180
snytro, noun, f., wisdom, 47, 75, 230
Solmonaþ, noun, m., February, 36a
sona, adv., immediately, straightaway, 1, 3, 4, 5, 8, 13, 15, 16, 26, 33, 38, 41, 51, 56a, 59, 60, 63, 68, 75, 76, 77, 88, 90, 94, 108, 109, 113, 116, 117, 118, 120, 121, 122, 126, 130, 131, 134, 136, 140, 145, 147, 152, 166, 178, 180, 181, 190, 209, 210, 211, 217, 219, 220, 221, 223, 225, 232, 234
soþ, adj., true, 4, 8, 12, 56a, 121, 122
soþfæstnes, noun, f., truth, 127
soþlice, adv., truly, 58, 73, 77
soþlufu, noun, f., love, charity, 122
gespannan, st. vb. VII, to harness, 65
spearca, noun, m., spark, 162
sped, noun, f., wealth, 127, 190
spere, noun, n., spear, 225, 238
spiwan, st. vb. I, to spew, to vomit, 6, 54
spraec, noun, f., speech, 73ap, 81
gespræc, noun, n., speech, 73
sprecan, st. vb. V, to speak, 1, 21, 26, 49, 63, 66, 73, 88, 100, 103, 118, 157, 198, 209, 215
springan, st. vb. III, to burst, 162
stalu, noun, f., theft, 70
stan, noun, m., stone, 3, 4, 5, 19, 51, 53, 56a, 58, 70, 72, 99, 130, 136, 145, 198, 200, 222
stancræftiga, noun, m., stone-mason, 222 [R]
standan, st. vb. VI, to stand, 4, 41, 49ap, 50, 51, 58, 60, 73, 79, 82, 94, 97, 111a, 117, 124, 136, 144, 150, 156, 157, 163, 181, 186, 187, 190, 194, 199, 221, 227, 228, 235, 238
gestandan, st. vb. VI, to stand, 60, 79, 186, 221
stangefeall, noun, n., fallen stones, 231 [R]

GLOSSARY

stanscræf, noun, n., rocky cave, 1, 133, 209 [R]
stanweall, noun, m., stone wall, 56a
gestaþelian, wk. vb. II, to establish, 204
gestællan, wk. vb. I, to stable, 20
stænan, wk. vb. I, to stone, 33, 157, 198
stænen, adj., made of stone, rocky, 58, 88, 124, 178, 228
stæning, noun, f., stoning, 4 [R]
stær, noun, n., history, 92
stefn, noun, f., voice, 35, 65, 67, 73, 76, 97, 122, 127, 157, 162, 198
stefnan, wk. vb. I, to direct, 134
stenc, noun, m., smell, 4, 5, 13, 56a, 77, 103, 140, 145, 181, 220, 233
steng, noun, m., pole, 27, 149, 195
steoran, wk. vb. I, to direct, to steer, 134ap
steorra, noun, m., star, 83a, 221a
stician, wk. vb. II, to prod, to stab, to pierce, 1, 53, 225
stigan, st. vb. I, to rise, 16
stillan, wk. vb. I, to calm, 223
gestillan, wk. vb. I, to calm, 65
stincan, st. vb. III, to smell, 210, 217
stingan, st. vb. III, to sting, to stab, 53ap, 150, 226
storm, noun, m., storm, 223
stow, noun, f., place, 17, 19, 26, 27, 56, 61, 63, 67ap, 72, 78, 79, 80, 81, 97, 102, 109, 111a, 122, 127, 145, 157, 167, 184, 207ap, 210, 211, 212, 217, 225
stræl, noun, m., arrow, 27, 82, 113, 198, 225
strang, adj., strong, 41, 60, 79, 88, 219
stranglice, adv., forcefully, severely, strongly, 39, 67, 79
stream, noun, m., stream, 80, 125, 203, 219
gestreon, noun, n., expense, treasure, 122, 136
gestrind, noun, f., progeny, descent, origin, 113 [R]
gestrynan, wk. vb. I, to conceive, 186
stycce, noun, n., piece, 173
sulh, noun, f., plough, 40
sum, pron., adj., some, certain, 1, 2, 3, 4, 12, 26, 30, 37, 41, 42, 49, 51, 60, 66, 70, 73, 74ap, 75, 87, 89, 90, 100, 102, 109, 115, 116, 117, 118, 124, 125, 131, 133, 136, 137, 144, 145, 147, 152, 155, 163, 164, 173, 178, 181, 183, 187, 192, 193, 195, 196, 198, 203, 204, 208, 209, 210, 211, 214, 217, 219, 220, 221, 222, 225, 226, 228, 230, 231, 232, 235, 236, 238
sumer, noun, m., summer, 21, 41, 83a, 111a
gesund, adj., healthy, 4, 26, 59, 80, 112, 148ap, 149, 166, 199, 223
sungihte, noun, n., solstice, 111a [R]
Sunnandæg, noun, m., Sunday, 97, 178ap
Sunnanniht, noun, f., Saturday night and Sunday morning, 178
sunnanuhta, noun, m., Sunday morning, 178
sunne, noun, f., sun, 1, 40, 41, 50, 56a, 64, 97, 111, 111a, 135, 156, 225, 226, 233b, 238
sunu, noun, m., son, 1, 4, 29, 30, 65, 86, 101, 102, 108, 113, 123, 129, 130, 135, 140, 144, 156, 166, 186, 190, 194, 215, 229
suþ, adv., to the south, 53
suþ, adj., south, southern, 221
suþaneastan, adv., from the southeast, 68
swa, adv., conj., so, as if, as, 1, 2, 3, 5, 9, 16, 21, 22, 23, 27, 30, 36, 38, 40, 41, 46, 48, 50, 51, 53, 54, 56, 56a, 57, 58, 59, 60, 61, 64, 66, 67, 68, 70, 73, 75, 77, 79, 80, 86, 88, 97, 102, 103, 108, 110, 111, 111a, 112, 113, 114, 115, 116, 117, 121, 122, 125, 127, 130, 133, 136, 137, 138, 140, 148, 151, 152, 153, 154ap, 156, 157, 160, 168, 170, 173, 176, 178, 180, 181, 184, 186, 187, 190, 191, 193, 194, 197, 198, 209, 210, 211, 217, 221, 222, 226, 227, 229, 230, 232, 234, 236, 238
swaþu, noun, f., track, trace, 79, 110
swætan, wk. vb. I, to toil, 235
geswætan, wk. vb. I, to sweat, 227
swæþ, noun, n., track, 79
sweart, adj., black, 22, 51, 59, 98, 162
swefen, noun, n., sleep, dream, 60, 142
sweg, noun, m., noise, 68, 88, 226
sweger, noun, f., mother-in-law, 156
swelc, adj., pron., such, 1, 13, 30, 60, 73b, 88ap, 180, 218, 221, 226
swelce, adv., conj., like, as if, 1, 13, 56a ap, 66ap, 68ap, 80ap (see also Appendix 2), 97,

98, 162, 180, 211
sweltan, st. vb. III, to die, 54, 76, 112, 113, 126, 138, 140, 154, 161, 162, 166, 181, 184, 229, 233
swencan, wk. vb. I, to torment, 102, 121
geswencan, wk. vb. I, to disturb, to affect, to trouble, 38, 127, 186
sweora, noun, m., neck, 3, 26, 70, 79, 110, 130, 195, 220, 228
sweorban, noun, n., neck, 90 [R]
sweord, noun, n., sword, 30, 39, 57, 60, 65, 90, 99, 103, 114, 122, 135, 184, 185, 187, 190, 199, 216, 227, 235, 238
sweostor, noun, f., sister, 11, 15, 47, 61, 166, 184
gesweostor, noun, f., sisters, 59, 125
sweostorsunu, noun, m., nephew, 108, 215 [R]
swerian, st. vb. VI, to swear, 64, 136, 140, 181
swete, adj., sweet, 4, 56a, 233
swetnes, sweetness, noun, f., sweetness, 5
geswican, wk. vb. I, to stop, 115
swift, adj., swift, 31
swigian, wk. vb. II, to be silent, 31
geswigian, wk. vb. II, to be silent, 231
swimman, st. vb. III, to swim, 52
swincan, st. vb. III, to work hard, to mortify, 121
swinen, adj., of pork, 140
swingan, st. vb. III, to beat, to flog, 22, 64 (see Appendix 1), 79ap, 107, 122, 150ap
swingel, noun, f., whipping, beating, 115
swiþ, adj. right (as opposed to left), 58, 156
swiþe, adv., very, 2, 3, 17, 33, 34, 36, 38, 40, 41, 46, 59, 60, 73ap, 80, 89, 90, 94, 100, 107, 112, 113, 115, 116, 117, 120, 121ap, 126, 127, 130, 136, 142, 151ap, 152, 157, 180, 184, 186, 191, 198, 220, 221, 226, 232, 235, 237
swiþlic, adj., very great, 221ap
swote, adv., sweetly, 217
syl, noun, f., column, 111a
symbel, noun, n., feast, 176, 203, 232
symbeldæg, noun, f., feastday, 75
symble, adv., always, 50, 80, 112
syn, noun, f., sin, 73, 122, 127, 133, 163, 210

synfull, adj., sinful, 149
gesyngian, wk. vb. II, to sin, 50
synnicge, noun, f., sinner, 133 [R]
synnig, adj., sinful, 190, 235

tacn, noun, n., sign, 1, 4, 63, 113, 225
tacnian, wk. vb. II, to mark, to signify, 1, 56a, 142, 226
getacnian, wk. vb. II, to signify, 9, 12, 28, 63, 74, 111, 142ap
getæcan, wk. vb. I, to inform, to show, 107, 203, 217
tælan, wk. vb. I, to rebuke, 186
teah, noun, f., bag, 209
tear, noun, m., tear, 6, 42, 115, 122, 210
teon, st. vb. II, to draw, to pull, 6, 48, 51, 154, 235
geteon, st. vb. II, to draw, 204
teona, noun, m., abuse, 112
geteorian, wk. vb. II, to be exhausted, 235
teoþa, teogeþa, numeral, tenth, 16, 84, 101, 123, 151, 200b, 234
tid, noun, f., time, feastday, hour, 3, 5, 6, 7, 10, 11, 14, 16, 17, 19, 20, 23, 27, 28, 29, 33, 34, 36a, 41, 43, 44, 47, 49, 58a, 59, 61, 62, 64, 65, 67, 69, 71, 72, 73ap, 73a, 74, 77, 78, 79, 84, 89, 90, 93, 94, 94a, 97, 98, 100, 101, 104, 105ap, 107, 110, 112, 115, 116a, 120, 124, 127, 128, 129, 131, 132, 133, 139, 139a, 140, 142, 143, 145, 146, 150, 151, 155, 156, 157, 158, 159, 160, 162, 163, 164, 165, 166, 167, 169, 170, 171a, 172, 174, 176, 177, 179, 182, 184, 190, 193, 195, 197, 198, 200, 200a, 202, 203, 206, 212, 213, 215, 217a, 218, 219, 224, 225, 226, 228, 230, 232, 233, 233a, 235, 236, 238
tidernes, noun, f., weakness, illness, 160
getigan, wk. vb. I, to tie, to bind, 238
tilian, wk. vb. II, to strive, to labour, to try, 111, 234
tima, noun, m., time, 143ap
timbran, both wk. vb. I and wk. vb. II forms occur in the *Old English Martyrology*, to build, 56, 79, 110, 122ap, 127, 203, 210, 226

getimbran, both wk. vb. I and wk. vb. II forms occur in the *Old English Martyrology*, to build, to establish, 17, 21, 86, 100, 107, 112, 122, 139b ap, 199, 210ap, 231, 238

tin, numeral, ten, 3, 36a, 58, 73a, 150ap, 171a, 217a

tindiht, adj., spiked, 150 [R]

tintregian, wk. vb. II, to torture, 67, 73, 151

to, prep., to, 1, 2, 3, 4, 5, *etc.*

to, adv., too, 46

tobeatan, st. vb. VII, to smash, 231

toberan, st. vb. IV, to carry off, 4

toberstan, st. vb. III, to burst, 3, 26, 51, 160, 181, 190

tobrecan, st. vb. IV, to break, 19, 57, 65, 182, 222

tobregdan, st. vb. III, to pull to pieces, 220

tobrengan, wk. vb. I, to bring, 49

toceorfan, st. vb. III, to cut to pieces, 173, 223

tocumend, adj., passing by, visitor (used as a noun), 186, 228

tocyme, noun, m., coming, 57ap, 140

todæg, adv., today, 160, 235

todælan, wk. vb. I, to separate, to hand out, 196, 198, 227

todragan, st. vb. VI, to pull to pieces, 154ap

todreosan, st. vb. II, to fall apart, 238

tofeallan, st. vb. VII, to fall to pieces, 41, 56a, 147ap

togædere, adv., together, 162ap

togeare, adv., this year, 1, 83

toglidan, st. vb. I, to disappear, to collapse, 197

tohwon, pron., why, 1, 71, 136, 211, 234

tol, noun, n., tool, 222ap

tomorgen, adv., tomorrow, 225

torcyrre, adj., hard to convert, 116 [R]

torr, noun, m., tower, 130

tosamne, adv., together, 22, 116, 162, 225

tosceadan, st. vb. VII, to separate, 45, 48

toslean, st. vb. VI, to smash to pieces, 148

toslitan, st. vb. I, to tear to pieces, 116, 219, 231, 235

tostregdan, st. vb. III, to disperse, 187

toþ, noun, m., tooth, 73

toþon, prep., for, to, 48

toweard, adj., future, 190, 210

toweorpan, st. vb. III, to overthrow, 71, 108, 139b, 147, 162

tredan, st. vb. V, to tread, 79, 230

treow, noun, n., tree, 1, 23, 52, 56, 56a, 77, 219

treowen, adj., wooden, 56a

getrymman, wk. vb. I, to found, to establish, 139b

trymnes, noun, f., strength, 69

tun, noun, m., town, 21, 38, 71, 38, 100, 145, 211, 220, 225

tunece, noun, f., tunic, 138, 210

tunge, noun, f., tongue, 103, 114, 209

tungerefa, noun, m., reeve, 151, 154

tungol, noun, m., star, 46, 50, 140, 226, 232

tungolcræft, noun, m., astronomy, 232

tungolcræftiga, noun, m., astronomer, 12

tusc, noun, m., tusk, 73

tuwa, adv., twice, 196

twegen, tu, twa, numeral, two, 1, 3, 5, 6, 12, 13, 16, 22, 29, 31, 45, 46, 47ap, 48, 51, 52, 56a, 59, 61, 73, 74, 76, 83, 87, 88, 89, 95, 100, 105, 106, 108, 110, 114, 116, 117, 121, 133, 138, 139, 148, 160, 166, 170, 173, 181, 186, 187, 190, 191, 196, 203, 210, 212, 221a, 222, 223, 224, 225, 227, 231, 233, 233b, 238

twelf, numeral, twelve, 12, 26, 28, 34, 40, 58a, 66, 97, 110, 130, 157, 200a, 220

twelfta, numeral, twelfth, 11, 17, 42, 86, 153, 233b

twentig, numeral, twenty, 17, 22, 38, 40, 48, 88, 91, 112, 134, 145, 180, 183, 184, 222

twentigoþa, numeral, twentieth, 27, 30, 31, 33, 34, 35, 48, 50, 52, 53, 55, 56, 57, 58, 66, 67, 68, 69, 71, 72, 90, 91, 92, 93, 108, 110, 111, 112, 113, 114, 132, 133, 135, 136, 137, 138, 160, 162, 164, 165, 166, 168, 189, 190, 191, 192, 194, 196, 197, 198, 199, 211, 212, 214, 215, 227, 228, 230, 231, 238

tweogan, wk. vb. II, to hesitate, 211

getweogan, wk. vb. II, to doubt, 41, 236

getwin, noun, m., twin, 23, 107, 196, 238

GLOSSARY

þa, adv., conj., then, when, 1, 2, 3, 4, 5, *etc.*

geþafian, wk. vb. II, to consent to, 8, 20, 23, 32, 41, 64, 72, 73, 76, 83, 86, 87, 103, 107, 109, 113, 123, 140, 183, 186, 187, 203, 211, 217, 220, 227

þanc, noun, m., thanks, 101ap, 184

geþanc, noun, m., thought, 110ap, 122ap

þancung, noun, f., thanks, 149, 151

þanon, adv., from there, 19, 21, 57, 97, 162, 207, 221, 233

þær, adv., conj., there, where, 3, 4, 5, 13, 16, 17, 19, 21, 22, 26, 29, 30, 31, 32, 33, 38, 40, 41, 49ap, 51, 56, 56a, 57, 58, 59, 60, 61, 65, 66, 68, 70, 73, 74, 76, 77, 79, 80, 81, 82, 83, 86, 88, 89, 94, 97, 98, 99, 102, 103, 107ap, 108, 109, 110, 111a, 112, 116, 122, 124, 127, 131, 133, 136, 139, 144, 145, 148, 153, 155, 156, 157, 161, 162, 167, 168, 173, 173, 176, 178, 180, 181, 184, 186, 190, 193, 194, 195, 196, 198, 199, 201, 203, 208, 209, 210, 211, 215, 217, 218, 220, 221, 222, 225, 226, 228, 230, 234, 235, 238

þæron, adv., therein, 1

þærto, adv., thereto, 31, 217

þærute, adv., outside, 117

þæs, adv., after, afterwards, later, 17, 40, 63, 80, 94, 110, 196

þæt, conj., that, so that, 1, 2, 3, 4, 5, *etc.*

þeah, adv., conj., though, however, although, 23, 57, 73ap, 79, 149, 166ap, 173, 198

þeahhwæþre, adv., nevertheless, 124, 166

þearfend, pres. part. of **þearfan**, needy, poor, 130, 151, 221, 223

þearlwislic, adj., severe, 115 [R]

þeaw, noun, m., custom, 68, 101, 115, 130, 131, 136, 168, 186

þeccan, wk. vb. I, to cover, 162ap

þegen, noun, m., man, follower, 4, 22, 40, 49, 58, 66, 74, 79, 83ap (see also Appendix 2), 88, 89, 101, 122, 135, 162, 182, 187, 190, 233, 238

þegenscipe, noun, m., service, 38

þegnian, wk. vb. II, to serve, 3, 20, 112

þegnungweorod, noun, n., a body of attendants, 235 [R]

þencean, wk. vb. I, to think, to have in mind, to intend, 21, 59, 186, 198

geþencean, wk. vb. I, to intend, to wish, 222

þenden, conj., while, 47, 50

þeod, noun, f., people, nation, 3, 35, 49, 60, 73, 73b, 81, 88ap, 92, 100, 101, 109, 112, 135, 146, 162, 171, 238

geþeodan, wk. vb. I, to join, to unite, 30, 116

geþeode, noun, n., language, 8, 8a, 9, 12, 36b, 58b, 73b, 74, 88, 94b, 101, 111a, 116b, 120, 138, 139b, 171b, 196, 200b, 210, 212, 217b, 233b, 238

þeodscipe, noun, m., teaching, 17, 140

þeoh, noun, n., thigh, 136, 178

þeostre, adj., dark, 56a, 57, 162

þeotan, st. vb. II, to howl, 22, 211

þeow, noun, m., servant, 37, 51, 65, 78, 89, 117, 131, 154, 166, 186, 190, 210ap, 226

þeowdom, noun, m., service, 20

þeowen, noun, f., female servant, handmaid, 38, 78, 130, 149, 210, 226

þeowian, wk. vb. II, to serve, 3, 13, 103, 112, 211, 232

þerscold, noun, m., threshold, 211

þerscan, st. vb. III, to thrash, 27, 40

þicce, adj., thick, 157

þicgan, st. vb. V, to eat, 22

þider, adv., there, 8, 31, 37, 38, 83, 145, 209, 217, 228, 238

þiderleodisc, adj., of the local people, 196 [R]

þignen, noun, f., female servant, handmaid, 210

þing, noun, n., thing, 51ap, 101ap, 110, 198ap

þingere, noun, m., intercessor, 235

þingian, wk. vb. II, to ask favour, 78

geþingian, wk. vb. II, to intercede, 42, 193

þingung, noun, f., intercession, 67ap

geþingung, noun, f., intercession, 67, 73

geþoht, noun, m., thought, mind, determination, 9, 38, 39, 110, 122, 232, 236

þolian, wk. vb. II, to allow, to suffer, 71ap, 193ap

þonne, adv., conj., then, when, than, 1, 2, 5, 6, 9, 20, 21, 22, 23, 26, 36a, 39, 47, 49, 50, 56, 56a, 58, 58a, 65, 67, 69, 70, 73, 73a, 73b,

355

74, 78, 79, 80, 83a, 86, 88, 94a, 94b, 102, 111, 111a, 112, 114, 116a, 117, 122, 124, 125, 127, 131, 133, 139a, 146, 157, 160, 162, 166, 168, 170, 171a, 191, 197, 200a, 203, 209, 213, 215, 217a, 221a, 222, 229, 232, 233a, 234

þorn, noun, m., thorn, 53, 154, 173

þreagan, wk. vb. II, to pressurise, to torment, to trouble, 19, 67, 71, 83, 109, 115, 122, 126, 127, 157

þreat, noun, m., host, crowd, 16, 156

þreatian, wk. vb. II, to urge, to pressurise, to threaten, 7, 30, 65, 67ap, 71ap, 122ap, 163, 170, 220, 235

þreoteoþa, numeral, thirteenth, 18, 43, 154, 235

þreotyne, numeral, thirteen, 10, 28, 30, 136, 234

þri, þreo, numeral, three, 1, 3, 12, 14, 16, 22, 23, 26, 33, 34, 52, 53, 56a, 58, 67, 74, 76, 78, 91, 102, 110, 111a, 121, 126, 127, 132, 136, 144, 149, 160, 176, 180, 192, 196, 198, 199, 205, 210, 223, 226, 227, 228

þridda, numeral, third, 5, 10, 12, 34, 36b, 48, 50ap, 59, 76, 78, 97, 115, 127, 145, 174, 181, 196, 199, 201, 205, 207

Þrimilce, noun, m., name for the month of May, 'Three Milkings', 73b, 94a

geþristlæcan, wk. vb. I, to dare, 136

þritig, numeral, thirty, 8a, 12, 36b, 44, 53, 56a, 58b, 73b, 94b, 116b, 133, 139b, 171b, 200b, 217b, 226, 228, 233b

þritigoþa, numeral, thirtieth, 94, 116, 139, 170, 171, 200, 217, 233

þriwa, adv., three times, 60, 73b, 130, 145, 227

þrowere, noun, m., martyr, 154

þrowian, wk. vb. II, to suffer, 59, 62, 93, 98, 99, 103, 105, 109, 120, 123, 125, 127, 128, 129, 132, 168, 170, 184, 187, 188, 197, 198ap, 205, 209, 219, 224, 229, 234, 238

geþrowian, wk. vb. II, to suffer, to suffer martyrdom, 3, 10, 28, 29, 30, 31, 38, 39, 54, 62ap, 65, 86, 109ap, 112, 118, 134, 135, 140, 150, 183, 189, 195, 198, 201, 225, 227, 236

þrowung, noun, f., passion, suffering, martyrdom, 4, 13, 30, 31, 32, 38, 41, 54, 70, 73, 76, 83, 85, 86, 87, 102, 103, 105, 106, 109, 114, 120, 122, 123, 125, 127, 134, 143, 144, 147, 148, 149, 153, 155, 168, 183, 185, 187, 190, 191, 201, 209, 212ap, 216, 217, 220, 222, 227, 230, 231, 234

þruh, noun, f., pipe, 173

þryccan, wk. vb. I, to press, 79

þrymm, noun, m., power, host, 57, 79, 153

þrymsetl, noun, n., throne, 73, 234

geþuhtsum, adj., abundant, 145 [R]

þunor, noun, m., thunder, 70

þunorrad, noun, f., thunderclap, 33

þurh, prep., through, 1, 2, 4, 8, 12, 23, 28, 38, 41, 47, 48, 50, 54, 56, 59, 67, 71, 75, 77, 79, 88, 89, 90, 97, 100, 109, 110, 116, 118, 124, 125, 127, 130, 132, 134, 136, 139, 140, 142, 144, 145, 149, 152, 154, 166, 173, 186, 192, 195, 198, 199, 210, 211, 219, 221, 222, 223, 228, 230, 232

þurhfaran, st. vb. VI, to travel through, 238

þurhsmeagan, wk. vb. II, to study carefully, 232

þurhwunian, wk. vb. II, to last, 176

þurhstingan, st. vb. III, to stab, to pierce, 190, 238

þurst, noun, m., thirst, 186

þus, adv., thus, 30, 35, 57ap, 67, 123ap, 127, 209, 213ap, 233, 238

þusend, numeral, thousand, 1, 12, 166, 191

þyrel, noun, n., hole, 79, 221

þyrnen, adj., thorny, 162

geþyrst, adj., thirsty, 186 [R]

þyrstan, wk. vb. I, to thirst, 49, 133, 186

ufan, adv., from above, above, 65, 72, 79, 80, 88ap, 125

uhta, noun, m., dawn, early morning, 83a

uhtsang, noun, m., matins, 110

unalifed, adj., unlawful, not allowed, 9, 22

unalifedlic, adj., unlawful, not allowed, 51

geunarian, wk. vb. II, to dishonour, 67, 234 [R]

GLOSSARY

unasecgendlic, adj., indescribable, 54, 67, 73ap, 126, 151

ungebrosnod, adj., uncorrupted, undecayed, 110, 146

unbyrged, adj., unburied, 31 [R]

unclæne, adj., unclean, impure, not chaste, 9, 22, 70, 127, 197, 211, 227

uncuþ, adj., unknown, 21, 133

uncyst, noun, f., vices, 133

under, prep., under, 4, 72, 75, 79, 80, 88, 98, 103, 211, 226, 231

underfon, st. vb. VII, to receive, 136

undern, noun, m., the third hour of the day, 78, 83ap

undernrest, noun, f., rest in the morning or at midday, 49

understregdan, st. vb. III, but wk. form occurs in the *Old English Martyrology*, to scatter underneath, 19 [R]

underþeodan, wk. vb. I, to subject, 31, 53, 146

uneaþe, adv., hardly, with difficulty, 80, 180

ungeendod, adj., unstoppable, 144

unforhtlice, adv., fearlessly, 185

ungyrwan, wk. vb. I, to undress, 89, 187ap

unhire, adj., cruel, grim, 184

ungehirsumnes, noun, f., disobedience, 115

ungeleaffull, adj., unbelieving, 36

unlibbende, adj., not alive, dead, 180

unlifigende, adj., not alive, dead, 70ap

unlucan, st. vb. II, to unlock, to open, 56a ap

unmæte, adj., immense, 79

ungemolsnod, adj., uncorrupted, undecayed, 80

unriht, adj., wrongful, 190

unrihthæmed, noun, n., illicit sex, adultery, fornication, 116, 186, 190ap, 211

unrihtlice, adv., wrongfully, unjustly, 89

unrihtwisnes, noun, f., unrighteousness, iniquity, 116

unrim, noun, n., countless number, 51, 57, 157, 210ap, 211, 215

ungerim, noun, n., countless number, 12, 51ap, 215ap

unrot, adj., sad, 151, 180, 198

unsceþþende, adj., innocent, 209

unsceþþig, adj., innocent, 235

unscod, adj., not wearing shoes, 89

unsmeþe, adj., rough, uneven, 231

unstrang, adj., not strong, feeble, 155

unsynnig, adj., innocent, 108

untrum, adj., weak, ill, sick, 1, 4, 56a, 70, 145, 152, 186, 217

geuntrumian, wk. vb. II, to fall ill, to become weak, 80, 120

untrummes, noun, f., illness, weakness, infirmity, 49, 67, 198

untweogende, adj., undoubting, 56a

untynan, wk. vb. I, to open, 153

upastigennes, noun, f., ascension, ascent, 74, 78, 79, 88, 108, 133, 190, 215, 233, 238

upcuman, st. vb. IV, to come from, to originate, 211

uplic, adj., heavenly, celestial, 17, 46, 156, 160

upp, adv., up, 4, 56a, 65, 71, 77, 83a, 107, 109, 110, 111, 145, 151, 164ap, 217, 221a, 222, 226, 228, 230, 238

upweard, adv., upwards, 190

ut, adv., out, 2, 22, 40, 51, 54, 56a, 59, 64, 70, 97, 98, 144, 145, 211, 238

utan, adv., prep., outside, from outside, about, 46, 78, 80ap (see also Appendix 2), 157ap, 238

ute, adv., outside, 221

utera, adj., outer, 22, 162, 184

utgang, noun, m., outgoing, departure, 211

uton, aux. vb. (inf. **witan**), let us, 181

wa, noun, m., woe, 71

wacian, wk. vb. II, to watch, to wake, 30, 131, 184

wanian, wk. vb. II, to decrease, to cut back, 48, 50, 108

gewanian, wk. vb. II, to decrease, 48ap, 50

wanung, noun, f., reduction, 79

waroþ, noun, m., shore, beach, 26, 75, 228, 230

wægn, noun, m., waggon, carriage, 4

wælgrim, adj., cruel, 135, 208, 235

wælgrimlice, adv., cruelly, 140ap

wæpen, noun, n., weapon, 40

wæstm, noun, m., produce, harvest, crops, 69

GLOSSARY

wæte, noun, f., liquid, 52, 56a
wæter, noun, n., 2, 3, 12, 16, 22, 32, 41, 49, 52, 53, 68, 83, 88, 102, 109, 121, 122, 125, 130, 137, 173, 217, 225, 228
geweald, noun, m., power, 139, 228
wealdleþer, noun, n., rein, 238
wealh, noun, m., servant, 235
weall, noun, m., wall, 116, 160, 209
weallan, st. vb. VII, to boil, 83, 234
weallhus, noun, n., building in a wall, 209ap [R]
weard, noun, m., guard, 41
wearm, adj., warm, 41
weax, noun, n., wax, 197, 238
weaxan, st. vb. VII, to grow, to increase, to wax, 1, 48, 50
geweaxan, st. vb. VII, to grow, 1, 139b
webgeweorc, noun, n., weaving, 180 [R]
webwyrhta, noun, m., fuller, 30, 108 [R]
wedan, wk. vb. I, to rage, 208
weg, noun, m., way, road, 3, 20, 30, 51, 65, 76, 79, 86, 91, 151, 166, 176, 186, 205
wel, adv., well, fairly, 5, 38, 122
welig, adj., wealthy, 86, 140, 198
gewemman, wk. vb. I, to defile, to pollute, 38, 112
wen, noun, f., chance, probability, 122
wenan, wk. vb. I, to think, to believe, 59
wendan, wk. vb. I, to turn, 151ap, 209ap
gewendan, wk. vb. I, to turn, to return, 53, 121ap, 160, 201
gewenge, noun, n., cheek, 113
Weodmonaþ, noun, m., August, 'Weedmonth', 139b, 171a
weofod, noun, n., altar, 190, 194
weorc, noun, n., work, 55, 78, 80, 87, 100, 115, 221, 222
weorod, noun, n., group, host, 13, 37, 57, 75, 108, 187, 191
weorpan, st. vb. III, to throw, 3, 4, 31, 41, 51, 72ap, 99, 125, 130, 137, 187, 193, 195, 216, 217, 222, 230
weorþan, st. vb. III, to become, to turn, to happen, 1, 3, 4, 5, 41, 56, 56a, 101, 160ap, 182, 208ap, 223

geweorþan, st. vb. III, to be made, 52, 56, 88, 114, 116, 120, 129, 145, 178, 194, 195, 197, 222
weorþian, wk. vb. II, to honour, to worship, 1, 97, 130, 157, 160, 182, 203, 212, 218, 225, 238
wepan, st. vb. VII, to cry, to weep, 30, 38, 39, 40, 57, 64, 78, 80, 106, 115, 127, 133, 138, 139, 151, 210, 221, 228
wer, noun, m., man, 1, 3, 12, 13, 29, 32, 38, 39, 40, 41, 49, 51, 57, 67, 70, 73, 78, 90, 98, 99, 100, 103, 106, 110, 111, 112, 113, 114, 120, 121, 124, 128, 130, 139, 145, 148, 152, 160, 161, 166, 173, 176, 178, 182, 187, 191, 193, 195, 196, 207, 210, 211, 222, 224, 227, 232
werlic, adj., male, manly, 9, 39, 160
westdæl, noun, m., west, 135
westen, noun, n., desert, 16, 22, 65, 97, 133, 136, 211
westensetla, noun, m., hermit, 89
wicgerefa, noun, m., official, 190 [R]
wid, adv., widely, 101, 114
gewider, noun, n., weather, 69
widewa, noun, f., widow, 123, 129, 144, 225, 229
widsæ, noun, f., ocean, sea, 26, 31, 140
wif, noun, n., woman, wife, 2, 12, 22, 29, 30, 38, 39, 43, 53, 57, 76, 78, 87, 94, 99, 102, 106, 111, 117, 118, 122, 128, 164, 168, 173, 183, 190, 194, 198, 203, 207, 210, 217, 220ap, 225, 228, 231, 233
wifmann, noun, m., woman, 3, 211, 217ap
wilddeor, noun, n., wild animal, 53, 65, 83, 97, 157
wilde, adj., wild, 31, 65, 83, 97ap, 139, 154, 157ap, 186, 193
willa, noun, m., will, 226, 235
willan, anom. vb., to wish, to desire, not to wish (with neg.), 3, 4, 6, 7, 9, 19, 21, 26, 30, 39, 51, 57, 65, 68, 70, 73, 76, 79, 82, 86, 102, 103, 111, 112, 114, 123, 124, 127, 133, 137, 139, 140, 152, 168, 170, 181, 193, 194, 195, 197, 203, 209, 211, 212, 217b, 221, 225, 227, 230, 232, 235, 236

wille, noun, f., well, spring, surge, 88, 109
wilm, noun, m., boiling, surge, 102, 228
wilnian, wk. vb. II, to desire, 51
gewilnian, wk. vb. II, to desire, 51ap
win, noun, n., wine, 12, 49, 108, 127, 178, 205
wind, noun, m., wind, 38, 41, 56, 79, 88, 94b
windwian, wk. vb. II, to winnow, 40
winter, noun, m., winter, year, 16, 21, 118, 122ap, 157, 209, 211, 221a, 223
Winterfylleþ, noun, m., October, 'Winter Full Moon', 200b, 217a
wirrest, adj., worst, 87, 197
wisdom, noun, m., wisdom, 17, 42, 75, 121
wise, noun, f., way, manner, 9, 40, 60, 79, 122
witan, pret. pres. vb., to know, not to know (with neg.), 5, 52, 80, 89, 116, 140, 191, 210, 234
gewitan, st. vb. I, to go, to depart, to migrate, 3, 16, 21, 22, 36, 49ap, 51ap, 56a, 59ap, 63, 70ap, 78, 79, 97, 110ap, 127ap, 133, 136, 142ap, 156ap, 157, 160ap, 196ap, 199, 207ap, 210, 211, 215, 226, 235
wite, noun, n., torment, punishment, 2, 31, 57, 64, 67, 71, 73, 83, 89, 102, 106, 109, 122, 123, 126, 127, 140, 149, 151, 157, 176, 185ap, 189, 193, 217, 220, 235
witega, noun, m., prophet, 111
gewitennes, noun, f., departure, death, 49ap, 51ap, 60ap, 63ap, 66ap, 68ap, 80ap, 81ap, 107ap, 110ap, 115, 136ap, 138ap, 141ap, 171ap, 178ap, 181ap, 186ap, 196ap, 204ap, 207ap, 211ap, 214ap, 221ap, 223, 226, 237
gewitnian, wk. vb. II, to punish, 26, 67
wiþ, prep., against, from, with, 3, 60, 67, 73, 97, 100, 102, 112, 176ap, 190, 195, 231
wiþceosan, st. vb. II, to reject, 41
wiþsacan, st. vb. VI, to reject, to deny, 2, 3, 19, 20, 23, 31, 32, 41, 59, 64, 65, 67, 76, 86, 102, 103, 107, 109, 181, 185, 186, 187, 210, 216, 227, 228, 232
wlitig, adj., beautiful, handsome, 94, 139, 180, 233
woh, adj., not straight 38
wop, noun, m., cry, 57, 196

word, noun, n., word, 13, 56, 71, 80, 115, 124, 146, 168, 211
woruld, noun, f., world, existence, 2, 17, 40, 46, 48, 50, 52, 53, 55, 57, 106, 127, 168, 180, 193
woruldbroc, noun, n., secular use, 143 [R]
woruldfægernes, noun, f., worldly beauty, 38 [R]
woruldgefeoht, noun, n., worldly war, 41 [R]
woruldlic, adj., worldly, 17, 40, 78, 127
woruldlif, noun, n., worldly life, secular life, 138
woruldsnotor, adj., wise in worldly matters, 52 [R]
woruldwela, noun, m., worldly wealth, 73ap, 210
woruldweorc, noun, n., mechanics, 232 [R]
woruldwis, adj., wise in worldly matters, 232
woruldwisdom, noun, m., secular learning, 232
woruldwise, noun, f., worldly fashion, 73 [R]
woruldgewrit, noun, n., secular literature, profane writings, 232 [R]
wracu, noun, f., vengeance, revenge, 178, 235
wræcsiþ, noun, m., foreign travel, pilgrimage, 53, 124
gewrecan, st. vb. V, to punish, to avenge, 108, 112, 219
wregan, wk. vb. I, to accuse, to denounce, to complain, 162, 222, 234
gewrit, noun, n., literature, writing, 77, 108, 163, 170, 198, 211, 222, 232, 238
writan, st. vb. I, to write, 37, 42, 70, 190, 207, 237
writbred, noun, n., writing tablet, 155 [R]
writingisen, noun, n., writing-style, metal pen [R]
writiren, noun, n., writing-style, metal pen, 155 [R]
wucu, noun, f., week 14, 121
wudu, noun, m., wood, forest, 52, 83, 98, 157, 219
wuldor, noun, n., glory, 16, 17, 56a, 73, 160, 162, 168, 210, 232

wuldorbeah, noun, m., crown, 41, 185
wuldorfæst, adj., glorious, 93
wuldorlic, adj., glorious, 2, 21, 106, 120, 130, 162ap
wuldorlice, adv., gloriously, 31
wuldrian, wk. vb. II, to glorify, 65
wulf, noun, m., wolf, 16, 22, 34, 187, 211
wund, noun, f., wound, 58, 110, 136, 190
wundian, wk. vb. II, to wound, 198, 235, 236
gewundian, wk. vb. II, to wound, 1, 58, 113
wundor, noun, n., wonder, 4, 5, 7, 12, 26, 36, 37, 49, 66, 72, 77, 81, 88, 92, 97, 98, 99, 100, 114, 116, 124, 129, 132, 133, 136, 137, 141, 146, 148, 149, 152, 154, 160, 171, 173, 178, 180, 181, 186, 189, 195, 198, 201, 204, 211, 215, 221, 222, 223, 225, 232
wundorlic, adj., wonderful, 13, 56a, 79, 93ap, 106ap, 130ap, 162, 226, 230
wundorlice, adv., amazingly, 111a,
wundrian, wk. vb. II, to wonder at, to be astonished, 73, 221
wundswaþu, noun, f., scar, 110ap [R]
gewunelic, adj., customary, 80, 94b
wunian, wk. vb. II, to live, to dwell, 2, 3, 13, 16, 22, 51, 52, 63, 65, 66, 80, 88, 127, 133ap, 176ap, 199, 210, 226
gewunian, wk. vb. II, to dwell, 51ap, 133
wyllen, adj., woollen, 108, 110
wynsum, adj., pleasant, beautiful, 2, 37, 56a, 77, 103, 181, 220
wynsumian, wk. vb. II, to rejoice, to be joyful, 156
wynsumnes, noun, f., plesantness, beauty, delight, joy, 133, 145
wyrcan, wk. vb. I, to make, 130, 190, 221
gewyrcan, wk. vb. I, to make, to work, to form, to perform, 52, 163, 238
wyrm, noun, m., vermin, 5, 83, 140
wyrmgaldere, noun, m., snake-charmer, 124 [R]
wyrt, noun, f., plant, 12, 38, 173, 181
wyrtdrenc, noun, m., herbal potion, 78
wyrtgemengnes, noun, f., spice, 233 [R]
wyscan, wk. vb. I, to wish, 229

yfel, adj., horrible, evil, 41, 100, 131
yfel, noun, n., evil, 122
yfellic, adj., horrible, 16, 53
yld, noun, f., age, 12
yldu, noun, f., old age, 53, 194, 196
ymb, prep., about, concerning, 21, 26, 49, 63, 78, 79, 100, 111a, 115, 121, 138, 154, 157ap, 192, 210, 228, 234
ymbehydelice, adv., carefully, 89ap [R]
ymbfon, st. vb. VII, to surround, 46
ymbhwyrft, noun, m., circle, space, 22
ymbsittan, st. vb. V, to besiege, 199
ymbsnidennes, noun, f., circumcision, 9
ymbsniþan, st. vb. I, to circumcise, 9
ymbstandan, st. vb. VI, to surround, to stand near, 235
ymbutan, prep., around, 157
ymbyrnan, st. vb. III, to surround, to run around, 80
geyppan, wk. vb. I, to reveal, 152
yrnan, st. vb. III, to run, 1, 4, 41, 65, 68, 136, 157, 166, 191, 198, 209ap, 221, 228, 238
geyrnan, st. vb. III, to run, 209, 225
yst, noun, f., storm, blast, 79
yþ, noun, f., wave, 52, 75, 127, 130, 210
yþian, wk. vb. II, to overflow, 210

Latin and Greek vocabulary

actus, noun, m., act, 207
alabaster, noun, m., box for perfumes, 133
altor, noun, m., foster-father, 42
alumnus, noun, m., foster-son, 42
anima, noun, f., soul, 146
apostolus, noun, m., apostle, 207
apparitio, noun, f., appearance, epiphany, 12
Aprilis, noun, m., April, 58b
arithmetica, noun, f., arithmetic, mathematics, 232
astrologia, noun, f., astrology, 232
astronomia, noun, f., astronomy, 232
Augustus, noun, m., August, 142

GLOSSARY

bellum, noun, n., war, 63
birrus, noun, m., cloak, 210
candidus, adj., white, 98
consolatio, noun, f., consolation, 101
coronatus, adj., crowned, 222
December, noun, m., December, 233b
Deus, noun, m., God, 14, 127ap, 146, 184ap
domus, noun, f., house, 74
Dominus, noun, m., Lord, 12, 38, 108, 127ap, 218
ecce, adv., here, there, 38
Epiphania, noun, f., Epiphany, 12
excelsum, noun, n., heaven, 14
Exomologesis, noun, f., Rogation, 69
filius, noun, m., son, 101
fornicatio, noun, f., fornication, adultery, 22
frater, noun, m., brother, 108
furtum, noun, n., theft, 70
geometrica, noun, f., geometry, 232
gloria, noun, f., glory, 14
gratia, noun, f., favour, thanks
hic, adv., here, 60
historia, noun, f., history, 81, 92, 201
Ianuarius, noun, m., January, 8a
in, prep., in 14
Iulius, noun, m., July, 116b
Iunius, noun, m. June, 94b
Kalendae, noun, f., the Calends, 142
lampas, noun, f., lamp, 74
larua, noun, f., ghost, mask, 59
laudabilis, adj., praiseworthy, 70
ledo, noun, f., neap tide, 48
Litania, noun, f., Rogation, 69, 78
Maius, noun, m., May, 73b, 77
maior, adj., greater, 69
malina, noun, f., spring tide, 48
Martius, noun, m., March, 36b
mechanica, noun, f., mechanics, 232
medicina, noun, f., medicine, 232
meretrix, noun, f., prostitute, 149
mille, numeral, thousand, 6
mimus, noun, m., actor, entertainer, 163
mima, noun, f., actress, female entertainer, 210
misereri, verb, to take pity, 146
mons, noun, m., mountain, 88ap

munus, noun, n., offering, 63
musica, noun, f. music, 232
(dies) natalis, noun, m., feastday, birthday, 218
niger, adj., black, 98
Nonae, f., the fifth or seventh day, 77
November, noun, m., November, 217b
obryzum, noun, n., pure gold, 5
Octember, noun, m., October, 200b
os, noun, n., mouth, 74
palatium, noun, n., palace, 71
podagra, noun, f., gout, 120
quattuor, numeral, four, 222
quintus, numeral, fifth, 77
(liber) sacramentorum, noun, m., sacramentary, 95, 158
Saluator, noun, m., Saviour, 9
September, noun, m., September, 171b
silua, noun, f., forest, wood, 98
solstitium, noun, n., solstice, 111a
Soter, noun, m., Saviour, 9
spiritus, noun, m., spirit, 22
terra, noun, f., earth, 111a
telonarius, noun, m., customs officer, 190
umbilicus, noun, m., navel, 111a
ursa, noun, f., female bear, 8
uenator, noun, m., hunter, 74

Bibliography

This bibliography includes only items cited in this edition. A more comprehensive bibliography of studies relating to the *Old English Martyrology* can be found in Rauer, 'An Annotated Bibliography'. The references to the primary texts below also indicate the method of citation (by pages, lines, chapters etc.) which is used in this edition for each individual item.

Primary Texts, Named Authors

Ado of Vienne, *Martyrologium*, PL 123, 139–436 (feastdays)

Adomnán, *De locis sanctis*, ed. L. Bieler, CCSL 175 (Turnhout, 1965), pp. 185–234 (books, chapters and lines)

Aldhelm, *De uirginitate* (prose), ed. R. Ehwald, MGH, AA 15 (Berlin, 1919), pp. 226–323 (pages and lines)

—, *Carmen de uirginitate*, ed. R. Ehwald, MGH, AA 15 (Berlin, 1919), pp. 350–471 (lines)

—, *Carmina ecclesiastica*, ed. R. Ehwald, MGH, AA 15 (Berlin, 1919), pp. 11–32 (sections and subsections)

Ambrose, *Epistola* 22 (*BHL* 3513), ed. M. Zelzer, CSEL 82.3 (Vienna, 1982), pp. 126–40 (pages)

Asser, *Life of King Alfred*, ed. W. H. Stevenson (Oxford, 1904) (chapters)

Augustine, *De ciuitate Dei*, ed. B. Dombart and A. Kalb, CCSL 47–8 (Turnhout, 1955) (books, chapters and lines)

—, Sermo 130, PL 38 (columns)

—, Sermo 281, PL 38 (columns)

—, Sermo 282, ed. I. Schiller, D. Weber and C. Weidmann, *Wiener Studien* 121, (2008), 260–4 (sections)

—, Sermo 309, PL 38 (columns)

Ælfric, *Catholic Homilies: The First Series*, ed. P. Clemoes, EETS ss 17 (Oxford, 1997) (lines)

—, *Catholic Homilies: The Second Series*, ed. M. Godden, EETS ss 5 (Oxford, 1979) (lines)

Bede, *Chronica maiora*, ed. C. W. Jones, CCSL 123B (Turnhout, 1977), pp. 463–544 (sections and lines)

—, *De temporibus*, ed. C. W. Jones, CCSL 123C (Turnhout, 1980), pp. 585–611 (sections and lines)

—, *De temporum ratione*, ed. C. W. Jones, CCSL 123B (Turnhout, 1977), pp. 263–460 (sections and lines)

—, *Historia abbatum*, ed. C. Plummer, *Venerabilis Baeda opera historica*, 2 vols. (Oxford, 1896), I, 364–87 (chapters)

—, *Historia ecclesiastica gentis Anglorum*, ed. B. Colgrave and R. A. B. Mynors (Oxford, 1969) (pages and lines)

—, *In Lucae euangelium expositio*, ed. D. Hurst, CCSL 120 (Turnhout, 1960), pp. 1–425 (pages and lines)

—, *In Marci euangelium expositio*, ed. D. Hurst, CCSL 120 (Turnhout, 1960), pp. 427–648 (pages and lines)

—, *Martyrologium,* excerpts ed. in H. Quentin, *Les martyrologes historiques du moyen âge* (Paris, 1908) (pages)

—, *Vita S. Cuthberti* (prose) (*BHL* 2021), ed. B. Colgrave, *Two Lives of Saint Cuthbert* (Cambridge, 1940), pp. 141–306 (pages and lines)

—, *Vita metrica S. Cuthberti* (*BHL* 2020), ed. W. Jaager, *Bedas metrische Vita Sancti Cuthberti* (Leipzig, 1935) (lines)

—, *Vita S. Felicis* (*BHL* 2873), PL 94, 789–98 (columns)

Caesarius of Arles, *Sermones*, ed. G. Morin, CCSL 103–4 (Turnhout, 1953) (pages and lines)

Dionysius Exiguus, *De inuentione capitis Joannis baptistae* (*BHL* 4290–1), PL 67, 419–54 (columns)

Ennodius, *Carmina*, ed. F. Vogel, MGH, AA 7 (Berlin, 1885) (pages, books and sections)

Eucherius, *Passio S. Mauricii* (*BHL* 5737), ed. B. Krusch, MGH, SRM 3 (Hanover, 1906), pp. 32–41 (pages and lines)

Eustochius, see Primary Texts, Hagiography below (Pelagia)

Evagrius, *Vita S. Antonii* (*BHL* 609), PL 73, 125–70 (columns), alternatively also in P. H. E. Bertrand, 'Die Evagriusübersetzung der *Vita Antonii*: Rezeption, Überlieferung, Edition' (PhD diss., University of Utrecht, 2005), electronic version at www.zevep.com

Felix, *Vita S. Guthlaci* (*BHL* 3723), ed. B. Colgrave, *Felix's Life of Saint Guthlac* (Cambridge, 1956) (pages and lines)

Gregory, *Homiliae in Euangelia*, ed. R. Étaix, CCSL 141 (Turnhout, 1999) (pages and lines)

—, *Dialogi*, ed. A. De Vogüé, SChr 251, 260, 265 (Paris, 1978–80) (books, chapters and lines)

—, *Moralia in Iob*, ed. M. Adriaen, CCSL 143, 143A and 143B (Turnhout, 1979–85) (books, sections and lines)

Gregory of Tours, *Miraculum Clementis* (*BHL* 1855), ed. Mombritius, I, 344–5 and 640 (pages and lines)

Haymo of Auxerre, *Sermones*, PL 118 (columns)

Helisachar of Trier, see Primary Texts, Hagiography below (All Saints)

Hrabanus Maurus, *Martyrologium*, ed. J. McCulloh, CCCM 44 (Turnhout, 1978) (feastdays)

Isidore, *De ortu et obitu patrum*, ed. C. Chaparro Gómez (Paris, 1985) (chapters and sections)

Iulius Obsequens, *De prodigiis*, ed. O. Rossbach, *T. Livi Periochae Omnium Librorum* (Leipzig, 1910), pp. 151–81 (sections)

Jerome, *Vita S. Hilarionis* (*BHL* 3879), PL 23, 29–54 (columns)

—, *Vita S. Pauli* (*BHL* 6596), ed. P. B. Harvey jr., CCSL (Turnhout, forthcoming) (chapters)

Orosius, *Historiae aduersum paganos*, ed. K. Zangemeister, CSEL 5 (Vienna, 1982) (books, chapters and sections)

Patrick of Dublin, *De signis et prodigiis*, ed. A. Gwynn, *The Writings of Bishop Patrick 1074–84*, Scriptores Latini Hiberniae 1 (Dublin, 1955), pp. 56–7 (sections)
Paul the Deacon, *Vita S. Gregorii* (*BHL* 3648), PL 75, 41–60 (columns)
Paulinus of Milan, *Vita S. Ambrosii* (*BHL* 377), ed. M. Pellegrino, *Vita di S. Ambrogio*, Verba seniorum ns 1 (Rome, 1961) (sections)
Petrus Chrysologus, *Sermones*, ed. A. Olivar, CCSL 24, 24A and 24B (Turnhout, 1975–82) (pages and lines)
Pseudo-Abdias, *Passio S. Iacobi minoris* (*BHL* 4089), ed. Fabricius, II, 591–608 (pages and lines)
—, *Passio S. Iohannis* (*BHL* 4316), ed. Fabricius, II, 531–90 (pages and lines)
—, *Passio S. Philippi* (*BHL* 6814), ed. Mombritius, II, 385 and 714 (pages and lines)
Pseudo-Ambrose, see *Passio S. Agnetis, Passio S. Geruasii, Passio S. Sebastiani*
—, *Sermones*, PL 17, 603–762 (columns)
Pseudo-Augustine, *Sermones*, PL 39 (columns)
Pseudo-Fulgentius, Sermo 6, PL 65, 740–1 (columns)
Pseudo-Gregory, *Liber responsalis*, PL 78, 725–850 (columns)
Pseudo-Isidore, *De ortu et obitu patrum*, ed. J. Carracedo Fraga, CCSL 108E (Turnhout, 1996) (chapters and sections)
—, *De ordine creaturarum*, PL 83, 913–54 (columns)
Pseudo-Jerome, *Martyrologium*, ed. J. B. De Rossi and L. Duchesne, AASS, Nov. 2.1 and ed. H. Quentin and H. Delehaye, AASS Nov. 2.2 (Brussels, 1894) (feastdays)
Pseudo-Maximus, *Sermones*, ed. A Mutzenbecher, CCSL 23 (Turnhout, 1962) (pages and lines)
Pseudo-Theotimus, see *Passio S. Margaretae*
Rufinus, *Historia ecclesiastica*, ed. T. Mommsen, in *Eusebius: Werke*, ed. E. Klostermann, II, Griechische christliche Schriftsteller 9.1–2 (Leipzig, 1903–8) (pages and lines)
Stephen of Ripon, *Vita S. Wilfridi* (*BHL* 8889), ed. B. Colgrave, *The Life of Bishop Wilfrid by Eddius Stephanus* (Cambridge, 1927) (pages and lines)
Sulpicius Severus, *Dialogi* (*BHL* 5614–16), ed. K. Halm, CSEL 1 (Vienna, 1866), pp. 152–216 (pages and lines)
—, *Vita S. Martini* (*BHL* 5610), ed. J. Fontaine, *Vie de Saint Martin*, SChr 133–5 (Paris, 1967), I, 248–344 (chapters and sections)
Usuard, *Martyrologium*, ed. J. Dubois, *Le Martyrologe d'Usuard*, SH 40 (Brussels, 1965) (feastdays)

Primary Texts, Anonymous
Aldhelm Glosses (prose *De Virginitate*, 13.1, Napier), ed. A. S. Napier, *Old English Glosses*, Anecdota Oxoniensia, Medieval and Modern Series 11 (Oxford, 1900) (gloss number)
Anglo-Saxon Litanies of the Saints, ed. M. Lapidge, HBS 106 (London, 1991)

Antwerp-London Alphabetical Glossary (Porter), ed. D. W. Porter, *The Antwerp-London Glossaries*, Publications of the Dictionary of Old English 8 (Toronto, 2011), I (lines)

Bible (Vulgate), ed. R. Weber, 4th edn (Stuttgart, 1994) (chapters and verses)

Blickling Homilies, ed. R. Morris, EETS os 58, 63, 73 (London, 1874–80) (pages and lines)

Cleopatra Glosses, ed. W. G. Stryker, 'The Latin-Old English Glossary in MS. Cotton Cleopatra A.III' (PhD diss., Stanford University, 1951) (gloss number)

Corpus Glossary, ed. J. H. Hessels, *An Eighth-Century Latin-Anglo-Saxon Glossary* (Cambridge, 1890) (letter and lines)

De descensu Christi ad inferos, ed. A. M. L. Fadda, '*De descensu Christi ad inferos*: Una inedita omelia anglo-sassone', *Studi medievali* 13 (1972), 989–1011, at 998–1010 (lines)

Euangelium Pseudo-Matthei (*BHL* 5334–42), ed. M. Clayton, *The Apocryphal Gospels of Mary in Anglo-Saxon England*, CSASE 26 (Cambridge, 1998), pp. 323–7 (sections and subsections)

Inuentio S. Crucis (*BHL* 4169), ed. Mombritius, I, 376–9 and 647 (pages and lines)

Kentish Hymn, ed. E. V. K. Dobbie, *The Anglo-Saxon Minor Poems*, ASPR 6 (New York, 1942), pp. 87–8 (lines)

Liber pontificalis, ed. L. Duchesne, 2 vols. (Paris, 1886) (volumes, pages and sections)

Occasional Glosses 82.5 (Gough), ed. J. Gough, 'Some Old English Glosses', *Anglia* 92 (1974), 273–90 (gloss number)

Old English Bede, ed. T. Miller, *The Old English Version of Bede's Ecclesiastical History of The English People*, EETS os 95, 96, 110, 111 (London, 1890–8) (pages and lines)

Old English Prose Life of Guthlac, ed. P. Gonser, *Das angelsächsische Prosa-Leben des hl. Guthlac*, Anglistische Forschungen 27 (Heidelberg, 1909) (pages)

Old English Homilies (Tristram), ed. H. L. C. Tristram, 'Vier altenglische Predigten aus der heterodoxen Tradition' (PhD diss., University of Freiburg i. Br., 1970) (homily and lines)

Old English Translation of Gregory's *Dialogi*, ed. H. Hecht, *Bischof Wærferths von Worcester Übersetzung der Dialoge Gregors des Grossen*, Bibliothek der angelsächsischen Prosa 5 (Leipzig, 1900–7), pp. 179–259 (chapters, pages and lines)

Vitae patrum (*BHL* 6527–9), PL 73, 851–1024 (columns)

Primary Texts, Hagiography (listed alphabetically by saint's name)

Passio SS. Abdon et Sennen (*BHL* 6), *AB* 51 (1933), 75–80 (pages and lines) [See also under *Passio S. Laurentii* (*BHL* 4753)]

Passio S. Afrae (*BHL* 108–9), ed. B. Krusch, MGH, SRM 3 (Hanover, 1906), pp. 55–64 (pages and lines)

Passio S. Agnetis (*BHL* 156), PL 17, 735–42 (columns)

Passio S. Alexandri (*BHL* 266), AASS, Maii 1, 371–5 (pages)

(All Saints), 'Legimus in ecclesiasticis historiis' (*BHL* 6332d), ed. J. E. Cross, '"Legimus in ecclesiasticis historiis": A Sermon for All Saints, and its Use in Old English Prose', *Traditio* 33 (1977), 101–35, at 105–21 (lines)

Passio S. Ananiae (*BHL* 397), AASS, Feb. 3, 492–5 (pages and sections)

Passio S. Anastasiae (*BHL* 118, 401, 8093), ed. P. F. Moretti, *La Passio Anastasiae: Introduzione, testo critico, traduzione*, Studi e Testi Tardo Antichi (Rome, 2006) (sections)

(Anastasius) *Miraculum Romae ad Aquas Saluias* (*BHL* 412), ed. C. V. Franklin, *The Latin Dossier of Anastasius the Persian: Hagiographic Translations and Transformations*, Studies and Texts 147 (Toronto), pp. 347–61 (lines)

Passio S. Anatholiae et Audacis (*BHL* 418), AASS, Iul. 2, 672–3 (pages)

Passio S. Andochii (*BHL* 424), ed. J. Van der Straeten, *AB* 79 (1961), 447–68 (pages and lines)

Passio S. Andreae (*BHL* 428), ed. Mombritius, I, 104–7 and 625 (pages and lines)

Passio S. Andreae (*BHL* 430), ed. Fabricius, II, 456–515 (pages and lines)

Passio S. Antonini (*BHL* 568), ed. J. E. Cross, 'Antoninus of Apamea and an Image in the *Old English Martyrology*', *NQ* 31 (1984), 18–22, at 21–2 (pages)

Passio S. Apollinaris (*BHL* 623), AASS, Iul. 5, 344–50 (pages)

Vita S. Audomari (*BHL* 763), ed. W. Levison, MGH, SRM 5 (Hanover, 1910), pp. 753–64 (pages and lines)

Passio S. Babylae (*BHL* 890), ed. Mombritius, I, 127–30 and 627–8 (pages and lines)

Passio S. Bartholomaei (*BHL* 1002), ed. Mombritius, I, 140–4 and 629 (pages and lines)

Passio S. Benigni (*BHL* 1153), ed. J. Van der Straeten, *AB* 79 (1961), 465–8 (pages and lines)

Vita S. Bertini (*BHL* 763), ed. W. Levison, MGH, SRM 5 (Hanover, 1910), pp. 765–9 and 778–80 (pages and lines)

Passio S. Caeciliae (*BHL* 1495), ed. R. K. Upchurch, *Ælfric's Lives of the Virgin Spouses* (Exeter, 2007), pp. 172–217 (sections)

Passio S. Caesarii (*BHL* 1511), AASS, Nov. 1, 106–17 (pages)

Passio S. Cassiani (*BHL* 1626), ed. Mombritius, I, 280 and 636 (pages and lines)

Vita S. Ceolfridi (*BHL* 1726), ed. C. Plummer, *Venerabilis Baeda opera historica*, 2 vols. (Oxford, 1896), II, 388–404 (pages and lines)

Passio S. Christinae (*BHL* 1748b), ed. J. E. Cross and C. J. Tuplin, 'An Unrecorded Variant of the *Passio S. Christinae* and the *Old English Martyrology*', *Traditio* 36 (1980), 161–236, at 173–87 (pages and lines)

Passio S. Christophori (*BHL* 1764), ed. A. Fábrega Grau, *Pasionario Hispánico*, 2 vols. (Madrid, 1953–5), II, 299–309 (sections)

Passio SS. Chrysanthi et Dariae (*BHL* 1787), ed. R. K. Upchurch, *Ælfric's Lives of the Virgin Spouses* (Exeter, 2007), pp. 218–49 (sections)

Passio S. Chrysogoni (*BHL* 1795), ed. P. F. Moretti, *La Passio Anastasiae: Introduzione, testo critico, traduzione*, Studi e Testi Tardo Antichi (Rome, 2006) (sections)

Passio S. Claudii et sociorum (*BHL* 1836), AASS, Nov. 3, 765–79 (pages)

Passio S. Clementis (*BHL* 1848), ed. Mombritius, I, 341–4 and 640 (pages and lines)

Passio S. Columbae (*BHL* 1892), ed. Mombritius, I, 370–1 and 645 (pages and lines)
Passio S. Cornelii (*BHL* 1958), ed. Mombritius, I, 373 and 646 (pages and lines)
Passio S. Cosmae (*BHL* 1970), AASS, Sept. 7, 474–8 (pages)
Acta S. Cypriani (*BHL* 2038), ed. R. Reitzenstein, *Die Nachrichten über den Tod Cyprians: Ein philologischer Beitrag zur Geschichte der Märtyrerliteratur*, Sitzungsberichte der Heidelberger Akademie der Wissenschaften, phil.-hist. Kl. 4 (1913), no. 14 (pages and lines)
Passio S. Cyrici (*BHL* 1802–8), AASS, Iun. 3, 28–33 (pages)
Passio S. Dionysii (*BHL* 2171), PL 88, 577–84 (columns)
Passio S. Donati (*BHL* 2289–92), ed. C. Lazzeri, *La donazione del tribuno romano Zenobio al vescovo d'Arezzo San Donato* (Arezzo, 1938), pp. 117–21 (pages and lines)
Passio S. Eleutherii (*BHL* 2451), ed. Mombritius, I, 443–6 and 658 (pages and lines)
Passio S. Erasmi (*BHL* 2582), ed. Mombritius, I, 485–8 and 665 (pages and lines)
Passio S. Eugeniae (*BHL* 2666), PL 73, 605–23 (columns)
Passio S. Eulaliae (*BHL* 2696), ed. C. Narbey, *Supplément aux Acta Sanctorum pour des vies de saints de l'époque mérovingienne*, 2 vols. (Paris, 1899–1900), II, 62–4 (sections)
Passio S. Euphemiae (*BHL* 2708), ed. Mombritius, I, 454–9 and 660–1 (pages and lines)
Passio S. Eupli (*BHL* 2729), ed. Mombritius, I, 448–9 and 659 (pages and lines)
Passio S. Eusebii (*BHL* 2748–9), ed. A. Ventilacini, *Miscellanea Augustana*, 2 vols. (Aosta, 1951–2), I, 145–62 (pages and lines)
Passio SS. Faustae et Evilasii (*BHL* 2833), AASS, Sept. 6, 144–6 (pages)
Passio S. Felicitatis (*BHL* 2853), ed. K. Künstle, *Hagiographische Studien über die Passio S. Felicitatis cum VII filiis* (Paderborn, 1894), pp. 60–3 (lines)
Passio S. Felicis Tubzocensis (*BHL* 2895b), ed. H. Quentin, *Les martyrologes historiques du moyen âge* (Paris, 1908), pp. 526–7 (pages and lines)
Passio S. Ferreoli (*BHL* 2903), AASS, Iun. 3, 7–8 (pages)
Vita S. Fursei (*BHL* 3213a), ed. W. W. Heist, *Vitae Sanctorum Hiberniae ex codice olim Salmanticensi*, SH 28 (Brussels, 1965), pp. 37–65 (sections and lines)
Passio SS. Gallicani, Iohannis et Pauli (*BHL* 3236, 3238), ed. Mombritius, I, 569–72 and 677 (pages and lines)
Passio S. Genesii (*BHL* 3304), ed. S. Cavallin, 'Saint Genès le notaire', *Eranos* 43 (1945), 150–75, at 160–4 (pages and lines)
Passio S. Genesii (*BHL* 3320), ed. W. Weismann, 'Die *Passio Genesii mimi* (*BHL* 3320)', *MJ* 12 (1977), 22–43, at 38–43 (sections)
Passio S. Georgii (*BHL* 3363), ed. W. Arndt, '*Passio Georgii martyris*', Berichte über die Verhandlungen der königlich sächsischen Gesellschaft der Wissenschaften zu Leipzig, philol.-hist. Kl. 26 (1874), 49–70 (pages and lines)
Passio S. Georgii (*BHL* 3379), ed. J. Matzke, 'Contributions to the History of the Legend of Saint George', *Publications of the Modern Language Association of America* 17 (1902), 464–535, at 525–9 (pages and lines)
Passio S. Geruasii (*BHL* 3514), PL 17, 742–7 (columns)

Vita S. Goaris (*BHL* 3565), ed. B. Krusch, MGH, SRM 4 (Hanover, 1902), pp. 411–23 (chapters)

Vita S. Gregorii (*BHL* 3637), ed. B. Colgrave, *The Earliest Life of Gregory the Great* (Cambridge, 1968) (pages)

Passio S. Hadriani et sociorum (*BHL* 3744), ed. Mombritius, I, 22–30 and 617–18 (pages and lines)

Vita S. Hilarionis (*BHL* 3879), PL 23, 29–54 (columns)

Passio S. Iacobi minoris (*BHL* 4093), *AB* 8 (1889), 136–7 (pages)

Passio S. Ianuarii (*BHL* 4132), ed. D. Mallardo, 'S. Gennaro e compagni nei più antichi testi e monumenti', *Rendiconti della reale accademia di archeologia, lettere e belle arti*, ns 20 (1940), 163–267, at 253–9 (pages and lines)

Passio SS. Irenaei et Abundii (*BHL* 4464), ed. H. Delehaye, *AB* 51 (1933), 95–6 (pages and lines)

Passio S. Iuliani (*BHL* 4529), ed. P. Salmon, *Le lectionnaire de Luxueil*, Collectanea Biblica Latina 7 (Vatican, 1944), pp. 27–56 (pages and lines)

Passio S. Iustinae (*BHL* 2047, 2050), ed. Mombritius, II, 70–5 and 669–70 (pages and lines)

Passio S. Iusti (*BHL* 4590), ed. M. Coens, 'Un fragment retrouvé d'une ancienne Passion de S. Just, martyr de Beauvais', *AB* 74 (1956), 94–6 (lines)

Passio S. Laurentii (*BHL* 4753), ed. H. Delehaye, *AB* 51 (1933), 72–98 (pages and lines) [This composite text also comprises the *Passio SS. Abdon et Sennen* (*BHL* 6) and the *Passio S. Sixti* (*BHL* 7801) which are given separate entries here]

Passio S. Luciae (*BHL* 4980), AASS, Iun. 5, 13–14 (pages)

Passio S. Luciae (*BHL* 4992), ed. Mombritius, II, 107–9 and 676 (pages and lines)

Vita S. Lupi (*BHL* 5087), ed. B. Krusch, MGH, SRM 7 (Hanover, 1919), pp. 295–302 (pages and lines)

Passio S. Mammetis (*BHL* 5194), ed. Mombritius, II, 126–9 and 681–2 (pages and lines)

Passio S. Marcelli (*BHL* 5245), AASS, Sept. 2, 196–7 (pages)

Passio S. Marcellini (*BHL* 5231), AASS, Iun. 1, 171–3 (pages)

Passio S. Marci (*BHL* 5276), AASS, Apr. 3, 347–9 (pages)

Passio S. Margaretae (*BHL* 5303), ed. M. Clayton and H. Magennis, *The Old English Lives of St Margaret*, CSASE 9 (Cambridge, 1994), pp. 194–218 (chapters)

Vita S. Mariae Magdalenae (*BHL* 5453), ed. J. E. Cross, 'Mary Magdalen in the *Old English Martyrology*: The Earliest Extant "Narrat Josephus" Variant of her Legend', *Speculum* 53 (1978), 16–25, at 21–2 (pages and lines)

Passio SS. Marii et Marthae (*BHL* 5543), AASS, Ian. 2, 216–19 (pages)

Vita S. Martialis (*BHL* 5551), ed. F. Arbellot, 'Étude historique sur l'ancienne *Vie de Saint Martial*', *Bulletin de la société archéologique et historique du Limousin* 40 (1892), 213–60, at 238–43 (pages and lines)

Miracula S. Martialis (*BHL* 5561), ed. F. Arbellot, 'Étude historique sur l'ancienne *Vie de Saint Martial*', *Bulletin de la société archéologique et historique du Limousin* 40 (1892), 213–60, at 243–8 (pages and lines)

Passio S. Matthei (*BHL* 5690), Fabricius, II, 636–68 (pages and lines)

Passio S. Mennae (*BHL* 5921), ed. R. Miedema, *De heilige Menas* (Rotterdam, 1913), pp. 105–21 (pages and lines)

Apparitio S. Michaelis (*BHL* 5948), ed. G. Waitz, MGH, SRLI (Hanover, 1878), pp. 541–3 (pages and lines)

Passio S. Nazarii (*BHL* 6039), ed. Mombritius, II, 326–34 (pages and lines)

Vita S. Pamphili (*BHL* 6418), AASS, Apr. 3, 585 (chapters)

Passio S. Pancratii (*BHL* 6421), ed. A. Z. Huisman, *Die Verehrung des Heiligen Pancratius in West- und Mitteleuropa*, Nederlandsche Bijdragen op het Gebied van Germaansche Philologie en Linguistiek 11 (Haarlem, 1939), pp. 16–18 (pages and lines)

Vita S. Pelagiae (*BHL* 6605, version A1), ed. F. Dolbeau, 'La réfection latine A'', *Pélagie la Penitente: Métamorphoses d'une légende*, ed. P. Petitmengin *et al.*, 2 vols. (Paris, 1981–4), I, 181–216, at 199–216 (sections)

Vita S. Pelagiae (*BHL* 6609, version B), ed. C. Lévy *et al.*, 'La réfection latine B', *Pélagie la Penitente: Métamorphoses d'une légende*, ed. P. Petitmengin *et al.*, 2 vols. (Paris, 1981–4), I, 217–49, at 231–49 (sections)

Passio SS. Perpetuae et Felicitatis (*BHL* 6633), ed. J. Amat, *Passion de Perpétue et de Félicité*, SChr 417 (Paris, 1996) (chapters and lines)

Vita S. Petronillae (*BHL* 6061), AASS, Maii 3, 10–11 (pages)

Passio S. Phocae (*BHL* 6838), ed. Mombritius, II, 417–22 and 718–19 (pages and lines)

Passio S. Procopii (*BHL* 6949), ed. W. Cureton, *History of the Martyrs in Palestine* (London, 1861), pp. 50–1 (pages and lines)

Passio et Inuentio S. Quintini (*BHL* 6999–7000), AASS, Oct. 13, 781–3 and 785–6 (pages)

Passio S. Saturnini (*BHL* 7495–6), ed. C. Devic and J. Vaissete, *Histoire générale de Languedoc*, 16 vols. (Toulouse, 1872–93), II (preuves), cols. 29–34 (sections)

Passio SS. Scillitanorum (*BHL* 7531), AASS, Iul. 4, 214 (pages)

Passio SS. Sebastenorum (*BHL* 7539), AASS, Mar. 2, 19–21 (pages)

Passio S. Sebastiani (*BHL* 7543), AASS, Ian. 2, 265–78 (pages and sections)

Gesta S. Siluestri (*BHL* 7725–32), ed. Mombritius, II, 508–31 and 736–7 (pages and lines)

Passio SS. Simonis et Iudae (*BHL* 7749–50), ed. Fabricius, II, 608–36 (pages and lines)

Passio S. Sixti (*BHL* 7801), ed. H. Delehaye, *AB* 51 (1933), 80–85 (pages and lines) [See also under *Passio S. Laurentii* (*BHL* 4753)]

Passio S. Speusippi (*BHL* 7828), AASS, Ian. 2, 74–6 (sections)

Reuelatio Stephani (*BHL* 7851), ed. E. Vanderlinden, '*Reuelatio Sancti Stephani, BHL* 7850–6), *Revue des études byzantines* 4 (1946), 190–216 (pages and lines)

Reuelatio Stephani (*BHL* 7855), ed. E. Vanderlinden, '*Reuelatio Sancti Stephani, BHL* 7850–6), *Revue des études byzantines* 4 (1946), 191–217 (pages and lines)

Vita S. Symeonis stylitae (*BHL* 7957, 7958), PL 73, 325–34 (columns)
Passio S. Symphoriani (*BHL* 7967–8), AASS, Aug. 4, 496–7 (pages)
Passio S. Symphorosae (*BHL* 7971), AASS, Iul. 4, 355 and 358–9 (pages)
Passio S. Theclae (*BHL* 8020n), ed. O. von Gebhardt, *Die lateinischen Übersetzungen der Acta Pauli et Theclae nebst Fragmenten, Auszügen und Beilagen*, TU 22 (Leipzig, 1902), pp. 3–127 (pages and lines)
Passio S. Theodoreti (*BHL* 8074), AASS, Oct. 10, 43–4 (pages)
Passio S. Thomae (*BHL* 8136), ed. K. Zelzer, *Die alten lateinischen Thomasakten*, TU 122 (Berlin, 1977), 3–42 (pages and lines)
Passio S. Valeriani (*BHL* 8488), AASS, Sept. 5, 21–2 (pages)
Passio S. Victoris (*BHL* 8559), AASS, Maii 3, 266–8 (pages)
Passio S. Victoris (*BHL* 8570), ed. C. Narbey, *Supplément aux Acta Sanctorum pour des vies de saints de l'époque mérovingienne*, 2 vols. (Paris, 1899–1900), II, 373–6 (sections)
Passio S. Victoris (*BHL* 8580), AASS, Maii 2, 288–90 (pages)
Passio S. Vincentii (*BHL* 8631), ed. M. Simonetti, 'Una redazione poco conosciuta della *Passio di S. Vincenzo*', *Rivista di archeologia cristiana* 32 (1956), 231–41 (sections)
Vita S. Winnoci (*BHL* 8952), ed. W. Levison, MGH, SRM 5 (Hanover, 1910), pp. 769–80 (pages and lines)

Secondary Literature
Abel, F.-M., 'Mélanges', *Revue Biblique* 33 (1924), 235–45
Aigrain, R., *L'hagiographie: ses sources, ses méthodes, son histoire*, SH 80 (Brussels, 2000)
Ambrasi, D., 'Rufo', *BSS*, XI, 485–7
—, 'Rufo e Carpoforo', *BSS*, XI, 488
—, 'Prisco da Capua', *BSS*, X, 1114–16
—, 'Prisco vescovo di Capua', *BSS*, X, 1116–17
—, 'Panfilo', *BSS*, X, 92–3
Amore, A., 'Eutichio, Plauto ed Eraclea', *BSS*, V, 488
—, 'Goar', *BSS*, VII, 64–5
—, 'Mamiliano', *BSS*, VIII, 617–19
Anderson, E. R., 'The Seasons of the Year in Old English', *ASE* 26 (1997), 231–63
Anderson, J., 'The Great Kentish Collapse', *Luick Revisited*, ed. D. Kastovsky and G. Bauer, Tübinger Beiträge zur Linguistik 288 (Tübingen, 1985), pp. 97–107
Anlezark, D., 'Three Notes on the Old English Metres of Boethius', *NQ* 51 (2004), 10–15
Bately, J., 'Grimbald of St. Bertin's', *MÆ* 35 (1966), 1–10
—, 'Old English Prose before and during the Reign of Alfred', *ASE* 17 (1988), 93–138
—, 'The Alfredian Canon Revisited: One Hundred Years on', *Alfred the Great: Papers from the Eleventh-Centenary Conferences*, ed. T. Reuter (Aldershot, 2003), pp. 107–20

—, 'The Place Which is Called "at X": A New Look at Old Evidence', *Essays for Joyce Hill on her Sixtieth Birthday*, ed. M. Swan, *Leeds Studies in English* ns 37 (2006), 343–59

—, 'Did King Alfred Actually Translate Anything? The Integrity of the Alfredian Canon Revisited', *MÆ* 78 (2009), 189–215

Bertram, J., ed., *The Chrodegang Rules* (Aldershot, 2005)

Bierbaumer, P., *Der botanische Wortschatz des Altenglischen*, 3 vols. (Frankfurt a. M., 1975–9)

Biggs, F. M., 'Inventio Sanctae Crucis', *SASLC*, pp. 12–13

—, ed., *The Apocrypha*, Instrumenta Anglistica Mediaevalia 1 (Kalamazoo, 2007)

Biggs, F. M., and J. H. Morey, 'Gospel of Nicodemus', *The Apocrypha*, ed. F. M. Biggs, Instrumenta Anglistica Mediaevalia 1 (Kalamazoo, 2007), pp. 29–31

Bischoff, B., and M. Lapidge, *Biblical Commentaries from the Canterbury School of Theodore and Hadrian*, CSASE 10 (Cambridge, 1994)

Blackburn, B., and L. Holford-Strevens, *The Oxford Companion to the Year* (Oxford, 1999)

Blair, J., 'A Handlist of Anglo-Saxon Saints', *Local Saints and Local Churches in the Early Medieval West*, ed. A. Thacker and R. Sharpe (Oxford, 2002), pp. 495–565

Blanton, V., *Signs of Devotion: The Cult of St. Æthelthryth in Medieval England 695–1615* (University Park, 2007)

Bollandists, ed., Acta Sanctorum, 1st edn, 68 vols. (1643–1940)

—, ed., *Bibliotheca Hagiographica Latina*, 2 vols. (Brussels, 1899–1901)

Bolton, W. F., 'The Background and Meaning of *Guthlac*', *Journal of English and Germanic Philology* 61 (1962), 595–603

Borst, A., *Die karolingische Kalenderreform*, MGH Schriften 46 (Hanover, 1998)

—, *Der karolingische Reichskalender und seine Überlieferung bis ins 12. Jahrhundert*, MGH Libri memoriales 2, 3 vols. (Hanover, 2001)

Bosworth, J., and T. N. Toller, *An Anglo-Saxon Dictionary* (Oxford, 1882–98)

Bratož, R., 'Die diokletianische Christenverfolgung in den Donau- und Balkanprovinzen', *Diokletian und die Tetrarchie: Aspekte einer Zeitenwende*, ed. A. Demandt, A. Goltz and H. Schlange-Schöningen, Millennium-Studien 1 (Berlin, 2004), pp. 115–40

Breeze, A., 'Locating *Ludica* in *The Old English Martyrology*', *NQ* 57 (2010), 168

Brooks, N., *The Early History of the Church of Canterbury* (Leicester, 1984)

Brown, M., 'Paris, Bibliothèque Nationale, lat. 10861 and the Scriptorium of Christ Church, Canterbury', *ASE* 15 (1986), 119–37

—, 'Mercian Manuscripts? The "Tiberius" Group and its Historical Context', *Mercia: An Anglo-Saxon Kingdom in Europe*, ed. M. P. Brown and C. A. Farr (London, 2001), pp. 279–90

Campbell, A., *Old English Grammar* (Oxford, 1959)

Campbell, J. J., 'The Dialect Vocabulary of the OE Bede', *Journal of English and Germanic Philology* 50 (1951), 349–72

—, 'To Hell and Back; Latin Tradition and Literary Use of the "Descensus ad inferos" in Old English', *Viator* 13 (1982), 107–58

Canart, P., 'Le nouveau-né qui dénonce son père', *AB* 84 (1966), 309–33
Caraffa, F., 'Panfilo', *BSS*, X, 93
—, ed., *Bibliotheca Sanctorum*, 13 vols. (Vatican, 1961–70)
Casiday, A., 'Thomas Didymus from India to England', *Quaestio Insularis* 4 (2003), 70–81
Catholic Encyclopedia, http://www.newadvent.org/cathen
Chapman, A., 'Reforming Time: Calendars and Almanacs in Early Modern England', (PhD diss., University of Pennsylvania, 2002)
Chardonnens, S., 'London, British Library, Harley 3271: The Composition and Structure of an Eleventh-Century Anglo-Saxon Miscellany', *Form and Content of Instruction in Anglo-Saxon England in the Light of Contemporary Manuscript Evidence*, ed. P. Lendinara, L. Lazzari and M. A. D'Aronco, Textes et Études du Moyen Âge 39 (Turnhout, 2007), pp. 3–34
Chenard, M., 'Narratives of the Saintly Body in Anglo-Saxon England' (PhD diss., University of Notre Dame, 2003)
Clayton, M., 'Feasts of the Virgin in the Liturgy of the Anglo-Saxon Church', *ASE* 13 (1984), 209–33
—, Review of Kotzor, ed., *Das altenglische Martyrologium*, *RES* 35 (1984), 347–9
—, *The Cult of the Virgin Mary in Anglo-Saxon England*, CSASE 2 (Cambridge, 1990)
—, *The Apocryphal Gospels of Mary in Anglo-Saxon England*, CSASE 26 (Cambridge, 1998)
Clayton, M., and H. Magennis, *The Old English Lives of St Margaret*, CSASE 9 (Cambridge, 1994)
Cockayne, T. O., *The Shrine: A Collection of Occasional Papers on Dry Subjects* (London, 1869)
Coens, M., 'Un fragment retrouvé d'une ancienne Passion de S. Just, martyr de Beauvais', *AB* 74 (1956), 94–6
—, 'Nouvelles recherches sur un thème hagiographique: la céphalophorie', in his *Recueil d'études bollandiennes*, SH 37 (Brussels, 1963), pp. 9–31
Coleman, J., *Love, Sex, and Marriage: A Historical Thesaurus*, Costerus ns 118 (Amsterdam, 1999)
Condie, V., 'Representations of the Nativity in the Art and Vernacular Literature of the Anglo-Saxons' (DPhil diss., University of Oxford, 2005)
Conner, P. W., 'On Dating Cynewulf', *The Cynewulf Reader*, ed. R. E. Bjork, BRASE 4 (New York, 1996), pp. 23–56
Cook, A. S., *Biblical Quotations in Old English Prose Writers: Second Series* (New York, 1903)
Corona, G., ed., *Ælfric's Life of Saint Basil the Great: Background and Context* (Cambridge, 2006)
Corradini, E., 'Leofric of Exeter and his Lotharingian Connections: A Bishop's Books c. 1050–72' (PhD diss., University of Leicester, 2008)
Cross, J. E., 'On the Blickling Homily for Ascension Day (no. XI)', *NM* 70 (1969), 228–40

—, 'De signis et prodigiis in versibus Sancti Patricii episcopi De mirabilibus Hibernie', *Proceedings of the Royal Irish Academy* 71C (1971), 247–54
—, Review of Pope, ed., *Homilies of Ælfric*, *Studia Neophilologica* 43 (1971), 569–71
—, '*De ordine creaturarum liber* in Old English Prose', *Anglia* 90 (1972), 132–40
—, 'Portents and Events at Christ's Birth: Comments on Vercelli v and vi and the *Old English Martyrology*', *ASE* 2 (1973), 209–20
—, 'Blickling Homily XIV and the *Old English Martyrology* on John the Baptist', *Anglia* 93 (1975), 145–60
—, '"Legimus in ecclesiasticis historiis": A Sermon for All Saints, and its Use in Old English Prose', *Traditio* 33 (1977), 101–35
—, 'Two Saints in the *Old English Martyrology*', *NM* 78 (1977), 101–7
—, 'Mary Magdalen in the *Old English Martyrology*: The Earliest Extant "Narrat Josephus" Variant of her Legend', *Speculum* 53 (1978), 16–25
—, 'Popes of Rome in the *Old English Martyrology*', *Papers of the Liverpool Latin Seminar: Second Volume 1979*, ed. F. Cairns, ARCA: Classical and Medieval Texts, Papers and Monographs (Liverpool, 1979), pp. 191–211
—, 'The Apostles in the *Old English Martyrology*', *Mediaevalia* 5 (1979), 1–59
—, 'Cynewulf's Traditions about the Apostles in *Fates of the Apostles*', *ASE* 8 (1979), 163–75
—, 'An Unrecorded Tradition of St. Michael in Old English Texts', *NQ* 28 (1981), 11–13
—, 'Eulalia of Barcelona: A Notice without Source in the *Old English Martyrology*', *NQ* 28 (1981), 483–4
—, 'Old English *leasere*', *NQ* 28 (1981), 484–6
—, '*Passio Symphoriani* and OE *cun(d)*', *NM* 82 (1981), 269–75
—, 'The Influence of Irish Texts and Traditions on the *Old English Martyrology*', *Procedings of the Royal Irish Academy.* 81 C (1981), 173–92
—, 'A Lost Life of Hilda of Whitby: The Evidence of the *Old English Martyrology*', *The Early Middle Ages*, ed. W. H. Snyder, Acta: Center for Medieval and Early Renaissance Studies 6 (Binghamton, 1982), pp. 21–43
—, 'A *Virgo* in the *Old English Martyrology*', *NQ* 29 (1982), 102–6
—, '*Passio S. Eugeniae et comitum* and the *Old English Martyrology*', *NQ* 29 (1982), 392–7
—, 'Saints' Lives in Old English: Latin Manuscripts and Vernacular Accounts: The *Old English Martyrology*', *Peritia* 1 (1982), 38–62
—, 'Columba of Sens in the *Old English Martyrology*', *NQ* 30 (1983), 195–8
—, 'Cosmas and Damian in the *Old English Martyrology*', *NQ* 30 (1983), 15–18
—, 'Euphemia and the Ambrosian Missal', *NQ* 30 (1983), 18–22
—, 'The *Passio S. Laurentii et aliorum*: Latin Manuscripts and the *Old English Martyrology*', *Mediaeval Studies* 45 (1983), 200–13
—, 'Antoninus of Apamea and an Image in the *Old English Martyrology*', *NQ* 31 (1984), 18–22
—, 'Pelagia in Mediaeval England', *Pélagie la Penitente: Métamorphoses d'une légende*, ed. P. Petitmengin *et al.*, 2 vols. (Paris, 1984), II, 281–93

—, 'Genesius of Rome and Genesius of Arles', *NQ* 31 (1984), 149–52
—, Review of Kotzor, ed., *Das altenglische Martyrologium*, *Anglia* 102 (1984), 518–21
—, 'Source, Lexis, and Edition', *Medieval Studies Conference Aachen 1983*, ed. W. D. Bald and H. Weinstock, Bamberger Beiträge zur Englischen Sprachwissenschaft 15 (Frankfurt a. M., 1984), pp. 25–36
—, 'On the Library of the Old English Martyrologist', *LLASE*, pp. 227–49
—, 'The Use of Patristic Homilies in the *Old English Martyrology*', *ASE* 14 (1985), 107–28
—, 'Identification: Towards Criticism', *Modes of Interpretation in Old English Literature: Essays in Honour of Stanley B. Greenfield*, ed. P. R. Brown, G. R. Crampton and F. C. Robinson (Toronto, 1986), pp. 229–46
—, 'The Latinity of the Ninth-Century Old English Martyrologist', *Studies in Earlier Old English Prose*, ed. P. E. Szarmach (Albany, 1986), pp. 275–99
—, 'The Use of a *Passio S. Sebastiani* in the *Old English Martyrology*', *Mediaevalia* 14 (1988), 39–50
—, 'English Vernacular Saints' Lives before 1000 A. D.', *Hagiographies: Histoire internationale de la littérature hagiographique latine et vernaculaire en Occident des origines à 1550*, ed. G. Philippart (Turnhout, 1996), II, 413–27
—, 'The Notice on Marina (7 July) and *Passiones S. Margaritae*', *Old English Prose: Basic Readings*, ed. P. E. Szarmach and D. A. Oosterhouse, BRASE 5 (New York, 2000), pp. 419–32
Cross, J. E., and C. J. Tuplin, 'An Unrecorded Variant of the *Passio S. Christinae* and the *Old English Martyrology*', *Traditio* 36 (1980), 161–236
Crowley, J., 'Anglicized Word Order in Old English Continuous Interlinear Glosses in British Library, Royal 2. A. XX', *ASE* 29 (2000), 123–51
Dekker, K., '"That most Elaborate one of Fr. Junius": An Investigation of Francis Junius's Manuscript Old English Dictionary', *The Recovery of Old English: Anglo-Saxon Studies in the Sixteenth and Seventeenth Centuries*, ed. T. Graham (Kalamazoo, 2000), pp. 301–43
—, 'Pentecost and Linguistic Self-Consciousness in Anglo-Saxon England: Bede and Ælfric', *Journal of English and Germanic Philology* 104 (2005), 345–72
—, 'Anglo-Saxon Encyclopaedic Notes: Tradition and Function', *Foundations of Learning: The Transfer of Encyclopaedic Knowledge in the Early Middle Ages*, ed. R. H. Bremmer jr. and K. Dekker, Mediaevalia Groningana ns 9 (Leuven, 2007), pp. 279–315
—, 'Eucherius of Lyons in Anglo-Saxon England: The Continental Connections', *Practice in Learning: The Transfer of Encyclopaedic Knowledge in the Early Middle Ages*, ed. R. H. Bremmer jr. and K. Dekker, Mediaevalia Groningana ns 16 (Leuven, 2010), pp. 147–73
Delehaye, H., *Étude sur le légendier romain: les saints de novembre et de décembre* (Brussels, 1936)
Dendle, P., *Satan Unbound: The Devil in Old English Narrative Literature* (Toronto, 2001)

diPaolo Healey, A., *et al.*, ed., *Dictionary of Old English Corpus* (Toronto, 2005), http://quodlib.umich.edu/o/oec

—, *et al.*, ed., *Dictionary of Old English: A-G on CD-ROM* (Toronto, 2008)

—, 'Old English *heafod* "head": A Lofty Place?', *Poetica* 75 (2011), 29–48

Doane, A. N., *Saints' Lives, Martyrologies, and Bilingual 'Rule of St. Benedict' in the British Library*, Anglo-Saxon Manuscripts in Microfiche Facsimile 19 (Tempe, 2010)

Dolbeau, F., 'Notes sur l'organisation interne des légendiers latins', *Hagiographie, cultures et sociétés, ive–xiie siècles*, ed. E. Patlagean and P. Riché (Paris, 1981), pp. 11–31

—, 'Naissance des homéliaires et des passionnaires', *L'antiquité tardive dans les collections médiévales*, ed. S. Gioanni and B. Grévin (Rome, 2008), pp. 13–35

Drobner, H. R., *Der heilige Pankratius: Leben, Legende und Verehrung* (Paderborn, 1988)

Dubois J., *Les martyrologes du moyen âge latin*, Typologie des sources du moyen âge occidental 26 (Turnhout, 1978)

Dumville, D. N., 'Liturgical Drama and Panegyric Responsory from the Eighth Century? A Re-examination of the Origin and Contents of the Ninth-Century Section of the Book of Cerne', *Journal of Theological Studies* ns 23 (1972), 374–406

—, 'The West Saxon Genealogical Regnal List: Manuscripts and Texts', *Anglia* 104 (1986), 1–32

—, *Saint Patrick, A.D. 493–1993* (Woodbridge, 1993)

—, 'English Script in the Second Half of the Ninth Century', *Latin Learning and English Lore: Studies in Anglo-Saxon Literature for Michael Lapidge*, ed. K. O'Brien O'Keeffe and A. Orchard, 2 vols (Toronto, 2005), I, 305–25

Falmagne, T., *Die Handschriften des Grossherzogtums Luxemburg*, 2 vols. (Wiesbaden, 2009)

Farmer, D. H., *The Oxford Dictionary of Saints*, 5th edn (Oxford, 2004)

Fisher, R. M. C., 'Writing Charms: The Transmission and Performance of Charms in Anglo-Saxon England' (PhD diss., University of Sheffield, 2011)

—, 'Genre, Prayers and the Anglo-Saxon Charms', *Genre, Text, Interpretation: Multidisciplinary Perspectives on Folklore and Beyond*, ed. K. Koski (Helsinki, forthcoming)

Flood, J., *Representations of Eve in Antiquity and the English Middle Ages* (New York, 2011)

Fontes Anglo-Saxonici: World-Wide Web Register, http://fontes.english.ox.ac.uk

Foot, S., 'Anglo-Saxon Minsters: A Review of Terminology', *Pastoral Care Before the Parish*, ed. John Blair and Richard Sharpe (Leicester, 1992), pp. 212–25

—, *Monastic Life in Anglo-Saxon England, c. 600–900* (Cambridge, 2006)

Förster, M., 'Zur altenglischen Quintinus-Legende', *Archiv für das Studium der neueren Sprachen und Literaturen* 106 (1901), 258–61

Forte, A. J., 'A Critical Edition of a Hiberno-Latin Commentary on Matthew 1–8 (Codex Vindobonensis 940)' (PhD diss., University of California, Los Angeles, 1991)

Frank, R., and A. Cameron, *A Plan for the Dictionary of Old English* (Toronto, 1973)

Frankis, J., Review of Kotzor, *Das altenglische Martyrologium*, *MÆ* 52 (1983), 313–15

Franklin, C. V., 'Theodore and the *Passio S. Anastasii*', *Archbishop Theodore: Commemorative Studies on his Life and Influence*, ed. M. Lapidge, CSASE 11 (Cambridge, 1995), pp. 175–203

—, *The Latin Dossier of Anastasius the Persian: Hagiographic Translations and Transformations*, Studies and Texts 147 (Toronto, 2004)

Frere, W. H., *Studies in Early Roman Liturgy*, Alcuin Club Collections 28 (London, 1930)

Fros, H., *Bibliotheca Hagiographica Latin: Novum Supplementum* (Brussels, 1986)

Fulk, R. D., 'Cynewulf: Canon, Dialect, and Date', *The Cynewulf Reader*, ed. R. E. Bjork, Basic Readings in Anglo-Saxon England 4 (New York, 1996), pp. 3–21

de Gaiffier, B., '*Sub Daciano praeside*: étude de quelques passions espagnoles', *AB* 72 (1954), 378–96

—, 'De l'usage et de la lecture du martyrologe: témoignages antérieurs au xie siècle', *AB* 79 (1961), 40–59

Galuzzi, A., 'Teodoreto', *BSS*, XII, 227

Gamber, K., *Sakramentartypen: Versuch einer Gruppierung der Handschriften und Fragmente bis zur Jahrtausendwende*, Texte und Arbeiten 49–50 (Beuron, 1958)

—, *Codices liturgici latini antiquiores*, 2nd edn (Fribourg, 1968)

Gioanni, S., 'Hagiographie d'Italie (300–550), II. Les Vies de saints latines composées en Italie de la Paix constantinienne au milieu du VIe siècle', *Hagiographies: Histoire internationale de la littérature hagiographique latine et vernaculaire en Occident des origines à 1550*, ed. G. Philippart (Turnhout, 2010), V, 371–445

Glaeske, K., 'Eve in Anglo-Saxon Retellings of the Harrowing of Hell', *Traditio* 54 (1999), 81–101

Gneuss, H., *Lehnbildungen und Lehnbedeutungen im Altenglischen* (Berlin, 1955)

—, 'Liturgical Books in Anglo-Saxon England and their Old English Terminology', *LLASE*, pp. 91–141

—, 'Guide to the Editing and Preparation of Texts for the *Dictionary of Old English*', *The Editing of Old English: Papers from the 1990 Manchester Conference*, ed. D. G. Scragg and P. E. Szarmach (Cambridge, 1994), pp. 7–26

—, 'Anglo-Saxon Libraries from the Conversion to the Benedictine Reform', in his *Books and Libraries in Early England* (Aldershot, 1996), item II

—, *Handlist of Anglo-Saxon Manuscripts: A List of Manuscripts and Manuscript Fragments Written or Owned in England up to 1100*, MRTS 241 (Tempe, 2001)

Godden, M., 'Old English Composite Homilies from Winchester', *ASE* 4 (1975), 57–65
—, 'Wærferth and King Alfred', *Alfred the Wise: Studies in Honour of Janet Bately on the Occasion of her Sixty-Fifth Birthday*, ed. J. Roberts, J. L. Nelson and M. Godden (Woodbridge, 1997), pp. 35–51
—, *Ælfric's Catholic Homilies: Introduction, Commentary and Glossary*, EETS ss 18 (Oxford, 2000)
—, 'Did King Alfred Write Anything?', *MÆ* 76 (2007), pp. 1–23
—, 'The Alfredian Project and its Aftermath: Rethinking the Literary History of the Ninth and Tenth Centuries', *Proceedings of the British Academy* 162 (2009), 93–122
Godden, M., and S. Irvine, ed., *The Old English Boethius*, 2 vols. (Oxford, 2009)
Good, J., *The Cult of Saint George in Medieval England* (Woodbridge, 2009)
Grant, R. J. S., ed., *Three Homilies from Cambridge, Corpus Christi College 41* (Ottawa, 1982)
Gretsch, M., *The Intellectual Foundations of the English Benedictine Reform*, CSASE 25 (Cambridge, 1999)
—, 'The Junius Psalter Gloss: its Historical and Cultural Context', *ASE* 29 (2000), 85–121
—, *Ælfric and the Cult of Saints in Late Anglo-Saxon England*, CSASE 34 (Cambridge, 2005)
—, 'Æthelthryth of Ely in a Lost Calendar from Munich', *ASE* 35 (2006), 159–77
Haessler, L., 'Old English *Bebeodan* and *Forbeodan*', *Language* 11 (1935), 211–15
Hagan, A., *Anglo-Saxon Food and Drink* (Hockwold-cum-Wilton, 2006)
Hagen, H., *Catalogus codicum Bernensium* (Bern, 1874)
Hall, J. R. C., *A Concise Anglo-Saxon Dictionary* (London, 1894)
Hall, T. N., 'The Ages of Christ and Mary in the Hyde Register and in Old English Literature', *NQ* 35 (1988), 4–11
—, 'Gospel of Pseudo-Matthew', *The Apocrypha*, ed. F. M. Biggs, Instrumenta Anglistica Mediaevalia 1 (Kalamazoo, 2007), pp. 23–5
—, 'Christ's Birth through Mary's Right Breast: An Echo of Carolingian Heresy in the Old English *Adrian and Ritheus*', *Source of Wisdom: Old English and Early Medieval Latin Studies in Honour of Thomas D. Hill*, ed. C. D. Wright, F. M. Biggs and T. N. Hall (Toronto, 2007), pp. 266–89
—, 'The Armaments of John the Baptist in Blickling Homily 14 and the Exeter Book *Descent into Hell*', *Intertexts: Studies in Anglo-Saxon Culture Presented to Paul E. Szarmach*, ed. V. Blanton and H. Scheck, MRTS 334 (Tempe, 2008), pp. 289–306
—, 'The Development of the Common of Saints in the Early English Versions of Paul the Deacon's Homiliary', *Anglo-Saxon Books and their Readers: Essays in Celebration of Helmut Gneuss's Handlist of Anglo-Saxon Manuscripts*, ed. T. N. Hall and D. Scragg (Kalamazoo, 2008), pp. 31–67
—, 'The Portents at Christ's Birth in Vercelli Homilies V and VI: Some Analogues from Medieval Sermons and Biblical Commentaries', *New Readings in the Vercelli Book*, ed. S. Zacher and A. Orchard (Toronto, 2009), pp. 62–97

—, 'Petrus Chrysologus', 2009, *Sources of Anglo-Saxon Literary Culture*, http://saslc.nd.edu/

Harbus, A., *Helena of Britain in Medieval Legend* (Cambridge, 2002)

Haubrichs, W., *Georgslied und Georgslegende im frühen Mittelalter: Text und Rekonstruktion*, Theorie, Kritik, Geschichte 13 (Siegen, 1979)

Henel, H., 'Altenglischer Mönchsaberglaube', *Englische Studien* 69 (1934–5), 329–49

Herzfeld, G., ed., *An Old English Martyrology*, EETS os 116 (London, 1900)

Hewish, J., 'Living on the Edge: A Study of the Translations of the Life of St Martin into Old English, Middle Irish, and Old Norse-Icelandic' (PhD diss., University College Dublin, 2005)

Hill, J., 'Saint George before the Conquest', *Report of the Society of the Friends of St George's and the Descendants of the Knights of the Garter* 6 (1985–6), 284–95

—, 'The *Litaniae maiores* and *minores* in Rome, Francia and Anglo-Saxon England', *Early Medieval Europe* 9 (2000), 211–46

—, 'Georgius', in E. G. Whatley, 'Acta Sanctorum', *SASLC*, pp. 229–31

—, 'Ælfric's Manuscript of Paul the Deacon's Homiliary: A Provisional Analysis', *The Old English Homily: Precedent, Practice, and Appropriation*, ed. A. J. Kleist, Studies in the Early Middle Ages 17 (Turnhout, 2007), pp. 67–96

Hofstetter, W., *Winchester und der spätaltenglische Sprachgebrauch: Untersuchungen zur geographischen und zeitlichen Verbreitung altenglischer Synonyme*, Münchener Universitätsschriften 14 (Munich, 1987)

Hogg, R. M., 'On the Impossibility of Old English Dialectology', *Luick Revisited*, ed. D. Kastovsky and G. Bauer, Tübinger Beiträge zur Linguistik 288 (Tübingen, 1985), pp. 183–203

Hohler, C., 'Theodore and the Liturgy', *Archbishop Theodore: Commemorative Studies on his Life and Influence*, ed. M. Lapidge, CSASE 11 (Cambridge, 1995), pp. 222–35

Hughes, K., Review of Gwynn, *The Writings of Bishop Patrick*, *MÆ* 26 (1957), 122–8

Huglo, M., 'Trois livres manuscrits présentés par Helisachar', *Revue Bénédictine* 99 (1989), 272–85

Incitti, I., 'Modelli agiografici femminili nel martirologio antico inglese' (MPhil diss., University of L'Aquila, 2008)

Irvine, S., ed., *Old English Homilies from MS Bodley 343*, EETS os 302 (Oxford, 1993)

Izzi, L., 'Representing Rome. The Influence of "Rome" on Aspects of the Public Arts of Early Anglo-Saxon England (c. 600–800)' (PhD diss., University of York, 2010)

—, 'Anglo-Saxons Underground: Early Medieval Graffiti in the Catacombs of Rome', *England and Rome in the Early Middle Ages: Piety, Politics and Culture*, ed. F. Tinti (Turnhout, 2013)

Jackson, P., and M. Lapidge, 'The Contents of the Cotton-Corpus Legendary', *Holy Men and Holy Women: Old English Prose Saints' Lives and their Contexts*, ed. P. E. Szarmach (Albany, 1996), pp. 131–46

John, C., and D. Attwater, *The Penguin Dictionary of Saints*, 3rd edn (Harmondsworth, 2005)

Johnson, R. F., *Saint Michael the Archangel in Medieval English Legend* (Woodbridge, 2005)

Jolly, K. L., 'On the Margins of Orthodoxy: Devotional Formulas and Protective Prayers in Cambridge, Corpus Christi College MS41', *Signs on the Edge: Space, Text and Margin in Medieval Manuscripts*, ed. S. L. Keefer and R. H. Bremmer jr, Medievalia Groningana 10 (Paris, 2007), pp. 135-83

Jordan, R., *Eigentümlichkeiten des anglischen Wortschatzes*, Anglistische Forschungen 17 (Heidelberg, 1906)

Kalbhen, U., *Kentische Glossen und kentischer Dialekt im Altenglischen*, Münchener Universitätsschriften 28 (Frankfurt a. M., 2003)

Karkov, C. E., 'Exiles from the Kingdom: The Naked and the Damned in Anglo-Saxon Art', *Naked before God: Uncovering the Body in Anglo-Saxon England*, ed. B. C. Withers and J. Wilcox, Medieval European Studies 3 (Morgantown, 2003), pp. 181–220

Karlin-Hayter, P., 'Passio of the XL Martyrs of Sebasteia: The Greek Tradition: the Earliest Account (*BHG* 1201)', *AB* 109 (1991), 249–304

Kastovsky, D., 'Semantics and Vocabulary', *The Cambridge History of the English Language: Volume I, The Beginnings to 1066*, ed. R. M. Hogg (Cambridge, 1992), pp. 290–408

Kelly, J. N. D., *The Oxford Dictionary of Popes*, 2nd edn (Oxford, 2005)

Ker, N. R., *Catalogue of Manuscripts Containing Anglo-Saxon* (Oxford, 1957)

Keynes, S., and M. Lapidge, trans., *Alfred the Great* (Harmondsworth, 1983)

—, 'King Alfred and the Mercians', *Kings, Currency and Alliances: History and Coinage of Southern England in the Ninth Century*, ed. M. A. S. Blackburn and D. N. Dumville, Studies in Anglo-Saxon History 9 (Woodbridge, 1998), pp. 1–45

—, 'The Control of Kent in the Ninth Century', *Early Medieval Europe* 2 (1993), 111–31

—, 'Between Bede and the *Chronicle*: London, BL, Cotton Vespasian B. vi, fols. 104–9', *Latin Learning and English Lore: Studies in Anglo-Saxon Literature for Michael Lapidge*, ed. K. O'Brien O'Keeffe and A. Orchard, 2 vols. (Toronto, 2005), I, 47–67

Kirschner, J., 'Die Bezeichnungen für Kranz und Krone im Altenglischen' (diss., University of Munich, 1975)

Klaeber, F., 'Notes on Old English Prose Texts', *Modern Language Notes* 18 (1903), 241–7

Kornexl, L., 'The Regularis Concordia and its Old English Gloss', *ASE* 24 (1995), 95–130

—, '"Unnatural Words"? Loan-Formations in Old English Glosses', *Language Contact in the History of English*, ed. D. Kastovsky and A. Mettinger, Studies in English Medieval Language and Literature 1 (Frankfurt a. M., 2001), pp. 195–216

—, 'Sprache der Glossen: Glossensprache?', *Mittelalterliche volkssprachliche Glossen*, ed. R. Bergmann, E. Glaser and C. Moulin-Fankhänel, Germanistische Bibliothek 13 (Heidelberg, 2001), pp. 109–35

Kotzor, G., 'St. Patrick in the Old English "Martyrology": On a Lost Leaf of MS. C.C.C.C. 196', *NQ* 21 (1974), 86–7

—, ed., *Das altenglische Martyrologium*, Abhandlungen der Bayerischen Akademie der Wissenschaften, phil.-hist. Kl. ns 88.1–2, 2 vols. (Munich, 1981)

—, 'The Latin Tradition of Martyrologies and the *Old English Martyrology*', *Studies in Earlier Old English Prose*, ed. P. E. Szarmach (New York, 1986), pp. 301–33

Kuhn, S. M., 'The Dialect of the Corpus *Glossary*', *Publications of the Modern Language Association of America* 54 (1939), 1–19

Lanéry, C., *Ambroise de Milan hagiographe*, Collection des Études Augustiniennes Série Antiquité 183 (Paris, 2008)

—, 'Hagiographie d'Italie (300–550), I. Les Passions latines composées en Italie', *Hagiographies: Histoire internationale de la littérature hagiographique latine et vernaculaire en Occident des origines à 1550*, ed. G. Philippart (Turnhout, 2010), V, 15–369

Langefeld, B., '*Regula canonicorum* or *Regula monasterialis uitae*? The Rule of Chrodegang and Archbishop Wulfred's Reforms at Canterbury', *ASE* 25 (1996), 21–36

—, ed., *The Old English Version of the Enlarged Rule of Chrodegang*, Münchener Universitätsschriften 26 (Frankfurt a. M., 2003)

Lapidge, M., 'Surviving Booklists from Anglo-Saxon England', *LLASE*, pp. 33–89

—, 'The Saintly Life in Anglo-Saxon England', *The Cambridge Companion to Old English Literature*, ed. M. Godden and M. Lapidge (Cambridge, 1991), pp. 243–63

—, 'Editing Hagiography', *La critica del testo mediolatino*, ed. C. Leonardi (Spoleto, 1994), pp. 239–58

—, 'Latin Learning in Ninth-Century England', in his *Anglo-Latin Literature 600–899* (London, 1996), pp. 409–39

—, 'Ælfric's Sanctorale', *Holy Men and Holy Women: Old English Prose Saints' Lives and their Contexts*, ed. P. E. Szarmach (Albany, 1996), pp. 115–29

—, 'Roman Martyrs and their Miracles in Anglo-Saxon England', *Miracles and the Miraculous in Medieval Germanic and Latin Literature*, ed. K. E. Olsen, A. Harbus, and T. Hofstra, Mediaevalia Groningana ns 6 (Leuven, 2004), pp. 95–120

—, 'Acca of Hexham and the Origin of the *Old English Martyrology*', *AB* 123 (2005), 29–78

—, *The Anglo-Saxon Library* (Oxford, 2006)

Lapidge, M., and M. Herren, trans., *Aldhelm: The Prose Works* (Ipswich, 1979)

Lapidge, M., and R. Sharpe, *Bibliography of Celtic-Latin Literature 400–1200* (Dublin, 1985)

Latham, R. E., *et al.*, ed., *Dictionary of Medieval Latin from British Sources* (London, 1975–)

Leinbaugh, T. H., Review of Kotzor, *Das altenglische Martyrologium*, *Speculum* 59 (1984), 172–4

—, 'St Christopher and the *Old English Martyrology*', *NQ* 32 (1985), 434–7

Lendinara, P., 'Pietro, apostolo, vescovo e santo nella letteratura anglo-sassone', *La figura di S. Pietro nelle fonti del Medioevo*, ed. L. Lazzari and A. M. Valente Bacci, Textes et études du moyen âge 17 (Louvain-la-Neuve, 2001), pp. 649–84

Leyser, C., '"A Church in the House of Saints": Property and Power in the Passion of John and Paul', *Religion, Dynasty, and Patronage in Early Christian Rome 300–900*, ed. K. Cooper and J. Hillner (Cambridge, 2007), pp. 140–62

Lifshitz, F., *The Name of the Saint: The Martyrology of Jerome and Access to the Sacred in Francia, 627–827* (Notre Dame, 2006)

Lionarons, J. T., 'From Monster to Martyr: The Old English Legend of Saint Christopher', *Marvels, Monsters, and Miracles: Studies in the Medieval and Early Modern Imaginations*, ed. T. S. Jones and D. A. Sprunger, Studies in Medieval Culture 42 (Kalamazoo, 2002), pp. 167–82

Love, R. C., ed., *Three Eleventh-Century Anglo-Latin Saints' Lives* (Oxford, 1996)

Lowe, K. A., 'On the Plausibility of Old English Dialectology: The Ninth-Century Kentish Charter Material', *Folia Linguistica Historica* 22 (2001), 67–102

Luongo, G., 'Erasmo di Formia', *Il grande libro dei santi*, ed. C. Leonardi, A. Riccardi and G. Zarri (Turin, 1998), pp. 612–16

Magennis, H., 'Occurrences of Nuptial Imagery in Old English Hagiographical Texts', *English Language Notes* 33 (1996), 1-9

Mara, M. G., *I martiri della Via Salaria*, Verba seniorum ns 4 (Rome, 1964)

Marsden, R., *The Cambridge Old English Reader* (Cambridge, 2004)

Matthew, H. C. G., and B. Harrison, ed., *Oxford Dictionary of National Biography* (Oxford, 2004), http://www.oxforddnb.com

McCulloh, J. M., 'Historical Martyrologies in the Benedictine Cultural Tradition', *Benedictine Culture 750–1050*, ed. W. Lourdaux and D. Verhelst, Mediaevalia Lovaniensia 11 (Leuven, 1983), pp. 114–31

—, 'Did Cynewulf Use a Martyrology? Reconsidering the Sources of *The Fates of the Apostles*', *ASE* 29 (2000), 67–83

Mitchell, B., *Old English Syntax*, 2 vols. (Oxford, 1985)

Mitchell, B. and F. C. Robinson, *A Guide to Old English*, 7th edn (Oxford, 2007)

Moretti, P. F., La *Passio Anastasiae: Introduzione, testo critico, traduzione*, Studi e Testi Tardo Antichi 3 (Rome, 2006)

Morey, J. H., 'Gospel of Nicodemus', *SASLC*, pp. 45–8

Nelson, J. L., S. Keynes, *et al.*, ed., *Prosopography of Anglo-Saxon England*, http://www.pase.ac.uk

North, R., *Heathen Gods in Old English Literature*, CSASE 22 (Cambridge, 1997)

Ó Broin, B. É., '*Rex Christus Ascendens*: The Christological Cult of the Ascension in Anglo-Saxon England (PhD diss., University of Illinois at Urbana-Champaign, 2002)

Oetgen, J., 'Common Motifs in the Old English Ascension Homilies', *Neophilologus* 69 (1985), 437–45

O'Leary, A. M., 'Apostolic *Passiones* in Early Anglo-Saxon England', *Apocryphal Texts and Traditions in Anglo-Saxon England*, ed. K. Powell and D. Scragg, Publications of the Manchester Centre for Anglo-Saxon Studies 2 (Cambridge, 2003), pp. 103–19

Olsen, K., 'Thematic Affinities between the Non-Liturgical Marginalia and the Old English Bede in Cambridge, Corpus Christi College 41', *Practice in Learning: The Transfer of Encyclopaedic Knowledge in the Early Middle Ages*, Mediaevalia Groningana ns 16 (Leuven, 2010), pp. 133–45

Orchard, A., *Pride and Prodigies: Studies in the Monsters of the Beowulf-Manuscript*, 2nd edn (Toronto, 2003)

Ortenberg, V., 'Le culte de sainte Marie Madeleine dans l'Angleterre anglo-saxonne', *Mélanges de l'École française de Rome: Moyen Âge* 104 (1992), 13–35

Page, R. I., 'The Lost Leaf of MS. C.C.C.C. 196', *NQ* 21 (1974), 472–3

Parker Library on the Web, http://parkerweb.stanford.edu

Pestell, T., *Landscapes of Monastic Foundation: The Establishment of Religious Houses in East Anglia c.650–1200*, Anglo-Saxon Studies 5 (Woodbridge, 2004)

Pfaff, R. W., 'The Hagiographical Peculiarity of Martha's Companion(s)', in his *Liturgical Calendars, Saints, and Services in Medieval England* (Aldershot, 1998), item IV

Philippart, G., *Les légendiers latins et autres manuscrits hagiographiques*, Typologie des sources du moyen âge 24–5 (Turnhout, 1977)

Philippart, G., and M. Trigalet, 'Latin Hagiography before the Ninth Century: A Synoptic View', *The Long Morning of Medieval Europe: New Directions in Early Medieval Studies*, ed. J. R. Davis and M. McCormick (Aldershot, 2008), pp. 111–29

Phillips, C., 'Materials for the Study of the Cult of Saint Agnes of Rome in Anglo-Saxon England: Texts and Interpretations' (PhD diss., University of York, 2008)

—, 'St Agnes of Rome: A Review of the Latin Sources Employed for her Entry in the Old English Martyrology', *NQ* 58 (2011), 177–81

Poncelet, A., 'Catalogus codicum hagiographicorum Latinorum Bibliotecae Nationalis Taurinensis', *AB* 28 (1909), 417–78

Pratt, D., 'Problems of Authorship and Audience in the Writings of King Alfred the Great', *Lay Intellectuals in the Carolingian World*, ed. P. Wormald and J. L. Nelson (Cambridge, 2007), pp. 162–91

The Production and Use of English Manuscripts 1060–1220, ed. O. Da Rold and others, http://www.le.ac.uk/english/em1060to1220

Quentin, H., *Les martyrologes historiques du moyen âge* (Paris, 1908)

Rauer, C., 'The Sources of the *Old English Martyrology* (Cameron B.19)', 1999, *Fontes Anglo-Saxonici: World-Wide Web Register* http://fontes.english.ox.ac.uk/
—, 'An Annotated Bibliography of Publications Relating to the *Old English Martyrology*', http://www.st-andrews.ac.uk/~cr30/martyrology
—, *Beowulf and the Dragon: Parallels and Analogues* (Cambridge, 2000)
—, 'The Sources of the *Old English Martyrology*', *ASE* 32 (2003), 89–109
—, 'Usage of the *Old English Martyrology*', *Foundations of Learning: The Transfer of Encyclopaedic Knowledge in the Early Middle Ages*, ed. R. H. Bremmer jr. and K. Dekker, Mediaevalia Groningana ns 9 (Leuven, 2007), pp. 125–46
—, 'Old English *blanca* in the *Old English Martyrology*', *NQ* 55 (2008), 396–9
—, 'Pelagia's Cloak in the *Old English Martyrology*', *NQ* 57 (2010), 3–6
—, 'Direct Speech, Intercession, and Prayer in the *Old English Martyrology*', *English Studies* 93 (2012), 563–71
—, 'Female Hagiography in the *Old English Martyrology*', *Writing Women Saints in Anglo-Saxon England*, ed. P. E. Szarmach (Toronto, 2013)
—, 'Errors and Textual Problems in the *Old English Martyrology*', *Neophilologus* 97 (2013), 147–64
—, 'The *Old English Martyrology* and Anglo-Saxon Glosses', *Latinity and Identity in Anglo-Saxon England*, ed. R. Stephenson and E. V. Thornbury (forthcoming)
Roberts, J., 'An Inventory of Early Guthlac Materials', *Mediaeval Studies* 32 (1970), 193–233
—, '*Fela martyra* "many martyrs": A Different View of Orosius's City', *Alfred the Wise: Studies in Honour of Janet Bately on the Occasion of her Sixty-Fifth Birthday*, ed. J. Roberts, J. L. Nelson and M. Godden (Cambridge, 1997), pp. 155–78
—, 'Hagiography and Literature: The Case of Guthlac of Crowland', *Mercia: An Anglo-Saxon Kingdom in Europe*, ed. M. P. Brown and C. A. Farr (London, 2001), pp. 69–86
—, *Guide to Scripts Used in English Writings up to 1500* (London, 2005)
Robinson, F. C., 'The Significance of Names in Old English Literature', *Anglia* 86 (1968), 14–58
Rollason, D. W., 'Lists of Saints' Resting-Places in Anglo-Saxon England', *ASE* 7 (1978), 61–93
—, Review of Kotzor, *Das altenglische Martyrologium*, *Yearbook of English Studies* 16 (1986), 233–4
Rowley, S. M., *The Old English Version of Bede's Historia ecclesiastica*, Anglo-Saxon Studies 16 (Cambridge, 2011)
Ruggerini, M. E., 'Saint Michael in the *Old English Martyrology*', *Studi e materiali di storia delle religioni* 65 (1999), 181–97
Rusche, P. G., 'The *Old English Martyrology* and the Canterbury Aldhelm Scholia' (forthcoming)
Rushforth, R., *Saints in English Kalendars before A.D. 1100*, HBS 117 (London, 2008)

Russcher, A., and R. H. Bremmer Jr., 'Fracture Treatment in Anglo-Saxon England', *Secular Learning in Anglo-Saxon England: Exploring the Vernacular*, ed. B. Carella and L. S. Chardonnens, Amsterdamer Beiträge zur älteren Germanistik 69 (Amsterdam, 2012), pp. 145–74

Salsano, M., 'Aristione', *BSS*, II, 424–5

Sanders Gale, J., 'John Joscelyn's Notebook: A Study of the Contents and Sources of BL Cotton MS. Vitellius D.vii' (MPhil diss., University of Nottingham, 1978)

Sauer, H., ed., *Theodulfi Capitula in England*, Münchener Universitätsschriften 8 (Munich, 1978)

Sauget, J. M., 'Procopio', *BSS*, X, 1159–66

Saxer, V., *Saint Vincent diacre et martyr*, SH 83 (Brussels, 2002)

Sayers, W., 'The Etymology of Late Latin *malina* "spring tide" and *ledo* "neap tide"', *MJ* 40 (2005), 35–43

Schabram, H., *Superbia: Studien zum altenglischen Wortschatz, Teil I* (Munich, 1965)

Scarfe Beckett, K., *Anglo-Saxon Perceptions of the Islamic World*, CSASE 33 (Cambridge, 2003)

Schleburg, F., *Altenglisch swa: Syntax und Semantik einer polyfunktionalen Partikel* (Heidelberg, 2002)

Shaw, P. A., 'Uses of Wodan: The Development of his Cult and of Medieval Responses to it' (PhD diss., University of Leeds, 2002)

Siegmund, A., *Die Überlieferung der griechischen christlichen Literatur in der lateinischen Kirche bis zum zwölften Jahrhundert*, Abhandlungen der Bayerischen Benediktiner-Akademie 5 (Munich, 1949)

Sievers, E., 'Miscellen zur angelsächsischen Grammatik', *Beiträge zur Geschichte der deutschen Sprache und Literatur* 9 (1884), 197–300

—, *Angelsächsische Grammatik*, Sammlung kurzer Grammatiken germanischer Dialekte 3, repr. of 3rd edn (Halle, 1921)

Sisam, C., 'An Early Fragment of the *Old English Martyrology*', *RES* 4 (1953), 209–20

—, Review of Kotzor, *Das altenglische Martyrologium*, *NQ* 30 (1983), 67–8

Sisam, K., 'Canterbury, Lichfield, and the Vespasian Psalter', *RES* 7 (1956), 1–10 and 113–31

Speidel, M. A., 'Die thebäische Legion und das spätrömische Heer', *Mauritius und die thebäische Legion*, ed. O. Wermelinger *et al.* (Fribourg, 2005), pp. 37–46

Stancliffe, C., 'Oswald: Most Holy and Most Victorious King of the Northumbrians', *Oswald: Northumbrian King to European Saint*, ed. C. Stancliffe and E. Cambridge (Stamford, 1995), pp. 33–83

Stiene, H. E., ed., *Wandelbert of Prüm: Vita et Miracula Sancti Goaris*, Lateinische Sprache und Literatur des Mittelalters 11 (Frankfurt a. M., 1981)

Stodnick, J., 'Bodies of Land: The Place of Gender in the *Old English Martyrology*', *Writing Women Saints in Anglo-Saxon England*, ed. P. E. Szarmach (Toronto, 2013)

Stossberg, F., 'Die Sprache des altenglischen Martyrologiums' (PhD diss., University of Bonn, 1905)

Swaen, A. E. H., 'Contributions to Anglo-Saxon Lexicography', *Englische Studien* 33 (1904), 176–8

Swanton, M., ed., *The Dream of the Rood*, rev. edn (Exeter, 1987)

Szarmach, P. E., 'Sulpicius Severus', *SASLC*, pp. 158–60

Thacker, A., 'Lindisfarne and the Origins of the Cult of St Cuthbert', *St Cuthbert, his Cult and his Community to AD1200*, ed. G. Bonner, D. Rollason and C. Stancliffe (Woodbridge, 1989), pp. 103–22

—, 'In Search of Saints: The English Church and the Cult of Roman Apostles and Martyrs in the Seventh and Eighth Centuries', *Early Medieval Rome and the Christian West*, ed. J. M. H. Smith, The Medieval Mediterranean 28 (Leiden, 2000), pp. 247–77

Thijs, C. B., 'Wærferth's Translation of the *Dialogi* of Gregory the Great' (PhD diss., University of Leeds, 2003)

Tinti, F., *Sustaining Belief: The Church of Worcester from c.870 to c.1100* (Farnham, 2010)

Toller, T. N., *An Anglo-Saxon Dictionary Supplement* (Oxford, 1908–21)

Toon, T. E., 'Old English Dialects', *The Cambridge History of the English Language: Volume I, The Beginnings to 1066*, ed. R. M. Hogg (Cambridge, 1992), pp. 409–51

Torkar, R., 'Die Ohnmacht der Textkritik, am Beispiel der Ausgaben der dritten Vercelli-Homilie', *Anglo-Saxonica: Beiträge zur Vor- und Frühgeschichte der englischen Sprache und zur altenglischen Literatur*, ed. K. R. Grinda and C.-D. Wetzel (Munich, 1993), pp. 225–50

Trahern, J. B., jr., 'Caesarius of Arles', 2008, *Sources of Anglo-Saxon Literary Culture*, http://saslc.nd.edu/

Tupper, F., 'Anglo-Saxon Dæg-Mæl', *Publications of the Modern Language Association of America* 10 (1895), pp. 111–241

Tyler, E. M., *Old English Poetics: The Aesthetics of the Familiar in Anglo-Saxon England* (York, 2006)

Upchurch, R. K., 'The Legend of Chrysanthus and Daria in Ælfric's *Lives of Saints*', *Studies in Philology* 101 (2004), 250–69

—, 'Virgin Spouses as Model Christians', *ASE* 34 (2005), 197–217

—, ed., *Ælfric's Lives of the Virgin Spouses* (Exeter, 2007)

—, 'Homiletic Contexts for Ælfric's Hagiography: The Legend of Saints Cecilia and Valerian', *The Old English Homily: Precedent, Practice, and Appropriation*, ed. A. J. Kleist, Studies in the Early Middle Ages 17 (Turnhout, 2007), pp. 265–84

Van Arsdall, A., *Medieval Herbal Remedies: The Old English Herbarium and Anglo-Saxon Medicine* (New York, 2002)

Vleeskruyer, R., ed., *The Life of St. Chad: An Old English Homily* (Amsterdam, 1953)

Waite, G., *Old English Prose Translations of King Alfred's Reign*, Annotated Bibliographies of Old and Middle English Literature 6 (Cambridge, 2000)

—, 'The Vocabulary of the Old English Version of Bede's *Historia ecclesiastica*' (PhD diss., University of Toronto, 1984)

Wasyliw, P. H., *Martyrdom, Murder and Magic: Child Saints and their Cults in Medieval Europe*, Studies in Church History 2 (New York, 2008)

Wenisch, F., *Spezifisch anglisches Wortgut in den nordhumbrischen Interlinearglossierungen des Lukasevangeliums*, Anglistische Forschungen 132 (Heidelberg, 1979)

Whatley, E. G., 'Acta Sanctorum', *Sources of Anglo-Saxon Literary Culture: Volume One*, ed. F. M. Biggs *et al.* (Kalamazoo, 2001), pp. 22–548

—, 'Eugenia before Ælfric', *Intertexts: Studies in Anglo-Saxon Culture Presented to Paul E. Szarmach*, MRTS 334 (Tempe, 2008), pp. 350–67

—, 'Textual Hybrids in the Transmission of the *Passio S. Eugeniae* (BHL 2666, 2667)', *Hagiographica* 18 (2011), 31–66

Williams, C., 'Perpetua's Gender', *Perpetua's Passions: Multidisciplinary Approaches to the Passio Perpetuae et Felicitatis*, ed. J. N. Bremmer and M. Formisano (Oxford, 2012), pp. 54–77

Williamson, C., ed., *The Old English Riddles of the Exeter Book* (Chapel Hill, 1977)

Wilson, R. M., 'The Provenance of the Vespasian Psalter Gloss: The Linguistic Evidence', *The Anglo-Saxons: Studies in Some Aspects of their History and Culture Presented to Bruce Dickins*, ed. P. Clemoes (London, 1959), pp. 292–310

—, *The Lost Literature of Medieval England*, 2nd edn (1970)

Wilson, S. E., *The Life and After-Life of St John of Beverley* (Aldershot, 2006)

Woolf, A., 'Reporting Scotland in the Anglo-Saxon Chronicle', *Reading the Anglo-Saxon Chronicle: Language, Literature, History*, ed. A. Jorgensen, Studies in the Early Middle Ages 23 (Turnhout, 2010), pp. 221–39

Wormald, F., *English Kalendars before A.D. 1100: Volume 1, Texts*, HBS 72 (London, 1934)

Wright, C. D., 'Vienna Commentary on Matthew', *SASLC*, pp. 104–5

—, 'Old English Homilies and Latin Sources', *The Old English Homily: Precedent, Practice, and Appropriation*, ed. A. J. Kleist, Studies in the Early Middle Ages 17 (Turnhout, 2007), pp. 15–66

Zanetti, U., 'Les passions des SS. Nazaire, Gervais, Protais et Celse', *AB* 97 (1979), 69–88

Zechiel-Eckes, K., 'Unbekannte Bruchstücke der merowingischen *Passio Sancti Iusti pueri* (*BHL* 4590c)', *Francia* 30 (2003), 1–8

Zelzer, M., 'Zur Überlieferung und Rezeption der *Passio Acaunensium martyrum*', *Mauritius und die thebäische Legion*, ed. O. Wermelinger *et al.* (Fribourg, 2005), pp. 325–3

Index of Persons Named in the *Old English Martyrology*

Numbers refer to text sections, not pages; numbers in bold indicate sections dedicated to the given saint. The list also includes names of persons who are named in error and those who are more correctly implied but not explicitly named in the text (often through reliance on an erroneous Latin tradition); readers are therefore also referred to the relevant Commentary sections. Names for Christ and God are not listed; references to populations and ethnic groups appear in the Index of Place-Names and Geographical Terms.

Abacuc, St, **29**
Abdon, St, **139**
Abundius, St, **164**
Adam, 50, 53, 57
Adrian, St, **38**
Afra, St, **149**
Agape, St, **59**, 61
Agapitus, St, **158**
Agnes, St, **30**, 33
Agricolaus, official, 41
Aidan, St, bp. of Lindisfarne, **171**
Alban, St, **109**
Alexander, St, bp. of Alexandria, 75
Alexander I, St, pope, **76**, 166
Alexander, St, b. of Sisinnius and Martyrius, **93**
Alexander, St, one of the Seven Brothers, **123**
Alexander, official, persecutor of Cyricus and Julitta, 127
Alexander, St, associate of Victor, 132
Alexander, official, persecutor of Mamas, 157
Alexandria, St, empress, **71**
All Saints, 218
Almachius, official, 64, 227
Almatheus, see Almachius
Alpheus, f. of James the Less, 108
Ambrose, St, bp. of Milan, **60**, 107
Ananias, St, **26**
Anastasia, St, **2**
Anastasius, St, **32**
Anatolia, St, **124**
Andochius, St, **195**
Andrew, St, **233**
Anna, k. of the E. Angles, 110

Anna, St, m. of Mary, 180
Anteros, St, pope, **10**
Antia, St, **65**
Antiochus IV, Seleucid king, 140
Antoninus Pius, Roman emperor, 14, 87, 123
Antoninus, St, **173**
Antony the Hermit, St, 16, **22**
Apollinaris, St, **134**
Arculf, informant in Adomnán's *De locis sanctis*, 67, 79, 111a, 200
Aristion, St, **174**
Arsenius, St, **131**
Artemius, St, **99**
Astachius, persecutor of Gervase and Protase, 107
Astaroth, pagan god, 162
Athanasius, St, bp. of Alexandria, 75
Auceia, St, suitor of Lucia, **112**
Audax, St, **124**
Audifax, St, **29**
Audomarus, St, **181**
Aufidianus, persecutor of Clement, 228
Augustine, St, archbp. of Canterbury, **92**
Augustine, St, bp. of Hippo, **167**
Augustus, Roman emperor, 139b
Aurelianus, persecutor of Alexander, Eventius, Theodulus and Hermes, 76, 166
Aurelian, Roman emperor, 195, 219, 220

Æthelburh, St, abbess of Barking, **204**
Æthelthryth, St, abbess of Ely, **110**
Æthelwald, St, hermit on Farne Island, **66**

Babylas, St, bp. of Antioch, **34**

INDEX OF PERSONS

Balbina, St, 202
Barnabas, St, **101**
Bartholomew, St, **162**
Basilla, St, **90**
Basilissa, St, **13**
Bede, 37, 237
Benedict of Nursia, St, **51**
Benedict Biscop, St, abt. of Monkwearmouth-Jarrow, **17**
Benignus, St, **220**
Bertinus, St, **178**
Blastus, St, **105**
Boniface IV, St, pope, 218
Bregoswith, m. of Hild, 226

Caecilia, see Cecilia
Caesarius, St, **219**
Calepodius, St, **85**, 205
Callistus I, St, pope, 10, 28, 143, 147, **205**
Calpurnius, f. of Patrick, 44
Calvisianus, official, 153
Candida, St, **99**
Candidus, St, **191**
Caritius, official, 238
Cassian, St, **155**
Cassius, St, **115**
Castitas, name of an apparition, 47
Castorius, St, one of the Four Crowned Ones, **222**
Cecilia, St, **227**
Cedd, St, b. of Chad, bp. of London, 37, **214**
Celsus, St, **137**
Ceolfrith, St, abt. of Monkwearmouth-Jarrow, **196**
Cerealis, St, 183
Chad, St, abt. of Lastingham, **37**, 214
Chionia, St, **59**, 61
Chosroes II, k. of Persia, 32
Christina, St, **130**
Christopher, St, **73**
Chrysanthus, St, **232**
Chrysogonus, St, **230**
Claudius, official, 103
Claudius II, Roman emperor, 213, 216

Claudius, St, one of the Four Crowned Ones, **222**
Clement I, St, pope, **228**
Cleonius, f. of Pancras, 86
Clovis II, k. of Neustria, 21
Colum Cille, see Columba of Iona
Columba, St, abt. of Iona, **100**
Columba, St, **8**
Commodus, Roman emperor, 3
Constantine I, Roman emperor, 113, 202, 207, 233
Constantius II, Roman emperor, 207, 233
Contablata, m. of Patrick, 44
Cornelius, St, pope, 86, **183**
Corona, St, **87**
Cosmas, St, **198**
Crescens, St, **129**
Cuthbert, St, bp. of Lindisfarne, **49**, 66, 80, 171
Cyprian, St, bp. of Carthage, **184**
Cyprian, St, associate of Justina, **197**
Cyriada, m. of Pancras, 86
Cyricus, St, **127**
Cyrilla, St, **216**

Damian, St, **198**
Daria, St, **232**
Datianus, official, persecutor of Eulalia and Vincent, 31, 234
Datianus, official, persecutor of George and Alexandria, 67, 71
Decius, Roman emperor, 28, 73, 125, 139, 147, 150, 151, 154, 183, 208, 216
Desiderius, St, 188
Didymus, see Thomas
Digna, St, 149
Diocletian, Roman emperor, 2, 26, 27, 59, 86, 97, 102, 106, 170, 187, 198, 224, 230, 235
Dionysius, St, bp. of Paris, **203**
Dominanda, St, one of the Seven Women at Sirmium, **62**
Donata, St, one of the Seven Women at Sirmium, **62**
Donatus, St, bp. of Arezzo, **148**

INDEX OF PERSONS

Dorotheus, persecutor of Marcellinus and Peter, 98
Dulcitius, official, 59

Eadberht, St, bp. of Lindisfarne, **80**
Eastorwine, St, bp. of Wearmouth, **40**
Ecgberht, St, 37
Ecgfrith, k. of the Northumbrians, 40, 110
Egeas, persecutor of Andrew, 233
Eglippus, associate of Matthew, 190
Eleusippus, St, **23**
Eleutherius, St, s. of Antia, **65**
Eleutherius, St, associate of Dionysius and Rusticus, **203**
Elizabeth, St, m. of John the Baptist, 111
Emerentiana, St, **33**
Emiliana, St, aunt of Gregory, **11**
Epolanus, St, 34
Erasmus, St, **97**
Eugenia, St, **3**, 90, 182
Eugenius, St, **129**
Eulalia, St, **234**
Eumenia, St, 149
Euphemia, St, 3, **187**
Ephinissa, w. of Eglippus, 190
Euplius, St, **153**
Eusebia, worshipper of Quentin, 217
Eusebius, St, bp. of Vercelli, **142**
Eutropia, St, 149
Eve, 50, 53, 57
Eventius, St, **76**
Evilasius, St, **189**
Evodius, St, **144**
Exsuperius, St, 191

Fabian, St, pope, **28**
Fausta, St, **189**
Felicia, m. of Justus, 209
Felicianus, St, associate of Victor, 132
Felicianus, St, **175**
Felicity, St, associate of Perpetua, **39**
Felicity, St, m. of the Seven Brothers, 123, **229**
Felix, St, Roman priest, **19**
Felix, St, one of the Seven Brothers, **123**
Felix, St, bp. of Thibiuca, **170**
Felix, St, associate of Andochius and Thyrsus, **195**
Ferreolus, St, **103**
Ferrucio, St, **103**
Festus, St, 188
Flaccus, suitor of Petronilla, 94
Flauianus, official, 121
Florentia, worshipper of Vitus and Modestus, 102
Fortunatus, St, 170
The Forty Soldiers of Sebastea, SS, **41**
The Four Crowned Ones. SS, **222**
Fursa, St, **21**

Gabriel, St, archangel, 56, 111, 194
Gaius, official, 149
Galerius, official, 184
Gallienus, Roman emperor, 90, 182
Gamaliel, worshipper of Stephen, 4, 145
Garsecg, personification of the sea, 162
Geminus, see Thomas
Genesius the Comedian, St, **163**
Genesius, St, **212**
George, St, **67**, 71
Germanus, St, bp. of Auxerre, **141**
Gervase, St, **107**
Gordianus, St, **84**
Gregory the Great, St, pope, 11, **42**, 117
Gregory Nazianzen, St, **47**
Gundaphorus, k. of India, 238
Guthlac, St, 15, **63**

Hadrian, Roman emperor, 65
Heliodorus, St, **224**
Heraclius I, Byzantine emperor, 32
Heraclius, official, 160
Hereric, f. of Hild, 226
Hermes, St, **166**
Herod, k. of Judaea, 6, 135, 168
Hewald, SS, two Northumbrian missionaries of the same name, 201
Higebald, St, abt. in Lindsey, 37, **237**
Hieronymus, see Jerome
Hilaria, St, m. of Afra, 149
Hilarina, St, one of the Seven Women at

INDEX OF PERSONS

Sirmium, **62**
Hilarinus, St, **148**
Hilarion, St, **211**
Hilary, St, bp. of Poitiers, **18**
Hild, St, abbess of Whitby, **226**
Hippolytus, St, 151, **154**
The Holy Innocents, SS, **6**
Hyacinth, St, **182**
Hyrtacus, official, 144
Hyrtacus, k. of Ethiopia, 190

Irenaeus, St, **164**
Irene, St, 59, **61**

James the Greater, St, **135**
James the Less, St, **108**
Januarius, St, one of the Seven Brothers, **123**
Januarius, St, bp. of Benevento, associate of Desiderius and Festus, **188**
Januarius, St, associate of Felix, 170
Jerome, St, **200**
Joachim, St, f. of Mary, 180
John the Baptist, St, 12, **36**, **111**, **168**, **194**
John the Evangelist, St, **5**, 135
John of Beverley, St, bp. of Hexham, **81**
John I, St, pope, **89**
John, St, associate of Paul, **113**
Judas, see Thaddeus
Julian, St, associate of Basilissa, **13**
Julian, Roman emperor, 54, 113
Julianus, St, s. of Symphorosa, **129**
Julitta, St, **127**
Julius Caesar, 116b
Justina, St, **197**
Justinus, St, s. of Symphorosa, **129**
Justinus, St, associate of Lawrence, 151, 216
Justinus, f. of Justus, 209
Justus, St, **209**

Lawrence, St, 150, **151**, 154
Leontius, official, 219
Licinius, Roman emperor, 41
Liutprand, k. of the Lombards, 167
Luceia, St, **112**
Lucianus, worshipper of Stephen, 145

Lucius, St, one of the Sixteen Soldiers, **213**
Lucy, St, **235**
Luke, St, **207**
Lupulus, St, **206**
Lupus, St, bp. of Troyes, **138**
Lysias, official, persecutor of the Forty Soldiers, 41
Lysias, official, persecutor of Cosmas and Damian, 198

Macedonius, St, **43**
The Machabees, SS, **140**
Macrinus, Roman emperor, 205
Magnus, St, **159**
Mamas, St, **157**
Mamilian, St, **186**
Marcellian, St, **106**
Marcellinus, St, **98**, 99
Marcellus I, St, pope, **20**
Marcellus, St, **176**
Marcus Aurelius, Roman emperor, 14
Marcus, St, one of the Sixteen Soldiers, **213**
Margaret, see Marina
Marina, St, **122**
Marius, St, **29**
Mark, St, pope, **202**
Mark, St, b. of Marcellian, **106**
Mark, St, evangelist, **70**
Martha, St, w. of Marius, **29**
Martial, St, bp. of Limoges, **116**
Martialis, St, one of the Seven Brothers, **123**
Martin, St, bp. of Tours, 18, **223**
Martinianus, St, **117**
Martyrius, St, **93**
Mary, St, 1, **9**, **56**, 57, **108**, **111**, **156**, 171, **180**, 215, 218
Mary, St, w. of Cleophas, m. of Simon, 215
Mary Magdalen, St, **133**
Maternus, St, bp. of Milan, 83
Matthew, St, **190**
Maurice, St, **191**
Maxentius, Roman emperor, 20
Maximian, Roman emperor, 38, 83, 97, 191, 235
Maximilla, w. of Egeas, 233

INDEX OF PERSONS

Maximinus, Roman emperor, 10
Maximus, St, associate of Valerianus and Tiburtius, **64**
Meleusippus, St, **23**
Mennas, St, **224**
Michael, St, archangel, 68, **82**, 97, 130, **199**
Milus, St, **225**
Modesta, St, **43**
Modestus, St, **102**
Moses, 88
Mygdeus, persecutor of Thomas, 238

Narcissus, St, bp. of Gerona, 149
Nazarius, St, **137**
Necitius, official, persecutor of Eugenia, Protus and Hyacinthus, 3, 182
Necitius, official, persecutor of Theodota, Evodius, 144
Nemesius, St, **129**
Nero, Roman emperor, 114
Nicander, St, **104**
Nicomedes, associate of Petronilla, 94
Nicomedes, St, **96**
Nicostratus, St, one of the Four Crowned Ones, **222**
Nonnus, St, 210
Numerian, Roman emperor, 34

Oceanus, personification of the sea, 162
Olibrius, official, 122
Omer, see Audomarus
Oswald, St, k. of the Northumbrians, **146**, 171
Owine, associate of Chad, 37

Pancras, St, **86**
Paschasius, persecutor of Lucia, 235
Paternianus, St, **175**
Patricia, St, **43**
Patrick, St, **44**
Paul the Hermit, St, **16**
Paul, St, apostle, 32, **35**, 101, **114**, 115, **119**, 161, 193, 207
Paul, St, associate of John, **113**
Paulina, St, one of the Seven Women at Sirmium, **62**

Paulina, see Virgo
Paulinus, official, 72, 236
Pega, St, **15**
Pelagia, St, **210**
Perpetua, St, **39**
Peter, St, apostle, 10, 14, 17, **25**, 40, 70, 76, 94, **114**, 115, 116, **119**, 134, 135, 166, 196, 228, 233
Peter, St, associate of Marcellinus, **98**, 99
Petronilla, St, **94**
Petrus, St, associate of Ananias, **26**
Petrus, associate of Christopher, 73
Petrus, St, one of the Sixteen Soldiers, **213**
Philip, St, apostle, **74**
Philippus, f. of Eugenia, 3
Philippus, St, one of the Seven Brothers, **123**
Phocas, St, bp. of Sinope, **126**
Pompeius, suitor of Basilla, 90
Praetextatus, 91, 147
Prilidianus, St, 34
Primitivus, St, **129**
Prisca, St, **24**
Priscilla, 20
Priscus, St, **95**
Priscus, St, bp. of Capua, **172**
Priscus, official, persecutor of Marcellus and Valerian, 176, 185
Priscus, official, persecutor of Euphemia, 187
Processus, St, **117**
Procopius, St, **121**
Protase, St, **107**
Protus, St, **182**
Publius, official, persecutor of the Seven Brothers, 123
Pyrrhus, official, persecutor of Mennas and Heliodorus, 224

Quentin, St, **217**
Quintus, St, **177**

Riciouarus, official, persecutor of Quentin, 217
Rizoalis, official, persecutor of Justus, 209
Rogatina, St, one of the Seven Women at Sirmium, **62**
Romana, godmother of Pelagia, 210

INDEX OF PERSONS

Romanus, St, **150**
Rufina, St, **125**
Rufus, St, **165**
Rusticus, St, **203**

Sabina, St, **169**
Sapientia, name of apparition, 47
Saturnina, one of the Seven Women at Sirmium, **62**
Saturninus, St, bp. of Toulouse, **231**
Saulus, see Paul the apostle
The Scillitan Martyrs, SS, **128**
Sebastian, St, **27**, 106, 118, 120, 152
Sebastianus, official, persecutor of Victor and Corona, 87
Secunda, St, 125
Sennes, St, **139**
Senneus, St, **225**
Septimus, St, 170
Serenus, official, persecutor of Marcellinus and Petrus, 98
Serotina, St, one of the Seven Women at Sirmium, **62**
The Seven Brothers, SS, **123**
The Seven Women at Sirmium, SS, **62**
Severiana, w. of Aurelianus, 76
Sigeberht, k. of the East Angles, 21
Silanus, St, one of the Seven Brothers, **123**
Silvester I, St, pope, **7**
Simeon Stylites, St, **136**
Simon, St, apostle, **215**
Simplicius, St, one of the Four Crowned Ones, **222**
Sinotus, St, **179**
Sisinnius, offical, persecutor of Agape, Chionia and Irene, 59, 61
Sisinnius, St, **93**
The Sixteen Soldiers, SS, **213**
Sixtus II, St, pope, **147**
Sosius, St, **192**
Sostenes, St, 187
Speratus, St, **128**
Speusippus, St, **23**
Stacteus, St, **129**
Stephen, St, 4, **145**

Stephen I, St, pope, **143**
Stratocles, b. of Egeas, 233
Symmachus, official, 89
Symphorian, St, **160**
Symphorianus, St, one of the Four Crowned Ones, **222**
Symphorosa, St, **129**
Symphronius, official, persecutor of Agnes, 30
Tarquinius, official, persecutor of Silvester and Timothy, 7, 161
Telesphorus, St, pope, **14**
Terentianus, official, persecutor of John and Paul, 113
Thaddeus, St, apostle, also known as Judas, 215
Thecla, St, **193**
Theoderic, k. of the Ostrogoths, 89
Theoderius, St, 132
Theodolus, St, **76**
Theodoret, St, **54**
Theodosius, St, one of the Sixteen Soldiers, **213**
Theodota, St, m. of Evodius, 2, **144**
Theodota, St, associate of Afra, 149 (in *C* only)
Thomas, St, apostle, also known as Didymus or Geminus, **238**
Thunor, pagan god, 182
Thyrsus, St, **195**
Tiburtius, St, b. of Valerianus, **64**
Tiburtius, St, associate of Sebastian, **152**
Timotheus, associate of Simeon Stylites, 136
Timothy, St, **161**
Tiu, pagan god, 147
Tondberht, h. of Æthelthryth, 110
Torquatus, persecutor of Tiburtius, 152
Trajan, Roman emperor, 42, 126, 166, 228
Tranquillinus, St, **120**
Tryphonia, St, **208**

Urban I, St, pope, **91**, 227
Urbanus, St, 34
Urbanus, f. of Christina, 130
Ursicinus, St, **236**

Valeria, St, 107
Valerian, St, **185**
Valerian, Roman emperor, 143, 184

Valerianus, St, **64**
Valerianus, official, persecutor of Vitus and Modestus, 102
Valerianus, official, persecutor of Abundius, Irenaeus and Hippolytus, 154, 164
Valerius, St, bp. of Saragossa, 31
Vespasian, Roman emperor, 134
Victor, St, associate of Corona, **87**
Victor, St, associate of Euphemia, 187
Victor Maurus, St, **83**
Victor of Marseilles, St, associate of Alexander, Theodorius and Felicianus, **132**
Vincent, St, **31**
Virgo, St, **99**
Vitalis, St, f. of Gervasius and Protasius, **72**, 107
Vitalis, St, one of the Seven Brothers, **123**
Vitus, St, **102**

Wilfrid, St, bp. of Northumbria, **68**
Winnoc, St, abt. of Wurmhout, **221**

Xerxes I, k. of Persia, 215

Zachary, St, f. of John the Baptist, 194
Zebedee, f. of James the Greater and John the Evangelist, 135
Zoe, St, **118**

Index of Authors and Texts

This index lists all primary texts which are referred to in this volume, and should not be understood as a list of sources used by the martyrologist. Numbers refer to text sections, not pages.

Authored Texts

Ado of Vienne, *Martyrologium*, 175

Adomnán, *De locis sanctis*, 1, 52, 53, 56, 58, 67, 79, 111a, 200

Ælfric, *Catholic Homilies*, 4, 229

Ælfric, *De falsis diis*, 50, 53

Aldhelm, *De uirginitate* (prose), 5, 7, 13, 16, 30, 47, 59, 75, 124, 130, 156, 173, 197, 198, 207, 232

Aldhelm, *Carmen de uirginitate*, 5, 7, 16, 30, 35, 47, 59, 75, 124, 125, 235

Aldhelm, *Carmina ecclesiastica*, 135

Ambrose, *Epistola* 22 (*BHL* 3513), 107

Augustine, *De ciuitate Dei*, 4

Augustine, *Sermones*, 39, 79, 184

Bede, *Chronica maiora*, 22, 32, 39, 167, 218

Bede, *De temporibus*, 1

Bede, *De temporum ratione*, 8a, 36a, 36b, 45, 46, 48, 50, 52, 53, 55, 58a, 58b, 73a, 73b, 83a, 94a, 94b, 116a, 116b, 139a, 139b, 171a, 171b, 200a, 200b, 217a, 217b, 221a, 233a, 233b

Bede, *Historia abbatum*, 17, 40, 196

Bede, *Historia ecclesiastica gentis Anglorum*, 21, 37, 81, 92, 100, 109, 110, 141, 146, 171, 201, 204, 214, 218, 226, 237

Bede, *In Lucae euangelium expositio*, 133

Bede, *In Marci euangelium expositio*, 133

Bede, *Martyrologium*, 18, 19, 34, 85, 148, 168, 188, 189, 192, 235

Bede, *Vita S. Cuthberti* (prose) (*BHL* 2021), 49, 66, 80, 171

Bede, *Vita metrica S. Cuthberti* (*BHL* 2020), 66

Bede, *Vita S. Felicis* (*BHL* 2873), 19

Caesarius of Arles, *Sermones*, 78, 111

Dionysius Exiguus, *De inuentione capitis Joannis baptistae* (*BHL* 4290–1), 36

Ennodius, *Carmina*, 137

Eucherius, *Passio S. Mauricii* (*BHL* 5737), 191

Eustochius, see Primary Texts, Hagiography below (Pelagia)

Evagrius, *Vita S. Antonii* (*BHL* 609), 22

Felix, *Vita S. Guthlaci* (*BHL* 3723), 15, 63

Gregory, *Homiliae in Euangelia*, 11, 56, 115, 117, 133, 229

Gregory, *Dialogi*, 51, 89, 148

Gregory, *Moralia in Iob*, 168

Gregory of Tours, *Miraculum Clementis* (*BHL* 1855), 228

Haymo of Auxerre, *Sermones*, 12

Helisachar of Trier, see Primary Texts, Hagiography below (All Saints)

Hrabanus Maurus, *Martyrologium*, 3, 126, 175, 189

Isidore, *De ortu et obitu patrum*, 5, 35, 108, 114, 135, 190, 207, 215, 233, 238

Iulius Obsequens, *De prodigiis*, 1

Jerome, *Vita S. Hilarionis* (*BHL* 3879), 173, 211

Jerome, *Vita S. Pauli* (*BHL* 6596), 16

Orosius, *Historiae aduersum paganos*, 1, 60

Patrick of Dublin, *De signis et prodigiis*, 1

Paul the Deacon, *Vita S. Gregorii* (*BHL* 3648), 42

Paulinus of Milan, *Vita S. Ambrosii* (*BHL* 377), 60

Petrus Chrysologus, *Sermones*, 6, 12, 111

Pseudo-Abdias, *Passio S. Iacobi minoris* (*BHL* 4089), 108

Pseudo-Abdias, *Passio S. Philippi* (*BHL* 6814), 74

Pseudo-Abdias, *Passio S. Iohannis* (*BHL* 4316), 5

Pseudo-Ambrose, *Sermones*, 30, 107, 137

Pseudo-Ambrose, *Passio S. Agnetis*, see Primary Texts, Hagiography below (Agnes)
Pseudo-Ambrose, *Passio S. Geruasii*, see Primary Texts, Hagiography below (Geruasius)
Pseudo-Ambrose, *Passio S. Sebastiani*, see Primary Texts, Hagiography below (Sebastianus)
Pseudo-Augustine, *Sermones*, 1, 57, 79
Pseudo-Fulgentius, *Sermones*, 184
Pseudo-Gregoy, *Liber responsalis*, 156
Pseudo-Isidore, *De ortu et obitu patrum*, 4, 5, 9, 35, 56, 70, 108, 114, 135, 190, 207, 215, 233, 238
Pseudo-Isidore, *De ordine creaturarum*, 46, 48, 50, 52, 53
Pseudo-Jerome, *Martyrologium*, 32, 118
Pseudo-Maximus, *Sermones*, 142
Pseudo-Theotimus, see Primary Texts, Hagiography below (Margaret)
Rufinus, *Historia ecclesiastica*, 6, 28, 75, 101, 108
Stephen of Ripon, *Vita S. Wilfridi* (*BHL* 8889), 68
Sulpicius Severus, *Dialogi* (*BHL* 5614–16), 223
Sulpicius Severus, *Vita S. Martini* (*BHL* 5610), 223
Usuard, *Martyrologium*, 3, 25, 167

Anonymous Texts, non-Hagiography

Bible (Vulgate), 1, 4, 5, 6, 7, 9, 12, 30, 35, 45, 46, 48, 52, 53, 55, 56, 58, 79, 88, 101, 114, 133, 135, 140, 168, 194, 228
Blickling Homilies, 57, 79
Catachesis celtica, 58
De descensu Christi ad inferos, 57
Euangelium Pseudo-Matthei (*BHL* 5334–42), 180
Glosses, 10
Hyde Breviary, 114
Inuentio S. Crucis (*BHL* 4169), 77
Kentish Hymn, 226
Liber pontificalis, 10, 14, 20, 28, 86, 89, 91, 143, 147, 202, 205, 228
Linz Homily Collection, 56
Meters of Boethius, 46
Old English Bede, 10, 138
Old English Homilies (Irvine), 50
Old English Homilies (Tristram), 199
Old English prose Life of Guthlac, 63
Old English Translation of Gregory the Great, *Dialogi*, 136
Vienna Commentary on Matthew, 56
Vitae patrum (*BHL* 6527–9), 131

Anonymous Texts, Hagiography (listed alphabetically by saint's name)

Passio SS. Abdon et Sennen (*BHL* 6), [See also under *Passio S. Laurentii* (*BHL* 4753)] 139
Passio S. Afrae (*BHL* 108–9), 149
Passio S. Agnetis (*BHL* 156), 30, 33
Passio S. Alexandri (*BHL* 266), 76, 166
(All Saints), 'Legimus in ecclesiasticis historiis' (*BHL* 6332d), 218
Passio S. Ananiae (*BHL* 397), 26
Passio S. Anastasiae (*BHL* 118, 401, 8093), 2, 59, 61, 144
(Anastasius) *Miraculum Romae ad Aquas Saluias* (*BHL* 412), 32
Passio S. Anatholiae et Audacis (*BHL* 418), 124
Passio S. Andochii (*BHL* 424), 160, 195
Passio S. Andreae (*BHL* 428), 233
Passio S. Andreae (*BHL* 430), 233
Passio S. Antonini (*BHL* 568), 173
Passio S. Apollinaris (*BHL* 623), 134
Vita S. Audomari (*BHL* 763), 181
Passio S. Babylae (*BHL* 890), 34
Passio S. Bartholomaei (*BHL* 1002), 162
Passio S. Benigni (*BHL* 1153), 220
Vita S. Bertini (*BHL* 763), 178
Passio S. Caeciliae (*BHL* 1495), 64, 227
Passio S. Caesarii (*BHL* 1511), 219
Passio S. Cassiani (*BHL* 1626), 155
Vita S. Ceolfridi (*BHL* 1726), 196
Passio S. Christinae (*BHL* 1748b), 130
Passio S. Christophori (*BHL* 1764), 73
Passio SS. Chrysanthi et Dariae (*BHL* 1787), 232

INDEX OF AUTHORS AND TEXTS

Passio S. Chrysogoni (*BHL* 1795), 230
Passio S. Claudii et sociorum (*BHL* 1836), 222
Passio S. Clementis (*BHL* 1848), 228
Miraculum S. Clementis (*BHL* 1855), 228
Passio S. Columbae (*BHL* 1892), 8
Passio S. Cornelii (*BHL* 1958), 183
Passio S. Cosmae (*BHL* 1970), 198
Acta S. Cypriani (*BHL* 2038), 184
Passio S. Cyrici (*BHL* 1802–8), 127
Passio S. Dionysii (*BHL* 2171), 203
Passio S. Donati (*BHL* 2289–92), 148
Passio S. Eleutherii (*BHL* 2451), 65
Passio S. Erasmi (*BHL* 2582), 97
Passio S. Eugeniae (*BHL* 2666), 3, 90, 182
Passio S. Eulaliae (*BHL* 2696), 234
Passio S. Euphemiae (*BHL* 2708), 187
Passio S. Eupli (*BHL* 2729), 153
Passio S. Eusebii (*BHL* 2748–9), 142
Passio SS. Faustae et Evilasii (*BHL* 2833), 189
Passio S. Felicitatis (*BHL* 2853), 123
Passio S. Felicis Tubzocensis (*BHL* 2895b), 170
Passio S. Ferreoli (*BHL* 2903), 103
Vita S. Fursei (*BHL* 3213a), 21
Passio SS. Galllicani, Iohannis et Pauli (*BHL* 3236, 3238), 113
Passio S. Genesii (*BHL* 3304), 212
Passio S. Genesii (*BHL* 3320), 163
Passio S. Georgii (*BHL* 3363), 67
Passio S. Georgii (*BHL* 3379), 67, 71
Passio S. Geruasii (*BHL* 3514), 72, 107, 236
Vita S. Goaris (*BHL* 3565), 186
Vita S. Gregorii (*BHL* 3637), 42
Passio S. Hadriani et sociorum (*BHL* 3744), 38
Passio S. Iacobi minoris (*BHL* 4093), 108
Passio S. Ianuarii (*BHL* 4132), 188, 192
Passio SS. Irenaei et Abundii (*BHL* 4464), 164
Passio S. Iuliani (*BHL* 4529), 13
Passio S. Iustinae (*BHL* 2047, 2050), 197
Passio S. Iusti (*BHL* 4590), 209
Passio S. Laurentii (*BHL* 4753) [This composite text also comprises the *Passio SS. Abdon et Sennen* (*BHL* 6) and the *Passio S. Sixti* (*BHL* 7801) which are given separate entries here] 139, 147, 150, 151, 154, 164, 208, 213, 216
Passio S. Luciae (*BHL* 4980), 112
Passio S. Luciae (*BHL* 4992), 235
Vita S. Lupi (*BHL* 5087), 138
Passio S. Mammetis (*BHL* 5194), 157
Passio S. Marcelli (*BHL* 5245), 176
Passio S. Marcellini (*BHL* 5231), 98, 99
Passio S. Marci (*BHL* 5276), 70
Passio S. Margaretae (*BHL* 5303), 122
Vita S. Mariae Magdalenae (*BHL* 5453), 133
Passio SS. Marii et Marthae (*BHL* 5543), 29, 105
Vita S. Martialis (*BHL* 5551), 116
Miracula S. Martialis (*BHL* 5561), 116
Passio S. Matthei (*BHL* 5690), 190
Passio S. Mennae (*BHL* 5921), 224
Apparitio S. Michaelis (*BHL* 5948), 82
Passio S. Nazarii (*BHL* 6039), 137
Vita S. Pamphili (*BHL* 6418), 186
Passio S. Pancratii (*BHL* 6421), 86
Vita S. Pelagiae (*BHL* 6605, version A1), 210
Vita S. Pelagiae (*BHL* 6609, version B), 210
Passio SS. Perpetuae et Felicitatis (*BHL* 6633), 39
Vita S. Petronillae (*BHL* 6061), 94
Passio S. Phocae (*BHL* 6838), 126
Passio S. Procopii (*BHL* 6949), 121
Passio et Inuentio S. Quintini (*BHL* 6999–7000), 217
Passio S. Saturnini (*BHL* 7495–6), 231
Passio SS. Scillitanorum (*BHL* 7531), 128
Passio SS. Sebastenorum (*BHL* 7539), 41
Passio S. Sebastiani (*BHL* 7543), 27, 106, 118, 120, 152
Gesta S. Siluestri (*BHL* 7725–32), 7, 161
Gesta S. Siluestri (*BHL* 7739), 7
Passio SS. Simonis et Iudae (*BHL* 7749–50), 215
Passio S. Sixti (*BHL* 7801) [See also under *Passio S. Laurentii* (*BHL* 4753)] 147
Passio S. Speusippi (*BHL* 7828), 23
Reuelatio Stephani (*BHL* 7851), 4, 145
Reuelatio Stephani (*BHL* 7855), 4, 145
Vita S. Symeonis stylitae (*BHL* 7957, 7958), 136

Passio S. Symphoriani (*BHL* 7967–8), 160
Passio S. Symphorosae (*BHL* 7971), 129
Passio S. Theclae (*BHL* 8020n), 193
Passio S. Theodoreti (*BHL* 8074), 54
Passio S. Thomae (*BHL* 8136), 238
Passio S. Valeriani (*BHL* 8488), 185
Passio S. Victoris (*BHL* 8559), 87
Passio S. Victoris (*BHL* 8570), 132
Passio S. Victoris (*BHL* 8580), 83
Passio S. Vincentii (*BHL* 8631), 31
Passio S. Viti (*BHL* 8714), 102
Passio S. Winnoci (*BHL* 8952), 221

Index of Place-Names and Geographical Terms

Numbers refer to text sections, not pages. Non-English terms are given in conventional Latin forms, except in cases where a conventional modern English form exists. Additional modern equivalents are also given for the more opaque Latin and Old English terms. References to populations and tribal groups are included in the entries for the relevant place- and country-names. For further information on place-names in the *Old English Martyrology*, see also Roberts, '*Fela martyra* "many martyrs"' and the commentary section in Kotzor, II, 277–375.

Achaea, 207, 233
Ad Ulmos, 83
Africa, 39, 167
Ager Veranus, 150, 151
Alexandria, 3, 22, 70, 75
Alticiotrum, 209 (see Commentary)
Ambeanis (Amiens), 217
Angeln, 73b
Anglia, 21, 37, 92, 110
Antioch, 13, 34, 54, 97, 122, 161, 197, 207, 210
Apamea, 173
Apulia, 65, 170
Aquae Saluiae, 32
Armenia, 215
Arretium (Arezzo), 148
Assyria, 173
Augusta (Augsburg), 149
Augustodunum (Autun), 160
Bactria, 238
Balbina, cemetery of, 202
Barcelona, 234
Bardney, 146
Bebbanburh (Bamburgh), 146
Beneuentum, 188
Bercingum (Barking), 204
Bethlehem, 1, 6, 200
Bethsaida, 74
Bisontium (Besançon), 103
Bithynia, 26, 144, 207
Bosphorus, 215
Byzantium, 38

Brytene (Britain), 17, 21, 40, 42, 49, 63, 73b, 80, 81, 92, 100, 109, 141, 146, 196, 201, 204, 226
Burgundy, 196
Cabillonum (Chalon), 176
Caesarea (city in Cappadocia), 157
Caesarea (city in Palestine), 121
Calamina, 238
Calepodius, cemetery of, 205
Callistus, cemetery of, 10, 28, 143, 147
Cantwarabyrg (Canterbury), 92
Caphargamala, 145 (see Commentary)
Cappadocia, 157, 191 (see Commentary)
Carthage, 39, 128, 184
Catacombs, 27, see also Balbina, cemetery of; Calepodius, cemetery of; Callistus, cemetery of; Praetextatus, cemetery of; Priscilla, cemetery of
Catina (Catania), 153
Chalcedon, 187
Cilicia, 87, 127
Cnobheresburh, 21 (see Commentary)
Colodesburh (Coldingham), 110
Constantinople, 56a, 207, 233
Crowland, 63
Cyprus, 101
Delagabria, 145
Derewudu (?Beverley), 81
Dorobernia (Canterbury), 92
Edessa, 238
Egypt, the Egyptians (Africans, Ethiopians), 1, 3, 22, 70, 87, 162, 190

INDEX OF PLACE-NAMES AND GEOGRAPHICAL TERMS

Ely, 110
Emesa, 36
England, the English, 17, 37, 92, 109, 141, 146, 196, 201, 214, 237
English Channel, 221
Ephesus, 5
Essex, 214
Ethiopia, see under Egypt
Farne Island, 66
Figlina, 213
Formiae, 97
Frisia, 201
Galilee, 74
Gaul, 21, 195, 217, 220, 223
Germany, 73b
Glæstingabyrig (Glastonbury), 171 (see Commentary)
Greece, 5, 10, 12, 14, 69
Gyrwan territory, 110
Hebron, 53
Heraclea, 199 (see Commentary)
Hibernia (Ireland), the Gaels (Scottas, inhabitants of Ireland and of Dál Riata), 21, 44, 100, 146, 171
Hierapolis, 74
Hierusalem (Jerusalem), 4, 56a, 58, 65 (the heavenly Jerusalem), 108, 111a, 145, 180, 210
Hispania (Spain), 31, 135, 234
Hyrcania, 238
Iconium, 193
Ila, 225
India, 162, 238
Iona, 100
Israel, 88
Italy, the Italians, 89, 97, 228
Jews, 157, 190
Jordan (River), 12
Læstenga yge, Læstinga ea (Lastingham), 37, 214
Lemouicum (Limoges), 116
Lerina (Lérins), 225
Libya, 70
Lichfield, 37

Lindisfarne, 80, 146
Lindsey, 37, 146, 237
Lingones (Langres), 23, 196
Lipara, 89
Lombardy, 167
Lucania, 102
Ludica, 97 (see Commentary)
Macedonia, 190
Maheldagdar, 225
Maiuma, 211
Marmarica, 70
Massilia (Marseilles), 132
Media, 238
Mediolana (Milan), 60, 83, 137
Mercia, 37
Misenum, 192
Mount Gargano, 82
Mount of Olives, 79, 210
Mount Sinai, 88
Narnia (Narni), 115
Nazareth, 56
Nazianzus, 47
Nerito, 215
Nicaea, 144
Nicomedia, 38
Northumbria, 49, 81, 110
Nursia, 51
Palestine, 121, 211
Parisius (Paris), 203
Parthia, 190, 238
Patrae, 233
Pentapolis (in North Africa), 70
Peronna (Péronne), 21
Persia, the Persians, 29, 32, 139, 215, 235
Phoenicia, 36
Phrygia, 74, 86 (see Commentary)
Picenum, 124 (see Commentary)
Pictauia (Poitiers), 18
Pictish territory, 100, 146
Pincian Hill, 19
Pontus, 126
Praetextatus, cemetery of, 91, 147
Priscilla, cemetery of, 20
Ravenna, 72, 89, 134, 236

INDEX OF PLACE-NAMES AND GEOGRAPHICAL TERMS

Razichitae, 225 (see Commentary)
Rhodanum, 212 (see Commentary)
Rome, 1, 2, 3, 7, 8a, 10, 12, 14, 17, 19, 24, 25, 27, 28, 29, 30, 32, 33, 60, 64, 65, 69, 76, 84, 86, 90, 91, 94, 98, 105, 108, 112, 113, 114, 116, 117, 118, 120, 123, 124, 125, 139, 139b, 143, 147, 150, 151, 152, 154, 158, 161, 164, 166, 169, 182, 183, 196, 202, 205, 217, 218, 222, 227, 235
Samos, 73
Saracen territory, the Saracens, 167
Sardinia, 167 (see Commentary)
Scotland, see under Hibernia
Scythia, 74, 233
Sequana (River Seine), 203
Sicily, 235
Siler (River Sele), 102
Sithiu, 178, 181
Somena (River Somme), 217
Spaniacum (Épagny), 220
Streoneshealh (Whitby), 226
Syracuse, 235
Syria, 62, 207
Tarsus, 127
Thabata, 211
Thessalonica, 61
Thibiuca, 170
Thracia, 199 (see Commentary)
Ticinum (Pavia), 167
Tiber (River), 3
Tolosa (Toulouse), 231
Trecassium (Troyes), 138
Triticum, 138
Turnum, 223
Turonica (Tours), 223
Tyrus (Tyre), 130
Valencia, 31
Venusia (Venosa), 170
Vercelli, 142
Verolamium (St Albans), 109
Via Appia, 91
Via Aurelia, 86
Via Latina, 3
Via Nomentana, 30, 76
Via Salaria, 20, 166
Via Tiburtina, 151
Vicus Longus, 72
Vulcania, 89
Wætlingaceaster (St Albans), 109
Wearmouth, 17, 40
Whitby, see Streoneshealh
Wormhout, 221

ANGLO-SAXON TEXTS

Volumes already published

1. *Wulfstan's Canon Law Collection*
edited by J. E. Cross (†) and Andrew Hamer

2. *The Old English Poem* Judgement Day II: *a Critical Edition with Editions of* De die iudicii *and the Hatton 113 Homily* Be domes dæge
edited by Graham D. Caie

3. Historia de Sancto Cuthberto: *A History of Saint Cuthbert and a Record of his Patrimony*
edited by Ted Johnson South

4. Excerptiones de Prisciano: *The Source for Ælfric's Latin-Old English* Grammar
edited by David W. Porter

5. *Ælfric's* Life of Saint Basil the Great: *Background and Context*
edited by Gabriella Corona

6. *Ælfric's* De Temporibus Anni
edited with a translation by Martin Blake

7. *The Old English Dialogues of Solomon and Saturn*
edited with a translation by Daniel Anlezark

8. *Sunday Observance and The Sunday Letter in Anglo-Saxon England*
edited with a translation by Dorothy Haines

9. *Anglo-Saxon Prognostics: An Edition and Translation of Texts from London, British Library, MS Cotton Tiberius A.iii*
edited with a translation by R. M. Liuzza

10. *The Old English Martyrology: Edition, Translation and Commentary*
edited with a translation by Christine Rauer

11. *Two Ælfric Texts: 'The Twelve Abuses' and 'The Vices and Virtues': An Edition and Translation of Ælfric's Old English Versions of* De duodecim abusivis *and* De octo vitiis et de duodecim abusivis
edited with a translation by Mary Clayton

12. *The Old English Metrical Calendar (*Menologium*)*
edited with a translation by Kazutomo Karasawa